THE

WORKS

OF

JOHN WHITGIFT, D.D.,

ARCHBISHOP OF CANTERBURY.

The Parker Society.

Instituted A.D. M.DCCC.XL.

For the Publication of the Works of the Fathers and Early Writers of the Reformed English Church.

THE

WORKS

OF

JOHN WHITGIFT, D.D.,

MASTER OF TRINITY COLLEGE, DEAN OF LINCOLN, &c.

AFTERWARDS SUCCESSIVELY

BISHOP OF WORCESTER AND ARCHBISHOP OF CANTERBURY.

THE SECOND PORTION,

CONTAINING

THE DEFENCE OF THE ANSWER TO THE ADMONITION, AGAINST THE REPLY OF THOMAS CARTWRIGHT:

TRACTATES VII—X.

EDITED FOR

The Parker Society,

BY THE

REV. JOHN AYRE, M.A.

OF GONVILLE AND CAIUS COLLEGE, CAMBRIDGE, MINISTER OF ST JOHN'S
CHAPEL, HAMPSTEAD.

CAMBRIDGE:

PRINTED AT

THE UNIVERSITY PRESS.

M.DCCC.LII.

161932

CONTENTS.

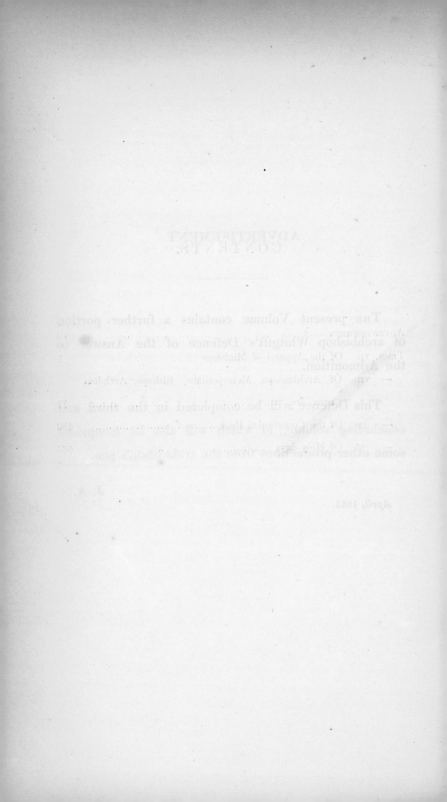

ADVERTISEMENT.

THE present Volume contains a further portion of archbishop Whitgift's Defence of the Answer to the Admonition.

This Defence will be completed in the third and concluding volume, in which will also be comprised some other productions from the archbishop's pen.

J. A.

April, 1853.

ADDENDA ET CORRIGENDA.

Vol. I. p. 35, marg. *for* 2 Chron. xxxix. *read* xxix.

p. 115, marg. *for* facing, *read* defacing.

p. 147, note 2, line 1, *for* from the first of the subsequent editions of the Admonition, *read* of the subsequent editions of the Admonition from the first.

p. 175, marg. *insert* 6 *after* Matt. vii.

p. 332, note 2. The crime of Birchet is probably referred to, who held that it was lawful to kill an enemy of the gospel. He therefore resolved to stab Christopher Hatton, the privy-councillor, but, mistaking his man, wounded the naval officer, Hawkins, afterwards so distinguished, Oct. 1573. See Strype, Parker, Book iv. chap. xxxiv.

p. 346, notes, line 7, *for* 346, *read* 347.

p. 351, marg. *insert after* argument *a.*

Vol. II. p. 495, note 2, *for* note 3, *read* note 4.

¶ Of the Apparel of Ministers.
Tract. VII.

The causes why they refuse the apparel examined.
Chapter i.   The First Division.
T. C. Page 52, Sect. 3.

The cap, the surplice, and tippet, are not the greatest matters we strive for, which notwithstanding hath been informed to the churches beyond sea, to the end that the judgments of some might be the easilier had against us.   Howbeit we think it an attire unmeet for a minister of the gospel to wear; and the surplice especially more than the other two; because such hurtful ceremonies are so much more dangerous, as they do approach nearer the service or worship of God.

Jo. Whitgift.

Yet in the beginning such was your pretence; neither was there anything else that you contended for; as it is well known to all men that had to deal with you, or heard of you.   I am certainly persuaded that, if the churches beyond sea did fully understand your proceeding, together with the state of this church of England, that they would as bitterly write against you, and as willingly condemn you, as ever they did the anabaptists.   But to your reasons against the apparel.

Chapter i.   The Second Division.
T. C. Page 52, Sect. 4.

The causes why we are loth to meddle with them are not, as many are borne in hand, because that we think any pollution so to stick to the things themselves, as that the wearing of them had any such power to pollute and make unclean the users of them ; neither yet only because the papists have superstitiously used them ; but because they, having been abominably abused by them, have no use nor profit in those things or ends wherein and whereunto they are now used: and further, that they are also hurtful, being monuments of idolatry, whereas to bring them in, and establish them, it behoveth that there should some manifest profit of them appear.   For it is not enough to say, it is indifferent in the own nature; ergo, meet to be done ; but, as the circumstances of the times and persons, and profit or hurt of our brethren, do require or not require, so must it be done or not be done. For, in these things which are called indifferent, God will have the use of them to be measured, that it be referred first to his glory, then to the profit of others.

This assertion is contrary to your practice.

Monuments of idolatry may be used if they have any profit.

Jo. Whitgift.

It is true that is commonly said, that such as be in error neither long agree with other, neither yet with themselves. Some of you have taught that " pollution doth stick in the things themselves, as that the wearing of them had power to pollute and make unclean the wearers:" and a number be carried away with that doctrine; else why do they refuse to come to our churches, our sermons, yea, to keep us company, or to salute us? why spit they in our faces, revile us in the streets, and shew such like villany unto us, and that only because of our apparel? Is not all this a manifest declaration, that they think us therewith to be so "polluted," that whatsoever we speak or do is "polluted," in like manner, even the word of God and his sacraments? And where have they learned this, but of you, and others your partners? Likewise, what was the chief ground of this opinion? how did you move the people to this extremity? and what have they yet to speak in the defence of their excessive raging? Forsooth that this gear came from the pope, was invented by antichrist, and therefore abominable, and not to be used. This only reason they have; and this is the common-place that you have hitherto bet upon. But now, being convinced by manifest reasons, and seeing the manifold absurdities that waiteth upon such assertions, you pass over the matter as though you had never been stained with it, and say, "the causes why" you "are loth to meddle with them are not, as many are borne in hand, &c." So that in effect this is now by you confessed, that those "things which the papists have superstitiously used, yea, which they have abominably abused, if they have any use or profit in those things or ends wherein and whereunto they are now used, be lawful, and not to be refused." And therefore we must, I think, have no more to do with this argument: "The pope invented them; *ergo*, they are not to be used;" but this must be the question, "whether they have any use or profit in those things or ends wherein or whereunto they are now used." And this shift is invented to take away all objections which may be of churches, of bells, of pulpits, and such like.

But let us proceed to the reasons. You have not yet proved that "they have no use, or that they profit not in those things and ends wherein and whereunto they are now

The apparel not refused because the papists use it.

used;" and therefore I will take that for no reason as yet: although I have sufficiently answered unto it, where I have spoken of ceremonies[1], and in this treatise also that followeth Tract. II. of this matter.

You say further, that "they are also hurtful, being monuments of idolatry, &c." Whereby you acknowledge that, notwithstanding they be monuments of idolatry, yet may they be brought in and established, "if some manifest profit of them appear:" so that this also is granted, that "monuments of idolatry may be brought in and established," upon this condition, if they be profitable.

That which followeth in this portion of your Reply touching "things indifferent" I consent unto, with this proviso, that it is not every man's part in the church to judge and determine what the circumstance of the times and persons maketh profitable or hurtful (for then should we never be quiet), but theirs only to whom the government of the church is committed; to the which proviso if you do consent, we are in this matter thus far agreed.

Chapter i.   The Third Division.
T. C. Page 52, Sect. 4, 5.

Now, that they are not profitable and hurtful, it also may appear, if we consider them by all the kinds of men in the realm.

The papists are either stubborn or weak, and in respect of both these they cannot be but hurtful. The weak I call those that have made some step from popery to the gospel, and of whom there is good hope that they may be fully gotten to the gospel; but these are harmed by the use of these vestiments, for they take occasion of falling at them, because they think that the sacraments get reverence by them, and the ministry is commended by such apparel-wearing, and think that the sacraments want something of that they should have, if they be not used: whereupon are heard[2] oftentimes these voices, I will not communicate unless he wear a surplice. But this offence and occasion of falling is confirmed by the use of these garments; therefore, in respect of such men, they are hurtful.

Jo. Whitgift.

All this is spoken without proof, and it is very untrue that the "weak papist is hurt" in any respect by wearing this apparel: they take such garments as things pertaining to comeliness and order, and so ought they to do. Neither did

[1 See Vol. I. pages 175, &c.]   [2 Hard, Def. A., and B.]

I ever in my life hear that these garments hindered one jot any from coming to the gospel. But admit all this were true (as it is most untrue), why should it not as well by doctrine and teaching be removed, as other superstitious opinions be in these things which you can be content still to remain?

These voices, "I will not communicate unless he wear a surplice," may sometimes come upon just cause, when the good subject seeth the minister, which ought to be an example of obedience, stubbornly and wilfully shew example to the contrary; and sometime it may come of waywardness, when men be disposed to contend. But surely I do not think that any man which is persuaded to communicate with us in the sacraments can think, that they be either the better or the worse for the external habit of the minister. They be dissuaded from far greater matters than that; and therefore it is not to be thought that they will stick in such trifles. But admit it were so, is it not as great an error to think that the sacraments be polluted with the apparel, as it is to think that they want something which they should have, if the apparel be lacking? Yes, truly; and therefore, to take away both the errors, I think it most convenient the apparel be used, and these errors by doctrine to be confuted.

Chapter i.   The Fourth Division.
T. C. Page 52, Sect. 6.

A silly cause.   *Again, although I have knowledge, and know that the wearing of a surplice is lawful for me, yet another which hath not knowledge is by my example edified or strengthened to wear a surplice, whereof he can tell no ground why he should wear it, and so sinneth against his conscience: and for this cause St Paul concludeth, that that which a man may* 1 Cor. viii. *do in respect of himself may not be done, and is not lawful to* 10, 13.[1] *be done, in respect of other.*

Jo. Whitgift.

The weak are not offended, but they which account themselves most strong.   If to wear "a surplice" were an offence to the weak, or if there were not manifest grounds in scripture (such I mean as command obedience to superiors) to prove "the wearing of the surplice to be lawful," then were it something that you say. But, seeing such only be offended therewith as account

[1 This marginal reference is inserted from Repl. 2.]

themselves most strong, and condemn other of infirmity; seeing also that obedience to magistrates in such indifferent things hath manifest grounds in scripture, and to doubt of obedience in such matters is in effect to pluck the magistrate his sword out of his hand; this reason hath not so much as any similitude of probability in it.   Is there any minister of the church (for of such only is the surplice required) that will rather be moved "to wear a surplice" by the example of another, than by the consideration of his duty towards the law and order of the church, by due authority in a lawful and indifferent thing appointed?   You might make the same reason serve to pluck down the church, the pulpit, the bells, yea, to overthrow all orders, and all laws in things indifferent, which all have the same ground of obedience that the surplice hath.

In the confession of the Dutch church in London, which is allowed by the church of Geneva, and divers other reformed churches (whereof I have made mention before), it is thus written of things indifferent: "Things otherwise indifferent of themselves after a sort change their nature, when by some commandment they are either commanded or forbidden; because neither they can be omitted contrary to the commandment, if they be once commanded, neither done contrary to the prohibition, if they be prohibited; as it appeareth in the ceremonial law[2]."   So that the ground why a man should wear the surplice (being an indifferent thing, as you confess it to be) cannot be unknown to any but such as know not the ground of their obedience towards authority.

Things indifferent change their nature being commanded or forbidden. Confess. Eccles. Belgio-German.

It is true that in some things indifferent a man must have respect to the weakness of his brother, and abstain from doing that which he might lawfully do, rather than to offend his brother.   But that is in such indifferent things as be not by any law commanded or forbidden, but left free to every man to do or not to do: as, if "to wear the surplice" were by no law commanded, but left to every man's own disposition, then surely, if there were any weak offended with the wearing of it, I ought to abstain for the weak his sake; but, being by lawful authority commanded to wear it, if I should refuse so to do, I should offend against the magistrate, and against

In what kind of indifferent things we ought to have a respect of the weak.

[2 Lib. Th. Bezæ Epist. Theolog. Genev. 1575. Ad Peregrin. in Angl. Fratr. Epist. xxiv. Ad Artt. v. vi. vii. viii. 6. pp. 142, 3.   See Vol. I. page 209, note 5.]

God, who by his apostle hath given this commandment: *Omnis anima potestatibus &c.:* "Let every soul be subject to the higher power, &c.;" which is to be understood in all things that are not against God. And therefore, if any man be offended with me in so doing, the offence is taken, it is not given.

Chapter i.   The Fifth Division.

T. C. Page 52, Sect. ult.

Again, for the stubborn papists, they take hereupon occasion to speak evil of and to blaspheme the truth of the gospel, saying that our religion cannot stand by itself, unless it lean upon the staff of their ceremonies, and persuade themselves that those were very well devised by their popes, that they that are their enemies to their religion cannot be without. And hereupon they take occasion to hope that their other trumpery and baggage will in the end come in again; which causeth them to be more frozen in their wickedness, and shut their ears unto[1] the truth, which possibly they would hear, if all hope of bringing in of their popery were cut off.

Jo. Whitgift.

This is but a mere fancy: for, first, it was brought into the church before their popes, whom they hold upon, invaded that seat; as it is afterwards declared. Secondly, they be not matters that they make any great account of. Thirdly, they know full well that we could be without them; and that we (but only for obedience' sake) do not much esteem of them. Wherefore this is an argument framed only upon light conjectures. But be it all this were true, shall we, for their fancy or fond judgment, refuse to do that which is lawful, which we may do, and which we are bound to do? Or, in making orders for the church, must we inquire what their opinion will be? Then pluck down churches, &c.; for of them they make a greater reckoning than they do of the surplice, or any other such like matter. I think verily that there is not one papist in England that doth take occasion upon any thing retained in this church "to hope that their other trumpery and baggage will in the end come in again;" neither is there any cause in respect of them why they should so hope; and, if they do, yet I doubt not but that they shall hop without that hope. But a man may imagine, if he will, that there is

[1 Against, Repl. 2.]

a man in the moon, with a tree on his back, &c.; and you cannot let him.

Chapter i.   The Sixth Division.

T. C. Page 53, Lin. 5.

And let it be observed, that throughout the realm there are none that make such clamours, and outcries, and complaints for these ceremonies, as they, and those that they suborn. They pretend, I confess, the queen's majesty's injunctions, and obedience unto them; but who is so blind as seeth not that they have another meaning? For I appeal unto the consciences of all that know them, whether they do it for any obedience towards her majesty, whose death should be a thousand times better news unto them than her grace's marriage.

Jo. Whitgift.

The more is the pity that they should have such just cause of "clamouring," and that those which should teach them obedience to God and their prince be examples to the contrary. A subtle and crafty papist will be glad of any cause of quarrelling: the more circumspect therefore ought the minister to be, in taking heed lest he give just cause of the same. But there be honest, godly, and zealous men also, that cannot abide such disorder and contempt, whom peradventure you would gladly stain with the note of papistry, as your manner is; and for my part I think it to be the part of all dutiful subjects to keep laws and orders appointed, and to see other keep them also, if they be thereunto called.

The clamours of papists should move the ministers to more circumspection.

Surely he that is a papist indeed cannot wish well "to her majesty;" but, if he communicate with us in the sacraments, hear the word preached, and come to our churches, I will think and hope the best of him. But, if he refuse so to do (as there be divers such), so long as he so continueth, I must count him an enemy to religion, to the church, and to the prince, be he papist, anabaptist, or whatsoever. For he that in heart and in deed misliketh the religion, cannot like well of such as maintain the same.

Chap. i.   The Seventh Division.

T. C. Page 53, Sect. 1.

*There are also numbers of those which have all antichristianity in
such detestation, that they cannot abide the least scrap of it, and, when
they see the ministers wear them, they are grieved in their hearts, and
they begin somewhat to fear, lest this communicating with the papists in
apparel should make some way to those which use them the easier to
admit other things, when they should be likewise commanded.   And these
brethren's minds are not to be lightly grieved; and the ministers, if they
think to profit them, must cut away all occasion whereby they may have
an evil opinion of them.*

Jo. Whitgift.

*The purity
which can
abide no im-
perfection is
devilish.
Calvin. adv.
Anabap.*

M. Calvin, in his book against the anabaptists, after he
had spoken something against the puritans and Donatists,
hath this saying worthy to be noted: "Here, therefore, we
may be admonished that, when, as under the pretence of the
study of perfection, we can tolerate no imperfection, either in
the body or in the members of the church, that then the
devil doth make us swell with pride, and doth seduce us by
hypocrisy, that he might provoke us to forsake the flock of
Christ; knowing assuredly that he doth obtain the victory
when he draweth us from the same.   For, seeing either remission of sins or health is in no other place, although we
outwardly bear the countenance of an angelical conversation,
yet, if we do with such boldness separate ourselves from the
christian fellowship, we are become devils[1]."   If this be to
be feared in such as shew this preposterous zeal against that
which is blameworthy; what shall we think of those that,
under the pretence of zeal, deface the minister and the word
that he preacheth for doing that which is lawful, and the
which of duty he ought to do?   If the minister should apply
himself to please the people, and such especially of whom you
seem to speak in this place, his greatest study had need to
be how to transform himself daily into a new shape.   But

[1 Hinc ergo moneamur, quum sub specie studii perfectionis imperfectionem
nullam tolerare possumus aut in corpore aut in membris ecclesiæ, tunc diabolum
nos tumefacere superbia et hypocrisi seducere, ut ad deserendum Christi gregem
nos instiget: certo sciens se victoriam obtinere, quum nos inde abduxit.   Quum
enim nusquam alibi sit aut remissio peccatorum, aut salus, tametsi vitæ plusquam
angelicæ speciem præ nobis feramus, tamen si tali audacia nos separemus a christiano cœtu, simus diaboli.—Calvin. Op. Amst. 1667-71.   Instr. adv. Anabapt.
Art. ii. Tom. VIII. p. 363.]

most certain it is that you study too much to please the people ;
and that is the occasion of so many novelties, whereby they
are most commonly delighted. *Est natura hominis novitatis
avida.*

Chapter i.   The Eighth Division.

T. C. Page 53, Sect. 2.

*Seeing that therefore this kind of ceremonies in apparel harden the
hearts of the papists, and cause them to be the stiffer in their popery, hinder
the weak from profiting in the knowledge of the gospel, grieve the minds of
the godly, are occasion of an evil opinion unto them of their ministers, we
think that these ceremonies are to be removed, as not only not profitable
(which they ought to be), but hurtful, if not to the ministers themselves that
use them, yet to their people to whom they are commanded by God to have
regard unto, in these things that are indifferent in their own natures. Now
I will come to that which you set down.*

Jo. WHITGIFT.

"Seeing that" not one word of that is true, and, if it were,
yet the error and false persuasion of the mind rather to be
reformed, than relented unto, I see no cause why this kind of
apparel (being commanded) ought not to be used, except you
will leave to every man liberty to do what him list, or suffer
the fancies of some to rule prince, council, bishops, church
and all.

¶ That Ministers were known in times
past by distinct apparel.

Chapter ii.   The First Division.

Admonition.

The eleventh :

^a1 Sam. ix. 28.² *In those days known ^aby voice, learning, and doctrine : now*
Matt. xxvi. 48.
Matt. xxvi. *they must be discerned from other by popish and antichristian*
73. *apparel, as cap, gown, tippet, &c.*

Answer to the Admonition, Page 53, Sect. ult., and
Page 54, Sect. 1, 2.

To prove that in those days ministers were known Vain and
childish alle-
by voice, learning, and doctrine, you cite the ninth of gations.³

[² 1 Sam. ix. 18. Adm.]   [³ This marginal note is not in Answ. 2.]

the first of Samuel, and the xxvi. of Matthew. In all
that ninth chapter of Samuel there is not one word
that maketh for this purpose, except you mean this,
that, when Saul asked of Samuel where the seer's house
was, Samuel answered again that he was the seer. If
this be to be "known by voice, learning, and doctrine,"
the ignorantest minister that is may soon be known by
his voice, learning, and doctrine; for, if you ask him,
Where is such a man? he can answer you, I am he. In
the xxvi. of Matthew, the first place, ver. 48, is this: "Now
he that betrayed him had given them a token, saying,
Whosoever I shall kiss, that is he: lay hold on him."
The multitude that came with Judas knew Christ by
Judas kissing of him; therefore in those days ministers
were "known by voice, learning, and doctrine." The
second place in that chapter alleged, ver. 73, is this:
"They that stood by said unto Peter, Surely thou art
also one of them; for even thy speech bewrayeth thee."
Peter was suspected by his speech to be a Galilean,
and therefore one of Christ's apostles; *ergo*, a minister

An argument
retorted[1]
upon the ad-
versary. was then "known by voice, learning, and doctrine." You
may as well of that place gather thus: Peter preached
not Christ then, but denied him; *ergo*, a minister must
be known by denying of Christ. Lord God, what dare
not these men allege for their purpose!

I know that the chief tokens whereby a minister
ought to be known is doctrine and learning; but you
childishly abuse the scripture, and play with the same.

A minister
may be
known by
his apparel. "Now," you say, "ministers must be discerned from
other by popish and antichristian apparel, as cap, gown,
tippet, &c." Do you think that, because a minister
ought to be known by his voice, learning, and doctrine,
therefore he may not be also known by his apparel?
John the Baptist had peculiar apparel, and was known
by it: Christ had distinct apparel from other; for his
coat had never a seam.

[☞ Calvin upon the xxiii. of Matthew proveth
out of the xiii. chap. of Zachary, that the prophets were
distinguished and known from other men by a certain
and peculiar form of cloaks; and addeth, that it is

[1 Arguments retorted, Answ. 2.]

not without reason that doctors should in gravity and *Apparel of ministers distinct.*
modesty of apparel differ from the common sort. ⟨⟩]²

T. C. Page 53, Sect. 3, 4.

The places alleged by the Admonition, with others which may be cited, howsoever you deride them, are notwithstanding probable conjectures* that ** They were quoted by the Admonition to prove that ministers were known by voice, learning, and doctrine; and you transfer them to apparel.*

neither Samuel, nor the apostles, nor our Saviour Christ, did wear any

1 Sam. ix. 18.³
Matt. xxvi. 73.³

distinct apparel from others which lived in their times.   For, if Samuel being then the seer had had a several apparel, which was proper to the seers, it is not like that Saul would have asked of himself where his house was.   And, if the apostles had worn a several apparel from the rest, they should not have been esteemed by so general and uncertain a note, as of speaking somewhat broadly, or, as I may term it, northernly; for it had been a surer note to have said, Thou art one of his apostles, because none weareth this apparel but his apostles; where there was a great number that spake Galilean-like, which were not of his apostles, nor disciples neither.   But let these go.   You say our

John xix. 23.³

Saviour Christ had a several apparel; because he had a coat without seam.   Assuredly you might use less scornfulness in rehearsing of other men's arguments, if for no other cause, yet for this, that they might take more pity of yours.

For what an argument is this! Our Saviour Christ did wear an under-garment, which could not be well parted, but with the spoil or marring of it; therefore he ware a several apparel from the rest.   It is true, John Bap-

Matt. iii. 4.³
2 Kings i. 8.³

tist had a several apparel; and, to help you, so had Elias, but to this end that, both by his unwonted apparel, and strange diet which he used of locusts and wild honey, the extraordinariness⁴ of his ministry might be set forth, and the people the rather moved to inquire of his office, whom they saw to vary so much from the common custom of other men.   But ministers now have no such extraordinary functions; therefore, by that reason of yours, they should not be severed from other men by any note of apparel.   You say you know that the chief notes of a minister are doctrine and learning : if you mean that the distinction of apparel must supply the rest, and that that also hath some force to com-mend their ministry, the prophets and apostles of our Saviour Christ left *A notable reason.*

us no perfect pattern of a minister, nor no sufficient glass to dress him by; whereof the most part never used any such several apparel, and none of them have left any commandment of it. *Untrue; as shall appear.*

Jo. Whitgift.

They be " conjectures " indeed, and mere " conjectures," *The unapt reasons of the Admonitors dissembled by T. C.*
but without all shadow of probability or reason; and, if you
will give me leave so to " conjecture," I will prove any thing.

[² This paragraph is inserted from Answ. 2.   See below, page 12.]
[³ These references are inserted from Repl. 2.]
[⁴ *Extraordinaries*, editt.; but, in the table of errata to Repl. 1, a notice is given to read *extraordinariness*.]

Apparel of ministers distinct.

But such slender "conjectures" argueth the slenderness of your proofs. The Admonition useth those places to prove that ministers were then "known by voice, learning, and doctrine;" which how they or you can conclude of them, I confess that I cannot imagine, except you will say, that Samuel said unto Saul, "I am the seer;" and they that stood by said unto Peter, "Even thy speech bewrayeth thee;" therefore, "ministers were known by voice, learning, and doctrine:" which is as much as though you would say, Saul knew Samuel by Samuel's own report; and a Welchman is known by his tongue; *ergo*, "ministers are known by voice, learning, and doctrine." Is not this a proper kind of reasoning? is this the reverence due to the scriptures, thus babishly to abuse them?

But say you, "if Samuel had had a several apparel proper to the seers, it was not like that Saul would have asked of him where his house was:" nay, you should rather have said, that it is like that Saul, being a rudesby, and brought up only in keeping of cattle, had never seen prophet before, and therefore could not know Samuel, what kind of apparel soever he had worn. And that this is true, that Saul did not know what a seer meant, and that he did never see any before, it may appear in the same chapter. And therefore saith

P. Martyr.

M. Martyr upon that 18. verse of the ix. chapter: "Saul is so rude in the commonwealth, and such a stranger from civil affairs, that he did not so much as know Samuel, although he were both judge of the people, and the magistrate, and prophet, and the captain of the host[1].

Prophets known by a distinct apparel. Calvin.

Moreover, M. Calvin, upon the xxiii. of Matthew, proveth out of the xiii. chapter of Zachary, that the prophets were distinguished and known from other men by a certain and peculiar form of cloaks[2]. And the very words of the text in the fourth verse of that chapter of Zachary doth evidently

Zech. xiii.

prove it; for there the Lord saith, "In that day shall the prophets be ashamed, &c.; neither shall they wear a rough

[1] Ita rudis est Saul in republica, et alienus ab omni luce civili, ut ne Samuelem quidem agnoscat, quamvis ille fuerit et judex populi, et magistratus, et propheta, et imperator militaris.—P. Martyr. Comm. in duos Libr. Samuel. Tigur. 1575. 1 Sam. cap. ix. fol. 54. 2.]

[2] Sed ex Zacharia apparet, prophetas certa pallii forma a reliquis fuisse distinctos. Nec vero ratione caruit doctores ita vestiri, ut in eorum habitu plus gravitatis et modestiæ quam in vulgari extaret.—Calvin. Op. Amst. 1667-71. Comm. in Harm. Euang. Matt. xxiii. Tom. VI. p. 257.]

garment to deceive." Upon the which words the note in the bible printed at Geneva is this: "They shall no more wear prophet's apparel, to make their doctrine seem more holy[3];" to the which also agreeth M. Calvin upon the same place, and addeth these words: "This is the sum, that this kind of vesture was not reproved in the false prophets; as some men unadvisedly do wrest this place to condemn long gowns, and whatsoever doth not please their waywardness, &c.[4]" Whereby it is evident, that the prophets did wear and were known by a peculiar kind of garment. If you inquire of the practice, we have divers examples; yea, even of Samuel, whom we now have in hand. For one thing, that persuaded Saul that he whom the witch had raised was Samuel, was the description of his apparel, 1 Sam. xxviii.: "There cometh up an old man with a mantle upon him; and Saul perceived that it was Samuel, &c." It cannot be thought that Saul conceived this opinion because she named an old man, but because she added his mantle and kind of attire. We read likewise of Elias, 2 *Reg*. i. and ii., that he had a hairy or rough mantle, agreeing to the description in the prophet Zachary, and a leather girdle, whereby he was known of Ahazia; and this is by you confessed. Elizeus succeedeth Elias both in office and vesture; and John Baptist did not only represent Elias his spirit, but also his kind of garment; for his rough garment of camel's hair, and leather girdle, are described by St Matthew, chap. iii. I suppose now that the manifest scripture, the opinion of learned interpreters, and the practice of so many notable prophets, do sufficiently justify my assertion, and are able to improve your "probable conjectures," as you term them.

Touching Peter, what kind of apparel soever he did wear, the matter is not great; it is the fond reason of theirs that I reprove, which is too too childish, as I have shewed before: and yet may it be supposed that Peter used all the means he could not to be known; and therefore, whether he cast off his uppermost garment, or changed it, it may be a question.

Margin notes: Apparel of ministers distinct. — 1 Sam. xxviii.

[3 The Bible transl. according to the Ebrew and Greeke, Lond. 1578. Zech. chap. xiii. fol. 375.]

[4 Hæc summa est, non reprehendi in pseudoprophetis vestem ipsam, quemadmodum quidam parum considerate arripiunt hunc locum, ut damnent et vestes oblongas, et quicquid displicet eorum morositati, &c.—Calvin. Op. Prælect. xxx. in Zach. cap. xiii. Tom. V. p. 552.]

Apparel of ministers distinct. Furthermore, it was in the night-time : finally, he was sus- pected by a maid to be one of Christ's disciples before he had spoken one word ; as it appeareth, John xviii. But, to let all this pass, what kind of reasoning call you this ? Peter was known by his voice ; *ergo*, he was not known by his apparel : or this ? Peter was known by his tongue to be a Galilean ; *ergo*, " ministers must be known by voice, learning, and doctrine ?"

The Admo- nition wanteth a proctor. Here you let slip, without any defence at all, that which is alleged by the Admonition out of the 48. verse of the xxvi. chapter of Matthew to the same purpose.

No man can deny but Christ's apparel differed from the rest, and that this was a rare kind of habit ; else would not the evangelist St John, chap. xix., have made so particular mention of it : wherefore that which I say is true, that even then ministers of the gospel might be known by their apparel, as Christ and John the Baptist ; and therefore not to be so strange a matter, that ministers should also now differ from other men in their apparel.

That which you speak of John Baptist confirmeth my saying, which is, that ministers of the gospel were then also known by their apparel ; and, if " unwonted apparel did set forth " John his " ministry, and moved them the rather to inquire of his office," why may it not have the same use now in like manner ? But I have used those examples only to shew the vanity of the Admonition, which would make the reader believe that in those days there was no distinction used in apparel.

Loose con- clusions of T. C. " Christ and his apostles have left a perfect pattern of a minister," touching conditions, qualities, and office ; so hath the scripture done of a magistrate, and of a subject also, of a master, and of a servant, &c. : but shall there be therefore no distinction in apparel betwixt them, or no external notes to discern them by ? What kind of argument call you this, " Christ and his apostles have left us a perfect pattern of the minister's office ;" *ergo*, the magistrate may not take any order for his apparel ? Truly these be loose conclusions, and (as you use to term them) " very pitiful arguments." Of the same force be these arguments : " Most of the apostles and prophets used no such several apparel ;" *ergo*, we may not use any several apparel ; and again : " None of them have left any commandment of it ;" *ergo*, it ought not to be.

The first reason hath thus many faults : first, the ante- Apparel of ministers distinct.
cedent is untrue; as I have shewed before out of this prophet
Zachary, and M. Calvin, &c. For the prophets were discerned from others by a certain kind of apparel; and it is not
able to be proved but that the apostles had several apparel
from the common sort of men. Secondly, it is no good
argument *a facto ad jus ;* but it is much worse, *a non facto* The ante-cedent of
ad non jus ; the which kind of argument Zuinglius divers T. C. infer-reth a con-
times reproveth in his treatises against the anabaptists; as I sequent against him-
have oftentimes said[1]. Thirdly, if some of the apostles, and self.
some of the prophets, did use several apparel (as the antece-
dent confesseth they did), though it doth not follow that we
must do so, yet it evidently proveth that we may do so,
being no commandment in the scripture to the contrary.

Your second argument is overthrown by your own self. The argu-ment of
For, page 13, you say that "many things are both commanded T. C. over-thrown by
and forbidden, of which there is no express mention in the his own as-sertion.
word; which are as necessary to be followed and avoided, Pag. 13. sect. 2.
as those whereof express mention is made :" which if it be
true (as it is most untrue), then things of less importance,
and not so necessary, though they be not expressedly commanded, yet may they be done. M. Calvin, in his book
against the anabaptists (for your arguments and theirs do
marvellously agree, and be builded upon the self-same founda-
tion), saith thus : " To disallow that which God never disallowed Calvin. adv. Anabap.
is, in a mortal man, a token of too much rashness and arrogancy.
But let us always hold this, that then the authority of God is
usurped, when that is condemned which he hath permitted.
But the scripture mentioneth in no place that the use of
armour is forbidden unto princes, &c.[3] " You may hereby
then perceive that M. Calvin doth not think this to be a
sound argument: It is not commanded; *ergo*, it is unlawful,
except it can be shewed to be prohibited : wherefore, if you
will condemn a several kind of apparel in ministers, you must

[1 H. Zvingl. Op. Tigur. 1581. Elench. contr. Catabapt. Pars II. foll. 9. 2,
13. See Vol. I. pages 179, note 5, 353, note 7.]

[2 See Vol. I. page 176.]

[3 Improbare autem quod nunquam improbavit Deus, nimiæ est, homini in-
quam mortali, temeritatis et arrogantiæ. Hoc autem perpetuo teneamus, usurpari
Dei auctoritatem, quum id quod permisit condemnatur. Nusquam vero scriptura mentionem facit, prohibitum esse principibus armorum usum adversus eos,
qui ipsis injuria molesti erunt.—Calvin. Op. Amst. 1667-71. Instr. adv. Anabapt.
Art. iv. Tom. VIII. p. 363.]

Apparel of
ministers
distinct.

shew some commandment or prohibition in the word of God
for the same; else are you "rash," and "arrogant," "usurping"
to yourself "God's authority;" as M. Calvin saith.

Chapter ii.   The Second Division.

Answer to the Admonition, Page 55, Sect. 1.

Eusebius saith that St John the apostle ware on his
head a leaf or thin plate like unto a bishop's mitre[1].

T. C. Page 53, Sect. ult.

*For want of store, and to make a long book, here is St John's mitre
rehearsed thrice in one leaf to the same purpose, and in the same words.
And, because it was not enough that M. Bullinger and M. Martyr should
speak of them, you have prevented them both, lest you should have seemed
to have brought nothing. If this be not coleworts twice sodden[2], I cannot
tell what is.*

But not once
digested or
answered.

Jo. Whitgift.

It is so often rehearsed, as you report, but by divers
authors, to shew their opinions of one and the self-same thing.
M. Gualter and M. Martyr, among other examples, use this of
St John to prove that in the ancient church there was a
peculiar fashion of apparel for priests.   I recite their words
as witnesses in this case worthy of credit; and by that
occasion this example of John is the oftener repeated; but this
is a sore matter to move such choler: you should quietly have
answered the reason, and left your heat of speech; but you
have done the contrary.

¶ That the Magistrate may appoint a
distinct apparel for Ministers.

Chapter iii.   The First Division.

Answer to the Admonition, Page 55, Sect. 1.

But what if none of the prophets, what if none of
the apostles (which you are not able to prove either of
the prophets or apostles) were known by their apparel?

Distinction
of apparel.[3]

[1 ... ἔτι δὲ καὶ Ἰωάννης ὁ ἐπὶ τὸ στῆθος τοῦ Κυρίου ἀναπεσών, ὃς ἐγενήθη
ἱερεὺς τὸ πέταλον πεφορεκώς, καὶ μάρτυς καὶ διδάσκαλος.—Euseb. in Hist.
Eccles. Script. Amst. 1695-1700. Lib. III. cap. xxxi. Lib. v. cap. xxiv. pp. 82,
155.]

[2 Crambe repetita.—Juv. VII. 154.]

[3 This marginal note is inserted from Answ. 2.]

May not therefore christian magistrates in christian commonweals, for order and decency, appoint a several kind of apparel, as well to ministers as to other states of men?

The magistrate may appoint apparel to ministers.

T. C. Page 54, Sect. 1.

You ask whether the christian magistrate may enjoin a several kind of apparel to the ministers. Either the cause is too weak which you defend, or else it hath gotten an evil patron, which would so gladly shift it, and change it with another: for this is another question, which you speak of. For, although that be granted unto you which you demand, yet you cannot conclude your cause. For, albeit the magistrate may command a several apparel, yet it followeth not that he may command this kind of popish apparel; and therefore what manner of argument is this of yours: The magistrate may command a several apparel; therefore he may command this? The college-walls will tell you that a man cannot conclude from the whole to the part affirmatively. So you see I might let you fish and catch nothing: but I am neither afraid nor ashamed to tell you the truth of that you ask; so far forth at least as I am persuaded. I think therefore it may be[4] such a kind of apparel as, the magistrate commanding it, the minister may refuse it, and such it may be as he may not refuse it. But, whatsoever apparel it be, this commandment cannot be without some injury done to the minister. For, seeing that the magistrate doth allow of him, as of a wise, learned, and discreet man, and trusteth him with the government of his people in matters between God and them, it were somewhat hard not to trust him with the appointing of his own apparel; and he is probably to be supposed that he hath discretion to wear his own gear comely and in order, that is able to teach others how they should wear theirs; and that he should be able to do that by his wisdom and learning, that others do without learning and great store of wisdom; and that he should keep order and decency in apparel, which hath learned in the school of Christ, which they do that had never other school-master than common sense and reason. And, if any minister be found to fault, in going either dissolutely, or too exquisitely and delicately, then the magistrate may punish him according to the disorder wherein he faulteth.

You might have learned other logic within the college-walls.

That is as much to say as, if you like it, you may use it.

You may say the like of judges.

Why may he not as well appoint him an order, as punish his disorder?

Jo. Whitgift.

If you had noted my order, and dealt sincerely, these words of yours might, with less discredit unto you, have been well forborne. For in this place I only prove that the ministers may be distinguished from other by a several kind of apparel. And I ask the question, whether a christian magistrate may appoint a several kind of apparel for order and decency. Of this apparel, which the Admonition calleth "an-

[4 He, Def. B.]

The magistrate may appoint apparel to ministers.

tichristian," I speak a little after. Your so usual kind of reasoning not *ad idem* argueth but lack of ability to answer the present purpose.

The question is incident to my cause; for, if the christian magistrate have authority to appoint a several kind of apparel to ministers, then it is also lawful for ministers to use it.

An argument holdeth from the whole to the part affirmatively sometime.

You say, "the college-walls will tell" me "that a man cannot conclude from the whole to the part affirmatively." Although my argument is neither *a genere*, nor *a toto*, but *ab oppositis relativis* (for it is this in effect: The magistrate may command it; *ergo*, the subjects must obey it), yet not "the college-walls" (which be dumb, and cannot speak), but the rules of logic telleth me, that, if by the whole you mean that which the logicians do call *genus*, then an argument from the whole to the part doth firmly hold affirmatively, if the whole be taken *universaliter*, "universally," as in this example: *Omne animal est sensibile; ergo, omnis homo est sensibilis. Omnis virtus est mediocritas; ergo, temperantia est mediocritas;* and so likewise: The magistrate hath authority to appoint any kind of habit for order or decency; *ergo*, he may appoint this or that kind of habit. If you mean by the "whole" that which the logicians do properly call *totum integrale*, as you seem to do, then the rules of logic tell you that *ab omni toto ad partes* (except it be *a toto in modo*) the argument is good affirmatively, and not otherwise. I am not disposed to boast of my knowledge in logic, nor to win any opinion thereof to myself by defacing or contemning of other. But, I thank God, I have sufficient to maintain whatsoever I have written, and to answer what you can reply to the contrary. But who would have thought that this spirit had been in T. C., a man supposed to be so mortified, &c.?

The magistrate's authority in appointing apparel abridged by T. C.

You answer my question indeed; but as good never a whit as never a deal the better. For in such sort you give the magistrate authority to command some kind of apparel to the minister, that he can command none unto him, "whatsoever it be, without some injury done to the minister;" which is a very strange answer. For first it restraineth the magistrate from having authority to command any kind of apparel; "for such," you say, "it may be, that the minister may refuse it:" then doth it accuse the magistrate of "doing injury," if he appoint even that kind of apparel that he may lawfully do. For you say, "whatsoever apparel it be, this commandment cannot be without some injury done to the minister." This is a very nice authority given to the magistrate : but let the reader well consider your words, and mark what authority you give to magistrates. One reason, whereby you would prove that the magistrate "doth the minister injury," if he command him to wear that kind of apparel which is lawful to be commanded, is this: "the magistrate doth allow of him as a wise, learned, and discreet man, &c. ;" and "therefore it were somewhat hard not to trust him with the appointing of his own apparel, &c." First, it is not true "that the magistrate doth allow of him, &c. :" for you will have him chosen by the parish ; and the magistrate cannot know what kind of ministers every parish doth choose. Secondly, if "the magistrate allow of him," it is upon condition that he be obedient to his laws. Thirdly, the magistrate may be deceived in him, and take him for another manner of man than he is. Last of all, how wise, how learned, how discreet soever he be, yet is it meet that he obey laws, and be subject unto good orders. May not other learned, wise, and discreet men allege this for themselves also, and say that they be able to govern themselves; what need they, like children, be prescribed what to do? And undoubtedly at this day this is the voice of divers; and this lesson of liberty belike they have learned of you.

The magistrate may appoint apparel to ministers.

I do most humbly desire those that have the care of this commonwealth but to consider what lieth hid even in these your words uttered in this place : they will then, no doubt, understand that you seek freedom from all laws of princes, and imagine that such perfection may be in men, that they shall not need to be governed by civil laws, but every man to be a law to himself.

Whereunto the assertion of the Replier tendeth.

And here your subtile dealing is worthy to be noted (which is very usual with you) in altering the case : for, whereas the kind of apparel is appointed to be a distinction from other men, and an external note of their calling, as it is in other sorts of men, as judges, serjeants, aldermen, &c., you (as though you knew not this) make your reader believe that the magistrate in appointing apparel doth mistrust the minister's "discretion in wearing his own gear comely, and in order ;" as if the meaning of the magistrate's commandment

herein were that ministers should not go either "dissolutely,"
or "disorderly," and not rather that all ministers should use
that form of decent apparel, whereby they might in one uniform order agree amongst themselves, and differ from other
states of people in her dominions. If you meant uprightly,
you would not so often deal in this order.

Chapter iii.   The Second Division.

Answer to the Admonition, Page 55, Sect. 1.

Judges, serjeants, aldermen, and citizens, are known
by their apparel; and why may not ministers be so likewise? are they not under subjection? be they not subject to civil laws and ordinances? ought they not to
obey their governors in all things not against the word
of God?

T. C. Page 54, Sect. 2.

*And, whereas you would prove that it may be done with the ministers
as it is done with judges, serjeants, aldermen, and sheriffs, the case is not
like. For, as for these which be in office, their robes and gowns may, as
their maces and swords, somewhat help to set forth the majesty and moderate pomp which is meet for the offices of justice which they execute, and
consequently to help to strike a profitable fear into their hearts which are
underneath them; which hath, nor can have, no place in the minister, whose
authority and power, as it is not outward, so can it not, nor ought not, to
borrow any credit of those[1] external shews. And the magistrate or the
city may seek some honour of the citizens, mustering as it were by numbers
in one livery: which ought not to be looked for at the minister's hand,
because he honoureth and serveth the magistrate another way, nor cannot
also, considering that they are scattered through all the land in every
town, one, or not so many as, being put in one livery, would make any
great shew to the honour and commendation of the town or city where they
remain.*

Jo. Whitgift.

I might as well answer for "judges, serjeants, &c.," as you
do for ministers, and say that, "seeing the magistrate doth
allow them as wise, learned, and discreet men, and trusteth
them with the government" of the commonwealth, "it were
something hard not to trust them with the appointing of their
own apparel:" but so should I reason fondly and seditiously;

[¹ These, Repl. 1 and 2.]

for it is meet that "learned, wise, and discreet men" should
be subject to laws; and, the wiser, the learneder, and the dis-
creeter they be, the more willing they are to obey the same.
And this kind of argument tendeth to nothing else but to the
animating of the subjects against the magistrate and against
the laws.

The magistrate may appoint apparel to ministers.

The subjects animated against the magistrate.

Though "the authority" that the minister ought to have
must come especially by his doctrine, good conversation, and
by his calling; yet is no outward means (being lawful) to be
refused, whereby the same may be helped; and he must labour
as much as he can, even by outward means (whether it be of
conversation, or of apparel, or any such like thing), to commend
his office and calling, and to procure reverence unto it.

A man might likewise say that princes, judges, and magistrates, are not to be reverenced for their apparel' sake, but
for the authority committed unto them by God; and yet is
it meet and convenient that they wear such kind of apparel
as may externally commend their authority.

The apparel of ministers declareth their modesty and
gravity, signifieth their calling and office, pertaineth to
comeliness and order, and therefore as convenient to be prescribed unto them as any other kind of apparel is to judges,
serjeants, or other civil magistrates. And, forasmuch as
ministers be members of the commonwealth, it is meet that
they should be subject to the orders of the same.

It is the honour of the prince to have all the states and
degrees of persons within her dominion in good order, be they
in city, or in town, together or separate; and therefore this
is nothing that you say, "the magistrate or the city may seek
some honour of the citizens, &c."

The judge, wheresoever he goeth, ought to be known by
his apparel, even so the minister; neither can you shew any
good reason to the contrary. M. Calvin upon the xxiii. of
Matthew saith, "it is meet that doctors should in gravity
and modesty of apparel differ from the common sort[2]."

Calvin.

[2 Calvin. Op. Amst. 1667-71. Comm. in Harm. Euang. Matt. xxiii. Tom. VI.
p. 257. See before, page 12, note 2.]

Distinction
of apparel
before the
pope's
tyranny.

Chapter iii. The Third Division.

T. C. Page 54, Sect. 3.

*And so you see your question answered, whereby appeareth they are
subjects, as other are, and to obey also sometimes, where the commandment
is not given upon good grounds.*

Jo. WHITGIFT.

It is answered indeed according to my expectation, but
neither according to the truth, nor the duty of a subject.

The distinction of apparel was appointed
for ministers before the pope's tyranny.

Chapter iv. The First Division.
Answer to the Admonition, Page 55, Sect. 2, 3.

Apparel ap-
pointed for
ministers
before the
pope's ty-
ranny[1].
If you doubt whether a particular kind of apparel,
differing from the laymen, were ever appointed for ministers in the church before the pope's tyranny, and
whether in these days it may be appointed in reformed
churches, or no, hear the judgment of Master Bullinger
and Master Gualter, in an epistle written by them to
Master N. and Master M. Their words be these:

Bullinger
and Gualter[2].
" That in the ancient church there was a particular
fashion of apparel for priests, it appeareth in the Ecclesiastical History of Theodoret, *Lib. ii. cap.* 27, and of
Socrates, *Lib. vi. cap.* 22. No man is ignorant, which
hath but lightly read over the monuments of the ancient
fathers, but that the ministers used a cloak in their service. And therefore I said before, that the diversity of
garments had not his original of the pope. Eusebius
citeth out of the ancient writers, that St John the apostle ware on his head a leaf or thin plate like unto a
Cyprian ware
white appa-
rel[3].
bishop's mitre. Pontius Diaconus witnesseth of St Cyprian the martyr that, when he offered his neck to the
executioner, he first gave him his cap, and the deacon
his upper garment, and so stood apparelled in white
Chrysostom[3].
linen. Moreover, Chrysostom maketh mention of white
apparel of ministers[4]." Hitherto Bullinger and Gualter.

[1 This note is inserted from Answ. 2.]
[2 Answer 2 has not *and Gualter.*]
[3 These marginal notes are inserted from Answ. 2.]
[4 Respondeo, In veteri ecclesia fuisse peculiarem presbyterorum vestitum

T. C. Page 54, Sect. 3, 4.

Distinction
of apparel
before the
pope's
tyranny.
The place of
Theodoret
falsified.

The place of Theodoret, cited by M. Bullinger, maketh mention of a golden cope, and that used by bishops of Hierusalem, and sold by Cyril, a good bishop; whereby he declared sufficiently his misliking of such garments in the ministry of the sacraments. In the place the which he citeth out of Socrates, there is one Sycinius, a Novatian bishop, is[5] said to have worn white apparel, and therefore is reprehended as for too much exquisiteness and fineness of apparel; and the bishop of Duresme, in a letter he wrote, allegeth the same place against the surplice[6]. A man would hardly believe that Master Bullinger should use these places to prove a distinction of apparel amongst the ministers. We are not ignorant but that a cloak hath been used of the ministers in their service; but that was no several apparel of the ministers, but common to all Christians[7], which with change of their religion changed also their apparel, as appeareth manifestly in Tertullian De Pallio.

As for the petalum that St John ware, I see not how it can be proved to be like a bishop's mitre. For the cap that St Cyprian gave the executioner argueth rather that it was the common apparel, which was customably worn; for else it would not have done him so much good. As for his upper garment, which he gave to his deacon, it was a token of his goodwill, which he would leave with him, as the practice hath been seen with us, and proveth nothing that it was any several apparel. As for the white linen garment which he suffered in, it cannot seem strange unto us which have seen the holy martyrs of the Lord executed in Smithfield and other places. And it is not to be thought that St Cyprian had so small judgment that, living in the time of persecution, he would, by wearing of some notable apparel from the rest, as it were betray himself into the hands of his enemies, unless all the Christians had done so too for clearer and more open profession of their faith, and greater detestation of the contrary religion;

apparet ex historia ecclesiastica Theodoreti, Li. 2. ca. 27 [See below, page 24, note 5]. Et Socratis Li. 6. ca. 22 [See below, page 25, note 7]. Pallio in sacris usos esse ministros, nemo ignorat, qui veterum monumenta obiter inspexit. Ideo antea submonui, diversitatem indumentorum non habere suam originem a papa. Eusebius certe testatur ex vetustissimis scriptoribus Johannem apostolum Ephesi petalum seu laminam gestasse pontificalem in capite [See before, page 16, note 1]. Et de Cypriano martyre testatur Pontius diaconus, quod cum jugulum carnifici præbere vellet, ei prius birrhum dedisse, diacono dalmaticam, atque sic ipsum in lineis stetisse indutum [See below, page 25, note 9]. Præterea vestis candidæ ministrorum meminit Chrysostomus [See below, page 24, note 2]. Ac certum est Christianos, cum a gentilismo converterentur ad evangelium et ecclesiam, pro toga induisse pallium. Ob quam rem cum ab infidelibus irriderentur, Tertullianus librum de Pallio scripsit eruditissimum [See below, page 24, note 1].—Bullinger's Letter to Sampson and Humphrey, 1566, in Strype, Annals, Vol. I. Append. No. xxiv. This letter is also printed by Burnet, Coll. Vol. III. Book vi. No. lxxvii.]

[5 Bishop which is, Repl. 2.]

[6 Bp. Pilkington's Works, Park. Soc. Edit. Letter to Earl of Leicester, p. 661.]

[7 All the Christians, Repl. 1 and 2.]

Distinction
of apparel
before the
pope's
tyranny. *as Tertullian and the Christians in his time did by the wearing of a cloak*[1] :
which reason may be also alleged of the petalum *of St John. It is true*
Chrysostom maketh mention of a white garment[2]*, but not in*
commendation of it, but rather to the contrary : for he sheweth Hom. 60.[3] ad
Pop. Antio-
chi.
that the dignity of their ministry, their safety and crown, was in
taking heed that none unmeet were admitted to the Lord's supper, not in
going about the church with a white garment. And it is easily to be seen
Scripture
fondly
alleged. *by Salomon, in his Ecclesiastes, that to wear a white garment* Eccles. ix. 8.[4]
was greatly esteemed in the East parts, and was ordinary to
those that were in any estimation, as the wearing of black with us; and
therefore was no several apparel for the ministers, or for to execute their
ministry in.

Jo. Whitgift.

Theod. Lib. ii.
cap. 27.
Constantius. The words of Theodoret be these : "But the tale, which
they had raised of Cyrillus, did chiefly displease the emperor.
For, whereas the most worthy king Constantine had, for the
honour of the church of Hierusalem, given unto Macarius,
bishop in the same city, a holy garment (precious and wrought
with gold) which he should wear when he ministered the
holy baptism, they reported that Cyril sold it, &c.[5]" Here
you see that Theodoret counteth it but a fable that Cyril
should make any such sale; and those that say he sold it
declare that it was not for any disallowing of the vesture,
Soz. Lib. iv.
cap. 25. but for necessity of the poor in the time of famine; as Sozo.
Lib. iv. cap. 25[6], testifieth.

You deal with M. Bullinger as you do with me, that is,
you pervert his meaning, and allege that out of Socrates that

[1 Gaude pallium et exulta, melior jam te philosophia dignata est, ex quo
Christianum vestire cœpisti.—Tertull. Op. Lut. 1641. De Pall. 5. p. 139.]

[2 Διὰ τοῦτο ὑμᾶς ὁ Θεὸς ἐτίμησε ταύτην τὴν τιμήν, ἵνα τὰ τοιαῦτα διακρί-
νητε· τοῦτο ὑμῶν ἡ ἀξία, τοῦτο ἡ ἀσφάλεια, τοῦτο ὁ στέφανος ἅπας, οὐχ ἵνα
λευκὸν χιτωνίσκον καὶ ἀποστίλβοντα παραβαλλόμενοι περιίητε.—Chrysost. Op.
Par. 1718-38. In Matt. Hom. lxxxii. Tom. VII. p. 789. Conf. Op. Lat. Basil.
1547. Ad Pop. Ant. Hom. lx. Tom. V. col. 397.]

[3 6, Answ. Def. A. and B.]

[4 The verse is added from Repl. 2.]

[5 Οὐχ ἥκιστα δὲ αὐτὸν χαλεπῆναι πεποίηκεν, ἃ κατὰ τοῦ Κυρίλλου συν-
τέθεικε. τὴν γὰρ ἱερὰν στολὴν ἣν ὁ πανεύφημος Κωνσταντῖνος ὁ βασιλεύς, τὴν
Ἱεροσολύμων ἐκκλησίαν γεραίρων, δεδώκει τῷ Μακαρίῳ τῷ τῆς πόλεως ἐκείνης
ἀρχιερεῖ, ἵνα ταύτην περιβαλλόμενος τὴν τοῦ θείου βαπτίσματος ἐπιτελῇ
λειτουργίαν· ἐκ χρυσῶν δὲ αὕτη κατεσκεύαστο νημάτων· πεπρακέναι τὸν Κύ-
ριλλον ἔφη, κ.τ.λ.—Theod. in Hist. Eccles. Script. Amst. 1695-1700. Lib. II.
cap. xxvii. p. 111.]

[6 ...λιμοῦ καταλαβόντος τὴν Ἱεροσολύμων χώραν, ὡς εἰς ἐπίσκοπον ἔβλεπε
τὸ τῶν δεομένων πλῆθος, τῆς ἀναγκαίας τροφῆς ἀπορούμενον· ἐπεὶ δὲ χρήματα
οὐκ ἦν οἷς ἐπικουρεῖν ἔδει, κειμήλια καὶ ἱερὰ παραπετάσματα ἀπέδοτο· κ.τ.λ.—
Soz. in eod. Lib. IV. cap. xxv. p. 474.]

he meant not, and keep that in silence which maketh directly Distinction of apparel before the pope's tyranny.
Lib. vi. cap. 22.
for this purpose. Socrates there sheweth how Sycinius being
a Novatian did wear white apparel, and, when he was for the
same reproved, he answered that it was nowhere written that
priests should wear black apparel, and bade them prove by
scripture that priests ought to wear black apparel[7]. Whereby
it is plain that ministers in those days did wear black apparel, and were thereby known, and that Sycinius being an
heretic refused so to do, using the same arguments that you
do, *scilicet*, that "it is nowhere commanded that priests
should wear such kind of vesture." Wherefore the story is
aptly alleged by Master Bullinger to prove a several kind of
apparel, and it insinuateth what manner of men those be that
contemn the common order in such matters, and love to be
singular, like unto Sycinius the Novatian heretic.

As for St John his *petalum*, you hear what these learned
men say, who no doubt have good ground of their judgment.
Neither would Eusebius have made any mention of it, if it
had not been a kind of apparel whereby St John was known.
The words of Eusebius, *Lib. iii. cap.* 31, be these: "John, Euseb. Lib. iii. cap. 31.
which leaned upon the breast of the Lord, being a priest, wore
a leaf or thin plate[8]." Whereby it is evident that this apparel was peculiar to St John in the respect that he was
a priest. That Cyprian his apparel was not usual and
"common" for other men to wear, it may appear by this,
that the names of his apparel be expressed; for that which
he gave to the executioner is called *birrus*, that is, "a thin
plate," and that which he gave to the deacon was called *dalmatica*, a garment with long sleeves: as for the white linen,
it is not there mentioned as any distinct kind of apparel[9].

The words of Chrysostom do manifestly declare that then
such kind of garment was used in the administration of the
sacraments; neither do his words tend anything at all to the
disallowing of it; for they be spoken by the way of com-

[7 ...ἄλλοτε δὲ Ἀρσάκιον τὸν ἐπίσκοπον κατὰ τιμὴν ὁρῶν, ἠρωτήθη ὑπό τινος
τῶν περὶ Ἀρσάκιον, διὰ τί ἀνοίκειον ἐπισκόπῳ ἐσθῆτα φοροίη, καὶ ποῦ γέγραπται
λευκὰ τὸν ἱερωμένον ἀμφιέννυσθαι· ὁ δὲ, σὺ πρότερον, ἔφη, εἰπὲ ποῦ γέγραπται
μέλαιναν ἐσθῆτα φορεῖν τὸν ἐπίσκοπον· κ.τ.λ.—Socr. in eod. Lib. vi. cap. xxii.
p. 270.]

[8 Euseb. in eod. Lib. iii. cap. xxxi. p. 82. See before, p. 16, note 1.]

[9 Et ita idem Cyprianus in agrum Sexti productus est, et ibi se lacerna birro
expoliavit, et genu in terra flexit, et in orationem se Domino prostravit. Et cum
se dalmatica expoliasset, et diaconibus tradidisset, in linea stetit, et cœpit spicu-
latorem sustinere.—Cypr. Op. Oxon. 1682. Cypr. Vit. præf. p. 13.]

Distinction
of apparel
before the
pope's
tyranny.
parison; and negatives by comparison are not simple negatives
(as I told you before), but by the way of comparison : and
therefore, when Chrysostom saith that "the dignity of their
ministry, &c. was in taking heed that none unmeet were
admitted to the Lord's supper, not in going about the church
with a white garment[1]," he doth not disallow going about the
church in a white garment, but he saith that it is not in
comparison of the other so greatly to be regarded.

T. C. doth
allege the
scripture
fondly and
carelessly.
If Salomon in that place meant any such matter, yet is
it no proof at all for this that you allege it for : there was a
great number of years betwixt Salomon his time and Chrysostom's, and all kind of customs much altered; and therefore
I marvel what you mean to bring in Salomon to prove that
the white apparel used by ministers of the church in the
administration of the sacraments in the time of Chrysostom
was "not several," but common and usual apparel. But that
the reader may understand your carelessness in alleging the
scriptures, I will set down the words of Salomon in that ix.
Eccles. ix.
chapter, and 8. verse: "At all times let thy garments be
white; and let not oil be lacking upon thine head." In the
which sentence, by the white garment is meant either in-
nocency of life, as Pellican doth interpret it[2], or joy and
mirth, as some other think[3]; but there can be nothing less
gathered thereof than that there was at that time any such
usual kind of apparel. And to what purpose should he have
so said, if it had been so ? The metaphors and figurative
kind of speeches that Salomon useth in those books cannot
be unknown to any. You do not trouble me with many
quotations; but those that be are passing strange. And surely
I cannot but marvel how you dare be so bold as thus to abuse
the scriptures.

Be it that this is the saying of belly-gods (according to
the note of the Geneva bible[4], whereupon I think you ground

---

[1 Chrysost. Op. Par. 1718-38. In Matt. Hom. lxxxii. Tom. VII. p. 789.
See before, page 24, note 2.]

[2 Conversatione honesta ornetur omnis habitus corporis tui.—Comment.
Biblior. Op. C. Pellican. Tigur. 1536-46. Eccles. cap. ix. 8. Tom. III. fol.
260. 2.]

[3 Omni tempore sint vestimenta tua candida, idem est ac si dicat, lætare, sis
hilari animo.—J. Brent. Op. Tubing. 1576-90. Explic. Eccles. Salom. cap. ix.
Tom. IV. p. 91.]

[4 Rejoice, be merry, and spare for no cost. thus speak the wicked belly-
gods.—The Bible, transl. according to the Ebrew and Greeke. Lond. 1578. Not. in
Eccles. ix. fol. 279. 2.]

your assertion), to move unto mirth and pastime; doth it there- Distinction of apparel before the pope's tyranny.
fore follow that this was an usual kind of apparel in Salomon
his time? Or, if it were then, must it be also in Chrysostom
his time? Or, if it were so in his time, might it not also be
used of the ministers in the administration of the sacraments,
as a comely and decent vesture, and differing from the rest?
If I had the gift of jesting, that you are so excellent in, what
sport could I make with this, and a number such like places!

Chap. iv. The Second Division.

Answer to the Admonition, Page 56, Sect. 1.

Peter Martyr likewise, in an epistle written to Master
Hoper, saith on this sort: " I will not grant that these P. Martyr[5].
diversities of vestures have their beginnings of the pope,
forsomuch as I read in the ecclesiastical history, how
that John the apostle wore at Ephesus, where he dwelled, John's apparel.
a bishop's apparel, terming it *petalum, seu lamina ponti-*
ficalis. As touching St Cyprian the holy martyr, Pontius
the deacon writeth, that a little before he should be be-
headed he gave unto him that was appointed to behead
him his vesture called *birrus,* after he had put it off, and
to the deacons he gave his other vesture called *dalma-*
tica, and so stood in linen. Chrysostom maketh mention
of the white vesture of the ministers of the church[6]."
Hæc ille.

T. C. Page 55, Sect. 1.

The reasons that M. Peter Martyr useth are the same before; and how
he hath also condemned [7] *them it shall appear, with M. Bucer's judgment*
of these things, in the end of the book [8].

Jo. Whitgift.

In the mean time you see how these notable learned men
agree in one truth against you; neither are you able to shew
any contrariety in this point uttered by him, or M. Bucer; as
I trust shall then appear.

[5] This note is not in Answ. 2.]

[6] P. Martyr's Letter to John Hoper Byshop, &c. at the end of A briefe
examination for the tyme, of a certaine declaration, &c.—Lond. Jugge, foll. B 4, C 1.
Conf. P. Martyr. Epist. Theolog. ad calc. Loc. Com. Heidelb. 1613. p. 1087.]

[7] Contemned, Def. B.]

[8] Cartwright here refers to some testimonies which he says he had collected
out of the later writers and placed at the end of his Reply.]

Distinction
of apparel
before the
pope's
tyranny.
Socrates[1].

Chap. iv.   The Third Division.

Answer to the Admonition, Page 56, Sect. 2, 3.

Socrates also, in the second book of his Ecclesiastical History, saith that the father of Eustathius, being bishop

of Cæsarea, did deprive the said Eustathius his son, being a priest, of his place and dignity, because he wore apparel not comely for a priest to wear, nor agreeable to his order[2].

Therefore it is certain that ministers, even from the apostles' time, have had a distinct and several kind of apparel from other men.

T. C. Page 55, Sect. 2.

As for Eustathius his deprivation because he did not wear apparel meet for a minister, it maketh not to this purpose one whit. For I have shewed that, if a[4] minister go like a ruffian or swash-buckler, or in the bravery of a courtier, that it is meet he should be punished according to the quantity of the fault. And that it is so to be understanded, it appeareth manifestly by the council of Gangris[5], which did therefore confirm the same deposing, because he ware a stranger apparel and the habit of a philosopher, and caused all his fellows to do so. Therefore I marvel what you mean to allege this place. It is also alleged of Nicephorus[6] : in Lib. ix. cap.*

No more is
there in my
Answer.

neither of the places there is any Eustathius, the son of Eusta- 45. *thius, but of Eulabius, or, as Nicephorus readeth, Eulalius. And therefore your conclusion is both untrue and uncertain, that since the apostles' times there hath been a distinct and several apparel of the ministers from the rest.*

Jo. Whitgift.

The words of Socrates, *Lib. ii. cap.* 43, be these : "Eustathius, the bishop of Sebastia in Armenia, was not admitted to make his defence, because he was deposed before of his father, bishop of Cæsarea in Cappadocia, for that he wore an undecent

garment[7]." The canon of the council of Gangris : "If any

[1] Instead of these names Answ. 2 has *Eustathius deposed for unorderly apparel.*]

[2] See below, note 7.]

[3] This marginal note is inserted from Answ. 2.]

[4] Any, Repl. 1, 2, and Def. A.]   [5] See below, note 8.]

[6] Niceph. Call. Eccles. Hist. Lut. Par. 1630. Lib. ix. cap. xlv. Tom. I. p. 795.]

[7] Εὐστάθιος δὲ ὁ τῆς ἐν Ἀρμενίᾳ Σεβαστείας, οὔτε εἰς ἀπολογίαν ἐδέχθη, διότι ὑπὸ Εὐλαλίου τοῦ ἰδίου πατρός, καὶ ἐπισκόπου Καισαρείας τῆς ἐν Καππαδοκίᾳ, ἤδη πρότερον καθήρητο, ἐπειδὴ ἀνάρμοστον τῇ ἱερωσύνῃ στολὴν ἠμφίεστο.—Socr. in Hist. Eccles. Script. Amst. 1695-1700. Lib. ii. cap. xliii. p. 128.]

man thinketh it to avail unto his holy purpose (to wit, of con- Distinction
tinency) that he wear a cloak, as if thereby he should attain of apparel
before the
unto righteousness, and reprehendeth or condemneth them pope's
tyranny.
which wear the ornament called *byrrhus*, and the other common and usual garment, let him be accursed. Dist. 30.[8]"
Both by Socrates, and also by this canon of the council, it
doth appear that Eustathius and his adherents were condemned for using a new and singular kind of apparel from
that which then was commonly and customably used of all
bishops. That in the conclusion of this council, which is
spoken of modest, simple, and decent apparel, against that
which is loose and dissolute[9], hath no colour of proving anything against Eustathius his contempt and singularity, neither
doth it in any one word signify that he was not deprived
for refusing to wear the ordinary and accustomed apparel to
priests.

You say that "in neither of the places there is any T. C. taketh
advantage
Eustathius, the son of Eustathius, but of Eulabius, &c." Gladly where none is
given.
would you have something to dally with, if possibly you
could tell how. Are you not ashamed thus to deal? Where
do I say that "Eustathius was the son of Eustathius?" Had
you not my book before you? Be not these my words:
"Socrates, in the second book of his Ecclesiastical History, saith
that the father of Eustathius, being bishop of Cæsarea, did
deprive the said Eustathius his son, being a priest, &c.?" I
neither name him Eustathius, nor Eulabius, nor Eulalius:
therefore my conclusion is both true and certain; and you do
but seek occasion of quarrelling.

[8 Εἴ τις ἀνδρῶν διὰ νομιζομένην ἄσκησιν περιβολαίῳ χρῆται, καὶ ὡς ἂν ἐκ
τούτου τὴν δικαιοσύνην ἔχων καταψηφίσοιτο τῶν μετ᾽ εὐλαβείας τοὺς βήρους
φορούντων, καὶ τῇ ἄλλῃ κοινῇ καὶ ἐν συνηθείᾳ οὔσῃ ἐσθῆτι κεχρημένων, ἀνάθεμα
ἔστω.—Concil. Gangrens. can. 12. in Concil. Stud. Labb. et Cossart. Lut. Par.
1671-2. Tom. II. col. 419. Conf. Corp. Jur. Canon. Lugd. 1624. Decret. Gratian.
Decr. Prim. Pars, Dist. xxx. can. 15. col. 147.]

[9 ...καὶ λιτότητα καὶ εὐτέλειαν ἀμφιασμάτων δι᾽ ἐπιμέλειαν μόνον τοῦ σώμα-
τος ἀπεριέργου ἐπαινοῦμεν· τὰς δὲ ἐκλύτους καὶ τεθρυμμένας ἐν τῇ ἐσθῆτι προό-
δους οὐκ ἀποδεχόμεθα.—Ibid. can. 21. col. 424. Conf. Decret. Gratian. Decr.
Prim. Pars, Dist. xli. can. 5. col. 200.]

That the apparel now used is not popish or
antichristian; and that things invented by evil men may be
used of Christians.

Chapter v.   The First Division.
Answer to the Admonition, Page 56, Sect. 4.

But "cap, gown, tippet, &c." you say, is "popish and
antichristian:" this is only said, and not proved. If you
call it popish and antichristian, because it was first invented by an antichristian pope, it is first to be considered whether that be true or no: then, if it be true,
whether everything so invented is of necessity to be
abolished.

T. C. Page 55, Sect. 3.

Then the
case is
altered of
late.

The matter lieth not in that, whether these things were first invented by
papists, or, being devised of others, were after taken by papists[1]; but the
matter standeth in this, that they have been used of the papists as notes and
marks and sacraments of their abominations.

Jo. Whitgift.

You alter the case as oft as it pleaseth you; and liberty
you have to affirm or deny what you list, when you list,
and where you list, without controlment: for hitherto I am
sure your chief grounds against the apparel hath been, that
the same was invented by popes and used by them. But
take your pleasure: that which followeth in my Answer to the
Admonition is directly against this your ground also, if you
will stand to it and not shrink.

Chapter v.   The Second Division.
Answer to the Admonition, Page 56, Sect. ult.

Stephanus, a
good bishop,
invented this
apparel[2].

It is certain that this apparel of ministers, which you
find yourselves so much grieved with, was appointed long
before the church of Rome declined from the purity of
Christ's religion: for Stephanus, bishop of Rome, who
lived the year of our Lord 256, is said to be the first

[1 By the papists, Repl. 1, 2, and Def. A.]
[2 Answ. 2 adds *of ministers*.]

which did appoint this kind of apparel for ministers[3]; neither are you able to shew that any antichristian pope invented the same.   But admit it were so, that this apparel was either borrowed of the Jews, or taken from the Gentiles, or invented and used by some antichristian pope; yet it followeth not but that the same may be well used of Christians in the church of Christ.

Things invented by evil men may be used of Christians.

Jo. Whitgift.

To this T. C. speaketh not one word, good or evil.

Chap. v.   The Third Division.

Answer to the Admonition, Page 57, Sect. 1; and Page 58, Sect. 1.

Augustine, in his epistle *Ad Publicolam,* hath this notable saying : *Et cum templa, idola, luci, et si quid hujusmodi data potestate evertuntur, quamvis manifestum est, cum id agimus, non ea nos honorare, sed potius detestari, ideo tamen in usus nostros privatos duntaxat et proprios non debemus inde aliquid usurpare, ut appareat nos pietate ista destruere, non avaritia. Cum vero in usus communes, non proprios ac privatos, vel in honorem Dei veri convertuntur, hoc de illis fit, quod de ipsis hominibus, cum ex sacrilegis et impiis in veram religionem mutantur. &c.[4]:* "When temples, idols, groves, and such like things, by authority be overthrown, although it is manifest when we do that we honour them not, but detest them; yet for all that we may not therefore convert them

Augustinus.

[3 Vestimenta ecclesiastica, quibus Domino ministratur, et sacrata debent esse, et honesta: quibus aliis in usibus non debent frui, quam in ecclesiasticis et Deo dignis officiis : quæ nec ab aliis debent contingi, aut ferri, nisi a sacratis hominibus.—Steph. Episc. Epist. i. in Corp. Jur. Canon. Lugd. 1624. Decret. Gratian. Decr. Tert. Pars, De Consecr. Dist. i. can. 42. col. 1900. Conf. Plat. De Vit. Pont. Col. 1551. Steph. I. p. 30.]

[4 Et cum &c. mutantur. Hoc Deus intelligitur docuisse illis testimoniis quæ ipse posuisti, cum de luco alienorum deorum jussit ligna ad holocaustum adhiberi ; et de Iericho, ut omne aurum, argentum, et æramentum inferretur in thesauros Domini. Quapropter etiam illud quod in Deuteronomio scriptum est, *Non concupisces argentum vel aurum illorum, nec accipies inde tibi, ne excedas propter illud, quoniam abominatio est Domino Deo tuo: &c.:* satis apparet aut ipsos privatos usus in talibus esse prohibitos, aut ne sic inde aliquid inferatur in domum ut honoretur : tunc est enim abominatio et exsecratio; non cum talium sacrilegus honor apertissima destructione subvertitur.—August. Op. Par. 1679-1700. Ad Public. Epist. xlvii. 3. Tom. II. col. 111.]

Things
wickedly
invented
may have
good use.
Private use
of idolatrous
things for-
bidden[1].

or use them to our own private uses only and commodity, that it may appear that we destroy them for religion'
sake, and not for covetousness. But, when they are converted, not into private and our own use, but into common uses, or to the honour of the true God, that is done
and brought to pass in them which is done and brought
to pass in men themselves, when of idolaters and wicked
persons they are changed into true religion. This hath
God himself taught in those testimonies, which thou thyself hast used, when as God himself commanded that of
that same grove which was dedicated to strange gods
there should be wood taken for his sacrifices; and, of
Hierico, that all the gold and silver and brass should be
brought into the treasury of the Lord. Wherefore that
also, which is written in Deuteronomy, 'Thou shalt not
covet their silver nor their gold, neither shalt thou take
anything thereof to thyself, lest thou offend; because it is
abomination unto the Lord thy God, &c.;' it manifestly
appeareth that either private uses is forbidden in such
things, or that nothing should so be brought into thy
house that it be honoured; for then it is abomination,
&c." Hitherto Augustine.

Idolatrous
things turned
to common
use.

By these words it doth manifestly appear that even
things altogether dedicated to idols, and used in idolatry,
may be converted to common uses, and used in the service of God and to his honour, but not to private uses,
nor superstitiously.

[Calvin upon the first of Matt. v. 37. *Purus est multarum rerum usus, quarum vitiosa est origo*[2]: "The use of
many things is pure, the original whereof is evil[3]."]

T. C. Page 55, Sect. 4.

This shift is
answered
afterward.

    *As for Augustine his place, it is to be understanded of such things as
have a necessary use, and therefore may not be taken away from us by the
superstition of men. For so we might also be deprived of the sun, which is
as it were the life of the world, because the sun hath been worshipped. But
that St Augustine did not like of this kind of retaining ceremonies, it may appear. "Do you ask," saith he, "how the pagans*
*may be won, how they may be brought to salvation? forsake their
solemnities, let go their toys; and then, if they agree not unto our*

August. Tom.
x. De Verbis
Domini in
Mattheum,
Serm. ix.[4]

[1 Private use forbidden of things idolatrous, Answ. 2.]
[2 Calvin. Op. Amst. 1667-71. Comm. in Harm. Euang. Tom. VI. p. 73.]
[3 This paragraph is inserted from Answ. 2.]   [4 Serm. 6, Repl. 1 and 2.]

truth, let them be ashamed of their fewness[5];" whereby he sheweth that the Things
nearest way to gain the papists is to forsake their ceremonies. And yet I wickedly
would be loth to say, either with you, or with Augustine, that it is not lawful may have
for a man to make a popish[6] surplice a shirt for himself, or to take the good use.
gold of a cope which he had[7] bought, and convert it to his private use.
And herein we do nothing disagree with St Augustine, which grant that
surplices, and copes, and tippets, and caps, may be applied to a good use,
either common or private, as they will best serve; but we deny that that
use is in distinguishing either the ministers from other men, or the ministers
executing their ecclesiastical function from themselves when they do not
exercise that office.

Jo. Whitgift.

The words of Augustine be plain, neither can they be so
shifted off. And it maketh evidently against your distinction
that he saith, "such things may not be converted into private
uses." A man may cavil with the most manifest authorities
either of scriptures or fathers that can be; but every shift
and cavil is not a sufficient answer. This proposition is by
these words of Augustine directly proved, "that things altogether dedicated to idols and used in idolatry may be afterward used in the service of God, and to his honour;" which is
the state of our question. And, because this is a material
point, and peradventure St Augustine his authority is not
much regarded of you, I will set down M. Calvin his opinion
also touching the same matter, who, in his Harmony upon the
books of Moses, upon these words in the xxiii. of Exodus, ver.
24, "Thou shalt utterly overthrow and break in pieces their
images," saith thus: "We make it not now any scruple of Calvin.
conscience to retain still those churches which were polluted
with idols, and to put them to better use, because that which is
added to the law *propter consequentiam* (as they term it)
doth not bind us. I grant that all those things which do tend
to the planting of superstition ought to be taken away, so that,
by precise urging of that which is of itself indifferent, we be
not in too much rigour superstitious[8]." The place is worth

---

[5] Si quæritis unde vincantur pagani, unde illuminentur, unde ad salutem
vocentur; deserite solemnitates eorum, deserite nugas ipsorum: et si non con-
sentiunt veritati nostræ, erubescant paucitati suæ.—August. Op. Par. 1679-1700.
De Verb. Evang. Matt. viii. Serm. lxii. cap. vii. 11. Tom. V. col. 362.]

[6] Of a popish, Repl. 1, 2, and Def. A.]

[7] Hath, Repl. 1, 2, and Def. A.]

[8] Neque enim nobis hodie religio est templa retinere quæ polluta fuerunt
idolis, et accommodare in meliorem usum: quia nos non obstringit quod propter

the noting, it fully overthroweth your grounds against the apparel.

St Augustine, in that sermon quoted in your margent, speaketh against such as professing Christianity did notwithstanding resort to the temples of the pagans at their solemnities and feasts, thinking it sufficient if they did in heart detest the idols, though in body they were present in their temples and at their feasts; much like unto those that think it sufficient to serve God in heart, though in body they be present at the mass and idolatrous service.   That this is the meaning of Augustine in that place, it may evidently appear to all such as will peruse it: upon this Augustine bringeth in these words:

"If you ask how the pagans may be overcome, won, and illuminated, how they may be brought to salvation; forsake all their solemnity, let go their toys; and then, if they agree not unto the truth, let them be ashamed of their fewness[1]." It was in St Augustine's time, as it is in some places at this day, where in some one city there be churches both for the gospel, and for the mass also: it is not meet that such as profess the gospel should resort to the mass; for, besides that they offend God in being present at idolatrous service, they also give occasion to the papists to think better of their mass, because they see it frequented of such as seem to profess the gospel, and thereby also persuade themselves of a greater multitude that embraceth their religion: wherefore one way to convert them is to abstain from their churches, that they may understand both our misliking of their service, and their own paucity also.   And that this is meant of by Augustine in that place, it may also appear by these words in the same sermon: "The pagans say in their hearts, Why forsake we our gods, seeing the Christians themselves worship them as well as we[2]?" And again: "Behold against what true God thou dost offend, whiles thou fallest down before false gods[3]."   St Augustine

consequentiam (ut loquuntur) legi additum est. Fateor quidem, quæcunque ad superstitionem fovendam spectant, e medio tollenda esse, modo ne præcise urgendo quod per se medium est, simus in nimio rigore superstitiosi.—Calvin. Op. Amst. 1667-71. Harm. in Quat. Libr. Mos. Sec. Præcept. Tom. I. p. 472.]

[1 August. Op. Par. 1679-1700. De Verb. Evang. Matt. viii. Serm. lxii. cap. vii. 11. Tom. V. col. 362. See above, page 33, note 5.]

[2 Dicunt enim in cordibus suis, Quare nos relinquamus deos, quos Christiani ipsi nobiscum colunt?—Id. ibid. cap. vi. 9. col. 360.]

[3 Ecce in quem verum Deum peccas, dum discumbis apud deos falsos.—Id. ibid. col. 361.]

speaketh not one word in all that sermon of "ceremonies," or Things wickedly invented may have good use. anything else taken from the gentiles, and by Christians converted to other uses; much less of any such matter as we have now in question. And therefore you do but abuse the reader by reciting certain words of St Augustine, without the circumstances which open the true meaning of them.

I praise your wit for saying that "such things may be converted to private uses;" for deny that (as St Augustine plainly doth), and I shall be bound unto you that your doctrine shall have the fewer fautors by three parts: for surely many that condemn your opinions in heart, for hope of private commodity that might come unto them by the dissolution of colleges, churches, &c., do seem very well to like of them. Wherefore teach them (if you be wise) that such things may be converted to their private uses, whatsoever Augustine saith to the contrary.

Augustine saith also that they may be converted *in honorem Dei*[4], "unto the honour of God." What say you to that? As for your "denying that that use is in distinguishing either the ministers from other men, &c.," because it is but your bare denial against all the proofs alleged, I will with affirming the contrary pass it over.

Chapter v. The Fourth Division.

Answer to the Admonition, Page 58, Sect. 2, 3.

Peter Martyr in the epistle before mentioned touching this matter writeth on this sort:

"But let us consider your other argument, that is to P. Martyr. say, it is not lawful to use these kind of vestures, because they were invented of[5] the pope's tyranny. In this point I do not well perceive how it may be affirmed for a surety, that we can use nothing that pertained to the pope, and is used in popery. Truly we must take good heed that we bring not the church of Christ into such bondage, that it may not use anything that the pope used. It is very true that our forefathers took the temples of idols, and turned them into holy churches, where Temples of idols converted to the worship of God[6].

[4 See above, page 31.]
[5 By, Def. A. and B.]   [6 Christ, Answ. 2.]

Things
wickedly
invented
may have
good use.
Revenues.

Christ should be worshipped; and they took also the
salary and revenues consecrated to the idols of the gentiles, to their wicked shews and plays, and to their holy
votaries virgins, and transposed it to find the ministers
of the church. And yet all these things did not only service unto antichrist, but unto the devil : yea, the holy

Phrases of
poets[1].

ecclesiastical writers did not stick to take the verses of
poets, which had been dedicated unto[2] Muses, and to
other divers gods and goddesses, for to be played in
plays, and spoken in shews, to obtain the favour of their
gods—I say, they did nothing stick or fear to use them,
when it seemed to them convenient, imitating Paul the
apostle, who stuck nothing at all to rehearse for his purpose Menander, Aratus, and Epimenides ; and that he did
in entreating the holy scripture apply profane words to

Wine, bread,
&c. conse-
crated[3] to
idols.

set forth God's religion. We read also how that wine
was consecrated unto Bacchus, bread unto Ceres, water
unto Neptune, oil unto Minerva, letters unto Mercury,
song unto the Muses and unto Apollo ; and many other
things Tertullian rehearseth in his book intituled *De
Coronâ Militis Christiani*[4], where almost he entreateth
this self-same argument : yet for all that we stick not to
use all these things freely as well in holy as in profane
uses, although at one time or other before they had been
consecrated to idols and to devils[5]." Hitherto Peter
Martyr.

T. C. Page 55, Sect. 5.

*To all these things that M. Martyr reckoneth up of revenues and wages,
verses, wine, bread, oil, water, which, being consecrated unto idols, are well
used, Tertullian answereth in the same book, whereout a number of these
are taken, when he saith that we ought to admit a participation of those
things which bring either a necessity or profit in the use of them*[6]. *But we*

[1 Phrases of speech of poets, Answ. 2.]   [2 To, Def. A. and B.]

[3 Wine and bread consecrated, Answ. 2.]

[4 Tertull. Op. Lut. 1641. De Coron. 8. p. 125.]

[5 Peter Martyr's Letter to John Hoper Byshop, &c. at the end of A briefe
examination for the tyme, of a certaine declaration, &c. Lond. Jugge, fol. B 4. 2 ;
where *applying profane*. Conf. P. Martyr. Epist. Theolog. ad calc. Loc. Comm.
Heidelb. 1613. p. 1087.]

[6 Hujusmodi quæstioni sic ubique respondeo, admittens quidem utensilium
communionem, &c. Dicimus enim ea demum et nostris et superiorum usibus, et
Dei rebus, et ipsi Christo competisse, quæ meras utilitates, et certa subsidia, et
honesta solatia necessariis vitæ humanæ procurant : &c.—Tertull. Op. De Coron.
8. p. 125.]

deny that these things thus used are either necessary or profitable. And therefore, instead of temples, tithes, wine, &c., if you would have matched the surplice well, you should have said, censers, tapers, holy bread, holy water, and such like.

Jo. Whitgift.

Master Martyr used these examples to prove that the "surplice" and other apparel of ministers now used (for that is the matter he handleth) may lawfully be retained and worn: whose judgment and authority with learned and wise men doth far overreach your naked denial. Neither doth Tertullian speak anything in his book *De Corona Militis*, that tendeth to the confutation of anything that Master Martyr hath here spoken, but to the confirmation of it rather; as he may perceive that with diligence readeth the book. Eusebius, *Lib. iv. cap.* 11, saith that Justinus Martyr preached the gospel of Christ being apparelled like an heathen philosopher[7]. St Augustine, *De Civit. Lib. xix. cap.* 19, writeth thus: "It appertaineth nothing to the city of God in what kind of apparel, or in what order of life, so that it be not against God, any man follow this faith whereby we come unto God. Therefore, when philosophers become Christians, the church compelleth them not to change their apparel or manner of living, which can nothing hinder religion, but only she compelleth them to change their false opinions[8]." Hilary also saith, *in Psal. lxvii.*, that "the spoils of the heathens taken from the devil are divided to the furniture and ornaments of the church of God[9]:" so that the saying of Master Martyr is very true, and confirmed by ancient authority, and the use of the church; as the testimonies of these fathers manifestly declare. Whereas you say that, if I "would have matched the surplice well," I "should have said censers, tapers, &c.," I tell you again, that

(marginal notes: Eusebius. Augustine. Hilary.)

[7] Μάλιστα δὲ ἤκμαζεν ἐπὶ τῶνδε Ἰουστῖνος, ἐν φιλοσόφου σχήματι πρεσβεύων τὸν θεῖον λόγον, κ.τ.λ.—Euseb. in Hist. Eccles. Script. Amst. 1695-1700. Lib. iv. cap. xi. p. 101.]

[8] Nihil sane ad istam pertinet civitatem quo habitu vel more vivendi, si non est contra divina præcepta, istam fidem, qua pervenitur ad Deum, quisque sectetur: unde ipsos quoque philosophos, quando Christiani fiunt, non habitum vel consuetudinem victus, quæ nihil impedit religionem, sed falsa dogmata mutare compellit.—August. Op. Par. 1679-1700. De Civ. Dei, Lib. xix. cap. xix. Tom. VII. col. 563.]

[9] Ad ecclesiæ enim decus detracta ab his diabolo gentium spolia dividuntur, atque etiam ex his spoliis domus pulcritudo perficitur, &c.—Hilar. Op. Par. 1693. Tract. in Psalm. lxvii. 12. col. 197.]

Things
wickedly
invented
may have
good use.
it is not I, but M. Martyr, a famous and notable man, that so
matched them, and at that time when the same matters were
in controversy, and his judgment required of them; and therefore could not be written of him but with great advisement.
Howbeit, that you may know something the more, you must
learn to put a difference between *adiaphora vera et pseudo-
adiaphora;* " those things that be indifferent indeed, and those
that are falsely accounted indifferent."

Chap. v.   The Fifth Division.

Answer to the Admonition, Page 59, Sect. 1, and Page 60, Sect. 1.

Bucer.
Bucer, in an epistle that he writ to John Alasco, is
of the same judgment: his words are worthy to be noted,
and be these : " For, if by no means it be lawful to use
those things, which were of Aaron's priesthood or of the
gentiles, then is it not lawful for us to have churches
nor holy-days.   For there is no express commandment by
word in the holy scriptures of these things.   It is gathered, notwithstanding, from the example of the old
people, that they are profitable for us to the increase of
What it is to
be a note of
antichrist[1].
godliness; which thing also experience proveth.   For any
thing to be a note of antichrist is not in the nature of
any creature in itself (for to that end nothing was made
of God), but it hangeth altogether of consenting to antichrist's religion and the professing thereof.   The which
consent and profession being changed into the consent
and profession of Christianity, there can stick in the
things themselves no note or mark of antichrist's reli-
The use or
abuse of
things indif-
ferent.
gion.   The use of bells was a mark of antichristianity in
our churches, when the people by them were called to
masses, and when they were rung against tempests !
Now they are a token of Christianity, when the people
by them are gathered together to the gospel of Christ,
Bucer's
opinion.
and other holy actions.   Why may it not then be that
the self-same garments may serve godly with godly men,
that was of wicked signification with the ungodly ?   Truly
I know very many ministers of Christ, most godly men,
who have used godly these vestures, and at this day do

[1 These marginal notes are not in Answ.]

yet use them; so that I dare not for this cause ascribe unto them any fault at all, much less so heinous a fault of communicating with antichrist; for the which fault we may utterly refuse to communicate with them in Christ. The priests of devils did celebrate in their sacrifices the distribution of bread and the cup; as Justinus Martyr[2] and Tertullian[3] make mention. What let is there why we may not use the same ceremonies also? You will say we have a commandment of the Lord touching this ceremony. Very well. And by the self-same it appeareth that same thing to serve among the children of God to the service of Christ, which the wicked abused in the service of devils, if the commandment of Christ be added thereto. But it is the commandment of Christ, that in our holy actions we institute and use all things so as comeliness and order be observed, that faith may be edified[5]."

Things wickedly invented may have good use.

The distribution of bread and wine in the sacrifices of devils[1]. Justinus Martyr[4].

The same M. Bucer, in another epistle written to M. Cranmer, archbishop of Canterbury, saith on this sort: "All true godly men may godly use those rites which wicked men have abused howsoever ungodly[6]."

T. C. Page 56, line 2, and Sect. 1.

It is true that M. Bucer saith that "it is not in the nature of any creature to be a note of antichrist;" but yet it followeth[7] not thereof that the creature that hath been accidentally, and through abuse, applied to idolatry, may be forthwith used as we shall think good. For neither the idols of the gentiles, nor the corruptions of those which offered, had not power[8] to make the beef or mutton that was offered no good and wholesome meat for the sustenance of man, neither cause that a christian man could not eat them as beef and mutton; but yet either to eat it at the table of idols before them, or else privately in his own house, when there was any

[2] Ὅταν γὰρ Διόνυσον μὲν υἱὸν τοῦ Διὸς...γεγενῆσθαι λέγωσι,...καὶ οἶνον ἐν τοῖς μυστηρίοις αὐτοῦ παραφέρωσιν, κ.τ.λ.—Just. Mart. Op. Par. 1742. Dialog. cum Tryph. Jud. 69. p. 167.]

[3] ...et si adhuc memini, Mithra signat illic in frontibus milites suos : celebrat et panis oblationem, &c.—Tertull. Op. Lut. 1641. De Præscr. Hæret. 40. p. 247.]

[4] This is inserted from Answ. 2.]

[5] M. Bucer, Letter to Joan. à Lasco, at the end of A briefe examination for the tyme, of a certaine declaration, &c. Lond. Jugge, fol. D 1; where *self-same garment may serve*.]

[6] The same to the Archb. of Canterbury, ibid. fol. A 3. Conf. Bucer, Script. Anglic. 1577. p. 682.]

[7] Yet followeth, Repl. 2.]   [8] Had power, Repl. 2.]

Things
wickedly
invented
may have
good use.

*weak by that thought it an abominable thing, was not lawful; and yet the
meat nevertheless the good creature of God, and which might be received with
thanksgiving: so the abuse of the surplice and cope, &c. cannot cause but
that they may be used as cloth and silk.*

*And, whereas he saith that they are changed, and made, of notes of anti-
christianity, marks of Christianity, I say that they cannot be changed so
by any decree or commandment; forasmuch as, notwithstanding that profession of change, the hearts of men, unto which every man must have
regard unto, are not changed. For not so soon as the magistrate will say
that these things shall be from henceforth used as things indifferent, forthwith men do use them so, but those only use them so which have knowledge;
both the ignorant and the weak take them still otherwise.*

JO. WHITGIFT.

The slender
answering of
T. C.

Your answer to these learned and famous men is not of
any moment at all; for their reasons you answer only with
words, when as indeed their only words (for their godliness',
experience', and learning' sake) ought to be of greater credit
than your reasons: but the aptness of your answers I refer
to the judgment of the reader, seeing he hath both their words
and yours before his eyes. This only I note, that something
you will say, how unaptly soever, lest you should seem to give
place to the plain truth. These vestures are neither "used
at the tables of idols," nor with the offence of "the weak;"
as I have shewed before: they are known of all men to be
notes of the ministers of the gospel, as well as the bell is known
to be rung to godly prayers and preachings, &c.; and therefore you have spoken, but answered nothing.

Chap. v. The Sixth Division.

Answer to the Admonition, Page 60, Sect. 2.

Bullinger and Gualter, in the epistle before alleged,
answering this question, whether we may wear such ap-

Bullinger
and Gualter.

parel as the papists do, say on this sort: "If we should
have nothing common with them, then must we forsake
all our churches, refuse all livings, not minister baptism,
not say the Apostles' or Nicene creed, yea, and quite cast
away the Lord's prayer; neither do you borrow any ceremonies of them. The matter of apparel was never taken
away at the beginning of reformation, and is yet retained, not by the pope's law, but by the king's commandment, as an indifferent thing of mere policy. Yea

truly, if you wear a cap or a peculiar kind of apparel, as a civil and politic thing, it smelleth neither of Judaism nor monachism.　For these will seem to separate themselves from the civil and common life, and account a meritorious deed in the wearing of a peculiar garment. So Eustathius[1], bishop of Sebastia, was not simply condemned for wearing a peculiar kind of garment ; but for that he did put religion in his garment.　The canons of the council of Gangren, Laodicen, and of the sixth council, are well known[2].　If in case any of the people be persuaded that these things savour of papism, monachism, or Judaism, let them be told the contrary, and perfectly instructed therein.　And if so be, through the importunate crying out hereon before the people by some men, many be disquieted in their conscience, let them beware which so do, that they bring not greater yokes on their own necks, and provoke the queen's majesty, and bring many faithful ministers in such danger, as they cannot rid themselves out [3]again[4]."　Hitherto Bullinger.

Things wickedly invented may have good use.

Superstition in garments condemned.

T. C. Page 56, Sect. 1, 2, 3.

The rest of those things which M. Bucer, and those which M. Bullinger and Gualter bring, are all of that sort whereunto answer is made.

[1 Eustachius, Answ.]

[2 Μηδεὶς τῶν ἐν κλήρῳ καταλεγομένων ἀνοίκειον ἐσθῆτα ἀμφιεννύσθω,... ἀλλὰ στολαῖς κεχρήσθω ταῖς ἤδη τοῖς ἐν κλήρῳ καταλεγομένοις ἀπονεμηθείσαις. —Concil. Quinisext. can. 27. in Concil. Stud. Labb. et Cossart. Lut. Par. 1671-2. Tom. VI. col. 1154.　Conf. Concil. Laod. cans. 21, 2. ibid. Tom. I. col. 1500; and see before, page 29, note 8.]

[3 Out of again, Answ.]

[4 Si nulla re cum illis communicare liceret, oporteret et templa omnia deserere, nulla accipere stipendia, non uti baptismo, non recitare symbolum apostolicum et Nicenum, adeoque abjicere orationem dominicam.　Neque vos mutuatis ab iis ullas ceremonias.　Res vestiari[a] ab initio reformationis nunquam fuit abolita, et retinetur adhuc, non lege papistica, sed vi edicti regii, ut res media et politica. Ita sane, si ut re civili utamini pileo et veste peculiari, hoc non redolet Judaismum neque monachismum.　Nam ii volunt videri a civili vita separari, et constituunt meritum in peculiari sua veste.　Sic Eustachius, Sebastiæ episcopus, damnatus est non simpliciter propter peculiarem vestem, sed quod in veste religionem constitueret.　Noti sunt Gangren. Concilii canones, Laodiceni et sexti synodi.　Quod si ex plebe nonnulli sunt persuasi redolere hoc papismum, Judaismum, et monachismum, admoneantur et recte de iis instituantur.　Quod si importunis quorundam clamoribus, hac de re ad vulgus profusis, multi inquieti reddantur, videant, qui hoc faciunt, ne graviora sibi onera imponant, regiamque majestatem irritent: denique multos fideles ministros in discrimine adducant; ex quo vix emergere queant.—Bullinger's Letter to Sampson and Humphrey, 1566, in Strype, Annals, Vol. I. Append. No. xxiv.]

Temples of idols converted to christian churches.

Only this they add, that, if the people do abuse and pervert those[1] ceremonies, they ought to be better instructed : which is a counsel not so convenient, that the ministers and pastors which have so many necessary points to bestow their time on, and to inform the people of, should be driven to cut off their time appointed thereto, to teach them not to abuse these things, which if they use never so well, they can gain nothing, and to take heed that they hurt not themselves at those things which in their best estate do no good, especially when one sermon of the taking of them away, joined with authority to execute it, may do more good than a thousand sermons without authority.

Besides that it is absurd that ceremonies, which ought to be helpers to promote the doctrine, should become lets and hinderances, whilst the minister is occupied in teaching to beware of the abuse of them and of superstition. And it is as much as if one should be set to watch a child all day long lest he hurt himself with the knife, when as by taking away the knife quite from him the danger is avoided, and the service of the man better employed. And so it followeth that, although the church may appoint ceremonies and rites, yet it cannot appoint these that have great incommodity and no commodity, great offence and no edifying.

Jo. Whitgift.

You have omitted divers things in the words of these learned men, whereunto you have not answered one word ; as the reader by conference may perceive ; and here you have also willingly passed over that which toucheth you something pinchingly, in these words of M. Bullinger and M. Gualter, *scil.:* "And if so be, through the importunate crying out hereon before the people, &c."

The reason returned upon himself.

If to preach the truth of the right use of these ceremonies be not so convenient, " because the pastors have so many necessary points, &c.," how cometh it to pass that you and your partakers have so pestered your sermons and books therewith, and so long time taught the people nothing else but contempt of all good order and obedience in such matters, and have stirred them up against the true preachers of the gospel, and against their magistrates and rulers for the selfsame thing ? Is it not as convenient for us to root out of the people's minds errors touching things indifferent, as it is for you to ingraft them ? or is not the doctrine of the true and lawful use of indifferent things, of due obedience towards laws and magistrates, a necessary doctrine ?

The doctrine of things indifferent necessary.

Where as you say, "It is absurd that ceremonies, which ought to be helpers to promote the doctrine, should become

[¹ These, Repl. 1 and 2.]

lets and hinderances, &c. ;" I will not say you speak ab- *Temples of idols converted to christian churches.* surdly, but undoubtedly you speak unadvisedly. For will you have things indifferent abrogated so soon as they be abused, "lest they should become lets and hinderances, whilst the minister is occupied in teaching, &c. ?" then take away tithes, lands, meats, &c.; the abuse whereof must of neces- *Things abused must not by and by be taken away.* sity oftentimes be reprehended in sermons, and the true use taught; and make all things common, that the preachers in their sermons may be occupied about great matters. Do you not see that doctrine of things indifferent is necessary? Understand you not that the taking away of the things from the eyes doth not by and by root the opinion out of the heart? Things abused must not always be taken away when they are abused, but the right use must be taught, and the abuse reproved.

The "child," when he hath discretion, and is able to be instructed, though he sometime "hurt himself with the knife," yet must not the same be altogether "taken from him," but he must be rebuked for using it so undiscreetly, and taught to use it better. Shall the rich and costly apparel be taken from princes, nobles, and men and women of estate, and they brought to a popularity therein, because there is great abuse oftentimes in such apparel, and many provocations to evil? No, truly; but such kinds of abuses are to be by the word of God reproved. Neither doth such instructions and doctrine in matters indifferent hinder preachers from weightier matters. Why did the apostles make their decree of abstaining *a suf-* *Acts xv.* *focato et sanguine,* "from that that is strangled and blood?" or St Paul, of praying bare-headed or covered? 1 Corinth. xi. Which things afterward might grow to abuse, if they had not thought the doctrine of ceremonies to be convenient.

Touching "the great incommodity and offence" that you imagine to be in this apparel, it is but your fancy, which take the apparel to be the cause of your niceness, contempt, disobedience, contention, and such like, remaining in you, when indeed it is nothing else but singularity, and preposterous zeal: wherefore that is to be removed out of the heart, rather than the apparel from the back. To be short, that which you imagine of any opinion of the religion in this apparel, or superstition, or any such like offence, it is but a mere imagination to cloke and cover the corruptions of the mind before mentioned.

Chapter v.   The Seventh Division.

Answer to the Admonition, Page 61, Sect. 1.

I have the rather set down these men's sayings at large, because they be both pithy, learned, and wholly to the confutation of your assertion.   Wherefore I conclude that a christian magistrate may retain any civil, politic, or ecclesiastical orders and rites, of whomsoever they were invented, or howsoever they have been abused, so that, first, they be not against the word of God; secondly, that justification and remission of sins be not attributed unto them; thirdly, that the church be not troubled with the multitude of them; fourthly, that they be not decreed as necessary, and not to be changed; and, last of all, that men be not so tied unto them but that by occasion they may be omitted, so that it be without offence and contempt.

T. C. Page 56, Sect. 4.

And, although they have all these properties which you recite, yet, if they be not to edifying, if not to God his glory, if not comely and agreeable to the simplicity of the gospel of Christ crucified, they may not be established.

Jo. Whitgift.

It is sufficient if they pertain to order and comeliness (as I have before declared); the judgment whereof doth not belong to every private man, but to such only as have authority in the church; to whose determination in such matters all other of duty are bound to submit themselves.

Chapter v.   The Eighth Division.

Answer to the Admonition, Page 62, Sect. 1.

A difference
between
worship-
ping of false
gods, and of
the true God
falsely[2].

Yet one thing I must admonish you of, that there is a difference to be made betwixt those things which were wholly dedicated to false gods, and to be used in the worshipping of them, and those things which were used in the false worshipping of the true God: for the papists

[1 *A* is not in Def. A.]
[2 A difference between the worshipping of false gods and the worshipping of the true God falsely, Answ. 2.]

herein differ from the gentiles, that they acknowledge
and confess the true God, and believe the same articles
of faith that we do, but yet worship him not aright, nor
believe on him in all points as the word of God prescribeth. And therefore, if things abused of the gentiles, and invented by them, may be used of Christians,
much more may things invented and abused by papists.

*Things
wickedly
invented
may have
a good use.*

T. C. Page 56, Sect. 4.

*Concerning your distinction, whereby you lessen the idolatry of the
papists, I have shewed the vanity thereof.*

Jo. Whitgift.

And I have answered whatsoever you have there said[3]:
but yet your reply in that place will not serve every circumstance of this place, except you will say with the Stoics, that
peccata sunt paria : "all sins are equal."

Chapter v.   The Ninth Division.

Answer to the Admonition, Page 62, Sect. 1.

But of this matter I mind also to speak something in
the second part of this Admonition.

T. C. Page 56, Sect. 5.

*But of this matter you say you will speak again. Indeed so you do,
and again, wherein you confound the memory and understanding of the
reader, and declare yourself not only ignorant of Aristotle's rule of καθόλου
πρῶτον (which is to speak of one thing generally and once for all), but even
to be void of that order, which men have commonly by the natural logic of
reason. Neither can you excuse yourself in saying that the Admonition
giveth you so oftentimes occasion to speak of them, and so to lay the fault
upon it, for that it, being written by divers persons of the same matters,
whereof one knew not of another's doing, cannot be blamed for the repetition of one thing twice, when as you cannot escape blame, which might have
gathered easily into one place that which is said of them in divers : which
thing although it be not so easy for me to do in your book as it was for
you to do in theirs, yet I will assay to do it both in this and in all other points
that follow ; not thinking thereby to bring this treatise of yours to any good
order (for that were to cast it new again, and then you would complain of
your mind perverted), but that I might remedy this so great disorder,
which may be done[4] without changing anything of that which you have
set down.*

*A manifest
untruth.*

[3 See Vol. I. pages 333, &c.]
[4 Disorder as far as may be done, Repl. 2.]

Jo. Whitgift.

I have done as you ought to have done, if you had meant plainly ; for I have followed *verbatim* the book that I confute in the same order that it is written, which I think he that confuteth ought to do. That the Admonition was "written by divers persons, the one not knowing of another's doing," cannot be true; for both the parts have one title, they be in one volume, they were printed in one letter, at one time, by one and the same printer, and came abroad together ; neither were they ever separated that I know or can understand. Moreover, this bewrayeth all, and condemneth you for one that hath no conscience in writing untruths, that in the beginning of the Admonition mention is made of both of these treatises in these words : " Two treatises you have here ensuing, beloved in Christ, which ye must read, &c.[1]" And in the end of both these treatises it is thus written : " We have thought good, in the latter end[2] of our book, for sundry considerations, to certify you, beloved brethren, of the reasons that have moved us, who are the authors of these treatises, to keep back our names, &c.[3]" Finally, the order and manner of both these treatises, the style, the quotations, &c. do manifestly convince you of false witness-bearing : but it is too usual with you.

I am not so cunning in Aristotle, that I can be so bold as to attribute that unto him which is not to be found in him; as you do in this place : for, though he speak much of this rule καθόλου πρῶτον[4], yet hath he no such thing as you father upon him in this place.

It is meet that he which writeth a book of any matters should of one matter speak fully in one place; but he that confuteth must follow his order whom he confuteth. Which if you had done in my book, as I have done in theirs, either would not your unfaithful dealing have been so much, or else must it sooner or easilier have been espied. Your taunts I leave to yourself that have so good a grace in them.

[1 See Vol. I. page 140.]
[2 *End* is not in Def. A.]
[3 Adm. to Parl. fol. C. i. 2 : where *this latter*.]
[4 Aristot. Op. Lut. Par. 1629. Analyt. Poster. Lib. II. capp. xvii. xviii. Tom. I. pp. 178, 9.]

Chapter v.   The Tenth Division.

T. C. Page 56, Sect. ult.

And, if there be any other arguments touching any of these points in other places, which I have not gathered together into one, the fault is in this, that I could not bestow so much time in making a harmony of the things which are at so great discord, and then that which is left out shall be answered in place where I shall find it.   Now let us see M. Doctor's δεύτερον πλοῦν, and second navigation touching apparel, whether it be any happier, or have any better success than the first.

Jo. Whitgift.

A proper excuse, if anything fall out in the whole book which you cannot answer; as there be divers which you have not answered.

Divers things concerning apparel in other places of the Answer[5].

Chapter vi.   The First Division.

Admonition.

Now we must have surplices devised by pope Adrian[6].

Answer to the Admonition, Page 105, Sect. 1, 2.

The impurities you find in the administration of baptism be these: " Surplice, &c.[7]" Touching the "surplice," and such like apparel, I have spoken before sufficiently: the first inventor of it (which you say to be pope Adrian) doth make it neither better nor worse; and yet it was used long before Adrian's time; neither can you prove him to be the first inventor thereof.   It is certain that such kind of vesture hath been used in the ministration of the sacraments long before any corruption of doctrine took place in the church; as it appeareth both by Hierome in his first book *Adversus*

[5 Cartwright has hitherto followed the order of Whitgift's Answer: here, as he has just apprised his readers, he collects from some later parts of the Answer matters which bear upon the subject of the apparel.   Whitgift of course in his Defence follows Cartwright's Reply.]

[6 This is only a portion of that paragraph of the Admonition which is inserted in the place from which the succeeding answer is taken.]

[7 Here we find in Answ. instead of &c. the sentence completed: *interrogatories ministered to the infant, godfathers and godmothers, holy fonts, crossing.*]

White gar-
ment used in
the minis-
tration [1].

Pelagianos, where he maketh manifest mention of a
white garment used in the administration of sacrifice by
the bishop, priest and deacon[2]; and also Chrysostom,
Hom. 6. to the people of Antioch, who speaketh of the
like garment worn in the church[3]. Those that answered
the Examiner do but childishly cavil at these two places,
which indeed be plain of themselves and evident; and so
is that of Hierome's also, upon the xliv. of Ezechiel:
"The religion of God hath one habit in the ministration,
and another in common use and life[4]." Read the place
considerately; and it shall easily appear that Hierome
meaneth as well of christian ministers as of Jewish
priests.

But of the use of this and other apparel prescribed
in this church to be worn by ministers, I have spoken
partly before, and am ready to speak more as occasion
shall be offered. In the mean time, the surplice is not
of the substance of baptism, neither required as necessary to the administration thereof, but as comely and
decent.

T. C. Page 57, Sect. 1.

In the 105. *page, M. Doctor, to prove the use of the surplice, to draw
out his book into some competent volume, borroweth certain places of the
Examiner; for answer whereunto I will refer the reader to that which is
answered unto the Examination[5], as to a full and sufficient answer,
wherein I will rest; and, when M. Doctor hath proved that which he saith,
that it is but a childish cavil, he shall then hear further.*

*In the mean season, it is but a slender reply to so learned an answer
(that proveth both out of other authors and out of those same which the
Examiner citeth, that by a white garment is meant a comely apparel, and
not slovenly) to say it is but a childish cavil, which a D. of Divinity and
of forty years of age cannot answer. The place of Hierome upon the*

[1 Of white garments in the church, Answ. 2.]

[2 Quæ sunt, rogo, inimicitiæ contra Deum, si tunicam habuero mundiorem;
si episcopus, presbyter, et diaconus, et reliquus ordo ecclesiasticus in administratione sacrificiorum candida veste processerint?—Hieron. Op. Par. 1693-1706.
Lib. I. Dialog. adv. Pelag. Tom. IV. Pars II. col. 502.]

[3 Chrysost. Op. Par. 1718-38. In Matt. Hom. lxxxii. Tom. VII. p. 789.
See before, page 24, note 2.]

[4 Porro religio divina alterum habitum habet in ministerio, alterum in usu
vitaque communi.—Hieron. Op. Comm. Lib. XIII. in Ezech. Proph. cap. xliv.
Tom. III. col. 1029.]

[5 The books meant are, A briefe examination, &c., already repeatedly referred to, and, An ansvvere for the tyme, to the examination put in print, &c.
Lond. 1566. The question of the habits is specially discussed in the latter from
p. 88 to the end.]

xliv. of Ezechiel, the more it be considered, the more shall appear the truth of the Answer.

Jo. Whitgift.

You have not answered one word of this, but only shifted it off : I purpose not at this time to unrip the answer to the Examiner, except you had taken the pains to set it down. Both the places of Hierome are to be seen : in the one he sheweth that "in the administration of the sacraments the bishop, priest, and deacon, did wear a white vesture [6];" and in the other he saith that "the religion of God hath one habit in the ministration, and another in the common use and life [7]." Join these two places together, and see whether the words of Hierome be manifest or no. And, that it may evidently appear that at this time wherein Hierome lived the manner was to wear white garments in the time of divine service and administration of sacraments, I will recite the words of the fourth council of Carthage, at the which there were present 214. bishops, among whom was St Augustine : *Diaconus tempore oblationis tantum vel lectionis alba induatur* [8]: "Let the deacon wear a white vesture only in the time of the oblation and reading." *Canone.* 41. And this may be a sufficient confutation to whatsoever is spoken of these places of Hierome in the answer to the Examiner.

A white garment in the ministration used in Hierome's time. Hier. Lib. i. advers. Pelag. in 44. Ezech.

Conc. Carth. iv. can. 41.

Chap. vi.   The Second Division.

Admonition [9].

Apparel. [10]   *And, as for the apparel, though we have been long borne in hand, and yet are, that it is for order and decency commanded, yet [11] we know and have proved that there is neither order nor comeliness nor obedience in using it.   There is no order in it, but confusion; no comeliness, but deformity; no obedience, but disobedience, both against God and the prince [12].*

[6 Hieron. Op. Lib. i. Dialog. adv. Pelag. Tom. IV. Pars ii. col. 502. See above, note 2.]

[7 Id. Comm. Lib. xiii. in Ezech.Proph. cap. xliv. Tom. III. col. 1029. See above, note 4.]

[8 Concil. Carthag. iv. can. 41. in Concil. Stud. Labb. et Cossart. Lut. Par. 1671-2. Tom. II. col. 1203 ; where *alba utatur.*]

[9 Here again, Whitgift, following Cartwright in his Reply, passes to another place of the Admonition and the Answer.]

[10 This is inserted from Adm. and Answ.]

[11 Commanded and yet, Adm.]

[12 The portions of the Admonition as far as *obstinate*, below, page 72, form one paragraph in Answ.]

Answer to the Admonition, Page 236, the last line but one,
and Page 237, Sect. 1.

To all this also I have answered before, I mean to all
the reasons here alleged; as for bare words, they prevail
with none but such as have respect to the persons, and
not to the matter. And therefore I omit these words of
pleasure which you use when you say that "in this
apparel there is no order, but confusion; no comeliness,
but deformity; no obedience, but disobedience, both
against God and the prince."

It is not every private man's part to define what is
order and comeliness in external matters being indifferent, but is proper to them only to whom God hath committed the government of his church; whose orders and
laws (not being against the word of God) whosoever
doth disobey, disobeyeth both God and the prince; as
you do in disobeying the prince's laws in these matters.

Disobedience to the prince in civil matters is disobedience to God.

Jo. WHITGIFT.

Nothing is said to this; although some part of it necessarily requireth an answer.

Chapter vi. The Third Division.

Admonition.

*We marvel that they could espy in the[1] last synod, that a grey amice,
which is but a garment of dignity, should be a garment (as they say) defiled with superstition, and yet that copes, caps, surplices, tippets, and such
like baggage, the preaching signs of popish priesthood, the pope's creatures,
kept in the same form to this end, to bring dignity and reverence to the
ministers and sacraments, should be retained still, and not abolished[2].*

Answer to the Admonition, Page 237, Sect. 2.

It is well that you seem to justify the "grey amice,"
because the bishops have disallowed of it "in their

[1 Their, Adm. and Answ.]
[2 Nullus nec decanus, &c. nec rector, nec quisquam ex illo ordine quocunque
nomine censeatur, utetur posthac amictu illo quem appellant graium amicium, aut
alia ulla veste simili superstitione contaminata. Sed in ecclesiis quisque suis
utentur tantum linea illa veste, quæ adhuc regio mandato retinetur, et scholastica
epomide, quæ suo cujusque scholastico gradui et loco conveniat.—Lib. Quorund.
Canon. Anno 1571. in A collection of Articles, &c. Lond. 1675. pp. 227, 8.]

synod." Truly this is your conscience and religion, to
be always *ad oppositum,* and to disallow that which law
and authority alloweth, and allow that which they disallow. The next way, as I think, to drive you unto
conformity in apparel were to make a strait law, that no
man should wear such kind of apparel; because you
love to be contrary to laws and good orders.

T. C. Page 57, Sect. 3, 4, 5.

*Now I will desire the reader to turn[3] unto the 237, 238, 239, 240, 242
pages, to see whether at this third voyage Master Doctor bringeth any better
merchandize. Where first he surmiseth an untruth, as though the Admonition misliked of the taking away of the grey amice, where it saith only
that there was less cause to take that away than the surplice, &c. Wherein
there is nothing but the truth said; for, because that was used in[4] few
churches, and but of few also in those few churches, therefore, if there were
cause to take away that, there was greater to take away the surplice. And
to take away the amice out of the church, and leave the surplice, &c. is to
heal a scratch, and leave a wound unhealed.*

Now, whereas you say that we are "always ad oppositum[5]*" and that,
if the law commanded straitly that we should[6] wear none of this apparel,
that then we would wear; if it should be answered again that you do
servire scenæ, that is, that you are a time-server, you see we might* I have served as few times as you. *speak with more likelihood than you. But we will not take (as you do)
the judgment of God out of his hands, but will attend patiently the revela-
tion and discovering of that which is now hid both in you and us[7].*

*And, although you will grant us neither learning nor conscience, yet
you might afford us so much wit, as that we would not willingly and of
purpose want those commodities of life, which we might otherwise enjoy as
well as you, if we had that gift of conformity which you have.*

Jo. Whitgift.

The words of the Admonition touching the grey amice be
these: "We marvel that they could espy in their last synod,
that a grey amice, which is but a garment of dignity, should
be a garment (as they say) defiled with superstition, and yet
that copes, &c." Do they not say that the amice "is but a
garment of dignity, &c." ? consider their words well, and you
shall see that Master Doctor hath said truly.

[3 Return, Def. B.]   [4 Used but in, Repl. 1 and 2.]
[5 So Repl. 2: the other editt. have *appositum.*]   [6 Would, Def. B.]
[7 Hid both in you and in us, Repl. 1 and 2: the word *hid* was printed *had*
in Repl. 1, and has been altered with a pen.]

The grey amice was justly taken away, because the use of it is not established by any law of this realm, as the use of other vestures be; and in mine opinion the bishops deserved commendation in so doing; for thereby they declared that they will not suffer any rites or ornaments to be used in this church, but such only as are by public authority established.

Some men delight to be contrary to times.

Experience hath taught me that divers men be of that nature, that they have a delight in opposing themselves to the present estate; and I see it by proof to be a great fault in divers of you.

I have hitherto "served" as few contrary "times" as you have done. As for "the gift of conformity," which you say I have, I thank God for it, I have learned to conform myself to the time in that sense that St Paul hath willed me so to do, Rom. xii., and to laws also and magistrates, as I am likewise commanded in the xiii. chapter of the same epistle.

Rom. xii.

Rom. xiii.

What "commodities" you "want" that I have, I cannot conjecture: your meat and drink is provided with less trouble and charges unto you, and in more delicate and dainty manner than mine is; your ease and pleasure ten times more; you do what you list, go when you list, come when you list, speak when you list at your pleasure. What would you have more? I know not why you should complain, except you be of the same disposition with the Franciscan friars, who, when they had filled their bellies at other men's tables, were wont to cry out and say, *O quanta patimur, &c.* Some men are delighted to be fed at other men's tables, and prefer popular fame before gold and silver.

The Faults wherewith the Admonitors
charge the apparel answered.

Chapter vii. The First Division.
Admonition.

But they are as the garments of the idol, to which we should say, Avaunt, and get thee hence. They are as the garments of Ba- laamites, of popish priests, enemies to God and all Christians. ʰ *Esay xxx. 22.*

Answer to the Admonition, Page 237, Sect. 3, 4;
and Page 238, Sect. 1.

But you say, "they are as the garments of the idol, to the which we should say, Avaunt, and get thee hence.

They are as the garments of Balaamites, of popish priests, enemies to God and all Christians." Be it so: so were all things in Hierico accursed and an abomination to the Lord; neither was it lawful for the Israelites to touch anything thereof; and yet was the gold, and the silver, and the brazen and iron vessels, carried into the treasure-house of the Lord, and consecrated unto him. Josue vi.

Temples of idols converted to christian churches.

Cursed things consecrated[1] to God.

Gedeon was commanded to take and sacrifice that ox of his father's to God, which his father had fed and brought up to be sacrificed to Baal, yea, and to burn that ox with the self-same wood that was consecrated and dedicated to the idol Baal. *Judic. vi.*

Gedeon sacrificed an ox consecrated to Baal[2].

Our forefathers took the temples dedicated wholly to idols, yea, to devils, and most abominably defiled with devilish and abominable service, and turned them into holy churches, where Christ should be worshipped.

T. C. Page 57, Sect. 6, 7.

Whereas you say that the accursed things of Jericho, and the ox that was fed to be sanctified unto Baal, and the wood consecrated unto the idol, were converted to the service of the living God; when you shall prove that the surplice is so necessary to the service of God as gold and silver and other metal, and as oxen and wood, whereof the first sort were such as without the which the temple could not be built, the other, such as were expressly commanded of God to be used in his service, then I will confess that this place maketh something for you. And yet, if your copes and surplices, &c. should have such a purgation by fire as those metals had, or ever the Lord would admit them into his treasure-house, and should be driven to pass from popery unto the gospel by the chimney, the fire would make such wrack with them, that they should need have better legs than your arguments to bring them into the church.

Here you disport yourself with your own imagination. No such purgation to be found in that place.

Moreover, do you not see here that you have not loosed the knot, but cut it? For the authors of the Admonition object the place of Esay xxx.; and you object again the places[4] of Deuteronomy, and of the Judges: this is to oppose sword against sword; in stead that you should have first holden out your buckler, and latched[5] the blow of your adversary. As for churches, it hath been answered that they have a profitable use, and therefore very evil compared with the surplice; which, beside that it bringeth no profit, hurteth also, as is before said.

Chap. xxx. 22,3

[1 Consecrate, Answ. 2.]
[2 Gedeon sacrificed to God an idolatrous ox, Answ. 2.]
[3 This reference is inserted from Repl. 2; which omits *xxx.* in the text.]
[4 Place, Def. B.]   [5 Latched: caught.]

Jo. Whitgift.

That "wood," that "gold," and that "ox," &c. was not so
"necessary," but that both God might have been served, and
"the temple builded without them;" and therefore that is no
answer. For, although "gold, wood, oxen, &c." be "necessary,"
yet the gold and silver found in Jericho, the ox reserved by
Gedeon's father, and wood that was consecrated to Baal, was
not so necessary; for there might have been other "gold,
silver, wood, oxen, &c." provided. In that God commanded
these things to be done, you know that St Augustine (in the
epistle *ad Publicolam*, in the words before rehearsed) doth
conclude a general doctrine, that things dedicated to idols
may be converted to common uses and to the honour of God[1].
For he useth the self-same places to prove the same, and
answereth that which may be alleged to the contrary out of
Deuteronomy. So doth it also the place of Esay, quoted in
the margent of the Admonition; which answer if it will not
satisfy you, then do I further refer you to that which I have
also before alleged out of M. Calvin, writing upon the xxiii.
of Exodus, verse 24.[2] But this place of Esay, and such like,
are unaptly alleged against the apparel now used, being
nothing of that nature that those things be whereof the
prophet in that place speaketh.

You say, "if our copes and surplices, &c. should have
such a purgation by fire, &c." I pray you, where read you
of any such "purgation by fire of those metals" before they
were admitted into the Lord's treasure-house? And what
"purgation by fire" could there be of the wood, or of the ox,
before they were used in the sacrifice and service of the Lord?
There is no such purging of the things taken in Jericho mentioned in that chapter, but the contrary; for thus it is written:
"After they burnt the city with fire, and all that was therein;
only the silver and gold, and the vessels of brass and iron,
they put into the treasure-house of the Lord;" and in the
place before, where Josua is commanded to reserve these
things, there is no commandment of any such purging.

As your common answer is this, that such things "have

[1 August. Op. Par. 1679-1700. Ad Public. Epist. xlvii. 3. Tom. II. col. 111.
See before, page 31, note 4.]
[2 Calvin. Op. Amst. 1667-71. Harm. in Quat. Libr. Mos. Sec. Præcept.
Tom. I. p. 472. See before, pages 33, 4, note 8.]

profitable uses," and therefore may be retained, though they were consecrated to idols (which is but a shift of your own, without any ground) so I say that these vestures have a decent and comely use, and be referred to order, and therefore may be retained likewise, although they were used in idolatry. And, if you shall answer and say that there may be other things used more comely and decently, then I reply that so there may be places as commodious as these churches; gold, silver, wood, &c. as good and as profitable as that. And, if you object that they be not comely and decent, then I say unto you that it is your part, and the part of all those that be obedient, to submit yourselves to the judgment of those that be in authority, except they command such things as be contrary to the commandment of God.

Chapter vii. The Second Division.

Answer to the Admonition, Page 238, Sect. 2, 3.

To be short, no devil, no idol, no pope, can so defile the nature or form (not being contrary to the scriptures) of any of God's creatures, that the liberty of a christian man should be taken away in using and not using them[4]. *No man can defile the nature and form of things[3].*

And I say again, with M. Bucer, that "for anything to be a note of antichrist is not in[5] the nature of any creature in itself (for to that end nothing was made of God), but it hangeth altogether of consenting to antichrist's religion, and the professing thereof. The which consent and profession being changed into the consent and profession of Christianity, there can stick in the things themselves no note or mark of antichrist's religion. The use of bells was a mark of antichristianity in our churches, when the people by them were called to masses, and when they were rung against tempests; now they are a token of Christianity, when the people by them are gathered together to the gospel of Christ, and other holy actions, &c.[6]" *Bucer.*

[3 The nature and form of things no man can defile, Answ. 2.]
[4 In using or not using of them, Answ.]   [5 Def. B. omits *in*.]
[6 M. Bucer, Letter to Joan. à Lasco, at the end of A briefe examination for the tyme, of a certaine declaration, &c.—Lond. Jugge, fol. D 1. See before, pages 38, 9.]

How the
apparel
serveth to
edification.

T. C. Page 57, Sect. ult.

*" To be short," saith M. Doctor, when he reciteth me almost a whole side
word for word, as he hath cited before, where he hath had his answer.*

Jo. Whitgift.

Surely this jesting spirit was never in any of the apostles
or martyrs of Christ's church that I can read; but, to pass it
over, M. Doctor's "short" is very shortly answered; the cause
whereof I refer to the reader. Howsoever you jest out the
matter, you have neither answered M. Doctor's "to be short,"
nor that which is translated.

Chapter vii.   The Third Division.
Admonition.

They serve not to edification.

Answer to the Admonition, Page 238, Sect. 3.

Ceremonies
do not edify
of them-
selves, but
tend[1] to edi-
fication.

You say also that they do not edify. If you say that
they do not edify of themselves, you say truly; for only
the Holy Ghost on this sort doth edify by the ministry
of the word. But, if you say they edify not at all, that
is, that they do not tend to edifying, as other ceremonies
and things used in the church (as pulpit, church, kneeling,
singing, and such like), which be appointed for order
and decency, do, then speak you that which you are not
able by sound arguments to justify.

Jo. Whitgift.

To this not one word.

Chapter vii.   The Fourth Division.

Answer to the Admonition, Page 238, Sect. ult.

Peter Martyr, in his epistle written to M. Hooper,
thinketh that they do edify, after a sort, as other ceremonies do. And so doth M. Bucer also, in his epistle
written to M. Alasco.

T. C. Page 57, Sect. ult.

*After this he setteth himself to prove that they do edify[2]; and first[3] by
M. Bucer's and M. Martyr's authority; and yet in their words before*

[1] But yet tend, Answ. 2.]
[2] They edify, Repl. 1 and 2.]   [3] And that first, Repl. 1, 2, and Def. A.]

alleged there is not a word of edifying.   If he gather it of their words, How the
the answer is already made. apparel
serveth to
edification.

Jo. WHITGIFT.

I tell you it is in their epistles, not in their "words before
alleged." M. Bucer's words be these : " Now, if any church Bucer.
judge and have experience (such as I doubt not there are
many at these days in Germany) that the use of such vesture
bringeth some commendation to the holy ministration, and
thereby helpeth somewhat in the way of comeliness and order,
to the increase of faith; what, I pray you, can be brought
out of the scriptures why that church is not left to her own
judgment in this matter, neither therefore to be contemned,
or to be called into question for her judgment' sake? That
church verily will keep in these things a mean agreeable to
the cross of Christ, and will diligently attend that no abuse
creep into it[4]." Hitherto M. Bucer. To the like effect also
writeth M. Martyr in the epistle before named[5].

Chapter vii.   The Fifth Division.

Answer to the Admonition, Page 239, Sect. 1.

Furthermore, that they do edify, it is manifest, first, The apparel
because they are by a lawful magistrate, by lawful doth tend to
edifying for
authority, for order and decency appointed in the three causes[6].
church, without any manner of superstition or suspicion
of the same.

T. C. Page 57, Sect. ult.

Then he bringeth reasons to prove it; whereof in the first he seemeth to
reason that, because it is commanded by a lawful magistrate, and lawful
authority, therefore it edifieth.   As though a lawful magistrate doth no-
thing at any time unlawfully, or as though a lawful and godly[7] magis-
trate doth not sometimes command things which are inconvenient and
unlawful.   Saul was a lawful magistrate, and did command unlawful
things.   David was a lawful and godly magistrate; and yet there slipped

---

[4 M. Bucer, Letter to Joan. à Lasco, at the end of A briefe examination for
the tyme, &c. Lond. Jugge, fol. D 1. 2 ; where *many this day in Germany,* and
church is not to be left.]

[5 P. Martyr's Letter to John Hoper Byshop, &c. ibid. fol. C 1. Conf. Epist.
Theolog. ad calc. Loc. Comm. Heidelb. 1613. pp. 1087, 8.]

[6 Ceremonies do edify by 3. reasons, Ans. 2.]

[7 And a godly, Repl. 1, 2, and Def. A.]

from him commandments which were neither lawful nor godly. But he addeth, that it is done " for order and for decency, without superstition or suspicion of it." This is that which is in controversy, and ought to be proved; and M. Doctor still taketh it as granted, and still faulteth in the petition of the principle, wherewith he chargeth others.

Jo. Whitgift.

That which is appointed in the church by a lawful magistrate, and by lawful authority, for order and decency, without any superstition or suspicion of superstition, doth edify, as other orders do; but it is certain that the apparel now used is so appointed; *ergo*, it doth edify, as other orders do.

You cavil at the major, and bring in the examples of "Saul and David," to prove that "a lawful magistrate did command unlawful things;" but you omit the other circumstances contained in the major, and therefore you answer not to the purpose. The minor, you say, is "in controversy," and I do "fault in the petition of the principle." Surely I do *petere* that *principium* that no good subject can deny. For the queen's majesty is a lawful magistrate: the authority of parliament is a lawful authority: her majesty by that authority hath appointed this apparel, and that, as it is protested, for comeliness and decency, without any superstition; *ergo*, the minor is true. If you will yet doubt of comeliness and decency, then I still say unto you that what is comely and decent is not every man's part to judge, but the magistrate's, and such as have authority in the church.

Chapter vii. The Sixth Division.

Answer to the Admonition, Page 239, Sect. 2.

Secondly, because we are by due proof and experience taught that such as have worn this apparel, and do wear it, by the ministry of the word have greatly edified, and do daily.

T. C. Page 58, Sect. 1.

The second reason is, that they that wear this apparel have edified, and do edify; which is as if a man would say: The midwives which lied unto Pharao did much good among[2] the Israelites; ergo, their lying did much good. If he will say, the comparison is not like, be- Exod. i. 19.[1]

[1 This reference is inserted from Repl. 2.]
[2 Amongst, Repl. 1, 2, and Def. A.]

cause the one is not sin in his own nature, whereas the other is sin, then take How ap-
this: One that stammereth and stutteth in his tongue edifieth the people; parel serv-
therefore stammering and stutting is good to edify.   For what if the fication.
Lord give his blessing unto his word, and to other good gifts, which he hath
that preacheth and weareth a surplice, &c.; is it to be thought therefore
that he liketh well of the wearing of that apparel?   This is to assign the
cause of a thing to that which is not only not the cause thereof, but some
hinderance also, and slaking of that whereof it is supposed to be a cause.
For a man may rather reason, that, forasmuch as they which preach with
surplice, &c. edify (notwithstanding that they thereby drive away some, They that
and to other some give suspicion of evil, &c.), then [3] *if they preached without* are driven
wearing any such things [4] *they should edify much more.   And yet, if a man* that cause
were assured to gain a thousand by doing of that which may offend, or picion of
cause to fall one brother, he ought not to do it. anabaptism.

Jo. Whitgift.

Indeed, if this apparel were of that nature that a lie is,
your similitude of the "midwives" had some shew in it;
and yet must you of necessity confess that their "lying" to
Pharao "did much good" *per accidens;* for otherwise the
men-children of the Israelites, and even Moses himself, had
been murdered; and you are not ignorant that divers writers
in this respect excuse that doing of theirs.   You know likewise
what the opinion of some is, touching that kind of lie that
is called *officiosum mendacium;* but, for my part, I am in
that point of St Augustine's judgment [5].   But your similitude
is not like; and, if it were, yet makes it against you; for
"their lying did good;" as I have said before.

Your other similitude of "stammering and stutting" is
ridiculous, and argueth your great contempt of lawful and
decent orders.   The laws of this church have prescribed this
apparel to the ministers of the word as decent, orderly, and
comely, the same laws have inhibited those to preach that
refuse to submit themselves unto such orders.   Wherefore,
seeing they be appointed as fit garments for preachers, and
none may preach except he receive them, they do edify, not

[3 Repl. 2. omits *then.*]   [4 Thing, Repl. 1 and 2.]

[5 Unde etiam sciri potest, utrum et tunc habeat aliquam caussam, sicut ipse
putat, officiosi mendacii, existimans falsa narratione hominem territum posse a
libidine cohiberi, atque hoc modo etiam ad spiritualia se consulere mentiendo
arbitretur?   Quo genere admisso atque approbato, omnis omnino fidei disciplina
subvertitur : &c.—August. Op. Par. 1679-1700. Lib. de Mendac. cap. viii. 11.
Tom. VI. col. 427.   Conf. ejusd. ad Hieron. Epist. xxviii. cap. iii. 3.   Tom. II.
cols. 46, 7.]

by themselves, as I have before declared, but *per accidens*; as all other such like things do. For neither the church, nor the pulpit, nor the bells, nor kneeling, and such other, do otherwise edify than *per accidens*.

Touching offence that is taken at the wearing of this apparel, I have shewed before that it is an offence taken, and not given; neither is it to be considered whether men be offended or no, but whether they have any just cause of offence. Many be offended with our churches, and will neither hear sermon nor receive the sacraments in them; we must not therefore pull down our churches, or cease to preach and administer the sacraments in them. You must remember the distinction of *scandalum acceptum* and *scandalum datum*, "an offence given," and "an offence taken."

Chapter vii. The Seventh Division.

Answer to the Admonition, Page 239, Sect. 3.

Thirdly, because also by experience we daily understand that such as consent in wearing this apparel consent also in all other points of doctrine, and keep the peace of the church, which is one of the principal causes of edifying; contrariwise, such as refuse the same apparel not only dissent and disagree among themselves, but fall into divers and strange opinions without stay, and slander the gospel with their contentiousness, and tear in pieces the church of Christ with their factions and schisms, and be the cause why both the word of God and christian magistrates be almost generally contemned.

T. C. Page 58, Sect. 2.

The third reason is, that they which consent in wearing the surplices consent also in all other points of doctrine, and they that do not wear it do not consent, not so much as amongst themselves. If this consent in the points of religion be in the surplice, cope, &c., tell us, I beseech you, whether in the matter, or in the form, or in what hid and unknown quality standeth it. If it be in that the ministers use all one apparel, then it is marvel that, this being so strong a bond to hold them together in godly unity, that it was never commanded of Christ, nor practised of prophets or apostles, neither[1] of no other reformed churches. I had thought wholly that those things

[1 Never, Repl. 1 and 2.]

which the Lord appointeth to maintain and keep unity with, and especially How ap-
the holy sacraments of baptism and of the Lord's supper, had been strong parel serv-
enough to have first of all knit us unto the Lord, and therefore also to his eth to edi-
fication.
doctrine, and then one of us to another, and that the dissentings[2] *in such a*
ceremony as a surplice, &c. neither should nor could in those that pertain
unto God break the unity of the Spirit, which is bound with the bond of
truth.   And, although there be which like not this apparel, that think
otherwise than either their brethren, or than indeed they ought to do, yet
a man may find greater dissent amongst those which are united in surplice
and cope, &c. than there is amongst those which wear them not, either with
themselves, or with them that wear them.   For how many there are that
wear surplices which would be gladder to say a mass than to hear a
sermon, let all the world judge.   And of those that do wear this apparel,
and be otherwise well-minded to the gospel, are there not which will wear
the surplice and not the cap ; other that will wear both cap and surplice,
but not the tippet ; and yet a third sort, that will wear surplice, cap, and
tippet, but not the cope ?   It hath been the manner always of wise and
learned men to esteem of things by the causes, and not by the event, and that
especially in matters of religion ; for, if they should be esteemed of the event,
Josh. viii.[3]
Judg. xx.[3] *who is there which will not condemn the Israelites' battle against*
Aye, and afterward against the Benjamites ? which, notwith-
standing, the cause, which was God's will, and God's commandment, justi-
fieth.   And therefore in a word I answer that, if there[4] *be such consent*
amongst those which like well of this apparel, and such jars amongst those
that like it not, as M. Doctor would make the world believe, neither is the
wearing of a[5] *surplice, &c. cause of that consent in them, nor the not wear-*
ing cause of that[6] *disagreement in the other.   But, as our knowledge and*
love is unperfect here in this world, so is our agreement and consent of
judgment unperfect.   And yet all these hard speeches of yours, or uncha-
ritable suspicions of papism, anabaptism, Catharism, Donatism, &c., where-
by you do as much as lieth in you to cut us clean off from you, shall not
be able so to estrange us or separate us from you, but that we will by God's
grace hold whatsoever you hold well, and keep that unity of spirit which
is the bond of truth, even with you, Master Doctor, whom we suppose, as
appeareth by this your book, to have set yourself further from us than
numbers of those which, although they be content to receive the apparel, and
bear with things, yet would have been loth to have set down that against
the sincerity of the gospel, and hinderance of reformation, which you
have done.

JO. WHITGIFT.

Such laws and orders as keep godly peace and unity in
the church do edify; but the laws for apparel keep godly
peace and unity in the church; *ergo*, they edify.   The minor

---

[2 Dissenting, Repl. 1 and 2.]

[3 These references are inserted from Repl. 2.]   [4 These, Def. B.]

[5 The, Repl. 1 and 2.]   [6 The, Repl. 1 and 2.]

I prove by experience of such as are subject to these laws, and by the event; which is a probable kind of reasoning, though it be not necessary; neither may the examples of a few improve that which is generally true almost in all.

These persons that you talk of, which be thus contrarily minded (if there be any such, as I think you do but feign), yet do they keep the peace of the church; they condemn not their brethren, neither yet the apparel that they themselves (peradventure for some special cause) wear not.

Some I know there are, which agree with us in wearing the apparel, and join with you in contention, subscribe to all our orders and articles, and yet in certain places and companies maintain your opinions; but of such we make no account, neither I think do you, further than they may serve your turn.

Again, I confess that there be some which have not received the apparel, and yet greatly mislike many of your opinions, and keep with us the unity of the church; whom I for my part have always reverenced, and do reverence, not only for their singular virtue and learning, but for their modesty also. Wherefore, when I speak either of the one or of the other, I speak not of all, but of the most part.

Certain it is that those things which "the Lord appointeth to keep unity with, and especially the sacraments," ought to be the especial bond of the same; and that nothing should separate those that are coupled and joined therein; but we see it fall out otherwise, such is the crooked and rebellious nature of man; and therefore hath God also appointed magistrates, and given them authority to make orders and laws to maintain the peace and unity of the church, that those, which of conscience and good disposition will not, by such laws and orders may be constrained at the least to keep the external peace and unity of the church. Do you take this to be a good reason: "The sacraments are bonds to keep and maintain the unity" of the Spirit; therefore there needeth no laws or magistrates to provide for the external peace and quietness of the church?

T. C. ima-
gineth such a
perfection as
is not to be
found.

Your imagination throughout your whole book is of such a perfection in men as though they needed no laws or magistrates to govern them, but that every man might be as it were a law to himself; which whereunto it tendeth may easily be conjectured.

I have not "set down" anything (I trust) "to the hinder- How ap-
ance of the gospel, or of reformation;" but I seek to reform parel serv-
such contentious spirits as be enemies unto both. And I believe fication.
that, when some other (not only such as you mean, but such
as you least think of) shall understand the depth of your
opinions, together with the strangeness, untruth, dangerous-
ness, and other circumstances joined with them, they will
think that I have spoken or written nothing either untruly
or unnecessarily. In the meantime I discharge my conscience
and duty, and so will do (God willing) as long as I can either
speak or write.

Chapter vii.   The Eighth Division.

Answer to the Admonition, Page 239, Sect. 4.

I here omit that which I might as justly bring for
this kind of apparel, as you do for sitting at the communion, I mean a fit and profitable signification; whereof
M. Martyr speaketh in the epistle before mentioned on
this sort : " I will not here say that they which stand to P. Martyr[1].
the defence of this matter may pretend some honest and
just signification of the apparel, and that not dissenting
from the word of God, which is this: the ministers of
the church (as the prophet Malachi witnesseth) be angels
and God's messengers; but angels for the most part
appeared being clothed in white garments. I pray you,
how shall we debar the church of this liberty, that it
cannot signify some good thing in setting forth their
rites and ceremonies, especially being so done that no
manner of God's honour is attributed unto them, and
that they be in sight comely and in number few, and
that christian people be not with them overburdened,
and matters of greater importance be omitted[2]?"

T. C. Page 59, Lin. 5.

The white apparel, which is a note and a true[3] representation of the Master
Acts i. 10.[4]   *glory and pureness in the angels, should be a lying sign and* words per-
pretence of that which is not in the ministers, which are miser- verted.

[1 This is not in Answ. 2.]
[2 P. Martyr's Letter to John Hoper Byshop, &c. at the end of A briefe examination for the tyme, &c. Lond. Jugge, fol. C 1. 2. Conf. Epist. Theolog. ad
calc. Loc. Comm. Heidelb. 1613. p. 1088.]
[3 And true, Repl. 2.]   [4 This reference is inserted from Repl. 2.]

How apparel serveth to edification.

able and sinful men. And our Saviour Christ, which was the minister of God and pure from sin, and therefore meetest to wear the marks[1] of pureness, used no such kind of weed, saving only for that small time wherein he would give to his disciples in the mount a taste of that glory which he should enjoy for ever, and they with him; where for the time his apparel appeared as white as snow. And, if it be meet that the ministers should represent the angels in their apparel, it is much more meet that they should have a pair of wings, as the angels are described to have, to put them in remembrance of their readiness and quickness to execute their office, which may and ought to be in them, than to wear white apparel, which is a token of pureness from sin and infection, and of a glory, which neither they have, nor can have, nor ought so much as to desire to have, as long as they be in this world. And, whereas the maintainers of this apparel have for their greatest defence that it is a thing mere civil; to let pass that they confound ecclesiastical orders with civil (which they can no more justly do than to confound the church with the commonwealth); I say, to let that pass, they do by this means not only make it an ecclesiastical ceremony, but also a matter of conscience. For, if so be that the white apparel of the minister have any force either to move the people or the minister unto greater pureness, or to any other godliness whatsoever, then it[3] is that which ought to be commanded, and to be obeyed of necessity, and to be retained, although the contrary were forbidden. And then also, if there be a virtue in a white garment, and the signification thereof be so strong to work godliness, it were meet that order were taken that the whitest cloth should be bought, that should[4] be often (at the least every week once) washed by a very good launder, and with soap; for, if the white help, more white helpeth more, and that which is most white helpeth most of all to godliness. Although the church have authority to make ceremonies (so they be according to the rules before recited of God's glory, and profiting the congregation), I could for all that never yet learn that it had power to give new significations, as it were to institute new sacraments. And by this means is taken clean away from us the hold which we have against the papists, whereby (against all the goodly shews which they make by the colour of these significations) we say that the word of God, and the sacraments of baptism, and of the supper of the Lord, are sufficient to teach, to admonish, and to put us in remembrance of all duty whatsoever. So we are now come to the superstition of the Grecians; for, as they will have neither graven nor carved image in their churches, but painted, so will we[5] neither have graven, nor carved, nor painted, but woven. And truly I see no cause why we may not have as well holy water and holy bread, if this reason which is here be good; for I am sure the significations of them are as glorious as this of the surplice, and call to remembrance as necessary things. And, if it be said that it may not be, lest the number of ceremonies should be too too great, it

Mark ix. 3.[2]

Isai. vi. 2.[2]

Here you play with a feather.

You understand not this topical place; for it holdeth in those things only, *quæ per se aliquid faciunt.*

[1 Mark, Repl. 1 and 2.]   [2 These references are inserted from Repl. 2.]
[3 *It* is not in Def. B.]
[4 That it should, Repl. 1 and 2.]   [5 We will, Repl. 1 and 2.]

may be easily answered, that these which we have may be taken away, and **How apparel serveth to edification.** *those set in place of them.   And therefore, although the surplice have a black spot, when it is whitest, yet is it not so black as you make it with your white significations, nor the cause so evil as you defend it.*

   If you press me with M. Martyr's and M. Bucer's authority, I first **An easy kind of answering.** *say they were men, and therefore (although otherwise very watchful) yet such as slept sometimes.   And then I appeal from their apocryphas unto their known writings, and from their private letters unto their public records.*

Jo. Whitgift.

I have here only set down M. Martyr's words to shew that I might as justly bring in a fit and profitable signification of the apparel, as the authors of the Admonition do of sitting at the communion.   I did not allow their signification of sitting, neither do I approve any such signification of apparel; but yet you will give me leave to set the one against the other, and to shew that I might as well do the one as they do the other.

   You pervert Master Martyr's words; for he saith that, **Mere civil things may have signification.** "forasmuch as angels appeared in white apparel, and the ministers of the church be angels and God's messengers, therefore the church may appoint to her ministers such apparel in signification of their office." Which you do not answer, but range up and down at your pleasure, like unto a spaniel not taught to follow his game.   M. Martyr doth not say that "the apparel is a sign of pureness" that is in the minister; and therefore all this that you write in confuting of that might have been cut off, and very well spared.   But, if **The form of apparel may put a man in mind of his duty.** Master Martyr should have said that it may be a sign of the pureness that ought to be in ministers, you are to seek for an answer as yet.   Christ, being purity itself, needed nothing to put him in mind thereof; but man, being impure, may have external instruments to bid him (as it were) remember what he ought to be.   I think that several kinds of habits be appointed to men of divers degrees and calling, partly for that purpose; and, if a man in grave apparel use himself lightly or wantonly, we use commonly to say, such behaviour becometh not that apparel, meaning that his habit and apparel ought to put him in mind of modesty and gravity; and this doth argue that even mere civil things may have significations; which overthroweth another argument of yours, whereby you would prove that the apparel must of necessity be "an ecclesiastical ceremony," because there is attributed unto it some signification.   Whether it be a matter "mere civil," or mere ecclesiastical, or mixed of both, is not now the question, neither yet whether "the church may be confounded with the commonwealth" or no ; and therefore I will not here deal with any of them, lest I should confound both the matter and the reader : only I speak of your argument which is confuted by common usage; for several habits in the universities signify several degrees in learning ; several kind of apparel, several callings and functions in the common-wealth ; and this apparel doth put every man in mind of his duty ; and yet they are not longer to be retained than the magistrate and the laws do permit, but are alterable accord-ing to times, places, and persons.   No man saith that there is virtue in such garments or power "to work godliness ;" and therefore your pretty jests builded upon that ground are vain and toyish, and your topical place not rightly under-standed ; for it is meant of such things *quæ per se aliquid faciunt*.

Everything that signifieth anything is not "a sacrament ;" for then were matrimony a sacrament; and so were laying on of hands, and such like.

The papists used unlawful signs, and attributed unto them life and death ; for they made them necessary to salvation.

"Images," whether they be "graven," "painted," or "woven," are against the express commandment of God ; and therefore these be unapt similitudes; neither would you have used them, if you had well considered M. Martyr's words.

The same I answer to your allegation of "holy water and holy bread :" they be *pseudo-adiaphora*, and have annexed unto them opinion of salvation and of worship ; all which we utterly remove from these orders.

Your answer to M. Martyr's and M. Bucer's authority is sure, but not greatly commendable ; for it is the easiest but the worst answer that can be to deny the authority of wise, learned, and famous men, and that without reason, and only by cavilling.   These be "their known writings," and they be written of purpose upon these controversies according to the circumstances of time, place, and person ; and therefore, if anything in "their public writings" seem to be against their judgments here, distinguish the time and other circumstances; and I doubt not but they will well agree with themselves. *Interim*, you do your endeavour to deface them.

Chapter vii.   The Ninth Division.

Admonition.

1 *Thess. v.* 22.[1]   *They have the shew of evil (seeing the popish priesthood is evil).*

Answer to the Admonition, Page 240, Sect. 2.

[You add and say that "they have the shew of evil (seeing the popish priesthood is evil)."[2]]

How apparel is a sign of evil, and how otherwise[3].

When they were a sign and token of the popish priesthood, then were they evil, even as the thing was which they signified; but now they be the tokens and the signs of the ministers of the word of God which are good, and therefore also they be good. No man in this church of England is so ignorant but that he knoweth this apparel not to be now the signs of a massing priest, but of a lawful minister; wherefore it is a shew of good; even as it is in the like manner in the universities a shew and sign of degrees in learning, and therefore a shew of good; except you will also condemn degrees of learning. Neither is it any strange matter for the self-same thing, in divers respects, and at divers times, to be the sign both of good and evil. The bells were a sign of evil, when they were rung to call to mass, and to stay storms and tempests; the self-same bells are now a sign of good, when they be rung to sermons and other godly actions. The churches themselves were a sign of evil, when idolatry was committed in them, and false doctrine preached; now they be a sign of good, when God is rightly worshipped in them, and his word truly preached. Many such examples I could bring; but a reasonable man can gather of these sufficiently to confute your error. Furthermore, when we be willed to abstain from all shew of evil, it is meant of evil life, and evil doctrine, lest we do anything with a scrupulous conscience.

[1 This reference is inserted from Adm. and Answ.]
[2 This sentence is added from Answ.]
[3 Signs of evil how apparel is, and how otherwise, Answ. 2.]

T. C. Page 59, towards the end.

M. Doctor proceedeth to prove that they are signs and shews of good, and not of evil, as the authors of the Admonition allege. To the proof where- of, although (according to his manner) he repeateth divers things before alleged, yet the sum of all he hath comprehended in an argument, which is that, forsomuch as the ministers are good which wear them, therefore they are also good ; and, because the ministers, whereof the apparel are notes and marks, be good, therefore those be good notes and good marks : so the rea- son is, they are notes, and notes of good ministers ; therefore Falla compo- *they be good notes of the ministers.   So I will prove the names* sitionis.[1] *of idols to be fit and convenient names for good men to be called by. Beltshaser, Saddrake, Misacke, and Abed-nego, were names of* Dan. i. 7.[2] *Daniel and his three companions, and they were the names of good men ; therefore they are good names of men.   And so the names of the Babylonian idols are by this reason of M. Doctor justified to be* Untruth. *good names.   Again, the golden calf was a sign.   Also it was a* Exod. xxxii. *sign of the true God ; therefore it was a true sign of God.   Con-* 4.[2] *cerning the notes of civil professions, and what difference is between those and this cause, I have spoken before.*

Jo. Whitgift.

The Admonition saith thus : "they have the shew of evil, seeing the popish priesthood is evil."   To this I answer that, "when they were a sign and token of the popish priest- hood, then they were evil, and a sign of evil, because the thing was evil which they signified ; but now they are tokens of the ministers of the gospel which are good, and therefore they are good," and the signs of good.   The reason is M. Bucer's[3] : I am not ashamed of my author; and it is stronger than you can overthrow.   For let me hear how you will an- swer this argument : Whatsoever signifieth and noteth that which is good is a sign of good ; but this apparel signifieth that which is good ; *ergo*, it is a sign of good.   The major is evident.   The minor is thus proved.   The ministry of the gospel is good ; but this apparel is a sign of the ministry of the gospel ; *ergo*, it is a sign of good.   All the logic you have cannot answer this argument, except you will deny the apparel to be the sign of the ministry of the gospel ; which were to deny that which is subject to the senses : the other examples that I have used doth make this matter more manifest.   I refer it to the reader to judge how fitly you have answered them.

[1 This is inserted from Repl. 1.]
[2 These references are inserted from Repl. 2.]   [3 See before, pages 38, 9.]

Whether they "be good signs," or no, is not now the question, but whether they "be signs of good;" for that the Admonition denieth. If you can conclude that they be evil, because they be signs of evil, why may not I likewise say that they be good, because they be signs of good? We commonly call that a good sign, which is a sign of good; neither can you place this reason in any fallation: it is a sign of good; *ergo*, it is a good sign; for it is called a good sign in this respect only, that it signifieth that which is good.

Those names, in respect of those whom they signified, were good; in respect of the idols, to whom they properly belonged, they were evil; for such external things in divers respects may be both good and evil. The "golden calf" was an idol made to be worshipped, no "sign of the true God;" and therefore undiscreetly here brought in.

External things may be both good and evil in divers respects.

Wheresoever I have before alleged these things you speak of, yet be they answered neither here nor there; and this the reader may note if he list, that, wheresoever you cannot answer, there either you frump and gird after your manner, or you cavil and confute your own imagination, or closely pass the matter over in silence, or post it over to some other place, where you speak nothing of it.

The divers shifts used by T. C. in answering.

Chapter vii.   The Tenth Division.

Admonition.

They work discord, they hinder the preaching of the gospel[4].

Answer to the Admonition, Page 241, Sect. 2.

This is an argument *a non causa ad causam;* [that is, when as that is put and taken for the cause, which is not the cause of the thing talked of. For[5]] it is not the apparel that worketh discord, or hindereth the preaching of the gospel; no, no more than it is the word of God that engendereth heresies, or wine that maketh drunk, or the sword that murdereth, or the law that worketh injury, &c. But it is the sinister affection, the

Non causa pro causa.

[4 This and other portions of the Admonition, to *obstinate*, page 72, which appeared in one paragraph in Answ., see above (page 50, note 1), are repeated in separate sentences in Answ. placed at the head of each paragraph thereof.]

[5 This is inserted from Answ. 2.]

rebellious nature, the contentious mind of man. For who began this contention, or when was it begun? Truly, if the law for apparel were utterly abrogated, yet would not your contention cease; nay, it would burst out much more[1] vehemently, and in far greater matters; as this your Admonition declareth. And therefore I think rather that the law for apparel will stay further contentions, especially if it be duly executed.

T. C. Page 60, Sect. 1.

You say the cause of disorder[2] is not in the apparel, but in the minds of men. You mean, I am sure, those that refuse the apparel; but, if you make them authors of discord, because they consent not with you in wearing, do you not see it is as soon said, that you are the causers of discord, because you do not consent with those which wear not? For, as there should be unity in that point if all did wear that apparel, so should there be if all did wear none of it. It is a very unequal comparison that you compare the use of this apparel with the use of wine, and of a sword, which are profitable and necessary; but it is more intolerable that you match it with the word of God. I could throw it as far down as you lift it up, but I will not do so. This only I will say, if there were no harm in it, and that it were also profitable, yet, forasmuch as it is not commanded of God expressly, but a thing (as you say) indifferent, and notwithstanding is cause of so many incommodities, and so abused (as I have before declared), it ought to be sufficient reason to abolish them; seeing that the Numb. xxi. brazen serpent, which was instituted of the Lord himself, and 8, 9.[3]
2 Kings xviii. contained a profitable remembrance of the wonderful benefit of 4.[3] God towards his people, was beaten to powder, when as it began to be an occasion of falling unto the children of Israel; and seeing that St Paul, after the love-feasts (which were kept at the administration of 1 Cor. xi. 22.[3] the Lord's supper, and were means to nourish love amongst the churches) were abused, and drawn to another use than they were first ordained, did utterly take them away, and commanded that they should not be used any more.*

It is as soon said, but not so truly; because the one retaineth order, and the other breaketh it.

Jo. WHITGIFT.

I may answer you almost in the self-same words and manner that M. Zuinglius answered one Balthazar, an anabaptist, who charged him then, as you charge us now in this place: "Consider," saith he, "who be the authors and causes of dissension; whether we, that attempt nothing of our own private authority, but have submitted ourselves to the judgment of the

Zuinglius ad Balt.

[1 Out more, Answ. 2.]   [2 Discord, Repl. 1 and 2.]
[3 The first two references and the verse of the third are inserted from Repl. 2.]

church, and of those that be governors of the same, or rather you, who so arrogantly, without any such authority, do what you list, speak what you list, allow and condemn at your pleasure[4]." But for further trial hereof I refer you to such notes as I have collected out of Zuinglius and others, and placed in the second edition of my Answer to the Admonition[5]. Pag. 19, &c.

Our consenting is according to our duty required of us by the word of God towards such as be in authority : your dissenting is contrary to your duty of obedience, in such cases enjoined unto you by the word of God. If all refused the apparel with you, yet would you not be quiet; for you make this the least cause of your schism. I do not compare " this apparel with the word of God," but by these examples I shew the unaptness of such arguments as be *a non causa ad causam.* You have " thrown it down as low " as you can, and, if you could cast it lower, your will is good; and therefore to say you " could " do it, and " will not," is as great an offence as was the midwives' lying to Pharao.

I have shewed in my Answer that, as the case now standeth, it is rather commodious ; as for abuses in it, as it is now used, you have hitherto shewed none ; and, if it were " abused," yet doth it not follow that therefore it is to be removed ; except the abuse could not be taken away without the abolishing of the thing, as it was in the " brazen serpent ;" which serpent though it was by God commanded to be set up, yet was it (as M. Martyr saith) but for that time[6], wherein power was given unto it to heal and cure those that were bitten of the serpents, Num. xxi. ; and therefore, being but temporal, and thus abused, was lawfully taken away ; neither would the idolatry committed unto it otherwise have ceased. But do you think that any man doth worship the apparel, as the Israelites did worship the serpent? St Paul, in that chapter of the 1 Cor., reproveth them for certain abuses about the " Lord's supper," whereof this was one of the chief, that they made it an occasion of feasting and banqueting; which manner Numb. xxi. 1 Cor. xi.

---

[4] H. Zvingl. Op. Tigur. 1581. ad Libell. Baltaz. Hvebm. Resp. Pars II. fol. 100. 2. See Vol. I. page 131, note 5.]

[5] See Vol. I. pages 125, &c.]

[6] ... nec erectum, ut esset perpetuo : verum potius ejus temporis calamitatum remedium, et venturi Messiæ typus esset : &c.—Melachim, id est Reg. Libr. Duo Post. cum Comm. P. Martyr. in prim. tot. et secund. priora xi. capp., et J. Wolph. in sec. quatuordecim ult. capp. Tigur. 1571. In II. Lib. cap. xviii. fol. 351.]

of feasting in the church was not only borrowed of the gentiles, as M. Bullinger saith, but occasion also of much contention, and very unseemly for that time and place[1]. And, as
Calvin. Master Calvin saith upon that place, "The Corinthians are reproved, because they had mingled profane banquets (and that also with the contumely of the poor) with that holy and spiritual feast[2];" and therefore expedient it was that they should "be taken away;" and, if you can shew the like uncurable abuse in the apparel, I will cry, away with it, as fast as you do.

Chapter vii.   The Eleventh Division.

Admonition.

They keep the memory of Egypt still amongst us, and put us in mind of that abomination whereunto they in times past have served, they bring the ministry into contempt, they offend the weak, they encourage the obstinate.

Answer to the Admonition, Page 241, Sect. 3, 4, 5.

You say, "they keep the memory of Egypt still amongst us, &c.[3]" No truly, no more than doth the church, the pulpit, the bells, &c.; but they teach us the true use of christian liberty, and that all things be clean to those that be clean; finally, that godly men may well use that which wicked have abused, howsoever ungodly.

"They bring the ministry into contempt." Only with you, and such as you (by your continual crying out against them) have deluded. Contemners of good orders, laws, and statutes, are to be severely punished for their contempt. Good laws, orders, and statutes, are not to be altered or dissolved, because by such as forget their duties they are contemned.

[1 Quoties ergo diebus statis mystica illa in ecclesia peragenda essent sacra, opulentiores instructis in cœtu sacro conviviis epulabantur pro more magis gentili quam christiano: pauperes vero qui in eundem congregabantur conventum vel invidebant, ut fit, ditioribus hanc felicitatem, vel nimis acerbe miseram illam sortem suam et deplorabant et execrabantur. Inde porro dissidia et factionum pullulabant studia, incalescebant contendentium jurgia, &c.—H. Bullinger. Comm. in Omn. Apostol. Epist. Tigur. 1539. In 1. Epist. ad Cor. cap. xi. p. 202.]

[2 Nunc taxat abusum qui in cœnam Domini obrepserat apud Corinthios: quod sacro et spirituali epulo profana symposia permiscerent, idque cum pauperum contumelia.—Calvin. Op. Amst. 1667-71. Comm. in Epist. 1. ad Cor. cap. xi. 20. Tom. VII. p. 180.]

[3 This sentence is not in Answ.]

"They offend the weak and encourage the obstinate." Those that be offended with them think themselves most strong, and glory therein with condemning of others. The obstinate be encouraged through the schisms and contentions that you trouble the church and slander the gospel with; which one day you will understand, if in time you do not repent.

[Admonition.

Therefore can no authority by the word of God, with any pretence of order and disobedience[4], command them, nor make them in any wise tolerable; but by circumstances they are wicked and against the word of God.

Answer [to the Admonition.]

Now you come to the point where you would have it: it is the mark you shoot at, to spoil the magistrate of all authority in things indifferent, especially in ecclesiastical matters. But you set it down only without proof; wherefore I will thus briefly answer to your bare words (until you bring some proof), that this your assertion is both anabaptistical, and papistical, and contrary also to the word of God, and all learning[5].] *Anabaptistical assertions.*

T. C. Page 60, Sect. 2.

The rest of that which followeth in this matter is nothing else but either that which hath been oftentimes repeated, or else reproachful words, or unjust accusations of contempt of magistrates, without any proof at all; and therefore are such as either are answered, or which I will not vouchsafe to[6] answer, especially seeing I mean not to give reproach[7] and reviling for reviling; and seeing that I have before protested of our humble submission, and loving fear or reverence, which we bear to the prince, and those which are appointed magistrates underneath her. *True; for you have given ten for one.*

Jo. Whitgift.

This is a short answer, to say you "will not vouchsafe to answer." What reproachful words or unjust accusations are here uttered by me? except this offend you, that I say, "contemners of good orders, laws, and statutes, are to be severely

---

[4 Obedience, Adm.]

[5 The paragraphs between brackets appear to be omitted in the Defence: they are inserted here from Answ.]

[6 The, Def. B.]

[7 Seeing that I mean not to give reproach for reproach, Repl. 1 and 2.]

punished for their contempt. Good laws, orders, and statutes are not to be altered and dissolved, because by such as forget their duties they be contemned." If this cast you into that choler, I cannot mend it: you must bear with me when I speak the truth.

Whether of us two have more offended in "reproachings and revilings," because we are both partial in our own causes, let us refer it to the indifferent readers. How far you are from performing that in deed to the magistrates, that you protest in word, is in another place declared.

Chapter vii.   The Twelfth Division.

T. C. Page 60, Sect. 3.

And therefore I will conclude that, forsomuch as the ceremonies of antichristianity are not, nor cannot be, the fittest to set forth the gospel, and for that they are occasions of fall to some, of hinderance to other some, of grief and alienation of minds unto others (the contrary of all which ought to be considered in establishing of things indifferent in the church); therefore neither is this apparel fittest for the minister of the gospel, and, if it were, yet, considering the incommodities that come of the use of it, it should be removed.

Jo. Whitgift.

This conclusion consisteth wholly upon false principles; whereof though some of them have been before spoken, yet not one of them proved: for trial whereof I refer the reader to that which we have both written of this matter.

Admonition[1].

The twelfth.

Then as God gave utterance [b] they preached the word only: now they read homilies, articles, injunctions, &c.

[b] John vi. 38.
John xii.
49.
1 Cor. xi.
23.

Answer to the Admonition, Page 62, Sect. 3.

Here you quote in the margent the sixth of John, verse 38; where Christ saith that he "came down from heaven not to do his own will, but the will of his Father that sent him." Likewise the twelfth of John, verse 49; where also he saith that he hath "not spoken of[2] himself,

[1 Here Reply takes up again the order which had been interrupted. See before, page 47, note 5.]

[2 So, Answ.]

but the Father that sent him gave him commandment
what he should say and what he should speak." And the
first to the Corinthians, xi. chapter, verse 23; where St
Paul saith that he "received of the Lord that which he
delivered unto them." No man denieth but that the word
of God only ought to be preached, and that as God
giveth utterance. But do you mean that we may not
study for our sermons, or that we may speak nothing
but the very text of scripture, without amplifying or *Scriptures may be amplified.*
expounding the same? When I know your meaning
herein, you shall understand more of my mind. In the
mean time, this I am sure of, that the homilies appointed
to be read in the church are learned, godly, agreeable
to God's word, and more effectual to edification, than a
number of your sermons, which consist in words only,
and intreat of little else but of cap, surplice, &c., archbishop, lord bishop, &c.; the end whereof is not edifi-
cation, but contention. Homilies read in the church *Homilies read in the church are commendable.*
have always been commendable, and usual even from
the beginning; look Augustine, Chrysostom, and others;
and why may not articles and injunctions, being collected to the setting forth of true religion and good
orders in the church, be read there also, as in a most
meet place? But I perceive you are enemies to reading, because you love so well to hear yourselves talking;
I will say no worse.

T. C. Page 60, Sect. 4.

*You know they allow studying for sermons, and amplifying and
expounding of the scriptures, and why then do you ask? But by this
question you would have your reader think, or at the least have the
authors of the Admonition in suspicion, that they liked not of study for
sermons. God make us more careful of the good name of our brethren,
than by such light and ungrounded suspicions, nay, without any suspicion,
nay, contrary to that which is daily seen and heard[3], to raise up such
slanderous reports of them. But homilies are smally beholding unto you,
which, to prove that they may be read in the church, allege that Augustine
and Chrysostom made sermons in their churches; for that which we call a
sermon, they called of the Greek word an homily; so that the argument is,
that Augustine and Chrysostom preached sermons or homilies in their
churches, therefore we may read homilies in ours. But peradventure you
have some better thing to say for them afterward.*

[³ Harde, Repl. 1 and 2; hard, Def. A.]

Jo. Whitgift.

I have heard some fautors of theirs earnestly reason against "studying for sermons;" and it is not long since it was almost in plain terms in the pulpit preached. I think they study for their sermons, but how diligently they study, or whether they would seem to study, or no, I know not: the words of the Admonition are very suspicious.

That which I speak of Augustine and Chrysostom aptly serveth for my purpose; for, although they were Augustine's and Chrysostom's sermons, yet in that they have both committed them to writing, and left them to their posterity, it argueth that they thought them to be very profitable for the church; neither do I see any cause why they should rather now be thought unlawful to be read, than they were then to be preached; but yet one thing we may note, that both Augustine and Chrysostom writ their homilies or sermons; and therefore it may be that they did also sometime read them in the church[1].

[1] Cartwright says that he had originally determined to answer this tractate; but, "considering after that this cause hath been so fully debated," "considering also" that he, Whitgift, "triumphs in his own shame," "considering that he hath almost nothing at all not before answered, and that he hath not fetched from any treasury of good learning, but as taken up by the highway-side, and considering that we have this question with very few (him, the papists, or those which have already cast an eye unto the papists only excepted,...), all these things considered, with that, that it may better appear we take not these things for the greatest matter we complain of; I thought good," he adds, "to tread this treatise under my foot, and to save some good hours, which might be lost in unripping this beggary."— Sec. Repl. pp. 402, 3.]

Of Archbishops, Metropolitans, Bishops, Archdeacons, &c.

Tract. VIII.

The reasons of T. C. answered, whereby he goeth about to take away the superfluous lop (as he termeth it) of these offices.

Chapter i.   The First Division.

Admonition.

The thirteenth and fourteenth[2].

^c 1 Tim. iii. 1.
^d Phil. iv. 11.
2 Cor. vi. 4, 8, 10.[3]

Then ^cit was painful; now gainful. ^dThen poor and ignominious[4]; now rich and glorious[5].

Answer to the Admonition, Page 63, Sect. ult.

It was then as it useth to be under the cross.   And it is now as it useth to be when God doth bless it with peace, quietness, and godly magistrates.   And yet surely even now it is more painful than gainful, more ignominious than rich and glorious; and that do those know that bear the heat of the day.   But it is the more painful and ignominious for you, who cease not with railing and spiteful words, in pulpits and at tables, to deprave and backbite your brethren, and to trouble the whole state with your factions, and daily-invented new opinions: the persecution of the sword ceaseth; but the persecution of the tongue is extreme hot: and we, who gain so much, and be so glorious, are molested as well by you as by the papist and atheist; and therefore not very glorious.

Scilicet, the ministry[6].

The ministry is now more painful than gainful.

T. C. Page 61, Sect. 1.

A hundred pounds by year is taken of some benefice, for which four sermons only are preached, and those sometimes by another.   If this be Prov. xxx. 15.[7] *"more painful than gainful," it is because "the horseleach hath two daughters, Give, give, &c."   And I cannot see how they can be more glorious, unless the palace were turned into a court, and their chair*

[2 Though "the fourteenth" is here mentioned, the examination of what is so called does not commence for a considerable space.]

[3 2 Cor. vi. 4, 4, 10, Adm.]

[4 Here Adm. adds *in the eyes of the world.*]

[5 Here Answ. continues the quotation from the Admonition, as far as *removed,* page 79.]

[6 This marginal note is not in Answ.]

[7 The verse of this reference is inserted from Repl. 2.]

into a throne.   There are divers places that God hath blessed with peace,

where the ministers take more pain, and have less gain, and Matt. xii.19.2
which make less noises[1] when they go in the streets.   We
have amongst us which have had bishoprics offered, and, as things unmeet
for a minister of the gospel, have refused them.   God be praised, the sun
shineth not so hot in this country now, that you need to complain of any
great heat; and, if you feel any heat, you have better shade than Jonas iv. 6.2
Jonas had by his gourd.

Jo. Whitgift.

It may be that he which hath "an hundred pounds by the year, for which four sermons only are preached, &c." (if there be any such) taketh more pains for the church, is more careful for the state of it, suffereth more opprobrious words, and false slanders (which is not the least kind of persecution), for doing his duty, and keeping himself within the lists of obedience towards God and his prince, than those do that glory most of persecution, and lack of living.   He that hath much is also occasioned to spend much; neither is his pains the less, but more, if he be once desirous to do his duty.   And, the higher he is in degree, the more subject to the envious backbiter, and to the slanderous tongue.

"Those that have such palaces, and make such noise when they go in the streets, &c.," I think verily take more pains and care in and for the church of God, profit their country more in one month, than you and all your company do in a whole year; nay, I would to God it might be said you profited. Their pomp and their palaces are by lawful authority committed unto them; and the true martyrs of God have occupied the same or the like before them, and yet martyrs too.

Who "amongst" you they be "that have had bishoprics offered" unto them, I know not; but, if they boast of their denial, and have suborned you to make it known, they have their reward.   It may be the bishopric was too little for them; and they looked for some greater, and so missed both; but I will not judge: surely this brag cometh here out of place.

The heat of the tongue and backbiter both I and other may "greatly complain of;" and I hope we get not our living by going up and down the streets, and feasting daily at other

[1 Noise, Repl. 1 and 2.]
[2 The verse of the first reference and the last altogether are inserted from Repl. 2.]

men's tables, or, as Diogenes did, by disdaining and contemning all others. *Melius est vinum bibere cum ratione, quam
aquam cum fastu et superbia :* " It is better to drink wine
with discretion, than water with haughtiness and pride." It
is also more acceptable to God to dwell " in a palace," and
live in abundance, with doing a man's duty toward God and
his church, than to lie in prison for disdain and contempt.
Godly men may enjoy preferment; and such as be arrogant
and wilful may seem to contemn the same.

Chapter i.   The Second Division.

Admonition[3].

*And therefore titles, livings, and offices by antichrist devised, are given
to them, as metropolitan, archbishop, lord's grace, lord bishop, suffragan,*
† Matt. xxiii. *dean, archdeacon, prelate of the garter, earl, county palatine,*
11, 12.
Luke xxii. *honour, high commissioners, justices of peace and quorum, &c.*
25.
1 Cor. iv. *All which together with their offices, as they are strange and*
1.
1 Pet. v. 2, *unheard of in Christ's church, nay, plainly* †*in Christ's*[4] *word*
3.   *forbidden, so are they utterly with speed out of the same to be*
removed.

Answer to the Admonition, Page 64, Sect. 2.

Here you are in your ruff, but you shew your ignorance and contemptuous stomach.   You have given sentence that " the names of metropolitan, archbishop, &c.,
and their offices, were devised by antichrist;" likewise that " they are strange and unheard of in Christ's
church;" also that " they be plainly in God's word forbidden;" and last, that " they are utterly with speed to
be removed."   If you can prove all these points, it is
time the church were transformed, and the whole kind
of government of this realm altered.   But, if you cannot
prove them, then is it high time that such insolency
should be repressed, and perturbers of churches and
commonwealths[5] reformed.   Well, I must do the best
I can to improve all these points, which I might do sufficiently, if I should as barely deny them as you have
affirmed them; but I will not deal so nakedly in so great
a matter.

[3 Answ. having completed this paragraph before (see above, page 77) here
introduces it again : *You add and say that " therefore &c."* Some words are
omitted in this repetition, and *God's word* found instead of *Christ's word.*]

[4 God's, Adm.]   [5 Common weals, Answ.]

T. C. Page 61, Sect. 2.

Of those[1] offices something hath been spoken before, where it hath been proved out of the words of Christ that neither the names, nor offices of archbishop or archdeacons, do agree to the ministry of the gospel. Now, as

Because they flourish more prosperously than the envious man can well bear.

M. Doctor bestoweth great cost here and travail, in digging about them, and laying (as it were) new earth to their roots, that they being half-dead, if it were possible, might be recovered and quickened again, so I (because these trees mount up so high, and spread their boughs and arms so broad, that for the cold shade of them nothing can grow and thrive by them) will, before I come to answer these things that are here alleged, set down certain reasons (as it were instruments) to take away the superfluous lop and spread of their[1] immoderate offices.

Jo. Whitgift.

T. C. maketh his chief quarrel against those in authority in the church, and why he so doth.

T. C. hath a special quarrel against archbishops, bishops, and other that have the name of authority and degree in the church. For he perceiveth that they be the principal stops and hinderances of his confused platform, and that also they be the enemies unto sects and contentions, wherewith he is so greatly delighted. Moreover, he and many of his adherents be of that nature whereof Cæsar and Pompey were reported to be: the one could abide no superior, the other no equal; even so is it with them, as it is well known to those that have been

What kind of equality is pretended.

conversant with some of them. And, although they pretend equality in words, yet, if you mark well their writings, it shall easily appear that they mean it in others, not in themselves; for they would have him to be the best rewarded, and most reverenced, that hath the most and best gifts, which every one of these chief captains persuaded himself to have; so that in the end there would be as great ado (after their manner) which of them should be the chief, as ever there was betwixt the bishop of Rome and other bishops, or betwixt Canterbury and York in times past. In the meantime you may easily understand, if you please, that, notwithstanding they themselves would be exempted from the jurisdiction of archbishop, lord bishop, &c., yet do they challenge unto themselves as great jurisdiction over their parishes, and as lofty dominion over prince, nobles, and all, as ever the pope did over the whole church; as shall (God willing) be more fully declared, when I come to speak of their seigniory and kind of government. Now to his Reply.

[1 These, Repl. 1 and 2.]

Where "hath something been spoken before of these offices and names?" Or what arguments have you hitherto used to prove that they do not "agree to the ministers of the gospel?" If you have so done, I trust you are fully answered in that same place. But I promise you I do not presently remember where you have hitherto done it. If you mean the places of Matth. xx., &c., you have your full answer.

I have "bestowed" the more cost and labour in this matter, because I see your chief force bent against it. For, mark you who will, all your drift is against superiors. But let us hear your reasons[2].

Chapter i.   The Third Division.
T. C. Page 61, Sect. 3.

And for the names first, I desire the reader that we be not thought studious of contention, because we strive about the name of archbishop, &c. For this is not to strive about words, unless it be counted a strife of words, which is taken for the maintenance of the word of God; as it hath before appeared out of the evangelists. Then it must be remembered which Aristotle saith very well in his Elenchs, that τὰ ὀνόματα τῶν πραγμάτων μιμήματα ἐστὶ[3], which is, that "names are imitations," or, as it were, express images "of the things whereof they are names," and do for the most part bring to him that heareth them knowledge of the things that are signified by them. Howsoever the thing be itself, yet oftentimes it is supposed to be as the name pretendeth; and thereupon followeth that a man may be easily deceived, when the names do not answer to the things whereof they are names. There may be, I grant, a free[4] and more licentious use of names; but that licence is more tolerable in any thing rather than in matters of the church and salvation. And, if there be some cases wherein names that are not so proper may be borne with, yet are there also which are intolerable. And[5] who can abide that a minister of the gospel should be called by the name of a Levite, or sacrificer, unless it be he which would not care much if the remembrance of the death and resurrection of our Saviour Christ were plucked out of his mind? Again, It is unlawful for any man to take upon him those titles which are proper to our Saviour Christ; but the title of an archbishop[6] is only proper to our Saviour Christ; therefore none may[7] take that unto him.   That it is proper to our Saviour Christ

If Christ be called an archbishop, then is not the title devised by antichrist.

[2 Cartwright says, "Unto the first and second division, being beside the question, I answer nothing." But, before advancing to the third, he reverts to the examination at length of the passages Matt. xx. 25, &c., Luke xxii. 25, &c. which had been discussed before (see Vol. I. pages 148, &c.).—Sec. Repl. pp. 404, &c.]

[3 The precise words have not been found; but for a very similar idea see Aristot. Op. Lut. Par. 1629. De Interp. cap. i. Tom. I. p. 37.]

[4 Freer, Repl. 1 and 2.]

[5 As, Repl. 1, 2, and Def. A.]   [6 Of archbishop, Repl. 1 and 2.]

[7 Therefore no man may, Repl. 1, 2, and Def. A.]

appeareth by that which St Peter saith, where he calleth him
ἀρχιποίμενα, which is "arch-shepherd," or archbishop; for bishop   1 Epist. v. 4.[1]
and shepherd are all one. And in the Hebrews, where he is   Heb. xiii. 20.[1]
called "the great Shepherd of the sheep;" and in the Acts, and   Acts iii. 15.[1]
                                                                    Acts v. 31.[1]
Hebrews, "arch-leader" of life and of salvation; which titles   Heb. xii. 2.[1]
are never found to be given unto any, but unto our Saviour Christ, and are
proper titles of his mediation, and therefore cannot be without bold pre-
sumption applied unto any mortal man.

Jo. Whitgift.

To contend about names, when there is an agreement of
the matter and substance, hath always been taken for a manifest note of a contentious sophister. But your answer is
ready, that you contend for the substance also, which being
true you might have cut off the most part of this section,
whereby you would excuse yourself for improving the name
of an archbishop. But, to come to the purpose, you say : " It
is unlawful for any man to take upon him those titles which
are proper to our Saviour Christ; but the title of archbishop
is only proper to our Saviour Christ; therefore, &c." The
minor you prove by the words of St Peter, 1 Epist. chap. v.,
where he calleth him *ἀρχιποίμενα*, and Acts iii., v., and xiii.
to the Hebrews, &c.; where he is called " the great Shepherd
of the sheep," " arch-leader," &c. But, before I come to your
minor, I must a little better search your major; for you
pass it over smoothly, as though there could be nothing said
unto it.

Names
proper to
God may in
some respect
be attributed
to other.

I grant that those names which be proper unto God cannot be given to any other, in that respect that they are proper
unto God; but that they can in no other respect be attributed
to any other, it is untrue, and against the manifest words of
the scriptures. What name is more proper unto God than
is this name " God?" And yet is the same also attributed
unto man. Moses, Exod. vii., is called " Pharao's god," because he was God's minister to speak nnto Pharao in his name,
and to execute his judgments upon him. *Nec vero*, as M.
Calvin saith, *quicquam sibi detraxit Deus &c.*[2] : " Neither
did God derogate anything from himself, in that he transferred

Calv. in
Harm.

[1 The verses are added from Repl. 2. In the third reference, Repl. 1 has
Acts ii.]

[2 Nec vero quicquam sibi detraxit Deus quod in Mosen transferret : quia sic
communicat cum servis suis quod sibi proprium est ut maneat semper integer.—
Calvin. Op. Amst. 1667-71. In Quat. Libr. Mos. Harm. Exod. vii. Tom. I. p. 278.]

(his name) unto Moses, because he doth so communicate that which is proper to himself with his servants, that he still remaineth whole." In the xxii. of Exod., the judges are called "gods;" and, in the lxxxii. Psalm, magistrates are called "gods" also. In the xxiii. of Matth., Christ speaketh of the names of "Master," "Father," and "Doctor," as proper to himself; for he saith: "Be not ye called Rabbi; for one is your Master, to wit, Christ, &c. And call no man your father upon earth; for there is but one your Father, which is in heaven. Be not called doctors; for one is your Doctor, even Christ;" and yet no man is so ignorant that he will deny these names to be common to others, though not in the same respects; as I have shewed before. Christ also calleth himself a "Pastor," John x.; and so doth St Peter call him "Bishop," and "Pastor," 1 Epist. ii.[3]; and so he is properly and of himself, and yet these names be communicated with other. In the viii. of John, he is called *Lux mundi*, which is a most proper name, aptly given unto him; and yet doth he himself give the same name to his disciples, Matth. v. Divers such examples might I shew for the improving of your major; but these be sufficient.

Thus therefore I answer in few words, both to your major and minor, that some names that be proper to God are also attributed unto man, but not in the same respect; for they belong unto God properly and *per se*, to man *per accidens*, and in respect that he is the minister of God, and such other like causes. And therefore, although this name "arch-shepherd," or (if you will) "archbishop," be proper to Christ in the respect that he is not only the chief Shepherd, but also the only Shepherd, to whom the sheep do properly pertain, and to whom all the other shepherds must of necessity submit themselves, and in whose name, and under whom only, the church is governed, yet, in the respect of the external policy of the church, and of pastors and bishops that are to be kept and directed in such things as pertain to their duty, the same name of archbishop may aptly and fitly be attributed unto him that hath the ordering and direction of the rest, in the external government of the church. *How the name archbishop may be transferred to other than Christ.*

But, whiles you confound the spiritual and the external regiment of the church, you confound both yourself and your reader also. In the spiritual regiment Christ is only the Pastor; *The spiritual and external government confounded.*

[[3] iii., Editt.]

6—2

and all other be his sheep: in the external regiment there be many other pastors. In the spiritual regiment Christ is only the Archbishop, and governeth all, to whom all other must make their account; but in the external government there be many archbishops, as the state of every church requireth. In the spiritual government Christ is only the Prince, the King, the Judge, and in respect of him all other be subjects; but in the external government there be several countries, several kings, princes, magistrates, judges. Again, in the spiritual kingdom of Christ, and regiment of his church, there is no respect of persons, but all be equal: in the external regiment and government there is and must be degrees of persons. To be short, in respect of Christ and his spiritual government, there is neither magistrate nor archbishop, &c.; but, in the respect of men, and the external face of the church, there are both, and that according to Christ's own order; as shall hereafter be declared. So that now you may perceive your error to be in not rightly distinguishing the states and times of the church and government[1].

Chapter i.   The Fourth Division.

T. C. Page 61, Sect. 4.

And, if any man will reply and say that it is not said that our Saviour Christ is only archbishop, I answer that he is not only said the head, and yet notwithstanding there is no more heads of the church but he. And, if it be further said that these archbishops are but under and as it were subordinate archbishops, I say that a man may as well say that men may be also under-heads of the church; which is the same which is alleged for the pope. Which thing is not only true in those words which do signify and set unlawful things before our eyes, but even in those names also which, having no corruption in their own nature, yet through the corrupt use of men have as it were gotten such a tack[2] of that corruption, that the use of them cannot be without offence.

[1 Cartwright rejoins that Whitgift's examples are unsatisfactory, asks if "a man which confesseth himself mortal may be called by the name of Jehovah, &c.," calls the answer "insufficient," and "full of disorder," and complains that "it confoundeth and shuffleth together the authority of our Saviour Christ, as he is the Son of God only before all worlds, co-equal with his Father, with that which he hath given of his Father, and which he exerciseth in respect he is Mediator between God and us."—Sec. Repl. pp. 408, &c.]

[2 Tack: spot, stain.]

Jo. Whitgift.

He is only " Archbishop " and Bishop in respect of his spiritual government, which he keepeth only unto himself, and in the respect that all other be under him, and have their authority from him.   But this name may also aptly be given unto those that have the oversight of other bishops in the external government of the church ; in the which, as I have said, magistrates be called gods.

How Christ is the only Head of the church.

Christ is "the only Head of the church," if by the head you understand that which giveth the body life, sense, and motion ; for Christ only by his Spirit doth give life and nutriment to his body : he only doth pour spiritual blessings into it, and doth inwardly direct and govern it.   Likewise he is only the Head of the whole church ; for that title cannot agree to any other.   But, if by "the head" you understand an external ruler and governor of any particular nation or church (in which signification head is usually taken), then I do not perceive why the magistrate may not as well be called the head of the church, that is, the chief governor of it in the external policy, as he is called the head of the people, and of the commonwealth.   And, as it is no absurdity to say that the civil magistrate is head of the commonwealth, next and immediately under God (for it is most true), so is it none to say that, under God also, he is head of the church, that is, chief governor, as I have before said.   Constantine, in an epistle that he writeth to the people of Alexandria, as it is reported by Athanasius, *Apol.* 2, calleth bishops *ecclesiarum capita*[3] : " the heads of their churches."   And yet is the pope's supremacy usurped, both because it taketh from magistrates that which is due unto them, and also usurpeth the authority of Christ in remitting and retaining sins, in making laws contrary to God's laws, which he saith be necessary to salvation, in making his supremacy a matter of salvation, and in challenging authority over the whole church of Christ, and an hundred such like presumptions.

How the magistrate may be called head of the church.

Bishops called heads of churches ; and yet the pope's supremacy is usurped.

The archbishop, being both under God and his prince, hath his name only in respect of his authority in certain causes

[3 Εἰ μὲν οὖν.... ἄχρι λόγων ἦσαν ἐνστάντες οἱ ἀληθῶς ἐπίσκοποι, ἢ τυχόντες ἦσαν ἄνδρες, ἀλλὰ μὴ ἐπισήμων πόλεων, καὶ κεφαλαὶ τοσούτων ἐκκλησιῶν, κ.τ.λ.—Athanas. Op. Par. 1698. Constant. Cæs. Epist. ad Pop. Alex. in Apolog. contr. Arian. 89. Tom. I. Pars ɪ. p. 204.]

above other bishops, and that but in one province or kingdom only ; neither can either the name or use of it (as it is in this church) offend any but such as be offended with all superiors, and think that none ought to be better than themselves[1].

Chapter i.   The Fifth Division.

T. C. Page 62, Sect. 1, 2.

In the primitive church the name of a pope was honest, and Tertullian,
Lib. De Pu-
dicitia: Cyp-
rian, Lib. ii.
7; Jerome in
his epistles to
August. *was all one with the name of a good pastor[2]; but now by the ambition of the man of Rome it is so defiled that every good man shaketh at the very mention of it.*

The name of a tyrant was first honourable, and the same with a king, and yet, through cruelty and unjust rule of certain, it is become now so hateful, that no upright and just-dealing prince, none that governeth with[3] equity, and to the commodity of his subjects, would bear to be called tyrant; whereby it may appear that it is not for nought that we do stand of these names.

JO. WHITGIFT.

A lawful
name may
remain,
though it
hath been
abused. *Papa* signifieth a father, and was in times past common to all bishops, but now it is proper to the bishop of Rome, and therefore hated for his sake, whom it now signifieth.   So *tyrannus* sometime signified a king generally, now it signifieth a cruel king, and a bloody governor, and therefore also abhorred.   But an archbishop, though the persons at some time have degenerated, yet the name hath continued in the same signification ; and therefore the reason is nothing like ; except you will also for the like cause condemn the name of a bishop, or of a king ; for there hath been many evil men called by the name of bishops, and many tyrants by the name of kings, and yet the names never the worse.   If names

[1 Cartwright here enters into a long disquisition "to prove the title head of the church to belong only to our Saviour Christ." He reverts to what Whitgift had said before (see Vol. I. page 392), declares that he has borrowed arguments from Harding, and cites Jewel's authority against him (Conf. Bp. Jewel's Works, Park. Soc. Edit. Vol. III. pp. 265, &c.).—Sec. Repl. pp. 411, &c.]

[2 ... bonus pastor et benedictus papa concionaris &c.—Tertull. Op. Lut. 1641. De Pudic. 13. p. 729. Optamus te, beatissime ac gloriosissime papa, &c.—Cypr. Op. Oxon. 1682. Cler. Rom. ad Cypr. Epist. xxx. p. 61.   Domino vere sancto et beatissimo papæ Augustino, Hieronymus in Christo salutem.—August. Op. Par. 1679-1700. Hieron. ad August. Epist. xxxix. Tom. II. col. 83.   Conf. cols. 156, 61, 8, 89, 612, 730. Et in Hieron. Op. Par. 1693-1706. Ad August. Epistt. lxvi., lxix., lxxi., lxxiv., lxxv., lxxix., lxxx. Tom. IV. Pars ii. cols. 604, 8, 11, 17, 29, 43, 4.]

[3 Governeth it with, Repl. 1.]

should be changed so oft as they be abused, some had need to have an office only to invent new names. There was a certain kind of heretics that called themselves "Apostolic;" and yet the name of an apostle is never the worse. A lawful name of a lawful office may remain together with the office, howsoever beforetime it hath been abused[4].

Chapter i.   The Sixth Division.

T. C. Page 62, Sect. 2.

Now, if the names ought to be odious, being both horribly abused, and also forbidden by our Saviour Christ, the things themselves must be in greater hatred; the unlawfulness whereof may thus appear.

Petitio principii; for you have not yet proved this.

Jo. Whitgift.

This is a manifest petition of the principle, and in no point as yet proved. But let us hear the reasons why the office should be condemned.

Chapter i.   The Seventh Division.

T. C. Page 62, Sect. 3.

First of all, the ministry is by the word of God, and heavenly, and not left to the will of men to devise at their pleasure; as appeareth by that which is noted of St John, where the Pharisees, coming to St John Baptist, after he[6] had denied to be either Christ, or Elias, or another prophet, conclude, "If thou be neither Christ, nor Elias, nor of the prophets, why baptizest thou?" which had been no good argument, if St John might have been of some other function than of those which were ordinary in the church, and instituted of God. And therefore St John, to establish his singular and extraordinary function, allegeth the word of God, whereby appeareth that, as it was not lawful to bring in any strange doctrine, so it was[7] not lawful to teach the true doctrine under the name of any other function than was instituted of[8] God.

John i. 25.[5]

Scriptures willingly falsified to make them serve his turn.

The Pharisees made false arguments; and so do you in following them.

Jo. Whitgift.

This is your first argument: "The Pharisees, coming to St John Baptist, after he had denied to be either Christ, or Elias,

[4 Cartwright rejoins, "The question is not whether the name of archbishop is, but whether it ought to be continued: &c." He then returns again to the discussion of Matt. xx.—Sec. Repl. pp. 420, &c.]

[5 This reference is inserted from Repl. 1 and 2; the former of which does not give the verse.]

[6 After that he, Repl. 1 and 2.]   [7 Was it, Repl. 1 and 2.]

[8 By, Repl. 1, 2, and Def. A.]

or another prophet, conclude, If thou be neither Christ, nor
Elias, nor of the prophets, why baptizest thou?" *Ergo,* there
may be no archbishops; which is your meaning. But, lest you
should think that I cavil, I will use your own conclusion, which
is this: *ergo,* "there was no other ordinary function in the
church." This argument hath neither head nor foot, form nor
matter; is this your exquisiteness in logic? First, your ante-
cedent is untrue, and builded upon the false allegation of the
scripture. For the Pharisees do not say unto him, "If thou
be neither Christ, nor Elias, nor of the prophets;" but these be
the words of the text, "If thou be not the Christ, nor Elias,
nor the prophet:" now there is a great difference betwixt these
two kind of speeches, "if thou be not of the prophets;" and,
"if thou be not the prophet." For the first signifieth that they
should ask him, whether he were any of the prophets; the
other, whether he were that prophet whom they looked for to
be such a one as Moses was, according to that which is written
Deut. xviii. verse 15; for else John would not have denied
himself to have been a prophet, seeing that Christ saith he was
one, Matth. xi. Moreover, they ask him not of those ordinary functions that were then in the church, but of such extraordinary persons as they looked for to come, as Christ,
Elias, or that prophet. Thirdly, they did not recite all the
ordinary functions, as Levite and priest; which were then
most ordinary and almost only at that time. So that your
reason hath neither form nor truth in it[1].

*The disor-
dered argu-
ment of the
Replier.*

Deut. xviii.

Matt. xi.

Chapter i.   The Eighth Division.
T. C. Page 62, Sect. 4.

*Let the whole practice of the church under the law be looked upon, and
it shall not be found that any other ecclesiastical ministry was appointed
than those orders of high priest and priests and Levites, &c., which were
appointed by the law of God; and, if there were any raised extraordinarily, the same had their calling confirmed from heaven, either by signs or
miracles, or by plain and clear testimonies of the mouth of God, or by extraordinary exciting and moving[2] of the Spirit of God. So that it appeareth that the ministry of the gospel, and the functions thereof, ought to
be from heaven, and of God, and not invented by the brains[3] of men:*

[1 Cartwright says that, though Whitgift declares there is "neither head nor
foot" in his reason, he can find both, and censures his exceptions to it as "vain."
—Sec. Repl. pp. 436, 7.]

[2 Movings, Repl. 1 and 2.]   [3 Brain, Repl. 1 and 2.]

from heaven, I say, and heavenly, because, although it be executed by earthly
men, and the ministers also are chosen by men like unto themselves, yet, be-
cause it is done by the word and institution of God, that hath not only
ordained that the word should be preached, but hath ordained also in what
order and by whom it should be preached, it may be well[4] accounted to
come from heaven and from God.

Jo. Whitgift.

Neither is there any new ministry or order appointed in The arch- bishop no
this church, because there be archbishops.   For archbishops new mi- nistry.
be ministers of the word and sacraments, and *quoad minis-*
terium do not differ from other pastors (in respect of whom
they are called archbishops) but touching order and government ; as you may read afterward in the Answer to the Admonition.   So that all this which is here spoken is grounded upon
a false principle.   For you would make the reader believe
that to institute an archbishop is to institute a new ministry ;
wherein you are marvellously overshot.   The Jews had government in their church, and superiority in the ecclesiastical
estate ; and so have we.   But you may not tie the church of
Christ to the pattern of the Jews' synagogue ; for that were
to make it servile.

Chapter i.   The Ninth Division.

T. C. Page 62, Sect. 5.

Seeing therefore that these functions of the archbishop and archdeacon Weak proofs
are not in the word of God, it followeth that they are of the earth, and so can must needs infer a weak
do no good, but much harm, in the church. And, if any man will say that conclusion.
we do the church great injury, because we do tie her to a certain number of
orders of ministers, as it were to a stake, so that she[5] may not devise new
functions ; I say that both the church and Christ doth accuse him again :
Christ esteemeth himself to have injury, because that by this means he is
imagined not to have been careful and provident enough for his church, in
that he hath left the ministry, wherein doth consist the life of the church
(being that whereby it is begotten), so rawly[6] and unperfect, that by per-
mitting it[7] to the ordering of men there is a great danger of error, which
he might have set without all danger, by a word or two speaking.

Jo. Whitgift.

Your proofs hitherto alleged are most insufficient to justify
this conclusion ; and yet do you boldly go on as though all

[4 Well be, Repl. 1 and 2.]   [5 We, Def. A. and B.]
[6 Raw, Repl. 2.]   [7 Permitting of it, Repl. 1 and 2.]

were sure.   This is but boldness and confidency, it is not
sound and pithy dealing.   I still deny that there is any other
ministry in the church, because there are archbishops, than is
by the word of God confirmed; but you have not yet proved,
by either scripture or reason, that there ought not to be
governors or superiors among the ministers of the gospel, to
whom any other names may be given than is expressed in
the word; which you ought to prove, else you do but dally,
and study with vain words to enlarge your book.

It is manifest that Christ hath left the government of his
church, touching the external policy, in sundry points in the
ordering of men, who have to make orders and laws for the
same, as time, place, and person requireth, so that nothing be
done contrary to his word; as it is before proved, Tract. ii.[1]
and shall be more hereafter.

Chapter i.   The Tenth Division.
T. C. Page 62, Sect. 6.

*The church of the other side riseth against him; for that he maketh
Christ less careful for her than he was for that under the law.   For, tell
me, in the whole volume of the testament is there any kind or degree of
ministry whereof God is not the certain and express author?   Was there
ever any man (I except Jeroboam and such profane men) either so holy, or
so wise, or of such great knowledge, that ever did so much as dream of instituting of a new ministry?   After the long wandering of the ark in the
wilderness, when it came to be placed in Jerusalem, tell me if any, besides
the Levites and priests, the ordinary ministers, and the prophets which were
immediately stirred up of God, were found to have ordained any office or
title which was not commanded, or whether there was at any time anything
added or enjoined to those offices of priesthood and Leviteship which was not
by the law prescribed.*

JO. WHITGIFT.

T. C. fault-
eth still in
the petition
of the prin-
ciple.

Surely here is nothing but vain repetitions of that false
principle, whereupon this tautology and multiplication of words
is builded, that is, that the institution of an archbishop is the
institution of a new ministry; as though the apostle St Paul,
when he placed Timothy at Ephesus and Titus at Creta, did
institute a new ministry, because he gave them authority and
jurisdiction over the rest, as it is afterward proved; or the
church, when it did appoint one among the bishops to govern

[[1] See Vol. I. pages 175, &c.]

the rest *in schismatis remedium*[2]: "to remedy schisms," as Hierome saith, and as it shall more at large hereafter be declared.   Neither can it therefore be said that Christ doth shew himself "less careful for his church than he did for that under the law."   For his carefulness appeareth and consisteth in this, that he hath now much more plainly set down the doctrine of salvation in all points, than it was in the law, and hath also ordained that there should be not only fit ministers to publish that doctrine, but offices also to govern the people in godliness.   As for names and titles and other external things variable according to divers circumstances, he hath left them to the liberty of his church; as I have before declared; which is one part of his singular goodness towards the church, in that it is not so servilely tied to external things, and to the letter, as it was under the law.

Christ is not less careful for this church than for that under the law.

And it is evident that under the law there were offices and titles in the church, which are not commanded in the scripture, nor whereof we read "God to have been the express author;" as, *archisynagogus*, Mark v.; *scribæ*, or *legis doctores*, or στρατηγοὶ τοῦ ἱεροῦ, *magistratus seu duces templi*, Luke xxii. ver. 52; and those *seniores populi*, and that συνέδριον whereupon you ground your seigniory.   For M. Calvin upon the xviii. of Matth. saith that this συνέδριον was appointed after the children of Israel returned from the captivity of [4]Babylon[5].

Titles and offices in the church under the law whereof[3]God is not the chief author.

[2 Quod autem postea unus electus est, qui cæteris præponeretur, in schismatis remedium factum est: ne unusquisque ad se trahens Christi ecclesiam rumperet. —Hieron. Op. Par. 1693-1706. Ad Evang. Epist. ci. Tom. IV. Pars ii. col. 803.]

[3 This word is corrected from the list of errata in Def. A.: both A. and B. have *where* in the text.]

[4 Scimus ex quo reversi fuerunt ab exilio Babylonico Judæi, delecto concilio quod vocabant Sanhedrin, Græce Synedrion, mandatam fuisse censuram morum et doctrinæ.—Calvin. Op. Amst. 1667-71. Comm. in Harm. Euang. Matt. xviii. 16. Tom. VI. p. 212.]

[5 Cartwright makes a long rejoinder to this division.   He first sets himself to prove that "the archbishopric" is "a new ministry."   Here among other arguments he says: "Whereas a bishop may be ordained by two or three other bishops, the archbishop must be ordained by all the bishops of the province, either present, or at the least consenting.   Now, seeing the ordination is of the form of their ministry, and these formal causes be divers, it followeth that these offices must needs be divers.   And that the substantial and essential form of a bishop is different from that of the archbishop, it is plain also by that they are members of one division, and therefore of necessity differ in the substantial form; as a man differeth from a brute beast, not in circumstance, but in that he is of another nature. &c."   He further says that Timothy and Titus "shall never be proved to have

Chapter i.   The Eleventh Division.
T. C. Page 63, Sect. 1.

All men know that the ark of Noah was a figure of the Gen. vi. 14,
church.   Noah was both a wise and a godly man; yet what 22.[1]
doth the Lord leave to his wisdom, when as he appointeth the matter, the
form, the length, the breadth, the height, the wood, the kind and sort of wood?

Jo. Whitgift.

Uncertain reasoning of figures and allegories.

Something left to Noah not commanded.

Gen. viii.

Calvin. in vi. Gen.

"All men know" how uncertain a reason it is that is grounded upon figures and types, except the application thereof may be found in the scriptures.   For a man may apply them as it pleaseth him, even as he may do allegories; and yet was there many things required to the ark, whereof there is no express mention made, and namely nails or pins to join it together; neither is it expressed whether the window was of glass, or of crystal, or of neither.   Moreover, he is not prescribed to make a cover for it; and yet it had one, as is declared *cap. viii.* The overseers and masters of the work likewise are not there appointed, but left to the discretion of Noah.   There are many other things required to the making of such an ark, whereof there is no express mention in that place.   To conclude, Noah being in the ark did things which the scripture doth not express that he was commanded to do; as when he sent out the raven and the dove, &c. *cap. viii.*   Wherefore I say with M. Calvin, *Arcam fuisse ecclesiæ imaginem certum est, teste Petro, verum singulas ejus parteis ad ecclesiam aptare minime consentaneum est*[2]: "It is certain that the ark was a figure of the church by the testimony of Peter, but it is not meet to apply every part thereof unto the church."

had any such authority over the rest, and, if they had, yet it falleth not on the archbishop's side; seeing they were no bishops, but evangelists, &c." Then he exclaims that "there is great injury done unto the church, great dishonour done unto our Saviour Christ:" if "he is said to have done less in appointing the outward government of his church now than under the law," he "is robbed" of part "of his kingly office." Afterwards he censures what is said about the "servile tie" as "papistical and anabaptistical," and declares "the examples brought as exceptions against the certain and commanded ministry" are such as to set Whitgift's cause "in the mockery and laughter of all men."—Sec. Repl. pp. 438, &c.]

[1 This reference is inserted from Repl. 2.]
[2 Calvin. Op. Amst. 1667-71. Comm. in Gen. cap. vi. Tom. I. p. 43.]

Chapter i.   The Twelfth Division.

T. C. Page 63, Sect. 4.

Exod. xxvi.[4]   *In the tabernacle the church is yet more expressly*[3] *shewed*
Exod. xxxi.   *forth.*   *Moses that was the overseer of the work was a wise*
3, 6.[4]   *and godly*[5] *man, the artificers that wrought it, Bezalael and*
Aholiab, most cunning workmen; and yet observe how the Lord leaveth
nothing to their will, but telleth not only of the boards, of the curtains, of
Exod.xxxix.   *the apparel, but also of the bars, of the rings, of the strings, of*
42.[4]   *the hooks*[6]*, of the besoms, of the snuffers, and of the things, the*
matter, and the form.

Jo. Whitgift.

It is well known that the Israelites had long continued Why God appointed so many ceremonies to the Israelites. among the Egyptians, a most superstitious kind of people, without any law of God written, and therefore now being delivered from them, and yet inclined to their idolatry, God (as most writers think) of his infinite wisdom did so charge them with ceremonies of his own institution, that they should neither have leisure to use any other, nor yet desire the Egyptiacal kind of worshipping.

Touching the tabernacle and the particular description of things pertaining to the same, I say with Pellican : "These Pellican. things are particularly described according to the word of the Lord, that the people might know that they ought not so much to obey Moses' precepts as the will of God, in building the tabernacle, and in freely offering to the same their gold, their silver, their brass, their purple, &c.; the which otherwise they would have abused to their own vanities; and that also they might not be without that beauty in ceremonies and worshipping of God, which they see among the gentiles; moreover, that they might have matter to occupy them with, lest they should fall to slothfulness and idleness[7]." So that

---

[3 Expressedly, Repl. 1 and 2.]
[4 These references are inserted from Repl. 2.]
[5 And a godly, Repl. 1 and 2.]   [6 Books, Def. A. and B.]
   [7 Hæc sigillatim sic descripta sunt, juxta verbum Domini, ut populus non tam Mosis institutis, quam divinæ voluntati se obsequi debere sciret : tabernaculum extruendo, et pretiosa quæque sponte largiendo, quibus alioqui abusi fuissent ad suas vanitates : et ne carerent suis ceremoniis, et splendore divini cultus, quem apud ethnicos passim admirari et concupiscere consueverunt, ut haberet is populus occupationes contra iners otium, utque prudentiores in populo essent in majori authoritate, quibus obedirent libentius ad bonum suum.—Comment. Biblior. Op. C. Pellican. Tigur. 1536-46. Exod. cap. xxv. Tom. I. foll. 99, 100.]

of this place it may be well gathered, that nothing wherein the worship of God doth consist is to be used without his prescription; but how you can[1] aptly apply this figure to the external government and policy of the church, I cannot well understand; and, if you may so use it, yet do you but allegory; which is no good kind of proof, because allegories may be applied according to every particular man's invention. But all that can be truly gathered of this figure is (as I have said before) that no kind of worship may be brought into the church of God which is not grounded upon his word; and therefore M. Calvin, speaking of this tabernacle, saith that God "gave precepts of the tabernacle, and things pertaining to it;" *ne externa pietatis exercitia, quæ videmus fuisse admodum necessaria, populum deficerent*[2]: "lest the people should want the outward exercises of godliness, which we see to have been very necessary." And again he saith that, when Moses in the mountain, did see the example of the tabernacle, he was then instructed *de vero Dei cultu et mysteriis*[3]: "of the true worship of God and of heavenly mysteries." And again, speaking of this tabernacle, he saith: *Lex Judæos ad spiritualem solum Dei cultum instituit, sed ceremoniis vestitum, ut ferebat temporis ratio*[4]: "The law did institute the Jews only to the spiritual worship of God, but yet covered with ceremonies, as the time required." Therefore in this figure there was only expressed what should be done in the worshipping of God, and not in the external policy and government of the church.

Calvin. xxxv. Exod. in expos. 2. præcepti.

Chapter i.   The Thirteenth Division.

T. C. Page 63, Sect. 3.

Let us come to the temple, which as it was more near the time of Christ, so it doth more lively express the church of God which now is. Salomon,

---

[1 Can you, Def. B.]

[2 Et probabile est, ex quo Deus fœdus suum pepigerat, statim de tabernaculo, ejusque appendicibus præcepta dedisse: ne &c. quæ vidimus &c.—Calvin. Op. Amst. 1667-71. In Quat. Libr. Mos. Harm. Sec. Præcept. Tom. I. p. 408.]

[3 Nunc si quis objiciat, compositum fuisse tabernaculum ad exemplar quod Moses viderat in monte: in promptu est solutio, Mosen non tunc primum in monte fuisse edoctum de vero Dei cultu et cœlestibus mysteriis, &c.—Id. ibid. p. 409.]

[4 Id. ibid. p. 410.]

1 Kings iii.
12.⁵
1 Chr. xxviii.
11, &c. 19.⁵

1 Kings vi.⁵
2 Chron. iii.
iv. v.⁵
Ezek. xl.⁵ *the wisest man that ever was, or shall be, doth nothing in it,
neither for the temple, nor for the vessels of the temple, nor for
the beauty of it, but according to the form that was enjoined him ;
as appeareth in the first of the Kings, and the second[6] of the
Chronicles[7]. And in the restoring of that temple Ezechiel is
witness how the angel by the commandment of God doth, part
by part, appoint all to be done both in the temple and in the furniture
thereof.*

Jo. Whitgift.

These two examples of the "tabernacle," and of the
"temple," tend to one end, and might more aptly have been
alleged in the title of ceremonies than of the government of
the church, because, whatsoever is here spoken of either of
them pertaineth to ceremonies, and to the worshipping of God,
and not to external policy and government of the church, and
therefore most unaptly alleged against archbishops, &c.

But what need I labour much in this matter, when you
yourself, in the 22. page of your book, "offer, for one thing
that I shall bring left to the order of this church, to shew me
that the Israelites had twenty that were undecided by the
express word[8]?"

The Replier confuted by his own words. Pag. 22, sect. 1.

And it is certain that both David and Salomon appointed
orders, the one about the tabernacle, the other about the temple, which we read not in scripture they were commanded to
do. And David appointed degrees of officers in the temple,
and Salomon workmen and overseers, whereof we do not read
that they had any special commandment[9].

1 Chron. xxiv.

Chapter i.   The Fourteenth Division.

T. C. Page 63, Sect. 4.

*Now, if the Holy Ghost in figures and tropes doth so carefully and (as
a man may speak) curiously comprehend all things, in the truth itself how
much more is it to be thought that he hath performed this ! If in the*

[5 These references are inserted from Repl. 2.]
[6 And second, Repl. 1.]   [7 In the Kings and Chronicles, Repl. 2.]
[8 See Vol. I. page 270.]
[9 Cartwright maintains at length that his reasonings hold in this and the two
preceding divisions, calls Whitgift's citations inconclusive, and accuses him of
inconsistency, because he had before said (see Vol. I. pages 263, 4), "neither was
there the least thing to be done in the church omitted in the law."—Sec. Repl.
pp. 444, &c.]

*shadows, how much more in the body! If he have done this in earthly
things, and which shall perish, how[1] is it to be thought that he hath not
performed it in heavenly, and those which abide for ever? And then tell
me what are those times of which it was said, "the Messias when
he cometh will tell us all?" Is it a like thing that he, which did* John iv. 25.[2]
*not only appoint the temple and the tabernacle, but the ornaments of them,
would not only neglect the ornaments of the church, but also that without
the which (as we are borne in hand) it cannot long stand? shall we think
that he, which remembered the bars there, hath forgotten the pillars here?
or he, that there remembered the pins, did here forget the master-builders?
how he should there remember[3] the besoms, and here forget archbishops, if
any had been needful? that he should there[4] make mention of the snuffers
to purge the lights, and here pass by the lights themselves? and, to conclude, that he should make mention there of the motes, and here say nothing
of the beams? there reckon up the gnats, here keep silence of the camels?
What is this else but that which Aristotle saith, τὰ μικρὰ ὁρᾶν καὶ τὰ με-
γάλα παρορᾶν[5], that is, "to look to small things, and not to look to great;"
which if it cannot fall into the Lord, let it be a shame to say that the chief
pillar and upholder of the church is not expressed in the scripture, nor
cannot be concluded of it?*

Jo. Whitgift.

T. C. an-
swered[7] by
his own
assertion.
You have before confessed, page 15,[6] that "certain things
are left to the order of the church, because they are of that
nature which are varied by times, places, persons, and other
circumstances, &c.;" which is sufficient to answer whatsoever
you have here spoken of "the carefulness of the Holy Ghost
in the truth itself, above figures and tropes." Although there
is no doubt but the Holy Ghost was as careful in the one as
in the other, and loved the one people as well as the other;
and therefore it may be an argument *a paribus,* but not
a minori; as you seem to make it. I have told you before
also why God did more particularly prescribe every ceremony
to the Israelites in the law, than he hath done to his people
in the gospel.

God hath in his gospel performed and fulfilled all "the
tropes and figures" of the law whatsoever. Christ which is
the Messias hath told us all things that are necessary to sal-

---

[1 Which are perished how, Repl. 2.]

[2 This reference is inserted from Repl. 1 and 2 : in the former the verse is
not given.]

[3 Should he there remember, Repl. 2.]   [4 Needful? there, Repl. 2.]

[5 ... οἳ μικρὰς ὁμοιότητας ὁρῶσι, μεγάλας δὲ παρορῶσι.—Aristot. Op. Lut.
Par. 1629. Metaphys. Lib. XII. cap. vi. Tom. II. p. 979.]

[6 See Vol. I. page 195.]   [7 Answereth, Def. A.]

vation, John xx.; and so is that place in the iv. of John to be John xx. understanded[8].

We make not an archbishop necessary to salvation, but profitable to the government of the church, and therefore consonant to the word of God; as shall be declared. We know the church of Christ is not builded upon any man, either as upon foundations[9], or "pillars," if we speak properly, but upon Christ himself, and his word, which remain unmoveable: we know also that the same church may stand without the external help of man. But yet hath God appointed functions in his church both ecclesiastical and civil, as means to keep it in external peace, discipline, and order; and, though he hath not expressed the names, yet hath he allowed the offices. Among men the chief "pillar" that upholdeth the church is the christian prince and magistrate; and yet where have you in the gospel any such express mention made thereof, as there is in the appointing of the tabernacle "of besoms, snuffers, &c."? which examples you use in derision; such is your modesty and reverence. We know that all things necessary to salvation are much more plainly expressed in the gospel than in the law: we are also well assured that Christ in his word hath fully and plainly comprehended all things requisite to faith and good life; but yet hath he committed certain orders of ceremonies, and kind of government, to the disposition of his church, the general rules given in his word being observed, and nothing being done contrary to his will and commandment therein contained; as I have proved before.

Chapter i.   The Fifteenth Division.

T. C. Page 63, Sect. 5.

Moreover, these[10] ministries, without the which the church is fully builded A dangerous *and brought to perfection and complete unity, are not to be retained in the* major. *church; but without the ministries of archbishop, &c., the church may be* An untrue *fully builded and brought to perfection; therefore these ministries[11] are not* minor. *to be retained.*

Jo. Whitgift.

Your minor is untrue. For the church, in a kingdom

[8 " That out of St John xx. is spoken of the miracles our Saviour did, not of his doctrine; and is thrust in by strong hands in this place."—Sec. Repl. p. 447.]
[9 Foundation, Def. A.]   [10 Those, Repl. 2.]   [11 Ministers, Def. B.]

The place in the iv. Ephes. discussed.

where it hath an external government, where it includeth both good and bad, where it is molested with contentious persons, with schisms, heresies, &c., cannot enjoy complete unity, nor

The major tendeth to the shutting out of the civil magistrate. The church must not only be brought to perfection, but also be preserved therein.

be perfectly governed touching the external form and government, without such offices and governors. Your major also containeth dangerous doctrine, including as well the christian magistrate as the archbishop. And it is in effect all one with this argument: "The church is fully builded and brought to perfection and complete unity" without the christian magistrate; therefore christian magistrates "are not to be retained;" which is the very argument of the anabaptists against christian magistrates. You must therefore understand that the church must as well be preserved and kept in perfection, peace and unity, as builded and brought thereunto, and that such offices and functions are lawful as tend to that end, and be therefore by lawful authority appointed, howsoever some wayward persons think the contrary[1].

Chapter i.   The Sixteenth Division.
T. C. Page 63, Sect. 6.

And that without these ministries the church may be complete, it appeareth by that which is in the fourth to the Ephesians[2], where Eph. iv. 11, 12.4 *it is said that Christ "gave some apostles, some[3] evangelists, some pastors and doctors, to the restoring of the saints unto the work of the ministry, until we all come to the unity of faith, and of the knowledge of the Son of God, and unto a perfect man."*

Jo. WHITGIFT.

The place in the iv. Ephes. discussed.

In that place to the Ephesians there is no mention made of deacons and widows, nor of your elders; and therefore it maketh as much against them as it doth against archbishops. Moreover, it hath apostles, evangelists, and prophets; all which you seclude from the state of this church. Thirdly, it containeth those ministries only which are occupied in the word and administration of the sacraments, not those which pertain

---

[1 Cartwright rejoins that, as the "question is, what ecclesiastical ministries are sufficient, the mention therefore of the civil magistrate is absurd." He adds, " Beside that, hereby at unawares he confesseth 'that the church may be fully builded, and accomplished without a christian magistrate;' which is against that he saith, ' the magistrate is the head of the church.' "—Sec. Repl. p. 448.]

[2 Is in the Ephesians, Repl. 2.]

[3 Apostles, some prophets, some, Repl. 1 and 2.]

[4 This reference is inserted from Repl. 2.]

to order and discipline; as you afterward yourself confess. And
therefore I understand not how that place can help you anything at all.

Chapter i.   The Seventeenth Division.

T. C. Page 63, Sect. ult.

*The learned writers have thus reasoned against the pope: that, foras-
much[5] as apostles, prophets, &c. are sufficient for the building of the church,
therefore there ought to be no pope.   The argument and necessity of the
conclusion is as strong against the archbishop, and all one.   For by the
same reason that the pope is cast away as a superfluous thing, for that
these offices are able to make perfect the church, is the archbishop likewise
thrown out of the church, as a knob or some lump of flesh, which being no
member of the body doth both burden it and disfigure it.   And, as they say
that God gave no pope to his church, therefore the pope can do no good;
so we may well say God gave no archbishop to his church, therefore the
archbishop can do no good.*

JO. WHITGIFT.

If there were no stronger places than this against the
pope of Rome his usurped authority, it might stand still, for
anything that I know; because this place speaketh only of the
offices occupied in preaching the word and administrating the
sacraments, as I have said, not of any office of government.
Neither is it a perfect pattern; because it hath omitted those
offices before mentioned.   I have told you before that a negative argument from the scripture (except it be in matters of
salvation) is but weak; likewise that an archbishop is no new
ministry, but may well be contained in the number of those
of whom the apostle there speaketh.   For the name of a pastor doth comprehend both archbishops and bishops.   The
name doth but signify an office of government convenient for
the state of the church in the external policy of it.   And, if it
did prevail against the pope, yet doth it not so against the
archbishop.   For the pope doth challenge his authority by
succession from Peter; so doth not the archbishop.   The pope
saith that he is the head of the universal church of Christ; so
doth not the archbishop.   The pope saith that to be subject to
him is necessary to salvation; the archbishop thinketh no such
matter.   The pope challengeth power to remit and retain sins,
to dispense with the word of God, to make new articles of

The great dif-
ference be-
twixt the
pope and the
archbishop.

[5 Forsomuch, Repl. 1 and 2.]

The place
Ephes. iv.
discussed.

faith, &c.; so doth not the archbishop. To be short, the pope claimeth authority over kings and princes, and saith that they have authority from him; but the archbishops (if you speak of ours) acknowledge themselves to be subject to their prince, and to have that authority and jurisdiction from her, which they practise over and above that that other bishops do; and therefore you must needs be reproved here, either of great lack of discretion, or else of gross ignorance, or purposed malice. You might say that God gave no magistrate in that place to his church; *ergo*, the magistrate can do no good. Surely I think that, if you should well consider how near your arguments approach to the anabaptists, you would either more circumspectly use them, or else quite cast them away[1].

Chapter i.   The Eighteenth Division.

T. C. Page 64, Sect. 1.

Neither did God give any archdeacon to his church; therefore he cannot profit the church. But it will be said that this argument followeth not, because no mention is made here of the deacon or of the elder, which notwithstanding are both necessary in the church; and therefore that there are functions profitable in the church whereof no mention is made here. But

It is easily
known and
as easily for-
gotten again
of you; as ap-
peareth after-
wards.

how easily do all men know that the apostle speaketh of those functions here only which are conversant in the word, and have to do with the preaching thereof, and therefore made here no mention of the deacon or elder. It is said again that in the epistle to the Corinthians St Paul speaketh only of apostles, prophets, and doctors, leaving out   1 Cor.xii.28.[2] *evangelists and pastors, and yet evangelists and pastors necessary; and so, although archbishops are not spoken of in the place to the Ephesians, yet they may not therefore be[3] shut out as unnecessary. But they that say so should have considered that the diversity of the matter which the apostle handleth in these two places bred a diverse kind of speech. For, in the epistle to the Corinthians, going about to condemn the ambition of men which will thrust themselves into other men's callings, and take upon them to do all themselves, and to be as it were eye, and ear, and hand, and all; St Paul proveth that the church is a body wherein there are many mem-*

[1 Cartwright says that "it is Calvin which reasoneth of the place of the Ephesians" that "there ought to be no pope;" and that, though Whitgift may consider this slender reasoning, he will find " that it is weighty." He insists that it is equally conclusive against an archbishop, and adds: " Therefore this difference between the archbishop and pope, being accidental, and not touching the nature of the government whereof we have to enquire, is unskilfully alleged."—Sec. Repl. pp. 449, 50.]

[2 The verse is inserted from Repl. 2.]

[3 Be therefore, Repl. 1, 2, and Def. A.]

bers, and the same diverse one from another, and that it is not one member The place
only. And, to prove that, it was sufficient to say that he placed some Ephes. iv.
apostles, some prophets, some doctors, without rehearsing all the kinds[4] *of* discussed.
functions. But, in the epistle to the Ephesians, meaning to shew the libe-
rality of our Saviour Christ in giving those which should be able by doc-
trine and teaching to make perfect and absolute his church, it was neces-
sary that he should reckon up all those functions whereby that work is
done.

Jo. Whitgift.

You have in this place yourself answered your former T. C. hath
reasons touching the place to the Ephesians. For I have told answered himself
you that the names of archbishops and archdeacons be names touching the
of jurisdiction and government, not of any new ministry; and place, Eph. iv.
therefore such bishops and ministers as be so called to have
those names, not in respect of the ministry of the word, but of
order and policy.

The objection made of the place of[5] the 1. to the Corinth.
cap. xii. is of more weight than you can be able to remove with
all the might you have. For the apostle there as well declareth
the diversity of offices in the church, as he doth in that epistle
to the Ephesians; yea, and more perfectly too; as the place
itself and the very order that the apostle keepeth doth declare.
Your distinction is but in vain invented for a shift only,
against both reason and authority; against reason, because, the
apostle having before made a perfect division of gifts in the
church, it is not like but now speaking of offices he doth the
same. Moreover, he doth rehearse them in order, saying,
first apostles, then prophets, thirdly doctors, &c. Lastly, he
reciteth here more offices than he doth there; for here he reciteth eight, and there only five at the most. Authority, both
of learned writers, and of the manifest words of the apostle
himself, is against it. Peter Martyr saith that in this place
Recenset......singulatim quas parteis habeat hoc corpus[6] : P. Martyr in
" he rehearseth particularly what parts this body hath," 1 Cor. xii.
meaning the church. And the apostle himself, reciting the
divers parts of the body and functions of the same, to declare
the divers functions that be in the church, doth no doubt
make as perfect a division here as he doth in any other place;
so that this shift cannot serve your turn; and, if it did, yet

[4 Kind, Def. B.]   [5 To, Def. B.]
[6 P. Martyr. Comm. in D. Pauli prior. ad Corinth. Epist. Tigur. 1572. cap.
xii. 28. fol. 182.]

The place
Ephes. iv.
discussed.
have you proved nothing by it, for you yourself have given the solution, saying that "in the place to the Ephesians he only speaketh of such functions as are conversant in the word;" which is true[1].

Chapter i.   The Nineteenth Division.

T. C. Page 64, Sect. 2.

But how cometh it to pass that St Paul, neither in the one place, neither in the[2] other, nor elsewhere, maketh mention of the archbishop, which is said to be the chiefest pillar and undersetter of the church?   Now I hear what is said to this, that under the pastor is contained bishop: he is not contained, but is the same that bishop[3].   How then?   Forsooth, say they, an archbishop is bishop: well then, of bishops some are archbishops, some[4] are

You imagine
that they are
hanged, and
therefore
help before
you be de-
sired.
what?   Here I see that they are hanged in the bush, but I will help them. Of bishops some are archbishops, some are by the common name bishops. For, if they answer not thus, what have they to say?   But what an absurd thing were that to say, that St Paul comprehended an archbishop under a pastor or bishop, which neither was at that time nor certain hundred years after!   This were not to divide, but to prophesy.   And how is it that they never marked that St Paul speaketh of those functions which were in the church, and not of those which should be afterward?   and of those that God had given, and not of those which he would give?   For the words are, "and he hath given."

JO. WHITGIFT.

No man can deny but a bishop may aptly be comprehended under this name pastor, and archbishop under the name of a bishop; and it may as well be said that "of bishops some be called archbishops, and some by the name of bishops," as it may be said of kings, some be called emperors, some by the common name of kings; of dukes, some archdukes, some by the common name of dukes; of justices, some chief justices, some by the common name of justices.

Things may
be lawful
which were
not in Paul's
time.
What if the name of an archbishop were not in St Paul's time?   Doth it therefore follow that the thing signified by the name was not in his time?   This word ὁμοούσιος was not in St Paul's time, but afterward invented in the council of Nice.   Yet was the thing thereby signified in St Paul's time,

---

[1 Cartwright makes light of what Whitgift says in this division, and accuses him of keeping to "his old wont; which is to cut the knot, and not to loose it."— Sec. Repl. pp. 450, &c.]

[2 Neither the, Repl. 1.]   [3 That pastor, Repl. 2.]

[4 Archbishops and some, Repl. 1 and 2.]

and from the beginning.   Other names there be also which The place
Ephes. iv.
discussed. were invented since the apostle's time, and yet both lawfully and necessarily used.   The authority and thing whereof the archbishop hath his name was in Paul's time, and therefore the name lawful; and, if it had not been in St Paul's time, yet were both the name and the office lawful; because it pertaineth to the external policy and regiment of the church, which is variable according to the place, time, person, and other circumstances.   Shall not the authority that christian princes have in matters ecclesiastical be thought lawful, because there were no such princes in St Paul's time?   Or shall not they have the chief authority in ruling and governing the church in external policy and regiment, because there is no such express mention of them in those two places of St Paul?

But you shall answer yourself, for you say that "in those places St Paul speaketh of such functions as were then in the church, not of such as should be afterward;" which is true. And therefore I conclude that, as all those offices (by your own confession before) are not necessary for all times in the church, so are they not only for all times of the church, but other may be brought in meet for the government of the same.   I know your meaning is nothing less; yet this is my collection which I think you will very hardly answer.

How many hundred years the name of archbishop was after the apostle's time shall appear in another place[5].

Chapter i.   The Twentieth Division.

T. C. Page 64, Sect. 3.

Moreover, if so be under the pastor the apostle comprehended an arch-bishop, then the archbishop is necessary, and such as the church cannot be without, and commanded of God, and therefore not taken up by the policy of the church for the time, country[6], and other circumstances, and such also as cannot be put down at the will of the church; which is contrary to the judgment of those which are the archbishop's patrons.

[5 Cartwright denies that "our kind of bishop should be comprehended under St Paul's pastor."   He afterwards goes on to say : "And, although the word consubstantial were not in St Paul's time, yet words of the same weight were.   If you can shew therefore words of the same value with archbishop, although you shew not this, it shall be sufficient: if you cannot, then this example maketh against you."   He also accuses Whitgift of reasoning as Harding did against bishop Jewel.—Sec. Repl. pp. 452, &c.]

[6 Time and country, Repl. 1 and 2.]

JO. WHITGIFT.

Your argument, if it be thus framed, Pastors are necessary at all times, in all estates of the church, and in all places, and cannot be put down at the will of the church: archbishops are pastors; therefore they be necessary at all times, &c.——I deny your argument, because the major in the first figure cannot be particular. If you make your major universal, then I do deny it, and put you to the proof. If you say that to preach the word and to administer the sacraments (which is the office of a pastor) is necessary at all times, then I confess it to be true, and distinguish the minor on this sort; that an archbishop, in respect of the ministry of the word and sacraments, is at all times necessary, not in the respect of policy and government, in consideration whereof he hath the name of an archbishop[1].

Chapter i.   The Twenty-first Division.
T. C. Page 64, Sect. 3, 4, 5.

You mislike
that against
yourself now,
which before
you were
glad to use as
a shift for
yourself.
Here he con-
futeth his
own shadow.

The last refuge is, that the apostle made mention of those functions which have to do with the ministering of the word and sacraments, and not of those which have[2] to do with order and discipline.

Speak in good earnest, had the apostles nothing to do with discipline and order? With what face can you take away the reins of government out of the apostles' hands, and put them in the archbishops' and archdeacons' hands? what a perverseness is this, that the ministries invented by men should be preferred to all the ministries appointed and commanded of God!

The apostles, forsooth, have in common with the archbishops and archdeacons the power of ministering of the word and of the sacraments, of binding and loosing; and thus far as good as the archbishops and archdeacons. But for discipline and order the apostles have nothing to do, but herein archbishops and archdeacons are above them, and better than they.

JO. WHITGIFT.

You wonderfully forget yourself, for it is your own distinction, as it appeareth in the 5. line of the same page of your book[3]; and thereby you shifted off the objection of deacons and elders. I know no man that "taketh the reins of govern-

[1 Cartwright declares that, "all shifts and colours failing him," Whitgift has here changed his argument. He re-states it, and insists that the answer is absurd and inconsistent with what had been before set down.—Sec. Repl. pp. 454, &c.]

[2 Hath, Repl. 1.]   [3 See before, page 100.]

ment out of the apostles' hands," and giveth it to any to whom it is not due by the word of God. But is your meaning that the apostles should now execute it themselves? else, *Quorsum hæc?* Surely you are so full of passions that you forget the matter. I know the apostles had in their time, together with the ministry of the word and sacraments, power to exercise ecclesiastical discipline and order. But truly I understand not your meaning; for never any such thing as you here fancy entered once into my cogitation. I rather say that, because in the apostles there was joined the administration of discipline with the ministry of the word and sacraments, therefore it may be so likewise now in archbishops and bishops. For that authority of discipline and government that the apostles had in their time is now, for the most part, executed by archbishops and bishops; which is the overthrow of your whole assertion[4].

Chapter i.   The Twenty-second Division.
T. C. Page 64, Sect. ult.

Now, sir, if I would follow your vein of making so many exclamations, as, "O the impudency," "O the insolency," with twenty other such great "Os," you see I have occasion both here and elsewhere. But I would not gladly declaim, especially when I should dispute, nor make outcries instead of reasons.   Indeed you have made yourself occasion.

Jo. Whitgift.

Where have I used these exclamations? or what cause have you so suddenly to burst into them at this time? except it be to set some countenance upon your evil-favoured reasons. But I will let you alone in such toys, and suffer you to play with yourself.

Chapter i.   The Twenty-third Division.
T. C. Page 65, Sect. 1.

But, to come to this distinction, I had thought before this time that the 1 Cor. iii. 10.[5] *apostles had been the chief builders in setting up the church, now* Surely the *I perceive you make the archbishops and archdeacons the chief* man is in a dream. *builders, and the apostles under-carpenters or common masons, to serve*

[4 Cartwright retorts: "... before you have said once or twice 'that the office and authority of an archbishop was in the apostles' times.' Which if it be true, how doth the archbishop receive his authority of order and government by their death? for, having it before, he cannot receive it by their departure."—Ibid. p. 457.]

[5 The verse is added from Repl. 2.]

and to take the commandment of the archbishop and archdeacon. And, whereas it is said that the ministries which St Paul speaketh of are in the word[1] *and sacraments, binding and loosing only, and that there be other which are besides these occupied in the order and discipline of the church (of which number are archbishops and archdeacons), let us mark a little what deep divinity here is.*

Jo. Whitgift.

Surely you wander you know not whither: without doubt your mind when you writ this was upon some other thing than upon my book. For where have I made this comparison betwixt the apostles and archbishops? or what have I spoken sounding that way? I would have you to deal honestly and plainly. If you mean the book in Latin[2], whereof you afterward speak, the words of that book sounding anything this way be these: *Archiepiscopi ab episcopis quoad ministerium non differunt (omnes enim pari potestate docendi, baptizandi, ligandi et solvendi præd1ti sunt), sed quoad ordinem et politiam; ordinis enim et politiæ causa quædam ultra episcopos archiepiscopis concessa sunt:* "Archbishops differ not from bishops in respect of the ministry (for they are all endued with equal authority to teach, to baptize, to bind and loose), but in respect of order and policy. For some things are granted to archbishops for order and policy's sake above the bishops." And further, answering that place to the Ephesians, it saith: *Apostolus eo in loco eos tantum ministros et ministeria enumerat, quæ in precibus, verbo, et administratione sacramentorum versantur, non eorum quæ ad ordinem et disciplinam instituuntur, qualia sunt archiepiscoporum et archidiaconorum:* "The apostle in that place doth only recite those ministers and ministries which are occupied in prayer, the word, and the administration of the sacraments, not of them which are instituted for order and discipline, such as are the functions of archbishops and archdeacons." The which self-same distinction for that place you use in the beginning

Pag. 64, lin. 5.

of the 64. page of your book[3], these only words excepted

[1 Words, Def. A and B.]

[2 The book intended is very probably that which Strype mentions, Life of Parker, Book iv. chap. xli., namely the Reply to a treatise, De Disciplina, which treatise Walter Travers had put forth, and which the archbishop was anxious to have answered. It does not appear by whom the Reply was composed; and, according to Strype, Parker kept "it some time by him, and would have more judgments before he put it out."]

[3 See before, page 100.]

(*qualia sunt archiepiscoporum et archidiaconorum*); as I have
before shewed, and your own words declare. And I am sure
these words do not "make the archbishops and archdeacons
chief builders, and the apostles under-carpenters," as it pleaseth you to collect; but this is your modesty.

Chapter i. The Twenty-fourth Division.
T. C. Page 65, Sect. 2.

*And, first of all, I would gladly ask them with what advice they have
laid on a greater burden and weight of the archbishops' and archdeacons'*
shoulders than the apostles were able to sustain.

What bur-
den? who
hath laid it
on?

Jo. Whitgift.

When you have told where "they have laid on this
greater burden and weight," or what "the burden and weight
is," that you say "they have laid on," or who they be that
have laid it on, then shall your question be answered: in the
mean time, let this suffice the reader, that you do but forge
matter to increase your volumes, and to sport yourself.

Chapter i. The Twenty-fifth Division.
T. C. Page 65, Sect. 3.

*Secondarily, I ask with what boldness, and upon the confidence of what
gifts, any man dare take upon him both that which the apostles did, and
more too?*

Jo. Whitgift.
To this I answer as to the former.

Chapter i.   The Twenty-sixth Division.
T. C. Page 65, Sect. 3.

*Then I say that it is too too unskilfully done to separate order and
discipline from them that have the ministry of the word in hand, as though
the church without archbishops and archdeacons were a confused heap*
Rom.xii.4,5.[4] *and a disordered lump; when as St Paul teacheth it to be
without them a body consisting of all his parts and members,
comely knit and joined together, wherein nothing wanteth nor nothing is
too much.*

Jo. Whitgift.

"Order and discipline" are not "separated from the ministry
of the word;" although all such as be ministers of the word

Authority to
execute dis-
cipline is

[4 This reference is inserted from Repl. 2.]

not equally given to all. have not the like authority to execute them. For as it is said in that Latin book, "for order and policy's sake more is granted to the archbishop than to the bishop [1];" neither will any learned man so greatly marvel at this, seeing the practice thereof was in the apostle's time. For Paul had more large and ample authority than Timothy, and Timothy than the rest of the ministers of Ephesus.

What if "the church without archbishops and archdeacons" were perfect in St Paul's time, and may be perfect at other times? doth it therefore follow that the church in no time or state may have them, or, rather, that they be not necessary at some time for the church? In St Paul's time apostles, prophets, workers of miracles, gifts of healing, diversity of tongues, were counted necessary, and principal parts of this body; which notwithstanding you confess now to be cut off, and yet the body perfect: so that you see this is no reason at all, to say that the church in St Paul's time was a perfect body without archbishops and archdeacons; *ergo*, they are not necessary in the church of Christ. For I might as well reason thus: The church of Christ in St Paul's time was not perfect without apostles, prophets, doers of miracles, gifts of healing, diversity of tongues; therefore it is not now perfect being without them. And likewise: It was then perfect without christian magistrates; *ergo*, christian magistrates are to be removed from the church.

The unskilful reasoning of T. C. openeth a door to anabaptism. This kind of reasoning, as it is unskilful, because it doth not distinguish the times of the church, neither considereth necessary circumstances, so it is most perilous, and openeth a door to anabaptism and confusion.

The office of the archbishop expressed in scripture. Moreover, I told you before that, although this name archbishop is not expressed in the scripture, yet is the office and function, as it is evidently to be seen in the examples of Timothy and Titus, yea, and in the apostles themselves, whose office of planting churches through the whole world is ceased, but their care for the good government of those churches which were planted, and their authority over those pastors whom they placed, doth and must remain in such places where there are churches. And therefore M. Bucer, writing upon

Bucer in iv. Ephes. the fourth to the Ephesians, saith thus : *Miletum presbyteros ecclesiæ Ephesinæ convocat ; tamen, quia unus inter eos præerat aliis et primam ecclesiæ curam habebat, in eo pro-*

[1 See before, page 106, note 3.]

prie residebat nomen episcopi[2] : " In the Acts, Paul calleth the same men bishops and elders, when as he called together the ministers of the church of Ephesus unto Miletum ; yet, because one amongst them did rule over the rest, and had the chief care of the church, the name of bishop did properly remain in him." So that this superiority and jurisdiction which we speak of was even in the apostle's time, as it is more at large afterward proved[3].

Chapter i.   The Twenty-seventh Division.

T. C. Page 65, Sect. 3.

1 *Cor. xii.* 28.[4]
Col. ii. 19.[4]

   Doth it not pertain to order that the apostle saith, that God hath set "first apostles, secondly prophets, thirdly teachers"? are not these words, "first," "second," "third," differences of order? If this be not order, surely I know not what order is. And yet neither archbishop nor archdeacon author of this; and it was kept also before they were hatched.

Jo. Whitgift.

Yes, but will you have the same "order" now? then must you have apostles and prophets, which you deny; so that this order you see is not perpetual; wherefore from time to time that "order" among the ministers of the word must be observed that is most convenient for the state of the church. *That order must be observed which is convenient for the state.* Neither is any against such order but those that will not live in order. Did ever any man deny but that there was "order" in the apostles' time? All this is but to make the reader believe that some such thing is in that Latin book, when there

[2 Et in Actis Paulus eosdem vocat episcopos et presbyteros, cum Mileti presbyteros &c.—M. Bucer. Prælect. in Epist. ad Ephes. Basil. 1562. cap. iv. p. 107.]

[3 Cartwright says that his reason is not answered. "For, if the church without the archbishop and archdeacon be a body consisting of all the parts comely knit together, wherein nothing wanteth, nor nothing is too much, then it followeth that these offices bring neither ornament nor accomplishment to the church, but make only an unprofitable knob and lump of flesh, to the both disfiguring and hinderance of the growth of the body." He goes on to except against Whitgift's inferences : "For, considering that the perfection of the body must be measured by the will of him whose the body is, that is, Christ; as when he gave apostles, evangelists, &c., he made it appear that he would not have his body perfect without them ; so, when he took them away from his church, he made it known that the body was perfect without them. &c." He adds: "If M. Bucer speak as you make him, I can by no means subscribe unto him."—Sec. Repl. pp. 459, 60.]

[4 These references are inserted from Repl. 2.]

is not one word whereof any such thing can be gathered. Is this your simplicity?

Chapter i.   The Twenty-eighth Division.
T. C. Page 65, Sect. 4.

Let us see of discipline and government, which we may see to be committed to those which have the preaching of the word, and to others also which did not preach the word, when St Paul saith that " the elders which govern well are worthy double honour, especially 1 Tim. v. 17.[1] *those which travail in the word;" where he appointeth the government to the ministers of the word, and to those also that were not ministers of the word.   And thereupon it followeth that the ministers of the church are not severed one from another as you, because[2] some have the ministration of the word and sacraments only, and some with the administration of the sacraments and word have also the government and discipline in their hands; but clean contrariwise St Paul distinguisheth them, and sheweth that all the ministers in the church have the government, but all have not the word to handle; so that he distinguisheth the ministry into that which is occupied in the word and government, and into that which is occupied in the government only.   But in this distinction you do not only forget St Paul, but you forget yourself.   For, if St Paul speak in that place of* those that meddle with the ministering of the word and sacraments only, why doth the bishop, which is one of the ministers that St Paul speaketh of (being the same that pastor is), why, I say, doth he meddle with the discipline and order of the church, seeing that belongeth not to him by your distinction? why doth also the archbishop (whom you say is a bishop) meddle with it?   And thus you see you need no other adversary than yourself to confute you.*

You falsify my words, by displacing the word 'only.'

JO. WHITGIFT.

The reader should better have understood what you had gone about, if you had set before his eyes the words that you confute.   Now I scarce understand your meaning myself.   You shoot altogether without a mark[3].   I know no man that denieth "discipline and government to be committed to those that have the preaching of the word, and to others also which preach not the word."   But, if you mean that either all kind

[1 The verse is added from Repl. 2.]
[2 As you sever them because, Repl. 2.]
[3 "The mark I shoot at is certain, that is, to confute your distinction of ministries of the word and sacraments only, and ministries of government and order; and it seemeth I shot so nigh, that I have driven you away from the mark. For you wander, and tell us of things that have neither head nor foot; and which, if they were true, make neither hot nor cold unto this question."—Sec. Repl. pp. 460, 1.]

of ecclesiastical discipline and government is committed to all
such as preach the word, or in as ample manner to one as
to another, you have not yet proved it, neither will you be
able to prove it with all the learning that you think yourself
to have.

That in 1 Tim. v. doth prove no such matter, as you pre- What it is to
rule well.
tend. For what doth St Paul mean there by "governing
well"? *Christo et ecclesiæ suæ tum doctrina tum integritate
vitæ fideliter inservire, non sua sed quæ Dei sunt quærere:*
"To serve Christ and his church faithfully both in doctrine
and integrity of life, to seek not those things which are his,
but those which are God's." Thus do the learned interpreters
expound *bene præesse* in this place. Is not the office of
teaching, exhorting, reproving, an office of ruling and governing? But you say that the apostle doth make two kind of
governors, one that travaileth in the word, the other that doth
not. And what then? he, that diligently doth that office that
is committed unto him, whether it be in preaching the word,
providing for the poor, visiting the sick, or any such like
function, doth rule well. But doth it therefore follow that all
have like authority, or that there is no kind of ecclesiastical
government or discipline but that which is common to all the
ministers of the word? Certain it is, that every pastor that All ministers
govern, but
not alike.
doth his duty in preaching ruleth well; and so do they also
that duly and truly administer the sacraments, relieve the
poor, visit the sick, privately admonish, &c. But is there
therefore none that hath superiority over them, to procure
that those things be done accordingly, to correct them if they
be not done, to see that every man be kept in order, be obedient to laws, teach true doctrine, break not unity, &c.? This
place therefore helpeth you not. For, although all ministers
of the word rule and govern, after a sort, yet do they not all
so, in all kind of government, nor equally, for they also must
have governors.

But consider your reason, or at the least the end of your Whereunto
the drift of
the Replier
tendeth.
drift. "All ministers of the word govern" their parishes by
preaching the word, rebuking sin, &c.; *ergo*, they must have
none to govern them, and keep them in order, and see that
they do their duty: it is all one with this: Every master of
a family ruleth over his family; and therefore he must have
no superior to rule over him; or: Every chief officer of cities or

towns be rulers and governors of those places; therefore they must have none to rule and govern either their cities and towns, or themselves. Indeed this is a plausible doctrine, to make every pastor chief governor within his own parish, and to make every city and town a kingdom within itself; but it is a pestilent doctrine; for in short time there would be as many popes as pastors, as many religions as parishes, as many sects as families, and in the end an overthrow both of religion, the church, and the kingdom. Neither could there possibly have been invented a more readier way for the pope to make his entry in hither again.

Of your distinction of *presbyter* I will speak in a more fit place.

I have not "forgot myself;" but you neither understand (as it appeareth) my writings, neither yet your own, for hitherto you have fought without an adversary.

And yet I must put you in mind of your falsehood and subtle dealing; for, whereas I say that the apostle in the iv. Ephes. "speaketh only of those ministers and ministries, which are occupied in prayers, the word, and administration of the sacraments," you, by displacing the word "only," make your reader believe that I affirm the apostle to speak in that place "of those that meddle with the ministering of the word and sacraments only;" as if I should seclude the ministers of the word from all kind of government.

Chap. i.   The Twenty-ninth Division.

T. C. Page 65, Sect. 5.

The book is named; but yet you have confuted your shadow and not the book, as hath appeared.

And, lest any man should say I confute my[1] own shadow, I must let him to understand[2] that there is a pamphlet in Latin, which is called the Book of the doctors, which goeth from hand to hand, and especially (so far as they could bring it to pass) to those only that they thought to favour that opinion; in the which book all these answers unto the place of the Ephesians are contained, and almost all that which is comprehended in this defence of archbishops and archdeacons, with other things also which are found in this book of M. Doctor's; and therefore it is very likely that he, having no other way to vent his rhapsodies and rackings[3] together, thought he would bring them to light after this sort. But how much better had it been that this misshapen thing had had the mother's womb for the grave, or being brought out had been hidden as the former is, in some

[1 Mine, Repl. 1 and 2.]   [2 Him understand, Repl. 2.]
[3 Rakings, Repl. 1 and 2.]

bench-hole or dark place, where it should never have seen any light, nor no man's eye should ever have looked of it!

Jo. Whitgift.

It had been much for your credit if you had set down the words of that book, the which you and your fautors in derision call " the Book of doctors[4];" which you have only named, and not confuted. The book dare abide the light, and the author also; but so dare not you. To the rest of your words my answer is only this, that you bewray your spirit: for further proof hereof I refer the reader to the third chapter of St James, from the tenth verse to the end.

Chapter i.   The Thirtieth Division.
T. C. Page 65, Sect. 5.

And thus, all these clouds being scattered by the sun of the truth[5], you see that the place to the Ephesians standeth strong against the archbishop and archdeacon.

Jo. Whitgift.

Nothing less; but the contrary for any thing that you have spoken yet.

Chapter i.   The Thirty-first Division.
T. C. Page 65, Sect. 5; and Page 66, Sect. 1.

Now I will[6] reason also after this sort out of the place of the Ephesians and Corinthians joined together.   There is no function but hath gifts fit and apt to discharge it annexed and given unto it; whereupon the apostle, by a metonymy, doth call the apostles, prophets, &c., " gifts," because they have always gifts joined with them.   This being granted (as no man can deny it) I reason thus:

Those functions only are sufficient for the church, which have all the Syllogism *gifts needful, either for the ministering of the word and sacraments, or for* without all *the government of the church; but all these functions reckoned of St Paul* form. *to the Ephesians, with those which St Paul calleth* ἀντιλήψεις *and* Eph. iv. 11.[7] κυβερνήσεις *(which are the deacons and elders), have the gifts needful either for the government of the church, either else* 1 Cor. xii. 28.[7] *for the ministering of the word and sacraments; therefore these functions only are sufficient for the church.   For it is a superfluous thing to make more offices than there be gifts to furnish them; for so they that should have them should rather be idols than officers.   And therefore,*

[4 See before, page 106, note 3.]
[5 Sun of truth, Repl. 2.]   [6 Will I, Repl. 2.]
[7 These references are inserted from Repl. 2.]

forasmuch as there is no gift which falleth not into some of these functions,
it is altogether a vain and unprofitable thing to bring more offices and
functions into the church besides these.

JO. WHITGIFT.

In what
sense every
function is
said to have
gifts to dis-
charge it.

You say " there is no function but hath gifts apt and fit
to discharge it annexed and given unto it." If you mean that
there is no function but there is gifts meet for it, which God
hath in his power to bestow, it is most true; but, if your
meaning be that the gifts be so annexed to the function, that
of necessity whosoever is called to that function must also have
those gifts, it is most untrue. For experience doth teach that
every man hath not gifts according to his function, although
he be lawfully thereunto called, touching his external calling;
for the inward calling none knoweth but God himself, and a
man's own conscience. But you put me in remembrance of
that which Master Bullinger writeth of the anabaptists, *Lib. v.*
cap. 1; where he (confuting the reason they use to prove
that Christians ought not to have magistrates, because Christians be so perfect of themselves that they can govern themselves, and therefore need not to be subject to any other

Bulling. Lib.
v. advers.
Anabapt.
cap. 1.

superior authority) saith thus: *Solent autem anabaptistæ*
libenter ea imaginari et animo suo fingere, quæ nunquam
fuerunt, neque extant, aut posthæc futura sunt[1]: "The anabaptists willingly use to imagine and conceive those things in
their minds, which never hath been, nor are, nor hereafter
shall be." Even so I say unto you that, in imagining the
" gifts " pertaining " to every function so to be annexed unto
the function," that he which hath the one must of necessity
have the other, you fancy that which never was, is, or shall
be; and in so reasoning what do you else than use that argument against superiority in the ecclesiastical estate, which the
anabaptists use both against ecclesiastical and civil magistrates?

Idem.

But I answer you as M. Bullinger answered them: " Except
you were blinded with pertinacy, you might easily see in
yourself just cause why there should be magistrates and
superiors."

Moreover, God doth not tie his gifts to any certain and

[1 Solent, &c. et in animo suo confingere, &c. posthac futura sunt. Nam nisi
pertinacia excæcati essent, facile hoc ipsum in seipsis experiri et deprehendere
potuissent.—H. Bullinger. adv. Anabapt. Libri VI. Tigur. 1560. Lib. v. cap. 1.
fol. 158.]

definite number of names or titles of offices, but bestoweth them
as it pleaseth him, to the commodity of his church, upon such
as be meet to use them, by what name or title soever they be
called. Wherefore this assertion of yours is either unadvisedly
avouched, or else doth it contain some secret poison not yet
uttered.

This being said to the ground that you have laid, thus I *The de-*
answer to your argument: it is in no "mode," and indeed too *formed ar-*
bad for any boy to use in his sophisms. It is in form the *gument of*
T. C.
same with this: Those things only are sufficient for salvation which are contained in the scriptures; but all those
things in the *Ave Maria* are contained in the scriptures;
therefore those things only which are in the *Ave Maria* are
sufficient to salvation. Or this: Those only are men which are
endued with reason; but all the costardmongers in London are
endued with reason; therefore the costardmongers of London
only are men. Besides this, the major is particular, which is
against all form of syllogism in the first or second figure.
To be short, in your major you have this word "only" in
your *medium;* and in the minor it[2] is left out. And therefore
your conclusion followeth not, except you had said in your
minor that only "these functions reckoned of St Paul to the
Ephesians, &c. have all gifts needful for the ministering of
the word and sacraments, and for the government of the
church." And yet, if it were so, your argument should be of
no force, being *ex solis particularibus.* So that in your
syllogism there is no manner of form, and therefore not
worthy of any other answer until it be better framed.
Although I could say unto you that all those functions have
gifts necessary for them; but not only those functions; because there be other not mentioned of you which have gifts
necessary also, and which the apostle rehearseth, 1 Cor. xii.
So likewise could I answer that most of those functions (according to your own opinion) be not perpetual, but for a time;
and therefore your reason is no good reason. Likewise, that
the apostle hath not made in either of these places any perfect
division of offices which were, even at that time, in the church.
For in the first to the Corinthians, the xii. chap., he leaveth
out evangelists, pastors, bishops, deacons, widows; and in the
fourth to the Ephesians, deacons, widows, workers of miracles,

[2 Def. A. omits *it.*]

8—2

&c. So that he hath not left any perpetual pattern of offices, or names, in either of those two places. To conclude, I could tell you that God hath left to his church authority to appoint both names and offices, as shall be for the same most convenient and profitable; the which authority the church hath also from the beginning used, as in appointing catechists, lectors, and such like, not superfluous but most necessary offices, and profitable for the church in those times wherein they were[1].

Chapter i.   The Thirty-second Division.
T. C. Page 66, Sect. 2.

And so it may be thus reasoned: If men may make and erect new ministries, they must either give gifts for to discharge them, or assure men that they shall have gifts of God, whereby they may be able to answer them. But they can neither give gifts, nor assure men of any gifts necessary to discharge those functions; therefore they may make or erect no new ministries.

Jo. Whitgift.

First, there is no " new ministry erected." But among the ministers some are appointed to govern the rest, and to have the chief direction of them; and such are chosen to that superiority, upon whom God (as far as man can judge) hath bestowed gifts meet for the same. Secondly, it is not necessary that those that appoint any office should be able to give gifts incident thereunto. For then no man might appoint any office. It is therefore sufficient if he appoint such persons as God hath endued with gifts meet for such an office, and such offices as there may be persons meet to execute; which being observed, your argument is soon answered.

[[1] "My words have light enough to have kept you from this wandering, but that you take pleasure in untruth. For, beside that the scope of my disputation doth beat you from that vagary, my words are plain. For I say not that 'every one that occupieth a ministry in the church hath gifts sufficient for his calling;' but, 'any function, or ministry of the church, hath gifts sufficient, &c.'...This is that I said, 'every function hath proper gifts for the execution of it;' and that, forsomuch as now there is no gift necessary for the ecclesiastical ministry not contained in these, and that all these fall into the ordinary ministry instituted and specified in the scripture, therefore these ordinary ministries specified in scripture are sufficient." Cartwright goes on to accuse Whitgift of changeableness in his interpretation of 1 Cor. xii., and maintains that his own argument excepted against "is as good as I can make any."—Sec. Repl. pp. 461, &c.]

Chapter i.   The Thirty-third Division.

T. C. Page 66, Sect. 3.

Last of all, to[2] conclude against these made and devised ministries of *archbishops and archdeacons after this sort: If men may add ministries* *they may also take away; for those both belong to one authority: but they* *cannot take away those ministries that God hath placed in his church;* *therefore they cannot add to those that are placed in the church. And* *this foundation I thought first to lay or ever I enter[3] into M. Doctor's not* *reasons, but authorities, not of God, but of men, in confuting of which* *there will fall forth other[4] arguments against both these offices of arch-* *bishop and archdeacon.*

The major untrue. The minor ambiguous.

Jo. Whitgift.

Your whole book is for the most part builded upon that false-founded argument, that is called *petitio principii*. For this will not be granted unto you, which you have so often-times repeated, and whereupon all your arguments are grounded, that "to appoint archbishops or archdeacons is to appoint a new ministry." It is (as I told you before) but to keep an order in the ministry, and in the church, and to execute that office of government which the apostles themselves did. When Hierome said, "That for the avoiding of schisms the ministers appointed one among themselves to govern the rest[5]," did he mean that they instituted a new ministry? A man may see by this how unable you are to defend your cause; seeing you are enforced to frame principles unto yourself, against the which you may reason, that the ignorant reader may think your quarrel to be just. But now to your argument. The major is not true; for men "may add ministries" to those that be, and break not the will and commandment of God; because they may be helps and furtherances to those ministries that God hath appointed[6]. But he "cannot take away such ministries as God hath placed in his church" to be perpetual, without breach of his will and commandment. Moreover, besides those ministries that God hath appointed in his word as necessary at all times, there may be some added

The Reply grounded upon the petition of the principle.

[2 I, Repl. 2.]   [3 Entered, Repl. 1, 2, and Def. A.]
[4 Forth also other, Repl. 1, 2, and Def. A.]
[5 Hieron. Op. Par. 1693-1706. Ad Evang. Epist. ci. Tom. IV. Pars II. col. 803. See before, page 91, note 2.]
[6 "... the papists may as well answer thus for the multiplying of their sacra-ments, as the D. for increase of the ministries."—Sec. Repl. p. 465.]

that be convenient for some times; and yet the church, that hath authority "to add these," hath not the like authority "to take away" the other; so that your major lacketh proof. Your minor also is ambiguous; for man "cannot take away those ministries that God hath appointed" to be perpetual in the church, but he may take away those that be but temporal, as occasion serveth.

If your "foundation" be no sounder than this that you have hitherto laid, surely your building cannot long stand, and M. Doctor's "authorities" may well enough encounter with all your "reasons."

¶ That the names of Metropolitan, Archbishop, &c., be not antichristian.

Chapter ii. The First Division.

Answer to the Admonition, Page 65, Sect. 1.

First, therefore, I prove that the names of metropolitan and archbishop, &c., be not antichristian names, that is, names invented by antichrist, but most ancient; yea, that they were in the church long before the gospel was publicly embraced by any prince or in any kingdom.   Polydore Vergil, *Lib. iv. de Inventoribus Rerum*,
cap. 12, saith that Clement, in his book entituled *Compendiarium Christianæ Religionis*, testifieth that the apostle Peter did in every province appoint one archbishop, whom all other bishops of the same province should obey.   He saith also that the same archbishop was called *primas, patriarcha,* and *metropolitanus*[2].   Peter

[1 This marginal note is inserted from Answ. 2.]

[2 ..placuit auctore apostolo Petro, *sicut D. Clemens in suæ Christianæ religionis compendiario libello perhibet*, ut similiter in singulis gentium, quæ religionem in posterum complecterentur, urbibus in locum flaminum episcopi substituerentur, et in qualibet provincia archiflaminis vice, unus archiepiscopus constitueretur, cui reliqui illius regionis episcopi subessent :...Ii archiepiscopi modo primates, modo Græca voce patriarchæ, h. e. patrum principes dicti, quatuor principio fuere,...Verum posthac...plures creati sunt,...Et quoniam hisce pontificibus sedes in iis præsertim locis, qui insigniores essent, datæ sunt, idcirco et metropolitanos vocamus &c.—Polyd. Verg. De Invent. Rer. Amst. 1671. Lib. IV. cap. xii. pp. 273, 4. Conf. Clement. ad Jacob. Epist. i. in Concil. Stud. Labb. et Cossart. Lut. Par. 1671-2. Tom. I. col. 91 ; et Corp. Jur. Canon. Lugd. 1624. Decret. Gratian. Decr. Prim. Pars, Dist. lxxx. cans. 1, 2. cols. 381, 2.]

.was not antichrist ; *ergo,* the name of an archbishop is no antichristian name.

T. C. Page 66, Sect. 4, 5, 6, 7 ; and Page 67, Sect. 1, 2.

Now I will come to the examining of your witnesses ; whereof some of them are so bored in the ears and branded in their foreheads, that no man need to fear any credit they shall get before any judge, wheresoever or before whomsoever they come, but in the Romish court, and the papists only excepted.   For, to let go Polydore Vergil, because whatsoever he saith he saith of the credit of another, let us come to Clement, which is the author of this you speak.   And what is he?   Is there any so blind that knoweth

Phil. iv. 3.[3]
Tertull. de
Præscript.
advers.
Hæret.

not that this was nothing less than Clement of whom St Paul speaketh, and which some think was the first bishop of Rome ordained by Peter[4], and not rather a wicked hell-hound into whom the Lord had sent Satan to be a lying spirit in his mouth, to deceive them for their unthankful receiving of the gospel?   And he must witness for the archbishop ; a worthy witness.   For, as all that popish hierarchy came out of the bottomless pit of hell, so, to uphold the archbishop the neck of it, whereupon the[5] Romish monster standeth, are raised up from hell bastards, Clemens and Anacletus, and indeed, as it may appear, the very natural sons of Satan, and the sworn soldiers of antichrist.

A man would have thought that the bishop of Salisbury, M. Jewel, had so pulled off the painting off the face of this Clement, that all good men would have had him in detestation ; so far off would they have been to have alleged out of him to prove anything that is in controversy.

In the Reply
to M. Hard-
ing, fol. 7.[6]

The bishop allegeth both Eusebius and St Hierome to prove that none of those works which go in his name are his[7] ; and, although the proofs be strong which the bishop useth, being the witness of unsuspected witnesses, yet, because the law, although it allow two witnesses, notwithstanding doth like the better[8] of three, I will set

Lib. iii.
cap. 3.

down here also Irenæus, which was a great while before them both, and followed hard after the time[9] of the true and uncounterfeit Clement, and therefore could best tell of him and of his writings ; and yet he maketh mention but of one epistle, which upon occasion amongst the Corinthians he wrote to them[10].   Indeed in another

---

[3 The verse is added from Repl. 2.]

[4 Hoc enim modo ecclesiæ apostolicæ census suos deferunt : sicut Smyrnæorum ecclesia Polycarpum ab Ioanne conlocatum refert : sicut Romanorum, Clementem a Petro ordinatum itidem.—Tertull. Op. Lut. 1641. De Præscr. Hæret. 32. p. 243.]

[5 That, Repl. 1 and 2.]   [6 The fol. is added from Repl. 2.]

[7 See Bp. Jewel's Works, Park. Soc. Edit. Vol. I. pp. 111, 12.]

[8 Like better, Repl. 1 and 2.]   [9 Times, Repl. 1 and 2.]

[10 Ἐπὶ τούτου οὖν τοῦ Κλήμεντος στάσεως οὐκ ὀλίγης τοῖς ἐν Κορίνθῳ γενομένης ἀδελφοῖς, ἐπέστειλεν ἡ ἐν Ῥώμῃ ἐκκλησία ἱκανωτάτην γραφὴν τοῖς Κορινθίοις, εἰς εἰρήνην συμβιβάζουσα αὐτούς, κ. τ. λ.—Iren. Op. Par. 1710. Lib. III. cap. iii. 3. p. 176.]

*place of that book he sheweth that it is very probable that Clement also
either wrote or turned the epistle to the Hebrews[1].   Now, if that epistle
to the Corinthes were extant[2], we should easily see, by comparing those that
are now in his name with that, what a misshapen thing this is.*

*And, if so be that Irenæus' conjecture be good, that Clement was the
author or interpreter of the epistle to the Hebrews, then what horrible
injury is done to the Holy Ghost, while the same is supposed the writer of
this book to the Hebrews, which is the author of such beggary as this
Clement brought into the world! And, I pray you, do you hold that it is
the true christian religion which that book containeth? Could none of
these considerations drive you from the testimony of this Clement? It
goeth very hard with the archbishop, when these Clements and Anacletuses
must be brought to underprop him.*

*But what if there be no such book as this is which you name (when you
say " in his book entituled* Compendiarium Religionis Christianæ")*? it is
like you know not him nor what he saith, when you cannot tell so much as
his name. Only, because Polydore writeth that Clement saith this in a certain
short and summary book of christian religion, you have set down that he
writeth thus in a book entituled* Compendiarium Christianæ Religionis ;
*where there is no such title neither in the Councils, where his epistles are,
neither yet in all other his works.*

*Thought you to disguise him with this new name of the book, that he
should not be known? or meant you to occupy your answerer in seeking
of a book, which because he should never find he should never answer?
The place which Polydore meaneth is in the first epistle which he writeth
unto James, the brother of the Lord, which is, as the rest are, both ridiculous
in the manner of writing, and in the matter oftener times wicked and
blasphemous; which I speak to this end, that the reader, through the commendation that M. Doctor hath given to this Clement, in taking him as
one of his witnesses in so great a matter, be not abused.*

Jo. Whitgift.

Here is much more labour spent than is necessary. No
man denieth but that the epistles attributed to Clement are
counterfeit ; neither do I otherwise allege him or Anacletus, or
any such like, than both M. Calvin, M. Jewel, and many
other learned men do ; as it is evident in their writings. That
testimony which I use is out of Polydore ; and therefore have
I quoted both the book and chapter. Polydore writeth as
other do that entreat of such matters ; and, forasmuch as

[1 It would seem that Cartwright is here in error. No such place has been
found in Irenæus. But see Euseb. in Hist. Eccles. Script. Amst. 1695-1700.
Lib. III. cap. xxxviii. p. 88 ; where the probability of Clement's having translated
the epistle to the Hebrews is maintained.]

[2 This epistle is extant, having been first printed from the Codex Alexandrinus in 1633.]

he was learned, and of purpose gave himself to the searching The name
of arch-
bishop and
metro-
politan. out of such things, his report is not lightly to be rejected. But (God be thanked) neither the name nor the authority of an archbishop dependeth upon these witnesses; neither do I use them as sure grounds, but as probable testimonies of the antiquity of the name. You have cited the Canons of the Apostles thrice at the least in this your book, and Higinus likewise, and used them as proofs; and yet is there as great suspicion in the counterfeiting of them as there is of this book of Clement's. I pray you, therefore, give me that liberty in reciting authors that you take to yourself, and that no man refuseth when they serve to his purpose. For I protest unto you that I have as evil an opinion of many of them, and think as great corruption to be in them, as any man doth; and that not only because I have so read in other men's writings of them, but also for that I myself in reading of them have noted the same. But I am well assured that Polydore meant that Clement which is supposed to be "the first bishop of Rome:" how he was therein deceived (being so learned a man) I leave it to others to judge.

It is not like that Polydore meant that epistle, for he knew what difference there was betwixt an epistle and a book; neither doth the length or the matter of that epistle give any occasion that it should so be called: wherefore it is like that Polydore had it out of some book attributed unto Clement under that title, though the same be not extant. For there be divers works of ancient fathers, which be not now extant in print, and yet in some places to be had. But I will not stand longer in this matter. The words of Polydore be these: *Sicut D. Clemens in suo Christianæ Religionis Compendiario libello perhibet, &c.*[3]

[3 "The Answerer in defence of his forged doctors is like unto one which to defend him from the cold covereth himself with a wet sack. For before his ignorance might have in part excused him: now by this maintenance of his Answer he hath doubled his folly. For first, to make himself clean, he defileth as much as he can Master Calvin, and the bishop of Salisbury; both which he neither sheweth to have used this Clement; and, if they do, yet their use of him or such like is so far from lessening his fault, that it maketh it more appear. For they use them against the papists, which for the most part attributing unto them as great weight of authority as to the scriptures themselves are so set up. &c."—Sec. Repl. pp. 465, &c. It is most probable that Polydore Vergil meant the spurious epistle which has been cited. See before, page 118, note 2.]

Chapter ii.   The Second Division.

T. C. Page 67, Sect. 3.

For answer unto him, although he be not worth the answering, I say, first[1], it may be well said here of the office of the archbishop, that the father of it was an Amorite and mother an[2] Hittite; that is, that it cometh of very infamous parentage, the beginning thereof being of the idolatrous nations.

JO. WHITGIFT.

These be but words of pleasure : it will appear in this discourse that the parents and authors both of the office and of the name be such as ought with greater reverence to be spoken of, and with greater signification of duty.

Chapter ii.   The Third Division.

T. C. Page 67, Sect. 4.

And, whereas Clement maketh St Peter the apostle to make it as it were his adopted son, thereby to wipe away the shame of his birth, it doth[3] St Peter shameful injury.   For, besides that it was far from St Peter to take this authority to himself, not only of making archbishops throughout every province, but also instituting a new order or office, without the counsel of the rest of the apostles, which none else of the apostles did, and which is contrary to the practice of St Peter both in the first and sixth of the Acts, contrary also to the practice[4] of the apostles ; which after shall appear—I say besides this, is it like that St Peter would graff the noblest plant, as it is said, of the ministry of the gospel, in such a rotten stock of that which was most abominable in all idolatry?   For the greater they were in the service of the idols the more detestable were they before God.

JO. WHITGIFT.

I do not take upon me the defence of Clement's words in that epistle, or of Polydore in the book and chapter before recited, in all things that they spake touching the matter. But I cannot suffer your vain reasons to serve for an answer. For, if St Peter did thus place archbishops, yet did he not appoint any "new order or office;" as you have been often-times told.   Of all bishops there is one order or ministry, but divers degrees.   Between an archbishop and a bishop there is only a difference of degree and dignity, not of order

[1 Say that first, Repl. 1 and 2.]   [2 A, Repl. 1 and 2.]
[3 So editt.; but according to list of errata in Repl. 1 *he doth*.]
[4 Practices, Repl. 1 and 2.]

or ministry; as divers learned men give unto Peter, above **The name of archbishop and metropolitan.** the rest of the apostles, the preeminence of honour for order's sake, but not of power. Moreover, Peter, in appointing them without the consent of the other apostles, did no otherwise than the apostle St Paul, when he placed Timothy at Ephesus, and Titus at Creta. It may be also that in some places where there were before *archiflamines* he placed such as were called archbishops, &c.; which might be done in respect of the city and place, and not in respect of the idolatrous priests. For *archiflamines* were but in great cities, which, being converted unto Christ, might have in the place of their *archiflamines* godly and learned archbishops, to oversee and direct the rest of the bishops and preachers, that unity and order might be observed. Thus Paul did at Ephesus and Creta. And why might not Peter do it in other places likewise[5]?

Chapter ii.   The Fourth Division.

T. C. Page 67, Sect. 5, 6, 7, 8.

Levit. xix. 27.7
Deut. xxii. 11, 12.7
Levit. xi.7
Deut. xiv.7

Eph. ii. 14.7

The Lord, when he would give laws of worshipping to[6] his people in the things that were indifferent, of shaving and cutting, and apparel-wearing, saith to his people, that they should not do so and so, because the gentiles did so; yea, even in those things, the use whereof was otherwise very profitable, and incommodious to forbear, he would have them notwithstanding to abstain from, as from swine's flesh, coneys, &c., to the end that he might have them severed, as appeareth by[8] St Paul, by a great and high wall from other nations.

And therefore it is very unlike that St Peter would frame the ministry of the gospel (which is no ceremony, but of the substance of the gospel) by the example of the heathenish and idolatrous functions.

If one had said that the Lord had shapen his[9] commonwealth by the pattern of other commonwealths, although it had been most untrue (all other flourishing commonwealths of Athens, Lacedemon, and Rome borrowing their good laws of the Lord's commonwealth), yet had it been more tolerable; but to say he framed the ministry of the gospel by the priesthood of idolatry is to fet[10] chastity out of Sodom, and to seek for heaven in hell.

[5 Cartwright makes a long reply to this division, contending that Whitgift contradicts here what he has elsewhere asserted, and that his reasoning is inconclusive.—Sec. Repl. pp. 467, &c.]

[6 Unto, Repl. 1 and 2.]

[7 The first four references, and the verse of the last are inserted from Repl. 2.]

[8 In, Repl. 1 and 2.]

[9 This, Def. A. and B.]   [10 Fetch, Repl. 1 and 2.]

The name of arch- bishop and metro- politan.

And, if so be that the Lord had delighted in this hierarchy, he would rather have taken of his own than borrowed of others, of his own church than of the synagogue of Satan. For under the law besides the Levites there were priests, and above them a high priest.

Jo. Whitgift.

The Israel- ites had some things like to the gentiles.

God gave unto the Israelites a king, though other nations had so in like manner. And he ordained degrees of priests among them to offer unto him sacrifices, though the gentiles had the like[1]; and what inconvenience could there come by placing archbishops (which should faithfully preach the word of God, and carefully govern the church of Christ) even in those places where there were *archiflamines*, who did deface Christianity and persecute the Christians? For by these means there could no harm come unto them, as there might have done to the Israelites by using of such things of the gentiles as he forbad unto them, but the contrary; for this was a means to pluck them from all their superstition and idolatry. Neither is this in any respect a "framing of the ministry of the gospel by the examples of idolatrous and heathenish functions." Except you will say also that, because the gentiles had *flamines*, and the Christians had bishops, therefore the christian bishops were framed according to the example of the gentiles' *flamines*. If you cannot say so truly in bishops, neither can you justly affirm it of archbishops; for the reason is all one. Do you think this to be a good collection? Where in the pope's time there was a massing priest, now is there placed a minister of the gospel; *ergo*, the ministry of the gospel is framed according to the example of massing priests. And yet thus do you conclude, that, because there are now-a-days archbishops where before there were *archiflamines*, therefore "the ministry of the gospel is framed according to the heathenish and idolatrous functions."

[1 " The Lord's priests and sacrifices were before the priests and sacrifices of the gentiles; therefore that exception ('God instituted priests and sacrifices though the gentiles had the like') is vain to prove that there may be archbishops, as there were archflamines."—Sec. Repl. p. 470.]

Chapter ii. The Fifth Division.

T. C. Page 68, Sect. 1.

And to say that Peter appointed archbishops and bishops by the example of idolaters[2] is after a sort to make the law to come out of Egypt or Babylon, and not out of Sion or Jerusalem, as the prophet saith.

Essay ii. 3.[3]

The name of archbishop and metropolitan.

No man hath said so.

Jo. WHITGIFT.

Neither Clement in that epistle, nor Polydore in that book, nor Gratian, *Dist.* 80, saith "that Peter appointed archbishops and bishops by the example of idolaters;" but this only they say, that in those cities, where there were before *archiflamines,* there were placed archbishops, and, where there were *flamines,* there bishops[4]. There is great difference betwixt their kind of speech and yours. Howsoever the authors please you, or displease you, yet report their words truly. M. Fox, Tom. I. p. 14, is of this judgment, that, where before there were *archiflamines,* &c., there were placed patriarchs, &c. His words be these: "Thus it is made plain how the bishop of the first seat, or first bishop, or primate, is none other but he which then was called patriarch, and belonged not only to the church of Rome, but to all such cities and places where as before among the gentiles were *primiflamines,* &c. *Dist.* 80, cap. *Urbes et loca; et, In illis[5]*." Hitherto M. Fox.

M. Fox, Tom. I. fol. 14.

Chapter ii. The Sixth Division.

T. C. Page 68, Sect, 1, 2, 3.

You say after that James was an archbishop: if he were, he was the first, and placed over the Jews.

And, although St Peter might, to gain the gentiles, be content to use their idolatrous functions with a little change of their names, yet there is none so mad to think that he would translate any such function from the gentiles to[6] the Jews; which were never before accustomed with any such flamines or archiflamines. And this I dare generally and at once say against you and your Clement, that the Lord translated divers things out

---

[2] Of the idolaters, Repl. 1 and 2.]

[3] The verse is added from Repl. 2.]

[4] See before, page 113, note 2.]

[5] Fox, Acts and Monuments, Lond. 1684. Vol. I, p. 12; where *he which was called.*]

[6] Unto, Repl. 1 and 2.]

The name
of arch-
bishop and
metro-
politan.

צדיקים
צדקה[2]

of the law into the gospel, as the presbytery or eldership, ex- Mat. v. 22.[1]
communication, and the office of deacons (as it is thought); for
that the Sadducees, of whom so often mention is made in the John ix. 22.[1]
gospel, are thought to have had that office to provide for the poor; for those
that know the Hebrew tongue do understand that Tsadikim *and* Tsidkah
do not only signify justice[3] and just men, but also alms and almsmen—I
say these and others more translated from the law unto the gospel; but
neither you nor your Clement shall ever be able to shew that the Lord ever
translated anything from gentilism into the gospel.

We read in the Acts that all the gentiles were commanded Acts xv. 29.[1]
to conform themselves unto the Jews in the abstaining from
blood and strangled meat for a time; but we can never find that the Jews
were commanded to conform themselves[4] to the gentiles in their ceremonies;
the reason whereof is, because the one was sometime[5] the law of God, and
therefore he that had conscience in it was to be borne with; and the other
came from men and out of their forge, which the Lord would never give so
much honour unto, as to make other men by any means subject unto them.

Jo. Whitgift.

If you had not learned that point of sophistry which is
called *petitio principii* (whereof I have so oftentimes told you),
without doubt you had lacked much matter, and your book
would have been very thin. For all this added in this place
is nothing but descanting upon a false plain-song. The
offices of an archbishop and bishop are no "idolatrous functions," but christian, and meet both for Jew and gentile converted unto Christ; neither are they translated from the
gentiles, but grounded upon the word of God, practised in
the apostles' time, approved by the best councils, as is declared in the Answer to the Admonition; and shall be more
amply hereafter, occasion being offered. Wherefore all this
that you have here said (the ground being taken away)
serveth to no purpose.

Your conjecture of the deaconship to be taken from the
Jews is but a mere conjecture; if there had been any such
office in the law, it would have been specified in one place or
other of the old testament[6].

[1 The verses are inserted from Repl. 2.]
[2 The words in the margin are not in Repl. 1 or 2.]
[3 Justices, Def. A. and B.]   [4 Them, Repl. 1 and 2.]
[5 Sometimes, Repl. 1 and 2.]
[6 "Here he hath at one push thrust the archbishop quite out of the church.
For if this be a good reason, there were no deacons amongst the Jews, because they
were not specified in the old testament, then it is likewise true that, forasmuch as

Touching your eldership, we shall see what you have to say for it in place. I will not trouble myself and the reader with by-matters not incident to this question. And yet I would gladly learn of you in what portion of the law your presbytery is commanded or prescribed; for I told you before, out of M. Calvin, that it was appointed after the return of the Jews from the captivity of Babylon.

The name of arch-bishop and metro-politan.

Your reason why there should be no orders or ceremonies taken from the gentiles is not sufficient; for it is a negative reason *ab auctoritate*. But to speak of that matter is now from the purpose, because I have denied these offices to be taken from the gentiles.

Chapter ii.   The Seventh Division.
T. C. Page 68, Sect. 4.

But what if there were no such offices among[7] *the gentiles and pagans as* archiflamines *and*[8] protoflamines? *whereof before I shew the conjectures which I have, I must give thee, gentle reader*[9], *to understand that I am not ignorant that there are divers which say there were such offices among*[7] *the gentiles, and namely here in England that there were 25. flamines and three* archiflamines, *whereof were made three archbishops, of London, Canterbury, and York, and 25. bishops; as Platine hath in the chapter Eleutherius*[10]. *And Galfridus Monemutensis in his second book and first chapter*[11]. *And, as I think, Gildas*[12] *also*[13]; *and Lombard in his fourth book*[14] *speaketh of it, as a*[15] *general thing that was in all places where paganism was. But, if so be that the religion of other pagans did follow and was like unto that of the Romans (which is very probable), they being then the rulers of the whole world in a manner, unto whose example all men do lightly conform themselves even without commandment, then there is great likelihood there were no such* archiflamines *or* protoflamines *out of Tully, which sheweth that there were among*[16] *the Romans divers kinds*

there is no archbishop specified in the new testament, there was no archbishop in the apostles' times."—Sec. Repl. pp. 470, 1.]

[7 Amongst, Repl. 1 and 2.]   [8 Or, Repl. 1 and 2.]

[9 The gentle reader, Editt.; Repl. 2., however, has *the (gentle reader)*, "the" evidently standing here, as it often does, for "thee."]

[10 Erant tum in Britannia pontifices quinque et viginti, quos flamines vocabant. Inter hos autem tres archiflamines habebantur, quorum in loco archiepiscopi tres constituti sunt, ut Ptolemæus ait. Protoflaminum vero loco primitiva ecclesia patriarchas instituit.—Plat. De Vit. Pont. Col. 1551. Eleuth. fol. 21.]

[11 Galfrid. Monemut. De Orig. et Gest. Brit. 1517. Lib. II. cap. i. fol. 33.]

[12 There does not seem to be anything to the point in Gildas. His treatise De Excid. Brit. may be seen in Biblioth. Vet. Patr. Stud. Galland. Venet. 1765-81. Tom. XII. pp. 192, &c.]

[13 The six preceding words are not in Repl. 2.]

[14 P. Lombard. Libr. Sentent.Col. Agrip. 1576. Lib. IV. Dist. xxiv. M. fol.396.]

[15 As of a, Repl. 1 and 2.]   [16 There was amongst, Repl. 1 and 2.]

The name
of arch-
bishop and
metro-
politan.

of priests[1], whereof some were called flamines, *of a several attire which they ware always on[2] their heads, other* pontifices, *and a third sort were called* Salii, *and the[3] chief of those* flamines *was called* flamen dialis, *who was also distinguished from the rest by a white hat; but of any* archiflamines, *or* protoflamines, *he maketh no mention at all; and therefore it is like that there was never any such office amongst the pagans.*

JO. WHITGIFT.

Whether "there were such offices among the gentiles" or no, the matter is not great, nor worthy of deciding. But that there were such it is manifest, if any credit is to be given to so many histories and writers both ecclesiastical and pro-

Archi-
flamines.

fane, not only those whom you have reported, but Gratian, Polydore[4], and others. But, as a sufficient confutation of all this that you have here written, and as an argument of your unskilfulness in stories, I will set down the words of Master

M. Fox,
Tom. I. fol.
146.

Fox, Tom. I. p. 146, which be these: "Let us return to Eleutherius, the good bishop, who, hearing the request of the king, and glad to see the godly towardness of his well-disposed mind, sendeth him certain teachers and preachers, called Fugatius, or by some Fagamus, and Damianus or Dimianus, which converted first the king and people of Britain, and baptized them with the baptism and sacrament of Christ's faith. The temples of idolatry and other monuments of gentility they subverted, converting the people from their divers and many gods to serve one living God. Thus, true religion with sincere faith increasing, superstition decayed with all rites of idolatry. There were then in Britain 28. head priests which they called *flamines*, and three archpriests among them which were called *archiflamines*, having the oversight of their manners, as judges over the rest. These 28. *flamines* they turned to 28. bishops, and the three *archiflamines* to three archbishops, having then their seats in three principal cities of the realm; that is, in London, in York, and in Glamorgantia, *videlicet, in Urbe Legionum,* by Wales[5]." Your "conjecture" therefore is but vain, and cannot countervail so many witnesses.

[1 See Cic. De Orat. Lib. III., De Harusp. Respons., De Leg. Lib. II. 8.]
[2 Of, Repl. 1 and 2.]   [3 And that the, Repl. 1 and 2.]
[4 See before, page 118, note 2. Conf. Polyd. Vergil. Anglic. Hist. Basil. 1555. Lib. II. p. 41.]
[5 Fox, Acts and Monuments, Lond. 1684. Vol. I. p. 118; where *of this king, Faganus, and all other monuments, all other rites, arch-flamines,* and *manners and as judges.*]

Moreover, your argument is negative from human au- The name thority; for you argue that there were no *archiflamines* of arch-
bishop and among the pagans, because Tully maketh no mention of them; metro- and therefore of no credit.   Besides, why might not the politan. Grecians call those *archiflamines* whom Tully called *flamines diales?* But the matter is not worthy the labour; and there- fore thus briefly to have answered it shall suffice: only I would have the reader by the way to note the antiquity of archbishops here in England, even from the first beginning of the public profession of Christianity, which was *anno* 180, Archbishops
in England. or thereabout[6]. An. Dom.
180.

Chapter ii.   The Eighth Division.
T. C. Page 68, Sect. 5.

And, if there were, I have shewed how wicked it is to say that Peter framed the ministry of the gospel by it.   Now let it be seen of all men how strongly you have concluded, that the names of archbishops are not anti-christian, when as it is most certain that he was a pillar of antichrist upon whom your reason is grounded.

Jo. Whitgift.

Though it be certain "that Peter framed not the ministry of the gospel by any custom of the pagans," yet your argu- ments are of no force to prove that he did not place ministers of the gospel where there were before priests of the pagans, call them by what other name you will; or that in the chief cities he placed not such as might direct and govern the rest; seeing it is the consent of all writers that the apostles, when they had planted churches, did place bishops and other minis- ters in the churches which were planted[7].

Whether he were "a pillar" or no "of antichrist," by whom I have hitherto proved "the names of archbishops not to be antichristian," I leave it to the learned to judge.   If you mean Clement, of whom Polydore doth borrow his report,

[6 Cartwright replies at considerable length, discrediting Whitgift's authori- ties, and exposing the story of Lucius and Eleutherius as a fable.   And he adds (but not truly) that bishop Jewel in his controversy with Harding had rejected it (See Bp. Jewel's Works, Park. Soc. Edit. Vol. III. p. 163).—Sec. Repl. pp. 471, &c.]

[7 " You shall not be able to shew 'that the bishops which the apostles planted were other' than which with the elders had the oversight of one particular congregation; and therefore your proofs are always by other things, as doubtful as the question in hand."—Ibid. p. 476.]

The name of archbishop and metropolitan.

it is evident that Polydore meaneth that Clement that was one of the first bishops of Rome, who was no "pillar of antichrist," but a godly bishop. If you mean Polydore himself, upon whose credit I take the report, then surely, howsoever in divers points of papism he erred, yet is he one that hath greatly detected and opened their superstitions, and whose authority neither yourself nor any other learned man in many things will refuse.

Reports of antiquity may be taken from infidels.

But, if all this were true that you say, yet may we take reports of antiquities even from Turks, pagans, papists, or else must we condemn the most part of histories.

Chapter ii. The Ninth Division.

Answer to the Admonition, Page 65, Sect. 2.

Volusianus.

Volusianus, bishop of Carthage, who lived *anno Dom.* 865, in one of his epistles which he writ[1] to Nicholas the first, in the defence of the marriage of priests, saith that Dionysius Areopagita, St Paul's scholar, was by St Paul made archbishop of Athens[2].

T. C. Page 68, Sect. ult.

The times wherein Volusianus lived declare sufficiently how little credit is to be given to his testimony; which were when the mass had place, if not so wicked as it was after, yet notwithstanding far differing from the simplicity of the supper which was left by our Saviour Christ. And Eusebius is of more credit in this than Volusianus, which, in the third Eus. iii. Lib. 4.[3] *book and fourth chapter, and in the fourth book and three and* Eus. iv. *twenty chapter, saith, of the report of Dionysius, bishop of* Lib. 23.[3] *Corinth, that St Paul made Dionysius Areopagita bishop of Athens[4]:*

A notable argument.

he saith not archbishop, but bishop, although he spake[5] twice of it; and in

[1 Write, Def. A. and B.]

[2 Quod et Dionysius Areopagita theosophus, id est, Deum sapiens, Pauli apostoli discipulus, et ab eo Atheniensium archiepiscopus ordinatus, &c.—Volus. Epist. ii. in Fox, Acts and Monuments, Lond. 1684. Vol. II. p. 396. For an account of this epistle and the author see Oudin. Comm. de Script. Eccles. Lips. 1722. Tom. II. cols. 247, &c.]

[3 These references are inserted from Repl. 2, which omits any notice in the text of the places in Eusebius.]

[4 Ἐπὶ τούτοις καὶ τὸν Ἀρεοπαγίτην ἐκεῖνον, Διονύσιος ὄνομα αὐτῷ...τὸν ἐν Ἀθήναις ἐκκλησίας πρῶτον ἐπίσκοπον, ἀρχαίων τὶς ἕτερος Διονύσιος...ἱστορεῖ γεγονέναι.—Euseb. in Hist. Eccles. Script. Amst. 1695-1700. Lib. III. cap. iv. p. 59. Conf. Lib. IV. cap. xxiii. p. 116.]

[5 Speake, Repl. 2.]

the preface before his works it is said that after his conversion he went The name
to Rome to Clement, and was sent with others of Clement into the west of arch-
parts, and that he came to Paris and was there executed[6]. *Whether soever* bishop and
of these opinions is true, that falleth which Volusianus affirmeth. And, if metro-
either Volusianus or you will have us believe that Dionysius Areopagita politan.
was archbishop of Athens, you must shew some better authority than
Eusebius, or Dionysius bishop of Corinth; and then your cause shall have
at the least some more colour of truth.

Jo. Whitgift.

Thus indeed may you easily wipe away all authority of
histories and fathers. But this shift will not serve your turn
with wise and learned men. Volusianus was very well learned,
and a very godly bishop in his time; neither is it to be thought
that he would write anything in such a matter which he had
not certainly learned of worthy writers. Your reason, brought
out of Eusebius to prove the contrary, faileth in two respects.
First, because it is negative from authority, and that of man;
for thus you conclude: "Eusebius did not call him archbishop;" *ergo*, he was no archbishop; which kind of argument
is never good in any respect, when it is taken from the authority of man. Secondly, your argument faileth, because
histories be not so curious in calling men by their several
titles. They think it sufficient, if they use the common and
most usual name; even as it is the common use amongst us
to call the archbishops of Canterbury and York oftener by
the names of bishops of Canterbury and York, than by the
names of archbishops. So that indeed, your argument being
denied, you are not able by any sound reason to confirm it.
If Eusebius or Dionysius had denied him to be an archbishop,
your argument had been good[7].

[6 Maximus says that Dionysius was made bishop of the Athenians. See
Dion. Areop. Op. Antv. 1634. S. Max. Prolog. Tom. I. p. xxxv. Conf. Vit. S.
Dion. per Sym. Metaphrast. ibid. Tom. II. pp. 193, 4, 9; where he is said to have
been first bishop of Athens, and afterwards to have gone to Rome and Paris.
The works extant under his name are of a later age.]

[7 Cartwright rejoins that Volusianus could not have learned of "worthier
writers in this behalf than Denis bishop of Corinth, and Eusebius." He goes on
to say: "Likewise when the bishop of Salisbury made this challenge after performed, that it could not be shewed out of any allowed writer 600. years after Christ,
that there was any mention of such and such things maintained by popery, the
Answ. hath, with one word, wiped away the profit of all those travails. For it
may be answered that such things were, although none made mention of them."
—Sec. Repl. pp. 476, 7.]

The name
of arch-
bishop and
metro-
politan.

Erasmus[1].

Chapter ii.   The Tenth Division.

Answer to the Admonition, Page 65, Sect. 3.

Erasmus, in his argument of the epistle to Titus,
saith that Paul made Titus archbishop of Creta[2]. [The
same saith Pellican in his argument upon the epistle to
Titus[3].][4] But antichrist was not in Paul's time; *ergo,*
the name of an archbishop was not invented by antichrist.

T. C. Page 69, Sect. 1.

*Erasmus followeth, which saith Titus was archbishop of Crete; whom
I could answer with his own words.   For I am sure he will grant me,
that Titus and Timothy had one office, the one in Ephesus, the other in
Crete; but it appeareth by Erasmus his own words that Timothy was but*

A slender
proof.

*bishop of Ephesus; therefore Titus was but bishop of Crete.   For Erasmus,
in his argument upon the first epistle of Timothy, saith that St Paul did
inform Timothy of the office of a bishop, and of the discipline of the
church[5].   If either he had been an archbishop, or an archbishop had been
so necessary as it is made, he would have instructed him in that also.*

Jo. Whitgift.

This maketh wholly against yourself; for hereby it appeareth that the writers use not any great curiosity in observing proper titles, but they think it sufficient if that name
of office be used that comprehendeth all.   Where doth Erasmus say, "that Timothy was but a bishop[6]?"   Will you not
learn to deal plainly?   But let us hear your argument:
"Erasmus saith that St Paul did inform Timothy of the office
of a bishop, and of the discipline of the church;" *ergo,* Erasmus saith that Timothy was no archbishop.   Undoubtedly

[1 This word is inserted from Answ. 2.]

[2 Titum...insulæ nobilissimæ Cretæ præfecerat apostolus, et illinc abiens
archiepiscopum consecrarat.—Erasm. Op. L. Bat. 1703-6. In Epist. ad Tit. Arg.
Tom. VII. cols. 1067, 8.]

[3 Titum discipulum suum, ac filii loco habitum ob eximias dotes, insulæ
nobilissimæ Cretæ præfecerat apostolus, et illinc abiens archiepiscopum consecrarat.—C. Pellican. Comm. in Omn. Apost. Epist. Tigur. 1539. In Epist. ad
Tit. Arg. p. 577.]

[4 This sentence is inserted from Answ. 2.]

[5 Quoniam autem huic [Timotheo] ecclesiarum curam delegarat [Paulus],
sicut et Tito, quas ipse non poterat adire, instituit eum in functione episcopali, et
in disciplina ecclesiæ.—Erasm. Op. In Epist. ad Timoth. prior. Arg. Tom. VII.
cols. 1033, 4.]

[6 "If a spade be but a spade, and a fig but a fig; then a bishop is but a
bishop."—Sec. Repl. p. 479.]

you had need bear with other men's unskilfulness in logic, if
you use such reasons in good earnest.   This argument also is
negative *ab humana auctoritate*.   Whatsoever is necessary
for a bishop is necessary for an archbishop; and the office of
a bishop is the office of an archbishop.   There is no difference
of bishop and archbishop, but only this, that the archbishop
hath authority over other bishops, to call them together when
occasion serveth, to see that they walk according to the laws
and rules prescribed, to keep unity and concord in the church,
and such like.   There is no difference, *quantum ad ministerium :* "in respect of their ministry and function," but only
quoad politiam et ordinem : "in respect of policy and order ;"
as I have said before.

The name of archbishop and metropolitan.

The difference betwixt an archbishop and a bishop.

Chapter ii.   The Eleventh Division.
T. C. Page 69, Sect. 2.

*And, I pray you, tell me whether Erasmus or the Greek scholiast be
more to be believed in this point, out of whom is taken that which is in the
latter end of the epistles to Timothy and Titus, where they both are called
the first elected bishops that ever were, either of Ephesus or Creta[7] : for my
part, I think they were neither bishops nor archbishops, but evangelists ;
as shall appear afterwards.   But it may be sufficient to have set against
Erasmus' authority the authority of the scholiast.   And here, if[8] you will
cavil, and say that the scholiast, which saith he was bishop, denieth not but
that he also was an archbishop, because an archbishop is a bishop, it may
be answered easily, that the scholiast did not speak nor write so unproperly
as to call them by the general name of bishop, whom he might as easily
have called (if the truth would have let him) by a more proper and particular name of archbishop.   And further, in this division of the ministers,
the archbishop and the bishop are members of one division, and therefore
one of them cannot be affirmed and said of another; for that were contrary
to the nature of a true division.*

This is often promised, but never performed.

This division is not so strange as you make it.

Jo. Whitgift.

I tell you that "Erasmus" and "the Greek scholiast," do
very well agree, and the one doth expound the other.   I tell
you also that your negative arguments are not worth a rush,
use them as oft as you list.   What you "think" of Timothy

[7 See the notes at the end of the second epistle to Timothy and of that to Titus,
in editions generally of the Greek Testament. Conf. Œcumen. Op. Lut. Par. 1631.
Comm. cap. ix. in II. Epist. ad Tim. Tom. II. p. 283; in Epist. ad Tit. cap. vi.
p. 300 ; where in the former passage πρῶτον does not appear.]

[8 If here, Repl. 1 and 2.]

The name of arch- bishop and metro- politan.
or Titus being archbishops or bishops is not material; but of what force your reasons are shall be considered when you utter them. If Erasmus and the Greek scholiast were of divers judgments in this point (as they be not), yet were it an unlearned answer to set the one against the other[1].

He that calleth an archbishop a bishop speaketh properly; for so he is in the respect of his ministry and substance of his office; the name of archbishop he hath only in respect of order and policy. "Archbishop and bishop are members of one division;" as chief justice and justice is. Every chief justice is a justice; but every justice is not a chief justice: even so, every archbishop is a bishop; but every bishop is not an arch- bishop; neither is this such a strange division as you think it to be. For Aristotle did in like manner divide πολιτείαν in *regnum, aristocratiam,* and πολιτείαν, that is, that which is commonly called πολιτεία[2].

Chapter ii.　The Twelfth Division.

T. C. Page 69, Sect. 3.

And yet I have a further answer both to Erasmus and Volusianus, and whatsoever other have written after this sort, that they spake[3] and gave titles to those men they wrote of, not according to that which they were, but according to the custom and manner of that age wherein they wrote. And so we may read that Vincentius and Nicephorus, Vinc. x. Lib. *writing of Victor, speak far otherwise of him than Eusebius* cap. 124. Niceph. iv. *doth; which notwithstanding wrote of the same man which they* Lib. cap. 38. *did. The one calleth Victor the pope of Rome[4]; and the other saith*

Nicephorus falsified.
that in glory he passed all the bishops before him[5]; which Eusebius never maketh any word of. Even so Volusianus and Erasmus, living in the times when as they which were the most esteemed in the ministry were called archbishops, call Titus and Dionysius archbishops, upon whom depended the chief care of those churches which they governed.

[1 "I will also refer to the reader's judgment, what 'unlearnedness' it is 'to confute authority' by better 'authority;' and in what place the D. will have us receive men's authority, when he will not have them controlled by other men."— Sec. Repl. p. 480.]

[2 Ἐπεί...διειλόμεθα, τρεῖς μὲν τὰς ὀρθὰς πολιτείας, βασιλείαν, ἀριστο- κρατίαν, πολιτείαν· κ. τ. λ.—Aristot. Op. Lut. Par. 1629. De Rep. Lib. IV. cap. ii. Tom. II. p. 364. Conf. ibid. Lib. III. cap. vii. p. 346.]

[3 Speake, Repl. 2.]

[4 Ea tempestate Eleutherio papæ Romæ Victor successit. &c.—Hugo Flori- acens. cit. in Vincent. Biblioth. Mund. Duac. 1624. Lib. x. cap. cxxiv. Tom. IV. p. 412.]

[5 See below, note 7.]

JO. WHITGIFT.

This is no answer at all, first, because Erasmus would then have given to Timothy the same title also; secondly, because Erasmus, being a man of so singular knowledge and judgment, would not otherwise than truly report of any man, especially in such a case, and handling matters of divinity; thirdly, because when he wrote there was neither bishop nor archbishop at Creta, as there was at Rome when Vincentius and Nicephorus writ. And, if this were true that you say, then should Eusebius when he wrote of Victor have termed him a "patriarch," or an "archbishop," or "metropolitan" at the least. For those names were usual in Eusebius his time[6].

But why do you untruly report of Nicephorus? for in that book and chapter he giveth unto Victor no other name and title than the same that Eusebius doth, for he calleth him by the bare name of Victor, without any other title; neither doth he say, "that in glory he passed all the bishops before him;" but this he saith, that the other bishops which were with him did dissuade him from excommunicating the bishops of Asia, and addeth: *Et acrius severiusque cum illo qui gloria eos anteiret egerunt*[7]: "They dealt more sharply and severely with him that excelled them in glory." Therefore he saith that he did excel in glory those bishops that were then, not those which were before him. But what is this to your purpose? If he had given unto Victor any other title than was usual when he lived, doth it therefore follow that Erasmus and Volusianus had done so in like manner? Will you answer such learned and notable men's authority with so vain and childish conjectures?

[6 "Let him shew one approved author for the name of archbishop, or patriarch once only used in Eusebius' time, or before, to note the superiority of one bishop over all his fellows; and we will all clap our hands unto him: if he cannot, then it is shame to say, 'those names were usual in Eusebius' time.'"—Sec. Repl. p. 481.]

[7 ... καὶ πληκτικώτερον δὲ προσεφέροντο τῆς προτέρας ἐχομένῳ δόξης.— Niceph. Call. Eccles. Hist. Lut. Par. 1630. Lib. IV. cap. xxxviii. Tom. I. p. 339. Whitgift appears to have followed an old Latin translation. Conf. Niceph. Call. Eccles. Hist. Op. J. Langi in Lat. Serm. transl. Par. 1574. col. 227; where the words stand exactly as here cited.]

The name
of arch-
bishop and
metro-
politan.

Chapter ii.   The Thirteenth Division.

Answer to the Admonition, Page 65, Sect. 4 ; and Page 66, Sect. 1.

Anacletus[1].

I omit Anacletus, a godly bishop and martyr, who lived *anno Domini* 85, which in his epistle, *Tom. i. Concil.*, divers times maketh mention of archbishops, patriarchs, primates, metropolitans, and saith that St James, which was called Justus, was the first archbishop of Jerusalem[2].

St James, archbishop[1].

I omit also Anicetus, who lived *anno Domini* 155, which likewise in his epistle maketh mention of archbishops[3]; because these epistles are not without just cause suspected either to be none of theirs, or else in divers points corrupted.

T. C. Page 69, Sect. 3.

There followeth Anacletus, another of these witnesses which must depose that the name of an archbishop is not antichristian, of whom as of Clement that went before, and Anicetus which followeth after, the common proverb may be verified: Ask my fellow if I be a thief. And, although the Answerer be ashamed of him, and saith therefore he will omit him,

This is untrue, as will appear in the end.

yet even very need driveth him to bring him in, and to make him speak the uttermost he can. And this honest man saith that James was the first archbishop of Jerusalem; but Eusebius saith James was bishop, Lib. ii. 23. *not archbishop of Jerusalem, and appointed by the apostles[4].*

It is the 11. chapter.

And, in the third book, 22. chapter, he saith[6] that the apostles Lib. iii. 22.[5] *did appoint after his death Simeon the son of Cleophas bishop of Jerusalem[7]. And Irenæus, in his fourth book, 63. chapter, saith[8]* Lib. iv. 63.[5] *that the apostles in all places appointed bishops unto the churches[9]; whereby it may appear what an idle dream it is of Clement,*

[1] These marginal notes are inserted from Answ. 2.]

[2] Porro et Hierosolymitarum primus archiepiscopus beatus Iacobus, qui justus dicebatur, &c.—Anaclet. Epist. ii. 1. ad Episc. Ital. in Concil. Stud. Labb. et Cossart. Lut. Par. 1671-2. Tom. I. col. 521. Conf. ibid. 4. col. 524.]

[3] Nulli archiepiscopi primates vocentur, nisi &c.—Anicet. Epist. 2. ad Episc. Gall. in eod. ibid. col. 531.]

[4] ... ἐπὶ Ἰάκωβον, τὸν τοῦ Κυρίου τρέπονται ἀδελφὸν, ᾧ πρὸς τῶν ἀποστόλων ὁ τῆς ἐπισκοπῆς τῆς ἐν Ἱεροσολύμοις ἐγκεχείριστο θρόνος.—Euseb. in Hist. Eccles. Script. Amst. 1695-1700. Lib. ii. cap. xxiii. p. 50.]

[5] These references are added from Repl. 2.]

[6] And in another place he saith, Repl. 2.]

[7] Συμεὼν ὁμοίως δεύτερος μετὰ τὸν τοῦ Σωτῆρος ἡμῶν ἀδελφὸν, τῆς ἐν Ἱεροσολύμοις ἐκκλησίας κατὰ τούτους τὴν λειτουργίαν ἐγκεχειρισμένος ἦν.— Id. Lib. iii. cap. xxii. p. 73. Conf. cap. xi. p. 69; where the appointment of the apostles is more particularly noted.]

[8] And Irenæus saith, Repl. 2.]

[9] Iren. Op. Par. 1710. Lib. iv. cap. xxxiii. 8. p. 272. See below, page 138.]

Volusianus, and Anacletus, either that Peter did this by his own authority,   The name
or that the primitive church was ever stained with these ambitious titles   of arch-
of patriarch, primate, metropolitan, or archbishop; when as the stories   bishop and
make mention that, throughout every church, not every province, not by   metro-
Peter or Paul, but by apostles, a bishop, not an archbishop, was ap-   politan.
pointed.

Jo. Whitgift.

If they be the Anacletus, or Clemens, or Anicetus that
commonly they are taken for, and these writings were theirs
uncorrupted, then were their witness sufficient, although they
were bishops of Rome.   But I neither will defend their writings, neither do I think them to be worthy any defence, only I
require but that liberty of using them that no learned man
refuseth when they serve his turn.   Master Calvin doth allege
this Anacletus his authority to prove that the people's consent
was required in the appointing of ministers. *Instit. cap. viii.* Calvin.
sect. 61.[10]   So doth M. Fox, Tom. I. page 12, who writeth
thus : "Wherefore, as we must needs grant the bishop of Rome M. Fox.
to be called a metropolitan, or an archbishop, by the council of
Nice, so we will not greatly stick in this also to have him numbered with patriarchs or primates ; which title seemed in old
time to be common to more cities than to Rome, both by the
epistle of Anacletus, of pope Stephanus, and pope Julius, and
Leo, &c.[11]"

Master Jewel also himself doth use his authority in that M. Jewel.
sort that I do[12].   But what need you be so curious, who have
so often alleged the canons of the apostles ; and in your 95. Page 95. Sect.
page you use the authority of Higinus or Pelagius, as great a 4.
counterfeit as this Anacletus is.   I speak not this to win any
credit to Anacletus his epistles or decrees, but to avoid your
cavils, and to shew that, in citing him in this manner and form
that I do, I do no otherwise than other godly and learned
men have done.   You shall understand ere I come to an end
that I have not alleged him for any need.

Your argument to prove that James was no archbishop,
because Eusebius and other do call him " bishop, and not arch-

[10] Quanquam in presbyteris quoque semper exigebatur civium consensus:
quod etiam testatur canon primus dist. 67. (Conf. Anaclet. Epist. ii. 1. in Concil.
Stud. Labb. et Cossart. Tom. I. col. 521) qui Anacleto tribuitur.—Calvin. Op. Amst.
1667-71. Inst. Lib. IV. cap. iv. 10. Tom. IX. p. 288.]

[11] Fox, Acts and Monuments, Lond. 1684. Vol. I. p. 11 ; where *to be a metropolitan or archbishop,* and *seemeth in the old time.*]

[12] See Bp. Jewel's Works, Park. Soc. Edit. Vol. IV. p. 1299.]

The name
of arch-
bishop and
metro-
politan.
bishop," is of the same nature that your other arguments be, that is, *ab auctoritate negativè*; and therefore must be sent away with the same answer.

Whether the "apostles placed James and Simeon at Jerusalem," or no, is not the question. But you are something deceived in your quotation, for you should in the place of the 22. chapter of Eusebius have noted the 11. chapter.

Irenæus.
The place of Irenæus, though it make not against any thing that I have spoken, if it were as you do allege it, yet must I tell you that it is by you not truly understood. For Irenæus doth not say that the apostles did together in every place appoint bishops, but he saith: *Secundum successiones episcoporum, quibus illi eam quæ in unoquoque loco est ecclesiam tradiderunt*[1] : "According to the succession of bishops, to whom they committed the church that was in every place." Meaning that every one of the apostles did appoint bishops in those churches which they had planted; as St Paul did at Ephesus and Creta[2]. And, notwithstanding that in some
Sometime
one apostle
did appoint
bishops.
churches the apostles together did place bishops, yet that in other churches which they planted they did the same severally, it is manifest, not only by these examples of Timothy and Titus, but of sundry other, whereof we may read in ecclesiastical histories, and namely of Polycarpus, made bishop of
Tertull. de
Præscript.[3]
Smyrna by St John. And you yourself testify the same of St John out of Eusebius, even in the next section. Moreover, it cannot be gathered either out of the words of Irenæus, or any other ecclesiastical history, that the apostles did place bishops anywhere but in the chief and principal towns and cities, committing unto them the government of other villages and towns, and the appointing of several pastors for them; as it is also evident in the foresaid examples of Timothy and Titus; and the words of Irenæus import the same. But, if they had in every hamlet placed pastors, yet doth it not follow but that there might be some one in a diocese or province by whom these pastors should be directed, as Timothy at Ephesus, Titus at Crete.

[1 Iren. Op. Par. 1710. Lib. iv. cap. xxxiii. 8. p. 272.]

[2 "For the exposition of Irenæus, which interpreteth (they) ' every one severally,' if they severally ordained bishops every one in his circuit, so it be understanded with the church's consent, as is before declared, I am well content."—Sec. Repl. p. 482.]

[3 Tertull. Op. Lut. 1641. De Præscr. Hæret. 32. p. 243. See before, page 119, note 4.]

The name of archbishop and metropolitan.

Chapter ii. The Fourteenth Division.

T. C. Page 69, Sect. ult.

And here you put me in remembrance of another argument against the archbishop, which I will frame after this sort. If there should be The major false. *any archbishop in any place, the same should be either in respect of the person or minister, and his excellency, or in respect of the magnificence of the place; but the most excellent ministers that ever were, in the most famous places, were no archbishops, but bishops only; therefore there is no cause why there should be any archbishop; for, if there were ever minister of a congregation worthy, that was James. If there were ever any city that ought to have this honour, as that the minister of it should have a more honourable title than the ministers of other cities and towns, that was Jerusalem, where the Son of God preached, and from whence the gospel issued out into[4] all places. And afterward that Jerusalem decayed and the church there, Antioch was a place where the notablest men were that ever have been since; which also deserved great honour, for that there* Acts xi. 26.[5] *the disciples were first called Christians; but neither was that called the first and chiefest church, neither the ministers of it called the arch or principal bishops.*

Jo. Whitgift.

It is a strange matter that you should so grossly err in making arguments, seeing you have taken upon you so great skill in that art. But I will not be occupied in examining the form of it. Your major is not true; for such offices may be appointed rather in the respect of the time, and of the persons that are to be governed, than of the worthiness of "the minister," or the dignity of "the place:" and therefore your major doth not contain a perfect and sufficient distribution. Again, the worthiness of "the person" and the dignity Why these offices are appointed. of "the place" be not at all the causes why such offices should be appointed in the church, but the suppression of sects, the peace of the church, and the good government of the same. The worthiness of the person may make him meet for such an office; and the place may be convenient for such officers to remain in; but neither of them both can be a sufficient cause why such offices should be appointed. I know the worthiest cities have had the pre-eminence in such matters, but it was because they were the most meetest places for that purpose; and the place doth only add one piece of title to the office, but it is not the cause of the office. Lastly, you have not yet

[4 Unto, Repl. 2.]   [5 This reference is inserted from Repl. 2.]

proved that there was no archbishops in those places, or that
James had not that office.

Chapter ii.   The Fifteenth Division.

T. C. Page 70, Lin. 9.

This is con-
trary to that
which was
immediately
affirmed
before.

*And Eusebius, to declare that this order was firm and durable, sheweth
in the third book, 23. chapter, that St John the apostle, which*
overlived the residue of the apostles, ordained bishops in every
city [2]. Eus. iii. 23. [1]

Jo. Whitgift.

This is no reason at all : " St John ordained bishops in
every church ;" therefore there was no one bishop superior
unto them to govern and direct them in matters of discipline,
order, and doctrine, if occasion served.   I think that St John
himself was director and governor of them all, and in effect
their archbishop.   And that doth manifestly appear in that
third book and 23. chapter of Eusebius.   For thus he saith :
" In those days John, the apostle and evangelist, whom the
Lord loved, lived as yet in Asia, which did govern the
churches there, after he was returned out of the isle from
banishment, after the death of Domitian [3]."   And a little after
he saith that " he went, being desired, *ad vicina gentium
loca, ut partim constitueret episcopos, partim totas ecclesias
componeret, partim clerum ex his quos Spiritus Sanctus judi-
casset sorte deligeret [4]:* unto the places of the gentiles adjoining, partly that he might appoint bishops, partly that he
might establish whole churches, partly that he might by lot
choose such into the clergy as the Holy Ghost should assign."
So that, whether he had the name of archbishop, or no, certain it is that he had the government and direction of the rest,
and that he appointed bishops and other ministers.   Eusebius
doth not say that " he ordained bishops in every church ;"
for his words be as I have reported them.   But, if he had so

The office of
an arch-
bishop in St
John.

Euseb. Lib.
iii. cap. 23.

[1] This reference is inserted from Repl. 2 ; which omits any notice in the text
of the place, and reads *sheweth that.*]

[2] Church, Repl. 1 and 2.]

[3] Ἐπὶ τούτοις κατὰ τὴν Ἀσίαν ἔτι τῷ βίῳ περιλειπόμενος, αὐτὸς ἐκεῖνος ὃν
ἠγάπα ὁ Ἰησοῦς, ἀπόστολος ὁμοῦ καὶ εὐαγγελιστὴς Ἰωάννης, τὰς αὐτόθι
διεῖπεν ἐκκλησίας, ἀπὸ τῆς κατὰ τὴν νῆσον μετὰ τὴν Δομετιανοῦ τελευτὴν ἐπανελθὼν φυγῆς.—Euseb. in Hist. Eccles. Script. Amst. 1695-1700. Lib. III.
cap. xxiii. p. 73.]

[4] Id. ibid.]

said, it had not made anything to your purpose, but against you. The name of arch-bishop and metropolitan.
For he appointed them; not all the apostles, nor the people;
and he governed and directed them as their archbishop[5].

Chapter ii.   The Sixteenth Division.

T. C. Page 70, Sect. 1, 2.

These two, Anacletus and Anicetus, you say are "suspected": why do I say not only sus-pected, but that they "are not without just cause suspected."
you say " suspected," when as they have been convinced and condemned, and
stand upon the pillory with the cause of forgery written in great letters,
that he which runneth may read?   Some of the papists themselves have
suspected them; but those which maintain the truth have condemned them
as full of popery, full of blasphemy, and as those in whom was the very
spirit of contradiction to the apostles and their doctrine.

And do you mark what you say when you say that these are but sus-
pected?   Thus much you say, that it is suspected or in doubt whether the
whole body of popery and antichristianity were in the apostles' time, or
soon after, or no.   For Clement was in the apostles' time, and their
scholar; and so you leave it in doubt whether the apostles appointed and
were the authors of popery or no.   I think, if ever you had read the
epistles, you would never have cited their authorities, nor have spoken so
favourably of them as you do.

Jo. Whitgift.

I say that they "are not without just cause suspected;"
which you have left out, and therefore it appeareth that you
have laid aside sincerity.   I have alleged them with as little
credit unto them as either Master Calvin or any other doth.
You yourself have sundry times in this Reply used (as I have
said) as forged authors as these be, with less defacing of them:
Turpe est doctori, &c.   I can shew good proof that I " have
read their epistles;" but I am not disposed either to boast
of my own reading, or to deface other men's.   I leave that
to you.

Chapter ii.   The Seventeenth Division.

Answer to the Admonition, Page 66, Lin. 5, and Sect. 1, 2, 3.

But that notable and famous council of Nice must
be, and is of all wise and learned men, next unto the

[5 " This archbishop, said to be the officer of order, confoundeth all order, and
changeth all ; an evangelist into a bishop, a bishop into an archbishop, an archbishop into an apostle, an apostle into an archbishop ; which follies are before
confuted."—Sec. Repl. p. 482.]

The name of archbishop and metropolitan.

Concil. Nice.

scriptures themselves, reverenced, esteemed, and embraced. That council, celebrated *anno. Domini* 330. (when as the bishops of Rome were as yet learned and godly men), doth not only allow of the name, but also of the office of metropolitan, archbishop, archdeacon, &c.

Metropolitan.

In the sixth canon of that council it is thus written : " This council doth determine him to be no bishop, which is made without the consent *metropolitani episcopi*[1] : "of the metropolitan."

Archdeacon.

In the 13. canon mention is made of a patriarch and of an archdeacon, divers times, and his office there in divers points declared; as it is also in the seventh canon of the same council. In the 25. canon is named both

Patriarch.

patriarch and archbishop, and declared what authority they had in their provinces, and in admitting of bishops. So is it likewise in the 26. and 27. canons of the same council[2].

T. C. Page 70, Sect. 3.

You come after to the council of Nice; wherein I will not stick with you that you say it was holden the 330. *year of the Lord, when it*[3] *may appear by Eusebius his computation that it was holden* anno Domini 320.

Jo. Whitgift.

Variety concerning the time of the Nicene council.

I know that there is some variety among the writers for the time of this council. Musculus, in his Common Places, saith that it was celebrated *anno Dom.* 313:[4] the writers of the Magd. History, *Centu. iv. cap.* 9, affirm (as they say) out of Eusebius, that it was *anno Dom.* 320.[5] Master Fox, Tom.

[1 Concil. Nic. can. 6. in Concil. Stud. Labb. et Cossart. Lut. Par. 1671-2. Tom. II. col. 32. See below, page 144, note 1.]

[2 The canons, to which Whitgift here referred, Cartwright afterwards (see below, pages 150, &c.) declared were not genuine, and were, some matters in them at least, not to be found according to the numbers here given. Whitgift rejoins that in different lists of the canons the numbers vary. For the things substantially which he meant see Concil. Nic. cans. Arab. 5, 6, 7, 33, 39, 71. Tom. II. cols. 293, 4, 301, 3, 14.]

[3 When as it, Repl. 1 and 2.]

[4 Contra hanc impietatem...pugnarunt aliquot concilia, utpote Nicenum, anno salutis 313, &c.—Wolfg. Muscul. Loc. Comm. Theolog. Basil. 1599. De Ministr. Verb. Dei, p. 211.]

[5 Convocata fuit synodus œcumenica...Christi vero anno, juxta Eusebii annotationem, trecentesimo et vigesimo, Constantini imperatoris decimo septimo.— Centur. Eccles. Hist. Basil. 1560, &c. Cent. iv. cap. ix. col. 617.]

1. fol. 12, thinketh that it was *anno Dom.* 340 ;[6] and so doth The name
of arch-
Illyricus himself, in his defence of the Magd. History,[7] though bishop and
he seem to be of a contrary judgment in the history itself. metro-
politan.
Pantaleon, in his Chronography, placeth it *anno Dom.* 330.[8]
Some there be that say it was 324, &c. So that to differ in the
year is no such matter as deserveth any such nip. But, if all
circumstances be well considered, it will fall out that Eusebius
himself confirmeth that which I have set down touching the
time of that council. For Constantine began his reign, according to Eusebius his Chronicle, *anno* 311;[9] and this is noted also
Cent. iv. fol. 62.[10] But the Nicene council, according to the
said Century, fol. 617, was holden *anno* 17. *Constantini.*[11] So
that it must needs be, by their own collection, *anno* 328, or
very near. But, if we admit Eusebius' Chronicle for the beginning of Constantine's reign, *videlicet anno* 311, it will fall
out by Eusebius himself upon the time which I have appointed ;
for, *Lib. iv. de Vita Constantini,* he saith that the Nicene
council was holden *anno vicesimo imperii Const.*[12] So that it
must needs be *anno* 330, or in the beginning 331. at the uttermost ; but under it cannot be.

Chapter ii. The Eighteenth Division.

T. C. Page 70, Sect. 3.

*And here you take so great a leap that it is enough to break the
archbishop's neck, to skip at once 300. years without any testimony of any
either father or story of faith and credit which maketh once mention of
an archbishop.*

Jo. Whitgift.

This "leap" shall not hurt him one whit. For, if there Archbishops
and metro-
were no other testimony but that council, it were of sufficient politans long
before the Ni-
cene council.

[6 Fox, Acts and Monuments, Lond. 1684. Vol. I. p. 11. See below, page 144,
note 3.]

[7 ... usque ad Nicænum concilium, nempe usque ad annum Domini 340, &c.—
Illyr. Flac. De Primat. Papæ Hist. ad calc. Refut. Invect. Bruni contr. Cent.
Eccles. Hist. Basil. 1566, p. 203.]

[8 H. Pantal. Chronogr. Christ. Eccles. Basil. 1561, p. 28; where different
dates are mentioned as assigned by different authors.]

[9 Euseb. Cæsar. Chronic. Hieron. Interp. in Chronic. Basil. 1536. fol. 82.]

[10 Centur. Eccles. Hist. Cent. IV. cap. iii. col. 62.]

[11 Ibid. cap. ix. col. 617. See above, note 5.]

[12 Ἀλλ' ἡ μὲν ἐπινίκιος [σύνοδος] ἦν, ἐν εἰκοσαετηρίδι τῆς βασιλείας, κ.τ.λ.—
Euseb. in Hist. Eccles. Script. Amst. 1695-1700. De Vit. Constant. Lib. IV. cap.
xlvii. p. 454.]

credit and ability both to save his neck and his body from all kind of harm. For—seeing it is thus written in the sixth canon of that council: *Antiqua consuetudo servetur per Ægyptum, Libyam, et Pentapolim, ut Alexandrinus episcopus horum omnium habeat potestatem; quia et urbis Romæ episcopo par illis mos est. &c.*[1]: " Let the ancient custom be kept throughout Egypt, Libya, and Pentapolis, that the bishop of Alexandria have the government of all these; for the bishop of the city of Rome hath the same order. Likewise in Antioch and other provinces let every church retain her privileges. But this is generally plain that, if any be made bishop without the consent of his metropolitan, the great synod hath decreed that he ought to be no bishop;" and in the seventh

canon: *Quia consuetudo obtinuit et antiqua traditio, ut Æliæ episcopus honoretur, habeat honoris consequentiam, salva metropolis dignitate*[2]: " Forasmuch as custom and ancient tradition hath been such that the bishop of Jerusalem be honoured, let him have honour accordingly, not impairing the dignity of the metropolitan city"—it is plain that archbishops and their office were long before the council of Nice; for else why should the canon say, " Let the old custom be observed, &c. ?" And M. Fox, Tom. i. page 12, reporting

these two canons, saith thus: " First in the council of Nice, which was the year of our Lord 340, and in the sixth canon of the said council, we find it is so decreed that, in every province, or precinct, some one church and bishop of the same was appointed and set up to have the inspection and regiment of other churches about him, *secundum morem antiquum,* that is, ' after the ancient custom;' as the words of the council do purport. So that the bishop of Alexandria should have power of Libya and Pentapolis in Egypt; forasmuch as the bishop of the city of Rome hath the like or same manner[3]."

[1 Τὰ ἀρχαῖα ἔθη κρατείτω, τὰ ἐν Αἰγύπτῳ καὶ Λιβύῃ καὶ Πενταπόλει, ὥστε τὸν Ἀλεξανδρείας ἐπίσκοπον πάντων τούτων ἔχειν τὴν ἐξουσίαν. ἐπειδὰν καὶ τῷ ἐν τῇ Ῥώμῃ ἐπισκόπῳ τοῦτο σύνηθές ἐστιν· ὁμοίως δὲ καὶ κατὰ τὴν Ἀντιόχειαν, καὶ ἐν ταῖς ἄλλαις ἐπαρχίαις, τὰ πρεσβεῖα σώζεσθαι ταῖς ἐκκλησίαις. καθόλου δὲ πρόδηλον ἐκεῖνο, ὅτι εἴ τις χωρὶς γνώμης τοῦ μητροπολίτου γένοιτο ἐπίσκοπος, τὸν τοιοῦτον ἡ μεγάλη σύνοδος ὥρισε μὴ δεῖν εἶναι ἐπίσκοπον.—Concil. Nic. can. 6. in Concil. Stud. Labb. et Cossart. Lut. Par. 1671-2. Tom. II. col. 32.]

[2 Ἐπειδὴ συνήθεια κεκράτηκε καὶ παράδοσις ἀρχαία, ὥστε τὸν ἐν Αἰλίᾳ ἐπίσκοπον τιμᾶσθαι, ἐχέτω τὴν ἀκολουθίαν τῆς τιμῆς, τῇ μητροπόλει σωζομένου τοῦ οἰκείου ἀξιώματος.—Ibid. can. 7. ibid.]

[3 Fox, Acts and Monuments, Lond. 1684. Vol. I. p. 11; where *find it so decreed.*]

Now, if I might as safely allege the canons of the apostles as The name
you do, then could I tell you that in the 33. canon (which of arch-
bishop and
canon is alleged as good authority against the supremacy of metro-
politan.
the bishop of Rome) you shall find archbishops. For that
canon, setting an order among bishops, willeth the bishops of
every nation "to know their first or chief bishop, and him to
be taken for the head of them." The words of the canon be
these : *Cujusque gentis episcopos oportet scire, quisnam inter* Can. Apost.
33. alias 35.
ipsos primus sit, habereque ipsum quodammodo pro capite,
neque sine illius voluntate quicquam agere insolitum[4]: "The
bishops of every country must know who is chief among them,
and must take him as it were for their head; neither must
they do any unaccustomed thing without his will; and every
one must do those things alone by himself which belong to
his parish and to the places that be under him; but neither
must he do anything without the will of all them; for so shall
concord be kept, and God shall be glorified through our Lord
in the Holy Ghost." Now, I pray you, tell me what difference
there is betwixt "the first or chief bishop or head of the
rest," and "archbishop." And, lest you should think this
canon to be of small force (as suspected), you shall hear it
almost *verbatim* repeated and confirmed by the council of
Antioch : "In every country it is convenient that the bishops Concil. An-
tioch. can. 9.
should know that their metropolitan bishop beareth the care
of the whole province. Wherefore let all those that have any
business repair to the metropolitan city. And for this cause
it is thought good that he both should excel in honour, and
that the other bishops do no unaccustomed thing without him,
according to the ancient rule appointed of our fathers, saving
those things only which belong to their own diocese and to
the places that are under them. For every bishop hath
power over his own parish to rule them according to reverence meet for every one, and to provide for all the country
that are under his city, so that he ordain both priests and
deacons, and contain all things with his judgment. But further let him attempt nothing without the metropolitan; neither

[4 Τοὺς ἐπισκόπους ἑκάστου ἔθνους εἰδέναι χρὴ τὸν ἐν αὐτοῖς πρῶτον, καὶ
ἡγεῖσθαι αὐτὸν ὡς κεφαλὴν, καὶ μηδέν τι πράττειν περιττὸν ἄνευ τῆς ἐκείνου
γνώμης. ἐκεῖνα δὲ μόνα πράττειν ἕκαστον, ὅσα τῇ αὐτοῦ παροικίᾳ ἐπιβάλλει, καὶ
ταῖς ὑπ' αὐτὴν χώραις. ἀλλὰ μηδὲ ἐκεῖνος ἄνευ τῆς πάντων γνώμης ποιείτω τί.
οὕτως γὰρ ὁμόνοια ἔσται, καὶ δοξασθήσεται ὁ Θεὸς διὰ Κυρίου ἐν ἁγίῳ Πνεύματι.
—Canon. Apost. 33. in Concil. Stud. Labb. et Cossart. Tom. I. col. 32.]

let the metropolitan do anything without the advice of the other[1]." You have now the canon of the apostles confirming archbishops, and the council of Nice and Antioch alleging "old custom" for them, and confirming them also. And a
little before I declared unto you out of M. Fox, that there were archbishops here in England *anno* 180[2]; so that their fall cannot be very great[3].

Chapter ii.   The Nineteenth Division.
T. C. Page 70, Sect. 3.

What! no mention of him in Theophilus, bishop of Antioch, none in Ignatius, none in Clemens Alexandrinus, none in Justin Martyr, in Irenæus, in Tertullian, in Origen, in Cyprian, none in all those old historiographers out of the which Eusebius gathereth his story? Was it for his baseness and smallness that he could not be seen among[4] the bishops, elders, and deacons, being the chief and principal of them all? Can the cedar of Lebanon be hid among[4] the box-trees? Aristotle, in his Rhetoric ad Theodecten, saith that it is a token of contempt to forget the name of another[5]. Belike therefore, if there were any archbishop, he had no chair in the church, but was as it seemeth digging at the metals; for otherwise they, that have filled their book[6] with the often mentioning of bishops, would have no doubt remembered him.

Jo. Whitgift.

And what then? is not the council of Nice and of Antioch of as good credit as all these? Shall not Athanasius,

[1 Τοὺς καθ᾽ ἑκάστην ἐπαρχίαν ἐπισκόπους εἰδέναι χρὴ τὸν ἐν τῇ μητροπόλει προεστῶτα ἐπίσκοπον, καὶ τὴν φροντίδα ἀναδέχεσθαι πάσης τῆς ἐπαρχίας, διὰ τὸ ἐν τῇ μητροπόλει πανταχόθεν συντρέχειν πάντας τοὺς πράγματα ἔχοντας. ὅθεν ἔδοξε καὶ τῇ τιμῇ προηγεῖσθαι αὐτόν, μηδέν τε πράττειν περιττὸν τοὺς λοιποὺς ἐπισκόπους ἄνευ αὐτοῦ, κατὰ τὸν ἀρχαῖον κρατήσαντα τῶν πατέρων ἡμῶν κανόνα, ἢ ταῦτα μόνα, ὅσα τῇ ἑκάστου ἐπιβάλλει παροικίᾳ, καὶ ταῖς ὑπ᾽ αὐτὴν χώραις. ἕκαστον γὰρ ἐπίσκοπον ἐξουσίαν ἔχειν τῆς ἑαυτοῦ παροικίας, διοικεῖν τε κατὰ τὴν ἑκάστῳ ἐπιβάλλουσαν εὐλάβειαν, καὶ πρόνοιαν ποιεῖσθαι πάσης τῆς χώρας τῆς ὑπὸ τὴν ἑαυτοῦ πόλιν, ὡς καὶ χειροτονεῖν πρεσβυτέρους καὶ διακόνους, καὶ μετὰ κρίσεως ἕκαστα διαλαμβάνειν· περαιτέρω δὲ μηδὲν πράττειν ἐπιχειρεῖν δίχα τοῦ τῆς μητροπόλεως ἐπισκόπου, μηδὲ αὐτὸν ἄνευ τῆς τῶν λοιπῶν γνώμης.—Concil. Antioch. can. 9. in eod. Tom. II. col. 565.]

[2 See before, page 128.]

[3 Cartwright replies that the ancient custom spoken of in the council of Nice did not necessarily imply any great space of time; and takes exception against the authority of that council, urging that some of the rules prescribed in it were "against the rule of St Paul."—Sec. Repl. pp. 483, &c.]

[4 Amongst, Repl. 1 and 2.]

[5 Ποιητικὸν δ᾽ ὀργῆς καὶ ἡ λήθη, οἷον καὶ ἡ τῶν ὀνομάτων οὖσα παρὰ μικρόν· ὀλιγωρίας γὰρ δοκεῖ καὶ ἡ λήθη σημεῖον εἶναι.—Aristot. Op. Lut. Par. 1629. Rhetor. Lib. II. cap. ii. Tom. II. p. 550.]

[6 Books, Repl. 2.]

Epiphanius, Ambrose, Hierome, Chrysostom, Sozomen, &c., The name of arch-bishop and metro-politan. countervail them? and yet, if you had read these authors, you might have learned that in the most of them the office of an archbishop is expressed; as my Answer following declareth. But still you use negative reasons *ab auctoritate*, and that human. Your taunts and frumps I let pass: they are confutation sufficient to themselves[7].

Chapter ii.   The Twentieth Division.

T. C. Page 70, Sect. 3, 4.

But let us hear what the council of Nice hath for these titles.

In the sixth canon mention is made of a metropolitan bishop[8]. *What is that to the metropolitan which now is*[9], *either to the name or to the office? Of the office it shall appear afterwards. In the name I think there is a great difference between a metropolitan bishop, and metropolitan of England, or of all England. A metropolitan bishop was nothing else but a bishop of that place which it pleased the emperor or magistrate to make the chief city of the diocese or shire; and, as for this name, it maketh no* An untruth, contrary to the manifest words of the council of Nice. *more difference between bishop and bishop than when I say a minister of London, and a minister of Newington. There is no man that is well advised, which will gather of this saying that there is as great difference in preeminence between those two ministers as is between London and Newington. For his office and preeminence we shall see hereafter.*

Jo. Whitgift.

For the full answering of this it shall be sufficient to set The judgment of learned writers of the 6.canon Conc. Niceni. down the judgment of certain of the learned writers of our time, touching the true meaning of that canon of the council of Nice; as the practice of the church before that time, at that time, and since that time, hath expounded it.

M. Calvin, in his Institutions, Chap. viii. sect. 54, saith Calvin. thus: "That every province had among their bishops an archbishop, and that the council of Nice did appoint patriarchs which should be in order and dignity above archbishops, it was for the preservation of discipline[10]." M. Calvin saith, the council of Nice did appoint patriarchs which should be in order and

---

[7 " ... a few such frumps will break the archbishop's back, if they be not better looked unto."—Sec. Repl. p. 487.]

[8 See before, page 144, note 1.]   [9 Which is now, Repl. 1 and 2.]

[10 Quod autem singulæ provinciæ unum habebant inter episcopos archiepiscopum : quod item in Nicena synodo constituti sunt patriarchæ, qui essent ordine et dignitate archiepiscopis superiores : id ad disciplinæ conservationem pertinebat. —Calvin. Op. Amst. 1667-71. Inst. Lib. IV. cap. iv. 4. Tom. IX. p. 286.]

The name
of arch-
bishop and
metro-
politan.
Illyricus.

dignity above archbishops. He saith also that every province had among their bishops an archbishop.

Illyricus in his Catalogue *testium veritatis*, speaking of this council, saith thus: *Constituit quoque hæc . . . . synodus, ut singularum provinciarum metropolitani potestatem habeant in suos episcopos, sacerdotes, et ecclesias, Alexandrinus in Ægypto, Antiochenus in Syria. &c.*[1]: "This synod also appointed that the metropolitans of every province should have authority over their bishops, priests, and churches; the bishop of Alexandria in Egypt, and the bishop of Antioch in Syria. &c." And in his book, that he intituleth "A Refutation of the Invective of Brunus against the Centuries," he doth interpret this canon on this manner: "Here we see plainly that the Nicene council first in this canon doth give a primacy to the metropolitan in every province, and doth make subject unto him all the bishops and priests of his province. Moreover, that it maketh all the metropolitan bishops, as of Alexandria, Rome, and Antioch, and of other provinces, altogether of equal authority amongst themselves. And last, that the subjects (if that I may so say) of another may not appeal to any other metropolitan. And after this manner the sixth council of Carthage doth understand, allege, and urge the foresaid canon in the former epistle[2]."

M. Fox, who hath very diligently and faithfully laboured in this matter, and searched out the truth of it as learnedly as I know any man to have done, in his first Tom. page 11, writeth thus: "Then followed the council of Nice, wherein it was decreed that, throughout the university of Christ's church, which was now far spread over the world, certain provinces and precincts to the number of four were appointed, every one to have his head church and chief bishop, called then[3] metropolitans or patriarchs, to have the oversight of

---

[1] M. Flac. Illyr. Catalog. Test. Basil. 1556. p. 47.]

[2] Hic clare videmus, Nicænam synodum primum in hoc canone primatum in singulis provinciis suo metropolitano dare, omnesque episcopos ac sacerdotes ei suæ provinciæ subjicere. Deinde, omnes metropolitanos episcopos, Alexandrinum, Romanum, Antiochenum, et aliarum provinciarum, inter sese plane exæquare, ita ut nullus alteri imperare in ulla plane re possit, aut debeat. Demum, ne ullius (ut ita dicam) subditi, ad alium metropolitanum appellare possint. Atque hoc modo etiam sexta Carthaginensis synodus prædictum canonem in præcedenti epistola intelligit, citat, et urget.—Illyr. Flac. De Primat. Papæ Hist. ad calc. Refut. Invect. Bruni contr. Cent. Eccles. Hist. Basil. 1566. p. 230.]

[3] Them, Def. A.]

such churches as did lie about him[4];" and, page 12, he speaketh to the same effect, as it may appear in his words which I have before recited[5]. And in the same page he saith: "Wherefore, as we must needs grant the bishop of Rome to be called a metropolitan or an archbishop by the council of Nice; so we will not greatly stick in this also, to have him numbered with patriarchs or primates; &c.[6]"

The name of archbishop and metropolitan.

But the very words of the canon itself doth condemn you of a great oversight. For this is the canon: *Antiqua consuetudo servetur per Ægyptum, Libyam, et Pentapolim, ita ut Alexandrinus episcopus horum omnium habeat potestatem; &c.[7]:* "Let the ancient custom be kept throughout Egypt, Libya, and Pentapolis, that the bishop of Alexandria have the government of all these; &c.;" as is said before.

T. C. condemned of untruth by the words of the canon. Can. 6.

How say you now? is not this "for the name and for the office" also of our metropolitans and archbishops? had not they jurisdiction of whole provinces, as ours have? were not all other bishops and ministers of the church subject to them, as they be to ours? were not they metropolitans of provinces and countries, as ours be? And is this no more to differ, "than a minister of London and a minister of Newington?" Truly I marvel that you can be carried unto so manifest untruths, and palpable errors. But, for the further declaration of the authority of a metropolitan bishop, though this which I have said be sufficient, it may please you to take pains to peruse in the council of Antioch the 9 canon: *Per singulas provincias episcopos convenit nosse metropolitanum episcopum solicitudinem totius provinciæ gerere[8]:* "In every province it is convenient that bishops should know, that the metropolitan bishop hath the caring for of the whole province. &c.;" as is mentioned before, in the first canon of the council of Ephesus. It is also evident that the "metropolitan of the province[9]" (for so is he there called) had authority over

The authority of the metropolitan.

Conc. Antioch.

---

[4] Fox, Acts and Monuments, Lond. 1684. Vol. I. pp. 9, 10; where *wherein was decreed, the whole university, over all the world, provinces or precincts,* and called them *metropolitan or patriarch.*]

[5] Id. ibid. p. 11. See before, page 144.]

[6] Id. ibid. See before, page 137.]

[7] Concil. Nic. can. 6. in Concil. Stud. Labb. et Cossart. Lut. Par. 1671-2. Tom. II. col. 32. See before, page 144, note 1.]

[8] Concil. Antioch. can. 9. in eod. ibid. col. 565. See before, page 146, note 1.]

[9] ...ὁ μητροπολίτης τῆς ἐπαρχίας.—Concil. Ephes. Act. VII. can. 1. in eod. Tom. III. col. 803.]

The name of archbishop and metropolitan.

M. Fox.

all the bishops in the same province. But, to make short, because I shall have other occasion to speak of this matter, M. Fox, in the treatise before recited, concludeth thus: "Whereby it is to be concluded, that to be false that Clement and Anacletus and Anicetus be reported (but falsely) to put a difference between primates or patriarchs, metropolitans or archbishops; whereas by sufficient authority it is to be proved that in the old church both primates, first bishops, bishops of the first seat, patriarchs, metropolitans, bishops of the mother-city, and archbishops, were all one. First, that primates and metropolitans were both one is before declared in the canons of the apostles, and by the council of Antioch aforesaid[1]."

Vilierius.

The same doth Vilierius affirm in his book *De Statu Primitivæ Ecclesiæ*, fol. 26, and proveth it out of Socrates, very manifestly; that is, that metropolitans and patriarchs were all one at the first[2]. I am not ignorant but there is some controversy among both the civilians and canonists, whether a metropolitan or an archbishop be all one or no, but in the end this is the opinion of the most, so far as I can read or learn, that they be *idem re*, "the same in deed," but differ *nomine*, "in name." For he is called an archbishop in respect of the other bishops of whom he is the chief. But he is called metropolitan in respect of the cities that be within his province. But of archbishops and metropolitans more must be spoken hereafter[3].

Chapter ii.   The Twenty-first Division.

T. C. Page 70, Sect. ult.

There are alleged, to prove the names of archbishops, patriarchs, archdeacons, the 13. 25. 26. and 27. canons of the council of Nice. For the 25. 26. and[4] 27. there are no such canons of that council; and, although there be a thirteenth canon, there is no word of patriarch or

These canons differ only in number, and not in matter, from those that are not counterfeit.

archdeacon there contained. And I marvel with what shame you can thrust upon us these counterfeit canons, which come out of the pope's mint;

[1 Fox, Acts and Monuments, Lond. 1684. Vol. I. p. 12; where *it is concluded, patriarchs and metropolitans*, and *declared by the canons.*]

[2 Aperte igitur Socrates omnes metropolitas, patriarchas appellat: et in his Alexandrinum, cujus patriarchiam reliquis comparat: ex quo intelligitur eam non multis partibus reliquis majorem fuisse.—Fr. Vilier. De Stat. Prim. Eccles. Hierap. 1553. p. 26. Conf. Socr. in Hist. Eccles. Script. Amst. 1695-1700. Lib. v. cap. viii. pp. 217, 18.]

[3 "The Answ. can never be holden in the rails of any lawful form of disputation. All men see that whatsoever he heapeth up toucheth not my reply. &c."
—Sec. Repl. pp. 487, 8.]

[4 Repl. 1 and 2 omit *and.*]

yea, and which are not to be found.   Theodoret saith that there are but The name
Lib. i. cap. 8. twenty canons of the council of Nice[5]; and those twenty are in of arch-
bishop and
the tome of the councils; and in those there is no mention of any metro-
Lib. i. cap. 6. patriarch, archbishop, archdeacon[6].   Ruffine also remembereth politan.
22. canons[7], very little differing from those other twenty but in length; and
in none of those are found any of these names of archbishop, archdeacon,
or[8] patriarch; and it is as lawful for M. Harding to allege the 44. Not so; for
canon of the council of Nice to prove the supremacy of the pope of Rome[9], that is re-
pugnant to
as it is for M. Doctor Whitgift to allege the 25. 26. 27. to prove the the true
canons, and
name of archbishop, archdeacon, patriarch; for they are all of one stamp, therefore
counterfeit.
and have like authority.

Jo. Whitgift.

I will not greatly stick in the defence of those canons : the Controversy
sixth and the seventh canon do sufficiently verify all that I about the
number of
have alleged out of the other; as is declared not only by the the canons
Concil.
words of the canons, but by the judgment of those whose Niceni.
learning and religion was never as yet stained.   I know that
there is no small controversy about the number of the canons
of that synod.   In the book of the councils there are only
twenty, in Ruffine 22.   Athanasius, in an epistle that he
(as some think) with the other bishops of Egypt, writ to
Marcus bishop of Rome (if any credit is to be given unto
that epistle), writeth that there were first 80. and afterwards the same brought into 70. canons[10].   Isidorus, in his Canons
preface to the council, saith that in the decrees of pope Julius ascribed to
the Nicene
there is mention made of 70. canons[11]; so that for the num- council not
found in the
ber of the canons there is great difference in the writers. number
extant.

[5 Αὖθις δὲ συνελθόντες εἰς τὸ συνέδριον, περὶ τῆς ἐκκλησιαστικῆς πολιτείας
νόμους ἔγραψαν εἴκοσι.—Theod. in Hist. Eccles. Script. Lib. i. cap. viii. p. 29.]

[6 Patriarch, archdeacon, archbishop, Repl. 1 and 2.]

[7 Hist. Eccles. Par. Lib. x. cap. vi. foll. 107, 8. There are only 20 canons
here recited. But see in Autor. Hist. Eccles. Basil. 1535. pp. 221-3 ; where
the number is 22.]

[8 *Or* is not in Repl. 1 or 2.]

[9 See Bp. Jewel's Works, Park. Soc. Edit. Vol. I. pp. 351, &c.]

[10 Sane præsentibus nobis, octoginta capitula in memorata tractata sunt synodo
semel,...Sed visum est trecentis decem et octo patribus,...ut decem capitula adu-
narentur aliis,...et ad formam septuaginta discipulorum...fierent capitula, &c.—
Athanas. Op. Par. 1698. Ad Marc. Pap. Epist. Tom. II. p. 665. This epistle is
spurious.]

[11 Scire autem vos...oportet, quod plura quam illa viginti capitula, quæ apud
nos habentur, Nicænæ synodi reperimus, et in decretis Julii papæ septuaginta
capitula ejusdem synodi esse debere legimus.—Isid. Mercat. Præfat. Concil. in
Concil. Stud. Labb. et Cossart. Lut. Par. 1671-2. Tom. I. cols. 6, 7. Conf. Jul.
Papæ I. Ad Episc. Orient. Epist. ii. ibid. Tom. II. cols. 484, &c. The epistle
of Julius is not genuine.]

The name
of arch-
bishop and
metro-
politan.
Conc. Arelat.
Hieronymus.

Ambrose.

The 25. 26. 27.
canons differ
only in
number, not
in substance,
from the true
canons.

Concilium Arelatense the second, canon the 24, doth recite a canon of the council of Nice, touching infamous libels[1];
which is not to be found among the 20.

Hierome, in his preface upon the book of Judith, saith
that the council of Nice did reckon that book in the number
of the holy scriptures[2]; and yet there is no such thing to be
found among those 20. canons.

Ambrose, *Lib. x.*, the epistle 82, attributeth another canon
to the council of Nice concerning second marriages in clerks[3].
I could recite more canons alleged by good writers out of that
council, which are not to be found in those 20. or 22; but it
shall not need.

Wherefore, though I have alleged more canons than are
to be found in the volume of councils, yet I have done
nothing which is strange, neither have I alleged any canon
that is not agreeable to the sixth and seventh, whereof there
is no doubt, and according to the true meaning of those two
canons as they be interpreted by the best-learned. And, in
very deed, the 25. 26. 27. canons by me alleged are the very
same with the 6. and 7, differing only in number; wherein I
followed the author that so placed them. And in the 13.
canon the name of archbishop is added; whereof more shall be
spoken hereafter (God willing).

M. Harding's 44. canon is plain repugnant to the sixth
canon, and therefore without all doubt a counterfeit. But
the canons that I have alleged agree both with the sixth and
seventh, and therefore not unlike to be truly attributed to
that council, in these points wherein I have alleged them[4].

[1] Eos qui falso fratribus suis capitalia objecisse convicti fuerint, placuit usque
ad exitum non communicare, sicut magna synodus ante constituit, nisi digna
satisfactione pœnituerint.—Concil. Arelat. ii. can. 24. ibid. Tom. IV. cols. 1013,4.
Conf. Concil. Arelat. i. can. 14. ibid. Tom. I. col. 1428; and Concil. Arelat. ii.
can. 24. in Crabb. Concil. Col. Agrip. 1551. Tom. I. p. 294, and not. in loc.]

[2] Sed quia hunc librum synodus Nicæna in numero sanctarum scripturarum
legitur computasse, acquievi postulationi vestræ, &c.—Hieron. Op. Par. 1693-
1706. Præf. in Lib. Judith, Tom. I. Pars ii. cols. 1169, 70. Conf. not. in loc.]

[3] Sed prius cognoscamus non solum hoc apostolum de episcopo et presbytero
statuisse, sed etiam patres in concilio Nicæni tractatus addidisse, neque clericum
quemquam debere esse, qui secunda conjugia sortitus sit.—Ambros. Op. Par.
1686-90. Ad Vercell. Eccles. Epist. lxiii. 64. Tom. II. col. 1037. Conf. not. in
loc.]

[4] Cartwright accuses Whitgift, in reply, of taking the same course with
"Pighius, Hosius, Harding, and their likes."—Sec. Repl. pp. 483, &c.]

Chapter ii.   The Twenty-second Division.

T. C. Page 71, Sect. 1.

I fear greatly some crafty dissembling papist had his hand in this book, who, having a great deal of rotten stuff which he could not utter under his own name, being already lost, brought it unto the author hereof, which hath upon his credit, without further examination, set it to sale. Peradventure you will think scorn to be censured and reprehended of a poor minister of the country; and therefore I will turn you over for your lesson in this behalf unto the bishop of Salisbury in his Reply against M. Harding, touching the article of the supremacy.

Jo. Whitgift.

" Fear" not ; I warrant you I have alleged nothing which I am not able by sufficient testimony to prove that I have read myself.   And therefore your surmise is but grounded upon your own practice.

Whatsoever the bishop of Salisbury saith, " in his Reply against Harding," touching the canon alleged by him is most true; and I do most willingly acknowledge it so to be[5], neither do I take any canon of that council as undoubtedly true, but these 20, specified in the first Tome of Councils ; the other I have only mentioned as probable, because they agree with them ; and yet all the canons that I have alleged be extant in print, and the book is commonly to be sold, and therefore I have not received them of any other.

Chapter ii.   The Twenty-third Division.

Answer to the Admonition, Page 66, Sect. 3.

Ambrose also, that old and learned father, both alloweth the name and office of an archbishop, *Lib. de Dignitate Sacerdotum, cap.* 5.[7]

[5 " The truth is, that you have done the best you can, to overthrow the whole defence of the bishop in that behalf."—Ibid. p. 490.]

[6 This note is not in Answ.]

[7 Quos si percunctari fideliter velis, quis eos præfecerit sacerdotes, respondent mox et dicunt : Ab archiepiscopo sum nuper episcopus ordinatus, centumque ei solidos dedi, ut episcopalem gratiam consequi meruissem, quos si minime dedissem, hodie episcopus non essem....Nempe hoc est, quod doleo, quia archiepiscopus carnaliter episcopum fecit.   Nam propter pecunias spiritaliter leprosum ordinavit.—Ambros. Op. De Dign. Sacerdot. cap. v. Tom. II. Append. cols. 362, 3.   This treatise is not by Ambrose.   It is attributed with considerable probability to pope Sylvester II.]

T. C. Page 71, Sect. 2.

The name
of arch-
bishop
and metro-
politan.

Ambrose is
little behold-
ing to you,
that cannot
be accepted
for a witness.

In those
words Am-
brose doth
not disallow
the office,
but the abuse
of it by the
person.

If all should be allowed of that St Ambrose allowed[1] of, then, besides other things which he holdeth corruptly, the marriage of the ministers[2] should go very hard; but it is worthy to be observed with i Lib. Offic. cap. 50. *what words Ambrose doth allow of the archbishop, that all men may understand how low it goeth with M. Doctor for his defence of the archbishop; and how the archbishop is so out of credit that there cannot be gotten any to be surety for his honesty. Ambrose, complaining of the ministers or bishops in those days, saith, "If a man ask them who preferred them to be priests, answer is made, by and by, that the archbishop for an hundred shillings ordained me bishop, to whom I gave an[3] hundred shillings that I might get the favour to be bishop, which if I had not given I had not been bishop;" and afterward he saith that this "grieved him, that the archbishop ordained bishops carnally or for some carnal respect." And this is all the allowance that Ambrose sheweth of an archbishop. Your archbishop taketh all things in good part; so that his very dispraise he expoundeth to his commendation.*

Jo. Whitgift.

I know no man whose writings and works are so perfect (the writers of the canonical scriptures excepted), that all things in their books are to be allowed. But God forbid that we should therefore reject that which they have well and truly spoken. You will do little for Ambrose, if you will not allow him for an historical witness of that which was in his time. This is therefore a shifting answer, but nothing commendable. It evidently appeareth by that place that in his time there were "archbishops;" for what though he reprove the abuse of some archbishops in ordaining bishops and ministers for money, doth he therefore disallow either the name or the office? Nay, this is rather to be concluded, that there were archbishops in Ambrose's time, which had authority to ordain bishops, because Ambrose doth reprove such archbishops "as for carnal respects ordained bishops[4]."

Your undutiful and arrogant frumps and scoffs I pass

[1 Alloweth, Repl. 1, 2, and Def. A.]

[2 Inoffensum autem exhibendum et immaculatum ministerium, nec ullo conjugali coitu violandum cognoscitis, &c.—Id. De Offic. Ministr. Lib. i. cap. 1. 258. Tom. II. col. 66.]

[3 A, Repl. 1 and 2.]

[4 Cartwright replies, that he did not refuse Ambrose "for an historical witness," he only questioned the genuineness of the treatise cited, assuring himself "that it is a false Ambrose, and therefore that testimony to be of no force."—Sec. Repl. p. 491.]

over.   It seemeth, by your so oft using them, that you are
afraid lest you should be taken for a modest Christian.

The name
of arch-
bishop and
metro-
politan.

Chapter ii.   The Twenty-fourth Division.

T. C. Page 71, Sect. 3.

And there is great likelihood that the archbishop, which Ambrose
maketh mention of, was no other than he which for the time ruled the
action wherein bishops were ordained, and after the action ended had no
more authority than the rest.

An unlikely
likelihood,
void of truth.

Jo. Whitgift.

If you had read any ancient story or father, yea, if you
had but perused M. Calvin's Institutions, the viii. chap.[5], or any
writer intreating of this matter, you would never have uttered
this vain conjecture, nor shewed so manifest a token of great
ignorance and no reading.   For it shall appear, by sufficient
testimony, that neither the name nor office of an archbishop
was anything at all strange in this time.   And the authors of
the Centuries, *Cent. iv.*, can tell you that Ambrose himself
was *metropolitanus...plurium conjunctarum ecclesiarum ad-*
ministratione fungens[6]: "a metropolitan governing many
churches adjoining together[7]."

Ambrose, a
metro-
politan.
Cent. iv.
cap. 10.

Your conjecture, that "this archbishop" should be "no
other than he which for the time ruled the action wherein
bishops were ordained, and after the action ended had no
more authority than the rest," is a mere fancy of your own,
contrary to all authority, and without any ground or similitude of reason; and yet you often repeat it, and make it the
foundation of this your building.   But let us hear your conjectures.

Chapter ii.   The Twenty-fifth Division.

T. C. Page 71, Sect. 4.

And I am moved so to think, first, because it is not like that one only
ordained bishops, being contrary to the old canons of the best councils;

[[5] Calvin. Op. Amst. 1667-71. Inst. Lib. iv. cap. iv. 4. Tom. IX. p. 286. See
before, page 147, note 10.]

[[6] Centur. Eccles. Hist. Basil. 1560, &c. Cent. iv. cap. x. col. 1150.]

[[7] Cartwright opposes to the opinion from the Centuries that of Coster (editor
of Ambrose's works), who says that he " was a bishop not of a whole province, or of
many cities, but of one only city."—Sec. Repl. p. 492. Conf. Ambros. Op. Basil.
1555. Ambros. Vit. per Joan. Coster. Tom. I. fol. C. 1. 2.]

*but that there were other, and that this whom Ambrose calleth archbishop
did gather the voices, &c.*

Jo. Whitgift.

I have shewed before that it was not so strange at this
time for the bishop alone to ordain ministers. And yet
Ambrose in this place signifieth that the people had somewhat

to do in this matter; for he calleth them *populum nugacem
et indoctum, qui talem sibi asciverunt sacerdotem*[1]: " a people that trifleth and is unlearned, that hath gotten unto them
such a priest." But, I pray you, where is now your distinction betwixt "election" and "ordination"? For Ambrose speaketh in this place of ordaining, and not of electing. If you
will needs so distinguish them that they may not be at any
time nor in any place confounded, then have you answered
yourself here, and with one conjecture overthrown another[2].
But, howsoever it is, conjectures cannot prevail against so
manifest a truth, being so silly conjectures. For tell me
where you ever read that he was called an "archbishop that
did" only "gather the voices," or that this name was attributed to any during the "action only," and no longer. This
is very new divinity, unheard of in any good author that I
have read, or can hear of.

Chapter ii.   The Twenty-sixth Division.

T. C. Page 71, Sect. 5.

*Secondly, because it was very unlike that there was any absolutely
above St Ambrose in those parts where he complaineth of evil bishops or
ministers made.*

Jo. Whitgift.

Why, to whom or for whom did Ambrose write this
book? for his own province or diocese only? Therein are you
deceived that you think Ambrose to have written this book
for his own province only, when he writ it to profit the whole
church; as it may appear in the first chapter of that book[3].

[1 Ambros. Op. Par. 1686-90. De Dign. Sacerdot. cap. v. Tom. II. Append.
col. 363; where *nugacem populum*. See before, page 153, note 7.]

[2 "... having nothing to answer, he speaketh in the clouds: where he is so far
from being understood of others, that I think he understood not himself."—Sec.
Repl. p. 493.]

[3 ... non jam ad subditum loquor vulgus, quod jugiter monere consuevi, sed

Neither doth he complain of such evil bishops or ministers as were under him (for then should he have complained of himself, being their metropolitan), but of such he complaineth as were in other places and provinces; as may be seen by these words of his: *Ita ut videas in ecclesia passim, quos non merita sed pecuniæ ad episcopatus ordinem provexerunt*[4]: "So that a man may see everywhere in the church such as are promoted to the order of a bishop, not by deserts but by money;" and therefore this conjecture is soon answered.

The name of archbishop and metropolitan.
De Dig. Sacer. cap. 5.

Chapter ii. The Twenty-seventh Division.
T. C. Page 71, Sect. 6.

Thirdly, for that Ambrose in another place (which you after cite) dividing all the church into the clergy and laity, doth subdivide the clergy into bishops, elders, and deacons[5]; and therefore it is not like that there was any which had any continual function of archbishop; but, as he was called χορήγος, or "leader of the dance," which cometh first, and after coming in again in the second or third place is no more so called, so that bishop was called archbishop, which for the time present did gather the voices of the rest of the bishops, which he, by and by, laid down with the dissolving of the meeting. And that this is not my conjecture only, that there was no ordinary or absolute archbishop, let the Centuries be seen which allege that place of Ambrose to prove that the office of an archbishop was not then come into the church, which was four hundred years after Christ, and more also.

Where, or which Century?
Untruth.

Jo. Whitgift.

This is a "dancing" device indeed, without any shadow of truth; as it may appear by that which already is alleged, and shall do more and more by that which followeth. You are marvellous circumspect in your quotations, lest you should be tripped, and therefore you say, "let the Centuries be seen," but you tell not where. Surely you do very untruly report the Centuries; for I have read them where they do allege that place of Ambrose; and there is not to be found any

ad ipsos jam prædicatores vulgi mea verba converto: et meis conservis velut obediens servus, id est, episcopus sacerdotibus, antistes pontificibus, audacter prædicare salutis commonitoria non retardabo.—Ambros. Op. De Dign. Sacerdot. cap. i. Tom. II. Append. col. 358.]

[4 Id. ibid. cap. v. col. 362.]

[5 Aliud est enim quod ab episcopo requirit Deus, et aliud quod a presbytero, et aliud quod a diacono, et aliud quod a clerico, et aliud quod a laico, vel a singulis quibusque hominibus.—Id. ibid. cap. iii. col. 360.]

The name of arch-bishop and metro-politan. Cent. iv. cap. 7.

such matter, but the clean contrary; as is to be seen in that place by you alleged of the fourth Cent. The words be these: *Episcopi et metropolitani dicebantur a præcipuis seu primariis civitatibus, sicut Basilium metropolitanum Cappadocum Zozomenus vocat, Lib. iii. cap.* 16; *et archiepiscopi, qualem Seleuciæ fuisse Simeonem idem retulit, Lib. ii. cap.* 8. *Patriarcha totius alicujus provinciæ dicebatur episcopus, ut Socrates indicat, Lib. v. cap.* 8[1]: "Bishops and metropolitans were named of the chief and principal cities; as Zozomenus calleth Basil the metropolitan of Cappadocia, *Lib. iii. cap.* 16; and archbishops, such as he reporteth that Simeon was of Seleucia, *Lib. ii. cap.* 8. Patriarch of some whole province was called a bishop; as Socrates sheweth, *Lib. v. cap.* 8." Wherefore it is too much boldness in you to avouch so manifest untruths. Neither is it any marvel though[2]

Forgery seeketh corners.

you quote not the places; for forgery seeketh corners[3].

And, although that which hath been hitherto alleged out of the councils of Nice and Antioch, with the judgment of so many learned men interpreting the same, might serve to persuade any reasonable man that the office and name of archbishop and metropolitan is both of great antiquity and not for one action only, or a "dancing" office (as you would have it), but fixed and permanent; yet, because I have to do with quarrellers, before I go any further in confuting, I will set down the judgment of other ancient and famous writers also, who allow both of these names and offices; and first I will recite such as have the names expressed with the offices, then such as speak of the very thing itself without the names. I will begin with councils.

Councils, of the name and office of metropolitan and arch-bishop, &c. Conc. Nicen. can. 4. 6. 7.

The council of Nice, as you have heard, hath the name of metropolitan, and doth limit unto him certain provinces, to govern and take the care of[4]. It hath been declared that

---

[1 Centur. Eccles. Hist. Basil. 1560, &c. Cent. IV. cap. vii. col. 489. Conf. Soz. in Hist. Eccles. Script. Amst. 1695-1700. Lib. III. cap. xvi., Lib. II. cap. ix.; Socr. Lib. v. cap. viii. pp. 427, 8, 371, 217, 8.]

[2 Through, Def. B.]

[3 "My quotation of the Centuries was easy to find...it is in the beginning of the chapter which you alleged."—Sec. Repl. p. 493.]

[4 Ἐπίσκοπον προσήκει μάλιστα μὲν ὑπὸ πάντων τῶν ἐν τῇ ἐπαρχίᾳ καθίστασθαι. εἰ δὲ δυσχερὲς εἴη τὸ τοιοῦτο,...τρεῖς ἐπὶ τὸ αὐτὸ συναγομένους,...τότε τὴν χειροτονίαν ποιεῖσθαι. τὸ δὲ κῦρος τῶν γινομένων δίδοσθαι καθ᾽ ἑκάστην ἐπαρχίαν τῷ μητροπολίτῃ.—Concil. Nic. can. 4. in Concil. Stud. Labb. et Cossart. Lut. Par. 1671-2. Tom. II. col. 29. Conf. cans. 6, 7. ibid. col. 32. See before, page 144, notes 1, 2.]

both M. Calvin, Illyricus, M. Fox, and others, do acknow- The name of arch-bishop and metropolitan.
ledge the names and office of patriarchs and archbishops, &c.,
in the same canon to be contained[5]. Neither do they, nor any
other learned writer, deny these names and offices to have been
in the primitive church, and that fixed to certain places and
persons, not moveable by actions, nor practised by course.

Likewise you have heard how that council, by this clause
Secundum morem antiquum : " according to the ancient custom," doth signify that these names and offices have[6] been in
the church of long time; or else it would not have been said to
be "an old custom."

Moreover, the ninth canon of the council of Antioch, before Conc. An-tioch. can. 9.
alleged, is most plain and evident, both for the name and the
thing, together with the long continuance of them in the church[7].

The 20. canon of the same council of Antioch saith di- Can. 20.
rectly that no bishops may call a several council without the
consent of their metropolitans[8].

In the sixth and 37. canons *Concilii Arelatensis*, mention Conc. Arelat. can. 6. & 37.[9]
is made of the metropolitan, of his authority in ordering of
bishops, and of the authority of his synod[10].

The like both for the name and the matter also touching Conc. Laod. can. 12.
ordaining of bishops is in the twelfth canon of the council of
Laodicea[11].

In the second council of Carthage, in the twelfth canon, it Conc. Carth. ii. can. 12.
is evident that there was a " primate " in every province, and
that without his commandment it was not lawful for any to be
ordained bishop[12].

In the 13. and 17, and divers other canons of the general Conc. Carth. can. 13. 17. &c.

[5 See before, pages 147, &c.]   [6 Hath, Def. B.]

[7 Concil. Antioch. can. 9. in Concil. Stud. Labb. et Cossart. Tom. II. col.
565. See before, page 146, note 1.]

[8 Μὴ ἐξεῖναι δέ τινας καθ᾽ ἑαυτοὺς ποιεῖσθαι ἄνευ τῶν πεπιστευμένων τὰς
μητροπόλεις.—Can. 20. ibid. col. 572.]   [9 17, Def. B.]

[10 Illud autem ante omnia clareat, eum qui sine conscientia metropolitani
constitutus fuerit episcopus, juxta magnam synodum esse episcopum non debere.—
Concil. Arelat. ii. can. 6. ibid. Tom. IV. col. 1012. Hoc etiam placuit custo-
diri, ut nihil contra magnam synodum metropolitani sibi æstiment vindican-
dum.—Ibid. can. 56 (al. 37). col. 1017.]

[11 Περὶ τοῦ τοὺς ἐπισκόπους, κρίσει τῶν μητροπολιτῶν καὶ τῶν πέριξ ἐπισκόπων, καθίστασθαι εἰς τὴν ἐκκλησιαστικὴν ἀρχὴν, ὄντας ἐκ πολλοῦ δεδοκιμασ-
μένους, ἔν τε τῷ λόγῳ τῆς πίστεως, καὶ τῇ τοῦ εὐθέος λόγου πολιτείᾳ.—Concil.
Laod. can. 12. ibid. Tom. I. col. 1497.]

[12 Concil. Carthag. ii. can. 12. ibid. Tom. II. cols. 1162, 3. This canon is
the same with that which follows.]

The name
of arch-
bishop and
metro-
politan.
Conc. Chal-
cedo.

council of Carthage, as it is in the Greek copy, the authority
of the "primate" is also expressed[1].

In the council of Chalcedon the name of "archbishop" is
sundry times used : Flavianus is there called "archbishop of
Constantinople," Dioscorus "archbishop of Alexandria," and
one Atticus, bishop of Nicopolis, doth call the said Dioscorus
archiepiscopum nostrum : "our archbishop." Leo is called
"archbishop of Rome," &c.[2]

Of the councils that followed there is no doubt; and it were
but superfluous for me to stand in reciting of them; and therefore this shall suffice for the councils, to shew that both the
name of "metropolitan or archbishop," and also the authority, is not unheard of in the church of Christ, or a flitting or
sliding office.

Fathers and
stories, of the
name and
office of arch-
bishop.
Epiphanius.

Now to the fathers and stories. Epiphanius, *Lib. ii.
Tom. ii. Hær.* 68, calleth one Peter "archbishop of Alexandria." And, that it may fully appear that it was both a
continual office and of great authority and jurisdiction, I will
set down his words:

*Et Meletius quidem in carcere detentus erat una cum
prædictis martyribus, ac Petro Alexandriæ archiepiscopo,
&c.*[3] : " And Meletius truly was kept in prison together with the
fore-named martyrs, and Peter the archbishop of Alexandria;
and Meletius seemed to excel the other bishops of Egypt, for
he had the second place after Peter in his archbishopric, as
being under him to help him, and looking to ecclesiastical

[1 ...ὀφείλει παρ' ἡμῶν τὰ ὁρισθέντα ἐκ τῶν πρὸ ἡμῶν, φυλαχθῆναι· ὧν τινων
ὡς ἔτυχεν ἀβούλως οἱ πρωτεύοντες τῆς οἰασδήποτε ἐπαρχίας οὐ κατατολμῶσι.
πολλοὶ οὖν ἐπίσκοποι συναχθέντες, ἐπίσκοπον χειροτονήσουσιν· εἰ δὲ ἀνάγκη
γένηται, τρεῖς ἐπίσκοποι ἐν οἰφδήποτε ἂν τόπῳ ὦσι, τῷ τοῦ πρωτεύοντος παρ-
αγγέλματι χειροτονήσουσιν τὸν ἐπίσκοπον.—Cod. Canon. Eccles. Afric. can.
13. ibid. col. 1055 ; see also can. 17. ibid. col. 1058. Conf. Synod. Carthag. cans.
13, 17. in Canon. Apost. Concil. &c. cum Comm. Theod. Balsam. Lut. Par.
1620. pp. 611, 27.]

[2 Concil. Calched. Act. I. in Concil. Stud. Labb. et Cossart. Lut. Par.
1671-2. Tom. IV. cols. 148, 9, 52.]

[3 ... καὶ ὁ μὲν Μελήτιος ἐν τῷ δεσμωτηρίῳ καθειργμένος ἦν, αὐτός τε καὶ οἱ
προειρημένοι μάρτυρες, ἅμα τῷ προειρημένῳ Πέτρῳ τῷ τῆς Ἀλεξανδρείας ἀρχι-
επισκόπῳ. ἐδόκει δὲ καὶ ὁ Μελήτιος τῶν [τὴν] κατὰ τὴν Αἴγυπτον προήκων, καὶ
δευτερεύων τῷ Πέτρῳ κατὰ τὴν ἀρχιεπισκοπήν, ὡς δι' ἀντιλήψεως αὐτοῦ χάριν,
ὑπ' αὐτὸν δὲ ὤν, καὶ ὑπ' αὐτὸν τὰ ἐκκλησιαστικὰ ἀναφέρων. τοῦτο γὰρ ἔθος ἐστί,
τὸν ἐν τῇ Ἀλεξανδρείᾳ ἀρχιεπίσκοπον πάσης τε Αἰγύπτου καὶ Θηβαΐδος, Μα-
ραιώτου τε, καὶ Λιβύης, Ἀμμωνιακῆς, Μαραιώτιδός τε καὶ Πενταπόλεως, ἔχων
τὴν ἐκκλησιαστικὴν διοίκησιν.—Epiph. Op. Par. 1622. Adv. Hær. Lib. II. Tom.
II. Hær. lxviii. 1. Tom. I. p. 717.]

matters under him. For this is the custom, that the bishop of Alexandria hath the ecclesiastical government of all Egypt, Thebais, and Mareota, and Libya, and Ammonica, and Mareotis, and Pentapolis." *The name of archbishop and metropolitan.*

In the same leaf he calleth this Peter archbishop three times. This Peter lived in the year of our Lord three hundred and four, twenty years at the least before the council of Nice. *Peter archbishop of Alexandria above twenty years before the council of Nice.*

The same Epiphanius, in the same book and tome, *Hær.* 69, writeth thus: *Quotquot enim ecclesiæ in Alexandria catholicæ ecclesiæ sunt, sub uno archiepiscopo sunt* [4] : "All the churches that are catholic churches in Alexandria are under one archbishop." And a little after he calleth Meletius "archbishop of Egypt," but yet subject to Alexander the archbishop of Alexandria [5]; and all this was before the council of Nice. *Idem.*

What can be spoken more aptly and more plainly to my purpose? And, if T. C. will cavil at the authority of the author (which is the poorest shift that can be, especially when the author is so generally allowed), then for brevity's sake I do refer him to the epistle of Janus Cornarius prefixed before this book [6], and to that which afterward I have alleged in his defence out of the Centuries.

Athanasius was called archbishop of Alexandria; and, that it may appear that it was not a bare title, but an office of government, you shall find these words in his second Apology:

Ischaras quidam, ut nequaquam clericus, ita moribus improbissimus conatus est sui pagi insulas decipere, jactans sese clericum esse. Id ubi rescivisset ejus loci presbyter, mihi tum ecclesias perlustranti renunciavit: ego igitur, &c. [7] "A certain man named Ischaras, as he was no clerk, so was he *Athanas. Apol. 2.*

[4 Id. ibid. Hær. lxix. 1. p. 727.]

[5 Ἀνήνεγκε τοίνυν εἰς τὰ ὦτα τοῦ ἀρχιεπισκόπου Ἀλεξάνδρου ὁ ἀρχιεπίσκοπος Μελήτιος ὁ κατὰ τὴν Αἴγυπτον, ὑπὸ δὲ χεῖρα Ἀλεξάνδρου ἐδόκει εἶναι.—Id. ibid. 3. p. 729.]

[6 Id. Contr. Octoag. Hær. Op. Panar. Iano Cornar. Interp. Basil. 1543. Præf. foll. a. 2, &c.]

[7 ... Ἰσχύρας τις οὕτω λεγόμενος, οὐ κληρικὸς, ἀλλὰ καὶ τὸν τρόπον πονηρὸς, ἐπεχείρει τοὺς ἐν τῇ ἰδίᾳ κώμῃ πλανᾷν, λέγων εἶναί τινα ἑαυτὸν κληρικόν. τοῦτο μαθὼν ὁ τῶν τόπων πρεσβύτερος, περιερχομένῳ μοι τὰς ἐκκλησίας ἀναγγέλλει, καὶ ἀποστέλλω σὺν αὐτῷ Μακάριον πρεσβύτερον καλέσαι τὸν Ἰσχύραν. εὑρόντες δὲ αὐτὸν νοσοῦντα καὶ κατακείμενον ἐν κελλίῳ, ἐντέλλονται τῷ πατρὶ αὐτοῦ παραγγεῖλαι τῷ υἱῷ, μηδέν τι τοιοῦτον ἐπιχειρεῖν, οἷον εἴρηται κατ' αὐτοῦ.—Athanas. Op. Par. 1698. Apolog. contr. Arian. 63. Tom. I. p. 181.]

most wicked in manners, who went about to deceive the isles of his precinct, boasting that he was a clerk; when the priest of that place understood thereof, he told it unto me when I was visiting my churches; so I sent the same man together with Macharius the priest to fetch unto me Ischaras, whom when they found sick in his chamber, they commanded his father to warn his son, that he attempted no such thing as was reported of him." And after in the same place followeth Ischaras'[1] letters of submission to Athanasius. In the same Apology there are letters of submission written by Arsennius bishop of Hipsell, and the ministers and deacons of the same diocese, to Athanasius: the beginning of the letters is this: *Et nos quoque diligentes pacem et unanimitatem cum ecclesia catholica, cui tu per Dei gratiam præfectus es, volensque ecclesiastico canoni pro veteri instituto subjici, scribimus tibi, papa dilecte, promittimusque in nomine Domini nos deinceps non communicaturos cum schismaticis. &c.*[2] "And we also, loving peace and concord with the catholic church, over which thou art by the grace of God appointed, and willing according to the old custom to be subject to the ecclesiastical canon, write to thee, loving father, and in the name of the Lord promise that we henceforth will not communicate with the schismatics."

By this it is plain that Athanasius had great jurisdiction over many bishops, and other ministers, and ecclesiastical persons. Again in the same Apology mention is made of an archbishop[3].

In the same book the priests and deacons of the churches of Mareota, in an epistle that they writ to the synod, besides that they call Athanasius *episcopum nostrum*[4]: "our bishop," they shew that he used to visit the church solemnly accompanied. Their words are worth the noting, and be these following: *Utpote qui non longis finibus ab episcopo distemus, et comites in lustranda Mariote ei cohæsimus; nunquam enim ille solus visitandi causa itinera obire solet, sed comites secum trahere, presbyteros et diaconos et non paucos ex plebe*[5]: "Because we dwell not far from the bishop, and we accompanied him whilst he visited Mariotes; for he is never

[1 Ischara, Def. B.]
[2 Ibid. 64. pp. 181, 2.]
[3 Ibid. 69. p. 185.]
[4 Ibid. 74. p. 190.]
[5 Ibid. p. 191.]

wont alone to take journeys in visitations, but to take companions with him, priests and deacons, and many of the people." And his own words a little before that epistle speaking of these priests and deacons be these : *Et mecum provincias lustrabant*[6]: "And they visited the provinces with me." Whereby also it is evident that he had a large jurisdiction, and that he did visit his provinces. The same Athanasius, in that Apology, declaring what this place called Mariotes is, saith : *Mariotes ager est in Alexandria, quo in loco nunquam fuit episcopus, imo ne chorepiscopus quidem ; sed universæ ejus loci ecclesiæ episcopo Alexandrino subjacent ; tamen ut singuli pagi suos presbyteros habeant*[7]: "Mariotes is a territory of Alexandria, where there was never bishop, no, not so much as a bishop's deputy ; but all the churches of that place are under the bishop of Alexandria ; yet so that every village have their priests."

The name of archbishop and metropolitan.

In his epistle *Ad solitariam vitam degentes*, he calleth "Lucius metropolitan of Sardinia," and "Dionysius metropolitan of Mediolane[8]."

Socrates, *Lib. v. cap.* 8, saith that in the council of Constantinople "they confirmed the faith of the Nicene council, and appointed patriarchs, assigning their provinces, that the bishops of one diocese should not intermeddle in other churches (for this before was indifferently used by reason of persecution). And to Nectarius was allotted Megalopolis and Thracia. &c.[9]"

Socrates.

The same is to be seen in the canons of that council of Constantinople[10].

I omit Justinian the emperor, who so often mentioneth these names and offices in his Constitutions[11]. I also omit that Illyricus calleth Cyprian "metropolitan of Carthage ;" and the

Justinian.
Illyricus, Cent. iv.

[6] ... καὶ ἐν τῇ περιοδείᾳ σὺν ἐμοὶ ὄντες, &c.—Ibid. p. 190.]

[7] Ibid. 85. p. 200.]

[8] ... Παυλῖνος ὁ ἀπὸ Τριβέρων τῆς μητροπόλεως τῶν Γαλλίων ἐπίσκοπος, καὶ Λουκίφερ ὁ ἀπὸ μητροπόλεως τῆς Σαρδινίας ἐπίσκοπος, Εὐσέβιός τε ὁ ἀπὸ Βερκέλλων τῆς Ἰταλίας, καὶ Διονύσιος ὁ ἀπὸ Μεδιολάνων, ἔστι δὲ καὶ αὕτη μητρόπολις τῆς Ἰταλίας.—Id. Hist. Arian. ad Monach. 33. Tom. I. p. 363.]

[9] ... ἐβεβαίωσάν τε αὖθις τὴν ἐν Νικαίᾳ πίστιν· καὶ πατριάρχας κατέστησαν, διανειμάμενοι τὰς ἐπαρχίας, ὥστε τοὺς ὑπὲρ διοίκησιν ἐπισκόπους ταῖς ὑπερορίοις ἐκκλησίαις μὴ ὑπερβαίνειν· τοῦτο γὰρ πρότερον διὰ τοὺς διωγμοὺς ἐγίνετο ἀδιαφόρως· καὶ κληροῦται Νεκτάριος μὲν τὴν Μεγαλόπολιν καὶ τὴν Θρᾴκην· κ. τ. λ.—Socr. in Hist. Eccles. Script. Amst. 1695-1700. Lib. v. cap. viii. pp. 217, 8.]

[10] Concil. Constant. cans. 1, 2. in Concil. Stud. Labb. et Cossart. Lut. Par. 1671-2. Tom. II. cols. 946, 7.]

[11] See below, page 166, note 5.]

The name
of arch-
bishop and
metro-
politan.
fourth Century, where Ambrose is called metropolitan, having
government of many churches[1]. Neither shall I need to repeat the places of Calvin[2], M. Fox[3], M. Beza, *Lib. Conf.
cap.* 5,[4] or other late writers' judgments, who directly confess
that these names were usual in the primitive church, and that
the office was permanent; for this that is spoken may suffice.

The office of
metropolitan
and arch-
bishop
without
the name.
I will come to those authors and places, where the office
and jurisdiction is spoken of, though the name be not expressed.

Cyprian.
Cyprian, *Lib. iv. Epist.* 8, saith that he had a large
province: *Habet enim Numidiam et Mauritaniam sibi cohærentes*[5]: "For it hath Numidia and Mauritania annexed
unto it." And Gregory Nazianzene, in the oration that he
Greg.
Nazi.
made in the commendation of Cyprian, saith that "he did rule
and govern not only the churches of Carthage or Afric, *sed
et Hesperiæ universæ; imo orienti fere ipsi ad finem usque
meridiei et septentrionis*[6]: but of all Spain, and almost of the
whole east, unto the end of the south and the north." And
what was this else but to be an archbishop?

Eusebius.
Eusebius, *Lib. vi. cap.* 1, saith that Demetrius was bishop
of the parishes of Alexandria, and of Egypt; and this Demetrius lived *anno Domini* 191. Eusebius testifieth there likewise
that one Julianus was before him in the same room[7].

Athanasius.
Athanasius, in an epistle that he writ *de sententia Dionysii
episcopi Alexand. contra Arianos*, affirmeth *ad Dionysium*

[1 Centur. Eccles. Hist. Basil. 1560, &c. Cent. IV. cap. x. col. 1150. See before,
page 155.]

[2 Calvin. Op. Amst. 1667-71. Inst. Lib. IV. cap. iv. 4. Tom. IX. p. 286. See
before, page 147, note 10.]

[3 Fox, Acts and Monuments, Lond. 1684. Vol. I. p. 11. See before, page 144.]

[4 Neque vero nos ignoramus quam multa sint a veteribus constituta de episcoporum, metropolitarum, et patriarcharum sedibus, idque optimo zelo, et de-
finitis cujusque limitibus, certaque attributa auctoritate.—Th. Bezæ Confess.
Christ. Fid. Genev. 1587. cap. v. 29. p. 142.]

[5 ... habet etiam Numidiam et Mauritanias duas sibi cohærentes.—Cypr. Op.
Oxon. 1682. Ad Cornel. Epist. xlviii. p. 91.]

[6 ... οὐ γὰρ τῆς Καρχηδονίων προκαθέζεται μόνον ἐκκλησίας, οὐδὲ τῆς ἐξ
ἐκείνου καὶ δι' ἐκεῖνον περιβοήτου μέχρι νῦν Ἀφρικῆς, ἀλλὰ καὶ πάσης τῆς ἑσπε-
ρίου, σχεδὸν δὲ καὶ τῆς ἑῴας αὐτῆς, νοτίου τε καὶ βορίου λήξεως, ἐφ' ὅσα ἐκεῖνος
ἦλθε τῷ θαύματι.—Gregor. Naz. Op. Par. 1778-1840. Orat. xxiv. 12. Tom. I.
p. 445. It appears that there was a Cyprian of Antioch; and Gregory seems to
have confused the two.]

[7 Δέκατον μὲν γὰρ ἐπεῖχε Σεβῆρος τῆς βασιλείας ἔτος· ἡγεῖτο δὲ Ἀλεξανδρείας καὶ τῆς λοιπῆς Αἰγύπτου Δαῖτος· τῶν δὲ αὐτόθι παροικιῶν τὴν ἐπισκοπὴν
νεωστὶ τότε μετὰ Ἰουλιανὸν Δημήτριος ὑπειλήφει.—Euseb. in Hist. Eccles.
Script. Amst. 1695-1700. Lib. VI. cap. ii. p. 164.]

Alexandriæ episcopum curam etiam ecclesiarum in Pentapoli *superioris Libyæ pertinuisse*[8]: " that unto Dionysius bishop of Alexandria the care of the churches in Pentapolis of the higher Libya pertained." And it is manifest in the same epistle, that these churches had their bishop besides. For Eusebius, *Lib. vii. cap.* 26, writeth that Basilides was bishop of the parishes of Pentapolis while Dionysius lived[9]; so that it is evident that Dionysius was an archbishop. And this is that Dionysius that is called *Alexandrinus*, whose works be extant, and is one of the most ancient writers. The same Eusebius saith that Gregory did govern the churches throughout Pontus[10].

The name of archbishop and metropolitan.

Euseb.

Sozomen, *Lib. vii. cap.* 19, saith that, " though there be many cities in Scythia, yet they have but one bishop[11]."

Sozom.

Theodoret, *Lib. iv. cap.* 11, testifieth that " Amphilochius, to whom the metropolitan city of Lycaonia was committed to be governed, did also govern that whole country, and did drive from thence the heresy of the Messalians." And in the same chapter we read that Letoius, governor of the churches of Militia, burned monasteries infected with that heresy[12]; which declareth that bishops had then great authority in government.

Theodoret.

Aurelius, bishop of Carthage, in the council of Afric, said that he had the oversight and care of many churches[13].

Conc. Afric. in can. 55, Græco.

---

[8] Ἐν Πενταπόλει τῆς ἄνω Λιβύης τηνικαῦτά τινες τῶν ἐπισκόπων ἐφρόνησαν τὰ Σαβελλίου·...τοῦτο μαθὼν Διονύσιος, αὐτὸς γὰρ εἶχε τὴν μέριμναν τῶν ἐκκλησιῶν ἐκείνων, πέμπει κ. τ. λ.—Athanas. Op. Par. 1698. Epist. de Sentent. Dionys. 5. Tom. I. p. 246.]

[9] Ἐπὶ τούτοις καὶ Βασιλείδῃ τῶν κατὰ Πεντάπολιν παροικιῶν ἐπισκόπῳ γράφων [Διονύσιος], φησὶν ἑαυτὸν εἰς τὴν ἀρχὴν ἐξήγησιν πεποιῆσθαι τοῦ Ἐκκλησιαστοῦ.—Euseb. in Hist. Eccles. Script. Lib. vii. cap. xxvi. p. 226.]

[10] ... ὧν ἐπισήμους μάλιστα ἔγνωμεν Θεόδωρον, ὃς ἦν αὐτὸς οὗτος ὁ καθ' ἡμᾶς ἐπισκόπων διαβόητος Γρηγόριος· τόν τε αὐτοῦ ἀδελφὸν Ἀθηνόδωρον·...τοσαύτην ἀπηνέγκαντο περὶ τὰ θεῖα λόγια βελτίωσιν, ὡς ἔτι νέους ἄμφω ἐπισκοπῆς τῶν κατὰ Πόντον ἐκκλησιῶν ἀξιωθῆναι.—Id. ibid. Lib. vi. cap. xxx. p. 187.]

[11] ... ἀμέλει Σκύθαι πολλαὶ πόλεις ὄντες, ἕνα πάντες ἐπίσκοπον ἔχουσιν.— Soz. in eod. Lib. vii. cap. xix. p. 595.]

[12] Λητόϊος μὴν οὖν, ὁ τῶν Μελετινῶν ἐκκλησίαν ἰθύνας, ἀνὴρ ζήλῳ θείῳ κοσμούμενος, πολλὰ τῆς νόσου ταύτης σπάσαντα θεασάμενος μοναστήρια, μᾶλλον δὲ σπήλαια λῃστρικὰ, ἐνέπρησε ταῦτα, καὶ τοὺς λύκους ἐκ τῆς ποίμνης ἐξήλασεν. ὡσαύτως δὲ καὶ ὁ πανεύφημος Ἀμφιλόχιος, τὴν Λυκαόνων μητρόπολιν νέμειν πεπιστευμένος, καὶ ἅπαν ἰθύνων τὸ ἔθνος, ἐπισκήψασαν αὐτόσε τὴν λύμην ταύτην μαθὼν, ἐξανέστησε πάλιν, καὶ τὰ ὑπ' αὐτοῦ νεμόμενα τῆς λώβης ἐκείνης ἠλευθέρωσε ποίμνιον.—Theod. in eod. Lib. iv. cap. xi. pp. 163, 4.]

[13] Αὐρήλιος ἐπίσκοπος εἶπεν·...ἐπειδὴ οἴδατε πολλῶν ἐκκλησιῶν καὶ χειροτονιῶν φροντίδα με βαστάζειν.—Cod. Canon. Eccles. Afric. can. 55. in Concil. Stud. Labb. et Cossart. Lut. Par. 1671-2. Tom. II. 1078, 9.]

But what need I labour so much in a matter that cannot
be unknown to any that is of any reading ? This therefore shall
suffice both for the name and office of an archbishop and metropolitan, &c., against the unlearned distinction that you have
used in answering St Ambrose[1].

Chapter ii.   The Twenty-eighth Division.

Answer to the Admonition, Page 66, Sect. 5.

Sozomenus, likewise, *Lib. ii.* of his ecclesiastical history, *cap.* 8, calleth Simeon archbishop of Seleucia[2],
and Basil the great metropolitan of Cappadocia, *Lib. iii.*
cap. 16.[3]

T. C. Page 71, Sect. ult.

"Basil," you say, "the great metropolitan of Cappadocia." I have shewed
what the word metropolitan signifieth, and how there was not then such a
metropolitan as we have now, and as the Admonition speaketh against.
You play as he which is noted as none of the wisest among[4] the merchants,
which thought that every ship that approached the haven was his ship.
For so you think that, wheresoever you read metropolitan or archbishop,
forthwith you think there is your metropolitan, or your archbishop, where
as it shall appear that, besides the name, they are no more like than a
bishop with us is like a minister.

Jo. Whitgift.

What this word "metropolitan" signifieth, what office
and jurisdiction he had, is before sufficiently declared, and
may more at large appear in the Constitutions of Justinian[5];
likewise, whether our metropolitans in office anything at all

[1 Cartwright considers that, "for this great shew the A. bringeth into the
stage, they are scarce worth the looking on." He will not allow any earlier authority than that of Epiphanius, "the first of ancient writers that gave this name
place in his writings." He maintains, therefore, that it was not "from the times
of the apostles;" and concludes : "So we see that, of all the testimonies the Answ.
hath mustered, there is not one that hath stricken one stroke, in the quarrel of
that antiquity of the name of archbishop."—Sec. Repl. pp. 494, 5.]

[2 ... καὶ διαβάλλουσι...Συμεώνην τὸν τότε ἀρχιεπίσκοπον Σελευκείας καὶ
Κτησιφῶντος, κ.τ.λ.—Soz. in Hist. Eccles. Script. Amst. 1695-1700. Lib. II.
cap. ix. p. 371.]

[3 ... ἀμέλει τοι καὶ Βασίλειος, ὁ τὴν Καππαδοκῶν μητρόπολιν μετὰ ταῦτα
ἐπισκοπήσας, κ.τ.λ.—Id. ibid. Lib. III. cap. xvi. pp. 427, 8.]

[4 Amongst, Repl. 1 and 2.]

[5 Corp. Jur. Civil. Amst. 1663. Auth. Coll. I. Tit. vi. Novell. vi. capp. 2, 3, 8,
Epil.; Auth. Coll. IX. Tit. vi. Novell. cxxiii. capp. 3, 10, 22. Tom. II. pp. 13, &c.,
169, 70, 73.]

differ from them. Surely, he that shall well consider your The name of arch-bishop and metro-politan.
unapt answers and your utopical jests, may think that you
wear the livery of those "merchants" you talk of, and may
very well sail in their ships.

Chapter ii.   The Twenty-ninth Division.
T. C. Page 72, Sect. 1.

I cannot tell whether you would abuse your reader here with the
fallation of the accent, because this word "great" is so placed between Basil
and metropolitan that it may be as well referred to the metropolitan as to
Basil, and so, you having put no comma, it seemeth you had as lief have
your reader read, "great metropolitan" as "great Basil." But, that the sim-
pler sort be not deceived thereby, it is not out of the way to let the reader
Soz. vi. Lib. *understand what a great metropolitan this was; which ap-*
c. 16. *peareth, for that, when he was threatened by the magistrate*
confiscation of his goods, answered that he was not afraid of the
threatenings, and that all his goods were " a very few books and an old
gown[6]*." Such were then those metropolitans, under whose shadows M.*
Doctor goeth about to shroud all this pomp and princely magnificence
of archbishops[7].

Jo. Whitgift.

You search very narrowly when you miss not a " comma,"
but you know what *nugator* signifieth[8].   All men of learning
can tell that Basil is in common speech called " Basil the
great."   And yet, if he were called " great metropolitan," the
title might very well agree unto him; for he had large and
ample jurisdiction, being bishop of Cappadocia; as Athanasius
doth also witness in his epistle written to Palladius[9].

The contention is for the name and the office, not for the
riches; although I think that there both are and have[10] been
bishops in England as poor as Basil, if they had been taken
so soon after they were placed in their bishoprics as Basil was
now at this time.

[6 ... εἴγε οὐσίαν μὲν οὐκ ἔχω, ῥάκως τε καὶ βιβλία ὀλίγα.—Soz. in Hist.
Eccles. Script. Lib. VI. cap. xvi. p. 535.]

[7 Of our archbishops, Repl. 1 and 2.]

[8 " ... he might know that, although a comma be but a little prick, yet it oft
maketh a great matter."—Sec. Repl. p. 496.]

[9 ... δοξαζέτωσαν τὸν Κύριον τὸν δεδωκότα τῇ Καππαδοκίᾳ τοιοῦτον ἐπίσκοπον, κ.τ.λ.—Athanas. Op. Par. 1698. Ad Pallad. Presb. Epist. Tom. I.
Pars II. p. 957.]

[10 Hath, Def. B.]

The name
of arch-
bishop and
metro-
politan.

An unadvised
answer.

Chapter ii.   The Thirtieth Division.
T. C. Page 72, Sect. 2, 3, 4.

As for Simeon, archbishop of Seleucia, I will not deny but at that time was the name of archbishops.   For then Satan had made, through the titles of archbishops, primates, and patriarchs [1], *as it were three stairs, whereby antichrist might climb up into his cursed seat, notwithstanding there wanted not good decrees of godly councils which did strike at these proud names, and went about to keep them down.   But the swelling waters of the ambition of divers could not by any banks be kept in, which, having once broken out in certain places, afterwards covered almost the face of the whole earth.*

This endeavour of godly men may appear in the council of Carthage, which decreed that the bishop of the first seat should not be called Conc. Carth. *ἔξαρχον τῶν ἱερέων ἢ ἄκρον ἱερέα ἢ τοιοῦτόν τι πότε* [2], *that is,* cap. 39. *"either the chief of the priests, or the high priest, or any such thing;" by which words "any such thing" he shutteth out the name of archbishop, and all such haughty titles.*

The same decree also was made in the African council [3] ; Conc. Tom. I. *and, if you say that it was made against the pope of Rome, or* cap. 6. *to forbid that any man should be called archbishop, shew me where there was either bishop of Rome, or any other that ever made any such title or challenge to be the general bishop of all at that time, when this council of Carthage was holden, when as the first of those which did make any such challenge was the bishop of Constantinople, which, notwithstanding, chal-*

An untruth.

lenged not the preeminence first over all, but that he might ordain bishops of Asia, Pontus, Thracia, which were before appointed by their synods; and this was in the council of Chalcedon [4], *which was long after that council of Carthage before remembered.*

Jo. Whitgift.

It is [5] before sufficiently declared that these names and offices were allowed and confirmed by the council of Nice [6], and therefore not brought in by Satan.   Moreover this Simeon, archbishop of Seleucia, lived, as it may appear by most chronicles, about the time of the council of Nice, and was martyred by Sapores the king of Persia.

[1 Of archbishop, primate, patriarch, Repl. 1 and 2.]

[2 Ὥστε τὸν τῆς πρώτης καθέδρας ἐπίσκοπον μὴ λέγεσθαι ἔξαρχον κ. τ. λ. τοιουτότροπόν τί ποτε.—Cod. Canon. Eccles. Afric. can. 39. in Concil. Stud. Labb. et Cossart. Lut. Par. 1671-2. Tom. II. col. 1070.]

[3 Concil. Afric. cap. 6. in Crabb. Concil. Col. Agrip. 1551. Tom. I. p. 503.]

[4 ... καὶ ὥστε τοὺς τῆς Ποντικῆς, καὶ τῆς Ἀσιανῆς, καὶ τῆς Θρᾳκικῆς διοικήσεως μητροπολίτας μόνους, ἔτι δὲ καὶ τοὺς ἐν τοῖς βαρβαρικοῖς ἐπισκόπους τῶν προειρημένων διοικήσεων χειροτονεῖσθαι ὑπὸ τοῦ προειρημένου ἁγιωτάτου θρόνου τῆς κατὰ Κωνσταντινούπολιν ἁγιωτάτης ἐκκλησίας.—Concil. Calched. Act. XVI. in Concil. Stud. Labb. et Cossart. Tom. IV. col. 798. Conf. col. 813.]

[5 If this, Def. B.]   [6 See before, pages 137, 44, &c.]

Which peradventure if you had understood, you would not have burst out into this heat of words; for then might you have made the same answer to Ambrose his authority which was long after him, and so kept secret your own fond device.

The council of Carthage and also of Afric was at that time, wherein the bishop of Rome, by his legates, did claim the right of hearing of appeals, from whomsoever they were made, and for his purpose alleged a counterfeit canon of the council of Nice. Wherefore it is most certain, that then the bishop of Rome began at the least to claim the superiority over all churches, and to take upon him as it were the name of universal bishop; and therefore this canon is made against him.

And that this is true, the epistle of the council of Afric written to Celestinus, then bishop of Rome, declareth. For, after that they have desired him that he would admit no such appeals, nor absolve such as they should excommunicate, because that was to do against the decrees of the council of Nice, and to abridge them of their jurisdiction and liberty; they add and say:

"Both because this privilege hath been taken from the church of Afric by no constitution of the fathers, and also the decrees of the council of Nice hath committed both the inferior clerks and the bishops themselves unto their metropolitans; for it was discreetly and rightly considered that all matters are to be determined in the places where they began, and that no province can lack the grace of the Holy Ghost, whereby the priest of Christ may be able both wisely to see, and also constantly to maintain the right; especially for that it is lawful for every man that shall mislike the discretion of the judges to appeal either to particular councils within the same province, or else to an universal council; unless perchance some man will think that God is able to inspire the trial of justice into one man alone, and will not inspire the same into a great number of priests meeting together in council. And how may such beyond-sea judgment be thought good, whereunto the persons of the witnesses which in trial of truth are thought necessary, either for that they be women, or for the infirmity of their age, or for many other incident lets, cannot be brought? Now that any should be sent abroad as it were from your holiness' side, we find it not decreed in any council."

The name of archbishop and metropolitan.

The name
of arch-
bishop and
metro-
politan.

And a little after : "And send you not any your clerks hither to execute justice at any man's request; lest we seem to bring the smoky puff of the world into the church of Christ. &c.[1]"

Whereby it is plain that they only prohibit that title of universality and of general jurisdiction that the bishop of Rome now claimed, and at that time began to claim, over all churches, and not the names of superiority due unto any in their own province. For that prerogative of jurisdiction over bishops and other ministers they acknowledge to be due to the metropolitan; as it is evident in the words of that same epistle which I have recited.

The name of
primate al-
lowed in the
council of
Carthage.

Moreover, it is manifest that this name "archbishop" was then used, and after that time continued and not disallowed by any; as it may appear by that which hath been hitherto written. And this name "primate" (which is as haughty as the name of archbishop) is allowed even in that council of Carthage, as may appear in the 13. 17. and 23. canons, as it

M. Fox.

is in the Greek copy[2]. Wherefore, in my opinion, M. Fox doth aptly decide this controversy, in that learned treatise of his first tome, where he, speaking of this same council and of this canon which you have recited (for I suppose you did

[1 Μὴ οὖν οἱ ἐν τῇ ἰδίᾳ ἐπαρχίᾳ ἀπὸ τῆς κοινωνίας ἀναρτηθέντες, παρὰ τῆς σῆς ἁγιωσύνης σπουδαίως καὶ καθὼς μὴ χρὴ φανῶσιν ἀποκαθιστάμενοι τῇ κοινωνίᾳ. καὶ τῶν πρεσβυτέρων δὲ ὁμοίως, καὶ τῶν ἑπομένων κληρικῶν τὰς ἀναιδεῖς ἀποφυγὰς, ὡς ἔστι σου ἄξιον, ἀποδιώξει ἡ ἁγιωσύνη ἡ σή· ἐπειδὴ καὶ οὐ διά τινος ὅρου τῶν πατέρων τοῦτο ἀπηγόρευται τῇ ἐν Ἀφρικῇ ἐκκλησίᾳ, ἢ τὰ ψηφίσματα τῆς ἐν Νικαίᾳ συνόδου, εἴτε κληρικοὺς τοῦ κατωτέρου βαθμοῦ, εἴτε αὐτοὺς τοὺς ἐπισκόπους τοῖς ἰδίοις μητροπολίταις φανερώτατα κατέπεμψαν. συνετῶς γὰρ καὶ δικαίως συνεῖδεν, ἅτινα δήποτε πράγματα ἀναφυῶσι, ταῦτα ἐν τοῖς ἰδίοις ὀφείλειν περατοῦσθαι τόποις· οὔτε γὰρ μιᾷ καὶ ἑκάστῃ προνοίᾳ ἐλογί-σαντο ἐλλείπειν τὴν χάριν τοῦ ἁγίου Πνεύματος, δι' ἧς ἡ δικαιοσύνη ἀπὸ τῶν τοῦ Χριστοῦ ἱερέων καὶ ὁρᾶται φρονίμως, καὶ κατέχεται σταθερῶς· μάλιστα, ὅτι ἑνὶ καὶ ἑκάστῳ συγκεχώρηται, ἐὰν περὶ τῆς δίκης τῶν διαγνωστῶν προΐσταται αὐτῷ πρὸς τὰς συνόδους τῆς ἰδίας ἐπαρχίας, ἢ ἔτι μὴν εἰς οἰκουμενικὴν σύνοδον ἐκκαλέσασθαι· εἰ μὴ ἄρα τίς ἐστιν, ὅστις πιστεύσει, ἐνὶ ᾡτινιδήποτε δύνασθαι τὸν Θεὸν ἡμῶν ἐμπνεῦσαι τὴν δικαιοσύνην, τοῖς δὲ ἀναριθμήτοις εἰς σύνοδον συνη-θροισμένοις ἱερεῦσιν ἀρνεῖσθαι. πῶς δὲ αὕτη ἡ περαματικὴ κρίσις βεβαία ἔσται, πρὸς ἣν τῶν μαρτύρων τὰ ἀναγκαῖα πρόσωπα, ἢ διὰ τὴν τῆς φύσεως, ἢ διὰ τὴν τοῦ γήρως ἀσθένειαν, ἢ πολλοῖς ἄλλοις ἐμποδισμοῖς ἐνεχθῆναι οὐ δύνα-ται ; περὶ γὰρ τοῦ τινας ὡσανεὶ ἐκ τοῦ πλευροῦ τῆς σῆς ἁγιωσύνης πέμπεσ-θαι, οὐδεμιᾷ τῶν πατέρων συνόδῳ ὁρισθὲν εὑρίσκομεν....ἐκβιβαστὰς τοίνυν κληρικοὺς ἡμῶν [al. ὑμῶν], τινῶν αἰτούντων, μὴ θέλετε ἀποστέλλειν, μήτε παραχωρεῖν, ἵνα τὸν καπνώδη τύφον τοῦ κόσμου δόξωμεν εἰσάγειν τῇ τοῦ Χριστοῦ ἐκκλησίᾳ, κ. τ. λ.—Cod. Canon. Eccles. Afric. Epist. ad Pap. Cælest. 138. in Concil. Stud. Labb. et Cossart. Lut. Par. 1671-2. Tom. II. cols. 1147, 50.]

[2 Ibid. cans. 13, 17, 23. cols. 1055, 8, 62.]

borrow it there), signifieth in effect that neither the name of
" primate, archbishop, or metropolitan," is by that canon prohibited, but rather these ambitious titles of " universal bishop,
prince of all priests, head of all priests," and such like[3].
Which names seem to derogate authority both of jurisdiction
and office from all other priests; and therefore a little after he
saith: " Thus then these titles above recited, as bishop, metropolitan, bishop of the first seat, primate, patriarch, archbishop,
that is to mean, chief bishop or head bishop to other bishops
of his province, we deny not but were then in old time applied, and might be applied to the bishop of Rome; like as the
same also were applied to other patriarchs in other chief cities
and provinces[4]." And in the same place, after he hath declared this title (*summus orbis pontifex*), as it is now used in
Rome, to be unheard of in the primitive time of the church,
that is five hundred years after Christ, he saith: " The like
is to be affirmed also of other presumptuous titles of like ambition, as, 'the head of the universal church,' 'the vicar of Christ
in earth,' ' prince of priests,' with such like, which be all new-
found terms, &c.[5];" so that it is plain that these general titles
of universal jurisdiction over all, and not the particular names of
superiority over several churches, is by this council forbidden.

This farther appeareth in the fifth council of Constantinople,
where John, not being content with the name of patriarch of
Constantinople, would needs have it ratified by the council
that he should be called *œcumenicus patriarcha*, that is,
"universal patriarch[6]." Against which title, not of " patriarch,"
but of " universal patriarch," both Pelagius and Gregory, at
that time bishops of Rome, the one succeeding the other, did
earnestly write. And this is the meaning of that canon. *Conc. Con-
stan. 5, alias
the 2.*

Ignatius, immediately after the apostles' time, calleth a
bishop *principem sacerdotum*[7]: " the prince of priests," or
chief priest; and so doth Ambrose in the fourth *ad Ephesios*[8]. *Ignatius
epist. ad
Smyrn.
Ambrose
in 4. Eph.*

---

[3] Fox, Acts and Monuments, Lond. 1684. Vol. 1. p. 12.]

[4] Id. ibid. p. 13; where *the bishop of the first see, that is to say chief bishop,*
and *were in the old.*]

[5] Id. ibid.; where *which all be.*]

[6] John had frequently this title given him in the council. See Constant.
Concil. sub Menna, in Concil. Stud. Labb. et Cossart. Act. v. Tom. V. col. 161.
Conf. col. 185.]

[7] ... τίμα μὲν τὸν Θεὸν,...ἐπίσκοπον δὲ, ὡς ἀρχιερέα.—Ignat. Interp. Epist.
ad Smyrn. 9. in Coteler. Patr. Apostol. Amst. 1724. Vol. II. p. 87.]

[8] Nam in episcopo omnes ordines sunt; quia primus sacerdos est, hoc est,

The name of arch-bishop and metro-politan.

But this they do not attribute to any one as having universal authority over all, but to every bishop in respect of such as be under him.

Touching "the bishop of Constantinople," you are deceived very much, and declare in him the same unskilfulness that you have done in the other. For it is evident that he required this name and title of "universal patriarch" ambitiously, as being desirous to be superior to all the patriarchs in the world. This to be true is manifest by the decree of Pelagius, *Distinct.* 99, *Canon Nullus*[1]; and by the epistles of Gregory[2], written purposely of that matter. Neither do I read in any approved author to the contrary.

Distinct. 99.

Again, you are deceived greatly in the council. For, though the bishop of Constantinople did challenge in the council of Chalcedon the right of ordering metropolitans in those places, yet doth he not in that council challenge the title of universal patriarch, which notwithstanding was offered to the bishop of Rome in that council of Chalcedon, but first given to the patriarch of Constantinople in the second council of Constantinople, or, as it is termed in the book of councils, the fifth, because it was the fifth general council, as it may appear in the same council. Moreover, whereas you say that "the bishop of Constantinople required that he might ordain bishops in Asia, &c.," if you mark the words diligently, you shall perceive that he required therein nothing but according to the sixth canon of the council of Nice, which is also there alleged for that purpose; but I have shewed before how the bishop of Rome made this challenge of universality in effect, and in deed, even in that council of Carthage, where this canon by you alleged is, and therefore I need not stand any longer upon this point[3].

Conc. Tom. II.

princeps est sacerdotum, &c.—Ambros. Op. Par. 1686-90. Comm. in Epist. ad Ephes. cap. iv. vv. 11, 12. Tom. II. Append. col. 241.]

[1 Nullus patriarcharum universalitatis vocabulo unquam utatur: quia si unus patriarcha universalis dicitur, patriarcharum nomen cæteris derogatur.—Pelag. II. in Corp. Jur. Canon. Lugd. 1624. Decret. Gratian. Decr. Prim. Pars, Dist. xcix. can. 4. col. 479.]

[2 Gregor. ibid. can. 5. cols. 479, 80. Conf. Op. Par. 1705. Epist. Lib. VIII. Indict. I. Ad Eulog. Episc. Epist. xxx., Lib. v. Indict. XIII. Ad Johan. Episc. Epist. xviii. Tom. II. cols. 919, 742, 3.]

[3 Cartwright makes a long rejoinder to this division, accusing Whitgift of having borrowed from Pighius, and of adducing arguments "partly vain and partly false."—Sec. Repl. pp. 496, &c.]

Chapter ii.   The Thirty-first Division.

Answer to the Admonition, Page 66, Sect. 6, 7, 8; and Page
67, Sect. 1, 2.

Damasus calleth Stephen an archdeacon[5].

Hierome in his epistle *ad Evagrium* hath this name
archdeacon[6].

Sextus in his decrees saith that Laurence the martyr
was an archdeacon[7].

Sozomenus, *Lib. vii. cap.* 19, maketh mention of an
archdeacon reading the scriptures[8].

Socrates in the seventh book of his ecclesiastical
history speaketh of one Timothy an archdeacon[9].

*Arch-
deacons[4]*

T. C. Page 72, Sect. 5, 6, 7.

*For to prove the lawfulness of the name of an archdeacon, the anti-
quity, the necessity of it, the testimonies of four are brought, which neither
speak of their lawfulness nor of their necessity, and they say not indeed
so much as, God save them; and two of these witnesses are popes, whereof
the first and best ordained that, if the metropolitan did not fetch his pall
at the apostolic see of Rome within three months after he be[10] consecrated,
that then he should lose his dignity; as Gratian witnesseth in the decrees
that he ascribeth unto Damasus[11].*

*T. C. faileth
in his ac-
count, and
telleth but
four, for five.*

*In what part
of Gratian?*

*I doubt not therefore that this is but a forger upon whom you would
father the archdeacon. For that Damasus, in whose place you put this
forger, lived anno 387; at what time the see of Rome had no such tyranny
as this and other things which are fathered of him do pretend. And, if*

[4 This word is not in Answ.]

[5 Hic omnem potestatem ecclesiæ dedit archidiacono suo Stephano, dum ad
passionem pergeret.—Ex Libr. Pont. Damas. in Vit. Lucii, in Concil. Stud. Labb.
et Cossart. Lut. Par. 1671-2. Tom. I. col. 719.]

[6 ... diaconi eligant de se, quem industrium noverint, et archidiaconum vocent.
—Hieron. Op. Par. 1693-1706. Ad Evang. Epist. ci. Tom. IV. Pars II. col. 803.]

[7 Et post passionem beati Sixti die tertio, passi sunt Laurentius ejus archi-
diaconus, &c.—Ex Libr. Pont. Damas. in Vit. Sixti Papæ II. in Concil. Stud.
Labb. et Cossart. Tom. I. col. 817. This, however, is merely an extract from the
Liber Pontificalis, untruly ascribed to Damasus.]

[8 Soz. in Hist. Eccles. Script. Amst. 1695-1700. Lib. VII. cap. xix. p. 596.
See below, page 176, note 2.]

[9 ... ἐπιμάχου δὲ γενομένης καὶ ἐνταῦθα τῆς ἐπισκοπῆς, οἱ μὲν ἐζήτουν
ἐνθρονισθῆναι Τιμόθεον ἀρχιδιάκονον· κ. τ. λ.—Socr. in eod. Lib. VII. cap. vii.
p. 280.]   [10 Were, Repl. 2.]

[11 ... placuit, ut quisquis metropolitanus ultra tres menses consecrationis suæ
ad fidem suam exponendam, palliumque suscipiendum ad apostolicam sedem non
miserit, commissa sibi careat dignitate, &c.—Pelag. in Corp. Jur. Canon. Decret.
Gratian. Decr. Prim. Pars, Dist. c. can. 1. col. 481. See not. in loc., where we are
told that some authors ascribe this decree to Damasus.]

Arch-
deacons.

This is
untrue; for
Sixtus is
more ancient.

this be enough to prove archdeacons, I can with better witness prove sub-deacons, acoluthes, exorcists, lectores[1], ostiarios; these doth Eusebius make mention of[2], an ancienter writer than any you bring; and, out of Ruffine[3], Theodoret[4], Sozomene[5], Socrates[6], &c., monks almost in every page; and hereupon it is more lawful for me to conclude that monks, subdeacons, exorcists, acoluthes, ostiarii, lectores, are necessary ecclesiastical orders in the church, as you conclude the necessity of the archdeacon.

What have
you else but
conjectures?

I perceive you care not whether the archdeacon fall or no, that you bestow so little cost of him, and leave him so nakedly. And, if I would be but half so bold in conjectures and divinations as you are, I could say that this slight[7] handling of the archdeacon, and sweating so much about the archbishop, is thereupon that you would be loth to come from being dean to be an archdeacon, and you live in some hope of being archbishop; but I will not enter so far. And surely, for anything that I see, you might have trussed up the archbishop as short as you do the archdeacon; for they stand upon one pin, and those reasons which establish the one establish the other. Whereupon also cometh to pass that all those reasons which were before alleged against the archbishop may be drawn against the archdeacon.

Jo. Whitgift.

The un-
toward deal-
ing of the
Replier, and
his un-
sufficient
answer.

My purpose in that place is (as you might have seen if you would) to prove that the "names of archbishops, archdeacon, &c." be not "antichristian names, that is, names invented by antichrist, but most ancient;" for those be my very words; and, as I have proved that to be most true in metropolitans and archbishops, by shewing that they were in the church before the pope was antichrist, so I do the like of archdeacons. And, where I have brought in five witnesses, you say I have brought in "four." Damasus, Hierome, Sixtus, Sozomen, and Socrates, be in number five; and of these five you have answered only two, and that after your usual manner, by rejecting the authors[8]. What is falsely attributed to Damasus in other matters is no answer to this, that he reporteth of archdeacons; which also the third Century allegeth as true[9]. And, though he were bishop of Rome, yet was he a virtuous, learned, and godly bishop. So was Sixtus in like manner, who lived bishop of Rome *anno* 265. So that Damasus was neither the first

[1] Lectors, Def. A. and B.]
[2] Euseb. in Hist. Eccles. Script. Amst. 1695-1700. Lib. vi. cap. xliii. p. 198.]
[3] Hyst. Eccles. Par. Lib. xi. capp. vi. viii. foll. 121. 2, 2.]
[4] Theod. in Hist. Eccles. Script. Lib. iv. capp. xxvi. xxvii. xxviii. pp.189, &c.]
[5] Soz. in eod. Lib. i. cap. xii. pp. 340, &c.]
[6] Socr. in eod. Lib. iv. cap. xxiii. pp. 190, &c.]   [7] Sleight, Editt.]
[8] "Affording you 'four witnesses,' I allowed you one too many, two of them being counterfeit."—Sec. Repl. p. 501.]
[9] Centur. Eccles. Hist. Basil. 1560, &c. Cent. iii. cap. vii. col. 150.]

nor the best. For Sixtus was martyred for the gospel; so was Arch-
deacons. not Damasus. They speak as much for archdeacons as I require, that is, that "their names were not invented by antichrist;" and, if there were then no such "tyranny in the church of Rome," as you here mislike, and yet this name in that church, it is not like to be a tyrannical name.

But I marvel you will deal so barely in this matter, knowing that Hierome, who lived in Damasus his time, hath this name archdeacon oftener than twice or thrice. Without doubt you do not well consider what you write.

This answer of yours was never as yet approved of any learned man. For what if "Eusebius make mention of subdeacons, acoluthes, &c." which were peradventure profitable offices in the church at that time, doth it therefore follow that it is unlawful to have archdeacons? I conclude no necessity of the archdeacon, but I conclude his antiquity; and, because you cannot answer that, you fall to scoffing and unseemly jesting, as your manner is, and so do you shift off three of my witnesses[10].

Chapter ii.　The Thirty-second Division.

T. C. Page 72, line 2, and Sect. 1.

Having therefore before proved the unlawfulness of them, I will here set down the difference between those archdeacons that were in times past and those which are now, whereby it may appear they are nothing like but in name.

Soz. vii. 19.[11]　*They were no ministers; as appeareth in Sozomen: ours are.* Untruth:
no such
thing ap-
peareth.

Jo. Whitgift.

What one reason have you used to prove the unlawfulness of them? If you mean such reasons as you have against archbishops, they be fully answered.

Not one word is there in the seventh book and nineteenth chapter of Sozomen, to prove that archdeacons either then "were not," or now may not be "ministers." For all that he speaketh in that chapter is this: "And this also is a strange thing in the church of Alexandria; whiles the gospels are a reading, the bishop doth not rise up; which I have

[10 "As for the anciety of the name archdeacon, it is not shewed before almost 400. years after Christ: which times how corrupt they were, hath in part, and will after more appear."—Sec. Repl. p. 502.]

[11 This marginal reference is introduced from Repl. 1 and 2.]

heard[1] of others. This holy book a monk that is an archdeacon readeth there; in other places deacons; in many
churches the priests only; but in principal feasts bishops[2]."
How you can conclude that archdeacons were not then
ministers by anything here spoken surely I know not. For, if
you mean, because he saith that in some churches only priests
did read; you can no more thereof conclude that archdeacons
were then no priests, than you may that they were no deacons,
or that bishops be no priests. Neither is it necessary that they
should be now ministers; it is sufficient if they be deacons:
yet may they be ministers, and meet it is that they should
so be; and you cannot prove the contrary[3].

Chapter ii.   The Thirty-third Division.

T. C. Page 73, Sect. 2.

They were tied to a certain church, and were called arch-   Conc. Urban.
deacon of such a congregation or church[4]: ours are tied to   Soz. vii. Lib.
none, but are called archdeacons of such a shire.   cap. 19.

Jo. Whitgift.

There is no other words in that book and chap. of Sozomen touching archdeacons, than these which I have before
recited: what they make for your purpose let the reader
judge. Your *Urbanum Concilium* is very obscure; for there
is none such to be found in all the volumes of councils. But,
to put you out of doubt, we have no archdeacons but such as
be "tied to one church," though they have the names sometimes of the shire wherein their jurisdiction lieth[5].

[1 Hard, Def. A. and B.]

[2 ... ξένον δὲ κἀκεῖνο παρὰ Ἀλεξανδρεῦσι τούτοις· ἀναγινωσκομένων γὰρ τῶν
εὐαγγελίων, οὐκ ἐπανίσταται ὁ ἐπίσκοπος· ὃ παρ' ἄλλοις οὔτ' ἔγνων οὔτε ἀκήκοα.
ταύτην δὲ τὴν ἱερὰν βίβλον ἀναγινώσκει ἐνθάδε μόνος ὁ ἀρχιδιάκονος. παρὰ
δὲ ἄλλοις, διάκονοι. ἐν πολλαῖς δὲ ἐκκλησίαις, οἱ ἱερεῖς μόνοι. ἐν δὲ ἐπισήμοις
ἡμέραις, ἐπίσκοποι, κ.τ.λ.—Soz. in Hist. Eccles. Script. Amst. 1695-1700. Lib. VII.
cap. xix. p. 596.]

[3 Cartwright asks: "Can there be plainer words to prove that the archdeacon
was no minister, than those whereby Sozomen putteth difference between an archdeacon, and an elder, making them several members?" He afterwards cites other
authorities to shew "that the archdeacon was not a priest, but a deacon."—Sec.
Repl. pp. 502, 3.]

[4 Ex Concil. Urban. II. hab. Placent. in Corp. Jur. Canon. Lugd. 1624.
Decret. Gratian. Decr. Prim. Pars, Dist. lxx. can. 2. col. 348. See Vol. I. page 480,
note 1. See also above, note 2.]

[5 "It is a simple exception against the council of Urban, that 'it is not to be
found in the tome of councils', especially when I cite it but for a story witness;

Chapter ii.   The Thirty-fourth Division.

T. C. Page 73, Sect. 3.

Jerom. to   *They were chosen by all the deacons of the church where*
Evagr.   *they be archdeacons*[6]*: ours are appointed by one man, and*
which is no deacon.

Jo. Whitgift.

There can be no such custom gathered of Hierome's words
in that place : only he, using an example to declare what the
manner of choosing their bishop was in the church of Alexandria, saith that " they elected one from among themselves,
whom they placing in an higher room called him a bishop ; as
if the soldiers should choose their captain, or deacons should
choose one of them whom they know to be painful, and name
him archdeacon." You can no more hereof conclude that it
was then usual for deacons to choose their archdeacon, than
you may that it was also usual for soldiers to choose their
captain ; neither can you hereby prove that our archdeacons
are not like unto theirs (if this were true), no more than you
can, that our captains are not like unto theirs, because the
soldiers do not choose them. But what great matter is it if
they were then chosen by deacons, and be not so now ? and
doth not the bishop appoint them ? and is not the bishop more
than a deacon ?

Chapter ii.   The Thirty-fifth Division.

T. C. Page 73, Sect. 4.

Conc. Nicen.   *They were subject to the minister of the word*[7]*: ours are*
can. 14. and
after Ruf. 20. above them, and rule over them.

Jo. Whitgift.

There is not one word of archdeacons in the fourteenth
canon of the council of Nice, nor in the 20. after Ruffine ;
and therefore you do but abuse the reader.   That which is

seeing there are some councils of more weight out of that book, than some in it."—
Ibid. p. 503.]

[6 ... presbyteri semper unum ex se electum, in excelsiori gradu collocatum,
episcopum nominabant : quomodo si exercitus imperatorem faciat : aut diaconi,
&c.—Hieron. Op. Par. 1693-1706. Ad Evang. Epist. ci. Tom. IV. Pars 11.
col. 803.   See before, page 173, note 6.]

[7 Concil. Nic. can. 18 [al. 14] in Concil. Stud. Labb. et Cossart. Lut. Par.
1671-2. Tom. II. cols. 37, 49.   This is the canon meant ; but, as Whitgift says,
it makes no mention of archdeacons.]

in that place is spoken of deacons only, and is at this day observed in this church.

Chapter ii.   The Thirty-sixth Division.

T. C. Page 73, Sect. 5.

Untruths; for neither of them speaketh of archdeacons in those places alleged to this purpose.

It was counted to them great arrogancy, if they preferred themselves to any minister or elder of the church[1]: ours will not take the best ministers of the church as their equals.   If therefore archdeacons will have any benefit by the archdeacons of old time, it is meet they should content themselves with that place which they were in.

Jerom. ad Evagr. Aug. Quæst. Novi et Vet. Test. q. 101.

Jo. Whitgift.

No such thing is in that epistle of Hierome : only he speaketh of deacons, touching that matter, whom he also sheweth in the church of Rome to have been in certain points preferred before ministers; neither is there one word of " archdeacons" in that book of Augustine's, but only of deacons. You must learn to make a distinction betwixt an " archdeacon" and a " deacon," and not to make the reader believe that the authors you quote in the margent speak of " archdeacons," when they only speak of " deacons." My witnesses, how few soever they be, are sufficient to withstand this cowardly assault of yours, wherein there is neither strength nor truth.

Chapter ii.   The Thirty-seventh Division.

Answer to the Admonition, Page 67, Sect. 3.

Deans.

Augustine, in his first book *de Moribus Ecclesiæ Catholicæ*, maketh mention of deans and their offices[2].

T. C. Page 73, Sect. 6.

Untruths.

As for the office of a dean, as it is used with us, it is therefore unlawful, for that he being minister hath no several charge or congregation appointed, wherein he may exercise his ministry ; and for that he is ruler and as it were master of divers other ministers in his college, which likewise have no several charges of congregations ; and for that (which is most intolerable) both he himself, oftentimes having a several church or

[1 Cæterum etiam in ecclesia Romæ, presbyteri sedent, et stant diaconi : licet paulatim increbrescentibus vitiis, inter presbyteros absente episcopo sedere diaconum viderim, et in domesticis conviviis, benedictiones presbyteris dare.—Hieron. Op. 1693-1706. Ad Evang. Epist. ci. Tom. IV. Pars II. col. 803.   Conf. August. Op. Par. 1679-1700. Quæst. ex utroq. (Vet. Test. et Nov.) mixt. Quæst. ci. Tom. III. Append. cols. 92, 3.   These Quæstiones are not reputed genuine.]

[2 See below, page 180, note 1.]

benefice (as they call it), is under the colour of his deanship absent from his church, and suffereth also those that are underneath him to be likewise absent from their churches. And, whereas M. Doctor allegeth St Augustine to prove this office to be ancient, indeed the name is there found, but besides the name not one property of that dean which we have. For Augustine, speaking of the monks of those days, saith that the money which they gat with the labour of their hands they gave to their dean, which did provide them meat, and drink, and cloth[3], and all things necessary for them; so that their[4] monks should not be drawn away from their studies and meditations through the care of worldly things: so that this dean which he speaketh of was servant and steward and cater to the monks, and therefore only called dean because he was steward and cater to ten monks. Now let it be seen what Augustine's dean maketh for the dean which is theirs[5], and what faith and trust M. Doctor useth in reciting of the old fathers.

Jo. Whitgift.

All this is but your own fancies taken for principles and grounds. For, first, it is untrue that every minister must of necessity have some "several charge;" as I have declared before[6]. Secondly, it is as untrue that a dean "hath no several charge or congregation wherein to exercise his ministry." For there is no cathedral church without "a congregation and charge." The third that followeth is builded of the same grounds that these two first be, and may as well be spoken against the masterships of such colleges in the universities wherein any preachers or ministers be maintained. Which argueth that you mean the same to colleges that you do to cathedral churches, and that you would have ministers free from subjection. Last of all, that which you say is "most intolerable," you speak without any tolerable reason; for Master dean and his prebendaries do more good both in the church of England generally, and in their several churches particularly, and take more pains in one month than you and your companions (whereof some notwithstanding are content, without doing any duty at all, to enjoy prebends more than one) in one whole year. And, if either Master dean or the prebendaries neglect their duties, there be superiors and laws to reform them.

The place of Augustine proveth the name of a dean: it proveth a college and society, whereof he is dean: it argueth a superiority and government; for he saith they be called

Tractat. iv.

[3 Clothe, Repl. 1.] [4 The, Repl. 2.]
[5 Now, Repl. 2.] [6 See Vol. I. pages 469, &c.]

Deans.

Decani, ideo quod sint denis præpositi[1] *:* " Deans, because
they are set over ten:" it sheweth an office to care and
provide for them, and see that they have all things necessary:
it declareth daily exercise of praying and teaching; for he

Aug. de
Moribus Ec-
clesiæ.

addeth thus : *Conveniunt autem diei tempore extremo de suis
quisque habitaculis, dum adhuc jejuni sunt, ad audiendum
illum patrem, et conveniunt ad singulos patres terna ad
minimum hominum millia : Nam*[2] *etiam multo numerosiores
sub uno agunt*[3] *:* " They come together at night every man
from his lodging, whilst yet they are fasting, to hear that
father; and they come together to every father, three thousand
men at the least; for a great many more live under one. &c."

Now, sir, if God of his singular goodness hath, to the
great and unspeakable benefit of his church, moved the hearts
of princes and men of wealth so to endue such places with
possessions and revenues, that they, having things necessary
provided for them, may bestow that time in studying, praying,
preaching, and other godly exercises, which these that St Augustine speaketh of did in labouring with their hands, is
Master dean's name or office ever the worse? Howsoever it
pleaseth you to term these companies that St Augustine here
speaketh of, yet were they godly societies, and do very aptly
set forth the utility and the antiquity of churches and colleges; the deans and masters whereof have indeed the chief
and special care of all external things pertaining to them,
whether it be lands, provisions, or any thing else that is
necessary; and therefore the liker to " St Augustine's dean;"
and the place more aptly alleged to prove the antiquity of
this name and office. If " Master Doctor" should use no more
" faith in reciting the doctors," than you do, I would he were
whipped at the cross in Cheap[4].

[1] Opus autem suum tradunt eis quos decanos vocant, eo quod sint denis præpositi, ut neminem illorum cura sui corporis tangat, neque in cibo, neque in
vestimento, &c.—August. Op. Par. 1679-1700. De Mor. Eccles. Cathol. Lib. i.
cap. xxxi. 67. Tom. I. col. 710.]

[2] Non, Def. B.]   [3] Id. ibid.; where *ut minimum.*]

[4] Cartwright rejoins that there was great difference between the deans of St
Augustine's time, and those then in the church, the former being monks, and so
not clergymen, nor established in any great town, nor appointed except in order
to provision for meat. He goes on: " Wherefore I will refer myself to the treatises of divers learned men, which have handled that matter ; that I be not compelled here to set upon this vermin, which the Ans. raiseth again from hell, to
help the office of the dean. &c." He afterwards attacks Whitgift for a citation
that he makes in another place from Beza.—Sec. Repl. pp. 504, &c.]

Chapter ii.   The Thirty-eighth Division.

Answer to the Admonition, Page 67, Sect. 4.

Hitherto antichrist had not invaded the church of Rome. But what should I trouble you with any more authorities? those that be learned may easily understand that these names, metropolitan, archbishop, archdeacon, primate, patriarch, and such like, be most ancient and approved of the eldest, best, and worthiest councils, fathers, and writers.

T. C. Page 73, Sect. 7.

And, unto the end that these testimonies might be more authentical and have some weight in them, Master Doctor addeth that hitherto antichrist[5] had not invaded the seat of Rome. You shall have much ado to prove that antichrist had not invaded the see of Rome when your Clement, Anaclete, Anicete, and Damasus wrote; nay, it is most certain that then he had possessed it. But what is that to the purpose, although there was no one singular head appeared or lifted up, yet corruption of doctrine and of the sacraments, hurtful ceremonies, dominion and pomp of the clergy, new orders and functions of the ministry, which were the hands that pulled him, the feet which brought him, the shoulders that lifted and heaved him up into that seat, were in the church. Neither, while you do thus speak, do you seem to remember that this monster needed not nine months, but almost nine hundred years, to be framed and fashioned, or ever he could with all his parts be brought to light. And, although the lover[6] of this antichristian building were not set up, yet, the foundations thereof being secretly and under the ground laid in the apostles' time[7], you might easily know that in those times that you spake[8] of the building was wonderfully advanced and grown very high. And, being a very dangerous thing to ground any order or policy of the church upon men at all, which indeed ought to have their standing upon the doctrine and orders of the apostles, I will shew what great injury M. Doctor doth to send us for our examples and patterns of government to these times which he doth direct us unto.

Jo. Whitgift.

These be but words: the same might be also spoken of the apostles' times. For even then Paul speaking of antichrist said, *Nam mysterium nunc agit iniquitatis:* "For the mystery of iniquity doth already work." And St John said that there

[5 Christ, Def. B.]

[6 Lover, loover, or louver : an open place at the top of the house to let out the smoke.]

[7 Times, Repl. 1 and 2.]   [8 Speak, Repl. 1 and 2.]

1 John ii. then began to be "many antichrists;" but doth this detract anything from the truth taught in that time? or shall we therefore refuse to take such examples of it as is convenient for our time? There is no man of learning and modesty, which will without manifest proof condemn any order, especially touching the government of the church, that was used and allowed during the time of the primitive church, which was the next 500. years after Christ; within the which time most of my authorities are contained. Neither was there any function or office brought into the church during all that time, allowed by any general council or credible writer, which was not most meet for that time, and allowable by the word of God.

I grant that antichrist was working all this time, and grew more and more; for else could there never have been so many sects and heresies from time to time spread in the church, which was the cause of so many singular and notable councils, so many profitable and necessary books, written by such learned and godly doctors, as did with might and main strive against them. Out of the which councils and fathers, as best witnesses what was done in those times, I have fetched my proofs——even out of them, I say, that did with might and main labour to keep out antichrist from the possession of the church, and therefore not to be suspected to consent to antichrist.

Antichrist
worketh in
England by
contentious
persons.

I know that those sects and heresies gave strength unto antichrist, and at the length were one special means of placing him in his throne; even as I am also persuaded that he worketh as effectually at this day by your stirs and contentions, whereby he hath and will more prevail against this church of England than by any other means whatsoever. Therefore it behoveth you to take heed how you divide the army of Christ, which should *unanimiter* fight against that antichrist. As for us, we must follow the examples of those good fathers, and labour accordingly, to restore unity, and to preserve it[1].

[1 Cartwright replies that he appealed "not unto the apostles' times only, but unto the doctrine and order established;" asks "what charter the Answ. can shew, that the first '500. years' (within compass whereof he hath brought his testimonies) be just the time of the primitive church, neither more nor less;" and says that within that time several unmeet functions were brought into the church.— Sec. Repl. pp. 507, &c.]

Chapter ii.   The Thirty-ninth Division.

T. C. Page 73, Sect. ult.

Eusebius out of Egesippus writeth that, " as long as the apostles lived,
Euseb. Lib.
iii. cap. 32.[2] *the church remained a pure virgin; for that, if there were any*
that went about to corrupt the holy rule that was preached,
they did it in the dark, and as it were digging underneath the earth. But,
after the death of the apostles, and that generation was past which God
vouchsafed to hear the divine wisdom with their own ears, then the placing
of wicked error began to come into the church[3]."

Jo. Whitgift.

It is evident in divers places of the scripture, namely, in
the first epistle to the Corinthians, and the epistle to the
Galatians, that there were many gross and great corruptions
openly professed in the church, by divers, not only in
matters, but also in doctrine, even in the apostles' time; and
Eusebius himself declareth that there was one Simon mentioned Acts viii., whom he calleth " the author of all heresy,"
Lib. ii. cap. xiii.[4] Likewise he sheweth, *Lib. iii.*, that Ebion,
Cerinthus, and the Nicholaites, all horrible heretics, were in
the apostles' time[5]. Wherefore, if this be a good reason, then
is it not safe for us to follow, no, not the apostles' time.

Corruptions
in the church
in the apo-
stles' time.

Euseb. Lib. ii.
cap. 13.
Idem, Lib. iii

Chapter ii.   The Fortieth Division.

T. C. Page 74, Sect. 1.

Lib. Stromat.
somewhat
after the
beginning. *Clement also in a certain place, to confirm that there was*
corruption of doctrine immediately after the apostles' time[6],
allegeth the proverb that there are " few sons like their fathers[7]."

[² This marginal reference is not printed in Repl. 1.]

[³ Ἐπὶ τούτοις ὁ αὐτὸς ἀνὴρ ['Ηγήσιππος] διηγούμενος τὰ κατὰ τοὺς δηλουμένους, ἐπιλέγει ὡς ἄρα μέχρι τῶν τότε χρόνων παρθένος καθαρὰ καὶ ἀδιάφθορος ἔμεινεν ἡ ἐκκλησία, ἐν ἀδήλῳ που σκότει φωλευόντων εἰσέτι τότε, τῶν, εἰ καί τινες ὑπῆρχον, παραφθείρειν ἐπιχειρούντων τὸν ὑγιῆ κανόνα τοῦ σωτηρίου κηρύγματος. ὡς δ' ὁ ἱερὸς τῶν ἀποστόλων χορὸς διάφορον εἰλήφει τοῦ βίου τέλος, παρεληλύθει τε ἡ γενεὰ ἐκείνη τῶν αὐταῖς ἀκοαῖς τῆς ἐνθέου σοφίας ἐπακοῦσαι κατηξιωμένων, τηνικαῦτα τῆς ἀθέου πλάνης τὴν ἀρχὴν ἐλάμβανεν ἡ σύστασις, διὰ τῆς τῶν ἑτεροδιδασκάλων ἀπάτης.—Euseb. in Hist. Eccles. Script. Amst. 1695-1700. Lib. iii. cap. xxxii. p. 84.]

[⁴ Πάσης μὲν οὖν ἀρχηγὸν αἱρέσεως, πρῶτον γενέσθαι τὸν Σίμωνα παρειλήφαμεν.—Id. ibid. Lib. ii. cap. xiii. p. 40.]

[⁵ Id. ibid. Lib. iii. capp. xxvii. xxviii. xxix. pp. 79, &c.]

[⁶ Times, Repl. 1 and 2.]

[⁷ Ἀλλ' οἱ μὲν τὴν ἀληθῆ τῆς μακαρίας σώζοντες διδασκαλίας παράδοσιν, εὐθὺς

Jo. Whitgift.

I can find no such thing in Clement[1]; but the matter is not great whether he say so or no. The argument is stark naught; for, if this follow, that we may take no "example," "pattern," or testimony "of government," out of that time, because it was corrupt, then by the same reason must we not take examples of any time, no, not out of the apostles' time, because that was also corrupt, as I have said. Your arguments be passing strong: surely I marvel with what boldness you write them.

Chapter ii. The Forty-first Division.

T. C. Page 74, Sect. 2.

And Socrates saith of the church of Rome and Alexandria, which were the most famous churches in the apostles' times, that about Lib. vii. cap. 11. *the year 430. the Roman and Alexandrian bishops, leaving the sacred function, were degenerate to a secular rule or dominion; whereupon we see that[2] it is safe for us to go to the scriptures and to the apostles' times for to fetch our government and order; and that it is very dangerous to draw from those rivers the fountains whereof are troubled and corrupted, especially when as the ways whereby they run are muddier and more fenny than is the head itself.*

Socrates falsified.

Jo. Whitgift.

You falsify the words of Socrates; for thus he saith: "For even till that time the Novatians flourished marvellously at Rome, and had many churches, and had gathered much people. But envy took hold of them, when as the bishopric of Rome and of Alexandria now a good while was passed beyond the limits of priesthood to an outward dominion[3]."

Socr. Lib. vii. cap. 11.

ἀπὸ Πέτρου τε καὶ Ἰακώβου, Ἰωάννου τε καὶ Παύλου, τῶν ἁγίων ἀποστόλων, παῖς παρὰ πατρὸς ἐκδεχόμενος· ὀλίγοι δὲ οἱ πατράσιν ὅμοιοι· ἧκον δὴ σὺν Θεῷ καὶ εἰς ἡμᾶς τὰ προγονικὰ ἐκεῖνα καὶ ἀποστολικὰ καταθησόμενοι σπέρματα.— Clement. Alex. Op. Oxon. 1715. Stromat. Lib. i. 1. Tom. I. pp. 322, 3.]

[1 Cartwright replies that Clement's place may easily be found.—Sec. Repl. p. 511.]

[2 See how that, Repl. 1 and 2.]

[3 ... ἄχρι γὰρ τούτου, Ναυατιανοὶ μεγάλως ἐπὶ τῆς Ῥώμης ἤνθησαν, ἐκκλησίας πλείστας ἔχοντες, καὶ λαὸν πολὺν συναθροίζοντες· ἀλλ᾽ ὁ φθόνος καὶ τούτων ἥψατο, τῆς Ῥωμαίων ἐπισκοπῆς ὁμοίως τῇ Ἀλεξανδρέων πέρα τῆς ἱερωσύνης ἐπὶ δυναστείαν ἤδη πάλαι προελθούσης. καὶ διατοῦτο, οὐδὲ τοὺς ὁμοφρονοῦντας οἱ ἐπίσκοποι ἐπ᾽ ἀδείας συνάγεσθαι συνεχώρησαν· ἀλλὰ πάντα λαβόντες αὐτῶν, μόνον διὰ τὴν ὁμοφροσύνην ἐπαινοῦσιν αὐτούς. οὐ μὴν οἱ ἐν

He saith not, " leaving the sacred function, were degenerate to a secular rule and dominion ;" as you translate it.

But why doth Socrates burst out into this reprehension of them? even because they expelled the Novatian heretics, of whom Socrates was a fautor[4]; as it may appear in Nicephorus[5]; wherefore he doth in that place affectionately[6] and unjustly reprove both the bishop of Rome, and Alexandria, for stoutly resisting those heretics and expelling them from their churches, especially they now increasing to so great a multitude, as it may seem by Socrates' words they did. And, although the words of Socrates which I have already recited justify this to be true, yet doth his words following declare the same more evidently. For he commendeth the bishop of Constantinople because he friendly entertained the Novatians, and suffered them quietly to remain within the city ; and yet it is certain that the bishop of Constantinople had as large authority as the bishop of Alexandria ; wherefore Socrates in this point is no more to be believed against those bishops, than you are against the bishops in this church, whose authority you malign upon the like occasion.

Socrates a favourer of the Novatians.

Niceph. Lib. vi. cap. 37, & Lib. ix. 13.

Socrates' doings agreeable to our time.

Chapter ii.   The Forty-second Division.

T. C. Page 74, Sect. 3, 4.

And, although M. Doctor hath brought neither scripture, nor reason, nor council wherein there is either name of archbishop or archdeacon, or proved that there may be ; and although he shew not so much as the name of them four hundred years after our Saviour Christ ; and although where he sheweth them they be either by counterfeit authors, or without any word of approbation of good authors ; yet, as though he had shewed all and proved all, having shewed nothing nor proved nothing, he clappeth the hands to himself, and putteth the crown upon his own head, saying that " those that be learned may easily understand that the names, archbishop, archdeacon, primate, patriarch, be most ancient, and approved of

Where is truth become?

Would you have better approbation than decrees for their authority, and continual practice?

Κωνσταντίνου πόλει τοῦτο πεπόνθασιν· ἀλλὰ μετὰ τοῦ στέργειν αὐτοὺς, καὶ ἔνδον πόλεως συνάγειν εἴασαν.—Socr. in Hist. Eccles. Script. Amst. 1695-1700. Lib. VII. cap. xi. pp. 283, 4.]

[4 "... a proof of the light esteem of authors which make against him."—Sec. Repl. p. 511.]

[5 ... Σωκράτης ὁ ἐκ Ναυάτου τὰ ἐκκλησιαστικὰ καὶ αὐτὸς συντάττων, κ. τ. λ.—Niceph. Call. Eccles. Hist. Lut. Par. 1630. Lib. VI. cap. xxxvii. Tom. I. p. 436. Conf. Lib. IX. cap. xiii. p. 700.]

[6 Affectionately : warmly, or partially.]

the eldest, best, worthiest councils, fathers, writers;" and, a little afterward,
that they are " unlearned and ignorant" which say otherwise.

Vanity.

Here is a victory blown with a great and sounding trumpet, that might
have been piped with an oaten straw : and, if it should be replied again,
that M. Doctor hath declared in this little learning, little reading, and
less judgment, there might grow controversies without all fruit.

JO. WHITGIFT.

If I were not acquainted with this spirit, it would make
me muse at such evident and manifest untruths, joined with
so profane jests and taunts. If I had alleged no more
authorities but only the council of Nice, it had been sufficient
to have disproved this so bold assertion of yours. But, seeing
I have alleged other testimonies also, which evidently prove
my purpose, I must needs think you not to be a man that
greatly careth for your own credit ; but, if you think they are
few, and therefore account them for none, I have now, I trust,
in this chapter, 25. division, supplied their want, and made up
the number[1].

What "scriptures" I have appeareth afterwards. It is
sufficient if I find there the office of an archbishop, as I doubt
not but I shall ; and therefore I say again, that to doubt of
the antiquity of these names and offices argueth great penury
of reading the ancient writers.

Chapter ii. The Forty-third Division.

Answer to the Admonition, Page 67, Sect. 4.

And, forasmuch as the original and beginning of
these names, metropolitan, archbishop, archdeacon, primate, patriarch, and such like[2] (such is their antiquity),
cannot be found (so far as I have read), it is to be supposed they[3] have their original from the apostles themselves. For, as I remember, St Augustine hath this rule

August.

in his 118. *Epist. ad Januar.:* "Those things that be
not expressed in the scriptures[4], and yet by tradition
observed of the whole church, come either from the
apostles, or from general councils ; as the observing of

[1 See before, pages 157, &c.]

[2 The clause from *names* is not in Answ.]

[3 Supposed that they, Answ.]   [4 Scripture, Answ.]

Easter, the celebrating of the day of the Ascension, and of the coming of the Holy Ghost, and such like[5]." [☞ And in his book *De Baptis. contra Donatistas, Lib. iv.*: *Quod universa tenet ecclesia, nec conciliis institutum, sed semper retentum est, non nisi auctoritate apostolica traditum rectissime creditur*[6]: "That which the whole church doth hold, not being appointed by councils, and yet is always observed, it is truly to be believed that it is no otherwise appointed than by the authority of the apostles." But these names and offices have been always generally observed of the whole church; neither is it to be found where they were first appointed in any council; therefore no doubt the apostles appointed them: &c. ☞]][7] Very unlearned therefore and ignorant be those which so boldly affirm that these names used in the purest time of the church be antichristian.

T. C. Page 74, Sect. 4, 5.

And, by and by, in saying that the archbishop's beginning is unknown, instead of a bastard which some brought into the church that hid themselves Modesty. *because they were ashamed of the child, he will make us believe that we have a new Melchisedec, without father, without mother, and whose generation is not known, and so concludeth with the place of St Augustine, as far as he remembereth, in the* 118. *epistle to Januarie, that the original of them is from the apostles themselves.*

Here M. Doctor seemeth to seek after some glory of a good memory, This is from *as though he had not Augustine by him when he wrote this sentence; and* the matter. *yet he marvellously forgetteth himself, for he used this place before in his* 23. *page, and citeth it there precisely and absolutely; where also I have shewed how unadvisedly that sentence of Augustine is approved, and how that thereby a window is open to bring in all popery and whatsoever other corrupt opinions. That the names of lords and honour as they are used in this realm are not meet to be given to the ministers of the gospel, there hath been spoken before.*

Jo. Whitgift.

This place of Augustine is of greater force and credit with those that be learned, than that it can be shifted off. I have answered whatsoever you say against it in that place, and shewed of what credit it is with some famous writers of

[5 August. Op. Par. 1679-1700. Ad Inq. Januar. Lib. i. seu Epist. liv. cap. i. 1. Tom. II. col. 124. See Vol. I. page 230, note 4.]

[6 Id. de Bapt. contr. Donatist. Lib. iv. cap. xxiv. 31. Tom. IX. col. 140.]

[7 The sentences between brackets are inserted from Answ. 2.]

our time, namely, with Master Zuinglius, Master Calvin, and
Master Gualter[1]. And surely I think no learned man doth
dissent from them.

Your jests are too usual and unseemly for a divine,
especially when you abuse the scripture to make sport withal.
I might have said also of you, that you "sought after some
glory of a good memory," when as you used the like kind of
speech in alleging of Gildas and Lombard, page 68,[2] but that
I am not delighted with such kind of eloquence.

Pag. 68,
Sect. 4.

Chapter ii.   The Forty-fourth Division.

Answer to the Admonition, Page 65, Sect. 5.

Civil offices
given to ec-
clesiastical
persons[3].

Whether that the name of prelate of the garter,
earl, county palatine, honour, high commissioner, justice
of peace and quorum, being necessary offices in this
commonweal, partly for the honour of the prince and
realm, but especially for good[4] government of all estates[5]
and degrees of persons, be antichristian, let those consider to whom God hath committed the sword of government: such insolent audacity against states and
lawful regiment is rather to be corrected with due punishment than confuted by argument.

T. C. Page 74, Sect. 6, 7, 8.

*As for prelate of the garter, if it be a needful office, there are enow to
execute it besides the ministers, which forasmuch as they be appointed to
watch over the souls of men purchased with the blood of Christ, all men
understand that it is not meet that they should attend upon the body, much
less upon the leg, and least of all upon the garter. It is not unlawful for
princes to have ministers of their honour, but also it is not lawful to take
those that God hath appointed for another end to use to such purposes.*

Untruth.

*Thou seest here, good reader, that M. Doctor keepeth his old wont, of
manifest perverting of the words and meaning of the authors of the Admonition. For, whereas they say that the name of earl, county palatine,
justice of peace and quorum, commissioner, are antichristian, when they
are given to the ministers[6] of the church, whose calling will not agree with
such titles, he concludeth simply, that they say they[7] be altogether unlawful
and simply antichristian; as if I should reason that it is not meet that*

[1 See Vol. I. pages 230, &c., 286, 7.]   [2 See before, page 127.]
[3 Civil offices given to prelates, Answ. 2.]
[4 For the good, Answ.]   [5 States, Answ.]
[6 To ministers, Repl. 1 and 2.]   [7 Say that they, Repl. 1 and 2.]

the queen's majesty should preach or minister the sacraments; therefore it
is not meet that there should be any preaching or ministering of the sacra-
ments.

Now, letting pass all your hard words and unbrotherly speeches, with
your uncharitable prognostications and cold prophecies, I will come to
examine whether you have any better hap in proving the office than you
have had [8] *in proving the name.*

Jo. WHITGIFT.

I see no cause why he that is "prelate of the garter"
may not also sufficiently discharge his duty in watching over
the soul; for I think the garter doth not require such continual or great attendance. "Those that are appointed to
watch over the soul" are not exempted from bodily service to
their prince; except you will take from the prince not only
authority in ecclesiastical matters, as you have done, but over
ecclesiastical persons also, as by this and such other like
assertions you seem to do. But hereof more in place. I
"pervert" not "the words of the Admonition," as appeareth
by their manifest words; what their meaning is God knoweth.
But how little authority these offices should have, if your
platform were framed, shall be declared when I come to your
seigniory; neither the names nor offices that come from a
christian prince, that detesteth antichrist, can be called antichristian, upon whomsoever they be bestowed. Whereunto
this your example tendeth of the queen's majesty, wise men
may easily conjecture. It smelleth of that papistical cavillation,
scilicet, that we give to her majesty authority to preach and
to administer the sacraments, because we acknowledge her
lawful authority in ecclesiastical causes.

I pray God my "prognostications" be not too true; the
more I consider of your book, the more I am driven to suspect
it. My "hard speeches" be within the bonds of modesty;
but yours may better beseem the order you talk of than a
man of your profession.

Chapter ii.   The Forty-fifth Division.

Answer to the Admonition, Page 68, Sect. 1, 2.

Lord's grace, lord bishop, honour, &c., be names of
reverence, teaching us to acknowledge our duty towards

[8 You had, Repl. 2.]

our superiors, and their authority over us. And it is
much more to be reprehended not to give honour to
whom honour is due, than to receive honour when it is
due. You may, and[1] you please, in very ancient histories
and in great learned fathers, see as honourable and reverent titles given unto bishops as these be. And surely
it is not antichristian to be called by names and titles
not ambitiously sought for, but orderly and lawfully
given, according to the condition and state of the place
wherein a man is. But it is antichristian, that is, proud,
presumptuous, disdainful, arrogant, and contemptuous,
to refuse to give to every one that name and title that
by law, civility, and duty of us is required, and expresseth our reverence, duty, and obedience.

Titles of dignity[2] in ministers not antichristian.

You would speak as much of names of honour and
reverence in other persons, if you durst be so bold with
them as you think you may be with some.

Jo. WHITGIFT.

Nothing is said to this[3].

The offices of Archbishops, &c., are not strange
or unheard of in Christ's Church: and of superiority
among the clergy[4].

Chapter iii.   The First Division.
Answer to the Admonition, Page 68, Sect. 3, 4;
and Page 69, Sect. 1.

Now it followeth to prove, that the offices signified
by these names are not strange and unheard of in

[1 And, or an: if.]

[2 Dignities, Answ. 2.]

[3 " Thus, after large promises of shewing the great antiquity of these names...
after high words against those which deny the pretended antiquity, after rifling
and ruffling up every dark corner where these great and glorious names might be
hidden, after hell itself hath been moved, and summoned to witness of this
antiquity; it is manifest that these names, nor no one of them, hath hitherto been
shewed in any one council, writer, or story before the council of Nice : &c."—Sec.
Repl. p. 513.]

[4 Before entering on the consideration of this chapter Cartwright says there
are "two questions" which seem "necessary to be decided:" "the one, whether
the word of God hath ordained that in every several congregation there should be a
bishop :" "the other...whether there were allowed in one city 2. or more bishops."
The affirmative of each of these he sets himself to prove at great length.—Ibid.
pp. 514-30.]

Christ's church; neither yet plainly in God's word forbidden; that they are not to be removed, but, as most
necessary, to be retained.

It is without all doubt that both these names and Antiquity of
the offices[5].
offices have been in Christ's church long before Nicene
council, and that they have had, in the same, continuance even to this day; as partly it may be gathered by
that which I have spoken before, and most manifestly
by all histories and learned writers from before that
council of Nice to this instant hour; and therefore
they little considered what they writ, when they set it
down that these names and offices were strange and Offices of
archbishops
unheard of in the church of Christ.   ancient[6].

These men, contemning ancient writers, never read
them; and that is the cause of such unlearned assertions.

T. C. Page 75, Sect. 1.

*And, whereas in the former treatise of the name of the archbishop, he
blew the trumpet before the victory, here in this of the office he bloweth it
before he cometh into the field or striketh one stroke, saying that " they little
consider what they write," that they are " contemners of ancient writers,"
and that they " never read them," and that they are " unlearned" which deny
these things which he affirmeth. Well, what we read, and how unlearned
we are, is not the matter which we strive for: the judgment thereof is first
with God, then[7] with the churches; and in their judgments we are content
to rest. But, if you be so greatly learned, and we so unlearned and smally
read, then the truth of our cause shall more appear that is maintained
with so small learning and reading, against men of such profound knowledge and great reading. And yet I know not why, if we be not too idle,
we should not be able to read as much as you, which may have leisure to
read a good long writer, or ever you can ride only to see and salute your
houses and livings, being so many and so far distant one from another.
And, if we be so unlearned and hold such dangerous opinions of papistry
and anabaptism[8], as you bear men in hand we do, why do you not, by
the example of the ministers in Germany, procure a public disputation,
where you may both win your spurs, and such detestable opinions with the
ignorance of the authors may be displayed unto the whole world? But
let us hear what is said.*

Jo. WHITGIFT.

I have said nothing of the authors of the Admonition,

[5 Antiquity of offices, Answ. 2.]
[6 This marginal note is inserted from Answ. 2.]
[7 God and then, Repl. 1 and 2.]   [8 Anabaptistry, Repl. 1 and 2.]

which their own doings proveth not to be true; and, if you will also take it unto yourself, who can let you. If, notwithstanding all my journeys "to see and salute my houses and livings," I be found to discharge my duty there, and also to have read as much as you that have such leisure, it is at the least an argument that I am not idle. I love not to boast of myself. Your too too arrogant and contemptuous speeches provoke me further than modesty requireth. I am not ashamed of my reading, and yet I will make no comparisons.

Conference offered hath been refused. I have sundry times, both privately and publicly, as I am able to prove by sufficient testimonies, and you cannot deny, offered you conference by writing of these matters; I have earnestly moved you unto it; and you have always refused it. This had been a quiet and the best and most assured way; for litera scripta manet: "That which is set down in writing remaineth." Howbeit I refuse no way that shall be thought convenient to the magistrate, neither am I afraid of your stout brags, for I know what substance is in you; but yet by the way this may be noted, what you hunt after and seek for, when you refuse private conference by writing offered unto you, and cry out for public disputation, scilicet popularem laudem: "popular praise." But therein do you follow the vain brags of other sectaries. &c.

Chapter iii.   The Second Division.

Answer to the Admonition, Page 69, Sect. 2, 3; and Page 70, Sect. 1.

Of the office of an archbishop.[1] Cyprianus, Lib. i. Epist. 3. ad Cornelium, speaking of the office of an archbishop, saith on this sort: Neque enim aliunde hæreses obortæ sunt, aut nata...schismata, quam inde quod sacerdoti Dei non obtemperatur, nec unus in ecclesia ad tempus sacerdos, et ad tempus judex vice Christi cogitatur; cui si secundum magisteria divina obtemperaret fraternitas universa, nemo adversus sacerdotum collegium quicquam moveret[2]: "Neither have heresies nor[3] schisms risen of any other occasion, than of that,

---

[1] Instead of this marginal note Answ. 2 has *Cyprian.*]

[2] Cypr. Op. Oxon. 1682. Ad Cornel. Epist. lix. p. 129; where *adversum sacerdotum collegium quidquam moveret.*]

[3] Or, Answ.]

that the priest of God is not obeyed, neither one priest Cyprian.
for the time in the church, and one judge for the time
in the stead[4] of Christ thought upon; to whom if the
whole brotherhood would be obedient according to
God's teaching, no man would move anything against
the college of priests.

Cornelius, being bishop of Rome, and having ex- Cyprian expounded.
communicated certain notorious wicked men, and afterward being threatened and ill used at their hands,
began to faint and to be weary of his office: Cyprian,
hearing thereof, wrote comfortably unto him, and willed
him in any wise to proceed, shewing further what sects
and schisms ensueth in any province or diocese where as
the bishop's authority is despised. For in these words
he speaketh not of the usurped authority of the bishop
of Rome over all churches, but against the insolency of
some, which, despising their metropolitan or archbishop,
did with their factiousness trouble the church. For he
would have an archbishop in every province, which should
bear the chief rule over the rest of the clergy; and so
do the godliest and best-learned expound Cyprian.

The same Cyprian, writing to one Florentius Pu- Authority of archbishops.
pianus, speaking in his own behalf being bishop of
Carthage, saith on this sort: *Unde schismata et hæreses
obortæ sunt et oriuntur, [nisi] dum episcopus qui unus est,
et ecclesiæ præest, superba quorundam præsumptione con-
temnitur, et homo dignatione Dei honoratus ab hominibus
indignis judicatur*[5]? "From whence have heresies and
schisms sprung heretofore, and whereof spring they now,
but that the bishop, which is one and governeth the
church, by the presumptuous disdain of certain is despised, and a man preferred by God's allowance is
examined and judged by unworthy men." For it is
the chief and principal office of an archbishop to keep
unity in the church, to compound contentions, to re-
dress heresies, schisms, factions, to see that bishops,
and all other of the clergy which be under him do their
duty, &c.

[4 Instead, Answ.]
[5 Inde enim schismata &c. indignus ab hominibus judicatur.—Id. ad Florent.
Pup. Epist. lxvi. p. 167.]

T. C. Page 75, Sect. 2, 3.

Cyprian.

"Cyprian," saith he, "speaking of the office of an archbishop, &c."

This is rather to make sport than to confute.

Unless, good reader, thou wilt first believe that Cyprian speaketh of an archbishop, and hast before conceived a strong imagination of it, M. Doctor can prove nothing. Aristotle saith that uncunning painters write the names of the beasts which they paint in their tables, for because otherwise it could not be known what they paint[1]: so M. Doctor, mistrusting that the archbishop will not be known by his description, writeth first the name of that he will paint out.

This is it which we strive about, whereof the controversy is ; and this M. Doctor taketh for granted. He accuseth the authors of the Admonition for faulting in the petition of the principle, or desiring to have that granted which is denied ; and yet I am sure that in the whole Admonition there is not such a gross petition as this is. Where or in what words doth St Cyprian speak of the office of an archbishop ?

Jo. Whitgift.

The principal office of an archbishop.

It is the chief and principal office of the archbishop, to provide that peace and unity be kept in the church, to suppress schisms and heresies, &c. This doth Cyprian in this place signify in plain words.

That he meaneth of an archbishop and metropolitan, though he express not the name, it is evident by his words ; for, in the first place, he speaketh of Cornelius, then bishop of Rome, who had government over that whole province. And, in the second place, he speaketh of himself, who had a very

Cyprian a metropolitan.

ample and large jurisdiction. For, being bishop of Carthage, he had the charge and oversight in[2] the churches in Afric, in Numidia, and in both the Mauritanies ; as he himself doth testify, *Lib. iv. Epist.* 8.[3] And, as I have before shewed out of Gregory Nazianzene[4], he did not only rule the church of Carthage, but also of Afric, of Spain, and almost of the

Cap. ii. Div. 25.

whole east parts ; for the which cause Illyricus, as I also said before, doth call him metropolitan[5]. And therefore I have truly affirmed that in those places he speaketh of the office of a metropolitan or archbishop ; neither is this a "petition of

[1 ...ἀλλὰ καθάπερ τὰ τῶν ἀρχαίων γραφέων, εἰ μή τις ἐπέγραψεν, οὐκ ἂν ἐγνωρίζετο τί ἐστιν ἕκαστον.—Aristot. Op. Lut. Par. 1629. Topic. Lib. VI. cap. ii. Tom. I. p. 243.]   [2 Of, Def. A.]

[3 Cypr. Op. Oxon. 1682. Ad Cornel. Epist. xlviii. p. 91. See before, page 164, note 5.]

[4 Gregor. Naz. Op. Par. 1778-1840. Orat. xxiv. 12. Tom. I. p. 445. See before, page 164, note 6.]

[5 Fuit metropolitanus Carthaginensis.—Catalog. Test. Genev. 1608. col. 118. Conf. Centur. Eccles. Hist. Basil. 1560, &c. Cent. III. cap. vii. col. 159.]

the principle," but a true principle; but it is strange to see how you forget yourself; for afterwards, in the 95. page of your book, you acknowledge that Cyprian was a metropolitan bishop, which sufficiently justifieth my second place out of Cyprian[6].

Cyprian.

Pag. 95, sect. 2.

Chapter iii.   The Third Division.
T. C. Page 75, Sect. 3.

And here by the way it is to be observed of the reader, how near akin the pope and the archbishop be. For this office is confirmed by the same places that the pope's is. The places and arguments which are brought against him are soluted with the same solutions that they use which maintain the papacy. For these places of Cyprian be alleged for the pope's supremacy; and indeed they make as much for the pope as the[7] archbishop. For, although they be two heads, yet they stand upon one neck; and therefore the reformed churches which cut right did strike them both[8] off at one blow.

Truly.

Falsely.

Indeed you know this is untrue.

Jo. Whitgift.

This argueth either wilful ignorance, or professed malice; for you cannot but know that Cyprian meaneth of the subjection that ought to be given to Cornelius in his own province, and that the papists wrest the same to prove his universal jurisdiction over all Christendom. Now, if a man may not allege that truly, according to the true sense and meaning of the author, which the papists abuse to serve their turn, then must we abstain from alleging divers places of the scripture.

It is true that the papists use this place "for the pope's supremacy," but falsely; for Cyprian only meaneth of the superiority of metropolitan or bishop in his province or diocese. And the papists themselves have given over their hold, that they took of those places of Cyprian, confessing that he meant of every several bishop in his own diocese or province; as appeareth in Dorman's and Harding's latter books, and others. And is this kind of reason so "near akin" to the papists, which utterly overthroweth one of their strongest arguments? Surely I marvel that your desire is so much to write against the person, that in the mean time you neglect

[6 Cartwright denies that the authorities which Whitgift cites bear out his assertions, and says that "the jurisdiction bishops had in times past, out of their certain congregations, was nothing but a reverent estimation, purchased by opinion of singular learning, and godliness, whereby others willingly would both ask and follow their advice, in government of their churches."—Sec. Repl. pp. 530, &c.]

[7 As for the, Repl. 2.]

[8 *Both* is not in Def. B.]

Cyprian.

the common cause, and give strength as much as lieth in you to the reason of the adversary, whilst you say that this place "maketh as much for the pope as it doth for the archbishop." But the truth of this your reply shall appear when I have answered your other cavils.

Chapter iii.   The Fourth Division.

T. C. Page 75, Sect. 3.

In neither of the sentences here alleged out of Cyprian, nor in all his works, as hath been before noted, is there one word of an archbishop; and yet M. Doctor saith that he speaketh of an archbishop. Before he sheweth[1] the name without the office, and now he goeth about to shew the office without the name; so that he can never make both the name and the office[2] meet together. To shape out an archbishop here, you must needs interpret the words "bishop" and "priest" archbishop and high priest; for Cyprian maketh mention of no other name of ministry in those places. And, if you may have this scope of interpreting, it will not be hard for you to prove that stones be bread, and that chalk is cheese.

Jo. Whitgift.

Epiphanius.

Conc. Chalced.

Epiphanius, *Lib. ii. Tom. 2. hær.* 69., doth call the bishop of Alexandria sometime bishop, and sometime archbishop[3]. The council of Chalcedon in like manner calleth the same men, as Flavianus, Dioscorus, Leo, and other, sometimes bishops, and sometimes archbishops[4]: the like is to be seen in other authors and writers. So that the omitting of the title is no reason at all to disprove the thing. It is certain that in Cyprian's time the name *papa* was a common name to many bishops, those especially that were of fame; as M. Fox at large declareth, Tom. i. fol. 11.[5] And yet doth not Cyprian use that title commonly when he writeth to Cornelius, or to any other bishop. This therefore is but a feeble argument.

Chapter iii.   The Fifth Division.

T. C. Page 75, Sect. 3.

Let us see what is a bishop or priest; I use the name of priest against my will; but, because it is sacerdos, *and you so translate it, that it may*

[1 Shewed, Repl. 1, 2, and Def. A.]   [2 And office, Repl. 1 and 2.]
[3 Epiph. Op. Par. 1622. Adv. Hær. Lib. ii. Tom. ii. Hær. lxix. 3, &c. Tom. i. pp. 729, &c.]
[4 Concil. Calched. Act. i. in Concil. Stud. Labb. et Cossart. Lut. Par. 1671-2. Tom. IV. cols. 148, 9, 52, &c.]
[5 Fox, Acts and Monuments, Lond. 1684. Vol. I. p. 9.]

better be[6] understanded what I answer to you, I am content to follow you so far. I say, let us consider what is a bishop or priest by St Cyprian, and thereby we shall know what an archbishop he setteth forth unto us, which thing may appear manifestly, by that which he saith in the same epistle, that "the bishop that is appointed into the place of him that is dead is chosen peaceably, by the voice of all the people[7]." I think you will not say that all the people throughout the whole province, or throughout a whole diocese (as we count a diocese) met together; for that had been both a great disorder and confusion, a great charge to the church, and, in the time of persecution as that was, to have offered the whole church in all the province into the mouth of the wolf.

Jo. Whitgift.

If you had read ecclesiastical histories, then should you understand that the metropolitans and bishops of every province and diocese were chosen in the presence of the people of that place and city whereof they had their names, and that the consent of no other of the people in that province or diocese was required[8]. So Cyprian himself, though he had so ample a charge as I have shewed before, yet was he chosen only by the people of Carthage. The same is to be seen also in other such elections ; and especially of the bishop of Rome, after that he was in his greatest glory. And therefore this is a poor argument : the bishop of Rome, or of Carthage, were chosen by the consent of the citizens only, and not of the people in other places of the province ; *ergo*, their authority and jurisdiction extended no farther than these cities. And yet the whole diocese, that is, the Christians in the diocese (such I mean as were appointed for that purpose), might have met in that time without peril, or any other such inconvenience as you speak of, for such a purpose, as well as they did in the same time to synods, which were frequent both in Cyprian's time and before.

Chapter iii.   The Sixth Division.

T. C. Page 75, Sect. ult.

And, lest peradventure you should have this hole to hide yourself in,

[6 Be better, Repl. 1 and 2.]

[7 Cæterum...quando episcopus in locum defuncti substituitur, quando populi universi suffragio in pace deligitur, &c.—Cypr. Op. Oxon. 1682. Ad Cornel. Epist. lix. p. 130.]

[8 "Which is a gross answer. For, although the stories of later times (wherein it is not denied but these offices were) make such mention, yet what is that to our cause ? whose controversy is whether it were so in Cyprian's times, as in times that followed."—Sec. Repl. p. 534.]

saying that it might be procured that in every church or parish through-out either the province or diocese, the consent of the people might be asked, and they tarry in their places where they dwell, Cyprian in the next epistle doth put the matter out of all question, saying that "the priest" (whom he after calleth bishop) "is chosen in the presence of the people, and in the eyes of all." So that Cyprian's bishop, whom you will needs have an arch-bishop, had neither province nor diocese as we call a diocese, but only a church or congregation, such as the ministers and pastors with us, which are appointed unto several towns; which may further appear in that Cyprian saith that out of one province there were ninety bishops which condemned Privatus[1]. Now, if there were ninety bishops in one province met[2], and yet not all that were in that province (as may appear out of the same epistle), all men do understand that the scope, that Cyprian's bishop or archbishop, as you will have him, had, was no such thing as a diocese or a province. I could bring infinite testimonies out of Cyprian to prove that the bishop in his time was nothing else but St Paul's bishop, that is, one that had cure and charge of one flock, which was so placed as it might be taught of him, and overseen by him, and governed by him, and of whom in matters pertaining to God it might depend.

Jo. Whitgift.

Your proofs go very low when you use such slender ones : the words of Cyprian in that epistle be these : *Quod et ipsum videmus de divina auctoritate descendere, ut sacerdos, plebe præsente, sub omnium oculis deligatur, &c.[3]:* "The which thing we see to descend from the authority of God, that the priest be chosen, the people being present, before them all, &c." What can you else gather of this, but that a priest must be chosen in presence of the people, and that then he is said to be chosen *sub omnium oculis:* "before all their eyes," when he is chosen publicly and openly in the sight of many. But what is this to the straitening of his charge? A man might as well reason thus : All the citizens of Rome were not at Cornelius' election; therefore he is not bishop of all the city of Rome[4]. But, to the end that you may understand the vanity of this your assertion, and that it may appear that Cyprian maketh the bishop in degree to be above a priest, and also that at the election of the bishop of Rome more were

[1 See below, pages 200, 1, note 1.]

[2 Province which met, Repl. 2.]

[3 Cypr. Op. Oxon. 1682. Ad. Cler. Hisp. Epist. lxvii. pp. 171, 2.]

[4 " I have no where ' reasoned that one should not be rightly chosen bishop, if any be absent that have interest in the election:' my reason is that, forsomuch as all the people of Cyprian's bishop was by the ecclesiastical discipline ap-pointed to be present at his choice, and by no good order of discipline the whole diocese or province could be so appointed, therefore the whole people of Cyprian's bishop was neither the people of a diocese nor province."—Sec. Repl. p. 537.]

present than those of the city, I will set down his words as Cyprian. they be, *Lib. iv. Epist.* 2: "I come now unto the person of our fellow Cornelius, that you may more truly know him, as well as we, not by the lies of malicious men and backbiters, but by the judgment of God, which made him bishop, and by the testimony of his fellow-bishops, the whole number whereof through all the world did jointly agree.   For (which thing did greatly commend our well-beloved Cornelius unto God, and to Christ, and his church, and also to all his fellow-ministers) he did not suddenly come to the bishopric, but, being promoted by all the ecclesiastical offices, he ascended to the high dignity of priesthood by all degrees of religion. Then afterward he neither desired nor would have the bishopric itself, neither, as others use which are puffed up with pride and arrogancy, did he invade the see by force; but, being quiet and modest, and such a one as they use to be which are chosen unto this place by God, for the moderation of his chaste conscience, and the humbleness of his natural and preserved shamefacedness, he did not (as some men do) use violence, that he might be made bishop, but suffered violence, that he might by compulsion be driven to receive the bishopric.   And he was made bishop of many of our fellow-bishops which were then at Rome, and which sent very honourable and commendable letters unto us of his ordination.   But Cornelius was made bishop by the judgment of God and his Christ, by the testimony almost of all clerks, by the suffrages of the people which was then present, and by the college of the ancient priests and of good men [5]."

Marginal notes:

Cyprian.

Cyp. Lib. iv. Ep. 2.

All the bishops agreed to Cornelius his election.

A bishop above a priest in Cyprian's time.

Cornelius chosen by others than the Romans.

[5 Venio jam nunc, frater carissime, ad personam Cornelii collegæ nostri; ut Cornelium nobiscum verius noveris, non de malignorum et detrahentium mendacio, sed de Domini Dei judicio, qui episcopum fecit; et coëpiscoporum testimonio, quorum numerus universus per totum mundum concordi unanimitate consensit. Nam, quod Cornelium carissimum nostrum Deo, et Christo et ecclesiæ ejus, item consacerdotibus cunctis laudabili prædicatione commendat; non iste ad episcopatum subito pervenit, sed per omnia ecclesiastica officia promotus, et in divinis administrationibus Dominum sæpe promeritus, ad sacerdotii sublime fastigium cunctis religionis gradibus ascendit.   Tum deinde episcopatum nec ipse postulavit, nec voluit, nec ut ceteri, quos arrogantiæ et superbiæ suæ tumor inflat, invasit; sed quietus et modestus, et quales esse consueverunt, qui ad hunc locum divinitus eliguntur, pro pudore virginalis conscientiæ suæ, et pro humilitate ingenitæ sibi et custoditæ verecundiæ, non ut quidam, vim facit ut episcopus fieret; sed ipse vim passus est, ut episcopatum coactus exciperet.   Et factus est episcopus a plurimis collegis nostris, qui tunc in urbe Roma aderant, qui ad nos literas honorificas, et laudabiles, et testimonio suæ prædicationis illustres de ejus

In these words first it is to be noted that he saith Cornelius was made bishop "by the testimony of his fellow-bishops; *quorum numerus universus per totum mundum concordi unanimitate consensit:* the whole number whereof through all the world did jointly agree." Secondly, that he was promoted "to the high dignity of priesthood, *per omnia ecclesiastica officia et cunctis religionis gradibus:* through all ecclesiastical offices, and by all degrees of religion;" and then afterward was "made bishop." Thirdly, that Cornelius was made bishop "by the judgment of God and Christ, by the testimony almost of all clerks, and by the suffrages of the people which was then present, and by the college of ancient priests and good men." How far these things differ from your collections, and how far from Cyprian's meaning you gather your conjectures, let the reader judge. I have before sufficiently proved by ancient testimonies, that the bishop of Rome, Carthage, and other, had not one city only to govern, or one parish, but divers places, whole provinces and countries; as Cyprian's own words before rehearsed maketh manifest. Wherefore all this you do but speak of pleasure.

If you had told me in what place "Cyprian saith that out of one province there was 90. bishops that condemned Privatus," I would have said something to it; but, seeing you have kept the place secret to yourself, you give your reader occasion to suspect, either that it is forged, or else not faithfully alleged. If it be that which is *Lib. i. Epist.* 3, then, truly, *antiquum obtines.* For these be Cyprian's words:

Per Fœlicianum autem significavi tibi, frater, venisse Carthaginem Privatum veterem hœreticum, in Pambesitana colonia, ante multos fere annos, ob multa et gravia delicta, 90. *episcoporum sententia condemnatum, antecessorum etiam nostrorum (quod et vestram conscientiam non latet) Fabiani et Donati literis severissime notatum,* &c.[1]: "I have signified unto you by Felicianus, that Privatus, an old heretic, is come to Carthage, being condemned in the city Pambesia many years since, for many and grievous trespasses, by the sentence of 90. bishops, and being also most sharply reprehended by the

ordinatione miserunt. Factus est autem Cornelius episcopus de Dei et Christi ejus judicio, de clericorum pene omnium testimonio, de plebis quæ tunc affuit suffragio, et de sacerdotum antiquorum et bonorum virorum collegio.—Cypr. Op. Oxon. 1682. Ad Anton. Epist. lv. pp. 103, 4.]

[1 Id. ad Cornel. Epist. lix. p. 132; where *Lambesitana colonia.*]

letters of my predecessors, Fabianus and Donatus (as your Cyprian. conscience knoweth)."

Here is not one word of so many bishops being in one province, neither yet any province or diocese mentioned wherein they should be.   Surely this is too much, so often to offend in falsifying². But, be it there were so many bishops in one province, what conclude you thereof, that bishops then had but one town or parish limited unto them? As though there be not provinces of that largeness that they may contain so many bishops, and yet the several parishes furnished with peculiar pastors. Massæus, *Lib. xvi.*, saith that there are 160. bishoprics subject to the patriarch of Antioch³.

But there can no such thing as you affirm be gathered of Cyprian's words; neither shall you ever be able to prove out of Cyprian, or any other ancient writer, that such bishops as Cyprian and Cornelius were had only government of one town, or, as we call it, parish; but the contrary is most evident, as I have before declared.

Chapter iii.   The Seventh Division.
T. C. Page 76, Sect. 1.

Furthermore, to shape the archbishop by these places of Cyprian, you must be driven to expound this word "church" province. The papists which cite this place for the pope as you do for the archbishop, they expound the word "church" here to be the whole church universal and catholic. And indeed, although it be falsely expounded so in this place, yet may they do it with more probability and likelihood, than to expound it a province; forsomuch as these words, "the church," is oftener read both in the scripture and old writers to signify the whole church than any province of one realm. But let Cyprian expound himself what he meaneth by a church here; although that may easily appear by that which is spoken of St Cyprian his bishop. Where as Cyprian declareth that Cornelius the bishop of the church which was in Rome would not let Felicissimum, a Novatian heretic, being cast out by the bishops of Afric, to enter into

[² "... the truth is, Cyprian saith not they were of one province. But, forsomuch as Privatus was of the same province with Cyprian, and controversies rising in every province were for the most part voided by bishops of the same; unless a general council can be shewed, a provincial is presumed. Beside that, it is unlike that Cyprian, to the intent he might draw Privatus into greater hatred, would have omitted that circumstance of general council, if it had been."—Sec. Repl. pp. 538, 9.]

[³ ...liberaverunt...Antiochiam, quæ sub se habuit olim centum sexaginta episcopatus, in se vero 360. ecclesias.—Massæ. Chronic. Libr. Antv. 1540. Lib. XVI. p. 225.]

the church, he declareth sufficiently that he meaneth that company of the faithful which were gathered together at Rome, to hear the word, and to communicate at the sacraments.   For it was not Cornelius' part to shut him out of the province; neither indeed could he himself, being not able without hazard, by reason of the persecution that then was, to tarry in any part of the province.   Again, speaking against the Novatian heretic, he sheweth that, through his wicked opinion of denying of repentance to those that were fallen, the confession of faults in the church was hindered. Now it is manifest that confession was not made throughout the province, but in that particular church where the party dwelt that committed the fault. Therefore Cyprian understandeth by the name of "the church" neither diocese, as we call diocese, and much less a whole province.   And in the same epistle, speaking of those which had fallen, he saith that they durst not come so much as to the threshold or entry of the church; where he also opposeth the church to the province, saying that they rove about the province, and run about to deceive the brethren[1].

Jo. Whitgift.

I expound "this word church" in this place no otherwise than all learned writers expound it, that is, for that province and diocese whereof Cornelius was bishop; and it is no unaccustomed thing to call the church which is extended through a province by the name of the chief city or metropolitan seat of the province; as the church of Rome, all that that is subject to the bishop of Rome; the church of Carthage, all that that is belonging to the bishop of Carthage.   And this is truly to expound the places of Cyprian, and may be justified both by examples and authorities; as I have proved before; whereas your interpretation hath no shadow or shew

of truth.   But you had rather justify the papists' interpretation, than seem to relent to the authority of an archbishop. Such is your zeal.

Cyprian's words touching Cornelius' dealing with Felicissimus the Novatian be these: "Likewise that thou mightest know of Felicissimus, the author of the sedition; who also is contained in the letters of our fellow-bishops, written of late unto thee; which Felicissimus is not only driven from hence by them, *sed abs te illic nuper de ecclesia pulsus est:* but is there of late expelled by thee out of the church[2]."   Of

---

[1 Denique quia conscientiam suam norunt, nec nos audent adire, aut ad ecclesiæ limen accedere; sed foris per provinciam circumveniendis fratribus, et spoliandis pererrant: &c.—Cypr. Op. Oxon. 1682. Ad Cornel. Epist. lix. p. 138. Felicissimus and his companions are here meant.]

[2 ... item Felicissimum signiferum seditionis recognosceres, qui et ipse in

these words you gather this argument: Cyprian signifieth Cyprian.
that Cornelius had banished Felicissimus from the church of
Rome; *ergo,* Cornelius was bishop but of one parish or city;
or, therefore a church in that place signifieth one only particular congregation to gather[3] together in one town.   What
kind of conjectures call you these?   And what though " Cornelius could not shut him out of the province?" might he not
therefore by excommunication seclude him from the congregation of the faithful throughout the province? do you think
that he forcibly shut him out of the local church of Rome, or
rather dealt with him according to the ecclesiastical censures?
You may delude simple readers that believe whatsoever you
say; but such as be able to examine your doings cannot (if
they will search) but find passing forgery.

  Again, you say, " speaking against the Novatian heretics,
&c."   Cyprian's words touching that matter be these: *Quibus* Ibidem.
etiam non satis fuit ab evangelio recessisse, spem lapsis The Novatian
heresy.
satisfactionis et pœnitentiæ sustulisse, fraudibus involutos
vel adulteriis commaculatos, et sacrificiorum funesta con-
tagione pollutos, ne Deum rogarent, ne in ecclesia exomolo-
gesin criminum facerent, ab omni sensu et fructu removisse[4]:
" To whom it was not enough to have departed from the
gospel, to have taken away hope and satisfaction and repentance from those that have fallen, to have removed from
all feeling and fruit of repentance those that are taken in
snares, or defiled with adulteries, or polluted with deadly
contagion of sacrifices, that they should not pray to God, nor
make confession of their sins in the congregation."   What
doth Cyprian else mean by these words, but that Novatus
denied repentance to such as were fallen, and would not
receive them again into the church, that is, not this or that
parish, but the church of Christ, the congregation of the
faithful? For that was Novatus' heresy, *negare veniam lapsis:*
" to deny forgiveness to those that fell."   And therefore also
he denied unto them the fruits of repentance, as confession of
their offences in the congregation of the faithful, &c.   For
Novatus' opinion was not that such should only be secluded
from this or that congregation, but generally from the church

iisdem coëpiscoporum nostrorum factis ad te pridem literis continetur: qui non
tantum ab iis istic abstentus, sed abs te &c.—Id. ibid. Epist. lix. pp. 131, 2.]

 [3 Congregation gathered, Def. A.]

 [4 Id. ibid. p. 135; where *satis non fuit, vel sacrificiorum,* and *omni et sensu*
et fructu pœnitentiæ removisse.]

of Christ and hope of salvation. And therefore in that place of Cyprian is meant that church, *extra quam non est salus:* "without the which there is no salvation."

And to what purpose do you proceed and go on forward, saying that "the same epistle, speaking of those that had fallen, &c.?" What proveth it, but that those heretics had cast them into such a despair of forgiveness, that they durst not offer themselves to be received into the church, that is to repentance; and that the same heretics, being themselves excommunicated, wandered up and down, sowing the pestilent seed of their doctrine? This is to oppose heretics and schismatics (which run up and down in corners) to the true members of the church. But it is not "to oppose the church to the province." For the province (if it be christened) is the church, although it contain in it several congregations, which be also churches, and yet, being members of it, are subject to one bishop; and so doth the whole epistle of Cyprian declare; neither can there anything be gathered out of it to the contrary: for a testimony whereof I call to witness these your weak collections; which you would not have used, if you could have found any better [1].

Chapter iii.   The Eighth Division.
T. C. Page 76, Sect. 2.

A weak conclusion of false principles *Seeing therefore the bishop which Cyprian speaketh of is nothing else but such as we call pastor, or as the common name with us is parson; and his church whereof he is bishop is neither diocese nor province, but a congregation which meet together in one place, and to be taught of one man; what should M. Doctor mean to put on this great name of archbishop upon so small a bishopric? as it were Saul's great harness upon David's [2] little body, or as if a man should set a wide huge porch before a little house.*

JO. WHITGIFT.

Where the premises be naught, how should the conclusion be good? I would to God your argument were in his right form, that we might see upon what substantial posts your conclusion doth stand. But let the reader consider your grounds which I have opened before.

I might here tell you again, that Cyprian in plain and

[1 Cartwright complains that Whitgift boasts in this division of authorities which he does not produce, and goes on to argue at length that the word church could not be applied to a province.—Sec. Repl. pp. 540, &c.]

[2 David his, Repl. 1, 2, and Def. A.]

manifest words, *Lib. iv. Epist.* 2, doth make a bishop superior in *Cyprian.*
degree to him that you call pastor : his words I have repeated
before[3].   I might also put you in mind of Cyprian's jurisdiction over the churches of Carthage, Numidia, and Mau-
ritanie, according to his testimony, *Lib. iv. Epist.* 8[4] ; in which
respect Illyricus doth call him metropolitan[5].   Likewise I
might tell you that the most writers of that age, as Tertullian,
De Coro. Militis, et De Fuga in Pers.[6], Origen, *Hom. 2. in
Numer. et* 11. *in Hierem*[7]., do make three degrees of ministers, deacons, priests, and bishops.   To be short, I could
bid you look Eusebius, *Lib. vi. cap.* 1 ; and you should find
that Demetrius who lived *anno* 191. was bishop *parœciarum
Alexandriæ et Ægypti*[8] : " of the parishes of Alexandria and
Egypt," and refer you to many such examples used before,
which utterly overthrow this conclusion, and even hiss it out
of the doors[9].

Chapter iii.   The Ninth Division.
T. C. Page 76, Sect. 3.

*And, lest that M. Doctor should say that, notwithstanding the bishops
had but several churches, yet one of them might have either a title more
excellent than the rest, or authority and government over the rest; that
shall likewise be considered*[10] *out of Cyprian.   And first for the title and
honour of archbishop, it appeareth how Cyprian held that as a proud*

Lib. iv.   *name, for he objecteth to Florentius*[11] *as a presumptuous thing,*
Epist. 9.   *for that, in believing certain evil reports of him, and misjudg-
ing of him, he did appoint himself* " *bishop of a bishop, and judge over him
which was for the time appointed of God to be judge.*"

[3 Cypr. Op. Oxon. 1682. Ad Anton. Epist. lv. pp. 103, 4. See before pages
199, 200, note 5.]

[4 Id. ad Cornel. Epist. xlviii. p. 91. See before, page 164, note 5.]

[5 See before, page 194, note 5.]

[6 Sed quum ipsi auctores, id est ipsi diaconi, presbyteri, et episcopi fugiunt,
&c.—Tertull. Op. Franek. 1597. De Fug. in Pers. 11. p. 586. Conf. De Cor.
Mil. 9. p. 182.]

[7 Et unde est quod sæpe audimus blasphemare homines, et dicere, ecce qualis
episcopus, aut qualis presbyter, vel qualis diaconus ?—Orig. Op. 1733-59. In
Numer. Hom. ii. 1. Tom. II. p. 278. Conf. in Jerem. Hom. xiv. (al. xi.) 4.
Tom. III. p. 210.]

[8 Euseb. in Hist. Eccles. Script. Amst. 1695-1700. Lib. vi. cap. ii. p. 164. See
before, page 164, note 7.]

[9 Cartwright rejoins: " I would you would ' omit ' nothing which might make
for your purpose ; but I would wish you would not repeat one thing so often."
He goes on to charge Whitgift with having " unfaithfully reported Eusebius."—
Sec. Repl. pp. 542, &c.]

[10 Shall be likewise considered, Repl. 1 and 2.]

[11 The preceding nine words are not printed in Repl. 1 : Repl. 2 has *for that
he objecteth.*]

Jo. Whitgift.

Pupianus, to whom Cyprian wrote that epistle, had greatly misused Cyprian, in believing certain false rumours and reports of him, and upon the same giving sentence against him : for this cause Cyprian reproveth Pupianus, saying : *Quis autem nostrum longe est ab humilitate, utrumne ego, qui quotidie fratribus servio, et venientes ad ecclesiam singulos benigne, et cum voto et gaudio suscipio ; an tu, qui te episcopum episcopi, et judicem judicis ad tempus a Deo dati constituis?* &c.[1] : "Whether of us is further from humility, I, which serve my brethren daily, and receive every one that cometh unto the church gently, and with desire and joy, or thou, which makest thyself the bishop of the bishop, and the judge of the judge given of God for the time ?"   It appeareth rather in these words that Florentius is reproved for taking upon him to judge Cyprian, to whom he ought obedience ; so that this place doth not derogate any thing from any lawful authority that one bishop hath over another, but it condemneth the rash and presumptuous judgment of those that will take upon them rashly to give sentence of their superiors and betters ; as Pupianus did.   For, in that he findeth fault with him, for making himself (as it were) "bishop of the bishop, and judge of the judge," he plainly declareth that he himself was both bishop and judge of Pupianus ; neither doth "he object this to Pupianus as a proud name," but as a proud deed.

Chapter iii.   The Tenth Division.

T. C. Page 76, Sect. 4.

And herein also I may use the same reasons, which the godly writers of our time[2] *use against the pope, to prove that he had no superiority in those days over other bishops, for that the other bishops called him brother, and he them, called him fellow-bishop, and he them.   For so doth Cyprian call the bishops of that province in his epistle his fellow-bishops, and in divers places his brethren*[3]*.   And, in the sentence which he spake in the council of Carthage, he saith : "None of us doth*[4] *take himself to be bishop of bishops."*

[1 Cypr. Op. Oxon. 1682. Ad Florent. Pup. Epist. lxvi. p. 166.]
[2 Times, Repl. 1 and 2.]
[3 Id. ad Januar. et cet. Episc. Num. Epistt. lxii. lxx. ad Nemes. et cet. co-episc. Epist. lxxvi.; ad Cypr. Nemes. et cet. Epist. lxxvii. pp. 146, 89, 230, 4, 5.]
[4 Both, Def. B.]

JO. WHITGIFT.　　　　　　　　　　Cyprian.

Every bishop was chief in his own province, and not subject to any. The bishop of Rome had no jurisdiction over the bishop of Carthage, but they were of equal power and authority; as others were also of the like seats. In that Cyprian called the bishops of his province "fellow-bishops" and "brethren," he declared that the function and ministry was all one; he likewise uttered his humble mind and spirit. But this proveth not that he had no superiority over them. St Peter, in his first epist. chap. v., calleth himself "fellow- 1 Pet. cap. 5. minister" with those whom he then exhorted, which were all pastors, and such as were ministers of the word; and yet you acknowledge an apostle to be the highest in the church, and above all the other degrees mentioned, *ad Eph. iv.*

Cyprian's words in the council of Carthage I have spoken of in another place: he meaneth the title of universal bishop, and such as seek tyrannically and unlawfully to rule, and especially such as will of necessity bind all other men to their opinions in all things; for his words be: *Tyrannico terrore ad obsequendi necessitatem collegas suos adigit[5]:* "None of us enforceth his fellows by tyrannical fear to the necessity of obeying."

Chapter iii.　The Eleventh Division.

T. C. Page 77, Sect. 1.

Now, that there was no authority of one bishop over another, and that there was none such as, when controversies rose, took upon him the compounding of them, or any one to whom it appertained to see the unity of the church kept, and to see that all other bishops and the clergy did their duty, as M. Doctor beareth us in hand, it may clearly be seen in divers places of Cyprian; and first of all in that sentence which he spake in the council of Carthage, where he proceedeth further after this sort, that "none of them did by any tyrannical fear bind his fellows in office, or any fellow-bishops, to any necessity of obedience; seeing that every bishop hath for his free liberty and power his own judgment and[6] discretion, as one which cannot be judged of another, as he also himself cannot judge another; but," saith he, "we ought to tarry and wait for the judgment of our Lord Jesus Christ, which only and alone hath power to set us over his church, and to judge of our doing." And in the same epistle, whereout the first place is taken by M. Doctor, he saith that "unto every one a portion of the flock is appointed, which every one must rule and govern, as he that shall render

[5 Adigat, Editt. See next page, note 3.]　　　[6 Or, Repl. 1 and 2.]

Cyprian. *an account of his deed unto the Lord[1]." And in another place* Lib. ii.
he saith: "We do not use any compulsion or violence over any, Epist. 1.
nor appoint no law to any; seeing that every one that is set over the church
hath in the government the free disposition of his own will, whereof he shall
give an account unto the Lord[2]." And yet Cyprian was the bishop of the
metropolitan or chief seat, and one whom for his learning and godliness
the rest no doubt had in great reverence, and gave great honour unto.

Jo. Whitgift.

The words of
Cyprian dis-
cussed.

Because so much ado is made of the words of Cyprian
in that erroneous council of Carthage, wherein Cyprian himself also was the chief author of the error, I will recite the
Tom. i. Conc.
Carth.
words as I do there find them: *Neque enim quisquam nos-*
trum episcopum se [esse] episcoporum constituit, aut tyran-
nico terrore ad obsequendi necessitatem collegas suos adigit,
cum habeat omnis episcopus licentiam libertatis, et potestatis
suæ arbitrium proprium, tanquam judicari ab alio non
possit, cum nec ipse possit alterum judicare; sed expectemus
universi judicium Domini nostri Jesu Christi, qui unus et
solus habet potestatem, et præponendi nos in ecclesiæ suæ
gubernatione, et de actu nostro judicandi[3]: "Neither doth
any of us make himself bishop of bishops, or enforceth his
fellows to the necessity of obeying by tyrannical fear; because
every bishop hath freedom of liberty and free judgment of
his own power, as he who can be judged of no other, neither
can himself judge another bishop; but let us all wait for the
judgment of our Lord Jesus Christ, who alone hath power
both to place us in the government of the church, and to
judge of our doing."   It were very absurd to think that
Cyprian's words are generally to be understanded of all kind
of judgment, or that a bishop in all things should be left to
his own free liberty and discretion, or that he is free from
all controlment.   For what if he be an heretic? what if he
be otherwise criminous? shall he not be judged by man, but

[1 Nam cum statutum sit omnibus nobis, et æquum sit pariter ac justum, ut
uniuscujusque causa illic audiatur, ubi est crimen admissum, et singulis pastoribus
portio gregis sit adscripta, quam regat unusquisque et gubernet, rationem sui
actus Domino redditurus; oportet utique eos quibus præsumus non circumcur-
sare...sed agere illic causam suam, ubi et accusatores habere et testes sui criminis possint; &c.—Cypr. Op. Oxon. 1682. Ad Cornel. Epist. lix. p. 136.]

[2 See below, page 210, note 1.]

[3 Neque &c. adigit; quando habeat omnis episcopus pro licentia libertatis
et potestatis suæ, arbitrium proprium; tamque judicari ab alio non possit, quam
nec ipse potest judicare. Sed &c.—Ibid. Concil. Carthag. pp. 229, 30.]

left only to the judgment of Christ? The words of Cyprian, *Cyprian.* if they be as you understand them, take authority of judg- *The meaning of Cyprian.* ment as well from synods as from archbishops. Cyprian therefore meaneth, as the words themselves do teach, that one bishop should not tyrannically rule over another, and at his pleasure abridge the liberty of another in uttering his judgment, especially in a synod, or rashly condemn another. For Cyprian in that council, propounding the controversy of re-baptization, requireth every man's judgment thereof, protesting (as it were) not to condemn, or to excommunicate any that should dissent from him in that matter, and thereupon saith, *Neque enim quisquam nostrum &c.;* so that he meaneth that to be *tyrannicum,* to compel other bishops necessarily to agree to his opinion in all things; and these words *licentia libertatis et potestatis suæ arbitrium proprium,* are not meant of jurisdiction, but of judgment and opinion. For one man is not of necessity bound to frame himself to the judgment and opinion of another, but therein hath freedom and liberty; neither will any man allow this authority in any archbishop.

Touching jurisdiction, every bishop in this church hath free government over his flock in all things that belongeth unto him: if anything happen that he cannot end, then the archbishop intermeddleth: if that will not serve, it is referred to a synod. The words of Cyprian can in no respect derogate anything from the jurisdiction of archbishops. For concerning jurisdiction they be bound to laws themselves, and do but execute laws made, not of their own private authority, but by parliament and by the prince. Neither can they control the worst minister in their diocese, if he observe the laws and rules prescribed. Therefore, except your meaning be to have bishops and ministers free from all laws, and from all subjection to any superior, prince or other (which is most like), I do not know why you should take this saying of Cyprian in that sense you do. Sure I am that the words do not favour your anarchy; and that may the reader easily perceive.

In that Cyprian saith, "unto every one a portion of the flock is appointed[4]," he saith truly, but yet doth he not thereby exempt bishops, pastors, and ministers, from obedience and subjection to their lawful governors. For due

[4 See above, note 1.]

obedience doth not hinder any duty that is owing towards their flock.

In the place that you allege out of Cyprian's second book and first epistle, you have omitted that which goeth before, and declareth what Cyprian meaneth by the words that you have recited. His words be these: *Cæterum scimus quosdam quod semel imbiberunt nolle deponere, nec propositum suum facile mutare, &c.*[1]: "But we know that certain will never lay away that which once they have taken, neither easily change their purpose, but do retain certain things peculiar to themselves, which once they have used, yet not breaking the bond of peace and concord among their fellows; wherein we neither compel any man, nor appoint any law; since every governor hath free judgment of his will in the government of the church, and shall render an account of his deed to the Lord." Cyprian, in the words before, sheweth his opinion concerning such as being ministers of the word had sacrificed to idols, and, when he hath so done, thus he speaketh to Stephen, to whom he writ the epistle: *Hæc ad conscientiam tuam, frater carissime, &c.* Then followeth, *Cæterum scimus &c.;* as I have before recited; wherein Cyprian signifieth that he will not take upon him to judge or to condemn other churches, which have a contrary custom, so that they keep the bond of peace. But he meaneth undoubtedly such churches and bishops as he had nothing to do with; else it is manifest that within his own charge he would not have suffered any such thing to be done; and this place answereth all that Cyprian hath spoken anywhere touching not receiving into the ministry such as had sacrificed to idols; whereof I have spoken [2]before[3].

[1 Et iccirco satis est talibus revertentibus veniam dari. Non tamen debet in domo fidei perfidia promoveri...Hæc ad conscientiam tuam, frater carissime, et pro honore communi, et pro simplici dilectione pertulimus, &c....Ceterum &c. imbiberint &c. mutare, sed salvo inter collegas pacis et concordiæ vinculo, quædam propria, quæ apud se semel sint usurpata, retinere. Qua in re nec nos vim cuiquam facimus aut legem damus, cum habeat in ecclesiæ administratione voluntatis suæ arbitrium liberum unusquisque præpositus, rationem actus sui Domino redditurus.—Cypr. Op. Oxon. 1682. Ad Steph. Epist. lxxii. pp. 197, 8.]

[2 See Vol. I. pages 324, 5.]

[3 Cartwright rejoins at length to this and the former division, accusing Whitgift of arguing inconclusively and begging the question.—Sec. Repl. pp. 545, &c.]

Chapter iii. The Twelfth Division.

T. C. Page 77, Sect. 2, 3, 4.

And, whereas it is said, for the preservation of unity one must be over
Lib. iv.   *all, St Cyprian sheweth that the unity of the church is con-*
Epist. 9.   *served not by having one bishop over all, but by the agreement*
of the bishops one with another. For so he writeth, that "the church is
knit and coupled together as it were with the glue of the bishops' con-
senting one with another[4]." *And, as for the compounding of contro-*
versies, it is manifest that it was not done by one bishop in a province,
but those bishops which were near the place where the schism or heresy
sprang.

For, speaking of the appeasing of controversies and schisms, and shew-
Lib. i.   *ing how divers bishops were drawn into the heresy of Novatus,*
Epist. 4.   *he saith that "the virtue and strength of the Christians was not*
so decayed or languished, but that there was a portion of priests which
did not give place unto those ruins and shipwrecks of faith[5]."

Lib. iii.   *And in another place he saith: "Therefore, most dear brother,*
Epist. 13.   *the plentiful body and*[6] *company of the priests are as it were*
with the glue of mutual concord and band of unity joined together, that,
if any of our company be author of an heresy, and go about to destroy
and rent the flock of Christ, the rest should help, and as profitable and
merciful shepherds gather together the sheep of the Lord[7]." *Whereby it is*
manifest that the appeasing and composing of controversies and heresies,
was not then thought to be most fit to be in one bishop's hand, but in as
many as could conveniently assemble together, according to the danger of
the heresy which sprang, or deep root which it had taken, or was like
to take.

Jo. Whitgift.

The bishops agree not one whit the worse[8], when they
have a superior by whom they may be called together and

[4 ... quando ecclesia quæ catholica una est, scissa non sit, neque divisa ; sed sit utique connexa, et cohærentium sibi invicem sacerdotum glutino copulata.— Cypr. Op. Ad Florent. Pup. Epist. lxvi. p. 168.]

[5 Non sic tamen, quamvis novissimis temporibus, in ecclesia Dei aut evangelicus vigor cecidit, aut christianæ virtutis aut fidei robur elanguit, ut non supersit portio sacerdotum, quæ minime ad has rerum ruinas, et fidei naufragia succumbat.—Id. ad Cler. Hisp. Epist. lxvii. p. 174.]

[6 Or, Repl. 1, 2, and Def. A.]

[7 Iccirco enim, frater carissime, copiosum corpus est sacerdotum concordiæ mutuæ glutino atque unitatis vinculo copulatum, ut si quis ex collegio nostro hæresin facere, et gregem Christi lacerare et vastare tentaverit, subveniant ceteri, et quasi pastores utiles et misericordes, oves dominicas in gregem colligant.—Id. ad Steph. Epist. lxviii. p. 178.]

[8 "Albeit they agree never the worse, yet, if they agree never the better, he ought as an unprofitable tree, which occupieth place in the Lord's orchard, be rooted out."—Sec. Repl. p. 549.]

Cyprian. put in mind of their office and duty. Neither doth Cyprian deny this, when he affirmeth the other. For, though the chief cause of unity is the consent and "agreement of the bishops one with another," yet to have one that shall have the chief care thereof must needs be a great help thereunto; even as it is in other societies. For, if the bishops were divided among themselves, and at variance, and had no superior, who should compound the controversies?

How far our archbishops deal in controversies. Our archbishops do not take upon them (neither can they) to decide any controversy in doctrine and religion of their own authority, but therein do they deal either according to the laws of the church provided for that purpose, or else expect a new parliament or synod. Neither doth any bishop in his diocese otherwise meddle in such matters than by the common consent of the church is appointed unto him; and yet it was never otherwise taught by any, but that a bishop in his own diocese, or an archbishop in his province, might use persuasions to end controversies, and execute the laws provided for the same; other kind of deciding controversies by any private authority I know none in this church of England. Wherefore all these allegations be but in vain; for surely not in Cyprian's time was the determining of such controversies committed to the pastor and seigniory of every parish; neither doth Cyprian make mention of any such matter: if he did, yet for government the diversity of the time and state of the church is to be considered; as I have before noted[1].

Tract. II. and III.

Chapter iii.   The Thirteenth Division.

T. C. Page 77, Sect. 4.

And that there was in his time no such authority given, as that any one might remove the causes or controversies which rose, as now we see there is when the bishop of the diocese taketh the matters in controversy, which rise in any church within his diocese, from the minister and elders, to whom the decision pertaineth, and as when the archbishop taketh it away from the bishop, it may appear in the same third epistle of the first book, where he saith after this sort: "It is ordained, and it is equal and right, that every man's cause should be there heard, where the fault was committed." And a little after he saith: "It is meet to handle the matter there where they may have both accusers and witnesses of the fault[2];" which

[1 See Vol. I. pages 175, &c., 378, &c.]   [2 See before, page 208, note 1.]

although it be spoken of them which fled out of Afric unto Rome, yet Cyprian.
*the reason is general, and doth as well serve against these ecclesiastical
persons, which will take upon*[3] *them the deciding of those controversies
that were done a hundred mile off them.*

Jo. Whitgift.

Cyprian, as I said, speaketh not one word of your
seigniory, and, in that place by you alleged, he speaketh of
the several province or diocese of every bishop, and would
have every matter ended in that province or diocese where it
is committed; and therefore he speaketh there of such as
"fled out of Africa" into Italy, to have their matters heard; so
that this place is soluted by your own self. "It is meet that
the matter should be there handled where there may be had
both accusers and witnesses." And that was one of the
reasons that the council of Africa used against the bishop of
Rome claiming interest in hearing appeals from thence. But
there is no province in England so large but that both the
accusers and witnesses may be brought into any part of it
from any other part. This reason of yours may serve better
against Westminster Hall, which is but one place to serve the
whole realm for deciding of controversies; and yet I think it
very necessary.

You may not wrest that to your purpose or proof of
seigniory, or authority thereof, which Cyprian speaketh of
divers provinces, yea, divers countries and nations. This is
no good reason: Cyprian misliked the translating of causes
from Africa to Rome; *ergo*, there may be no causes removed
from Northampton to London.

Chapter iii. The Fourteenth Division.
T. C. Page 77, Sect. 5.

*And, whereas M. Doctor in both places of Cyprian seemeth to stand
much upon the words "one bishop and priest," the reason thereof doth*
Lib. iii.   *appear in another place of Cyprian most manifestly, and that*
Epist. 13.   *it maketh no more to prove that there ought to be one archbishop over a whole province, than to say that there ought to be but one
husband proveth that therefore there should be but one husband in every
country or province, which should see that all the rest of the husbands do
their duty*[4] *to their wives. For this was the case: a Novatian heretic,*

[³ Unto, Repl. 1, 2, and Def. A.]
[⁴ Duties, Repl. 1, 2, and Def. A.]

Cyprian.

being condemned and cast out of the churches of Africa by the consent of the bishops, and not able by embassage sent to them to obtain to be received to their communion and fellowship again, goeth afterwards to Rome, and, being likewise there repelled, in time getteth himself, by certain which favoured his heresy, to be chosen bishop there at Rome[1] (Cornelius being the bishop or pastor of those which were there godly-minded); whereupon it cometh that Cyprian urgeth "one bishop, one priest in the church," because at Rome there was two, whereof one was a wolf, which ought not to have been there, considering there was but one church which was gathered under the government of Cornelius; and therefore by that place of Cyprian it cannot be gathered that there ought to be but one bishop in one city, if the multitude of professors require more, and that all cannot well gather themselves together in one congregation to be taught of one man; much less can it serve to prove that there should be but one in a whole diocese or province. I grant that in later times, and which went more from the simplicity of the primitive church, they took occasion of these words to

This is to prefer your own judgment before the judgment of worthy councils.

decree that there should be but one bishop in a city; but that can never be concluded of Cyprian's words, if it be understood why he urgeth "one bishop and one priest." If therefore neither word, "bishop" nor "priest," do make anything to prove an archbishop, nor this word "church" doth imply any province, nor in these words, "one bishop, one priest," there is nothing less meant than that there should be one archbishop over all the bishops and clergy in a province; and if Cyprian will neither allow of the title of an archbishop[2], nor of the authority and office, but in plain words speaketh against both; we may conclude that M. Doctor hath done very unadvisedly to lay so great weight of the archbishop upon St Cyprian's shoulders, that will not only not bear anything of him, but which hath done all that could be to make him go afoot and hand in hand with his fellows.

Jo. Whitgift.

M. Doctor "standeth" not "upon these words, 'one bishop and one priest,'" although the words serve very well for his purpose; neither is your shift of "a Novatian being chosen bishop in Rome" any thing to the matter. For, though it might seem partly to interpret Cyprian's meaning, in his epistle to Cornelius, yet can it not pertain to that that he writeth of Florentius Pupianus. And, be it that Cyprian

[1 ...cum Novatianus ipse, quem sequitur [Marcianus], olim abstentus et hostis ecclesiæ judicatus sit: et cum ad nos in Africam legatos misisset, optans ad communicationem nostram admitti, hinc a concilio plurimorum sacerdotum qui præsentes eramus sententiam retulerit; se foris esse cœpisse, nec posse a quoquam nostrum sibi communicari, qui episcopo Cornelio in catholica ecclesia de Dei judicio et cleri ac plebis suffragio ordinato, profanum altare erigere, et adulteram cathedram collocare, et sacrilega contra verum sacerdotem sacrificia offerre tentaverit.—Cypr. Op. Oxon. 1682. Ad Steph. Epist. lxviii. p. 177.]

[2 Of archbishop, Repl. 1 and 2.]

meant to seclude Novatus, when he said, *Dum episcopus* Cyprian.
qui unus est, &c.[3] : " When as the bishop which is one, &c. :"
what can be spoken more to my purpose ? For Cyprian
would have but one bishop in one city to govern the church ;
as his words manifestly declare.

And, whereas you say that " it cannot be gathered by
that place of Cyprian, that there ought to be but one bishop
in one city, if the multitude of professors require more, &c. ;"
the epistle of Cornelius, in Eusebius, *Lib. vi. cap.* 43, doth Euseb. Lib.
vi. cap. 43.
convince you of vanity in so saying. For in that epistle he The number
of Christians
declareth that there was then in Rome 46. priests, seyen in Rome
great in Cy-
deacons, seven subdeacons, 42. acoluths, 52. exorcists, readers, prian's time.
door-keepers, 1500. widows and diseased[4]; and therefore it is
to be presupposed that the number of other Christians there
was very great, seeing that the clergy and those which were
found of the church amounted to the number of 1654. ; and
most like that there were several congregations ; for it was
not possible for them to meet in one place ; and yet was there
then but one bishop. For Cornelius, in the same epistle,
speaking of Novatus, saith : *Itaque vindex ille evangelii igno-*
ravit unum esse debere episcopum in catholica ecclesia[4] :
" This defender of the gospel was ignorant that there ought
to be one bishop in a catholic church."

The old canons and ancient fathers do testify that in one
city there ought to be but one bishop. Chrysostom told
Sisinius that one city must have but one bishop ; as we read,
Lib. vi. cap. 22. of Socrates[5]. Neither are you able to shew Socrat. Lib.
vi. cap. 22.
from Christ's time, that ever there was allowed to be two
bishops in one city. Wherefore the words of Cyprian are
yet in force (for anything you have alleged to the contrary)
to prove the office of an archbishop or metropolitan to be to
compound schisms, and to provide that there be unity in the
church. &c.[6]

[3 Id. ad Florent. Pup. Epist. lxvi. p. 167. See before, page 193, note 5.]

[4 Ὁ ἐκδικητὴς οὖν τοῦ εὐαγγελίου, οὐκ ἠπίστατο ἕνα ἐπίσκοπον δεῖν εἶναι ἐν
καθολικῇ ἐκκλησίᾳ· ἐν ᾗ οὐκ ἠγνόει, πῶς γάρ; πρεσβυτέρους εἶναι τεσσαράκοντα
ἕξ· διακόνους ἑπτά. ὑποδιακόνους ἑπτὰ, ἀκολούθους δύο καὶ τεσσαράκοντα. ἐξορ-
κιστὰς δὲ καὶ ἀναγνώστας ἅμα πυλωροῖς δύο καὶ πεντήκοντα· χήρας σὺν θλιβομέ-
νοις, ὑπὲρ τὰς χιλίας πεντακοσίας.—Euseb. in Hist. Eccles. Script. Amst. 1695—
1700. Lib. VI. cap. xliii. p. 198.]

[5 ...οὐ δύναται ἡ πόλις δύο ἐπισκόπους ἔχειν, κ.τ.λ.—Socr. in eod. Lib. VI.
cap. xxii. p. 270.]

[6 " In all these places which the Ans. hath brought out of Cyprian, Eusebius,

Cyprian.

Chapter iii.   The Fifteenth Division.

T. C. Page 78, Line 26.

This argument is of your own coining, and not M. Doctor's.

There are other reasons which M. Doctor useth, as this, a notable one: St Cyprian "speaketh not of the usurped power of the bishop of Rome;" therefore he speaketh of the office of an archbishop and metropolitan. It is hard to call this argument to any head of fallation, for it hath not so much as a colour of a reason.   I think[1] it can deceive nobody but yourself.

Jo. Whitgift.

I tell you that the place is not to be understood of the usurped authority of the bishop of Rome, but of the authority of the archbishop in his province, or bishop in his diocese.   I do not make any argument of it : doth it grieve you to hear that Cyprian doth not speak of the usurped authority of the bishop of Rome? or doth every man make an argument when he doth interpret?   But this dealing of yours is not strange; I must be content to bear with it.

Chapter iii.   The Sixteenth Division.

T. C. Page 78, Line 30 ; and Sect. 1, 2, 3, 4.

Another reason is that " all the godliest and best-learned men do expound" the place of Cyprian, in the third epistle of the first book, of an archbishop. The vanity of this saying, that " the godly and learned writers so expound it," I have shewed before; and here it cometh to be considered again. I will not say that no godly nor learned writer expoundeth the place of Cyprian of the authority of an archbishop.

But, first, I desire M. Doctor to set down but one, and then I will leave it to thy consideration, gentle reader, to think whether M. Doctor hath read any learned or godly man's exposition to be such, when he hath not read those which are nearest him, I mean our own countrymen. I say he hath not read them, because I would think charitably so of him, rather than that he should have read them, and yet speak untruly of them, and father those things of them which they never spake[2].

Untruth, as will appear.

M. Jewel, the bishop of Salisbury, expounded this place, In his first book, 4. article, and in division 5. *and yet did never expound it of the office and authority of an archbishop of all the bishops and clergy of the province, but, clean contrariwise, applieth it to the authority that every bishop had in his diocese. His words are these: " Now therefore to draw that thing by*

Socrates, it is manifest that "one bishop" is opposed unto heretic bishops. Whereby may appear how like it is which I have alleged, that by one bishop is understanded not the unity of number, but of truth in religion."—Sec. Repl. p. 553.]

[1 And I think, Repl. 1 and 2.]   [2 Speake, Repl. 2.]

violence to one only bishop, that is generally spoken of all bishops, is a Cyprian.
guileful fetch to mislead the reader, and no simple nor plain dealing[3]."
Here you see that M. Jewel doth not understand this of any archbishop,
but of every bishop.

First book *M. Nowel, dean of Paul's, having occasion to talk[4] of this* M. Nowel
against Dor- *place, saith on this sort: " So that, when he speaketh (meaning* will witness
man, and 25. *Cyprian) of one bishop, one judge, in the church, for the time,* against you.
leaf.
*or of the bishop which is one, and ruleth the church absolutely, he meaneth
every bishop in his own diocese, without exception: if he speak specially,
he meaneth the bishop of the city or diocese whereof he entreateth, whether
it be the bishop of Rome, Carthage, or any other place[5]."*

1 Tom. *M. Fox also expoundeth this of every bishop within his*
Fol. 93.[6] *own church or diocese[7]. You hear the judgment of these three
writers, that cannot pick out neither the name nor the office of an archbishop out of Cyprian's place; and yet I think you will not deny but these
were learned and godly writers.*

*Now I have shewed you three. I ask once again of you one godly
and learned writer that expoundeth it as you do. And by this time I
suppose all men understand what a small friend St Cyprian is either to
the name or office of an archbishop. Let us hear whether Hierome make
any more for the archbishop than did Cyprian.*

Jo. Whitgift.

M. Jewel, bishop of Sarisbury, expounding the place of
Cyprian, in the fourth article, 5. division, 228. page of his
first book, hath these words: " Upon occasion hereof he shew- M. Jewel.
eth (meaning Cyprian) what hurt and confusion of sects and
schisms ensueth in any province or diocese where as the
bishop's authority and ecclesiastical discipline is despised[8]."
I pray you, what call you that bishop that hath government
of a "province?" Is he not a metropolitan, or archbishop?
and doth not my L. of Sarisbury as well speak of a province
as he doth of a diocese? I do not deny but that Cyprian's
words may be fitly applied to every bishop in his diocese; but

[3] Bp. Jewel's Works, Park. Soc. Edit. Vol. I. p. 348; where *it is a guileful
fetch*, and *simple or plain.*]

[4] Speak, Repl. 1 and 2.]

[5] And therefore when St Cyprian nameth one bishop in the catholic church,
or of a catholic church, he meaneth the bishop of that special diocese which he
entreateth of, of what country so ever it be, as here he meaneth Cornelius: and
by the like words in other places, he meaneth other bishops, and of other dioceses.—
A Reprovfe, written by Alexander Nowell, of a booke entituled, A Provfe of Cer-
tayne Articles in Religion denied by M. Iuell, set furth by Thomas Dorman,
Lond. 1565. fol. 24.]

[6] So Repl. 2: the other editt. have only *Fol.* 93.]

[7] See below, page 219, note 7.]

[8] Bp. Jewel's Works, Park. Soc. Edit. Vol. I. p. 348.]

is the archbishop therefore secluded, seeing he of whom Cyprian did write was a metropolitan, or archbishop? That, which is the office of the archbishop in his province, is also the office of a bishop in his diocese; and therefore that which is spoken of the province, in respect of the archbishop, is also spoken of the diocese, in respect of the bishop. And page 230.

he saith that *universa fraternitas* is "taken for one whole particular brotherhood, within one province or diocese[1];" so that your first witness testifieth with me, else would he not have named a province.

M. Nowel, fol. 22. 23. 24., doth expound this place of the authority of every bishop in his own diocese[2]; which is sufficient for me, and is as much against you as can be; for you would have no bishops over dioceses, but only pastors in several towns. That which he speaketh of a bishop in his diocese he also meaneth of an archbishop in his province, whose both name and office he doth allow; as it is manifest in these words of his in his third book against Dorman, fol. 320.; where he, answering this question of Dorman's, whether he will condemn the whole church for making of archbishops,
saith thus: "I answer, I much commend the church for so doing; so far off is it that I will condemn the whole church therefore[3]." But what shall I need to use any circumstances; seeing he doth most evidently apply this place of Cyprian to that purpose which you will not acknowledge, yea, even unto the office of an archbishop in his province? for thus he writeth, fol. 33. of his first book (speaking of this epistle of Cyprian to Cornelius, and confuting Dorman's argument taken out of it for the pope's supremacy, which is grounded upon this place: *Non aliunde hæreses obortæ sunt, &c.*): "Concerning the avoiding and quieting of schisms and troubles in the church, we say that, as the several kings of every kingdom, the several governors of every country and city, &c., are able to oversee their several charges, and to keep their people in civil order and peace, so are the several bishops of every diocese, and the several chief prelates of every province, able to avoid, or to appease (if they rise) all schisms and troubles eccle-

[1 Id. ibid. p. 350.]   [2 A Reprovfe, &c. Lond. 1565. foll. 22, 3, 4.]
[3 A Confutation, as wel of M. Dormans last Boke entituled A Disproufe. &c. as also of D. Sander his causes of Transubstantiation, by Alexander Nowel. Lond. 1567.   Conf. of M. Dorman's 7 chap. fol. 320. 2.]

siastical; as St Cyprian, out of whom this reason is borrowed Cyprian. and falsely wrested by them to another purpose, doth most plainly teach, saying thus: *Cum statutum sit omnibus nobis &c.*[4]" What call you "chief prelates of every province?" Be they not archbishops? Likewise, fol. 60. and 61., in the same book, speaking of this and such like places, he saith: " And further, whatsoever M. Dorman, either out of Deutero., or any other place of scripture, doth untruly apply to the proof of the supremacy of one head, to wit, the bishop of Rome, the same doth St Cyprian, M. Dorman's own usual witness, everywhere allege for the proof of the superiority of every bishop in his own diocese, and for the obedience due unto him there; he doth never apply it, as doth M. Dorman, to the supremacy of one bishop over all other, but rather against such supremacy of one; and it agreeth very well with the estate of the Jews, that as they[5] being one nation had one chief priest, so is it good likewise that every christian nation have their chief priest or bishop: it agreeth not that, because the Jews (one nation) had one high priest to govern them in doubts, therefore all nations throughout the world should have one high priest over all other; for not only the unlikelihood between these two, but the impossibility of the latter, is most evident[6]."

The words of M. Fox in that place, speaking against the papistical interpretation of Cyprian's words, be these: " when M. Fox. their meaning is otherwise, how that every one catholic fol. 93. church or diocese ought to have one bishop over it[7];" which also justifieth my interpretation. For, if it be understanded of one bishop over one diocese, then is it in like manner of one archbishop over one province. For the reason is all one; and you deny them both alike; for you would have no bishops but in several parishes. Now therefore you see that even these authors, whom you would abuse against me, do make wholly and fully against you, and with me. For they confess the two places of Cyprian to be meant of Cornelius and of himself, who were both archbishops and metropolitans, and had ample jurisdiction, especially Cyprian; as I have declared. And

[4] A Reprovfe, &c. fol. 33. 2. Conf. Cypr. Op. Oxon. 1682. Ad Cornel. Epist. lix. pp. 129, 36.]

[5] That they, Def. B.]　　　[6] Ibid. foll. 60. 2, 61; where *later* for *latter*.]

[6] Fox, Acts and Monuments, Lond. 1684. Vol. I. p. 71.]

M. Fox himself, Tom. I. fol. 21, saith that "the see of Rome was a patriarchal see appointed by the primitive church, and the bishop thereof an archbishop, limited within his own bordering churches[1];" so that, the one place being meant of Cornelius, archbishop of Rome, the other of Cyprian, archbishop of Carthage (for so they were indeed, though they were not in those places so called), St Cyprian may well be said in both places to speak of an archbishop, though he express not his name. And that, which is there spoken of Cornelius or Cyprian within their provinces, may most aptly also be understood of every bishop within his diocese; and therefore my L. of Sarum expounding this place speaketh of them both under these names of "province" and "diocese;" and so doth M. Nowel, under the name of "chief prelate" and "province;" and M. Fox also under the word "diocese;" being plain and evident that they allow of the office.

That learned man and godly martyr, M. Philpot, as it is recorded in the book of Acts and Monuments, in his fifth examination answering this place of Cyprian, objected unto him by D. Saverson, answereth most plainly in these words:

"And now for the understanding of that place, you do misconstrue it, to take the high priest only for the bishop of Rome, and otherwise than it was in his time. For there were by Nicene council four patriarchs appointed, the patriarch of Jerusalem, the patriarch of Constantinople, the patriarch of Alexandria, and the patriarch of Rome; of which four the patriarch of Rome was placed lowest in the council, and so continued many years, for the time of seven or eight general councils; as I am able to shew. Therefore St Cyprian, writing to Cornelius, patriarch of Rome, whom he calleth fellow-bishop, findeth himself offended that certain heretics, being justly excommunicated by him (as the Novatians were), did fly from his diocese, which was their chief bishop (refusing to be obedient unto him and to be reformed), to the bishop of Rome, and to the patriarch of Constantinople, and there were received in communion of congregation, in derogation of good order and discipline in the church, and to the maintaining of heresies and schisms. And that heresies did spring up and schisms daily arise hereof, that obedience was not given to the priest of God,

[1 Wherefore, seeing the see of Rome is a patriarchal see &c. bishop thereof and archbishop, &c.—Id. ibid. p. 18.]

nor once considered him to be in the church for the time the priest, and for the time the judge in Christ's stead (as in decree of Nicene council was appointed); not meaning the bishop of Rome only, but every patriarch in his precinct, who had every one of them a college or a cathedral church of learned priests, in hearing of whom, by a convocation of all his fellow-bishops, with the consent of the people, all heresies were determined by the word of God; and this is the meaning of St Cyprian[2]." Hitherto M. Philpot. Thus the reader may easily perceive how you have dallied about this place of Cyprian, and that this interpretation is not mine alone[3].

Chapter iii. The Seventeenth Division.

Answer to the Admonition, Page 70, Sect. 1, 2, 3; and Page 71, Sect. 1.

And therefore Hierome, writing upon the first to Titus, saith that "in the beginning a bishop and a priest was all one. But, after that there began to rise[4] factions in religion, and some said they held of Apollo, some of Paul, some of Cephas, and some of Christ, it was decreed that one should be chosen to bear rule over the rest; to whom the chief care of the church should appertain, and by whom sects and schisms should be cut off[5]." Hierome.

[2] Philpot's Fifth Examination, ibid. Vol. III. p. 469. Conf. The examinacion of the constaunt Martir of Christ, Johñ Philpot Archediacon of Winchestre &c. s. l. & a. foll. 36. 2, 37, and Philpot's Examinations and Writings, Park. Soc. Edit. pp. 43, 4. There are several verbal differences in all these editions. The metropolitans of Alexandria, Rome, Antioch and Jerusalem were mentioned at the council of Nice.]

[3] Cartwright complains that Whitgift has misrepresented Jewel; that Nowel probably meant otherwise than is here alleged: "howbeit (he adds), because the author himself is alive, and knoweth best what he meaneth, I am well content the meaning of his words be such as himself shall best like of;" that "out of M. Fox he cannot find so much as a fig-leaf;" and that Philpot, "attributing unto Cyprian a diocese, declareth that he esteemed him a bishop, not an archbishop." He proceeds: "Albeit the truth is, that the appointment of those 4. patriarchal seats was not by the council of Nice, but of Chalcedon." He afterwards goes on to animadvert on authorities which Whitgift has produced in a much later portion of his book.—Sec. Repl. pp. 554, &c.]

[4] Arise, Answ.]

[5] Idem est ergo presbyter qui episcopus: et antequam diaboli instinctu, studia in religione fierent; et diceretur in populis, Ego sum Pauli, ego Apollo, ego autem Cephæ, communi presbyterorum consilio, ecclesiæ gubernabantur.

Here a man may reason thus. The distinction of degrees began in the church, when men began to say, I hold of Paul, I hold of Apollo, &c. But this was in the apostles' time, the[1] 1 Cor. i. Therefore these distinctions of degrees began in the apostles' time.

The same Hierome, in his epistle *ad Evagrium*, teacheth that the cause why one was chosen amongst[2] the bishops to rule over the rest was *in schismatis remedium, ne unusquisque ad se trahens Christi ecclesiam rumperet*[3]: "to meet with schisms; lest every one according to his own fancy should tear in pieces the church of Christ;" and saith further that, "in Alexandria, from St Mark unto Heracla and Dionysius, bishops, the ministers used to elect one among themselves, whom they, placing in a higher degree, called a bishop; even as an army should choose their captain, or deacons should choose one of themselves whom they knew to be painful, and call him an archdeacon." *Hæc Hieronymus.*

In all these places Hierome doth not maintain the authority of one man over the whole church, but thinketh it necessary that in every province there be one to be chief over the rest, for unity' sake, and for rooting out of contentions and sects. And therefore, *contra Luciferianos*, he saith that, unless this superiority were, "there would be as many schisms in the church as there be priests[5]."

Causes of superiority amongst ministers[4].

Postquam vero unusquisque eos quos baptizaverat suos putabat esse, non Christi, in toto orbe decretum est, ut unus de presbyteris electus superponeretur cæteris, ad quem omnis ecclesiæ cura pertineret, et schismatum semina tollerentur.— Hieron. Op. Par. 1693-1706. Comm. in Epist. ad Tit. cap. i. Tom. IV. Pars I. col. 413.]

[1 *The* is not in Answ.]   [2 Among, Answ.]

[3 Quod autem postea unus electus est, qui cæteris præponeretur, in schismatis remedium factum est: ne unusquisque ad se trahens Christi ecclesiam rumperet. Nam et Alexandriæ a Marco evangelista usque ad Heraclam et Dionysium episcopos, &c.—Id. ad Evang. Epist. ci. Tom. IV. Pars II. col. 803. See before, p. 177, note 6.]

[4 This marginal note is inserted from Answ. 2.]

[5 Ecclesiæ salus in summi sacerdotis dignitate pendet: cui si non exors quædam et ab omnibus eminens detur potestas, tot in ecclesiis efficientur schismata, quot sacerdotes.—Id. adv. Lucifer. Tom. IV. Pars II. col. 295.]

T. C. Page 79, Sect. 1, 2.

The Hebrews do derive the name of time of a verb which signifieth to corrupt, because indeed it doth corrupt all; and, as the times are, so are men which live in them; that even very good men carry the note of the infection of the times wherein they live. And the stream of the corruption thereof, being so vehement and forcible, doth not only drive before it light things, but it eateth also and weareth the very hard and stony rocks; and therefore there is not to be looked for such sincerity at Hierome's hand[6], which we found in St Cyprian, considering that he lived some ages after Cyprian, what time Satan had a great deal more darkened the clear light of the sun of the gospel than it was in St Cyprian's time. For, as those that came nearest unto the apostles' times, because they were nearest the light, did see best, so those that were further off from these lights had, until the time of the manifestation of the son of perdition, their heavens more dark and cloudy, and consequently did see more dimly; which is diligently to be observed of the reader, both the better to understand the state of this question, and all other controversies which lie between us and the papists.

And, although Hierome, besides his other faults, might have also in this matter spoken more soundly, yet we shall easily perceive that he is a great deal further from either the title or office of an archbishop, or else from the authority that a bishop hath with us, than he is from the simplicity of the ministry, which ought to be, and is commended unto us by the word of God.

This is your usual practice, when you cannot answer, to cavil at the credit of the author.

Jo. Whitgift.

This is but a poor refuge, when you cannot answer, to discredit the author: it is evident that Hierome saith nothing touching this matter but that which is both consonant to the scriptures and confirmed by the practice of the church, long before his time; as appeareth by that which is said before. And, I pray you, what difference is there betwixt that which Hierome speaketh in this place, and that which Cyprian hath said before? For Cyprian said that "heresies and schisms have sprung and do spring of this, because the priest of God is not obeyed, &c." And, "because the bishop, which is one, and is set over the church, is through the proud presumption of some contemned, &c.[7]" And Hierome saith that the cause, why among the bishops one was chosen to govern the rest, was "to remedy schisms." Do you not perceive how these two fathers join in one truth, and directly affirm the self-same matter? It is true that "time corrupteth;" and therefore

[6] At Jerome his hand, Repl. 1 and 2.]

[7] Cypr. Op. Oxon. 1682. Ad Cornel. Epist. lix. p. 129; ad Florent. Pup. Epist. lxvi. p. 167. See before, pages 192, 3, notes 2, 5.]

much more occasion is offered to appoint government according to the times, lest the corruptions prevail and get the upper hand ; and for this cause Hierome saith that upon these corruptions of time the church was constrained to appoint this order [1].

Chapter iii.   The Eighteenth Division.

T. C. Page 79, Sect. 3.

A frivolous
digression
from the
matter.

And here I must put M. Doctor in remembrance how unfitly he hath dedicated his book unto the church, which hath so patched it and pieced it of a number of shreds of the doctors, that a sentence of the scripture either truly or falsely alleged is as it were a phenix in this book. If he would have had the church believe him, he ought to have settled their judgment and grounded their faith upon the scriptures, which are the only foundations whereupon the church may build. Now he doth not only not give them ground to stand of, but he leadeth them into ways which they cannot follow, nor come after him. For, except it be those which are learned, and besides have the means and ability to have the books which are here cited (which are the least and smallest portion of the church), how can they know that these things be true which are alleged ; and, as I have said, if they could know, yet have they nothing to stay themselves upon, and quiet their conscience in allowing that which M. Doctor would so fain have them like of. Therefore he might have much more fitly dedicated his book unto the learned and rich, which have furnished libraries.

Jo. WHITGIFT.

Tract. II.

M. Doctor hath brought more scriptures than you have answered, as in the sequel it will fall out, although (as I said before) [2] in such matters the scripture hath not expressly determined any certainty, but hath left them to the church, to be appointed according to the circumstances of time, place, and person ; as I have proved both out of the scriptures and learned writers, and intend to do hereafter more particularly, when I come to entreat of your seigniory. If all other men should do as you have done, that is, borrow the sayings of the doctors out of other men's collections, and not read the

---

[1 Cartwright rejoins "that Jerome's bishop is lower by head and shoulders than they for whom his authority is holden out." He afterwards says : "I willingly give testimony unto those governors, or at least the most of them, that they had a good meaning in that invention of man ; but that it was remedy against the corruptions I deny," and declares "that even from the first day, wherein this devise was established, the corruption in the church was not diminished, but grew."—Sec. Repl. pp. 568, 9.]

[2 See Vol. I. pages 175, &c.]

authors themselves, a few books will serve, and with very small charges they might be provided.

The "patches, pieces, and shreds of doctors," that be in my book, are taken out of the doctors themselves, and they be whole sentences faithfully alleged. But the "shreds of doctors," that your book is stuffed with, you have borrowed of other; you have falsified them, and cut them off by the half; you have fathered upon them that which is not to be found in them; and the words of late writers you have set down under the name of ancient fathers; and the scriptures you have falsely alleged and untruly translated: I would not gladly have burst out into this accusation at this time, being from the matter, but that you have urged me thereunto.

Chapter iii. The Nineteenth Division.

T. C. Page 79, Sect. 4, 5, 6.

Hierome saith that "*at the first a bishop and an elder (which you call a priest*[3]) *were all one, but afterward, through factions and schisms, it was decreed that one should rule over the rest*[4]." *Now I say, against this order that the bishop should bear rule over all, that which our Saviour Christ saith unto the Pharisees,* "*From the beginning it was not so;*" *and therefore I require that the first order may stand, which was that a bishop and elder were all one. And, if you place so great authority against the institution of God in a mortal man, hear what Tertullian saith unto you:*

Contra Prax.   "*That is true whatsoever is first; and that is false whatsoever is*[5] *latter*[6]."

Hierome and you confess that this was first, that the bishop was all one with the elder, and first also by the word of God: then I conclude that that is true. You both do likewise confess that it came after, that one bare rule over the rest: then I conclude that that is false; for all that is false that is latter[6]. *Furthermore, Hierome in the same place of Titus saith after this sort:* "*As the elders know themselves to be subject by a custom of the church unto him that is set over them, so the bishops must know that they are greater than the elders rather by custom than by any truth of the institution of the Lord*[7];" *and so they ought to govern the church in common.*

     Tertullian's meaning falsified.

[3 Call priest, Repl. 1 and 2.]   [4 See before, page 221, note 5.]
[5 See below, page 226, note 2.]   [6 Later, Repl. 1 and 2.]
     [7 Sicut ergo presbyteri sciunt se ex ecclesiæ consuetudine ei qui sibi præpositus fuerit, esse subjectos: ita episcopi noverint se magis consuetudine, quam dispositionis dominicæ veritate, presbyteris esse majores. — Hieron. Op. Par. 1693-1706. In Epist. ad Tit. cap. i. Tom. IV. Pars I. cols. 413, 4.]

Jo. Whitgift.

It followeth after in my Answer to the Admonition, that there was superiority among the ministers of the word, even in the apostles' time; which I prove by the scriptures and other testimonies: it is also evident that great factions and schisms did arise in the church even in the apostles' time; and therefore most like these that Jerome speaketh of, to have been then determined. The which to be true, his words *ad Evagrium*, touching the church of Alexandria, doth evidently declare; for he saith that this order was kept therein from St Mark[1]. But admit these were not true (which you will never be able to prove), yet your argument is of no force; and the place of Tertullian is not understanded; for Tertullian in that book, after he hath repeated the rule of faith, "which is to believe in one God, and in his Son Jesus Christ, &c.," he saith: "That this rule hath come from the beginning of the gospel, even before all former heretics, much more before Praxeas that was but yesterday, as well the posterity of all heretics as the very novelty of Praxeas, which was of late, will prove. Whereby judgment may hereof be indifferently given against all heresies, that that is true whatsoever is first, and that counterfeit whatsoever is last[2]." Whereby it is evident that Tertullian's rule is to be understanded in matters of salvation, and of faith, and not in matters of ceremonies and kinds of government; which thing he himself in plain words declareth, in his book *De Virginibus Velandis*; where in like manner, after he hath recited this rule of faith, he addeth: "This law of faith remaining, other things of discipline and conversation admit newness of correction, the grace of God working and going forward, even to the end[3]." So that Tertullian thinketh that matters of ceremonies and dis-

Tertull. contra Prax.

Wherein Tertullian's rule is to be understood.

Tertull. de Virgin. Veland.

[1 See above, page 222, note 3.]

[2 Nos vero et semper, et nunc magis, ut instructiores per Paracletum deductorem scilicet omnis veritatis, unicum quidem Deum credimus : sub hac tamen dispensatione, quam œconomiam dicimus, ut unici Dei sit et Filius sermo ipsius, &c. Hanc regulam ab initio evangelii decucurrisse, etiam ante priores quosque hæreticos, nedum ante Praxeam hesternum, probabit tam ipsa posteritas omnium hæreticorum, quam ipsa novellitas Praxeæ hesterni. Quo peræque adversus universas hæreses jam hinc præjudicatum sit, id esse verum quodcunque primum; id esse adulterum, quodcunque posterius.—Tertull. Op. Lut. 1641. Adv. Prax. 2. p. 635.]

[3 Hac lege fidei manente, cetera jam disciplinæ et conversationis admittunt novitatem correctionis, operante scilicet et proficiente usque in finem gratia Dei.— Id. de Virg. Veland. 1. p. 192.]

cipline may be altered (the rule of faith remaining inviolable), notwithstanding his former rule.

If you will not have this to be the meaning of Tertullian, then will I reason thus. In the beginning there were apostles; therefore there must be apostles now: in the beginning it was forbidden to eat that which was strangled; *ergo*, we may not eat it now: in the beginning there were no christian magistrates; *ergo*, there must be none now: in the beginning the apostles baptized in rivers, the communion was ministered to 12. only, &c. *Ergo quod posterius falsum* : "that which is latter is false." These be as good arguments as yours. But it is manifest that Tertullian speaketh of matters of faith, and necessary to salvation; and therefore these arguments, and yours also with such like, be stark naught[4].

The reason of the Replier retorted against himself.

Chapter iii.   The Twentieth Division.

T. C. Page 79, Sect. ult.

Now, seeing that Hierome confesseth that a bishop and an elder by God his institution are all one, and that custom of the church hath altered this institution, for the taking away of this custom, and restoring of the Matt. xv. 3.[5] *Lord's institution, I say as our Saviour Christ said, "Why do you break the commandments of God, to establish your own traditions?"   For the one is the institution of God; and the other the tradition of the church; and, if a man's testimony be so much with M.* De Veland. *Doctor, let him hear what the same Tertullian saith : "What-* Virg. *soever savoureth against the truth shall be accounted heresy, even although it be an old custom[6]."*

Jo. WHITGIFT.

Your whole book is grounded upon the sands, that is, upon foundations not proved, as this is. For you should first have proved that Christ hath so commanded equality of ministers in government and ecclesiastical policy, that one of

---

[4 Cartwright rejoins that, " as one whose forehead is more hard than adamant, he shameth not still to affirm that this manner of bishop and archbishop was in the apostles' time; notwithstanding the author out of whom he draweth his proofs confesseth that at the first there was no difference between a bishop and an elder." He goes on to say that " the answer to Tertullian is absurd."—Sec. Repl. pp. 569, 70.]

[5 The verse is added from Repl. 2.]

[6 Quodcunque adversus veritatem sapit, hoc erit hæresis, etiam vetus consuetudo.—Tertull. Op. De Virg. Veland. 1. p. 192.]

them may not be above the other : the contrary is to be seen in scripture, both in words and examples ; as I have after declared ; so far off is it that you can shew any commandment to the contrary.   This text of the xv. of Matt. did the anabaptists object unto Zuinglius in the like case ; as it appeareth in his book *De Baptismo*.   But he answered them

as I must answer you : "I speak not as you feign me to speak : I speak only of external and indifferent things ; whereof there be many which are neither commanded nor forbidden by any express word of God, &c.[1]"   And again : "For this that we speak of is not necessary unto salvation ; but it is external ; of the which things many may be found omitted in the scriptures. &c.[2]"   Wherefore, except you can prove that we bring into the church something as necessary unto salvation, which is not expressed in the scriptures, this text is no more aptly applied by you against me, than it was by the anabaptists against Zuinglius.

The words of Tertullian are true, and make nothing for your purpose ; for you must first prove that these degrees be against the truth.

Chapter iii.   The Twenty-first Division.

T. C. Page 80, Line 3.

Now I will turn M. Doctor's own argument upon his head after this sort.   In the apostles' times there were schisms and heresies, but in their times there were no archbishops ordained to appease them ; therefore the best means of composing of controversies and keeping concord is not by having an archbishop to be over a whole province.

Jo. WHITGIFT.

I will severally answer your arguments, that the reader

may the better understand the pith of them.   And first I deny this argument, because it is neither in mode nor figure. For, first, you must call to memory that, in the third figure, where you would seem to place it, the minor may not be negative as yours is.   Secondly, there is more in the con-

[1 H. Zvingl. Op. Tigur. 1581. De Bapt. Lib. Tract. III. Pars II. fol. 85. 2. See Vol. I. pages 255, 6, note 3.]

[2 Id. ibid. fol. 87. 2.   See Vol. I. pages 256, 7, note 1.]

[3 See before, page 183.]

clusion than there is in the premises; which is against all rules of syllogisms. If you had concluded according to your former propositions, you should have said thus; *ergo,* when there are archbishops there are no schisms. For this is the true conclusion of that false syllogism. Thirdly, *minus extremum* should be *subjectum conclusionis;* and in this argument it is *prædicatum.* Seeing therefore that your argument hath no true form in any respect, I deny it until it be better framed.

Chapter iii. The Twenty-second Division.

T. C. Page 80, Line 7.

That there was none in the apostles' times, thus it may appear. If there were any, they were either ordained by the apostles and their authority, or else without and besides their authority. If there were any without and besides their authority, then they are therefore to be condemned the more, because in their time[4] they start up without their warrant. And, if the apostles did ordain them, there was some use of them to that whereunto they were ordained; but there was no use of them to that whereunto they were ordained; therefore the apostles did not ordain them. The use, whereunto M. Doctor saith they were ordained, was to compose controversies and end schisms, but to this they were not used; whereupon it followeth that if there were any they were unprofitable. That they were not used to any such end, it shall be perceived by that which followeth.

Jo. Whitgift.

This should be the proof of your former minor, if the argument had been good; but be it as you would have it, here is yet no sufficient proof of your minor. They are but only your own bare words, which may as easily be rejected as they be barely by you affirmed. But, lest the ignorant reader should think that I shift off matters with such quiddities as they understand not, I will set aside the deformed face of your argument, and come to the matter, and (as I think) your meaning, which is this: Controversies were compounded in the apostles' time without an archbishop; *ergo,* they may likewise be so now; so that there is no need of any archbishop. This is the controversy, whether the church be bound to the same kind of external government at all times that was used in the apostles' times. I have proved hitherto that it is not. And more is to be said of the same afterwards. In the meantime this I give you to understand, that, although the

The office of an archbishop in the apostles.

[4 Times, Repl. 1 and 2.]

apostles had not this name of archbishop among them, yet they had the same authority and office.   For they had the government and direction of divers churches, both in matters

Acts xiv. xv. xviii.
1 Cor. iii. iv. v. xi.

of doctrine and discipline : they ended controversies, repressed errors, kept them in quietness, ordained them bishops, and visited them ; as appeareth, Acts xiv. xv. xviii.; 1 Cor. iii. iv. v.

Utraque ad Tim.
Ep. ad Tit.
Euseb.
Lib. iii. cap. 23.

xi., and in the epistle to Timothy, and Titus.   Euseb., *Lib. iii. cap.* 23., declareth of John the evangelist, that, after he returned from Pathmos, he visited and governed sundry churches, and ordained them ministers[1].   The like doth

Epipha. Lib. i. Tom. ii.

Epiphanius report of Peter in Pontus and Bithynia, *Lib. i. Tom. ii.*[2]   And what other office than those hath the archbishop?   Therefore, though the name of archbishop was not among the apostles, yet was his office and function.   And, notwithstanding that part of the office of the apostles is ceased which consisted in planting and founding of churches throughout the world, yet this part of government and direction of churches remaineth still, and is committed to bishops.

Ambro in iv. Ephes.

Therefore, saith Ambrose, in the *iv. ad Ephe.* : *Apostoli episcopi sunt*[3] : " Apostles are bishops ;" because bishops do succeed them in preaching the word, and governing the church.

Superiority among the apostles.

Now, if I shall also prove by good authority that among the apostles themselves, and in their times, there was one chief (though he were not called archbishop), then I suppose that it will not seem strange unto you, that in this state of the church it should be convenient to have the like in every province or diocese.   Jerome, in his first book *adversus*

Jerom. adv. Jovi. Lib. i.

Jovinianum, saith thus : " Yet among the twelve one is chosen, that a head being appointed occasion of schism might be removed[4]."   And, lest ye should wipe this away with your

[1 Ἐπὶ τούτοις κατὰ τὴν Ἀσίαν ἔτι τῷ βίῳ περιλειπόμενος, αὐτὸς ἐκεῖνος ὃν ἠγάπα ὁ Ἰησοῦς, ἀπόστολος ὁμοῦ καὶ εὐαγγελιστὴς Ἰωάννης, τὰς αὐτόθι διεῖπεν ἐκκλησίας, ἀπὸ τῆς κατὰ τὴν νῆσον μετὰ τὴν Δομετιανοῦ τελευτὴν ἐπανελθὼν φυγῆς.—Euseb. in Hist. Eccles. Script. Amst. 1695-1700. Lib. III. cap. xxiii. p. 73.]

[2 Ὁ μὲν γὰρ Παῦλος καὶ ἐπὶ τὴν Ἰσπανίαν ἀφικνεῖται, Πέτρος δὲ πολλάκις Πόντον τε καὶ Βιθυνίαν ἐπεσκέψατο.—Epiph. Op. Par. 1622. Adv. Hær. Lib. I. Tom. II. Hær. xxvii. 6. Tom. I. p. 107.]

[3 Ambros. Op. Par. 1686-90. Comm. in Epist. ad Ephes. cap. iv. vv. 11, 12. Tom. II. Append. col. 241.]

[4 ... tamen propterea inter duodecim unus eligitur, ut capite constituto, schismatis tollatur occasio.—Hieron. Op. Par. 1693-1706. Adv. Jovin. Lib. I. Tom. IV. Pars I. col. 168.]

accustomed depraving of the author, I will join unto him the
testimony of M. Calvin, in his Institutions, *cap.* 8. who writeth
thus: "That the twelve apostles had one among them to Calvin.
govern the rest it was no marvel; for nature requireth it,
and the disposition of man will so have it, that in every company (although they be all equal in power) yet that there be
one as governor, by whom the rest may be directed. There
is no court without a consul, no senate without a prætor, no
college without a president, no society without a master[5]."
M. Bucer likewise, in his book *De Regno Christi*, hath these
words: "Now we see by the perpetual observation of the Bucer.
churches, even from the apostles themselves, that it hath
pleased the Holy Ghost that, among the ministers to whom
especially the government of the church is committed, one
should have the chief care, both of the churches and whole
ministry, and that he should go before all other in that care
and diligence; for the which cause the name of a bishop is
peculiarly given to such chief governors of churches: &c.[6]"
Again, upon the iv. to the Ephe. he saith, as before is alleged,
"Paul in the Acts called the same men bishops and ministers, Idem.
when he called for the ministers of Ephesus to Miletum; yet,
because one among them did rule, and had the chief care of
the church, the name of a bishop did properly belong unto
him. Neither was his age always considered, so that he were
virtuous and learned; as we have an example in Timothy
being a young man[7]." Thus then you see that, even among
the apostles themselves, and in the churches in their times,

[5] Quod duodecim unum habuerint inter se qui omnes regeret, nihil mirum.
Hoc enim fert natura, hoc hominum ingenium postulat, ut in quovis cœtu, etiamsi
æquales sint omnes potestate, unus tamen sit veluti moderator, in quem alii
respiciant. Nulla est curia sine consule, nullus consessus judicum sine prætore
seu quæstore, collegium nullum sine præfecto, nulla sine magistro societas.—
Calvin. Op. Amst. 1667-71. Inst. Lib. IV. cap. vi. 8. Tom. IX. p. 296.]

[6] Jam ex perpetua ecclesiarum observatione, ab ipsis jam apostolis, videmus,
visum et hoc esse Spiritui sancto, ut inter presbyteros, quibus ecclesiarum procuratio potissimum est commissa, unus ecclesiarum et totius sacri ministerii curam
gerat singularem, eaque cura et solicitudine cunctis præeat aliis. qua de causa
episcopi nomen, hujusmodi summis ecclesiarum curatoribus est peculiariter
attributum : tametsi hi, sine reliquorum presbyterorum consilio nihil statuere
debeant: &c.—M. Bucer. De Regno Christi Libr. II. Basil. 1557. Lib. II. cap. xii.
p. 98.]

[7] Et in Actis &c. Nec ætas semper in illis spectabatur, modo singularis
probitas, et rerum cognitio adesset: ut est exemplum in Timotheo, alioquin
adolescente.—Id. Prælect. in Epist. ad Ephes. Basil. 1562. cap. iv. p. 107. See
before, pages 108, 9, note 2.]

there were some that had the chief authority over the rest, and to this end especially, that schisms and contentions might be compounded, and the rest might be directed; which are the chief parts of the archbishop's office; and therefore all this that you have here said falleth flat to the ground. And yet still I do affirm that, if it had not been so in the apostles' time, yet might it have been both lawfully and necessarily at other times[1].

Chapter iii.   The Twenty-third Division.

T. C. Page 80, Sect. 1.

At Antioch there rose a great and dangerous heresy, that Acts xv. 2.[2]
had in a manner infected all the churches, which shaked the very foundation of the salvation of God's children, that was, whether faith were sufficient to justify without circumcision. The matter was disputed of both sides; it could not be agreed of. What do they now? Do they ordain some archbishop, arch-prophet, arch-apostle, or any one chief, to whom they will refer the controversy, or upon whom they will depend? Nothing less. And, if they would have had the controversies ended by one, what divine was there ever or shall there be more fitter for that purpose than St Paul, which was amongst them? Why do they send abroad for remedy, when they had it at home? Why with great charges and long journeys, which they might have had without charges, or one foot set out of the door? What do they then? They send Paul and Barnabas to Jerusalem: as if the lesser towns should send to the churches of the universities and of London, to desire their help in the determining of the controversy. And what is Paul and Barnabas' ambassage? is it to desire the judgment or mind of some one? It must needs be answered with St Luke, that they came to know the resolution of the church; Acts xv. 23.[2]
and yet there were the apostles, whereof every one was better able both sharply to see, and to judge incorruptly without affection, than any archbishop that ever was. If therefore, in so great abundance and overflowing of the gifts of God, and in that time when as controversies might have been referred without danger of error unto one only, this ministry of one above all was not thought good; now, when the gifts are less and the danger of error more, to make an archbishop for the deciding of controversies and avoiding of schisms is a thing so strange that I am not able to see the reason of it. For, to which soever of the apostles the controversy had been referred, it is certain that he would have given a true sentence of it.

[1 Cartwright rejoins that "to prove the apostles' authority in the churches (which is not in question) he hath made a great muster of testimonies; to prove the archbishop's not a word;" and characterizes the reason afterwards brought as "more favourable to the pope than to the archbishop."—Sec. Repl. pp. 572, 3.]

[2 These marginal references are inserted from Repl. 2.]

Jo. Whitgift.

It was told you before that an archbishop of himself Supr. div. 12.
alone doth not take upon him to determine matters of doctrine
in controversy[3]; but, if any such contention arise, either he
determineth the matter according to the law and rule already
by the church established, or else with the consent of the
prince doth he set an order in the same by a provincial and
lawful synod; in the which he is the chief, as some one of the
apostles were in such like assemblies, according to that which
I have before declared; and therefore all this speech might
well have been spared.   Your argument also is faulty in two
respects: first, it is *ab auctoritate negativè*, or *a non facto
ad non jus*, which is good *neque in divinis neque in
humanis*: "neither in divine nor in human matters." Secondly, you go about to conclude an universal doctrine of one
particular and singular example; which at no time nor in any
matter is tolerable.

Moreover, it rather justifieth my assertion, for it evidently The example
proveth that every parish within itself hath not absolute of T. C. is rather
authority to end controversies, but that it behoveth them in against him than for him.
such weighty matters to resort to the chief church, as they
now did to Jerusalem.   This example therefore, if you well
consider it, is directly against you; neither doth it in any
respect prove that there was then no chief governor, or guide
of the rest, to supply that place and office which now the
archbishop hath.

Chapter iii.   The Twenty-fourth Division.
T. C. Page 80, Sect. 2.

And, if any can shew me one man in these times, of whom we may be The arch-
assured that he will pronounce the truth of every question which shall bishop hath cause to
arise, he shall make me somewhat more favourable to the archbishop than thank you for your gen-
presently I am.   For, although there were found one such as could not tleness.
err, yet I could not consent that the matter should lie only upon his hand;
seeing that the apostles, which could not err in these matters, would not
take that upon them; and seeing that by that means the judgment of the
church should be contemned; and, further, for that the judgment of one
man in a controversy is not so strong to pull up errors that are rooted in
men's minds, as the judgment and consent of many.   For that the judg-
ment of many is very apt either to confirm a truth, or to confute false-

[3 See before, page 212.]

hood, it is evident that St Paul doth hold forth, as it were a   _{1Cor. xi. 16.¹}
buckler against the frowardness of certain, the authority of the   _{1Cor. xiv. 33.¹}
church.

Jo. Whitgift.

You take great pains in fighting without an adversary, and, because otherwise (as it should seem) you lack matter to lengthen your book, therefore you devise matter of your own to strive against. For who hath affirmed that which you so earnestly seek in this place to overthrow? It hath been told twice already, that neither of our archbishops taketh upon him to compound controversies in doctrine by himself alone; neither is it their office so to do. The archbishop's authority in this church is to provide by lawful and ordinary means that unity be observed in the church; that contentions and schisms be cut off; that the religion and orders of the church, by the whole consent of the church agreed upon, be maintained; that every bishop in his province do his duty according to the same: this is his principal charge (as I take it), against the which you have not as yet spoken any thing, but devise with yourself² to improve that which no man affirmeth: this is but very shifting and dallying.

The authority of archbishops in our church.

Chapter iii.   The Twenty-fifth Division.

T. C. Page 80, Sect. 3.

Furthermore, if this distinction came up in the apostles' time, and by them, how cometh it to pass that they never mention it? nay, how cometh it to pass that even St Paul, in that very epistle where these voices are found, "I hold of Paul, I of Apollo, I of Cephas," which are   _{1Cor. xiv. 29.³} *said to be the cause of the archbishop, ordaineth a clean contrary to this that M. Doctor commendeth? For, when two or three prophets have expounded the scriptures, he appointeth that all the rest that are there should judge whether they have done well or no.*

A place far-fetched, to improve the office of the archbishop.

Jo. Whitgift.

I contend not that the name of the archbishop was in the apostles' time; but you have not yet proved that the office was not then, or that there was then no superiority among the clergy, which you notwithstanding deny. Your negative reason proveth nothing; as you have been oftentimes told.

[¹ These references are inserted from Repl. 2.]

[² You self, Def. B.]   [³ The verse is inserted from Repl. 2.]

The place in the 1 Cor. xiv. is far-fetched : it speaketh not of government and discipline, or external policy of the church, but of expounding the scriptures. And what a reason call you this? St Paul saith, 1 Cor. xiv.: *Prophetæ duo aut tres loquantur, cæteri dijudicent:* "Let two or three prophets speak, and let the other judge;" *ergo,* he speaketh against an archbishop!   Surely, if the authors of the Admonition had not been detected of their unskilful allegations of scriptures, I should have had as much ado with you in that point; for, even of these few which you have used, there is not almost one rightly and truly applied. St Paul in that place to the Corinthians sheweth that the hearers must judge of the doctrine of the prophets, whether it be according to the word of God or no[4] ; as those did which are commended in the xvii. of the Acts. But what is this to an archbishop?

T. C. faulteth with the Admonition in unapt allegations of scripture.

Chapter iii.   The Twenty-sixth Division.
T. C. Page 81, Sect. 1.

And how cometh it to pass that St Paul, being at Rome in prison, and looking every day when he should give up his last breath, com- *Eph. iv.11.[5]* *mended unto the church a perfect and an absolute ministry, standing of five parts, wherein he maketh mention not one word of an archbishop; and saith, further, that that ministry is able to entertain the perfect unity and knitting together of the church? Do not all these things speak, or rather cry, that there was not so much as a step of an archbishop in the apostles' times?*

How oft hath this been repeated.

Jo. Whitgift.

How oft have you alleged this place to the same purpose[6]? If I should do the like, you would bestow one whole side in jesting at it. But I answer you as I did before. In this place the apostle, as you confess, reciteth offices that be but temporal, as " apostle, prophet, &c.:" he leaveth out those offices which you say are perpetual, as " deacon" and "senior." Therefore it is no such perfect pattern as you would have it.

The place Eph. iv. no perfect pattern.

[4 " Howbeit, if he had conferred the text, he should have found that the apostle speaketh of the prophets, and not of the whole church....Therefore the D. corrupteth the place, &c."—Sec. Repl. p. 576.]

[5 The verse is added from Repl. 2.]

[6 " If it be a fault in me to allege one place often upon divers occasions, what is it in him to allege one thing so continually upon the same occasion? If he would have opened his eyes, he should have seen that I used an argument proper to this place, and not used before."—Ibid.]

And, if you say that these offices are contained under the names of " pastors and doctors," then I say that "bishops and archbishops" be so in like manner.   If you will have the apostles to speak of these ministries only which are occupied in the word and sacraments, then I say unto you that an "archbishop" is a name of jurisdiction and government committed to a bishop, pastor, or minister of the word, as necessary for the good government of the church, but not as any new ministry; as you untruly, both now and also before, have surmised. But to let all this pass: in those offices which St Paul here reciteth is the office of an archbishop contained, though it be not named, and namely under the apostles and pastors; as I have before shewed.

Archbishop
a name of
jurisdiction,
not of a new
ministry.

Chapter iii.   The Twenty-seventh Division.

T. C. Page 81, Sect. 1.

And, if you will say that the apostles did ordain archbishops (as you have indeed said and do now again), when as there is not one word in the writings of them, I pray you, tell us how we shall hold out of the church the unwritten verities of the papists? For my part, if it be true that you say, I cannot tell what to answer unto them. For our answer is to them, the apostles have left a perfect rule of ordering the church written; and therefore we reject their traditions, if for no other cause, yet because they are superfluous and more than need. Now, this degree of archbishop being not only not mentioned in the scriptures, but also manifestly oppugned, it is too bold and hardy a speech (that I say no more) to fet[1] the pedigree of the archbishop from the apostles' times, and from the apostles themselves.

Jo. Whitgift.

I must answer you still as Zuinglius answered the anabaptists in the like objection, and as I have answered you before[2]: the papists make their traditions necessary unto salvation; and therefore they are to be rejected, because the word of God containeth all things necessary to salvation.   I make those offices part of decency, order, ecclesiastical government and policy, which admitteth alteration as the times and persons require, and are not particularly expressed in the scriptures, no more than divers other things be in the same kind; as I have proved before.   And, that this may seem no strange matter, or anything favouring " the papists' unwritten

[1 Fetch, Repl. 1 and 2.]   [2 See Vol. I. pages 255, 6, 7.]

verities," you may call to remembrance that which M. Calvin
saith of such traditions upon these words, 1 Cor. xi., *Quemadmodum tradidi vobis instituta tenetis.* "I do not deny Calvin.
(saith he) but that there were some traditions of the apostles
not written, &c.[3];" as I have before recited, speaking of cere- Tract. ii.
monies not expressed in the word.   And you may see that
wise and learned men are not so scrupulous in apostolical
traditions not written, so that they be not such as are made
necessary unto salvation; neither is any learned man of contrary judgment.   And therefore archbishops may well be
brought from the apostles' times, without any danger of
admitting "the unwritten verities of the papists."   You have
not yet proved that either the name or office of archbishops
is in any respect " oppugned " in the word of God ; and therefore that is but feigned.

Chapter iii.   The Twenty-eighth Division
T. C. Page 81, Sect. 1.

*But all this time M. Doctor hath forgotten his question, which was to
prove an archbishop ; whereas all these testimonies which he allegeth make
mention only of a bishop; and therefore this may rather confirm the state
of the bishop in this realm than the archbishop.   But in the answer unto
them it shall appear that, as there is not in these places so much as the
name of an archbishop mentioned, so, except only the name of a bishop,
there shall be found very little agreement between the bishops in those days
and those which are called bishops in our time and with us.*

Jo. WHITGIFT.

M. Doctor remembereth that the authors of the Admonition as well deny the office of " a bishop " as the office of
" an archbishop," and he is not ignorant that the proof of the
one is the confirmation of the other, and therefore he useth
such testimonies as pertain to them both ; of the which nature
those places be that he hath hitherto alleged.   For you must
understand that I spake before of the name, and now, according to my promise, I speak of the office, which is not so
far distant from the bishop's, but that in most things they be
confounded.   But let us now hear how you perform your
promise.

[3 Calvin. Op. Amst. 1667-71. Comm. in Epist. i. ad Cor. cap. xi. Tom. VII.
p. 177. See Vol. I. page 221, note 7.]

Chapter iii.   The Twenty-ninth Division.

T. C. Page 81, Sect. 2.

And consequently, although M. Doctor thought with one whiting-box to have whited two walls (by establishing our archbishop and bishop by the same testimonies of the fathers), yet it shall be plain that, in going about to defend both, he left both undefended.

Jo. Whitgift.

Words of pleasure, too too usual with T. C., but of small weight (God be thanked), and of less truth.

Chapter iii.   The Thirtieth Division.

T. C. Page 81, Sect. 2, 3.

Let us therefore come first to examine Jerome's reasons why one must be over the rest; for in the testimony of men that is only to be regarded which is spoken either with some authority of the scripture, or with some reason grounded of the scripture: otherwise, if he speak without either scripture or reason, he is as easily rejected as alleged. " One (saith he), being chosen to be over the rest, bringeth remedy unto schisms:" how so? "Lest every man (saith he) drawing to himself do break the church in pieces."

Here you confound a monarchy and a tyranny.

Not so, if that one do govern by law. Your similitudes hold not.

Untruth.

A good proctor for contention.

But I would ask if the church be not in as great danger when all is done at the pleasure and lust of one man, and when one carrieth all into error, as when one pulleth one piece with him, another another piece, and the third his part also with him.   And it is harder to draw many into an error than one, or that many should be carried away by their affections than one; which is evident in water, which if it be but a little it is quickly troubled and corrupted, but being much it is not so easily.   But by this ecclesiastical monarchy all things are kept in peace. Nay, rather it hath been the cause of discord and well-spring of most horrible schism ; as it is to be seen in the very Decretals themselves[1].   And admit it were Decret. par. ii. c. 9. q. 3. et *so, yet the peace which is without truth is more execrable than* Can. Apost. 33. et alibi *a thousand contentions.   For as by striking of two flints to-* passim. *gether there cometh out fire, so it may be that sometimes by contention the truth which is hidden in a dark peace may come to light, which by a peace in naughtiness and wickedness, being as it were buried under the ground, doth not appear.*

Jo. Whitgift.

T. C. discrediteth the author whom he cannot answer

Jerome, being a man of such singular learning and great credit, among those that be learned, in a matter of history as this (for he reporteth when one bishop was placed over the

[1 See before, page 222, note 3 ; also below, pages 241, 2, notes 4, 1, 2.]

rest, and for what cause), is more to be believed without "reasons" than you with all your popular and frivolous arguments. Let the reader again consider whether this be your manner or no, by vain reasons to shake the credit of the author, when you cannot otherwise answer[2].

The reasons, that you use for the popular or aristocratical government of the church, when they come among the people, will be easily transferred to the state of the commonweal, and peradventure breed that misliking of civil government, that you would now have of ecclesiastical, to a further inconvenience and mischief than you and all yours will be able to remedy. In the meantime you utterly overthrow the queen's authority in ecclesiastical matters, given unto her by the laws of God; as hereafter shall be proved. For, if the state must either be popular or aristocratical, then must there be no one supreme governor in church-matters. But I will come to your reasons.

T. C. overthroweth the authority of the prince in matters ecclesiastical.

First you ask, "whether the church be not in as great danger when all is done at the pleasure and lust of one man, and when one carrieth all into error, &c." Here you do either ignorantly or wilfully confound *monarchiam* with tyranny[3]. For betwixt a king and a tyrant this is one difference, that a king ruleth according to the laws that are prescribed for him to rule by, and according to equity and reason; a tyrant doth what him list, followeth his own affections, contemneth laws, and saith, *Sic volo, sic jubeo: stat pro ratione voluntas*[4]: "So I will, so I command: my pleasure standeth for reason." Now, therefore, to use those reasons to overthrow a lawful monarchy, which are only proper to wicked tyranny, is either closely to accuse the government of this church of England of tyranny, or maliciously, by subtile dealing and confounding of states, to procure the misliking of the same in the hearts of the subjects. There is neither prince nor prelate in this land that ruleth "after their pleasure and lust," but according to

Difference betwixt a king and a tyrant.

The ecclesiastical government in this church not tyrannical but lawful.

[2 "The D. saith 'I refuse Jerome in a matter of story,' yet I deny no part of his story : wherein he seemeth to have lost all common sense. For who (in whom there is any light of judgment) would say it is matter of story, ' whether the appointing of one in every church over the rest is a remedy against heresy or no ?' ...If this be ' a matter of story,' story hath a larger kingdom than ever I heard of."—Sec. Repl. p. 577.]

[3 Cartwright rejoins here : "it is but a vain shifting-hole."—Ibid. p. 578.]

[4 Juvenal. Sat. vi. 222.]

those laws and orders that are appointed by the common
consent of the whole realm in parliament, and by such laws
of this monarchy as never hitherto any good subject hath
misliked; and therefore, your ground being false, how can the
rest of your building stand? It hath been said before that
the archbishop hath not this absolute authority given unto
him, to do all things alone, or as him lust. He is by law
prescribed both what to do, and how to proceed in his doings.
Moreover, this church of England (God's name be praised
therefore) hath all points of necessary doctrine certainly determined, ceremonies and orders expressly prescribed, from
the which neither archbishop nor bishop may swerve, and
according to the which they must be directed, to the observing of the which also their duty is to constrain all those that
be under them. So that whosoever shall wilfully and stubbornly sever himself from obedience either to archbishop or
bishop in such matters may justly be called a schismatic, or
a disturber of the church[1]. And in this respect is that saying
of Cyprian now most true: "For neither do heresies arise,
nor schisms spring of any other thing, but hereof, that the
priest of God is not obeyed[2]." And so is this of Jerome's in
like manner: *Ecclesiæ salus in summi sacerdotis pendet
dignitate; cui si non exors et ab omnibus eminens detur
potestas, tot in ecclesia efficiuntur schismata, quot sacerdotes*[3]:
"The safety of the church dependeth upon the dignity of the
high priest; to whom unless a singular and peerless power be
given, there will be as many schisms in the church as there
be priests."

*Lib. i.
Epist. 3.*

*Contra Luci-
ferianos.*

You say that "it is harder to draw many into an error
than one, &c.;" which is not true when that one ruleth and
governeth by law. For the mind of man, even of the best,
may be overruled by affection; but so cannot the law. Wherefore a wicked man directed by law governeth more indifferently than multitudes without law, be they never so godly.

*The govern-
ment of one
by law more
safe than of
many with-
out law.*

[1 Cartwright calls the answer here "as much to the question as if he had
answered of the weather. For the question is not of the estate of our church, but
of all generally; nor whether we have the truth of doctrine, &c., but by what way
it is best kept."—Sec. Repl. p. 578.]

[2 Cypr. Op. Oxon. 1682. Ad Cornel. Epist. lix. p. 129. See before, page 192,
note 2.]

[3 Hieron. Op. Par. 1693-1706. Adv. Lucifer. Tom. IV. Pars II. col. 295.
See before, page 222, note 5.]

Moreover, one godly wise and learned man is much more hardly moved to any error than is the multitude, which naturally is prone and bent to the same; in whom not only philosophers, but singular divines also, have noted great inconstancy and a disposition most unmeet to govern.

Your similitude of water holdeth not; for a little water in a gravelly or stony well or river is not so soon troubled and corrupted as are multitudes of waters in fennish and marish grounds. Again, a little water in a running river or ford is at all times more pure and clear than is a great quantity in standing puddles. To be short, is not the water of those little springs and conduit-heads (which, being safely locked up, and inclosed in stone and lead, do minister great relief to whole cities), much more pleasant, hardlier corrupted, less troubled, than the great waters in the Thames? Therefore is a little water proceeding from a good fountain, by stones and lead kept from things that may hurt it, hardlier putrefied and corrupted than all the fennish waters in a whole country, than mighty pools, yea, than the Thames itself. So is one wise and prudent man, governed and directed by order and by law, further from corruption and error in government, than whole multitudes of people, of what sort soever they be.

The similitude of water returned against the Replier.

You further say that "this ecclesiastical monarchy hath been the cause of discord, &c." I answer, that it hath been the cause of the contrary, until such time as it was turned into tyranny; as by all ecclesiastical stories and writers it may appear, and namely by these two, Cyprian and Jerome.

In all that Decretal, part ii. *C. 9. Quæst.* 3, noted in your margent, there is nothing against any form of government used by the archbishop in this church of England, but in plain and manifest words both the name and office of the archbishop is there maintained and approved. And I wish that the learned reader would peruse over all that part of Gratian, then should he easily perceive your faithfulness in alleging authorities. And, though it be somewhat tedious, yet, that the unlearned also may have some taste of your dealing, I will set down some canons contained in that part of Gratian. Out of the council of pope Martin he citeth this canon: *Per singulas provincias oportet episcopos cognoscere &c.*[4]: "In every province the bishops must know their metro-

The places cited by T. C. maketh for the archbishop.

[4 Per singulas &c. cognoscere metropolitanum tantum suum, et ipsum pri-

politan to have the chief authority, and that they ought to
do nothing without him, according to the old and ancient
canons of our forefathers; for the which cause also the metropolitan must take upon him nothing presumptuously without
the counsel of other bishops." And out of the council of
Antioch he hath this: *Per singulas provincias episcopos
singulos scire oportet &c.*[1] : "In every province the bishops
must know their metropolitan which governeth to have the
chief care of the whole province; and therefore those that
have any causes must resort to the metropolitan city. &c."
In all the rest of the canons he manifestly attributeth superiority and government to the archbishop and metropolitan,
even the same that we do in this church, only he denieth that
the metropolitan or archbishop hath such absolute authority,
that he can deal anything in criminal causes against a bishop,
or in other common matters, without the consent of other
bishops; which is not against anything by me affirmed, or
contrary to any authority claimed by the archbishop; for it
hath been from the beginning denied that the archbishop of
his own absolute authority can determine anything in matters
doubtful and not determined by the laws and orders of this
church, to the which the whole realm hath consented.

  The 33. canon of the apostles quoted in the margent is
Can. Apost.
33. this: *Episcopos singularum gentium scire convenit quis
inter eos primus habeatur, quem velut existiment &c.*[2] : "It
behoveth the bishops of every province to know who is chief
among them, whom they must esteem as their head, and do
nothing without his knowledge, save such things only as appertain to their own parish and villages which are under it;
neither shall he do anything without the knowledge of all.
For so shall unity be kept; and God shall be glorified through
Christ in the Holy Ghost." What have you gotten by this
canon? You see here manifestly that in every province or
nation there must be one chief bishop, that is archbishop; to

matus curam suscipere, nihil autem agere reliquos episcopos præter eum, secundum quod antiquitus a patribus nostris constitutum continetur in canone.
Propter quod metropolitanus episcopus nihil præsumptive assumat absque consilio cæterorum.—Concil. Martin. Papæ, cap. 4. in Corp. Jur. Canon. Lugd. 1624.
Decret. Gratian. Decr. Sec. Pars, Caus. IX. Quæst. iii. can. 1. col. 871.]

 [1 Ex Concil. Antioch. c. 9. ibid. can. 2. cols. 871, 2. See before, pages 145, 6,
note 1.]

 [2 Can. Apost. 33. in Concil. Stud. Labb. et Cossart. Lut. Par. 1671-2. Tom. I.
col. 32. See before, page 145, note 4.]

whom the rest must submit themselves, and do nothing without his knowledge.   This is as much as I require.   And, if this canon was made by the apostles (whereof you seem not to doubt), then is the name and authority of an archbishop of greater antiquity than you would gladly have it, and the reason and saying of St Jerome most true.

Both of this canon, and of the canon of the council of Antioch confirming it, I have spoken before.   Your *passim* in the margent, if it be meant of such like places as this, I grant it; but, if of any other popular or aristocratical state and kind of government, or to the improving of the office and authority of an archbishop, it will fall out to be *nusquam*. You say that "it appeareth in the Decretals themselves that this kind of government hath been the well-spring of most horrible schism."   Shew one place : why are you not ashamed to utter manifest untruths?   Shew one sentence there tending to that end.   I have recited some canons out of that place, and I have shewed the intent of Gratian both in them and in the rest.   They all signify that an archbishop may not do anything of his own authority without the consent of the other bishops; which no man denieth; and this is the whole scope of that question[3].

Our peace is in truth and due obedience : we have the true doctrine of the word of God, and the right administration of the sacraments; and therefore to make contention in this church, and to disturb the quietness and peace, cannot be but mere schismatical, I will say no worse.   Zuinglius in his Ecclesiastes saith that the anabaptists went about to defend their contentions then after the same manner that you do yours now.   But I answer you as he answered them : your contention is not against infidels, papists, and such like; but

[3 Cartwright rejoins : "After, where I quoted certain places out of the decrees, and other canons, to prove the contention for these offices, the Ans. acknowledgeth 'nothing' there 'that carrieth any sound that ways.'   Albeit the sound was clear enough, if he had not been deaf of that ear."   He then goes on to argue that the decrees and canons of councils prove that there was "continual war" "who should be the first," and concludes : "Whereby it appeareth, that this metropolitanship was the very apple of contention, in scambling for which, the church was miserably haled in pieces.   Therefore, forasmuch as the apostle sheweth that the truth is kept by the bond of unity, and it being most manifest that these smoky titles of honour were cause of contention, it followeth that, so far they are from that pretended, of being bulwarks against heresies and schisms, that they were the principal hooks that pulled them in."—Sec. Repl. pp. 580, 1.]

against the faithful, against the true professors of the gospel,
and in the church of Christ; and therefore, as it is of itself
wicked, so is it the cause of contempt, disobedience, and much
other ungodliness[1].   And "the two flint-stones" may be in
such time and place "stricken together," that the sparks of
fire which cometh from them may consume and burn the
whole city and country too.   And surely he is but a mad
man that will smite fire to light a candle to see by at noon-
day when the sun shineth most clearly.

Chapter iii.   The Thirty-first Division.
T. C. Page 81, Sect. 4.

*If therefore superiority and domination of one above the rest have
such force to keep men from schisms, when they be in the truth, it hath
as great force to keep them together in error; and so, besides that one is
easier to be corrupted than many, this power of one bringeth as great
incommodity in keeping them in error, if they fall into it, as in the truth,
if they are in it.*

Jo. Whitgift.

This is as though you should say that, if a monarchy be an
excellent kind of government, and indeed the best, when the
laws rule and not man[2] (as Aristotle saith), then also is it the
worst when affection ruleth and not the law, which is true;
for that is the worst state of government which is opposed to
the best.   But, if you will therefore conclude that a monarchy
is not the best state, your argument hath no reason in it:
even so is it in the government of the church, if the chief
governor thereof should follow his own appetite and be
ruled by his private affections; but it is far otherwise when
he ruleth according to the laws whereunto he himself is
subject.

Chapter iii.   The Thirty-second Division.
T. C. Page 81, Sect. 4.

*Moreover, if it be necessary, for the keeping of unity in the church of
England, that one archbishop should be primate over all, why is it not as
meet that, for the keeping of the whole universal church, there should be*

A popish
reason.

[1 H. Zvingl. Op. Tigur. 1581. Ecclesiast. Part II. foll. 44. 2, 54. See Vol. I.
pages 127, note 8, 128, 9, note 3.]

[2 See Aristot. Op. Lut. Par. 1629. De Rep. Lib. iii. cap. xv. Tom. II.
pp. 357, &c.]

one archbishop or bishop over all, and the like necessity of the bishop over
all Christendom, as of the bishop of all England? unless peradventure it
be more necessary that there should be one bishop over the universal church
than over the church of England; forasmuch as it is more necessary that
peace should be kept, and schisms be avoided in the universal church, than
in the particular church of England.

Jo. Whitgift.

This is the reason of the papists for the pope's supremacy; and you have borrowed it from them. Wherefore I will answer you as M. Calvin answereth them in his Institutions, *cap. viii. sect.* 95 : "That which is profitable in one nation cannot by any reason be extended to the whole world; for there is great difference betwixt the whole world and one nation[3]." And a little after : "It is even as though a man should affirm that the whole world may be governed by one king, because one field or town hath but one ruler or master[4]." And again : "That which is of force among few may not by and by be drawn to the whole world; to the government whereof no one man is sufficient[5]." M. Nowel also answereth Dorman (making the same reason that you do) in these words : "To your third question," saith he, speaking to Dorman, "the lewdest of all, why the same proportion may not be kept between the pope and the rest of the bishops of Christendom, that is, between the archbishop and the other bishops of the province? I answer, you might as well ask, why the same proportion may not be kept between one emperor of all the world and all the princes of the world to be under him, that is between the king of one realm and his lords under him? The reason that the same proportion cannot be kept is, first, because there is no like proportion at all between the ability of man's wit and power (being but weak) to govern one province, and his ability to govern the whole church and all churches throughout the world, which no one man can have knowledge of, much less can have ability to rule them. Secondly, you can bring no such pro-

The reasons serve not for the pope that serve for the arch-bishop.

Calvin.

M. Nowel, Lib. iii. fol. 321.

[3] Primum, quod in natione una fuit utile, id in universum orbem extendere nulla ratio cogit: imo gentis unius et totius orbis longe diversa erit ratio.—Calvin. Op. Amst. 1667-71. Inst. Lib. iv. cap. vi. 2. Tom. IX. p. 295.]

[4] Perinde enim est acsi quis contendat totum mundum a praefecto uno debere regi, quia ager unus non plures praefectos habeat.—Id. ibid.]

[5] Sed quod inter paucos valet, non protinus trahendum ad universum orbem terrarum, ad quem regendum nemo unus sufficit.—Id. ibid. 8. p. 296.]

portion of antiquity for your pope to be chief head of the whole church, as is to be shewed for archbishops to be the chief bishops in their own provinces, &c.[1]" Hitherto M. Nowel. I marvel that ye will join with the papists in so gross a reason.

Chapter iii.   The Thirty-third Division.
T. C. Page 82, Sect. 1.

If you say that the archbishop of England hath his authority granted of the prince, the pope of Rome will say that Constantine or Phocas, which was emperor of all Christendom, did grant him his authority over all churches.   But you will say that is[2] a lie; but the pope will set as good a face, and make as great a shew therein, as you do in divers points here. But admit it to be, yet[3] I say further, that it may come to pass, and it hath been, that there may be one christian Cæsar over all the realms which have churches.   What if he then will give that authority to one over all, that one king granteth in his land? may any man accept and take at his hands[4] such authority?   And, if it be not lawful for him to take that authority, tell me what fault you can find in him which may not be found in them.

Jo. WHITGIFT.

The pope doth challenge much of his temporalties from Constantinus and Phocas; but his supremacy and jurisdiction over all churches he claimeth from Peter and from Christ; wherein his claim is more intolerable, being most false, and his jurisdiction more usurped, being wrongfully challenged: you err therefore in that point greatly. The archbishop doth exercise his jurisdiction under the prince and by the prince's authority. For, the prince having the supreme government of the realm, in all causes and over all persons, as she doth exercise the one by the lord chancellor, so doth she the other by the archbishops.

Your supposition of one Cæsar over all realms that have churches is but supposed, and therefore of no weight; but admit it were true, yet is there not the like reason for one archbishop to be over all those churches, and over one province: the reasons I have alleged before out of M. Calvin

[1 A Confutation, as wel of M. Dormans last Boke entituled A Disproufe. &c. as also of D. Sander his causes of Transubstantiation, by Alexander Nowel. Lond. 1567. Conf. of M. Dorman's 7 chap. fol. 321; where *the same proportion that you speak of cannot be kept.*]

[2 That it is, Repl. 2.]

[3 But admit it to be a lie (as indeed it is touching Constantine) yet, Repl. 2.]

[4 Hand, Repl. 1 and 2.]

and other; neither is there any man not wilfully blinded, or papistically affected, that seeth not what great diversity there is betwixt one province, and many kingdoms, the government of the one, and the government of the other.   *Si unus duo-* Inst. cap. 8. *decim hominibus præfuit, an propterea sequetur unum debere centum millibus hominum præfici*[5] *?*   "If one was over twelve men, shall it therefore follow that one may be appointed over an hundred thousand men?" saith M. Calvin.

Chapter iii.   The Thirty-fourth Division.
T. C. Page 82, Sect. 2.

It will be said that no one is able to do the office of a bishop unto all the whole church. Neither is there any one able to do the office of a bishop to the whole church of England: for, when those which have been most excellent in knowledge and wisdom, and most ready and quick in doing and dispatching matters, being always present, have found enough to do to rule and govern one several congregation, what is he which absent is able to discharge his duty toward so many thousand churches? And, if you take exception that, although they be absent, yet they may do by under-ministers, as archdeacons[6]*, chancellors, officials, commissaries, and such other kind of people, what do you else say than the pope, which saith that by the cardinals*[7]*, and archbishops, and legates, and other such like, he doth*[8] *all things? For with their hands he ruleth all, and by their feet he is present everywhere, and with their eyes he seeth what is done in all places. Let them take heed therefore, lest, if they have a common defence with the pope, that they be not also joined nearer with him in the cause than peradventure they be aware of. Truly it is against my will that I* Who can be-*am constrained to make such comparisons; not that I think there is so* lieve you *great diversity between the popedom and the archbishopric, but because,* mean good *there being great resemblance between them, I mean having regard to the* faith? *bare functions, without respecting the doctrine good or bad which they uphold, that I say, there being great resemblance between them, there is yet, as I am persuaded, great difference between the persons*[9] *that execute them. The which good opinion conceived of them, I do most humbly beseech them, by the glory of God, by the liberty of the church purchased by the precious blood of our Saviour Christ, and by their own salvation, that they would not deceive, by retaining so hard such excessive and unjust dominion over the church of the living God.*

Jo. Whitgift.
But one man may do the office of an archbishop in one

---

[5] Calvin. Op. Amst. 1667-71. Inst. Lib. iv. cap. vi. 8. Tom. IX. p. 296; where *propterea consequetur*.]

[6] As by archdeacons, Repl. 1 and 2.]

[7] By his cardinals, Repl. 1, 2, and Def. A.]   [8] Doeth, Repl. 2.]

[9] Parsons, Repl. 1 and 2.]

province, every several diocese whereof hath a bishop.   And
one man may do the office of a bishop in one diocese, every
several parish whereof hath a several pastor.   The archbishop
hath a general charge over the province to see that unity be
kept among the bishops, and that the bishops do their duties
according to the laws and orders of the church, or else to see
them reformed according to the said laws and orders, if they
shall be complained of to have neglected the same.   The like
care have the bishops over the several pastors of their diocese,
and other persons.   Neither doth their office consist in preaching only, but in governing also; in the respect whereof they
are over and above the rest.   This office of government may
be well executed in one province, so much and so far as by
the laws is required, and as is convenient for the state of the
church; but it could not be so over all Christendom.

It may be that some pastors, having small charges and
busy heads, may find and procure more matters and controversies than either they be able or willing to compound : such
busy pastors there be in England; but their unquietness or
lack of ability to dispatch those controversies, which they
themselves are the authors and causes of, doth not prove but
that either the archbishop or bishop may do those things
sufficiently and well that do appertain to their office and
calling[1].

So much may they do "by under-ministers, as archdeacons, chancellors, &c.," as by the rules of the church are
permitted unto them[2], and may be convenient for the time
and persons.   But the office of preaching, of ordaining ministers, of suppressing heresies and schisms, with such like, they
do not commit unto them, but execute them themselves; the
which because they cannot do throughout all churches, as
they may in one province, therefore your reason is no reason.
Moreover, a bishop of one diocese or province may have conference with his archdeacons and chancellor, and be privy to

[1] " I make my argument of all; and he answereth of some : I of the most fit
and sufficient pastors; and he of unfit.   If he have any better answer, we will
attend after it; if not, then the archbishop is here again taken by default."—Sec.
Repl. p. 584.]

[2] "... it is his continual fault, that he should prove by the law of God he
proveth by the laws of our church, yea, and by those which remained of the estate
which was in popery.   I might much better allege the laws of the reformed
churches, which have abolished them."—Ibid. p. 585.]

all and singular their doings: so cannot the pope with "his cardinals, archbishops, and legates, &c." dispersed throughout whole Christendom. And therefore an archbishop or bishop may well govern a province or diocese, and use the help of archdeacons, chancellors, &c.; but so cannot the pope do whole Christendom, what help or deputies soever he have.

If "against your will" you were "constrained to make such comparisons," why do you make them when there is no cause? why do you forge that which is untrue? why do you join together offices which in no point are like. The pope challengeth authority over all Christendom; so do not our archbishops. The pope exalteth himself above kings and princes; so do not our archbishops, but with all reverence acknowledge their subjection to the prince. The pope saith that to be subject unto him is of necessity to salvation; so do not our archbishops. The pope maketh his decrees equal to the word of God; our archbishops think nothing less of theirs. To be short, the pope oppresseth and persecuteth the gospel; they earnestly profess it, and have suffered persecution for it. Therefore your comparison is odious, and your riotous speech more presumptuous than becometh a man pretending your simplicity[3].

Difference between the pope and our archbishops.

Your "good opinion conceived of them" is well uttered in your book: what spirit hath taught you thus to dissemble? Surely even the same that hath falsified scriptures and writers in your book, that hath uttered so many proud and contemptuous speeches against your superiors, that hath moved you to make contention in the church, even *spiritus mendax, spiritus arrogantiæ et superbiæ:* "a lying spirit, the spirit of arrogancy and pride;" for such fruits cannot proceed from any other spirit.

Chapter iii.   The Thirty-fifth Division.

T. C. Page 82, Sect. 3, 4.

But Jerome saith that this distinction of a bishop, and a minister or elder, was from St Mark his time unto Dionysius his time[4]; whereby M. Doctor would make us believe that Mark was the author of this dis-

[3 "The differences between the pope and the archbishop serve but for stuffing."—Ibid. p. 587.]

[4 Dionysius time, Repl. 1, 2, and Def. A.]

*tinction. But that cannot be gathered by Jerome's words[1]. For, besides
that, things being ordered then by the suffrages of the ministers and elders,
it might (as it falleth out oftentimes) be done without the approbation of
St Mark, the words "from Mark" may be rather taken exclusively, to shut
out St Mark, and the time wherein he lived, than inclusively, to shut him
in the time wherein this distinction rose.*

*Howsoever it be, it is certain that St Mark did not distinguish, and
make those things divers, which the Holy Ghost made all one. For then
(which the Lord forbid) he should make the story of the gospel which he
wrote suspected.*

Jo. Whitgift.

This is no answer to Jerome's words, but a dallying with
them: the place is evident: he saith, "from the time of
Mark the Evangelist," whom undoubtedly he would not have
named, unless the same manner had been in his time. But
be it that the words "from Mark" "be taken exclusively"
(which no man of judgment will grant), yet doth it argue a
great antiquity of this distinction, even from the most pure
and best time of the church.

It is certain that these things were not otherwise "distinguished" than the Holy Ghost had appointed; and therefore
your "for then, &c." is an ungodly collection, and unbeseem-
ing your person in any respect to imagine of the glorious
gospel written by that holy evangelist.

Chapter iii.   The Thirty-sixth Division.
T. C. Page 82, Sect. 5.

*An absurd
collection.*

*Again, it is to be observed that Jerome saith it was so in Alexandria,
signifying thereby that in other churches it was not so. And indeed it
may appear in divers places of the ancient fathers, that they confounded
priest and bishop, and took them for all one; as Eusebius out* Lib. v. 26.
of Irenæus calleth Anicete, Pius, Telesphorus, Higinus, Xystus,
πρεσβυτέρους καὶ προστάντας: *"elders and presidents[2]." Cyprian con-* De Dignitate
foundeth priest and bishop in the epistles before recited[3]: so sacerdotali.
doth Ambrose in the place alleged before by M. Doctor[4]; and

[1 See before, page 222, note 3.]

[2 Καὶ οἱ πρὸ Σωτῆρος πρεσβύτεροι οἱ προστάντες τῆς ἐκκλησίας ἧς νῦν
ἀφηγῇ, Ἀνίκητον λέγομεν καὶ Πίον, Ὑγῖνόν τε καὶ Τελεσφόρον καὶ Ξύστον,
κ. τ. λ.—Euseb. in Hist. Eccles. Script. Amst. 1695-1700. Lib. v. cap. xxiv.
p. 156.]

[3 Cypr. Op. Oxon. 1682. Ad Cornel. Epist. lix.; ad Steph. Epist. lxviii.
pp. 129, 178. See before, pages 192, 211.]

[4 Ambros. Op. Par. 1686-90. De Dign. Sacerd. cap. v. Tom. II. Append.
col. 362. See before, page 153, note 7.]

yet it is one thing with us to be a priest (as M. Doctor speaketh), and another thing to be a bishop.

JO. WHITGIFT.

This argument passeth of all that ever I heard. Jerome The passing logic of T. C. saith, there was a bishop " in Alexandria" above the other ministers from St Mark's time ; therefore there was no bishop in any place else. God is the God of Abraham, Isaac, and Jacob ; *ergo,* he is nobody's God else : he is the God of the Jews ; *ergo,* not of the gentiles. There be bishops in England ; *ergo,* there are none in any other place. No marvel is it though you riot in your logic, when such stuff is set abroad. Like unto this are the other : " Eusebius out of Irenæus calleth Anicete, Pius, Telesphorus, &c., elders and presidents ; and Cyprian confoundeth priest and bishop ; and so doth Ambrose ;" *ergo,* every priest is such a bishop as Jerome here speaketh of. These be pretty arguments.

Every bishop is a priest, but every priest hath not the Difference betwixt bishop and priest. name and title of a bishop, in that meaning that Jerome in this place taketh the name of a bishop. For his words be these : *Nam Alexandriæ a Marco evangelista usque ad* Hieronymus ad Eva-grium. *Heraclam &c.[5] :* " At Alexandria, from Mark the evangelist until Heracla and Dionysius, bishops, the ministers always chose one from among themselves, and, placing him in a higher degree of dignity, called him a bishop ; as if an army should make a captain[6], &c." Neither shall you find this word *episcopus* commonly used but for that priest that is in degree over and above the rest, notwithstanding *episcopus* be oftentimes called *presbyter*, because *presbyter* is the more general name ; so that M. Doctor saith truly, that " it is with us one thing to be a bishop, another thing to be a priest ;" because every bishop is a priest, but every priest is not a bishop.

I know these names be confounded in the scriptures, but I speak according to the manner and custom of the church, even since the apostles' time. And this is not only my opinion, but other learned men affirm it in like manner ; as M. Bucer in his book *De Regno Christi*[7], and upon the iv.

[5 Hieron. Op. Par. 1693-1706. Ad Evang. Epist. ci. Tom. IV. Pars ii. col. 803. See before, page 222, note 3.]   [6 Capitain, Def. B.]

[7 M. Bucer. De Regno Christ. Libr. ii. Basil. 1557. Lib. ii. cap. xii. p. 98. See before, page 231, note 6.]

Ephes.[1]; whose words I have before rehearsed. Thus you see that M. Doctor's distinction is with better authority confirmed than you have any to overthrow it.

Chapter iii. The Thirty-seventh Division.

T. C. Page 82, Sect. ult.

Jerusalem was a famous church; so was Rome, as the apostle witnesseth; so was Antioch and others; where also were Rom. i. 8.2 *great contentions, both in doctrine and otherwise; and yet for avoiding* of contention and schism there there was no one that was ruler of the *rest. Therefore we ought rather to follow these churches, being many, in keeping us to the institution of the apostles, than Alexandria, being but one church and departing from that institution; and, if there had been any one set over all the rest in other places, it would have made much for the distinction that Jerome had recited.*

An untruth

Jo. WHITGIFT.

Bishops at Jerusalem in the apostles' time.

James was bishop of Jerusalem, and in authority above all other ministers there.   Eusebius so reporteth of him out of Egesippus, who lived immediately after the apostles' time : his words out of Egesippus be these : *Ecclesiam gubernandam post apostolos Jacobus frater Domini accepit*[3] : "James the brother of the Lord had the government of the church after the apostles," *Lib. ii. cap.* 23.   And, in the beginning of that chapter, Eusebius, speaking of this James, saith thus : *Cui Hierosolymis ab apostolis episcopalis sedes concredita fuerat*[4] : "To whom the bishop's seat at Jerusalem was committed by the apostles."   In the first chapter of that book he saith, out of Clement, that Peter and John, after the ascension of Christ, *constituerunt Jacobum Justum Hierosolymorum episcopum*[5] : "did appoint James the Just bishop of Jerusalem."   The same thing do all ecclesiastical histories and writers (that make any mention of this matter) affirm of him.   After James was Simeon the son of Cleophas appointed bishop there ; as the same Eusebius reporteth, *Lib. iii. cap.* 11, and *Lib. iv.*

Eusebius, Lib. ii. cap. 23.

Lib. ii. cap. 1.

Idem.

[1 Id. Prælect. in Epist. ad Ephes. Basil. 1562. cap. iv. p. 107.   See before, pages 108, 9, note 2.]

[2 The verse is added from Repl. 2.]

[3 Euseb. in Hist. Eccles. Script. Amst. 1695-1700. Lib. ii. cap. xxiii. p. 50.]

[4 Id. ibid.]

[5 Πέτρον γάρ φησι καὶ Ἰάκωβον καὶ Ἰωάννην μετὰ τὴν ἀνάληψιν τοῦ Σωτῆρος...Ἰάκωβον τὸν Δίκαιον ἐπίσκοπον τῶν Ἱεροσολύμων ἐλέσθαι.—Id. ibid. cap. i. p. 30.]

cap. 22.[6]   Therefore you are greatly deceived in saying that there "was no one over the rest" at Jerusalem; although, if there had been none, yet would it not have served your turn; because, the apostles as yet being alive, this office of bishops was less needful.   But it is certain that they placed bishops in all great and famous churches after they had planted them; as Zuinglius saith in his Ecclesiastes[7]; and ancient authors do testify.

Linus was bishop of Rome; as Eusebius witnesseth, *Lib. iii. cap.* 2;[8] and he lived in the apostles' time; Timothy bishop at Ephesus, Titus at Creta, Dionysius Areopagita at Athens, &c.; as he also writeth in the same book, *cap.* 4.[9]   But this thing is so manifest and so well known to all that read ecclesiastical histories, that I am sure they will marvel at your gross oversight in denying the same.   Wherefore Jerome's distinction standeth.

Other bishops in the apostles' time. Eus. Lib. iii. cap. 2 & 4.

Chapter iii.   The Thirty-eighth Division.

T. C. Page 83, Lin. 2.

But against this distinction of St Jerome I will use no other reason than that which Jerome useth in the same epistle to Evagrius.   Jerome in that epistle taketh up very sharply the archdeacon that he preferred himself before the elder; and the reason is, because by the scripture the deacon is inferior to[10] *the elder.   Now therefore, Jerome himself confessing that by the scripture a bishop and an elder are equal, by Jerome's own reason the bishop is to be sharply reprehended, because he lifteth himself above the elder.*

Jerome speaketh not of an archdeacon, but of a deacon.

Jo. Whitgift.

Without doubt you forget yourself, else would you not reason in this manner : The archdeacon is inferior to the elder ; therefore the bishop is not superior to the elder in any respect.   I see no sequel in this reason, neither yet any likelihood[11].   Besides that, you untruly report of Hierome ;

[6 Id. Lib. iii. cap. xi.; Lib. iv. cap. xxii. pp. 69, 115. See before, page 136, note 7.]

[7 Quoties vero se fidem alicubi plantavisse, et eandem succrescere videbant [apostoli], mox vigiles et episcopos constituebant, &c.—H. Zvingl. Op. Tigur. 1581. Ecclesiast. Pars II. p. 48.]

[8 Euseb. in Hist. Eccles. Script. Lib. iii. cap. ii. p. 57.]

[9 Id. ibid. cap. iv. pp. 58, 9.   See before, page 130, note 4.]

[10 Unto, Repl. 1, 2, and Def. A.]

[11 "Notwithstanding I trust there is none that hath but his common sense, which doth not easily understand that it is no more lawful for those which are

for he speaketh of a deacon and not of an archdeacon. But it[1] is your manner so to deal: surely I marvel that you will utter so manifest untruths. But, if Hierome should so say, yet is your argument nothing; for, though an archdeacon be inferior to a minister (whom you call " elder "), yet doth not that prove but that there may be degrees among the ministers, and that the chiefest of them in authority may be called a bishop; as Hierome also in that epistle declareth. And, although Hierome confess that by scripture *presbyter* and *episcopus* is all one (as indeed they be *quoad ministerium*), yet doth he acknowledge a superiority of the bishop before the minister. For, besides these places that I have alleged in my Answer to the Admonition, he saith thus in the same epistle: *Presbyter et episcopus aliud ætatis, aliud dignitatis est nomen*[2]: " The one is a name of age, and the other of dignity." And a little after: *In episcopo et presbyter continetur*[3]: " The elder or minister is contained in the bishop." Therefore no doubt this is Jerome's mind, that a bishop in degree and dignity is above the minister, though he be one and the self-same with him in the office of ministering the word and sacraments; and therefore he saith, *Presbyter continetur in episcopo;* because every bishop is presbyter, but every presbyter is not bishop[4].

Ad Evagr.

Chapter iii.   The Thirty-ninth Division.

T. C. Page 83, Lin. 8.

But what helpeth it you that there was a bishop of Alexandria, which urge an archbishop, or what avantageth it you that there was one chief, called a bishop, in every several congregation, which would prove that there ought to be one bishop chief over a thousand congregations? What could have been brought more strong to pull down the archbishop out of his throne, than that which Jerome saith there, when he affirmeth that the

ordained equals by the scripture, to lift themselves one above another, than it is lawful for him that is appointed to be under, to exalt himself above his superior."—Sec. Repl. pp. 589, 90.]

[1] *It* is supplied from Def. A.]

[2] Hieron. Op. Par. 1693-1706. Ad Evang. Epist. ci. Tom. IV. Pars ii. col. 803.]

[3] Id. ibid.]

[4] Cartwright makes a long answer to this division, accusing Whitgift of " striving with the truth," of being " stricken with...a giddiness of spirit," of " oversight in his grammar," and " in logic," &c.—Sec. Repl. pp. 590, &c.]

*bishop of the obscurest village or hamlet hath as great authority and dignity
as the bishop of Rome? Erasmus did see this, and said, εἰρωνευόμενος, that
is, jestingly, that Hierome spake that of the bishops of his time [5]; but, "if he
had seen how the metropolitans of our age excel other bishops, he would
have spoken otherwise [6]." And what could have been more fit to have confuted the large dominion and superiority of our realm, than that that
Jerome saith, when he appointeth the bishop's see in an uplandish town,
or in a poor village or hamlet, declaring thereby that in every town there
was a bishop, and that the bishop that he speaketh of differeth nothing at
all from an elder, but that the bishop had the ordaining of the ministers?
Whereupon it doth appear (which I promised to shew) that by this place of
Jerome there is neither name of archbishop, nor so much as the shadow of
his authority, and that the bishops which are now have besides the name
no similitude almost with the bishops that were in Jerome's time. As for
his reason* ad Luciferanos, *it is the same which he hath* ad Evagr., *and
to Titus, and is already answered.*

But in the
same place
speaking in
earnest he af-
firmeth as
much as I
require.

Untrue.

JO. WHITGIFT.

If this be true that you say, why have you then hitherto
sought so to deface this worthy writer? why did you not in
the beginning tell us that this saying of Jerome made nothing
against you, because he only speaketh of pastors in several
parishes, and not of one to have charge and government over
one whole diocese? But full well knew you the vanity of
this your fancy, and how unlike it is to stand with Jerome's
words. For in his commentaries upon the epistle to Titus, he
saith that, *postquam unusquisque eos quos baptizaverat &c.*[7]:
"After that every one did think those to be his, and not
Christ's whom he had baptized, it was decreed throughout
the whole world that one of the ministers being chosen should
be set over the rest, unto whom the whole care of the church
should appertain, and the seeds of schisms be taken away."
Do you think that this is meant of the pastor of "every
town?" To what purpose should Jerome say so? For the
pastor of every several town had from the beginning his
authority over his flock without any such constitution. Moreover, there are not in every several congregation many pas-

Jerome's
bishop differ-
eth from an
elder in dig-
nity and rule.

Hier. in Tit. i.

<hr/>

[5 Times, Repl. 1 and 2.]

[6 Quod episcopo minus tribuit dignitatis, quam his temporibus videntur
possidere, non ad hanc tempestatem, sed ad eam, in qua vixit Hieronymus, referri
debet. Si nostros vidisset episcopos, longe aliud dixisset.—Hieron. Op. Par.
1534. Erasm. Schol. in Epist. ad Evagr. Tom. II. fol. 117. 2.]

[7 Id. Op. Par. 1693-1706. Comm. in Epist. ad Tit. cap. i. Tom. IV. Pars i.
col. 413. See before, pages 221, 2, note 5.]

tors or priests, over whom one should be placed as chief. But Jerome speaketh of a bishop that must govern the other priests, and procure that unity be kept among them; and therefore his jurisdiction must of necessity extend to many parishes, because it is over many pastors. He saith likewise that "the care of the whole was committed unto him." In his epistle *ad Evagrium* he uttereth his meaning as plainly.

Idem ad Evagr.

For he saith that "the priests did choose one among themselves, whom they, placing in a higher degree, called a bishop[1]." Whereby it appeareth that he had authority over many pastors, and therefore over many congregations; for you will not deny but that every *presbyter*, that is minister of the word, had his several flock. This he declareth more evidently by the examples there used, of soldiers choosing their captain; for, though the captain before was a common soldier, yet now, being thus preferred, he ruleth and governeth the rest of the soldiers; even so, the bishop being before a minister equal with other, yet, being chosen to that degree, he is their guide and governor; a governor, I say, of those that did elect him, that is of priests or ministers, and therefore of divers congregations.

Ibidem.

This doth yet more evidently appear in these words of the same epistle: "That one was afterwards chosen to rule the rest, it was a remedy against schisms, lest every one, drawing to himself the church, should break the same[2]."

Idem contra Lucifer.

And, in his book *contra Luciferianos*, he saith that, "except the chief authority were given to one, *tot essent schismata quot sacerdotes:* there would be as many schisms as priests[3]." By which places it is certain that Jerome's meaning is to have some one in a province or diocese over the rest (properly called a bishop), who should have chief authority, lest every man, in his own several parish being permitted to do what he list, might in the end fill the church with schisms, *ut tot essent schismata quot sacerdotes.* And surely it is unpossible to expound Jerome otherwise.

But you ask me, "what this helpeth for the archbishop, &c.?" Very much. For, if it be so necessary to have one

[1 Id. ad Evang. Epist. ci. Tom. IV. Pars II. col. 803. See before, page 222, note 3.]

[2 Id. ibid. See before, page 222, note 3.]

[3 Id. adv. Lucifer. Tom. IV. Pars II. col. 295. See before, page 222, note 5.]

bishop over divers priests in every several diocese, for the avoiding of schism and contention, it is also necessary in every province to have an archbishop for the direction of divers bishops, and the avoiding of schism among them. And therefore saith Jerome again in his epistle *ad Rusticum Monachum:* "Every ecclesiastical order is subject to her governors[4]."

Hier. ad Rusticum.

You ask, "what could have been brought more strong to pull down the archbishop out of his throne than that which Jerome saith there, when he affirmeth that the bishop of the obscurest village or hamlet hath as great authority and dignity as the bishop of Rome?" I answer that this nothing at all derogateth from the archbishop. For it is not denied but that every bishop and every minister are equal *quoad ministerium*, but not *quoad ordinem et politiam;* and this is that which Jerome saith, *Ejusdem sunt meriti et sacerdotii[5]:* "They be of the same merit and priesthood," that is, their ministry and office in preaching the word and administering the sacraments is all one; and their authority also toward such as were under their jurisdiction. But he doth not say that one bishop hath not more ample and large jurisdiction than the other; for the contrary of that is manifest. And in St Jerome's time there were metropolitans, archbishops, &c.; as you may read in the Defence of the Apology[6], Edit. 2. pa. 121.

Metropolitans, &c. in Jerome his time.

These obscure towns do derogate nothing from the authority of a bishop; for we see it oftentimes come to pass, that the bishop's seat is often in[7] obscure towns; as it is in divers places of England: and yet is the bishop's jurisdiction in his diocese no whit the less. If we respect the places, Canterbury is far inferior to London. And therefore Jerome's meaning is that the place neither addeth anything or taketh anything away from the worthiness, authority, and office of a bishop. Wheresoever a bishop is, in city or in town, he is of the same authority and worthiness.

Erasmus in his Scholies upon that epistle of Jerome hath these words: *Certe metropolitanus habet aliquid dignitatis,*

Erasmus.

[4] ... et omnis ordo ecclesiasticus suis rectoribus nititur.—Id. ad Rustic. Monach. Epist. xcv. Tom. II. Pars II. col. 775.]

[5] Ubiquumque fuerit episcopus...ejusdem meriti, ejusdem est et sacerdotii.— Id. ad Evang. Epist. ci. Tom. IV. Pars II. col. 803.]

[6] See Bp. Jewel's Works, Park. Soc. Edit. Vol. III. p. 292.]

[7] Is but in, Def. A.]

&c. [1] : " Surely the metropolitan hath some dignity and jurisdiction above the other bishops; therefore that he here maketh
the bishops of base cities equal with the rest, it is to be referred unto the deacons, which in some places were preferred
before the ministers, whom he doth in a manner make equal
with bishops. And in another place he saith that the ministers succeed into the place of the apostles, the bishop into the
place of Christ. In this thing therefore are bishops and
ministers equal, that, wheresoever they are, they are to be
preferred before deacons." Here Erasmus speaketh in good
earnest, howsoever he jested before. He sheweth that these
obscure villages or hamlets (as you term them) were cities,
and no doubt as good as either Ely or Peterborough; but, in
the respect of Rome, contemptible, as these be in respect of
London. And yet the bishops of every one of them *ejusdem
meriti et sacerdotii:* " of the same merit, priesthood, and
authority." Erasmus also here telleth in what respect he hath
made this comparison betwixt bishops and other ministers, in
the respect of deacons. For both bishops and priests are to
be preferred equally before deacons, because of their ministry
and office, which is above the office of a deacon. *Nam ex diacono ordinatur presbyter:* " For a minister or priest is made
of a deacon," not *ex presbytero diaconus* [2] : " the deacon of the
priest." It is most evident (neither can it be so unknown
unto you) that Jerome in all these places meaneth to have one
bishop governor of many priests. And therefore this interpretation of yours is without all probability, or shadow of
truth, that " Hierome's meaning is to have such a bishop in
every town."

The shift of
T. C. in his
answer to
Hierome.

I trust the reader will note with what vain reasons you
first went about to shake the credit of this writer; then, how
without reason you took upon you to answer his reasons;
and now, in the end, how unpossible an interpretation you feign

[1 Certe metropolitanus habet aliquid dignitatis, et jurisdictionis supra reliquos
episcopos. Itaque quod hic æquat humilium urbium episcopos cum aliis, ad
diaconos est referendum : qui nonnullis locis præferebantur presbyteris, quos
propemodum æquat episcopis. Et alicubi dicit, presbyteros in apostolorum vicem
succedere, episcopum in locum Christi. In hoc igitur æquales sunt episcopi et
presbyteri, quod, ubicunque sunt, diaconis sint præferendi.—Hieron. Op. Par.1534.
Erasm. Schol. in Epist. ad Evagr. Tom. II. fol. 117. 2.]

[2 Aut igitur ex presbytero ordinetur diaconus, ut presbyter minor diacono
comprobetur, in quem crescit ex parvo: aut si ex diacono ordinatur presbyter,
noverit se lucris minorem, sacerdotio esse majorem.—Id. Op. Par. 1693-1706. Ad
Evang. Epist. ci. Tom. IV. Pars ii. col. 803.]

of his words; which if he well consider, he shall note in you great audacity, small judgment, and no truth. For the author is of great learning and worthiness, his reasons strong, and his words plain and evident, for the authority of the bishop over the rest of the clergy [3].

Chapter iii.   The Fortieth Division.

Answer to the Admonition, Page 71, Sect. 2, 3.

Chrysostom, writing upon the twentieth of Matthew, saith that "the rebellious nature of man caused these distinctions of degrees, that one should be an apostle, another a bishop, another a minister, another a layman." And that, "unless there were such distinctions of persons, there could be no discipline [4]."

And upon the xiii. to the Romans he saith that, "because equality engendereth strife and contention, therefore superiority and degrees of persons were appointed [5]."

[☞ And in the *xiii. ad Hebr.*, expounding these words, *Parete his qui præsunt vobis, &c.* (which both he and all other writers understand of bishops), saith that there be three evils which overthrow the church and all other societies: the first is to have no superior, none to rule; the second, to have many disobedient; the third, to have evil rulers. The first he proveth by divers examples, as by a quire which is without a chanter, an army of soldiers without a captain, a ship without a

(marginal note: Chrysostom.)

[3 Cartwright rejoins at very great length to this division, maintaining that Whitgift cannot "prove that the bishop had any further reach than unto one only church." He adds, however, "I will not deny but in Jerome's times the bishops upon occasions before of me alleged had enlarged their bounds in such sort, that there were certain congregations which belonged to their oversight, and whereof they were called bishops. But I appeal first," he goes on, "to the institution of God, and use of the purer times after the apostles: and then I answer, that a diocese was not the twentieth part of that which they have now. &c."—Sec. Repl. pp. 593, &c.]

[4 Quod autem in hoc sæculo differentia dignitatis facta est inter sanctos, dignitatis dico, non sanctitatis, ut alter quidem sit apostolus, alter autem episcopus, vel minister, vel laicus: contumacia carnis coëgit,... nisi ergo sint quos timeant, solvitur disciplina.—Chrysost. Op. Par. 1718-38. Op. Imp. in Matt. Hom. xxxv. ex cap. xx. Tom. VI. p. cliii.]

[5 Ἐπειδὴ γὰρ τὸ ὁμότιμον μάχην πολλάκις εἰσάγει, πολλὰς ἐποίησε τὰς ἀρχὰς καὶ τὰς ὑποταγὰς, κ. τ. λ.—Id. in Epist. ad Rom. Hom. xxiii. Tom. IX. p. 686.]

master, a flock of sheep without a shepherd; as it may
in that place more at large be seen[1]. 🐚][2].

T. C. Page 83, Sect. 1.

*What is that to the purpose, that Chrysostom saith there must be
degrees? Who denieth that there are degrees of functions? We confess
there is, and ought to be, a degree of pastors, another of doctors, the third
of those which are called elders, the fourth of deacons. And, where he
saith, there should be "one degree of bishop, another of a minister, another
of the layman," what proveth that for the office of an archbishop, which is
your purpose to shew? How oftentimes must you be called ad Rhombum?
And that he meaneth nothing less than to make any such difference between
a bishop and a minister, as is with us, which you would fain make your
reader believe, I will send you to Chrysostom, upon the third chapter
1. Epistle to Timothy; where he saith: "The office of a bishop differeth
little or nothing from an elder's;" and, a little after, that "a bishop differeth nothing from an elder or minister but by the ordination only."
Still M. Doctor goeth forward in killing a dead man, that is, in confuting that which all men condemn, and proving that which no man
denieth; that there must be superiority amongst men, and that equality
of all men alike confoundeth all and overthroweth all.*

*It proveth
that there
are degrees
among
ministers of
the word ;
which you
deny.*

Jo. Whitgift.

Chrysostom in that place maketh degrees in the ministry,
and placeth the bishop in degree above the minister; which
utterly overthroweth your equality. As for your distinction
of degrees, it hath as small ground in the scripture to warrant
it as can be; and indeed it is but your own invention. For
the pastor, doctor, and elder in office are all one; as the most
and best writers think. Howsoever it is, you have them not
thus distinguished in the scripture, that the pastor should be
first, the doctor next, the elder third, and the deacon last;
and it is strange that you will invent a new order of ministers, without the express warrant of God's word, misliking the
same so much in other.

[1 Κακὸν μὲν ἡ ἀναρχία πανταχοῦ, καὶ πολλῶν ὑπόθεσις συμφορῶν, καὶ
ἀρχὴ ἀταξίας καὶ συγχύσεως· μάλιστα δὲ ἐν ἐκκλησίᾳ τοσοῦτον ἐπισφαλεσ-
τέρα ἐστὶν, ὅσον καὶ τὸ τῆς ἀρχῆς μεῖζον καὶ ὑψηλότερον. ὥσπερ γὰρ, ἂν
χοροῦ τὸν κορυφαῖον ἀνέλῃς, οὐχὶ κατὰ μέλος καὶ κατὰ τάξιν ὁ χορὸς ἔσται,
καὶ φάλαγγος στρατοπέδου τὸν στρατηγὸν ἂν ἀποστήσῃς, οὐκ ἔτι ῥυθμῷ καὶ
τάξει τὰ τῆς παρατάξεως ἔσται, καὶ πλοίου τὸν κυβερνήτην ἐὰν περιέλῃς,
καταδύσεις τὸ σκάφος· οὕτω καὶ ποιμνίου τὸν ποιμένα ἐὰν ἀποστήσῃς, πάντα
ἀνέτρεψας καὶ ἠφάνισας. κακὸν μὲν οὖν ἡ ἀναρχία, καὶ ἀνατροπῆς ὑπόθεσις.
κακὸν δὲ οὐχ ἧττον καὶ ἡ ἀπείθεια τῶν ἀρχομένων...ἀλλ' ἴσως ἐρεῖ τις ἡμῖν,
ὅτι ἔστι καὶ τρίτον κακὸν, ὅταν ὁ ἄρχων ᾖ κακός.—Id. in Epist. ad Hebr. cap.
xiii. Hom. xxxiv. Tom. XII. p. 311.]

[2 This paragraph is inserted from Answ. 2.]

This superiority that Chrysostom talketh of overthroweth that part of the Admonition that I confute; for they do not only disallow the office of the archbishop, but of the bishop also, and would have a mere equality among the ministers: this I refel, as well as the other; and indeed the overthrow of this is the overthrow of the other. And therefore this place of Chrysostom serveth my turn very well, and aptly.

Chrysostom, upon that iii. chapter of the first to Timothy, giveth as much superiority to the bishop as I do, and maketh as much difference betwixt him and the minister; for I grant that *quoad ministerium* they be all one, but that there be degrees of dignity; and so saith Chrysostom, that " there is little difference betwixt a bishop and a priest;" but that a bishop hath authority to ordain priests, and all other things that the bishop may do the priest also may do, that excepted[3]; so that Chrysostom here speaketh only of the ministry of the bishop, not of his authority in the ecclesiastical government; for of that he spake in the place before alleged, where he saith that " there is one degree of the bishop, and another In xx. Matth. of the minister, &c.[4];" which distinction of degrees was long before Chrysostom's time, as I have declared.

To prove these degrees of superiority among ministers is to prove that which both the Admonition and you " deny," and which is the ground of this controversy; and therefore I have not herein gone about to " kill a dead man," except you count the ground of your assertion " dead."

If " there must be superiority amongst men, and that equality of all men alike confoundeth all and overthroweth" (as you confess, and is most true), then equality of ministers confoundeth all among them; and therefore it is requisite that in that state also there be superiors to avoid confusion; which being granted, what have you to say, either against archbishops or bishops, except you have some new device of your own? which is not unlike, because nothing doth please you but your own.

[3 Ὅτι οὐ πολὺ μέσον αὐτῶν [πρεσβυτέρων] καὶ τῶν ἐπισκόπων...τῇ γὰρ χειροτονίᾳ μόνῃ ὑπερβεβήκασι, καὶ τούτῳ μόνον δοκοῦσι πλεονεκτεῖν τοὺς πρεσβυτέρους.—Id. in I. Epist. ad Tim. cap. iii. Hom. xi. Tom. XI. p. 604.]

[4 See before, page 259, note 4.]

Chapter iii.   The Forty-first Division.

T. C. Page 83, Sect. 2.

This is a notable argument: There must be some superior amongst[1]
men; ergo, one minister must be superior to another: again: There must
be in the ecclesiastical functions some degrees; ergo, there must be an arch-
bishop over the whole province, or a bishop over the whole diocese.   And,
albeit M. Doctor taketh great pain to prove that which no man denieth,
yet he doth it so evil-favouredly and so unfitly, as that, if a man had no
better proofs than he bringeth, the degrees of the ecclesiastical functions
might fall to the ground.   For here, to prove the degrees of the ecclesiastical
functions, he bringeth in that that Chrysostom saith there must be magis-
trate and subject, him that commandeth and him that obeyeth.

Jo. Whitgift.

Superiority
convenient
among mi-
nisters.

The argument is good, and followeth very well.   For, as
superiority and government is necessary in all other states
and degrees of men, so is it in the ministry also; for ministers
be not angels, nor they are not of that perfection that they
may safely be left in their own absolute government.   That
which Chrysostom in this place speaketh of government in
the civil state, the same doth he speak in the xiii. to the
Hebrews of the ecclesiastical in like manner; for, expounding

Chrysost.

these words, *Parete his qui præsunt vobis, &c.*, which is understood of bishops, he saith that there be three evils which
overthrow the church and all other societies.   The first
whereof is to have no superior, none to rule; and this he
proveth by divers examples, as of a quire without a chanter,
an army of soldiers without a captain, a ship without a master,
a flock of sheep without a shepherd[2].   Now, if superiority be
so needful among the clergy, then why may not one bishop
be over one diocese, and one archbishop over one province?
Wherefore I conclude thus: It is necessary that among the
clergy some should be in authority over the rest; and therefore there may be both archbishops and bishops.   But I know
you will answer that there may be government without these
degrees: then say I unto you again, Stand not so much in
your own conceit: this order is most ancient in the church, it
is confirmed by the best and noblest councils, it is allowed
by the best-learned fathers, it hath the pattern from the

[1 Among, Repl. 2.]

[2 Chrysost. Op. Par. 1718-38.   In Epist. ad Hebr. cap. xiii. Hom. xxxiv.
Tom. XII. p. 311.   See before, page 260, note 1.]

practice of the apostles (all which hath been shewed before), it is most meet for this state and kingdom; and therefore be not wilful in a new device, the trial whereof was never as yet, the manner whereof is unknown to yourself[3], and the end no doubt mere confusion. Your well-favoured and fit speeches, together with your accustomed contempt, I omit here, as I do in other places.

Chapter iii. The Forty-second Division.

T. C. Page 83, Sect. 3.

The most therefore that he can conclude of this, for the ministry, is that there must be minister that shall rule and people that shall be obedient; and hereby he cannot prove that there should be any degrees amongst the ministers and ecclesiastical governors, unless he will say, peradventure, that, as there are under-magistrates and a king above them all, so there should be under-ministers, and one minister above all[4]. But he must remember that it is not necessary in a commonwealth that there should be one over all; for that there are other good commonwealths, wherein many have like power and authority. And further, if, because there is one king in a land above all, he will conclude there should be one[5] archbishop over all, I say, as I have said, that it is not against any word of God which I know (although it be inconvenient) but that there may be one Cæsar over all the world; and yet I think M. Doctor will not say that there may be one archbishop over all the world.

Note this suspicious speech of the kind of government.

Jo. Whitgift.

Yes, I will conclude that there ought to be degrees of superiority among the ministers also, because they labour of imperfections as well as other men do, and especially of pride, arrogancy, vain-glory, which engender schisms, heresies, contentions; as the examples of all times and ages even from the apostles to this time declare.

Why there ought to be superiority among ministers as well as other.

I am persuaded that the external government of the church under a christian magistrate must be according to the kind and form of government used in the commonwealth; else how can you make the prince supreme governor of all states and causes ecclesiastical[6]? will you so divide the govern-

The government of the church in a christian commonwealth ough to be according to the form therein used.

[3 You self, Def. B.]
[4 Above them all, Repl. 1 and 2.]   [5 None, Repl. 1.]
[6 "His reason ('the prince cannot else be supreme governor of all estates and causes ecclesiastical'), to say no more, is senseless, and hath no knot with that whereunto it belongeth."—Sec. Repl. p. 604.]

ment of the church from the government of the commonwealth, that, the one being a monarchy, the other must be a
democraty, or an aristocraty? This were to divide one realm
into two, and to spoil the prince of the one half of her jurisdiction and authority. If you will therefore have the queen
of England rule as monarch over all her dominions, then must
you also give her leave to use one kind and form of government in all and every part of the same, and so to govern
the church in ecclesiastical affairs as she doth the commonwealth in civil.

T. C. speak-
eth suspici-
ously of go-
vernment.

But you say that I "must remember that it is not necessary in a commonwealth that there should be one over
all;" and I say that you must remember that in this commonwealth it is necessary that one should be over all,
except you will transform as well the state of the kingdom
as you would of the church; which is not unlike to be your
meaning; for not long after you add that the "commonwealth
must be framed according to the church, as the hangings to
the house, and the government thereof with her government,
&c.; and not contrary[1];" meaning that the government of the
commonwealth ought not to be monarchical, but either de-
mocratical, or aristocratical, because (as you say) the government of the church ought to be such. What this in time will
breed in this commonwealth, especially when it cometh to
the understanding of the people, who naturally are so desirous
of innovations, I refer it to the judgment of those that can
and ought best to consider it.

The unlikeliness that is betwixt "one Cæsar being over all
the world," and of "one archbishop being over all the world,"
I have shewed before: they be most unlike; and yet this is
but a frivolous and vain supposition; and M. Calvin, in his
Inst. cap. viii. sect. 96., doth say that it is *absurdissimum :*
"most absurd[2]."

[1 See Tract. XVII. Chap. ii. Div. 17.]

[2 Verum sit sane, ut volunt, bonum atque utile, orbem totum monarchia con-
tineri : quod est tamen absurdissimum. sed ita sit: non tamen propterea concedam
idipsum in ecclesiæ gubernatione valere.—Calvin. Op. Amst.1667-71. Inst. Lib.IV.
cap. vi. 9. Tom. IX. p. 296.]

Chapter iii.   The Forty-third Division.

Answer to the Admonition, Page 71, Sect. 4.

It is not to be denied but that there is an equality of all ministers of God's word *quoad ministerium :* "touching the ministry ;" for they have all like power to preach the word, to minister the sacraments : that is to say, the word preached, or the sacraments ministered, is as effectual in one (in respect of the ministry) as it is in another.   But, *quoad ordinem et politiam :* "touching order and government," there always hath been and must be degrees and superiority among them.   For the church of God is not a confused congregation, but ruled and directed as well by discipline and policy in matters of regiment, as by the word of God in matters of faith.

Equality among ministers touching ministry[3].

T. C. Page 84, Sect. 1, 2.

Now M. Doctor cometh to his old hole, where he would fain hide himself, and with him all the ambition, tyranny, and excess of authority which is joined with these functions of archbishop and bishop, as they are now used ; and this his hole is that all the ministers are equal with bishops and archbishops, as touching the ministry of the word and sacraments, but not as touching policy and government.   The papists use the very self-same distinction for the maintenance of the pope's tyranny and ambition, and other their hierarchy.

This distinction is allowed of those that be far from papistry.

M. Doctor hath put out the mark and concealed the name of the papists, and so with a little change of words, as it were with certain new colours, he would deceive us.   For the papists say that every sir John or hedge-priest hath as great authority to sacrifice and offer for the quick and the dead, and to minister the sacraments, as the pope of Rome hath, but for government and for order the bishop is above a priest, the archbishop above a bishop, and the pope above them all.   But I have declared before out of the scriptures, how vain a distinction it is ; and it appeareth out of Cyprian that, as all the bishops were equal one to another, so he saith that "to every one was given a portion of the Lord's flock," not only to feed with the word and sacraments, but "to rule and govern," not as they which shall make any account unto an archbishop, or be judged of him, but as they which cannot be judged of any but of God[4].   And Jerome upon Titus saith that the elder or minister did govern and rule, in common with the bishops, the church whereof he was elder or minister[5].

You have not yet declared it, neither can you.

But you conceal that which followeth.

[3 In what respect there is equality among ministers, Answ. 2.]

[4 Cypr. Op. Oxon. 1682. Ad Cornel. Epist. lix. p. 136. See before, page 208, note 1.]

[5 See next page, note 4.]

Jo. Whitgift.

The distinction *quoad ministerium*, and *quoad ordinem*, justified. Calvin.

The distinction is good and true, allowed of the best writers; though the papists wrongfully apply it. M. Calvin, upon the 2. Cor. x., hath the same distinction. *Quamvis ...* (saith he) *commune sit omnibus verbi ministris idemque officium, sunt tamen honoris gradus*[1]: "Although there is one office common to all the ministers of the word, yet are there degrees of honour." M. Beza likewise, *Lib.Conf. cap. vii.*, saith

Beza. Lib. Con. cap. vii. Art. 12.

thus: "That pastors in process of time were distinct into metropolitans, bishops, and those we now call curates, it was not in the respect of the ministry of the word, but rather in respect of jurisdiction and discipline. Therefore concerning the office of preaching the word and administrating the sacraments there is no difference betwixt archbishops, bishops, and curates. &c.[2]" The same distinction doth Hemingius use in

In the 72. division of this chapter.

his *Enchiridion*[3]; as shall be seen hereafter. What say you now? is this a starting-"hole," or rather a true distinction, allowed by such as are far from papistry? except you will accuse M. Calvin and Beza for papists. You are not able to improve this distinction with all the learning you boast of; and bitterness of words will not carry away the matter.

You "have declared" nothing tending to the improving "of this distinction;" and the words both of Cyprian and of Hierome do manifestly confirm it; for they both would have one chief among the ministers to govern the rest, as it is said before. You deal corruptly in reciting Hierome's words; for you have left out his purpose and meaning: I will set them

Hier ad Tit. i.

down as they be indeed: *Idem est ergo presbyter, &c.*[4]: "Wherefore the minister and bishop are all one; and, before that

---

[1 Calvin. Op. Amst. 1667-71. Comm. in Epist. ii. ad Corinth. cap. x. v. 8. Tom. VII. p. 261.]

[2 Nam quod pastores temporis progressu distincti sunt in metropolitas, episcopos, et quos nunc vocant curatos, id est singulis parœciis præfectos, id minime factum est respectu ministerii verbi, sed potius habita ecclesiasticæ jurisdictionis ac disciplinæ ratione. Itaque quod attinet ad verbi prædicandi munus, et sacramentorum administrationem, nullum est inter archiepiscopos, episcopos, et curatos discrimen.—Th. Bezæ Confess. Christ. Fid. Genev. 1587. cap. vii. 12. p. 238.]

[3 ... in ministris magna est diversitas. Quanquam enim potestas omnium eadem est ministrorum, quantum ad spiritualem jurisdictionem attinet...tamen dispares dignitatis ordines et gradus sunt.—N. Hemming. Opusc. Theol. 1586. Enchir. Theol. Class. iii. cap. x. col. 459.]

[4 Hieron. Op. Par. 1693-1706. Comm. in Epist. ad Tit. cap. i. Tom. IV. Pars i. col. 413. See before, pages 221, 2, note 5.]

through the instinct of the devil there were divisions in religion, and that it was said among the people, I hold of Paul, I of Apollo, and I of Cephas, the churches were ruled in common by the council of the ministers; but, after that every one accounted those whom he baptized to be his, and not Christ's, it was decreed throughout the whole world, that one being chosen from among the ministers should be placed over the rest, to whom the whole care of the church should appertain, and the seeds of schisms be taken away." Will you not leave off to deal thus guilefully with your reader? have you no care to deal plainly and simply? Jerome in that place verifieth this distinction, and sheweth that it was for order and policy, that among the ministers there was one bishop appointed, *ad quem omnis ecclesiæ cura pertineret, et schismatum semina tollerentur.* And what can be spoken more directly to the purpose? But one thing here I note, that you would be controlled of none but of God, that is, you would be exempted from all authority of man, even as the pope himself is.

Chapter iii.   The Forty-fourth Division.

Answer to the Admonition, Page 72, Lin. 4.

And therefore well saith M. Calvin, in his Institutions, *cap. viii.:* "That the twelve apostles had one among them to govern the rest, it was no marvel; for nature requireth it, and the disposition of man will so have it, that in every company (although they be all equal in power) yet that there be one as governor, by whom the rest may be directed: there is no court without a consul, no senate without a prætor, no college without a president, no society without a master[5]." *Hæc Calvin.*

Calvin alloweth superiority.

T. C. Page 84, Sect. 3.

After followeth M. Calvin, a great patron forsooth of the archbishop, or of this kind of bishop, which is used amongst us here in England. And here to pass over your strange citations and quotations which you make, to put your answerer to pain, sending him sometimes to Musculus' Common-places for one sentence, to Augustine's works, to Chrysostom's works, to Cyril, to M. Fox, and here sending him to the viii. chapter of the Insti-

[5 Calvin. Op. Amst. 1667-71. Inst. Lib. IV. cap. vi. 8. Tom. IX. p. 296. See before, page 231, note 5.]

As though
you know
not that
there are
divers
editions of
his Institu-
tions.

*tutions, as though you had never read Calvin's Institutions, but took the
sentence of somebody else, without any examination; whereby it seemeth
that you were loth that ever any man should answer your book—letting,
I say, all this pass, what maketh this either to prove that there should be
one archbishop over all the ministers in the province, or one bishop over
all in the diocese, that amongst twelve that were gathered together into one
place there was one which ruled the action for which they met?*

JO. WHITGIFT.

A practice
worthy the
noting.

This is to be observed throughout your whole book, as
I have noted in other places, that, when any authority is
alleged that pincheth you, then you fall to cavilling by and by.
I have nowhere referred you to "Justinian's code," to "Gratian's decrees," to "Augustine's works," to "divers councils,"
to "Theodoret," to the "Centuries," &c., without noting either
book, chapter, distinction, number, canon, or such like, as you
usually deal with me; and yet these be far more tedious to read
over than is the viii. chap. of Calvin's Institutions. I do not
remember that I referred you to Augustine, Chrysostom, or
any other writers, for any matter in controversy (Cyril,
Musculus, and M. Fox only in one place excepted), but I
quoted the places as particularly as I could[1]. And why will
you then so untruly report of me? undoubtedly I never read
a book, for the quantity of it, so pestered with slanderous reports, false accusations, and contentious deriding speeches, as
this your book is. But let it go.

This book of Institutions, which is distinguished into chapters and not into books, I read and noted through before you
(as it should seem) knew whether there were any such book
or no; and, because I have laboured in it, noted it, and am
well acquainted with it, therefore I use it, and follow it, and
Divers edi-
tions of Cal-
vin's Institu-
tions.
so will I do still; neither are you ignorant, I am sure, that
there be sundry editions of those Institutions[2], although you
seem to dissemble the matter in this place, I might say of
purpose (for you have answered after your manner places be-

[1 " Touching Augustine; that he was so alleged appeareth first, page 583
(an error for 581, see Tract. XIII. Chap. iii. Div. 1), and both he and Chrysostom, page 296 (see before, page 75). Where he saith he used that large quotation
only once in Muscul. Cyril. and M. Fox; he could hardly do it oftener in the
two last, considering that, as I remember, he allegeth them once only; but
touching Muscul. beside the place I charge him with, he left his adversary twice
to his wide works. &c."—Sec. Repl. p. 605.]

[2 The edition Whitgift used was that of 1553.]

fore, out of the same book quoted in like manner), but let it be of ignorance, you take occasion by it to utter your cynical rhetoric but to your own shame.

The place alleged maketh much for my purpose; for it proveth superiority to have been among the apostles, and therefore that it may be among ministers; which you deny, and I affirm; which also being granted (as it cannot be denied), whatsoever I affirm either of archbishops or bishops will soon be proved. But let us hear the proof of this new device of yours in soluting this, and such like places, that one " ruled the action, &c."

Chapter iii. The Forty-fifth Division.

T. C. Page 84, Sect. 2.

And, that it may appear what superiority it is which is lawful amongst the ministers, and what it is that M. Calvin speaketh of, what also the fathers and councils do mean, when they give more to the bishop of any one church than to the elder of the same church, and that no man be deceived by the name of governor, or ruler over the rest, to fancy any such authority and domination or lordship, as we see used in our church, it is to be understood that, amongst the pastors, elders, and deacons of every particular church, and in the meetings and companies of the mi-nisters or elders of divers churches, there was one chosen by the voices This is a de-
and suffrages of them all, or the most part, which did propound the vice never heard[3] of
matters that were to be handled, whether they were difficulties to be soluted, before.
or punishments and censures to be decreed upon those which had faulted, or whether there were elections to be made, or what other matter soever occasion was given to entreat of, the which also gathered the voices and reasons of those which had interest to speak in such cases, which also did pronounce according to the number of the voices which were given, which was also the mouth of the rest, to admonish, or to comfort, or to rebuke sharply, such as were to receive admonishment, consolation, or rebuke, and which, in a word, did moderate that whole action, which was done for the time they were assembled. Which thing we do not deny may be, but affirm that it is fit and necessary to be, to the avoiding of confusion.

Jo. Whitgift.

All this is spoken of your own head, and a device without proof or reason as yet, and contrary to the testimonies of all histories, councils, and fathers, affirmed by no learned writer; as it may appear by that which I have hitherto alleged out

[3 Hard, Def. A. and B.]

of the canons attributed to the apostles, the council also of
Nice, Antioch, Arelat., Carthage, Chalcedon, likewise out of
Cyprian, Eusebius, Epiphanius, Athanasius, Gregory Nazian.,
Ambrose, Jerome, Socrates, Sozom., Theodoret, Calvin, Illyricus[1].
All which manifestly declare that the office of an archbishop
and jurisdiction of a bishop is permanent, and affixed to certain places, not moveable, nor during one action only. And,
undoubtedly, I marvel what urgeth you to such absurd and
unlearned paradoxes, unless it be ignorance and lack of reading. But let us hear your reasons.

Chapter iii.   The Forty-sixth Division.

T. C. Page 84, Sect. 3.

A needless
proof.

*For it were an absurd hearing that many should at once attempt to
speak. Neither could it be done without great reproach that, many men
beginning to speak, some should be bidden to hold their peace; which would
come to pass if there should be no order kept, nor none to appoint when
every one should speak or not, to put them to silence when they attempted
confusedly to speak and out of order. Moreover, when many ministers
meet together, and in so great diversity of gifts as the Lord hath given to
his church, there be found that excel in memory, facility of tongue, and
expedition or quickness to dispatch matters more than the rest; and therefore it is fit that the brethren, that have that dexterity, should especially
be preferred unto this office, that the action may be the better and more
speedily made an end of.*

Jo. Whitgift.

Surely and your device of salving it is as absurd; for
there would be as great contention at such elections as there
is confusion in the former equality; and the rather because
there is none to direct them therein. For who shall call them
together before this election be made? where shall they meet?
who shall declare unto them the cause of their meeting? or
what remedy if they cannot agree of some one that hath this
dexterity, but are drawn into divers parts, some thinking one
most meet, and some another, other some the third, &c.?
How if there be sects and schisms among them, as there is at
this time? an hundred inconveniences are there in this device
of yours; and, to tell you the truth, it may be used in places
where there is no government, no laws, no form of a common-

[1 See before, pages 158, &c.]

wealth, no order; but in a kingdom, in a church under civil government, in a place of order, &c., it is the very highway to subversion and confusion.

Chapter iii.   The Forty-seventh Division.

T. C. Page 85, Sect. 1.

And, if any man will call this a rule or presidentship, and him that executeth this office a president or moderator, or a governor, we will not strive, so that it be with these cautions, that he be not called simply governor or moderator, but governor or moderator of that action, and for that time, and subject to the orders that others be, and to be censured by the company of the brethren, as well as others, if he be judged any way faulty. And that, after that action ended, and meeting dissolved, he sit him down in his old place, and set himself in equal estate with the rest of the ministers. Thirdly, that this government or presidentship, or whatsoever like name you will give it, be not so tied unto that minister, but that at the next meeting it shall be lawful to take another, if another be thought meeter.

And what scripture have you for this ?

Jo. Whitgift.

These cautions are meet for such a device, and apt for a tumultuous company and a congregation of proud and arrogant persons that cannot abide any superiority or government. This I am well assured of; and it is evident both by that which is already spoken, and that which is to be said hereafter, that there can neither pattern nor form be found of it in any church since the apostles' time, recorded in any writer of credit, but the clean contrary; for ecclesiastical writers do both call bishops "governors simply," and manifestly also declare that their office of government was not for one action only, but during their life, or, at the least, during their continuance in that seat or bishopric; and it is plain, by that which I have said before, that the office of the metropolitan (which was to call synods, and to moderate them, to ordain bishops, or, at the least, to consent thereunto, to suppress schisms, and such like) was affixed to the place and bishop of the same, as to Rome, Constantinople, Alexandria, &c. This do all the old canons declare; as the 6. and 7. canon of the council of Nice[2], the 9. of the council of Antioch[3], and the

Bishops, governors simply, not of one action only.

The office of the metropolitan fixed to a place.

[2 Concil. Nic. cans. 6, 7, in Concil. Stud. Labb. et Cossart. Lut. Par. 1671-2. Tom. II. col. 32. See before, page 144, notes 1, 2.]

[3 Concil. Antioch. can. 9. ibid. col. 565. See before, page 146, note 1.]

5. of the general council of Constantinople[1], the 12. of the second council of Carthage[2], the 21. *Concilii Milevitani*[3], the 11. of the general council of Chalcedon[4]; to be short, all these testimonies and examples alleged of me before out of Cyprian, &c., and the continual practice of the church. And therefore such new cautions here by you set down be only meet for such a strange and misshapen platform and kind of government as is by you and your faction devised.

Chapter iii.   The Forty-eighth Division.

T. C. Page 85, Sect. 2, 3, 4.

Of this order and policy of the church, if we will see a lively image and perfect pattern, let us set before our eyes the most ancient and gospel-like church that ever was or shall be.

In the first of the Acts[5], *the church being gathered together for the election of an apostle into the place of Judas the traitor, when as the interest of election belonged unto all, and to the apostles especially above the rest, out of the whole company Peter riseth up, telleth the cause of their coming together, with what cautions and qualities they* Acts i. 15.[6] *ought to choose another, conceiveth the prayer whereby the help of God in that election and his direction is begged, and no doubt executed the residue of the things which pertained unto the whole action.*

In the ii. of the Acts, all the apostles are accused of drunkenness. Peter answered[7] *for them all, wipeth away the infamy they were charged with. But you will say, Where are the voices of the rest, which did choose Peter unto this?*

What is this but a mere conjecture, or rather an imagined answer of your own?

First, you must know that the scripture setteth not down every circumstance, and then surely you do Peter great injury that ask whether he were chosen unto it; for is it to be thought that Peter would thrust in himself to this office or dignity, without the consent and allowance of his fellows, and prevent his fellows of this pre-eminence? undoubtedly,

---

[1 Τὸν μέντοι Κωνσταντινουπόλεως ἐπίσκοπον ἔχειν τὰ πρεσβεῖα τῆς τιμῆς μετὰ τὸν τῆς Ῥώμης ἐπίσκοπον, διὰ τὸ εἶναι αὐτὴν νέαν Ῥώμην.—Constant. Concil. can. 3. ibid. col. 947.]

[2 Concil. Carthag. II. can. 12. ibid. cols. 1162, 3. See before, page 159, note 12.]

[3 It will be sufficient to give the closing sentence of this canon : Si autem ille aliquam quæstionem retulerit, per episcopos judices causa finiatur, sive quos eis primates dederint, sive quos ipsi vicinos ex consultu primatis delegerint.— Concil. Milev. II. can. 21. ibid. col. 1542.]

[4 The 9th canon is probably that intended ; where we find : Εἰ δὲ πρὸς τὸν τῆς αὐτῆς ἐπαρχίας μητροπολίτην ἐπίσκοπος ἢ κληρικὸς ἀμφισβητοίη, καταλαμβανέτω ἢ τὸν ἔξαρχον τῆς διοικήσεως, ἢ τὸν τῆς βασιλευούσης Κωνσταντινουπόλεως θρόνον, καὶ ἐπ᾽ αὐτῷ δικαζέσθω.—Conc. Calched. Act. xv. can. 9. ibid. Tom. IV. col. 759.]

[5 In the Acts, Repl. 2.]   [6 This reference is inserted from Repl. 2.]

[7 Answereth, Repl. 1 and 2.]

if it had not been done arrogantly, yet it must needs have a great shew of arrogancy, if he had done this without the consent of his fellows. And here you shall hear what the scholiast saith which gathereth the judgment of Greek divines: ὅρα (speaking of Peter) πάντα μετὰ κοινῆς αὐτὸν γνώμης ποιοῦντα[8] : "Behold, how he doth all with their common consent." And, if any man hereupon will say that Peter exercised domination over the rest, or gat any arch-apostleship, beside that the whole story of the Acts of the Apostles and his whole course of life doth refute that, the same scholiast which I made mention of in the same place saith he did nothing ἀρχικῶς: "imperiously," nothing μετὰ ἐξουσίας: "with dominion or power :" further I will admonish him to take heed, lest if he strive so far[9] for the archbishop, he slide or ever he be aware into the tents of the papists, which use these places to prove that Peter had authority and rule over the rest of the apostles.

> This is not spoken of choosing Peter to be speaker, but of electing Matthias, which pertained not to Peter alone.

Jo. Whitgift.

This is a rod to beat yourself with ; for it is evident, even by these words of yours, that your devise is most farthest from the apostolical form ; for Peter in all such assemblies is the chief, speaketh the first and moderateth the rest ; in which respect most of the old ecclesiastical writers count him the chief of the apostles ; neither do the late writers dissent from them in that point ; and yet is there no danger " of sliding into the papists' tents," who by this would prove the pope's supremacy, whose arguments you have used and I have confuted before.

> Peter chief in apostolical assemblies.

To prevent subtilly that question which neither you do nor can answer, that is, where it is in scripture mentioned that, at every action, or at any time, Peter was chosen to speak before the rest, or to govern the action, you say that "first I must know that the scripture setteth not down every circumstance, and then that I do Peter great injury that ask whether he were chosen to it, &c." To the first, I answer that you ought to know how wicked and ungodly a thing it is to ground the alteration of any lawful kind of government so long continued, and in the best times of the church practised, upon your own fond device and conjectures, without any ground of scripture, yea, to make that your foundation which you cannot find in the whole scripture, but the clean contrary. For shew me one piece of a text that doth but insinuate Peter to have been at any time in any action

> Peter not chosen in every action to be chief.

[8 Ὅρα δὲ πάντα κατὰ κοινῆς κ. τ. λ. καὶ οὐκ ἀρχικῶς οὐδὲ μετὰ ἐξουσίας.—Œcumen. Op. Lut. Par. 1631. Enarr. cap. ii. in Act. Apost. Tom. I. p. 10.]

[9 Sore, Repl. 1 and 2.]

chosen to direct the action; I can shew you the contrary, especially in the second of the Acts, where Peter suddenly answered with a notable apology, in the presence of the apostles, the accusation of drunkenness laid against him and them: neither can it be that he should expect the voices of the rest to choose him to be the chief for that time in that action.

Whosoever shall well consider the first of the Acts, and the xv., and other places where mention is made of Peter's speaking, as he shall perceive that this was Peter's peculiar office, and always appertaining unto him from the ascension of Christ to his dying day, so shall he also easily understand that he was not at any time chosen to that office by voices, much less at every particular meeting or singular action. And dare you presume upon vain conjectures, without warrant of scripture, to build the foundation of your kind of government, which you before said is a matter of faith and salvation? Is not this to open a way to unwritten verities and fantastical interpretations? If your words be of such weight with the reader, that because you speak them therefore he will believe them, *per me licebit;* but this I will assure him of, that he shall believe that that is neither grounded upon scripture, nor any learned or ancient authority.

To the second, that is, that I " do Peter great injury, &c.," I say that I do him no injury at all when I affirm that of him that the scripture doth, and presume not of mine own brain for the maintaining of an evil cause to imagine that of him which I have myself devised besides the word of God; as you do most manifestly.

Peter did not " thrust himself into any office or dignity," which was not appointed unto him by God, neither did he otherwise use himself therein than his office and duty required; and it is impiety thus to dally and trifle in God's matters. We are well assured in scripture that Peter did this and had this pre-eminence; and therefore you must know that he was lawfully called unto it, and did lawfully execute it.

The scholiast playeth not the part which is laid upon him.

The Greek scholiast saith that Peter in such assemblies did conclude nothing without the consent of the rest; the which also the scripture itself doth plainly declare. But the Greek scholiast nowhere saith that Peter was at every assembly or at any time chosen by the voices of the rest, to speak first, and to moderate the action; which is your assertion. For, in

the place by you cited, he speaketh not of the election of
Peter to his prolocutorship, but of the choosing of Matthias to
the apostleship; wherein Peter took not that pre-eminence to
himself to appoint him alone, but communicated the matter
with the rest of the disciples. So that you have either wittingly or ignorantly applied the scholiast to a wrong matter.

It is true that "Peter did nothing imperiously, nothing
with dominion or power:" no more doth any man that executeth lawful jurisdiction, and governeth by law, equity, and
order, no, not the king himself; for in superiority there is
humility, and in rule and authority there is servitude; as I
have before shewed in the exposition of the places in the xx. Tract. I.
of Matth., xxii. Luke, &c.[1] And yet doth the Greek scholiast
in the same place say that "Peter rose up, and not James, as
being more fervent, καὶ ὡς τὴν προστασίαν τῶν μαθητῶν
ἐγκεχειρισμένος[2]: and as having received the presidentship
of the apostles." Your admonishment of "falling into the
tents of the papists," how necessary it is for yourself, which
use their manner of reasoning upon this example of Peter,
and upon devised interpretations of the scripture, I have
touched before. As for myself, I refuse no warning. But I
trust it is not so necessary; for I know what they have said,
and what they can say in that matter[3].

Chapter iii.   The Forty-ninth Division.

T. C. Page 85, Sect. 4.

*And, that it may be understood that this moderate rule, void of all
pomp and outward shew, was not perpetual, nor all was tied[4] unto one*
Acts xv. 13.[5] *man, which were the last points of the cautions I put before,
turn unto the xv. of the Acts; where is shewed how, with the
rest of the church, the apostles, and amongst them Peter, being assembled,
decide[6] a great controversy, James the apostle, and not Peter, moderated* This maketh
and governed the whole action, when as, after other had said their judg- against yourself; as will
appear.

[1 See Vol. I. pages 148, &c.]

[2 Ἀνίσταται ὁ Πέτρος οὐχ ὁ Ἰάκωβος, καὶ ὡς θερμότερος, καὶ ὡς κ. τ. λ.
—Œcumen. Op. Lut. Par. 1631. Enarr. cap. ii. in Act. Apost. Tom. I. pp. 9, 10.]

[3 In his reply to this division, Cartwright accuses Whitgift that, "although
he have never a spur of argument either to defend himself, or to offend his
adversary, yet" he "croweth as high as if the mastery were in his hand;" and
calls his reasoning "ridiculous," smelling "of anabaptistry," &c.—Sec. Repl.
pp. 607, &c.]

[4 Nor always tied, Repl. 2.]   [5 This reference is inserted from Repl. 2.]
[6 Assembled to decide, Repl. 2.]

ments, and namely Paul and Barnabas, and Peter, he, in the end, in the
name of all, pronounced the sentence, and that whereof the rest agreed, and
had disputed unto; and the residue rested in that judgment; the which
also may likewise appear in the xxi. of the Acts. Acts xxi. 20.[1]

Jo. Whitgift.

Peter moderator so long as the apostles remained together.

It is evident, by the story of the Acts of the Apostles, that this function remained to Peter so long as the apostles continued together, and that he did execute the same whensoever they met; and therefore it is untrue that this office was not " tied to one man :" the xv. of the Acts helpeth you nothing : for even there Peter keepeth his accustomed manner in making the first oration[2]; and in that place it may appear that he did it as chief in that assembly; for the text saith

Acts xv.

that, " when there had been great disputation, Peter rose up and said unto them, &c.;" so that Peter, as one having authority to appease the tumult and bitter contention, " rose up and said unto them, &c." Then spake Barnabas and Paul, after them James, not as moderator or governor of the whole action, but as one having interest to speak as the rest of the apostles had; and, because he had spoken that which the rest well liked of, therefore they consented to his opinion and judgment. This is no more to give pre-eminence to James in moderating that action, than it is to give the speakership in the parliament to him that speaketh last in a matter, and whose oration hath most persuaded, to whom also the whole house consenteth. So that Peter keepeth his prerogative still, for

The office of the speaker or moderator.

anything that is here spoken to the contrary; which may also evidently appear by this, that, when there was great contention among them about the matter, the cause whereof is like to be, for that they did not understand the state of the cause, Peter stood up, *et in hoc maxime insistit, ... ut statum quæstionis demonstraret*[3]: " and stood especially upon this point, that he might declare the state of the question," as M. Calvin saith ; which is the office of the speaker or moderator ; wherefore not James, but Peter, did moderate the action.

[1 This reference is inserted from Repl. 2.]
[2 "... which is untrue ; for there was great disputation of both sides before Peter spake ; therefore it must needs be that the cause was propounded by some before."—Sec. Repl. p. 611.]
[3 ... quare in hoc &c. demonstret, &c.—Calvin. Op. Amst. 1667-71. Comm. in Act. Apost. cap. xv. v. 7. Tom. VI. p. 136.]

But be it as you would have it, that "James did mode- The example
rate the action," it maketh most against you; for, if we believe of James
against the
the ancient writers, and namely the Greek scholiast upon the Replier.
xv. of the Acts, James was now bishop of Jerusalem[4]; and
therefore, the synod being within his charge, it was not unfit
that he, according to his office, should moderate the same; as
other bishops did in their several churches[5].

The xxi. of the Acts is nothing to your purpose; but Paul,
coming to Jerusalem, went with certain other in unto James,
and told him and all the rest that were gathered together
what God had wrought among the gentiles by his ministration.
What is this to prove your purpose? Peter is not here; and
James was now bishop of Jerusalem; as the note in the margent
of the bible printed at Geneva doth testify[6]. The place in no
respect proveth your assertion, but the contrary; for there is
no doubt but that James was the chief governor of the church
of Jerusalem in all actions during his life, after that he was
once placed in the bishopric.

You talk in another place of "raking of doctors to prove
my purpose;" but, if these be not rakings of scriptures,
gathered together to no purpose, for the confirming of your
fond devices, I know not what you should mean by the name
of "rakings."

Chapter iii.   The Fiftieth Division.
T. C. Page 85, Sect. 4.

*This is he which is called the bishop in every church, this is he also
whom Justin, whereof mention is made afterwards, called[7] προεστώς[8];
and, finally, this is that great archbishopric and great bishopric that M.
Doctor so often stumbleth on. This order and pre-eminence the apostles'
time, and those that were near them, kept; and the nearer they came to
the apostles' times the nearer they kept them to this order, and the farther
off they were from those times, until the discovering of the son of perdition,*

[4 Οὗτος ὁ Ἰάκωβος, ὁ τῶν Ἱεροσολύμων ὑπὸ Κυρίου προχειρισθεὶς ἐπίσκοπος υἱὸς Ἰωσὴφ ἦν τοῦ τέκτονος, κ. τ. λ.—Œcumen. Op. Lut. Par. 1631.
Enarr. cap. xxiii. in Act. Apost. Tom. I. p. 122.]

[5 "...if it be true that it is meet the bishop of the place where the synod is
holden should govern the synod, why hath he made this before (see before, pages
211, 2) a necessary cause of having an archbishop, to govern synods?"—Sec. Repl.
p. 612.]

[6 Who was the chief or superintendent of the church of Jerusalem.—The
Bible, transl. according to the Ebrew and Greeke. Lond. 1578. Not. in Acts xxi.
v. 18. fol. 61.]

[7 Calleth, Repl. 1 and 2.]   [8 Just. Mart. Op. Par. 1742. Apol. i. 67. p. 83.]

*the further off were they from this moderation, and the nearer they came
to[1] that tyranny and ambitious power which oppressed and overlaid the
church of God.*

Jo. Whitgift.

Indeed this is one part of the office of the archbishop
and bishop, but not the whole, no more than it was of James
being bishop of Jerusalem, nor of him whom Justin calleth
προεστώς. But your chief purpose now is to prove that this
office is not perpetual, but changeable at every action, and
durable only continuing that action; which how soundly you
have done, and with what strange arguments, every child that
hath discretion may judge.

Chapter iii.   The Fifty-first Division.

T. C. Page 86, Sect. 1.

*And therefore M. Calvin doth warely say, that one amongst the apostles
indefinitely, not any one singular person, as Peter, had the moderation and
rule of the other, and further shadoweth out what rule that was, by the*
example of the consul of Rome, whose authority was to gather the senate
together, and to tell of the matters which were to be handled, to gather the
voices, to pronounce the sentence.   And, although the antichrist of Rome
had perverted all good order, and taken all liberty of the church into his
hands, the cardinals', archbishops', and bishops', yet[2] there are some cold
and light footings of it in our synods, which are holden with the parliament, where, amongst all the ministers which are assembled out of all the
whole realm, by the more part of voices one is chosen which should go
before the rest, propound the causes, gather the voices, and be as it were
the mouth of the whole company, whom they term the prolocutor.   Such
great force hath the truth, that in the utter ruins of popery it could never
be so pulled up by the roots, that a man could never know the place thereof
no more, or that it should not leave such marks and prints behind it,
whereby it might afterwards recover itself, and come again to the knowledge of men.*

*The arch-
bishop con-
tenteth him-
self with less
authority
than the
consuls had.*

Jo. Whitgift.

It followeth in the same place of M. Calvin immediately:
Instit. cap. 8.   *Sic nihil absurdi esset si fateremur apostolos detulisse Petro
talem primatum.   Sed quod inter paucos valet non protinus
trahendum [est] ad universum orbem terrarum, ad quem regendum nemo unus sufficit[3]:* "So should it be no absurdity
if we should confess that the apostles did give this kind of
pre-eminence unto Peter.   But yet that which availeth among

[1 And nearer to, Repl. 2.]
[2 Into his the cardinals archbishops and bishops hands yet, Repl. 2.]
[3 Calvin. Op. Amst. 1667-71. Inst. Lib. iv. cap. vi. 8. Tom. IX. p. 296.]

few must not by and by be drawn to the whole world; to the ruling whereof no one man can suffice." You see, therefore, that M. Calvin speaketh of one singular person, even of Peter himself, and yet doth he not "slide into the tents of the papists," but teacheth rather how to beware of them, and yet to acknowledge the truth of Peter.

We give no greater authority either to archbishop or bishop than the consul or prætor had among the Romans, or a master or [4] president in a college; for the consuls (upon whose authority you seem so much to stay) were appointed to govern the commonwealth of the Romans, after they had banished their kings, and they were called consuls, *quia plurimum reipublicæ consulebant* [5]: "because they profited the commonwealth very much;" whose authority in this did differ from the authority of a king, that there might be appeal from them, and that they could not put to death any citizen of Rome without the consent of the people; but they might otherwise punish them, and cast them into prison: they had authority also to make free those that were in bondage, they were of the greatest honour (*si nullus esset dictator*), "if there were no dictator," in the commonwealth, and their authority was of force, not only in the senate, but elsewhere. And it is manifest that they had not only "authority to call the senate, to tell those matters that were to be handled, and to take their voices," but to command that none should depart out of the city that had any voice in the senate, and to elect senators, &c. It appeareth that you little knew what the office of a consul was, when you writ this. If you take advantage of this, that the office of the consul was annual, and not perpetual, yet it helpeth not you anything; for he was moderator and ruler not of one action only, but of so many as were by occasion, either ordinary or extraordinary, in the whole year of his consulship. For my part, I do not think that the archbishop either hath, or ought to have, that authority in his province that the consul had in Rome.

A master of a college (the which example also master Calvin doth use [6]) hath a perpetual office: he is chief governor

The example of T. C. against himself. Consuls, and their authority.

Masters of colleges, and their authority.

[4 And, Def. A.]

[5 Animo consulem esse oportet,......omni officio tuendo, maximeque, id quod vis nominis præscribit, reipublicæ consulendo.—Cic. Op. Lond. 1681. Orat. in C. Pison. Tom. II. p. 465. Conf. De Orat. Lib. II. Tom. I. p. 112.]

[6 Calvin. Op. Inst. Lib. IV. cap. vi. 8. Tom. IX. p. 296. See before, page 231, note 5.]

of that society; and all the members thereof owe duty and obedience unto him, as to their head: he hath authority to punish, and to see laws executed: neither do I think that either archbishop or bishop claimeth greater authority and jurisdiction over their provinces and diocese than is due to the master within his college. And therefore those examples of Master Calvin do confute your assertion, they do in no point confirm it.

In synods, though there be chosen a "prolocutor" for the inferior sort of the clergy, yet doth the archbishop retain still both his office, place, and authority[1]: even as the prince doth, or the lord-keeper, notwithstanding it be permitted to the lower house of parliament to choose them a speaker. And therefore this is nothing, nor alleged to any purpose; except you will say that in the civil state all was equal, and that there was no superior, but in every action some chosen by the multitude to govern the action, because in the lower house of parliament they choose a speaker, whose office continueth but during that parliament. You pass not what you allege, so you may seem to allege something.

Chapter iii.   The Fifty-second Division.
T. C. Page 86, Sect. 2.

Now you see what authority we allow amongst the ministers, both in their several churches, or in provincial synods, or national, or general, or whatsoever other meetings shall be advised of, for the profit and edifying of the church; and withal you see that, as we are far from this tyranny and excessive power which now is in the church, so we are by the grace of God as far from confusion and disorder; wherein you travail so much to make us to seem guilty.

Jo. Whitgift.

I see you "allow" much more "authority" in words, that is in the examples you have used, than you will willingly acknowledge: I see also that this authority, which you call "tyranny, and excessive," is moderate and lawful, and according both to the laws of God and man. To conclude, I see that you are as far from order, and a right form of government, as you are from modesty and due obedience, and that the end you shoot at is nothing else but a mere "confusion,"

[1 "... it sheweth that he is now but an idol, having put over the duty to other, for which he is supposed to have been so necessary."—Sec. Repl. p. 613.]

not only of the church, but of the commonwealth also; the government whereof you would have framed according to your platform of the church: that is, you would have it brought from a monarchy to a popular or aristocratical kind of government, even as you would have the church.

Chapter iii.   The Fifty-third Division.

Answer to the Admonition, Page 72, Sect. 1.

Paul was superior both to Timothy and Titus; as it may easily be gathered out of his epistles written unto them.

T. C. Page 86, Sect. 3.

M. Doctor reasoneth again, that Paul, an apostle, and in the highest degree of ministry, was superior to Timothy and Titus, evangelists, and so in a lower degree of ministry; therefore one minister is superior to another, one bishop to another bishop; which are all one office, and one function. As if I should say, my lord mayor of London is above the sheriffs; therefore one sheriff is superior to another.

They are not yet proved evangelists.

Jo. Whitgift.

There was no difference betwixt them in respect of preaching the gospel and administering the sacraments, but in respect of government[2]; therefore among ministers of the word and sacraments there may be degrees of dignity, and superiority, and one may rule over another; which is the ground of my assertion, and the overthrow of yours. And this doth the example of Paul prove evidently; even as the example of " my lord mayor" doth prove that there is superiority in government among the citizens. For thus you should have reasoned: as " my lord mayor" his authority above the rest of the citizens declareth that there is superiority in the civil state, and one subject to another, even so Paul's superiority over Timothy, Titus, and other ministers, declareth that there may be superiority in the state ecclesiastical, and that one of them may and ought to be subject to another. Thus you should have applied the similitude, if you had truly applied it[3].

The example of Paul proveth superiority among the ministers of the word.

[2 " Which is untrue, for they differed in both alike."—Ibid. p. 614.]

[3 Cartwright calls this "too ridiculous," and says "that, if there were any argument here, it is that, as my lord mayor ruleth over the citizens, so it behoveth the pastor to rule over his flock."—Ibid.]

Chapter iii.   The Fifty-fourth Division.
Answer to the Admonition, Page 72, Sect. 2.

Titus had superiority.

Titus had superiority over all the other pastors and ministers which were in Creta; for he had *potestatem constituendi oppidatim presbyteros: ad Tit. i.*[1] The which place M. Calvin expounding saith on this sort : *Discimus ex hoc loco, &c.*[2] : "We learn of this place (saith he) that there was not such equality among the ministers of the church, but that one both in authority and counsel did rule over another."

Calvin confesseth superiority among ministers[3].

T. C. Page 86, Sect. 3.

Again, another argument he hath of the same strength. Titus being an evangelist was superior to all the pastors in Crete, which was a degree under the evangelists; therefore one pastor must be superior unto another pastor. And that he was superior he proveth, because he had authority to ordain pastors; so that the print of the archbishop is so deeply set in his head, that hereof he can imagine nothing but that Titus should be archbishop of all Creta.

Jo. Whitgift.

Titus was a bishop, as it shall be proved; and you have not one word in scripture of his being an evangelist : it is Erasmus[4] and Pellican[5], two famous men, that "imagine Titus to have been archbishop of Creta:" scoff at them.

Chapter iii.   The Fifty-fifth Division.
T. C. Page 86, Sect. 4.

I have shewed before how these words are to be taken of St Paul. And, forsomuch as M. Doctor burdeneth us with the authority of Calvin so often, I will send him to Calvin's own interpretation upon this place; where he sheweth that Titus did not ordain by his own authority[6]. *For St Paul*

You shift off M. Calvin's place for

[1 *Presbyteros :* authority to ordain elders in every city, Tit. i., Answ. 2.]

[2 Discimus quidem ex hoc loco, non eam fuisse tunc æqualitatem inter ecclesiæ ministros, quin unus aliquis auctoritate et consilio præesset.—Calvin. Op. Amst. 1667-71. Comm. in Epist. ad Tit. cap. i. 5. Tom. VII. p. 497.]

[3 This marginal note is not in Answ.]

[4 Erasm. Op. L. Bat. 1703-6. In Epist. ad Tit. Arg. Tom. VII. cols. 1067, 8. See before, page 132, note 2.]

[5 C. Pellican. Comm. in Omn. Apost. Epist. Tigur. 1539. In Epist. ad Tit. Arg. p. 577. See before, page 132, note 3.]

[6 Sed videtur nimium Tito permittere, dum jubet eum præficere omnibus ecclesiis ministros. hæc enim fere regia esset potestas: deinde hoc modo et singulis ecclesiis jus eligendi, et pastorum collegio judicium tollitur: id vero esset totam sacram ecclesiæ administrationem profanare. Verum, &c.—Calvin. Op. Comm. in Epist. ad Tit. cap. i. 5. Tom. VII. p. 497. See Vol. I. page 427, note 9.]

would not grant Titus leave to do that which he himself would not, and *sheweth that to say that Titus should make the election of pastors by himself is to give unto him "a princely authority, and to take away the election from the church, and the judgment of the insufficiency of the minister from the company of the pastors; which were (saith he) to profane the whole government of the church."*

superiority amongst the clergy, by flying to another place of election of ministers.

JO. WHITGIFT.

This is to set Calvin against Calvin, and not to answer him; and yet this is nothing contrary to that which I have alleged out of him; for in the place that I have alleged he gathereth upon these words, *ut constituas oppidatim presbyteros, &c.*, "that there was not such equality among the ministers of the church, but that one both in authority and counsel did rule over another[7]." You, to avoid this testimony of Calvin for superiority, tell me that Calvin saith upon this place, that "Titus did not ordain ministers by his own authority, &c.;" which is no answer to the place that I have alleged, but a very quarrel picked out to avoid the answering of it. Master Calvin saith that among the ministers there "was one ruled over another *auctoritate et consilio*: by authority and counsel." And he doth gather it out of the text by me alleged. Either answer it, or give place unto it, or deny it. Of electing ministers I have spoken before: it is now out of place to speak of it again, and it is to no purpose, but to shift off an answer.

The shifts of the Replier.

Chapter iii. The Fifty-sixth Division.

T. C. Page 86, Sect. 5.

I marvel therefore what M. Doctor meaneth to be so busy with M. Calvin, and to seek confirmation of his archbishop and bishop at him, which would have shaken at the naming of the one, and trembled at the office of the other, unless it be because he would fain have his plaster where he received his wound. But I dare assure him that in his garden he shall never find the herb that will heal him. And, because that the scriptures, when they make for our cause, receive this answer commonly, that they served but for the apostles' times, and Master Calvin's authority will weigh nothing as I think with Master Doctor, when he is alleged by us against him, I will send him to the Greek scholiast, which upon this place of Titus saith after this sort: "He would not (speaking of St Paul) have the whole isle of Crete ministered and governed by one, but that every one should have his proper charge and care[8];" for so should Titus have a

[7 Id. ibid. See above, note 2.]

[8 Οὐ γὰρ ἐβούλετο πᾶσαν τὴν νῆσον τὴν Κρήτην μεγάλην οὖσαν, ἐπι-

lighter labour, and the people that are governed should enjoy greater at-
tendance of the pastor, whilst he that teacheth them doth not run about the
government of many congregations, but attendeth unto one, and garnisheth
that.

Jo. Whitgift.

What opinion Master Calvin hath of archbishops, and of
superiority amongst pastors and ministers, may appear in his
words that I have alleged in my Answer. I think Master
Calvin never uttered in word or writing his misliking of the
present government of this church of England by archbishops and bishops : what he hath spoken against the abuse
of them in the pope's church is not to be wrested against the
right use of them in the true church of Christ.

I have answered the scriptures by you alleged truly and
directly. You have not as yet urged me with that authority
of Master Calvin, that I have so shifted off, as you have done
this last.

The scholiast meaneth that every city should have his
pastor in the isle of Creta, and that Titus should govern

Titus, arch-
bishop. them as bishop, not as having the whole and sole charge of
every several town or city; which may evidently appear to
be true by these words of Theodoret placed in the same

Theodoret. in
arg. Epist.
Tit. apud
Scholiast. author : "Titus was a notable disciple of Paul, but was ordained bishop of Creta, which was a very large isle; and it
was permitted and committed unto him, that he might ordain
τοὺς ὑπ' αὐτοῦ ἐπισκόπους[1] : bishops that were under him."
Whereby it may be gathered that every city in Creta had a
bishop, which had the several charge, and that Titus governed
them as archbishop. The like doth Chrysostom (whom the
Greek scholiast doth especially follow) affirm of Timothy in

Chrysost. 1 Tim. v. upon these words, *Adversus presbyterum &c.* : *Ti-*
motheo credita fuerat ecclesia, imo gens fere tota Asiatica[2] :
"The church, yea, almost the whole people of Asia, was committed to Timothy." But what need I use many words, when
Chrysostom himself affirmeth the same directly of Titus, *i. ad*

τετράφθαι ἐνὶ ἐπισκόπῳ, ἀλλ' ἑκάστην πόλιν ἔχειν ἴδιον ποιμένα.—Œcumen.
Op. Lut. Par. 1631. Comm. cap. i. in Epist. ad Tit. Tom. II. p. 289. Conf.
Chrysost. Op. Par. 1718-38.   In Epist. ad Tit. cap. i. Hom. ii. Tom. XI. p. 737.]

[1 Ὁ Τίτος θαυμάσιός τις ἦν μαθητὴς τοῦ Παύλου. ἐπίσκοπος δὲ τῆς Κρήτης,
μεγίστης οὔσης, κεχειροτόνητο ὑπὸ τοῦ Παύλου. ἐπετέτραπτο δὲ τοὺς ὑπ'
αὐτὸν ἐπισκόπους χειροτονῆσαι.—Theod. ibid. p. 285.]

[2 Chrysost. Op. In i. Epist. ad Timoth. cap. v. Hom. xv. Tom. XI. p. 637.]

Titum: Neque ejus profecto illi &c.[3] : "Truly Paul would Idem.
not have committed the whole isle to him, neither would he
have commanded those things to be supplied which were
wanting (for he saith, 'that thou mightest correct those things
which are wanting'), neither would he have committed unto him
the judgment of so many bishops, if he had not trusted him
very well[4]."

Chapter iii.   The Fifty-seventh Division.
T. C. Page 87, Sect. 1.

*Now M. Doctor may see by this, that Titus was not[5], as he fancieth, the
archbishop of all Crete; but that he had one flock, whereupon for the time
he was there he attended; and that, where it is said he ordained ministers,
it is nothing else but that he was the chief and the moderator in the election
of the ministers; as I have declared before by many examples. And it is
no marvel although the rest granted him this pre-eminence, when he had
both most excellent gifts, and was a degree above the pastors, being an
evangelist.*

Jo. Whitgift.

This I "may see," that, first, you have no conscience in
falsifying and corrupting of authors: secondly, that you speak T. C. con-
trary to him-
self.
contraries, even in these few lines; for you say that "Titus had
one flock in Creta, whereupon he did attend for the time he
was there," which must needs prove him to be a pastor [6];
and yet you afterwards deny him to be a pastor, affirming him to be "an evangelist;" and you take the office of
an evangelist to be so distinct from the office of a pastor,
that they may not meet together in one man: thirdly, I see
that you confidently take upon you to expound Paul's meaning against his plain words, and against the judgment of the
old interpreters, and divers of the new; as I have shewn before

[3 Εἰ μὴ γὰρ ἦν δόκιμος, οὐκ ἂν αὐτῷ τὴν νῆσον ὁλόκληρον ἐπέτρεψεν,
οὐκ ἂν τὰ ἐλλειφθέντα ἀναπληρῶσαι προσέταξεν· ἵνα γάρ, φησι, τὰ λείποντα
ἐπιδιορθώσῃ· οὐκ ἂν τοσούτων ἐπισκόπων κρίσιν ἐπέτρεψεν, εἰ μὴ σφόδρα
ἐθάρρει τἀνδρί.—Id. in Epist. ad Tit. cap. i. Hom. i. p. 729.]

[4 Cartwright rejoins that the first two sections of this division are "shamefully" "said," and urges against the last that Timothy and Titus might have a more
extended charge "until the church there were fully established;" but, when "every
church had a lawful and complete ministry, the charge before general is now
restrained unto that one church where Titus made his abode."—Sec. Repl. p. 615.]

[5 Titus (by the judgment of the scholiast) was not, Repl. 2.]

[6 "... let him learn that to have charge in one church alone maketh not a
pastor, unless he be so tied that he cannot depart, without the church loose his
bond."—Ibid. pp. 615, 6.]

in the election of ministers. Besides these, I see nothing answered to this example of Titus.

Chapter iii. The Fifty-eighth Division.
Answer to the Admonition, Page 72, Sect. 3.

Timothy's
authority.

Timothy bare rule over all the other ministers of the church of Ephesus; for Paul saith unto him, 1 Tim. v. *Adversus presbyterum accusationem &c.*: "Against a minister receive no accusation, unless there be two or three witnesses." In which words Paul maketh him a judge over the rest of the ministers.

T. C. Page 87, Sect. 2.

Unto the place of Timothy, where he willeth him not to admit an accusation against an elder under two or three witnesses, I answer as I have done before to the place of Titus; that is, that, as the ordination of the pastors is attributed unto Titus and Timothy, because they governed and moderated that action, and were the first in it, so also is the deposing, or other censures of them; and that, forasmuch as he writeth his epistles unto Timothy and Titus, he telleth them how they should behave themselves in their office, and doth not shut out other from this censure and judgment. And it is more agreeable to the inscription of the epistles that he should say, admit not thou, or, ordain not thou, writing unto one, than if he should say, ordain not ye, or, admit not ye, as if he should write to many; for so should neither the ending agree with the beginning, nor the midst with them both. And, if this be a good rule, that, because Paul biddeth Timothy and Titus to judge of the faults of the pastors, and to ordain

A mere cavil.

pastors, therefore none else did but they, then, whereas St Paul biddeth Timothy that he should command, and teach, that, "godliness is 1 Tim. iv. *profitable to all things," and admonisheth him to "be an example* 8, 12.[1] *of the whole flock," by your reason he will have no other of the ministers of Ephesus, or of the isle of Creta, to teach that doctrine, or to be examples to their flocks, and an hundred such things in the epistles of Timothy and Titus; which although they be there particularly directed unto Timothy and Titus, yet do they agree, and are common to them with all other ministers, yea, sometimes unto the whole flock.*

Jo. Whitgift.

You have certain common shifts to put off such places as you cannot answer; among which this is one, that you use in this place. But it will not serve, being grounded neither upon authority nor reason. These words of St Paul indeed be not

[1 This marginal reference is inserted from Repl. 2.]

spoken to Timothy alone, but to all other bishops of like authority; for that which is prescribed to Timothy is also prescribed to all other in the like function; which argueth that this authority, given to Timothy over all the ministers of the church of Ephesus, doth pertain also to all other bishops over the ministers of their several diocese. But, as St Paul in these epistles writeth only to bishops and pastors, so are the precepts given therein properly pertaining to the office of bishops and pastors, and therefore not to be wrested to any other. And how can the papists more grossly abuse the scriptures, in interpreting them to serve their turn, and to shift off their authority alleged against them, than you do in this, and such other places, against the whole scope of the epistle, and the plain and evident words of the text? for what is this but to give Timothy superiority and government over the other ministers of Ephesus, to say unto him, *Adversus presbyterum:* "Against a minister receive no accusation, &c.?" And, as this authority of judgment is not only given unto Timothy, but to all bishops of like calling, so that also of teaching (that "godliness is profitable to all things," &c.) pertaineth to all ministers of the word generally, and not to Timothy alone. This is only the difference, that the first is common to Timothy with all other bishops of like jurisdiction; the other, common to him with all other ministers of the word.

You know that every pastor, or other minister of the word, hath not other pastors and ministers of the word under him, that it may be said unto him, *Adversus presbyteros &c.*, as it is here said to Timothy; for I have proved before that *presbyter* doth signify the ministers of the word and sacraments, and shall have occasion to speak more of it hereafter.

You say that there is "an hundred such things in the epistles of Timothy and Titus:" I think that there is not one hundred several precepts in all the three epistles. These stout and hyperbolical brags, with so manifest resisting of the plain sense and meaning of the scriptures, argueth an evil conscience, and a mind so addicted to error, that it will not be reformed. Many things in these epistles pertain to all Christians, many things be proper to bishops, such as Timothy was, and many common to all ministers. But this, *Adversus presbyteros &c.*, must needs be proper to those that have under them other ministers, committed to their government; which every pastor hath not[1].

Chapter iii.   The Fifty-ninth Division.

Answer to the Admonition, Page 72, Sect. 3.

And Epiphanius, *Lib. iii. Tom. i. contra Hæresim Aerii*, proveth Timothy his superiority[3] over the rest by this self-same place[4].

T. C. Page 87, Sect. 3.

As for Epiphanius, it is known of what authority he is in this place, when as by Aerius' sides he goeth about to prick at the apostle, whilst he goeth about to confute the apostle, which maketh a distinction and difference between those which the apostle maketh one, that is, a bishop and elder[5]; and, to spare the credit of Epiphanius, it were better lay that opinion upon some Pseud-epiphanius, which[6] we may do not without great probability, seeing Augustine saith that the true Epiphanius uttereth Ad Quod- *all after a story fashion, and doth not use any disputation, or* vult-deum. *reasoning for the truth against the falsehood; and this Epiphanius is very full of arguments and reasons; the choice whereof M. Doctor hath taken.*

Jo. Whitgift.

I have not heard any probable reason alleged of any why these books of Epiphanius should be suspected, whether they be his or no, seeing they be both learned and very ancient, mentioned also of sundry old writers. But, to omit all other proofs, I will only use the judgment (at this time) of the authors of the Centuries, who are to be credited in such matters, because they have diligently and carefully laboured in them: their opinion of these books of Epiphanius, *Cent. iv.* *cap.* 10. is this : *Nunc de scriptis &c.*[7]: "Now we will speak

[1 Cartwright rejoins to this that "it argueth that the D. is spent. For he knoweth that we hold that every pastor had his elders assistant : &c."—Sec. Repl. p. 616.]

[2 This word is not in Answ.]

[3 Titus' superiority, Answ. 1 ; Timothy's superiority, Answ. 2.]

[4 Epiph. Op. Par. 1622. Adv. Hær. Lib. iii. Tom. i. Hær. lxxv. 5. Tom. I. pp. 909, 10. See below, pages 291, 2, note 2.]

[5 And an elder, Repl. 1 and 2.]

[6 Pseud-epiphanius that is to say counterfeit which, Repl. 2.]

[7 Nunc de scriptis ejus dicemus : ex quibus nobilissimum opus illud est contra octuaginta hæreses, quod πανάριον ipse in epistola ad Acacium et Paulum presbyteros dixit, et in Anacephalæosi : ...De quo scripto Augustinus ad Quod-vult-deum hæc retulit : Noster, inquit, Epiphanius Cyprius episcopus, abhinc non

of his books; of the which that work against the four-score
heresies is most noble; which book he himself in his epistle
to Acacius and Paulus, ministers, and in his book called *Anacephaleosis*, calleth πανάριον, &c. Of the which writing Augustine, in his book *ad Quod-vult-deum*, maketh this mention.
' Our Epiphanius, bishop of Cy[p]rus (saith he), which died not
long since, speaking of four-score heresies, wrote also himself
six books making mention of all things after an historical
manner, and disputing nothing either against the falsehood,
or with the truth: they be but short books, and, if they were
all made in one, yet were it not to be compared to ours, or
to divers other men's books in length.' Out of the which
words it is evident that Augustine neither had, nor at any
time did see, that work which Epiphanius intituled *Panarium*;
for Epiphanius is very long in recounting the history, as concerning the beginning, the endeavour, and country of the heretics, the occasion of the heresy, the success, increase, and such
like, throughout every heresy. Then is he very long in confuting and condemning the heresies by true scriptures, and the
interpretation of them. Wherefore it should seem that Augustine had belike only the arguments prefixed before the tomes
of books of Epiphanius, which he doth therefore call short
books, or, at the least, had his book called *Anacephaleosis*"
(which is the sum of his work called *Panarium*). Cornarius, Cornarius.
that writeth the preface before this book of Epiphanius, is of
the same judgment, and addeth these words: " Wherefore
either Augustine did not see this work of Epiphanius; or the
right work of Augustine is not extant, but lost; or else Augustine did not indeed perform that which he promised[8]." I can

longe humanis rebus exemptus, de octoginta hæresibus loquens, sex libros etiam
ipse conscripsit, historica narratione commemorans omnia, nulla disputatione adversus falsitatem pro veritate decertans. Breves sane sunt libelli, et si in unum
librum redigantur, nec ipse erit nostris, vel aliorum quorundam libris longitu-
dine comparandus (August. Op. Par. 1679-1700. Lib. de Hær. ad Quodvultd.
Tom. VIII. col. 3). Ex quibus tamen verbis liquet, Augustinum id operis quod
Panarium Epiphanii inscripsit, non habuisse, neque vidisse. Nam Epiphanius
multus est in historia recensenda, quod ad originem, studia, patriam hæreticorum,
hæresis occasionem, successum, incrementum et alia attinet, per singulas adeo
hæreses. Deinde prolixus est in confutandis ac condemnandis hæresibus, per
veras scripturas, earumque interpretationes. Quare argumenta forsan sola, præfixa
tomis librorum Epiphanii, quæ sic vocet breves libellos, aut Anacephalæosin saltem
habuisse Augustinus videtur.—Centur. Eccles. Hist. Basil. 1560, &c. Cent. IV.
cap. x. cols. 1105, 6.]

[8 Aut igitur hoc Epiphanii opus Augustinus non vidit, aut justum opus

read of none that doubteth whether these books were Epiphanius his, or no. And certainly this kind of answering is next the worst, especially when it is used against such approved authors.

Aerius'
heresy in denying the
difference betwixt a
bishop and
priest.

And, because all men may understand what Epiphanius' words and reasons be (which indeed pinch you very near, for he calleth you heretics), I will declare them as I have there found them. First he setteth down the heresy of Aerius in

these words: "His talk was more outrageous than becomed a man; and he said, 'What is a bishop to a priest? he nothing differeth from him; for there is but one order, and the same honour and dignity. The bishop layeth on his hands; and so doth the priest: the bishop ministereth baptism; and so doth the priest: the bishop saith divine service; and so doth the priest: the bishop sitteth in his throne; and so doth the priest.' In this he hath deceived many; and they use him for their captain[1]." Then doth he a little after confute this heresy with Aerius' reasons on this sort: "To say that a bishop and a priest is equal, how can it be possible? for the order of bishops is the begetter of fathers, for it ingendereth fathers to the church: the order of priests, not being able to beget fathers, doth beget sons to the church, by the sacrament of baptism, but not fathers or teachers; and how is it possible for him to ordain a priest, not having imposition of hands to elect, or to say that he is equal with a bishop? but fantasticalness and emulation deceived the foresaid Aerius: he proveth his error, and the error of those that hear him, by this, that the apostle writ to priests and deacons, and did not write to bishops. And to the bishop he saith, 'Neglect not the gift that is in thee, which thou hast received by the hands of the presbytery.' And again, in another place he writeth to bishops and deacons: 'Wherefore (saith he) a bishop

Augustini non extat et periit, aut non præstitit Augustinus quod promisit.—Epiph. contr. Octoag. Hær. Op. Panar. Iano Cornar. Interp. Basil. 1543. Præf. fol. α 2.2.]

[1 ῏Ην δὲ αὐτοῦ ὁ λόγος μανιώδης μᾶλλον, ἤπερ καταστάσεως ἀνθρωπίνης. καί φησι, τί ἐστιν ἐπίσκοπος πρὸς πρεσβύτερον; οὐδὲν διαλλάττει οὗτος τούτου· μία γάρ ἐστι τάξις, καὶ μία, φησὶ, τιμή, καὶ ἓν ἀξίωμα. χειροθετεῖ φησὶ ἐπίσκοπος, ἀλλὰ καὶ ὁ πρεσβύτερος. λουτρὸν δίδωσιν ὁ ἐπίσκοπος, ὁμοίως καὶ ὁ πρεσβύτερος. τὴν οἰκονομίαν τῆς λατρείας ποιεῖ ὁ ἐπίσκοπος, καὶ ὁ πρεσβύτερος ὡσαύτως. καθέζεται ὁ ἐπίσκοπος ἐπὶ τοῦ θρόνου, καθέζεται καὶ ὁ πρεσβύτερος. ἐν τούτῳ πολλοὺς ἠπάτησε, καὶ ἀρχηγὸν τοῦτον ἐσχήκασιν.—Id. Op. Par. 1622. Adv. Hær. Lib. III. Tom. I. Hær. lxxv. 3. Tom. I. pp. 906, 7.]

and a priest is all one;' and he knoweth not, which is ignorant
of the sequel of the truth, and hath not read profound stories,
that, when the preaching was but newly begun, the holy
apostle writ according to the state of things as they were
then; for, where there were bishops appointed, he writ to
bishops and deacons; for the apostle could not by and by at
the first appoint all things; for there was need of priests and
deacons, because by those two ecclesiastical matters may be
complete. And, where there was not any found worthy a
bishopric, there the place remained without a bishop; but,
where there was need, and worthy men to be bishops, there
were bishops appointed. And, when there was not so many
that there could be found among them meet to be priests,
they were content with one bishop in an appointed place; but
it is unpossible for a bishop to be without a deacon; and the
holy apostle had a care that deacons should be where the
bishop was, for the ministry. So did the church receive the
fulness of dispensation, such was then the state and condition
of the places. For every thing had not the perfection from
the beginning, but in process of time those things which were
necessary to perfection were added. &c. The apostle teacheth
who is a bishop, and who is a priest, when he saith to Timothy,
that was a bishop, ' Chide not a priest, but exhort him as a
father:' what should a bishop have to do not to chide a priest,
if he had not authority above a priest? As he also saith
again, ' Against a priest admit no accusation suddenly, without
two or three witnesses;' and he said not to any priest, admit
no accusation against a bishop; neither did he write to any
priest, that he should not rebuke a bishop[2]." Thus mayest

[2 ... τὸ λέγειν αὐτὸν ἐπίσκοπον καὶ πρεσβύτερον ἴσον εἶναι. καὶ πῶς
ἔσται τοῦτο δυνατόν; ἡ μὲν γάρ ἐστι πατέρων γεννητικὴ τάξις· πατέρας
γὰρ γεννᾷ τῇ ἐκκλησίᾳ. ἡ δὲ πατέρας μὴ δυναμένη γεννᾷν, διὰ τῆς τοῦ λου-
τροῦ παλιγγενεσίας τέκνα γεννᾷ τῇ ἐκκλησίᾳ, οὐ μὴν πατέρας, ἢ διδασκά-
λους. καὶ πῶς οἷόν τε ἦν τὸν πρεσβύτερον καθιστᾷν, μὴ ἔχοντα χειροθεσίαν
τοῦ χειροτονεῖν; ἢ εἰπεῖν αὐτὸν εἶναι ἴσον τῷ ἐπισκόπῳ; ἠπάτησε δὲ τὸν
προειρημένον Ἀέριον ἡ αὐτοῦ ἐρεσχελία, καὶ ὁ ζῆλος. φέρει δὲ εἰς ἑαυτοῦ
πλάνην καὶ τῶν αὐτοῦ ἀκουόντων, ὅτι ὁ ἀπόστολος γράφει πρεσβυτέροις, καὶ
διακόνοις, καὶ οὐ γράφει ἐπισκόποις. καὶ τῷ ἐπισκόπῳ φησὶ, μὴ ἀμέλει τοῦ ἐν
σοὶ χαρίσματος, οὗ ἔλαβες διὰ χειρῶν τοῦ πρεσβυτερίου. πάλιν δὲ ἐν ἄλλῳ
τόπῳ, ἐπισκόποις καὶ διακόνοις ὡς εἶναι, φησὶ, τὸν αὐτὸν ἐπίσκοπον, τὸν
αὐτὸν πρεσβύτερον. καὶ οὐκ οἶδεν ὁ τὴν ἀκολουθίαν τῆς ἀληθείας ἀγνοήσας,
καὶ ἱστορίαις βαθυτάταις μὴ ἐντυχὼν, ὅτι νέου ὄντος τοῦ κηρύγματος, πρὸς
τὰ ὑποπίπτοντα ἔγραφεν ὁ ἅγιος ἀπόστολος. ὅπου μὲν ἦσαν ἐπίσκοποι ἤδη
κατασταθέντες, ἔγραφεν ἐπισκόποις, καὶ διακόνοις. οὐ γὰρ πάντα εὐθὺς ἠδυ-

thou see, good reader, that it is not for nought that T. C. so
storms against Epiphanius, and so unreverently useth him.

But I will give him as much cause to deal in like manner
with Augustine, who in this matter fully joineth with Epiphanius; and in that book of his, *De Hæresibus ad Quod-vult-*
deum (quoted by T. C. in his margent), attributeth this also
as heresy to the said Aerius, adding that the cause of this and
other of his heresies was, " because he himself was not made
¹bishop²."

Chapter iii.   The Sixtieth Division.

Answer to the Admonition, Page 72, Sect. 4.

That this word *presbyter* in this place of the apostle
signifieth a minister of the word, both Ambrose³,
Calvin⁴, and other learned writers declare.

νήθησαν οἱ ἀπόστολοι καταστῆσαι. πρεσβυτέρων γὰρ ἐγίνετο χρεία, καὶ δια-
κόνων. διὰ γὰρ τῶν δύο τούτων τὰ ἐκκλησιαστικὰ δύνανται πληροῦσθαι. ὅπου
δὲ οὐχ εὑρέθη τις ἄξιος ἐπισκοπῆς, ἔμεινεν ὁ τόπος χωρὶς ἐπισκόπου. ὅπου δὲ
γέγονε χρεία, καὶ ἦσαν ἄξιοι ἐπισκοπῆς, κατεστάθησαν ἐπίσκοποι. πλήθους
δὲ μὴ ὄντος, οὐχ εὑρέθησαν ἐν αὐτοῖς πρεσβύτεροι κατασταθῆναι, καὶ ἠρκέ-
σθησαν ἐπὶ τῷ κατὰ τόπον μόνῳ ἐπισκόπῳ. ἄνευ δὲ διακόνου, ἐπίσκοπον ἀδύ-
νατον εἶναι. καὶ ἐπεμελήσατο ὁ ἅγιος ἀπόστολος διακόνους εἶναι τῷ ἐπισκόπῳ
διὰ τὴν ὑπηρεσίαν, οὕτω τῆς ἐκκλησίας λαβούσης τὰ πληρώματα τῆς οἰκονο-
μίας. οὕτω κατ᾽ ἐκείνῳ [?] καιροῦ ἦσαν οἱ τόποι. καὶ γὰρ ἕκαστον πρᾶγμα οὐκ
ἀπαρχῆς τὰ πάντα ἔσχεν, ἀλλὰ προβαίνοντος τοῦ χρόνου τὰ πρὸς τελείωσιν
τῶν χρειῶν κατηρτίζετο.κ.τ.λ. καὶ ὅτι μὲν οὐ δύναται ταὐτὸν εἶναι, διδάσκει
ὁ θεῖος λόγος τοῦ ἁγίου ἀποστόλου, τίς μέν ἐστιν ἐπίσκοπος, τίς δέ ἐστι
πρεσβύτερος, ὡς λέγει Τιμοθέῳ ἐπισκόπῳ ὄντι, πρεσβύτερον μὴ ἐπιπλήξῃς,
ἀλλὰ παρακάλει ὡς πατέρα. τί εἶχε πρᾶγμα, ἐπίσκοπον πρεσβυτέρῳ μὴ
ἐπιπλήττειν, εἰ μὴ ἦν ὑπὲρ τὸν πρεσβύτερον ἔχων τὴν ἐξουσίαν; ὡς καὶ πάλιν
λέγει, κατὰ πρεσβυτέρου μὴ ταχέως κατηγορίαν δέχου, εἰ μή τι ἐπὶ δύο καὶ
τριῶν μαρτύρων. καὶ οὐκ εἶπέ τινι τῶν πρεσβυτέρων, μὴ δέξῃ κατηγορίαν κατὰ
ἐπισκόπου, οὐδὲ ἔγραψε [περὶ] τῶν πρεσβυτέρων τινὶ μὴ ἐπιπλήττειν ἐπισκόπῳ.
_Id. ibid. 4, 5. pp. 908, 9, 10.]

[¹ Aeriani ab Aerio quodam sunt, qui cum esset presbyter, doluisse fertur quod
episcopus non potuit ordinari.—August. Op. Par. 1679-1700. Lib. de Hær. ad
Quodvultd. 53. Tom. VIII. col. 18.]

[² Cartwright accuses Whitgift of taking the ground of Pighius; and maintains that Wicliffe, Luther, and the reformed churches generally in their confessions held other views: he also argues at length against the citation from
Epiphanius, who he says contradicted Augustine and Jerome, they teaching that
a bishop and an elder differed "not by the word of God but by custom;" while
Epiphanius made "a bishop and an elder differ by the apostles' institution."—
Sec. Repl. pp. 616, &c.]

[³ Ambros. Op. Par. 1686-90. Comm. in Epist. ad Timoth. prim. cap. v. vv.
17, 18, 19. Tom. II. Append. cols. 300, 1.]

[⁴ Calvin. Op. Amst. 1667-71. Comm. in Epist. ɪ. ad Timoth. cap. v. 19.
Tom. VII. p. 463.]

[☞ But, because some, desirous of contention, see- Timothy, ing certain points of their contentious doctrine mani- bishop. festly overthrown by the example of Timothy bishop of Ephesus, have, contrary to the opinion of all learned men, denied him to be bishop there, I purpose in few words to shew how desirous they are in this point (as in divers others) to be singular, and how manifestly they do decline from the truth.][5]

T. C. Page 87, Sect. 4.

And, whereas M. Doctor citeth Ambrose, Calvin, and other godly writers, to prove that the minister is understanded by the word elder or presbyter, he keepeth his old wont by bringing sticks into the wood, and proving always that which no man denieth; and yet with the minister of the word he also understandeth the elder of the church which ruleth and doth not labour in the word. But therein is not the matter; for I do grant that by presbyter *the minister of the word is understood, and yet nothing proved of that which M. Doctor would so fain prove.*

Jo. Whitgift.

I add this interpretation, that the reader may understand Timothy to have authority over bishops and ministers of the word, lest you by cavilling should shift off this place with your signification of seniors, which were not ministers of the word, as you say.

All this while have I looked for the performance of your That promise, to prove that Timothy and Titus were no bishops; was bishop. but, because I perceive that you are content to forget it, I will here perform mine (lest I fall into the same fault with you), repeating only that which I have before added to my Answer in the 2. edition, lest I should put the reader both to cost and pains in searching for it there.

First therefore, that Timothy was bishop of Ephesus, the   1. whole course of the two epistles written unto him declareth; the epistle. wherein is contained the office and duty of a bishop, and divers precepts peculiarly pertaining to that function, as it is manifest; neither were those epistles written to Timothy for the instruction of other only, but for the instruction of himself also; as the whole course of both the epistles do declare, and all learned expositors confess.

[5 Answ. 2 introduces here the paragraph between brackets, and proceeds (as noted by Whitgift) with what follows below, " First therefore &c." to " purpose," page 304.]

Secondly, the subscription of the second epistle is this:
Πρὸς Τιμόθεον δευτέρα, τῆς Ἐφεσίων ἐκκλησίας πρῶτον
ἐπίσκοπον χειροτονηθέντα, ἐγράφη ἀπὸ Ῥώμης, ὅτε ἐκ
δευτέρου παρέστη Παῦλος τῷ Καίσαρι Νέρωνι: "The second
(epistle) was written from Rome to Timothy, who was ordained
the first bishop of the church of Ephesus, when Paul appeared
before the emperor Nero the second time." Which although
it be left out in some Greek testaments, yet is it in the most,
the best, and the ancientest, yea, almost in all; neither is this
a sufficient answer to say that the subscription[1] of some one
or two epistles seem to be untrue, therefore this is untrue.
For the[2] subscription, as it is (no doubt) of great antiquity, so
is it consonant to all old ancient authority.

Thirdly, the universal consent of histories conclude him
to be bishop at Ephesus. Eusebius, *Lib. iii. cap. 4.*, saith
that "Timothy was the first bishop of Ephesus[3]."

Dorotheus, who lived in Dioclesian's time, writeth that
"Paul made him bishop of Ephesus[4]."

Nicephorus, *Lib. ii. cap. 34.*, saith that "Paul made him
bishop of Ephesus, before he writ his first epistle unto
him[5]."

Hierome, *in Catalog. Scripto. Eccles.*, saith that "he was
made bishop of Ephesus by Paul[6]."

Isidorus, *De Patribus novi Testamenti*, saith also that
"he was bishop of Ephesus[7]."

Antoninus[8], *Parte i. titulo vi. cap. i.*, affirmeth the same

---

[1 Subscriptions, Answ. 2.]   [2 This, Answ. 2.]

[3 Τιμόθεός γε μὴν τῆς ἐν Ἐφέσῳ παροικίας ἱστορεῖται πρῶτος τὴν ἐπισκοπὴν εἰληχέναι.—Euseb. in Hist. Eccles. Script. Amst. 1695-1700. Lib. III. cap. iv.
p. 58.]

[4 Timotheus Ephesiorum episcopus a Paulo constitutus, evangelium Domini
Jesu Christi Ephesi exorsus, Illyricum usque, et in universa Hellade prædicavit,
ubi et mortuus et honorifice sepultus est.—Doroth. de Vit. et Mort. Proph. et Apost.
Synops. in Magn. Biblioth. Vet. Patr. Col. Agrip. 1618-22. Tom. III. p. 148.
This Synopsis is spurious. See Cave, Script. Eccles. Hist. Lit. Oxon. 1740-3.
Vol. I. pp. 163, &c.]

[5 ... τὴν πρὸς Τιμόθεον πρώτην γράφει ἐπιστολήν· ὃν ἐπίσκοπον Ἐφέσου
πρότερον καταστήσειεν.—Niceph. Call. Eccles. Hist. Lut. Par. 1630. Lib. II.
cap. xxxiv. Tom. I. p. 189.]

[6 Timotheus autem Ephesiorum episcopus ordinatus a beato Paulo, ex gentibus erat, non ex circumcisione.—Hieron. Op. Par. 1533-4. Catalog. Script.
Eccles. 11. Tom. I. fol. 94. 2. This is an addition to Jerome's genuine catalogue.]

[7 Timotheus, Ephesiorum episcopus sanctus,...apud Ephesum, in monte, qui
vocatur Pion, cum magno honore sepultus, quiescit.—Isidor. Hisp. Op. Col.
Agrip. 1617. De Vit. et Mort. Sanct. 86. p. 366.]

[8 Antonius, Answ. 2.]

out of Polycrates[9]. So doth *Supplementum Chroni.*[10] So doth also Volaterane, *Lib. xx.;* where he calleth him *præsulem Ephesinum*[11]. And all the histories that I have read, which make any mention of him.

Historia Magdel., Centu. i. Lib. ii. cap. 10. *in vita Ioan. Evangel.*, hath these words : *Constat Paulum Ephesinæ ecclesiæ Timotheum dedisse pastorem*[12]: "It is certain that Paul appointed Timothy pastor of the church of Ephesus[13]."

Surely it is the general consent of all histories that Timothy was bishop of Ephesus.

Fourthly, the fathers affirm the same.

Dionysius Areopagita (so called of some men), who lived in the apostles' time, writeth his book *De Divinis Nominibus,* " to Timothy bishop of Ephesus[14]."

Epiphanius, *Lib. iii. Tom. i.,* affirmeth that " Timothy was bishop of Ephesus[15]."

Ambrose saith the same in his preface to the first epistle written to Timothy[16].

Chrysostom in his argument of the same epistle giveth this reason why Paul of all his disciples writ only to Timothy and Titus, " because he had committed to them the government and care of the church ; and the other he carried about with him[17]." The same Chrysostom, upon the fourth to the

[9] De eo sic scribit Polycrates presbyter. Timotheus...a Paulo apostolo edoctus est...devenit cum eo ad...Ephesinorum metropolim, a quo episcopatum ibidem consecutus est...At operarii diaboli indignati palis et lapidibus justum interfecerunt.—Antonin. Chronic. Op. Lugd. 1586. Pars I. Tit. vi. cap. xxviii. 6. p. 448. Conf. Bolland. Act. Sanct. Antv. 1643. Jan. xxiv. Tom. II. p. 566.]

[10] Timotheus Pauli apostoli discipulus, Ephesi episcopus ab eodem magistro ordinatus, &c.—Suppl. Chronic. Par. 1538. Lib. VIII. fol. 181.]

[11] Timotheus...præsul Ephesinus, &c.—R. Volater. Comm. Urban. Par. 1603. Lib. xx. col. 727.]

[12] Centur. Eccles. Hist. Basil. 1560, &c. Cent. I. Lib. II. cap. x. col. 569.]

[13] The translation of this sentence is not in Answ. 2.]

[14] Τῷ συμπρεσβυτέρῳ Τιμοθέῳ Διονύσιος ὁ πρεσβύτερος.—Dion. Areop. Op. Antv. 1634. De Div. Nom. cap. i. Tom. I. p. 437. Conf. Pachym. Paraphr. in Cœlest. Hierarch. cap. i. 1. ibid. p. 9. The works ascribed to Dionysius are not genuine.]

[15] Epiph. Op. Par. 1622. Adv. Hær. Lib. III. Tom. I. Hær. lxxv. 5. Tom. I. p. 909. See before, pages 291, 2, note 2.]

[16] Hunc ergo jam creatum episcopum instruit per epistolam quomodo deberet ecclesiam ordinare.—Ambros. Op. Par. 1686-90. Comm. in Epist. ad Timoth. prim. Prolog. Tom. II. Append. col. 289.]

[17] Τίνος οὖν ἕνεκεν Τίτῳ καὶ Τιμοθέῳ γράφει μόνοις ; ὅτι τούτοις ἤδη ἐκκλησίας ἦν ἐγκεχειρικὼς, ἐκείνους δὲ ἔτι μεθ' ἑαυτοῦ περιῆγε.—Chrysost. Op. Par. 1718-38. In Epist. I. ad Timoth. cap. i. Arg. Tom. XI. p. 547.]

Ephe., speaking of pastors and doctors, useth Timothy and Titus for an example[1].

Œcumenius likewise, upon the fourth to the Ephe., calleth Timothy and Titus bishops[2]. And upon 1 Tim. i. he saith that Paul ordained Timothy bishop of Ephesus[3]. And in the fifth chapter upon these words, *Manus cito nemini imponas*, he saith, *Mandat de ordinationibus, episcopo enim scribebat*[4]: "He giveth precepts of ordaining; for he wrote to a bishop[5]."

Theodoret, upon the first to Timothy, affirmeth in plain words that "Timothy had cure of souls committed unto him[6]."

But to be short, there is not one old writer which speaking of this matter doth not testify that Timothy was bishop of Ephesus.

Last of all, I prove him to be bishop there by the consent of the late writers.

Erasmus, in his Annotations, saith that Paul made him bishop; so saith he likewise in his Paraphr. 1 Tim. iv.[7]

Pellican saith the same, 1 Timoth. i.[8]

Zuinglius, in his book called *Ecclesiastes*, saith directly that "Timothy was a bishop[9]."

[1] Τί οὖν; οἱ ποιμένες καὶ οἱ διδάσκαλοι ἐλάττους; καὶ πάνυ, τῶν περιϊόντων καὶ εὐαγγελιζομένων οἱ καθήμενοι καὶ περὶ ἕνα τόπον ἠσχολημένοι, οἷον Τιμόθεος, Τίτος.—Id. in Epist. ad Ephes. cap. iv. Hom. xi. Tom. XI. p. 83.]

[2] Τοὺς τὰς ἐκκλησίας ἐμπεπιστευμένους λέγει, τοὺς ἐπισκόπους, οἷος ὁ Τιμόθεος, οἷος ὁ Τῖτος ἦν.—Œcumen. Op. Lut. Par. 1631. Comm. cap. vi. in Epist. ad Ephes. Tom. II. p. 36.]

[3] ... ἐνταῦθα δὲ [ἐν Ἐφέσῳ] αὐτὸν ἐπίσκοπον ἐκεχειροτονήκει.—Id. Comm. cap. i. in 1. Epist. ad Timoth. Tom. II. p. 210.]

[4] Καὶ περὶ χειροτονιῶν διαλαμβάνει. ἐπισκόπῳ γὰρ ἔγραφε.—Id. ibid. cap. xiii. p. 242.]

[5] The translation is not in Answ. 2.]

[6] Ταῦτα τοίνυν, φησὶ, γράφω, διδάσκων πῶς δεῖ πολιτεύεσθαι τοὺς ψυχῶν πεπιστευμένους κηδεμονίαν.—Theod. Op. Lut. Par. 1642-84. In Epist. 1. ad Timoth. cap. iv. v. 15. Tom. III. p. 477.]

[7] ... feci te episcopum, &c.—Erasm. Op. L. Bat. 1703-6. Adnot. in Epist. Paul. ad Timoth. 1. cap. i. v. 18. Tom. VI. col. 931. Te non ambitus aut hominum favor, sed divinus Spiritus per ora prophetarum significans Dei voluntatem ad id muneris designavit, ac mox presbyterorum auctoritas, rite tibi impositis manibus, episcopi functionem delegavit.—Id. Paraphr. in Epist. 1. ad Timoth. cap. iv. v. 14. Tom. VII. col. 1048.]

[8] Cui doctorem urbi [Epheso] Paulus Timotheum praefecit, &c.—C. Pellican. Comm. in Omn. Apost. Epist. Tigur. 1539. In 1. Epist. ad Timoth. cap. i. p. 467. Conf. p. 478.]

[9] H. Zvingl. Op. Tigur. 1581. Ecclesiast. Pars II. fol. 45. See below, page 300, note 3.]

Bucer saith the same, writing upon the iv. chapter of the epistle to the Ephe.[10]

Calvin upon 1 Tim. i. calleth him "pastor of the church of Ephesus[11]." And in the 1 Timoth. iv. expounding these words, *Ne donum quod in te est &c.*, he saith: *Spiritus sanctus oraculo Timotheum destinaverat, ut in ordinem pastorum cooptaretur*[12]: "The Holy Ghost by oracle did appoint Timothy, that he should be chosen into the order of pastors[13]." And in the 2 Timoth. iv. saith that he did excel *vulgares pastores*[14]: "common pastors," meaning that he was an excellent pastor, endued with more singular and notable gifts, and of greater authority than the common sort of pastors be. And in the same chapter, speaking of Paul's sending for Timothy from Ephesus to Rome, he saith that "there was no small cause why Paul sent for Timothy from that church which he ruled and governed, and that so far off: hereby we may gather (saith he) how profitable conference is with such men; for it might be profitable to all churches which Timothy might learn in a small time: so that the absence of half a year, or a whole year, is nothing in comparison of the commodity that cometh thereby[15]." And, again, in the same place he saith that "Paul sent Tychicus to Ephesus, when he sent for Timothy to Rome, in the mean time to supply Timothy's absence[16]." By all these places it is manifest that Calvin taketh Timothy to be pastor and bishop of Ephesus; as I have before said[17].

Bullinger, upon these words also, *Ne neglexeris quod in te est donum, &c.*, noteth three things to be observed in the ordering of a bishop, and proveth thereby that Timothy was lawfully called to his bishopric[18]. And upon these words,

[10] M. Bucer. Prælect. in Epist. ad Ephes. Basil. 1562. cap. iv. p. 107. See before, page 231, note 7.]

[11] Calvin. Op. Amst. 1667-71. Comm. in Epist. I. ad Tim. cap. i. 3. Tom. VII. p. 438. See Vol. I. p. 508, note 1.]

[12] Id. ibid. cap. iv. 14. p. 458. See Vol. I. page 508, note 2.]

[13] The translation is not given in Answ. 2.]

[14] Id. in Epist. II. ad Tim. cap. iv. 5. p. 490. See Vol. I. page 508, note 3.]

[15] Id. ibid. 9. p. 491. See Vol. I. page 508, note 4.]

[16] Id. ibid. 10. ibid. See Vol. I. page 509, note 5.]

[17] These five words are not in Answ. 2.]

[18] Colligimus autem nos ex hoc Pauli loco tria in cujusvis episcopi ordinatione necessaria esse. Primum ut habeat donum Dei, hoc est ut sit irreprehensibilis bonarum et literarum et rerum non tam studiosus quam peritus. Deinde ut juste et sancte, hoc est secundum verbum Dei eligatur ac vocetur. Postremo ut delecto et ecclesiæ quod aiunt præsentato imponantur manus.....Certe cum ea fiunt ex

2 Tim. i., *Quamobrem commonefacio te ut suscites donum
&c.*, he saith that, *per donum Dei,* "Paul understandeth the
gift of prophesying, *et functionem episcopalem :* the office
of a bishop; to the which the Lord called Timothy, but by the
ministry of Paul[1]." What can be spoken more plainer ?

Illyricus, in his epistle dedicatory to the new testament,
saith that "Paul praised Timothy his bishop[2];" and, in his
preface to the epistle written to Timothy, he calleth Timothy
and Titus *præstantes doctores, multarumque ecclesiarum
episcopos[3]:* "notable doctors, and bishops of many churches[4]."

Of the same judgment is Musculus, and all the rest of the
late writers that I have read, one only excepted[5]; who notwithstanding in effect confesseth also that he was bishop at
Ephesus; for in his annotations, 1 Tim. iv., upon these words,
usquedum venero, &c., he saith that, "when Paul sent for
the ministers of Ephesus to Miletum, Acts xx., he sent for
Timothy especially." *Cujus ministros* (meaning of Ephesus),
ac proinde Timotheum inprimis Miletum accersivit[6]. But
it is manifest, Acts xx., that they were all pastors and bishops;
therefore Timothy was a bishop. The same author, upon these
words, 1 Tim. v., *Adversus presbyterum &c.*, saith: *Timotheum
in Ephesino presbyterio tum fuisse* τὸν προεστῶτα, *i. antistitem, ut vocat Justinus[7].* And addeth that "it is manifest
by Cyprian, that the bishop did rule in the college of seniors."
Then, if he that was chief in the college of seniors was a
bishop, and Timothy was chief in the college of seniors, it
must needs follow that Timothy was a bishop.

institutione Domini fiunt. Et apostolus hinc magna petiit argumenta quibus
Timoth eum sui admoneret officii.—H. Bullinger. Comm. in Omn. Apost. Epist.
Tigur. 1539. In i. Epist. ad Timoth. cap. iv. p. 585.]

[1 Paulus in præsenti per donum Dei prophetiæ donum intellexit et functionem
episcopalem, ad quam vocarat Timotheum Dominus, sed per ministerium Pauli,
&c.—Id. Comm. in ii. Epist. ad Timoth. cap. i. p. 603.]

[2 Sic etiam idem [Paulus] laudat suum episcopum Timotheum, &c.—Nov.
Test. ex Vers. Erasm. cum Gloss. Comp. Flac. Illyr. Basil. 1570. Epist. Dedic.
fol. * 3.]

[3 Ibid. In Quat. Epist. Timoth. &c. inscr. Præf. p. 1036; where *plurima-
rumque.*]

[4 The translation is not in Answ. 2.]

[5 ... voluit eum [Timotheum] Paulus Ephesi subsistere, non ut illi ecclesiæ,
tanquam episcopus, addictus esset: sed ut ecclesia constituta, pseudapostolis occur-
reret: &c.—Nov. Test. cum Th. Bezæ Annot. H. Steph. 1565. In Epist. ad
Timoth. i. cap. i. v. 3. p. 454.]

[6 ... præter expectationem coactus est, mutato consilio, Ephesum prætervehi:
cujus tamen ministros &c.—Ibid. cap. iv. v. 13. p. 467.]

[7 Ibid. cap. v. v. 19. p. 470; where *fuisse* προεστῶτα *(id est antistitem)*.]

But it may appear how little learning and learned men Timothy,
bishop. be esteemed of those, which, to maintain contention, are not ashamed to deny that which all learned men agree upon.

Their reasons, as in number they be not many, so in substance they be nothing: I will recite the chief, and leave the rest to children to be discussed.

The first is taken out of the 2 Tim. iv.; where Paul saith The chief
reasons to the
contrary an-
swered. to Timothy, *Opus perage evangelistæ :* "Do the work of an evangelist." Their reason is this: Paul biddeth Timothy do the work of an evangelist; *ergo,* Timothy was not bishop.

First therefore we must search out what *opus evangelistæ* 1.
The place
2 Tim. iv. an-
swered. is, and then try whether it be incident to the office of a bishop, or no.

Bullinger upon that place saith that "he doth the work The work of
an evangelist. of an evangelist, which preacheth the gospel purely, and is not by any persecutions or adversity driven from his calling[8]."

Hemingius saith that *opus evangelistæ,* generally taken, is "to preach the gospel[9]."

Musculus, *in Locis Commun. titulo de verbi ministris,* saith that "he is *evangelista* either that preacheth or that writeth the gospel; and that Paul in the first sense speaketh to Timothy, saying, *Opus fac evangelistæ*[10]."

And in the same place, among other things that Paul requireth of a bishop, he affirmeth this to be one, *ut opus peragat evangelistæ*[11]. So saith Illyricus likewise[12].

Zuinglius also is of the same judgment in his book called *Ecclesiastes,* and proveth by that text of Paul, that "the work of an evangelist and of a bishop is all one[13]." Now how

[8] Opus evangelistæ peragit qui evangelium pure prædicat nec ullis persequutionibus aut adversitatum fluctibus depulsus clavum abjicit.—H. Bullinger. Comm. in Omn. Apost. Epist. In II. Epist. ad Timoth. cap. iv. p. 617.]

[9] ... Timothy, whom St Paul exhorteth to do the work of an "evangelist:" which work appeareth to have been enjoined to the apostles, in bestowing their travail in preaching the gospel everywhere.—N. Hemming, The Epistle to the Ephesians expovnded, transl. by A. Fleming, Lond. 1581. chap. iv. vv. 11, 12, 13. p. 137.]

[10] Evangelistam esse quid sit, varie exponitur. Breviter, vel est qui prædicat, vel qui literis mandat historias et doctrinam evangelii. Priore sensu Timotheo dicit apostolus: Opus fac evangelistæ, 2 Tim. 4.—Wolfg. Muscul. Loc. Comm. Theolog. Basil. 1599. De Ministr. Verb. Dei, p. 194.]

[11] Id. ibid. p. 196.]

[12] Tertio jubet, eum facere opus evangelistæ, quod pertinet potissimum ad doctrinam.—Nov. Test. ex Vers. Erasm. cum Gloss. Comp. Flac. Illyr. sup. II. Epist. ad Timoth. cap. iv. p. 1085.]

[13] See below, page 300, note 3.]

Timothy,
bishop.

this reason doth follow: Paul did bid Timothy preach the gospel purely and constantly; *ergo*, Timothy was not a bishop, let every man judge.

2.
The place
Ephes. iv.
answered.

The second reason is taken out of the fourth to the Ephe.: *Et ipse dedit alios quidem apostolos, alios vero prophetas, alios autem evangelistas, alios autem pastores ac doctores :* "He therefore gave some to be apostles, and some prophets, and some evangelists, and some pastors and teachers." The reason is framed on this sort: an evangelist and a bishop were distinct offices, and could not be both joined in one. But Timothy was an evangelist; *ergo*, he was not a bishop. This argument is very feeble in every part. For first

The major
false.

the major is utterly false; for those offices named by Paul were not so distinct but that divers of them may concur in one man; as may easily be proved. Paul was an apostle and also a doctor, 2 Timoth. i. Matthew and John being apostles were also evangelists; as the consent of all writers doth testify.

Timothy was according to M. Beza his judgment both an evangelist and also a prophet: look his notes in the iv. chapter of the first to Timothy[1].

Zuinglius, in his book called *Ecclesiastes*, saith that "an evangelist is nothing else but a bishop or a pastor, as it is manifest (saith he) by the words of Paul which he speaketh to Timothy, saying, *Opus fac evangelistæ ;* and Timothy, at that time when Paul writ his[2] epistle unto him, was a bishop; and therefore it is certain that according to Paul his sentence the office of an evangelist and of a bishop is all one[3]." These be the very words of Zuinglius.

Bullinger, expounding this place in the fourth to the Ephe., hath these words: "There is no man which seeth not these names to be confounded, and one to be taken for

[1] Nam probabilius est, quum jam haberet insigne prophetiæ donum, fuisse ex Spiritu sancti mandato illi impositas manus a presbyteris Ephesinis, id est ad prophetandum in illa ecclesia fuisse delectum, tantisper dum alio vocaretur a Domino : erat enim evangelista.—Nov. Test. cum Th, Bezæ Annot. H. Steph. 1565. Ad Timoth. I. cap. iv. v. 14. p. 467.]

[2] This, Answ. 2, and Def. A.]

[3] Nec etiam evangelistam alium, quam episcopum vel pastorem esse dicere possumus, quemadmodum ex Pauli verbis certo colligere licet, quibus Timotheum suum compellans ait,...opus perage evangelistæ...Atqui Timotheus tunc temporis, cum hæc illi Paulus scriberet, episcopum agebat. Unde constat juxta Pauli sententiam idem esse episcopi et evangelistæ officium.—H. Zvingl. Op. Tigur. 1581. Ecclesiast. Pars II. fol. 45.]

another; for an apostle is also a prophet, a doctor, an evan- Timothy,
bishop.
gelist, a minister, and a bishop ; and a bishop is an evangelist
and a prophet : a prophet is a doctor, a minister, and an
evangelist. Therefore the apostle Paul by these sundry names
doth signify these divers gifts which God hath bestowed upon
his church to salvation.   And, in that he so often useth this
disjunction, *alios atque alios*, he hath signified that all gifts
are not given to one man, but that divers men have divers
gifts of the Spirit; whereof he hath spoken more in the xii. to
the Rom., and the 1. to the Corinth. xii. chapter[4]." Hitherto
Bullinger.

Pellican in the same place is of the same judgment[5].

These offices therefore, or gifts, may well concur in one
man ; so that the major is false; and this conclusion followeth
not : Timothy was an evangelist; *ergo*, he was no bishop.

The minor (which is this : Timothy was an evangelist) is The minor
doubtful.
very doubtful. For first it may be doubted what an evangelist
is. The common opinion of old writers, and also of divers late
writers, is that those were properly called evangelists which
writ the gospels.   Other say that he is an evangelist which
preacheth the gospel.   Some say that he was an evangelist
that was occupied in teaching the people plainly and simply.
Calvin and some other think that they were next unto the
apostles in degree, and helpers of them, and such as supplied
their office oftentimes[6].   Divers other opinions there are of[7]
evangelists, and scarce two agree in one opinion touching the
office of an evangelist. The most say (which also the etymo-

[4 Nemo autem est qui non videat hæc vocabula invicem confundi et alterum
accipi pro altero. Nam apostolus etiam propheta, doctor, evangelista, presbyter
atque episcopus est. Et episcopus evangelista et propheta est. Propheta doctor,
presbyter, et evangelista. Proinde apostolus Paulus variis hisce vocabulis varia
illa dona significavit quæ Dominus ecclesiæ suæ impertiit ad salutem. Quod
vero dirimente particula subinde repetiit alios atque alios, significavit non uni
data esse omnia, sed alios aliis insignitos esse ornamentis Spiritus, non ut quæstum
faciant aut cæteris se præferant, sed dona sua in commune conferant. De qua re
pluribus disputavit in 12. capite ad Romanos, item in 1. ad Corinth. cap. 12.—H.
Bullinger. Comm. in Omn. Apost. Epist. Tigur. 1539. In Epist. ad Ephes. cap. iv.
p. 431.]

[5 C. Pellican. Comm. in Omn. Apost. Epist. Tigur. 1539. In Epist. ad
Ephes. cap. iv. v. 7. p. 383.]

[6 Iis [apostolis] proximi erant *evangelistæ*, et munus affine habebant : tantum
gradu dignitatis erant dispares...Ergo secundum apostolos istorum subsidiaria
opera usus est Dominus.—Calvin. Op. Amst. 1667-71. Comm. in Epist. ad Ephes.
cap. iv. 11. Tom. VII. p. 340.]

[7 There is of, Answ. 2.]

logy of the name doth import) that those were evangelists
which either preached or writ the gospel.

St Augustine, in his second book *contra Faustum Mani-
chæum*[1], writeth hereof on this sort: *Narratores ... originis,
factorum, dictorum, passionum Domini nostri Jesu Christi
proprie*[2] *dicti sunt evangelistæ*[3]: "They are properly called
evangelists which are the declarers of the birth, deeds, sayings, and sufferings of our Lord and Saviour Jesus Christ."
Which may be done both by preaching and writing the
gospel; as I said before.

Now, if Timothy be an evangelist because he preached the
gospel, there is no cause why he may not be a bishop also.
And it is certain that, when Paul said unto him, "Do the work
of an evangelist," he meant the preaching of the gospel.

If an evangelist be taken in any other signification, how
can it be proved that Timothy was an evangelist? For this
proveth it not, *Fac opus evangelistæ*: a man may do the work
of an evangelist, though he be not an evangelist: a man may
do the work of a pastor, though he be not a pastor.

To be short, the conclusion is not necessary, howsoever
the premises be true; for, although it should be granted that
both the major and minor were true, yet the conclusion doth
not follow; for Timothy might first be an evangelist, and after
a bishop; as Zuinglius, in his book called *Ecclesiastes*, saith
that "Philip the evangelist, being a deacon, was afterward
bishop and pastor of Cesarea: James the younger being an
apostle, as Hierome and all the old fathers do testify, was
after bishop of Jerusalem, and there remained; and divers of
the apostles, when they left off going from place to place,
became in the end bishops, and remained in one place; as it
appeareth in old histories[4]."

[1 Manichæ, Answ. 2, and Def. A.]　　　　[2 Propriæ, Answ. 2.]
[3 August. Op. Par. 1679-1700. Contr. Faust. Manich. Lib. II. cap. ii. Tom.
VIII. col. 185.]
[4 Quo in loco (Act. xxi.) illud nobis primo notandum est, Philippum hunc
Cæsariensis ecclesiæ evangelistam, episcopum vel pastorem fuisse, nec apostolum
a Luca dici, quamvis unus e septem illis esset, qui antea diaconi constituti
erant....Simul etiam illud notari debet, quod apostolorum nomen deposuerunt, ut
primum uni alicui ecclesiæ affixi, illius curam continuam habuerunt : cum nimirum
vel senecta impediti, vel morbis afflicti peregrinationum molestiis et periculis
amplius sufficere non potuerunt.　Tunc enim non apostoli amplius, sed episcopi
dicti sunt.　Possumus autem hujus rei exemplum, imo testem adducere divum
Jacobum, quem nos Minorem ab ætate dicimus.　Hunc enim Hieronymus

So that, although one man could not be both an evangelist *Timothy,* and a bishop at one time, and if it be granted that Timothy *bishop.* was an evangelist, yet doth it not prove but that he was a bishop also.

But certain it is that one man at one time might be both an evangelist and a bishop; and most certain it is that Timothy was a bishop, how certain soever it be whether[5] he were an evangelist or no.

But here it may be said that Timothy no more returned to Ephesus after he had been the second time with Paul at Rome, and therefore not to be like that he was bishop there. This argument is only conjectural, and of no force to prove any such matter. Howbeit, if we will credit stories, whereby in such cases we must be directed, it is certain that Timothy returned to Ephesus, and there died.

Dorotheus saith that he died at Ephesus, and was there buried[6].

Polycrates testifieth that he was stoned to death at Ephesus[7].

Isidorus, in his book *De Patribus Novi Testamenti,* writeth that he was buried at Ephesus in the mount Pyon[8].

Symeon Metaphrastes testifieth the same[9].

Nicephorus, *Lib. x. cap.* 11, testifieth that "Julian the apostata did torment one Artemius for translating the bones of Andrew, Luke, and Timothy from Patra, Achaia, and Ephesus, to Constantinople[10]." But it is certain that Andrew was crucified at Patra by Ægeas the proconsul; and ancient

[Hieron. Op. Par. 1693-1706. Catalog. Script. Eccles. 2. Tom. IV. Pars ii. col. 101.], et omnes simul vetusti patres, Hierosolymitanorum episcopum nominant, non aliam ob causam, quam quod ea in urbe sedem fixam posuisset.—H. Zvingl. Op. Tigur. Ecclesiast. Pars II. fol. 48.]

[5] It is whether, Answ. 2.]

[6] Doroth. de Vit. et Mort. Proph. et Apost. Synops. in Magn. Biblioth. Vet. Patr. Col. Agrip. 1618-22. Tom. III. p. 148. See before, page 294, note 4.]

[7] Polycr. in Antonin. Chronic. Op. Lugd. 1586. Pars I. Tit. vi. cap. xxviii. 6. p. 448. See before, page 295, note 9.]

[8] Isidor. Hisp. Op. Col. Agrip. 1617. De Vit. et Mort. Sanct. 86. p. 366. See before, page 294, note 7.]

[9] Sim. Metaphrast. Vit. Timoth. cap. ii. 10. in Bolland. Act. Sanct. Antv. 1643. Jan. xxiv. Tom. II. p. 568.]

[10] ... Ἀρτέμιον δὲ τὸν γενναῖον τῆς εὐσεβείας ἀγωνιστὴν...δι' ἑαυτοῦ ἐκολάσατο·...ὅτι περ τὰ τῶν θείων ἀποστόλων ὀστᾶ, ἐκ Πατρῶν καὶ Ἀχαΐας καὶ Ἐφέσου, Ἀνδρέου τε καὶ Λουκᾶ καὶ Τιμοθέου, ἀνήγαγεν ἐν τῇ Κωνσταντίνου.— Niceph. Call. Eccles. Hist. Lut. Par. 1630. Lib. x. cap. xi. Tom. II. p. 29. Conf. Lib. ii. capp. xxxix. xliii. Tom. I. pp. 199, 200, 210.]

writers testify that Luke was buried in Achaia; therefore the bones that were brought from Ephesus must needs be Timothy's.

Hereby it may appear that Timothy not only returned from Rome to Ephesus, but also continued there even to his death. And therefore certain it is that he was bishop at Ephesus. But now to my purpose.

Chapter iii.   The Sixty-first Division.

Answer to the Admonition, Page 72, Sect. ult.

Ignatius.

The bishops' authority[2].

Ignatius, who was St John his scholar, and lived in Christ's time, in his epistle *ad Trallianos*, speaketh thus of the authority of a bishop over the rest: *Quid aliud est episcopus quam quidam obtinens principatum et potestatem supra omnes*[1]*?* "What is a bishop but one having power and rule over all?" And, in his epistle *ad Smyrnenses*, he writeth on this sort: *Honora quidem Deum ut auctorem universorum et Dominum; episcopum autem, ut sacerdotum principem, imaginem Dei ferentem; Dei quidem per principatum; Christi vero per sacerdotium*[3]: "Honour God as the author and Lord of all things, and a bishop as the chief of priests, bearing the image of God; of God, because of his superiority; of Christ, by reason of his priesthood." And a little after: "Let laymen be subject to deacons, deacons to priests, and priests to bishops, the bishop to Christ[4]." And again: "Let no man do anything which pertaineth to the church without the consent of the bishop[5]." And again: "He, that attempteth to do anything without the bishop, breaketh peace, and confoundeth good order[6]." The

[1 Ignat. Interp. Epist. ad Trall. 7. in Coteler. Patr. Apost. Amst. 1724. Vol. II. p. 63.]

[2 The authority of bishops, Answ. 2.]

[3 Id. Interp. Epist. ad Smyrn. 9. ibid. p. 87. See before, page 171, note 7.]

[4 Οἱ λαϊκοὶ τοῖς διακόνοις ὑποτασσέσθωσαν. οἱ διάκονοι τοῖς πρεσβυτέροις· οἱ πρεσβύτεροι τῷ ἐπισκόπῳ· ὁ ἐπίσκοπος τῷ Χριστῷ, ὡς αὐτὸς τῷ Πατρί.—Id. ibid.]

[5 Μηδεὶς χωρὶς τοῦ ἐπισκόπου τι πρασσέτω τῶν ἀνηκόντων εἰς τὴν ἐκκλησίαν.—Id. Gen. Epist. ad Smyrn. 8. p. 36.]

[6 ... πόσῳ δοκεῖτε χείρονος ἀξιωθήσεται τιμωρίας, ὁ ἄνευ ἐπισκόπου τι ποιεῖν προαιρούμενος, καὶ τὴν ὁμόνοιαν διασπῶν, καὶ τὴν εὐταξίαν συγχέων;— Id. Interp. Epist. ad Smyrn. 9. ibid. p. 87.]

like saying he hath in his epistle *ad Magnesianos*[7]. These three epistles doth Eusebius make mention of *Lib. iii. cap.* 35 & 36,[8] and Hiero. *De Viris Illustribus*[9].

T. C. Page 87, Sect. 4.

It is no marvel, although you take up the authors of the Admonition for want of logic, for you utter great skill yourself in writing, which keep no order, but confound your reader, in that thing which even the common logic of the country, which is reason, might have directed you in; for what a confusion of times is this, to begin with Cyprian, and then come to Jerome and Chrysostom, and after to the scripture, and back again to Ignatius that was before Cyprian! which times are ill disposed of you, and that in a matter wherein it stood you upon to have observed the order of the times.

Jo. Whitgift.

Be patient awhile: the matter is not great, the authors be known, and the antiquity of them: my mind is of the matter; and there is reason why I should thus place them. Cyprian telleth the necessity of such superiority; and so doth Chrysostom; Hierome, the cause and the original: Paul, Timothy, and Titus be examples hereof: Ignatius and the rest are brought in as witnesses of the continuance of such offices and superiority in the church, even from the apostles. Now, first to prove the name of these offices not to be antichristian, then to shew the necessity of the offices, thirdly the cause, and last of all to declare the use of the same to have been in the church even from St Paul's time to this hour, is to keep a better order than you shall be able to disorder, with all the logic, rhetoric, and hot eloquence you have.

The order observed in placing the authorities in the Answer.

Chapter iii. The Sixty-second Division.

T. C. Page 87, Sect. 4.

But as for Ignatius' place, it is sufficiently answered before, in that which was answered to Cyprian his place[10]; for, when he saith "the bishop hath rule over all," he meaneth no more all in the province, than in all the world; but meaneth that flock and congregation whereof he is bishop or minister. And, when he calleth him "prince of the priests," although the

[7] Id. Interp. Epist. ad Magnes. 4. ibid. pp. 54, 5.]

[8] Euseb. in Hist. Eccles. Script. Amst. 1695-1700. Lib. iii. cap. xxxvi. p. 86.]

[9] Hieron. Op. Par. 1693-1706. Catalog. Script. Eccles. 16. Tom. IV. Pars ii. col. 108.]

[10] See before, pages 201, &c.]

*title be too excessive and big, condemned by Cyprian and the council of
Carthage [1], yet he meaneth no more the prince of all in the diocese as we
take it, or of the province, than he meaneth the prince of all the priests in
the world, but he meaneth those fellow-ministers [2] and elders that had the
rule and government of that particular church and congregation whereof
he is a bishop [3]; as the great churches have for the most part both elders
which govern only, and ministers also to aid one another; and the princi-
pality, that he which they called the bishop had over the rest, hath been
before at large declared.*

Jo. Whitgift.

You very lightly shake off Ignatius' words; but they have
more pith in them, if it please you better to consider of them.
For he maketh degrees of ministers, and the bishop to be the
chief: he placeth deacons under priests, and priests under
bishops, so that he giveth to the bishop superiority and government over both priests and deacons; which is the ground
of this cause; and, it being granted (as it must needs, neither
can this authority of Ignatius be avoided) Aerius' heresy falleth;
and so doth your whole assertion.

What is meant by "prince of priests," Ignatius himself
declareth, saying: *obtinens principatum et potestatem supra
omnes [4]:* "having chiefty and power over all."

How this name may be well used, I have shewed before,
where I have also declared the meaning of Cyprian's words,
uttered in the heretical council of Carthage, and therefore
not counted in the number of those councils.

Chapter iii.   The Sixty-third Division.
T. C. Page 88, Sect. 1, 2.

*But M. Doctor doth not remember that, whilst he thus reasoneth for
the authority of the bishop, he overthroweth his archbishop quite and clean.
For Ignatius will have none above the bishop but Christ; and he will have
an archbishop.*

*I see a man cannot well serve two masters, but either he must displease
the one and please the other, or by pleasing of one offend the other. For
M. Doctor would fain please and uphold both; and yet his proofs are such,
that every prop that he setteth under one is an axe to strike at the other.*

[1 Concil. Carthag. in Cypr. Op. Oxon. 1682. p. 229. See before, page 208,
note 3.]

[2 But those fellow-ministers, Repl. 2.]   [3 He was bishop, Repl. 2.]

[4 Ignat. Interp. Epist. ad Trall. 7. in Coteler. Patr. Apost. Amst. 1724. Vol. II.
p. 63. See before, page 304.]

Jo. Whitgift.

I remember it very well; and I know that an archbishop is a bishop, and that therefore there may be superiority among bishops, and yet nothing detracted from the words of Ignatius[5]. I know likewise that as well the one as the other is condemned by you, and I am well assured that the proof of the one is the proof of the other; and therefore M. Doctor may "well serve two masters;" but they be such as be not only not contrary one to the other, but so nearly linked and joined together, that whatsoever pleaseth the one doth also please the other. "M. Doctor's props and proofs" are such, as M. T. C. is compelled to use railing and flouting, instead of answering; which is a shift, but how honest and christian let the world judge.

Chapter iii. The Sixty-fourth Division.

Answer to the Admonition, Page 73, Sect. 1.

Justinus Martyr, one of the most ancient writers of the Greeks, in his second Apology *ad Antoninum Pium*, alloweth this superiority, and calleth him that bare rule over the other ministers προεστῶτα[7].

Justin Martyr.

T. C. Page 88, Sect. 2.

But that M. Doctor delighteth always, where he might fetch at the foun-
1 Tim. v. 17.[8] *tain, to be raking in ditches, he needed not to have gone to Justin Martyr for προεστώς, when as St Paul calleth the ministers and elders by this title. And, if this place of Justin make for an archbishop, then instead of an archbishop in every province we shall have one in every congregation. For Justin declareth there the liturgy or manner of serving God that was in every church used of the Christians. And I pray you let it be considered what is the office of that προεστώς, and see whether there be any resemblance in the world between him and an archbishop. For he placeth his office to be in preaching, in conceiving prayers, in ministering of the sacraments: of any commandment which he had over the rest of the ministers, or of any such privileges as the archbishop hath, he maketh not one word. It may be that the same might have the pre-*

[5] "... thereby he affirmeth that, albeit the bishop of the diocese were the highest bishop that could be upon earth, yet there might be another higher than he."—Sec. Repl. p. 620.]
[6] Justinus, Answ. 2.]
[7] Just. Mart. Op. Par. 1742. Apol. i. 65. p. 82.]
[8] The verse is added from Repl. 2.]

eminence of calling the rest together, and propounding the matter to the
rest of the company, and such like, as is before declared[1]. As soon as ever
you found προεστώς, you snatched that by and bye, and went your ways,
and so deceive yourself and others. But, if you had read the whole treatise,
you should have found that he was προεστώς of the people; for thus it is
written in the same Apology: ἔπειτα προσφέρεται τῷ προεστῶτι τῶν ἀδελφῶν
ἄρτος: "Afterward bread is brought to the president of the brethren,"
calling the people, as St Paul doth continually, brethren. And therefore

Nay, they
are yours,
and like to
the rest.

these are M. Doctor's arguments out of Martyr's place: There was a
minister which did stand before or was president of the rest in every par-
ticular church and congregation; therefore there was an archbishop over
all the province. And again: There was one which ruled the people in every
congregation; therefore there was one that ruled all the ministers through-
out the whole province. And, albeit things were in great purity in the

Antiquum
obtinet.

days that Justin lived, in respect of the times which followed; yet, as there
was in other things which appear in his works, and even in the ministra-
tion of the sacraments spoken of in that place, corruption, in that they
mingled water and wine together; so even in the ministry there began to
peep out something which went from the simplicity of the gospel, as that the
name of προεστώς, which was common to the elders with the ministers of
the word, was (as it seemeth) appropriated unto one.

Jo. Whitgift.

Though notable and famous doctors be "ditches" with
T. C., yet are they pleasant and clear rivers with men of more
liberal sciences. St Paul, 1 Tim. v., hath these words, οἱ καλῶς
προεστῶτες πρεσβύτεροι, &c., which derogate nothing from
anything that I have alleged, but justifieth the same; for
there it signifieth rule and government; but yet in Justin it
signifieth some one that had the chief rule and government
over the rest; as M. Beza noteth upon these words, 1 Tim. v.,

Beza.

Adversus presbyterum &c. Præterea notandum est ex hoc
loco Timotheum in Ephesino presbyterio tum fuisse προεσ-
τῶτα, id est, antistitem, ut vocat Justinus[2]: "Furthermore,
it is to be noted out of this place, that Timothy, in the presbytery or college of ministers at Ephesus, was προεστώς, that
is to say, the prelate or bishop; as Justinus[3] calleth it." You
may say unto him as well as to me, that he "delighteth, where
he might search at the fountain, to be raking in ditches," because he might have had the same words spoken of all ministers
in the same chapter of that epistle to Timothy.

[1] See before, pages 269, 278.]
[2] Nov. Test. cum Th. Bezæ Annot. H. Steph. 1565. In Epist. ad Timoth. I.
cap. v. v. 19. p. 470.]
[3] Justines, Def. B.]

Furthermore, that Justinus Martyr doth use this word for him that hath authority over the rest, not only of the people, but of such also as be *presbyteri*, the same M. Beza testifieth upon the first to the Philip. saying : *Hæc igitur olim erat episcoporum appellatio, donec qui politiæ causa reliquis fratribus in cœtu præerat, quem Justinus* προεστῶτα *vocat, peculiariter dici episcopus cœpit*[4]: " This therefore was the common name of bishops, until he, which for policy' sake did govern the rest in the company, whom Justin calleth προεστῶτα, began to be called peculiarly a bishop." In which words M. Beza testifieth that he whom Justinus called προεστῶτα did govern as well the other ministers as he did the people. And, whosoever doth duly consider Justin's words, and peruse that whole place, he shall easily understand that those whom he there calleth "brethren" were ministers and deacons ; for afterward, speaking of the people, he calleth them by the name of people, as it is there to be seen.

I know that Justin speaketh of their "manner of liturgy," but that doth not improve anything that I have affirmed ; for I speak of the name προεστῶς in that signification that Justin doth use it, which is for one that doth govern the rest. Wherefore this is my argument : There was one among the ministers in Justin's time that did rule and govern the rest ; *ergo,* there was then superiority among the ministers of the church, and one was above another ; which is the overthrow of your ground of equality, at the which I shoot ; and, the which being overthrown, the superiority of bishops and archbishops is soon proved. And, again, I say that in Justin's time there was one that governed the rest of the ministers ; *ergo,* there may be one to do the same now in like manner. These be my reasons ; as for yours, they be like to the rest of your own. But your best refuge is to discredit the author, which you do in Justin, as you have done in the rest. There is no antiquity of any credit with you, no, not in a matter of history, as this is. For Justinus doth but declare the manner used in the church in his time. It is well that in the end you confess this name προεστῶς to signify in Justin the authority of one minister : this because you are constrained to acknowledge, you will do it with nipping and biting the author, after your

Marginal notes:
προεστῶς over ministers as well as over the people.

Idem.

[4 Ibid. In Epist. ad Philip. cap. i. v. 1. p. 404 ; where τὸν προεστῶτα.]

manner. Ignatius, who was before Justin[1], as you have
heard, useth a more lofty word; for he doth call him, *princeps
sacerdotum*[2]: " the prince or chief of priests."

Chapter iii.   The Sixty-fifth Division.

Answer to the Admonition, Page 73, Sect. 1.

Cyrill.[4]

Cyrillus calleth him ἀρχιερέα[3]. [Tertullian in his book
De Baptis. saith that a bishop is *summus sacerdos*[5].][6]

T. C. Page 88, Sect. 3.

*Another of M. Doctor's reasons for to prove the archbishop is that
Cyril maketh mention of an high priest; whereunto I answer that he that
bringeth in a priest into the church goeth about to bury our Saviour
Christ; for, although it might be proved that the word "priest" were the same
with the Greeks' πρεσβύτερος, yet (as shall appear in his place) is the use
of this word "priest" for a minister of the gospel very dangerous.   And,
as for him that bringeth in an high priest into the church, he goeth about
to put our Saviour Christ out of his office, who is proved, in the* Hebr. vii.[7]
*epistle to the Hebrews, to be the only high priest, and that there
can be no more as long as the world endureth.   And yet, if all this were
granted, you are not yet come to that which you desire to prove, that is, an*
In what book? *archbishop.   For, if you look in Theodoret you shall find this word, ἀρχιε-
ρωσύνη, which signifieth the high priesthood, to be nothing else but a bishopric*[8]; *and in the seventh chapter of that book, and so forth
divers times, you shall have ἀρχιερεὺς taken for a bishop, as,* i Lib. 3.
cap.7
speaking of the council of Nice, he saith that there was 318.

[1] Cartwright, after calling Whitgift's arguments " pitiful" and " childish,"
proceeds : " Justin's writings, compared as I compared them with the holy scripture, are as I said a ditch : I added the reason, that there was in them not a little
mud of errors, which the D. could not answer."   Of the assertion that Ignatius
was before Justin, he says : " If he were the true Ignatius, he should indeed be
' before Justin;' but, to let pass other exceptions, with M. Calvin's sharp censure
of him, it is absurd to ascribe to Ignatius, St John's scholar, that vain boast of
being able to expound [Ignat. Interp. Epist. ad Trall. 5. in Coteler. Patr. Apostol. Amst. 1724. Vol. II. p. 23.] the orders of angels, &c."—Sec. Repl. pp.
621, 2.]

[2] Ignat. Interp. Epist. ad Smyrn. 9. in Coteler. Patr. Apost. Vol. II. p. 87.
See before, page 304.]

[3] The editor has not been able to find the passage intended.]

[4] This is not in Answ.]

[5] Dandi [baptismum] quidem habet jus summus sacerdos, qui est episcopus.—
Tertull. Op. Lut. 1641. De Bapt. 17. p. 263.]

[6] This sentence is inserted from Answ. 2.]

[7] These marginal references are inserted from Repl. 2.]

[8] Κατὰ τοῦτον δὲ τὸν χρόνον, τῆς μὴν Ῥωμαίων ἐκκλησίας Σίλβεστρος
κατεῖχε τὰς ἡνίας, Μιλτιάδην διαδεξάμενος, ὅς...τὴν τῆς αὐτῆς ἀρχιερωσύνης
χειροτονίαν ἐδέξατο.—Theod. in Hist. Eccles. Script. Amst. 1695-1700. Lib. i.
cap. iii. p. 8.]

ἀρχιερεῖς : high priests[9].   *Now I think you will not say there were* 318.
*archbishops ; if you do, you are confuted by all ecclesiastical writers that
ever I read, which, speaking of them, calleth*[10] *them bishops.*

Jo. Whitgift.

This name " priest" is usually applied to the minister of
the gospel, in all histories, fathers, and writers of antiquity.
And the most of the latest writers do use it, and make no
great scrupulosity in it; neither doth the name " priest" " bury
our Saviour Christ," as long as it is used for a minister of the
gospel; neither is there any danger in it at all, as long as the
office is lawful.

Not only Cyril useth this name " high priest," but Tertull. Tertull.
also in his book *De Baptismo*, where he saith that *episcopus*
is *summus sacerdos*[11]: " The bishop is the high priest ;" and in
like manner Theodoret, as you here say; and yet none of
them meant to derogate anything from the office of Christ.

I told you before how names proper to Christ may be
also attributed to men[12]: this being granted, I have as much
as I desire; for, as the bishop is called *ἀρχιερεύς*, in the respect of other priests that be inferior unto him, so is the chief
bishop called *archiepiscopus,* in respect of other bishops that
be governed and directed by him.   And, as among the ministers there is one chief which is called a bishop, so among the
bishops there is one chief also that is called an archbishop; and
this is that *ordo* that Augustine speaketh of[13]; as I have said
in my Answer to the Admonition, in the words of M. Fox.

Chapter iii.   The Sixty-sixth Division.

Answer to the Admonition, Page 73, Sect. 2.

Theodoretus, *Lib. v. c.* 28, writeth that Chrysostom, Theodoret
being the bishop of Constantinople, did not only rule that of Chryso-
church, but the churches also in Thracia, in Asia, and in stom[14].
Pontus [15].

[9] 'Οκτωκαίδεκα δὲ καὶ τριακόσιοι συνῆλθον ἀρχιερεῖς.—Id. ibid. cap. vii.
p. 24.]

[10] Call, Repl. 1 and 2.]   [11] See above, note 5.]

[12] "... absurd, and before confuted."—Sec. Repl. p. 622.]

[13] August. Op. Par. 1679-1700. De Civ. Dei, Lib. xix. cap. xiii. 1. Tom. VII.
col. 557. See below, page 334.]

[14] Answ. 2 has simply *Theodoretus*, and does not repeat the word in the
margin of the next paragraph, page 318.]

[15] Theod. in Hist. Eccles. Script. Lib. v. cap. xxviii. pp. 235, 6. See
below, page 313, note 5.]

T. C. Page 88, Sect. 4.

Chrysostom followeth, which, as M. Doctor saith, "ruled not only the church of Constantinople, but the churches of Thracia, Asia, and Pontus;" and he saith it out of Theodoret. But herein it may appear that either

Or else you pluck yourself by the nose.

M. Doctor hath a very evil conscience in falsifying writers, and that in the points which lie in controversy, or else he hath taken his stuff of certain at the second hand, without any examination of it at all. For here he hath set down, instead of "had care of the churches of[1] *Thracia, &c.,"*

The words of Theodoret clipped.

"ruled the churches:" the Greek is ἐποιεῖτο τὴν προμήθειαν : it is translated also prospexit; so that it appeareth he fetched it neither from Theodoret in Greek nor in Latin. And what is this to prove an archbishop, that he had care of these churches? there is no minister but ought to have care over all the churches through Christendom, and to shew that care for them in comforting or admonishing of them by writing or by

What scripture expresseth these conditions and cautions?

visiting them, if the necessity so require, and it is thought[2] *good by the churches, and leave obtained of the place where he is minister, upon some notable and especial cause, being some man of singular gifts, whose learning and credit may profit much to the bringing to pass of that thing for the which he is to be sent. After this sort St Cyprian,* As it appeareth by divers epistles of his. *being in Afric, had care over Rome in Europe, and wrote unto the church there*[3]*. After this sort also was Irenæus,* Euseb. Lib. v. cap. 3. & 4.

Untrue.

bishop of Lyons, sent by the French churches unto the churches in Phrygia[4]*; and after this sort have M. Calvin and M. Beza been sent from Geneva in Savoy to the churches of France.*

Jo. Whitgift.

The falsifying of Theodoret returned upon the Replier.

It shall appear, God willing, whether M. Doctor's memory or yours be worse; whether "he hath an evil conscience in falsifying writers," or you in slandering of him; whether "he taketh his stuff at the second hand," or you rather that have borrowed of other men's collections almost whatsoever you have heaped together in your book. All this I say shall appear, even to try your corrupt and untrue dealing in this place; and certainly I cannot but marvel what affection hath so gotten the upper hand of you, that it provoketh you to such outrageous speeches in a matter so manifestly counterfeit. If you have not seen the author, I will ascribe it to negligent ignorance; but, if you have seen him, I cannot ascribe it to any other thing than to unshamefast malice. The whole story

Theodor. Lib. v. cap. 28.

as it is in Theodoret is this: Ὁ δὲ μέγας Ἰωάννης τοὺς

[1 In, Repl. 1 and 2.]   [2 It be thought, Repl. 2.]
[3 Cypr. Op. Oxon. 1682. Ad Presb. et Diac. Rom. Epistt. ix. xx. xxvii. xxxv. pp. 18, 19, 42, &c. 52, 3, 69.]
[4 Euseb. in Hist. Eccles. Script. Amst. 1695-1700. Lib. v. capp. iii. iv. pp. 136, 7. See below page 314, note 1.]

ἐκκλησίας δεξάμενος οἴακας, τάς τε παρά τινων γινομένας
ἀδικίας σὺν παῤῥησίᾳ διήλεγχε, καὶ βασιλεῖ καὶ βασιλίδι
παρῄνει τὰ πρόσφορα, καὶ τοὺς ἱερέας ἠξίου κατὰ τοὺς
κειμένους πολιτεύεσθαι νόμους· τοὺς δὲ τούτους παραβαίνειν
τολμῶντας ἐπιβαίνειν τῶν ἀνακτόρων ἐκώλυεν, οὐ χρῆναι
λέγων τῆς μὲν τῶν ἱερέων ἀπολαύειν τιμῆς, τὴν δὲ τῶν
ἀληθῶν ἱερέων μὴ ζηλοῦν βιοτήν. καὶ ταύτην ἐποιεῖτο τὴν
προμήθειαν οὐ μόνον ἐκείνης τῆς πόλεως, ἀλλὰ καὶ τῆς
Θρᾴκης ἁπάσης, εἰς ἓξ δὲ αὐτὴ ἡγεμονίας διήρηται, καὶ τῆς
Ἀσίας ὅλης, ὑπὸ ἕνδεκα δὲ καὶ αὐτὴ ἀρχόντων ἰθύνεται,
καὶ μέντοι καὶ τὴν Ποντικὴν τούτοις κατεκόσμει τοῖς
νόμοις, ἰσαρίθμους δὲ καὶ αὐτὴ ἔχει τῆς Ἀσίας τοὺς ἡγου-
μένους[5]: "John the great, having received the stern of the
church, reproved the injuries of certain boldly, and counselled
the king and the queen things convenient, and exhorted the
priests to walk according to the laws appointed. But such as
were not afraid to break them he suffered not to come to the
table, saying it was not meet that those should enjoy the
honour of priests, which would not follow the conversation of
true priests. And this care he used not only over that city,
but also over whole Thracia, which containeth six provinces,
and over all Asia, which is governed under eleven rulers;
and moreover he governed the church of Pontus with these
laws, in which country are as many rulers as in Asia." First
he saith that " Chrysostom took the stern or government of
the church;" then that "he did freely reprehend vice;"
thirdly, that " he commanded the priests to live according to
the laws;" fourthly, that he did excommunicate and deprive
of their priestly honour such as durst transgress. Is not this
" to rule?" what archbishop in England doth execute greater
jurisdiction? Then it followeth immediately in Theodor.: "and
with this care he did provide for or embrace not only his
city, but the churches of Thracia, &c." Where it is to be
noted that Theodoret saith, "with this care, &c.," meaning
that, as he had the government of the church of Constantinople, and did there reprehend vice, commanded the priests
to live according to the laws, excommunicate them that did
not, and put them from their office, so did he also " in the
churches of Thracia, Asia, and Pontus." Theodoret's words

[5 Theod. in eod. Lib. v. cap. xxviii. pp. 235, 6; where τοὺς τῆς ἐκκλησίας,
and οὐ μόνης ἐκείνης.]

be καὶ ταύτην ἐποιεῖτο τὴν προμήθειαν, &c.; and you have
craftily left out ταύτην that you might the rather cloke
Theodoret's plain meaning.   Besides this, Theodoret saith in
plain words, that " he governed the churches in Pontus with
these laws :" the Greek word is κατεκόσμει τοῖς νόμοις.

I shall most heartily desire the reader to consider this
dealing of yours : surely I think few papists would have dealt
in like manner.   And, if the words of themselves were not
plain (as they be most plain), yet very reason might have
taught you that this was Theodoret's meaning; for, if he
should not have meant some special care of these churches,
wherefore should he rather make particular mention of them
than of other churches ? Do you not think that wise men can
easily espy your gross shifts ?

Cyprian's " care over Rome " was not like the care that
he had over his own churches : it could not be said that he
embraced Rome with the same care of government, of reproving, of excommunicating such as durst offend, &c., that
he did Carthage and other places committed unto him, as it
is here said of Chrysostom.

I omit your oversight in saying that Irenæus was sent to
the churches in Phrygia; for Eusebius, *Lib. v. cap.* 3, & 4.[1]
(which places you quote in your margent to prove it) hath
no such thing : only he saith that Irenæus was sent to Rome
to Eleutherius[2].

Chapter iii.   The Sixty-seventh Division.

T. C. Page 89, Sect. 1.

*Now, if you will conclude hereupon that Cyprian ruled the church of
Rome, or Irenæus the church*[3] *of Phrygia, or M. Calvin or M. Beza the
churches of France, or that they were bishops or archbishops of those places,
you shall but conclude as you were wont to do ; but yet all men understand*

[1 Euseb. in eod. Lib. v. capp. iii. iv. pp. 136, 7. It was only a letter that was
sent to the churches in Asia and Phrygia.]

[2 Cartwright answers this division at length, contending that "care doth not
necessarily draw jurisdiction or rule over that cared for," maintaining that he had
not corrupted or misalleged Theodoret, and adding : " Touching Irenæus' ambassage into Phrygia, the D. eye is not simple. For, after Euseb. had shewed that
there were ambassadors sent by the French churches to those of Phrygia, he addeth,
as an augmentation, that they were also sent to the bishop of Rome. &c."—Sec.
Repl. pp. 622, &c.]

[3 Churches, Repl. 1 and 2.]

that here is nothing less than an archbishop, or any such bishop as we Or else you are deceived.
have and use in our church.   And, if so be that Chrysostom should be
bishop or archbishop of all these churches which were in all Asia, Pontus,
Thracia, as you would give the reader to understand, you make him bishop
of more churches than ever the pope of Rome was when he was in his
greatest pride and his empire largest.   For there were six presidentships
in Thracia, and in Asia there were an[4] *eleven princes, and had several*
regions or governments, and in Pontus as many; and, if he were bishop or
archbishop of all the churches within these dominions, he had need of a
long spoon to feed withal.   It is certain therefore that he was bishop only An untruth, as will appear.
of the church in Constantinople, and had an eye and a care to those other
churches.   And that he was bishop of one city or of one church, it may
appear by that which I have before alleged out of the Greek scholiast upon
Titus, who citeth there Chrysostom, where it is said that St Paul "did not
mean to make one over the whole isle, but that every one should have The words of the scholiast perverted.
his proper congregation, &c.[5]" *And in another place he sheweth*
3. Hom. Act.[6] *the difference between the emperor and the bishop, that the one is*
over the world, and the other, that is the bishop, is over one city[7].

Jo. Whitgift.

Your examples prove nothing, neither be they anything Thracia, &c. annexed to the bishopric of Constantinople.
like to this of Chrysostom; for Theodoret doth mention these
churches as places annexed to the bishopric of Constantinople,
and properly appertaining to the care and charge of Chrysostom, the bishop of that city. Socrates, speaking of a council
assembled at Constantinople, saith thus: "They do again Socrates, Lib. v. cap. 8.
establish the faith of the council of Nice; and dividing provinces they appoint patriarchs; there was therefore allotted
unto Nectarius the great and ample city of Constantinople and
Thracia, &c.[8]" And this Nectarius was patriarch of Constantinople next before Chrysostom; so that it is manifest that
Chrysostom was patriarch, or archbishop, both of Constantin-
ople and also of Thracia, &c. Sozomenus sheweth evidently Sozom. Lib. VIII. cap. 6.
that Chrysostom had jurisdiction over all Asia, and of other
places also, and that he executed jurisdiction there accord-
ingly: "For he deposed to the number of 13. bishops, some Chrysostom exerciseth archiepiscopal jurisdiction in Asia.
in Lycia, some in Phrygia, some in Asia; because they sold

[4 A, Repl. 1 and 2.]

[5 Œcumen. Op. Lut. Par. 1631.   Comm. cap. i. in Epist. ad Tit. Tom. II.
p. 289.   See before, pages 283, 4, note 8.]

[6 Repl. 2 adds here *vi.*]

[7 Οὐχὶ τῆς οἰκουμένης ὁ βασιλεύων κρατεῖ, οὗτος δὲ πόλεως μόνης;—Chrysost.
Op. Par. 1718-38.   In Act: Apost. Hom. iii. Tom. IX. p. 29.]

[8 Socr. in Hist. Eccles. Script. Amst. 1695-1700. Lib. v. cap. viii. pp. 217, 8.
See before, page 163, note 9.]

benefices, and bestowed them for favour and for reward[1]."
And, if you were not either very ignorant or wilfully bent,
you might have read in ecclesiastical histories that one bishop
had authority and charge over divers churches, long before
Chrysostom's time; the which thing I have also before proved
by divers examples.

That Chrysostom was archbishop of all those churches
(although it be sufficiently proved by the testimony of Theodoret, a worthy writer and notable divine, and by Sozomen
also), yet will I add (as a full confutation of all your fancies
in this matter) the judgment of the writers and collectors of
the Centuries, who, being many, learned, and travailing especially in such matters, deserve great credit.   In their v.
Century, *cap. x.* they write thus of Chrysostom : *Non autem
tantum istius ecclesiæ pastorem egit, &c.*[2]: " But he was not
only pastor of this church (meaning Constantinople), but was
archbishop also, or overseer, of other churches in Thracia,
which was divided into six presidentships; in Asia, which
was ruled of eleven prætors; and in the region of Pontus,
which is likewise divided into eleven presidentships." If no
report of any historiographer will please you, what remedy?
though you remain wilful still, yet I trust the tractable reader
may here find sufficient to satisfy him.   For a further proof
that the bishops of Constantinople were called archbishops, I
could refer you to the general council of Chalcedon, which was
anno 453, where Flavianus is called archbishop of Constantinople sundry times[3].   Where also it appeareth that the
archbishop of Constantinople had the ordaining, allowing, and
disallowing of the bishops in Pontus, Asia, and Thracia[4]. You
are greatly deceived in saying that, " if he were archbishop

Marginal notes:
Cent. v. cap. 10.
Chrysostom, archbishop of Thracia, Asia, &c.

Act. xvi.

[1 Ὁ δὲ Ἰωάννης πυθόμενος...τοὺς μὲν, λήμμασι καὶ δωροδοκίαις, τοὺς δὲ χάριτι ὑπαγομένους τὰς ἱερωσύνας ἀπεμπωλεῖν, ἧκεν εἰς Ἔφεσον· καθελών τε δέκα καὶ τρεῖς ἐπισκόπους, τοὺς μὲν ἐν Λυκίᾳ καὶ Φρυγίᾳ, τοὺς δὲ ἐν αὐτῇ τῇ Ἀσίᾳ, ἑτέρους ἀντ' αὐτῶν κατέστησε.—Soz. in eod. Lib. VIII. cap. vi. p. 618.]

[2 Non &c. egit, sed et archiepiscopum seu inspectorem aliarum per Thraciam, quæ in sex præfecturas erat divisa: et per Asiam, quæ ab undecim prætoribus regebatur : et per regionem Ponti, itidem in undecim præfecturas distributam.—Centur. Eccles. Hist. 1560, &c. Cent. v. cap. x. col. 1171.]

[3 Concil. Calched. Act. i. in Concil. Stud. Labb. et Cossart. Lut. Par. 1671-2, Tom. IV. cols. 177, &c.]

[4 ... χρῆναι δὲ τὸν ὁσιώτατον ἀρχιεπίσκοπον τῆς βασιλίδος Κωνσταντι-νουπόλεως νέας Ῥώμης...ἐξουσίαν ἔχειν τοῦ χειροτονεῖν τοὺς μητροπολίτας ἔν τε τῇ Ἀσιανῇ, καὶ Ποντικῇ καὶ Θρακικῇ ταῖς διοικήσεσι, κ. τ. λ.—Act. XVI. ibid. col. 818. Conf. cols. 795, 8. See before, page 168, note 4.]

of all these churches, he was bishop of more churches than ever the pope was in his greatest pride;" for even all these churches, and all other churches, were made subject to him, when by Phocas he was made the head of the church and universal bishop; and, though he had not possession of all, yet did he claim interest in all, and jurisdiction over all, or, at the least, over so many of them as professed Christianity.

You say, "it is certain therefore that he was bishop only of the church in Constantinople, and had an eye and care to those other churches;" and against this your own certainty, without any ground or authority, I have brought in Theodoret, Sozomen, the council of Chalcedon, and the Centuries; although in effect you confess as much as I desire; for there is neither archbishop nor bishop in this church but he hath his peculiar see and church, and yet care of government over other also; even as Chrysostom had.

You have alleged nothing, neither can you, to prove that Chrysostom had not government over more churches than one. The Greek scholiast (whom I have answered) hath not one word to that purpose; for every several parish hath a pastor, notwithstanding the bishop hath the care of government of them; even as Titus had in Creta. The words of the author be: *Sed singulas civitates suum habere pastorem*[5]: "but every city should have her pastor." And you have translated it, that "every one should have his proper congregation;" whereby you mean scant good faith, but covertly go about to make your reader believe that the scholiast would have no ministers without a proper congregation. But of this and many other of your like corruptions I trust the reader is already sufficiently instructed.

The scholiast falsified by T. C., and to what purpose.

The words of Chrysostom be, *Hom. iii. in Act.*, these: *Nonne imperium orbis terrarum tenet imperator? Hic autem unius civitatis episcopus est*[6]: "Doth not the emperor govern the world? but this man is bishop of one city." The which words are spoken of Chrysostom in this sense, that he which is but bishop of one city is as much subject to afflictions and troubles as the emperor is that governeth the whole world. This to be Chrysostom's meaning the words following

[5 Œcumen. Op. Lut. Par. 1631. Comm. cap. i. in Epist. ad Tit. Tom. II. p. 289. See before, pages 283, 4, note 8.]

[6 Chrysost. Op. Par. 1718-38. In Act. Apost. Hom. iii. Tom. IX. p. 29.]

do declare ; wherefore he doth not in that place "shew any
difference betwixt the emperor and a bishop," in the largeness or straitness of their charges and places of government
(as you say), but in the troubles, in the opprobries and slanders that they be subject unto, wherewith the bishop of one
city is more tossed than the emperor of the whole world ;
which Chrysostom speaketh hyperbolically ; for there was not
one emperor over the whole world at any time, and he himself being bishop had the care and charge of divers cities ;
wherefore he must be understood *secundum subjectam mate-
riam :* "as the matter in hand requireth."

Chapter iii.   The Sixty-eighth Division.

Answer to the Admonition, Page 73, Sect. 3.

Theodoret.   *Theodoretus, episcopus Cyri,* in an epistle that he
wrote[1] to Leo, saith of himself, that he had government
over 800. churches[2].

T. C. Page 89, Sect. 2.

You nip those that are against you.   *Touching Theodoret, bishop of Cyrus, to let pass that which the bishops of
Egypt cried in the council of Chalcedon, that he was no bishop[3], In the 1. Act.
it is to be observed that which the emperors Theodosius and
Valentinian write unto Dioscorus, bishop of Alexandria, that In the same
he had commanded Theodoret, bishop of Cyrus, that he should Act.*
An untruth and foul over-sight. *keep himself unto his own church only[4] ; whereby it appeareth that he
meddled in more churches than was meet he should. Besides, that wanteth
not suspicion that he speaketh this of himself, especially when he saith that*
Untrue inter-pretation. *there was not in all those 800. churches one tare, that is, one hypocrite or
evil man.*

Jo. Whitgift.

Theodoret can have no credit either with the pa-pists or with the Replier.   In the convocation holden in the first year of queen Mary,
the testimony of this Theodoret being alleged against tran-
substantiation, D. Watson, because he could not answer the
authority, denied the author, accusing him to be a Nestorian.
To whom reply was made, that it was but a lewd refuge,

[1 Writ, Answ. and Def. A.]
[2 Theod. Op. Lut. Par. 1642-84. Ad Leon. Episc. Rom. Epist. cxiii. Tom.
III. pp. 986, 7. See below, page 320, note 5.]
[3 Concil. Calched. Act. I. in Concil. Stud. Labb. et Cossart. Lut. Par. 1671-2.
Tom. IV. col. 101.]
[4 Ibid. cols. 100, 1. See below, note 10.]

when he could not answer, to deny the author[5]. The same may be said to you, dealing in the self-same manner. For this Theodoret, as he is a notable historiographer, and of great credit in the reporting of things done by other, and before his time, so is there no cause at all why he should be suspected speaking of himself. And he himself doth report of himself in that epistle written by him to Leo, that he had not only governed these 800. churches, but "so governed them by the space of 26. years, that he sustained no reproach or blame of the bishops of Antioch[6];" whereof I might also truly gather that the bishop of Antioch was as it were his archbishop or metropolitan. This authority, or rather example, of Theodoret is so plain, that you are driven to[7] seek unlawful shifts[8] to deface a worthy writer; but let us see how justly.

You say that "the bishops of Egypt cried in the council of Chalcedon, that he was no bishop," and you note in the margent the first act. of that council; and I say unto you again, that the whole council of the 8. action cried out and said, *Theodoretus dignus est sede ecclesiæ : orthodoxum ecclesia pastorem recipiat[9]:* "Theodoret is worthy the seat of the church (that is the bishopric) : let the church receive him as a catholic pastor."

Act. viii. Conc. Chalced.

You add that "Theodosius and Valentinian writ unto Dioscorus, bishop of Alexandria, that he had commanded Theodoret, bishop of Cyrus, that he should keep himself to his own church only, &c." To this I answer, that you have here dealt as commonly you do, that is, very corruptly; for the words that follow in the same epistle do evidently declare that the emperors' meaning was, that Theodoret should keep himself at home, and not come to the synod, unless it should please the whole synod to accept of him, and to admit him[10].

The corrupt dealing of T. C.

[5] Fox, Acts and Monuments, Lond. 1684. Vol. III. p. 21. Conf. Philpot's Works, Park. Soc. Edit. p. 202.]

[6] See below, page 320, note 5.]   [7] So, Def. B.]

[8] "I could not here be 'put to shift,' seeing where our question is of 300. you fetch your proofs of 400."—Sec. Repl. p. 627.]

[9] Concil. Calched. Act. VIII. in Concil. Stud. Labb. et Cossart. Tom. IV. col. 622.]

[10] Θεοδώρητον μέντοι τὸν ἐπίσκοπον Κύρου τῆς πόλεως, ὃν ἤδη ἐκελεύσαμεν τῇ ἰδίᾳ αὐτοῦ μόνῃ ἐκκλησίᾳ σχολάζειν, θεσπίζομεν μὴ πρότερον ἐλθεῖν εἰς τὴν ἁγίαν σύνοδον, ἐὰν μὴ πάσῃ τῇ ἁγίᾳ συνόδῳ συνελθούσῃ δόξῃ καὶ αὐτὸν παραγενέσθαι τῆς αὐτῆς ἁγίας συνόδου.—Impp. Theod. et Valent. ad Diosc. Epist. ibid. Act. I. ibid. cols. 100, 1.]

The which also appeareth in another epistle of the emperor's
to Dioscorus, in that first act of the council of Chalcedon (in
the which epistle the emperor calleth the bishop of Jerusalem
archbishop)[1].   It appeareth that Theodoret was first by the
emperors' commandment inhibited from coming to that synod,
which was called the second council of Ephesus, and afterward that he was condemned in the same synod in his absence,
and not called to answer for himself; as he declareth in[2] his
epistle written to Leo[3].   But he was restored in this general
council of Chalcedon; and that second council of Ephesus was
afterward condemned; so that all this that you speak to the
discredit of Theodoret is but a frivolous, and yet a corrupt shift.

You do but as you are wont, when you expound that
which Theodoret speaketh of his 800. churches being without
tares, "of hypocrites and evil men." If you had read the
author yourself, I think you would not so grossly have erred[4]:
his words be these: "By God's help I delivered more than
a thousand souls from Marcion's heresy, and I converted many
to Christ the Lord from the sect of Arius and Eunomius, *et
ut in octingentis ecclesiis pastor essem, mihi sortito obtigit:
tot enim paroecias habet Cyrus:* and it was allotted to me
to be pastor in 800. churches; for Cyrus hath so many parishes:
in the which through your prayers there did not remain one
tare; *sed ab omni errore hæretico liberatus fuit grex noster:* but our flock was delivered from all heretical error[5]."
Theodoret therefore meaneth "heresy," he meaneth not

Theod. in Epist. ad Leonem.

How Theo-doret left no tares in his 800. churches.

[1 Imp. ad Diosc. Epist. ibid. col. 109.]   [2 Is, Def. B.]

[3 Ὁ γὰρ τῆς Ἀλεξανδρείας δικαιότατος πρόεδρος...κἀμὲ τὸν ἀπόντα ὁμοίως
καλάμῳ κατέσφαξεν, οὔτε καλέσας εἰς κριτήριον, οὔτε παρόντα κρίνας, κ.τ.λ.—
Theod. Op. Lut. Par. 1642-84. Ad Leon. Episc. Rom. Epist. cxiii. Tom. III.
p. 986.]

[4 "When I expounded 'tares,' hypocrites, I had not the book before me,
but, trusting therein to Theodoret's knowledge in the scripture, esteemed that he
meant them of whom the parable is understanded: &c."—Sec. Repl. p. 628.]

[5 Ἐξ γὰρ καὶ εἴκοσι ἔτη τὴν ἐγχειρισθεῖσάν μοι παρὰ τοῦ Θεοῦ τῶν
ὅλων ἐκκλησίαν ἰθύνας διὰ τὰς ὑμετέρας εὐχὰς, οὐκ ἐπὶ τοῦ μακαριωτάτου
Θεοδότου τοῦ τῆς ἀνατολῆς προέδρου, οὐκ ἐπὶ τῶν μετὰ ἐκεῖνον τῶν τὸν
Ἀντιοχέων διαδεξαμένων θρόνον, τὴν τυχοῦσαν μέμψιν ὑπέμεινα, ἀλλὰ τῆς
θείας μοι χάριτος συνεργησάσης πλείους μὲν ἢ χιλίας ψυχὰς ἠλευθέρωσα τῆς
Μαρκίωνος νόσου, πολλοὺς δὲ ἄλλους ἐκ τῆς Ἀρείου καὶ Εὐνομίου συμμορίας
προσήγαγον τῷ δεσπότῃ Χριστῷ. καὶ ἐν ὀκτακοσίαις ἐκκλησίαις ἔλαχον ποι-
μαίνειν· τοσαύτας γὰρ ἡ Κύρρος παροικίας ἔχει, ἐν αἷς οὐδὲ ἓν διὰ τὰς ὑμετέρας εὐχὰς μεμένηκε ζιζάνιον· ἀλλὰ πάσης αἱρετικῆς ἠλευθέρωται πλάνης
τὸ ἡμέτερον ποίμνιον.—Theod. Op. Ad Leon. Episc. Rom. Epist. cxiii. Tom.
III. pp. 986, 7.]

" hypocrisy :" there was not one heretic in all his bishopric, he doth not say " one hypocrite or evil man ;" so that you are far wide, and do Theodoret double injury; for you do both slander him and misconstrue him.

Chapter iii.   The Sixty-ninth Division.

T. C. Page 89, Sect. 3.

Now, that it may appear what great likelihood there is between this Theodoret and our lord bishops and archbishops, it is to be considered which he writeth of himself in the epistle unto Leo, that is, that he, having been 26. years bishop, was known of all those that[6] dwelt in those parts, that he had never house of his own, nor field, nor halfpenny, not so much as a place to be buried in, but had willingly contented himself with a poor estate[7] : belike he had a very lean archbishopric ; and, if the fat morsels of our bishoprics and archbishoprics were taken and employed to their uses of maintenance of the poor, and of the ministers, and of the universities, which are the seed of the ministry, I think the heat of the disputation and contention for archbishops and bishops would be well cooled.

Jo. WHITGIFT.

We speak of the office and authority, not of the living ; to the spoil of the which you and most of your fautors have more respect, than you have to the office, though you pretend the contrary ; and yet it followeth not but that Theodoret had living sufficient, and might have been more wealthy ; but as it seemeth he professed voluntary poverty of purpose, for he gave away that also which was left unto him of his parents, as he in that epistle testifieth, saying, *Sed sponte electam amplexus sum paupertatem:* "but I embraced poverty, which I chose willingly." His bishopric might be of large revenues, and yet he poor, seeing that he had chosen a professed poverty[8]. But, if bishops be better now provided for than they were then, it is their parts to be thankful unto God and the prince for it, and to use it well. It is not your

Comparison made in office, not in riches.

[6 All that, Repl. 1 and 2.]

[7 ... ὅτι τοσοῦτον χρόνον ἐπισκοπεύσας, οὐκ οἰκίαν ἐκτησάμην, οὐκ ἀγρὸν, οὐκ ὀβολὸν, οὐ τάφον, ἀλλὰ τὴν αὐθαισάμην πενίαν, καὶ τὰ παρὰ τῶν πατέρων εἰς ἡμᾶς ἐλθόντα μετὰ τὴν ἐκείνων τελευτὴν εὐθὺς διανείμας, ὡς ἴσασιν ἅπαντες οἱ τὴν ἑῴαν οἰκοῦντες.—Id. ibid. pp. 987, 8.]

[8 " Whereto I have little to reply, but that the D. for advantage spareth not the honour of his authors : it being a great reproach in so great wealth, as the D. supposeth he might lawfully have had, to be so beggarly."—Sec. Repl. p. 629.]

duty to envy their prosperity, because you are not in case yourself.

Chapter iii.   The Seventieth Division.

Answer to the Admonition, Page 73, Sect. ult.

But what shall I need to use such proofs in a matter so plain and evident to all such as have read anything of antiquity?   The best-learned men of our days, and diligentest preferrers of the gospel of Christ do with one consent (one or two of the latest writers excepted) acknowledge and confess that this distinction of degrees, and superiority in the government of the church, is a thing most convenient and necessary.

T. C. Page 89, Sect. 4.

Now, good reader, thou hearest what M. Doctor hath been able to rake together out of the old fathers, which he saith are so plain in this matter, and yet can shew nothing to the purpose.   Hear also what he saith out of the writers of our age, all which he saith (except one or two) are of his judgment, and allow well of this distinction of degrees.

Jo. WHITGIFT.

Well, what I have "raked together," and how you have carted these rakings away, I commit to the judgment of the learned.   These raking terms, in my opinion, are not seemly in him that would seem so much to justify himself, and to condemn other of immodesty.

Chapter iii.   The Seventy-first Division.

Answer to the Admonition, Page 74, Sect. 1.

Calvin in his Institutions saith on this sort: "That every province had among their bishops an archbishop, and that the council of Nice did appoint patriarchs which should be in order and dignity above archbishops, it was for the preservation of discipline.   Therefore for this cause especially were those degrees appointed, that, if anything should happen in any particular church which could not there be decided, it might be removed

Calvin. cap. viii. sect. 54.[1]

[1 *Sect.* 54 is not in Answ.]

to a provincial synod: if the greatness or difficulty of the cause required greater consultation, then was there added patriarchs together with the synods, from whom there was no appeal but unto a general council. This kind of government some called *hierarchiam*, an improper name, and not used in the scriptures; for the Spirit of God will not have us to dream of dominion and rule in the government of the church; but, if (omitting the name) we shall consider the thing itself, we shall find that these old bishops did not frame any other kind of government in the church, from that which the Lord hath prescribed in his word[2]." Calvin here misliketh this name *hierarchia*, but he alloweth the names and authority of patriarchs and archbishops, and thinketh the government of the church then used not to differ from that which God in his word prescribeth.

T. C. Page 89, Sect. ult. and Page 90, Sect. 1, 2.

M. Calvin first is cited to prove those offices of archbishop, primate, patriarch; the names whereof he cannot abide, and as for him he approveth only that there should be some which, when difficult causes arise which cannot be ended in the particular churches, might refer the matters to synods and provincial councils, and which might do the offices which I have spoken of before of gathering voices, &c.

But that he liketh not of those dominations and large jurisdictions, or at all of the bishops or archbishops, which we have now, it may appear plainly enough both in that place, when as he will have his words drawn to no other than the old bishops, shutting out thereby the bishops that now are, as also in other places, and, namely, upon the Philip-
Phil. i.   *pians, where, reasoning against this distinction between pastor and bishop, and shewing that giving the name of bishop to one man only in*

[2 Quod autem singulæ provinciæ unum habebant inter episcopos archiepiscopum : quod item in Nicena synodo constituti sunt patriarchæ, qui essent ordine et dignitate archiepiscopis superiores : id ad disciplinæ conservationem pertinebat. Quanquam in hac disputatione præteriri non potest quod rarissimi erat usus. Ob hanc igitur causam potissimum instituti sunt illi gradus, ut siquid in ecclesia qualibet incideret quod non posset bene a paucis expediri, ad synodum provincialem referretur. Si magnitudo aut difficultas causæ majorem quoque discussionem postularet, adhibebantur patriarchæ una cum synodis, a quibus non esset provocatio nisi ad universale concilium. Gubernationem sic constitutam nonnulli hierarchiam vocarunt, nomine (ut mihi videtur) improprio : certe scripturis inusitato. Cavere enim voluit Spiritus sanctus nequis principatum aut dominationem somniaret, quum de ecclesiæ gubernatione agitur. Verum si rem omisso vocabulo intuemur, reperiemus veteres episcopos non aliam regendæ ecclesiæ formam voluisse fingere ab ea quam Deus verbo suo præscripsit.—Calvin. Op. Amst. 1667-71. Inst. Lib. iv. cap. iv. 4. Tom. IX. p. 286.]

a church was the occasion why he afterward usurped domination over the rest, he saith after this sort : "Indeed I grant," saith he, " as the dispositions and manners of men are, order cannot stand amongst the ministers of the word unless one be over the rest ; I mean," saith he, " of every several and singular body, not of a whole province, much less of the whole world[1]."

Now, if you will needs have M. Calvin's archbishop, you must not have him neither over a province nor diocese, but only over one singular and particular congregation. How much better therefore were it for you to seek some other shelter against the storm than M. Calvin's, which will not suffer you by any means to cover yourself under his wings, but thrusteth you out always as soon as you enter upon him forcibly !

JO. WHITGIFT.

Calvin acknowledgeth the names, and the end of them, and alloweth the kind of government.

M. Calvin affirmeth directly that "every province among their bishops had an archbishop, and that the council of Nice did appoint patriarchs;" he saith that these degrees were appointed " for the preservation of discipline," and by calling of synods to end controversies that arise in particular churches : he well liketh this kind of government ; only he misliketh the name *hierarchia :* what can be plainlier spoken both of the name and office of the archbishop ? As for your fond device that it should be his office only " to gather voices, &c.," it is singular to yourself ; you have not one learned writer (that I can read) with you.

The bishops that now are in this church neither have, nor challenge to have, more jurisdiction than the old bishops had ; nay, they have not so much, as it is evidently to be seen in the old canons ; and therefore M. Calvin, allowing of them, doth allow of ours also.

His place to the Philippians maketh against you ; for he alloweth one to be superior amongst the ministers, and to rule the rest, and saith that, " as the nature and disposition of men now is, there could be no order except it were so ;" which doth utterly overthrow the equality that you and the Admonition dream of. He saith that he speaketh *de singulis corporibus ;* which he cannot understand of particular parishes ; for every

[1 Postea invaluit usus, ut quem suo collegio præficiebant in singulis ecclesiis presbyteri, episcopus vocaretur solus. id tamen ex hominum consuetudine natum est, scripturæ auctoritate minime nititur. Fateor quidem, ut sunt hominum ingenia et mores, non posse ordinem stare inter verbi ministros, quin reliquis præsit unus. De singulis corporibus loquor : non de totis provinciis, multo autem minus de orbe universo.—Id. Comm. in Epist. ad Philip. cap. i. 1. Tom. VII. p. 358.]

particular parish hath not many ministers; so that of necessity
he must have many several churches to make the body he
speaketh of; and therefore a diocese or a province.   I think
M. Calvin did think Geneva, and the towns thereunto adjoining and belonging, to be but one body; so do I think
London, and the diocese thereunto pertaining, to be but one
particular body.   And likewise the province of Canterbury,
distinguished into divers parts and members, to be but one
body in like manner.   Neither do I think that Master Calvin
ever shewed his misliking of these degrees in this church
as they be now used; for (as I said before) the great abuse
of them under the pope made him more to mislike of them
than he would have done; but in these words that I have
repeated of his he testifieth as much as I desire, that is, the
antiquity, and the cause, and use of those offices, and (that
which you omit and skip over) that "herein the old bishops
did frame no kind of government in the church diverse from
that which the Lord hath prescribed in his word;" which
neither you nor your adherents can abide to hear of[2].

T. C. letteth that slip that maketh against him.

Chapter iii.   The Seventy-second Division.

T. C. Page 90, Sect. 3.

*But here I cannot let pass M. Doctor's ill dealing, which, reciting
so much of Master Calvin, cutteth him off in the waist, and leaveth
quite out that which made against him, that is, which M. Calvin
saith in these words: "Although," saith he, " in this disputation it
may not be passed over that this office of archbishop, or patriarch, was
most rarely and seldom used;" which dealing seemeth to proceed of a very
evil conscience.*

Unjust accusation.

Jo. Whitgift.

I know not what perfection is in your book more than in
mine, but I am sure that I have followed mine own book
faithfully and truly, neither have I omitted one word that
maketh either with me or against me; and therefore you

[2 Cartwright insists that Calvin did mislike of these degrees in the church, and
says: "If I should use the advantage of that he spake, and I heard of undoubted
witnesses, that, although he had no pre-eminence before the lowest minister,
but only to propound the causes, gather the voices, &c. and was chosen thereunto
every two year, yet he misliked that that small pre-eminence should so long
remain with one, as which in time might breed inconvenience : &c."—Sec. Repl.
pp. 629, &c.]

have unjustly charged me. The book that I follow was printed *anno* 1553.; wherein there are no such words, "that this office of archbishop, or patriarch, was most rarely and seldom used[1]." Neither is there cause why M. Calvin should so say; for he could not but know that these offices have had continuance in the church, at the least, since before the council of Nice; for there are these words, *Mos antiquus perduret &c.*[2], and that they were continually affixed to the bishoprics of certain cities, as Rome, Antioch, &c.

Indeed in the last edition of his Institutions he hath these words: *Quanquam in hac disputatione præteriri non potest,*

The use of the patriarch rare, in what sense.

quod rarissimi erat usus; which words he referreth to the office of a "patriarch," whom he saith the Nicene council did place in dignity and order above archbishops, for the preservation of discipline. Neither doth he say that the office of a patriarch was moveable, or chosen at every action (for then should he affirm that which is repugnant to all histories, councils, and ancient writers that speak of patriarchs); but his meaning is, that there was but seldom times occasion offered for patriarchs to exercise the authority they had over archbishops; which is the occasion that the most authors do confound them, and think them to be all one. Other meaning than this his words neither can nor do admit[3].

Chapter iii.   The Seventy-third Division.

Answer to the Admonition, Page 74, Sect. ult.

Hemingius.

Hemingius, in his *Enchirid.*, sheweth that these degrees in the church be necessary, and that discipline cannot be kept without them. And he addeth that their church keepeth this form: *Nec movetur* (saith he)

[1] The editor has not succeeded in finding an edition of the date mentioned by Whitgift; but in another printed about the same time his reading appears: e. g. ...id ad disciplinæ conservationem pertinebat. Quanquam in hac disputatione præteriri non potest. Ob hanc igitur &c.—Inst. tot. Christ. Relig. J. Calvin. Auth. Genev. 1550. cap. viii. De Fide, 54. p. 242.]

[2] Concil. Nic. can. 6. in Concil. Stud. Labb. et Cossart. Lut. Par. 1671-2. Tom. II. col. 32. See before, page 144, note 1.]

[3] Cartwright declares that in the edition Whitgift used the former part of the sentence appeared, and that he ought to have seen that it was an omission of the printer; so that, "if there had been any love of the truth in him," he would have consulted a later edition.—Sec. Repl. p. 632.]

*anabaptistarum ac libertinorum effreni libidine, qui eccle-
siam Christi barbaricum quendam hominum cœtum, sine ordine fingunt,...cum habeat*[4] *nostra ecclesia non solum exemplum apostolicæ [et] purioris ecclesiæ, verum etiam mandatum
Spiritus sancti omnia ordinate et decenter ad œdificationem
faciendi*[5]: "Neither is our church moved with the licentious liberty of anabaptists and libertines, which feign
the church of Christ to be a barbarous confused society
without order; seeing that our church hath not only the
example of the apostolical and most pure church, but
also the commandment of the Spirit of God, to do all
things orderly and decently to edify."

T. C. Page 90, Sect. 4.

*Then followeth Hemingius, who, you say, approveth these degrees of
archbishop, metropolitan, bishop, archdeacon; for so you must needs
mean when you say he approveth these degrees, or else you say nothing; for thereupon is the question.　Now how untruly*
*you speak let it be judged by that which followeth.　First, he
saith that our "Saviour Christ, in St Luke, distinguisheth and
putteth a difference between the office of a prince and the office
of a*[6] *minister of the church, leaving dominion to the princes,
and taking it altogether from the ministers*[7]." *Here you see,*
not only how he is against you in your exposition in the place of St Luke,
which would have it nothing else but a prohibition of ambition, but also how
at a word he cutteth the throat of your archbishop and bishop as it is now
used.　And afterward, speaking of the churches of Denmark, he saith,
"they have Christ for their head, and for the outward discipline they have
magistrates to punish with the sword," and for to exercise the ecclesiastical
discipline they have "bishops, pastors, doctors, which may keep men under
with the word, without using any corporal punishment."　Here is no
mention of archbishops, primates, metropolitans.　And, although he sheweth
that they keep the distinction between bishops and ministers, against which
there hath been before spoken, yet he saith that the authority which they
have is "as the authority of a father, not as the power of a master;" which
is far otherwise here.　For the condition of many servants under their
masters is much more free than the condition of a minister under his
bishop.　And afterward he sheweth wherein that authority or dignity of
the bishop over the minister lieth, that is, in exhorting of him, in chiding of*

*Cap. x.
3. Class. Lib.
Enchirid.;
where also
among the
popish orders
he reckoneth
the archb.*

So is the con-
dition of a
good servant
under a good
master
much better
than the con-
dition of an
unruly son
under a wise
father.

[4] Habet, Answ. 2.]
[5] N. Hemming. Opusc. Theolog. 1586. Enchir. Class. III. cap. x. col. 462.]
[6] The, Repl. 1, 2, and Def. A.]
[7] Huc accedit, quod Dominus apud Lucam ministerium verbi ab officio
principum separat: huic dominationem relinquens, illi prorsus adimens: Reges,
inquit gentium dominantur ipsis, vos autem non sic.—Id. ibid. col. 460.]

him, as he doth the lay-people; and yet he will have also the minister,
although not with such authority, after a modest sort to do the same unto
the bishop.   And so he concludeth that they retain these orders, notwith-
standing the anabaptists.   Now let the reader judge whether Hemingius
be truly or faithfully alleged or no, or whether Hemingius do say that
they have in their church archbishops, primates, metropolitans, archdeacons,
or whether the bishops in the churches of Denmark are anything like ours.
For I will omit that he speaketh there against all pomp in the ministry, all

And there-
fore you cut
short and
clip sen-
tences.

worldly superiority or highness, because I love not to write out whole
pages, as M. Doctor doth, out of other men's writings, to help to make up
a book.

Jo. Whitgift.

Hemin. in that very place quoted in your margent hath

Hemingius
alloweth dis-
tinction of
degrees in
the ministry.

first these words: *Præterea cum hic cœtus &c.*[1]: "Furthermore, seeing this society is ruled by the word of God, there
are in it two sorts of men, that is to say, the preachers of the
word and their hearers, which do reverence and love one
another as fathers and children.   But in the ministers there
is great diversity; for, although the authority of all ministers
in respect of spiritual regiment is all one (for of external
discipline shall be spoken in the proper place), yet there are
divers orders and degrees of honour and dignity; and that
partly by the word of God, partly by the approbation and
allowance of the church."   Where first he alloweth this
distinction which you so greatly mislike, that all ministers be
equal touching spiritual jurisdiction, that is, their ministry,
but not concerning external discipline; then doth he allow
degrees of dignity and superiority among the clergy; the
which after that he hath proved by the scripture, as namely,
the iv. to the Ephesians, and by the examples of Paul, Timothy,
and Titus, he proceedeth and goeth on forward, and saith:

Hemingius
acknowledg-

Ecclesia, &c.[2]: "The church, to whom the Lord hath given

[1 Præterea cum hic cœtus verbo Dei regitur, duo sunt in eo genera hominum :
nimirum verbi præcones, et eorum auditores, qui non secus atque patres et filii se
invicem venerantur et colunt; verum in ministris magna est diversitas.   Quanquam enim potestas omnium eadem est ministrorum, quantum ad spiritualem
jurisdictionem attinet (de externa enim disciplina suo loco dicendum est) tamen
dispares dignitatis ordines et gradus sunt.   Idque partim jure divino, partim
ecclesiæ approbatione.—Id. ibid. col. 459.]

[2 Ecclesia, cui Dominus potestatem dedit in ædificationem, ordinem ministeriorum instituit pro commodo suo, ut omnia sint rite ordinata ad instaurationem
corporis Christi.   Hinc ecclesia purior secuta tempora apostolorum, fecit alios
patriarchas, quorum erat curare, ut episcopi cujusque diœcesios rite eligerentur,
et ordinarentur, ut suum munus episcopi singuli probe administrarent: ut cuique

power unto edification, hath ordained an order of ministers eth patriarchs in the primitive church.
for her profit, that all things might be rightly ordained for tive church.
the re-edifying of the body of Christ.   Hereof the primitive
church, following the times of the apostles, did appoint some The office of patriarchs in the primitive church.
patriarchs, whose office it was to provide that the bishops of
every diocese should be rightly ordained and elected; that
the bishops should do their duty truly; and that the clergy
and people should obey them in those things that pertained
to the Lord: it appointed also *chorepiscopos* (that is, coad-
jutors of bishops, whom we now call provosts), some pastors,
and catechists.   This was the ordination of the primitive
church." Wherein he plainly declareth these degrees that I
speak of (for under the name of patriarchs it is evident that
he comprehendeth archbishops or metropolitans) to have been
in the primitive church immediately after the apostles' time,
and in the purest time of the church; than the which what
can be spoken more directly for my purpose, whose chief
intent is to prove the antiquity of these names and offices?

After this he sheweth the abuses of these offices in the
corruption of doctrine under the pope, and he doth not only
name archbishops, but bishops also, curates, and other[3]; and
therefore the note in your margent is but a note of a special
spite against the archbishops. In the end, speaking of bishops,
pastors, and doctors, he saith thus: *Inter hos ministros &c.*[4]:

suus clerus et sua plebs in his, quæ Domini sunt, pie obsequerentur. Alios
chorepiscopos (coadjutores nimirum episcoporum, quos hodie præpositos appella-
mus) alios pastores et catechetas. Hæc fuit purioris ecclesiæ ordinatio.—Id. ibid.
cols. 459, 60.]

[3 Nam in regno papæ post corruptionem doctrinæ, monstrosa quædam ecclesiæ œconomia inventa est,...tum ordines ecclesiasticos septem numerant,...7. Presbyterorum, quorum plures gradus fecerunt. Alios enim vocarunt episcopos, alios
archiepiscopos, metropolitanos, parochos, antistites et præsides. &c.—Id. ibid.
col. 460.]

[4 ... ecclesia nostra Danica non est ἀκέφαλος sed agnoscit cum ecclesia
catholica unum Christum regem et sacerdotem. Deinde quantum ad disciplinam
externam attinet, agnoscit magistratum civilem jus gladii habere, quod exercere
debet secundum suas leges in reos. Agnoscit etiam ecclesiasticam disciplinam,
qua superiores legitime vocati ad ministerium, ut episcopi, pastores, doctores in
scholis, uti possunt ad coercendos contumaces verbo, sine vi corporali....Inter hos
ministros agnoscit etiam ecclesia nostra gradus dignitatis, et ordines pro diversi-
tate donorum, laborum magnitudine ac vocationum dignitate, ac judicat barbaricum esse, de ecclesia hunc ordinem tollere velle. Judicat cæteros ministros
suis episcopis oportere obtemperare in omnibus, quæ ad ædificationem ecclesiæ
faciunt, juxta verbum Dei, ac utilem ecclesiæ œconomiam. Judicat episcopos
jus habere in cæteros ministros ecclesiæ, non despoticum, sed patrium....judicat

"Amongst these ministers also our church acknowledgeth degrees and orders of dignity, for the diversity of gifts, the
greatness of labour, and the worthiness of their calling; and
judgeth it to be barbarous to will to take this order out of

the church. It judgeth that other ministers ought to obey
their bishops in all things that tend to the edification of the
church, according to the word of God, and the profitable
order of the church: it judgeth that the bishops have authority over the other ministers of the church, not such as is of
masters, but of fathers." Whereby he acknowledgeth distinction of degrees and superiority among ministers, and the
jurisdiction of bishops over other ministers: after all this he
concludeth with these words contained in mine Answer. Now
let the reader judge whether I have otherwise reported of
Hemingius than he himself in that chapter affirmeth; and
whether he consent unto me, that would have distinction of
degrees among the ministers, or to you, that would have an
equality, which he calleth an anabaptistical and barbarous
confusion.

Touching your notes gathered out of him, I will briefly
answer. First, in the exposition of the xxii. of Luke, he is not
against me; for I would not have archbishops or bishops, &c.,
to take from kings their rule and dominion, as doth the pope;
neither would I have them to reign over the people, as kings
and princes do. And I do not think but that the authority
and superiority that they have is a ministry for the quietness
of the church, and the commodity of other, and yet a govern-

ment too; for the apostle saith, *ad Hebr. xiii.* : *Obedite his
qui præsunt vobis :* " Obey them that bear rule over you,
&c." Hemingius in that place especially dealeth against the
two swords of the bishop of Rome and his excessive pomp.

For the kind of authority that the bishop hath over the
ministers, that it should be "of a father and not of a master,"
I agree with him; and I know that all you speak to the contrary in the government of this church is most untrue; for
undoubtedly, if they have offended in anything, it is in too
much lenity; which is a fault even in a father. The authority
that Hemingius giveth to the civil magistrate we acknowledge

recte facere episcopos, qui hortationibus et objurgationibus non solum laicos
(ut vocant) verumetiam presbyteros in officio retinent...si episcopi aliquid præce-
perint, quod non sit sui officii, hic modeste licet inferiori ministro quod imperatur
recusare.—Id. ibid. cols. 461, 2.]

with him to be most due; and I would to God you also did in heart and mouth confess the same. Thus you see that Hemingius and we agree, and that there is nothing ascribed unto him which is not plainly to be found in him.

Chapter iii.   The Seventy-third Division.

Answer to the Admonition, Page 75, Line 11, and Sect. 1.

[☞ Bucer, upon the iv. to the Ephesi., where he of Bucer. purpose speaketh of the church and the due reformation of the same, saith thus: "The third part of discipline is obedience, which is, first, to be rendered of all to the bishop and minister; then, of every clerk to those that be in degree above him, and to such as may help him to the well executing of his ministry; last of all, of bishops to synods, and to their metropolitan bishops, and to all other to whom a more ample charge of the church is committed[1]."

These words be plain: he would have all to obey the bishop and minister, every clerk to obey him that is in superior degree, and bishops to obey synods and their metropolitans.

In the same place he proveth by sundry examples and apt reasons that this superiority among ecclesiastical persons is convenient and necessary, and sheweth that these degrees in the church, bishop, archbishop, metropolitan, primate, patriarch, be not only most ancient but also necessary; and in the end he concludeth on this sort: *At quia omnino necesse est ut singuli cleri suos habeant proprios custodes et curatores, instauranda est ut episcoporum, ita et archidiaconorum, aliorumque omnium, quibuscunque censeantur nominibus, quibus portio aliqua commissa est custodiendi gubernandique cleri, auctoritas, potestas, sed et vigilantia, et animadversio, ne quis omnino sit in hoc ordine ἀφρούρητος[2]:* "Because it is necessary that every one of the clergy should have their rulers and governors, the authority, power, vigilancy, and se-

---

[1] Tertia pars hujus disciplinæ est, Traditio sui in singularem obedientiam, præstandam primum ab omnibus episcopo et presbytero: Deinde ab unoquoque clerico, iis qui sunt in clericatu gradus superioris, et a quo possunt ad recte obeundum ministerium suum adjuvari: Postremo ab episcopis, synodis, ac etiam suo modo, episcopis metropolitanis, cunctisque quibus amplior sit ecclesiarum cura demandata.—M. Bucer. Prælect. in Epist. ad Ephes. Basil. 1562. cap. iv. p. 129.]

[2] Id. ibid. p. 133 ; where *singuli clerici suos.*]

verity of bishops, archdeacons, and all other by what name soever they be called (to whom any portion of keeping and governing the clergy is committed), should and ought to be restored, lest there be any in this order out of rule, or without government."

Beza, *Lib. Confess. ca.* 5., seemeth to allow this superiority, and those names also : his words be these : " What was in old time decreed of calling provincial synods by the metropolitan, it manifestly appeareth in the old canons : *Neque vero nos hi sumus qui (si instauratæ essent ecclesiarum ruinæ) vel hunc vel alium non dissimilem ordinem repudiandum arbitremur*[1]: Neither are we those who (if the church were reformed) think either this or any other like order to be refused." The words be plain ; and in the seventh chapter of the same book he maketh two kinds of degrees used in the papistical church ; the one unknown to the apostles and to the primitive church ; the other taken out of the word of God and from the primitive church: in this second order he placeth archbishops, curates, canons, seniors or ministers, archdeacons, deans, subdeacons, clerks ; and, although, as he truly there saith, the papists have impudently abused those names, and that the light is no more contrary unto darkness than they be unto those whose names they challenge, yet, forasmuch as Master Beza confesseth that these names and degrees are derived from the scriptures and primitive church, he insinuateth his allowing of them, the papistical abuses being taken away, as they be (God be thanked) in this church of England[2].

In the same chapter he hath these words : " That pastors in process of time were distinct into metropo-

[1 Quod olim fuerit constitutum de provincialibus synodis a metropolitano cogendis, abunde liquet ex veteribus canonibus. Neque vero nos ii sumus &c.— Th. Bezæ Confess. Christ. Fid. Genev. 1587. cap. v. 22. p. 134.]

[2 Tertio, qui possunt isti merito dici apostolorum successores, quum præcipui gradus papisticæ hierarchiæ et apostolis et omnibus ecclesiis per tot secula penitus fuerint incogniti, et in iis gradibus quos ex verbo Dei et vetere ecclesia videntur desumpsisse, sola nomina retinuerint,...Numero autem in prima classe, papam universalem...cardinales, suffraganeos, officiales, procuratores curiæ ecclesiasticæ, vicarios, capellanos, præfectos, priores, cum tota ejusmodi monstrorum colluvie, quæ penitus ignoravit vetus ecclesia. In secunda vero classe recenseo archiepiscopos, curatos, canonicos, presbyteros, archidiaconos, diaconos, subdiaconos, clericos, et totam istam catervam, quorum nominibus isti tam impudenter abutuntur, &c.—Id. ibid. cap. vii. 12. pp. 230, 1.]

litans, bishops, and those whom they now call curates"
(that is, such as be appointed to every parish), "which
was not in the respect of the ministry of the word, but
rather in respect of jurisdiction and discipline. Therefore, concerning the office of preaching the word and
administering the sacraments, there is no difference
betwixt archbishops, bishops, and curates; for all are
bound to feed their flock with the same bread; and
therefore by one common name in the scriptures they
be called pastors and bishops. But what impudency is
there in those men" (meaning the papists) "to use those
holy names, and therefore to glory of the succession of
the apostles and true bishops[3]!" He calleth them "holy
names," reproveth the papists for abusing of them, and
truly saith that the distinction of these names and offices
is not in the ministry of the word and sacraments, but
in jurisdiction and discipline.

I might here use the authority of Gualter and Zan-
chus, both of them notable godly and learned men, who
in their epistles dedicatory to their books of late set
forth refuse not to give unto the archbishop of York his
title of archbishop, and that with all reverence[4].

But what should I use any more words in a matter
so generally avouched and allowed of all old writers,
stories, councils, churches, and disallowed of no learned
writers of our age (the abuses taken away as they be),
nor of any godly-wise man; but only of such as either
seek a confusion, or else a spoil; whose hearts I pray
God convert? ⟨symbol⟩][5]

Wherefore thus I conclude with the very words of
that worthy man (who hath so well deserved of this
church of England), Master Fox: "In the ecclesiastical
state[7] we take not away the distinction of ordinary

M. Fox.
Part. i.
Histo. pag.
20.6

[3 Nam quod pastores &c. discrimen [See before, page 266, note 2]. Omnes
enim tenentur suos greges eodem cibo pascere, ideoque communi nomine, pastores, et episcopi in scripturis passim vocantur. Quæ vero istorum impudentia
est sacra nomina usurpare, et propterea apostolorum et verorum episcoporum
successionem jactare?—Id. ibid. p. 238.]

[4 See Strype, Annals, Vol. II. Book i. chap. xxx. Zanchy afterwards wrote
to archbishop Grindal to congratulate him on his elevation to the see of Canterbury. Strype, Life of Grindal, Book ii. chap. viii.]

[5 The paragraphs between brackets are introduced from Answ. 2.]

[6 Def. A. and B. have only *M. Fox*.]   [7 Estate, Answ. and Def. A.]

degrees, such as by the scripture be appointed, or by the
primitive church allowed, as patriarchs or archbishops,
bishops, ministers, and deacons; for of these four we
especially read as chief: in which four degrees as we
grant diversity of office, so we admit in the same also
diversity of dignity; neither denying that which is due
to each degree, neither yet maintaining the ambition of
any singular person. For, as we give to the minister
place above the deacon, to the bishop above the minister,
to the archbishop above the bishop, so we see no cause
of inequality why one minister should be above another
minister, one bishop in his degree above another bishop
to deal in his diocese, or one [1] archbishop above another
archbishop; and this is to keep an order duly and truly
in the church, according to the true nature and defini-
tion of order by the authority of Augustine, *Lib. de Civi.*
.... *Ordo est parium dispariumque rerum sua cuique loca
tribuens dispositio* [2]. [Order is a disposition of things
equal and unequal, attributing to each their proper
places]." [3]   Hitherto M. Fox.

Now let the indifferent reader judge whether these
offices be strange and unheard of in the church of
Christ, or no.

T. C. Page 90, Sect. ult.

*M. Doctor closeth up this matter with M. Fox; but, either for fear
that the place should be found, that there might be answer, or for fear that
M. Fox should give me the solution, which hath given you the objection,
he would neither quote the place of the book, nor the book itself, he having
written divers. You cannot speak so much good of M. Fox which I will
not willingly subscribe unto; and, if it be any declaration of good-will
and of honour that one beareth to another, to read that which he writeth,*
I marvel this *I think I have read more of him than you. For I have read over his Book*
place could *of Martyrs, and so I think did never you; for, if you had read so dili-*
escape so di- *of Martyrs, and so I think did never you; for, if you had read so dili-*
ligent a *gently in M. Fox, as you have been hasty to snatch at this place,*
reader. *he would have taught you the forgery of these epistles whereout* Page 78. of
you fetch these [4] *authorities, and would have shewed you that* the book of
Acts.
the distinguishing of the orders of metropolitans, bishops, and other

[1] An, Def. A. and B.]
[2] Fox, Acts and Monuments, Lond. 1684. Vol. I. p. 18; where *patriarchs,
archbishops,* and *specially.* Conf. August. Op. Par. 1679-1700. De Civ. Dei, Lib.
XIX. cap. xiii. Tom. VII. col. 557.]
[3] The sentence between brackets is inserted from Answ. 2.]
[4] Your, Repl. 1, 2, and Def. A.]

degrees, which you say sometimes had their beginnings in the apostles' *times, sometimes you cannot tell when, were not in Higinus' time, which* *was 180.*[5] *years after Christ*[6]*.   I perceive you fear M. Fox is an enemy* A suspicious *unto your archbishop and primate, and therefore it seemeth you went* head. *about to corrupt him with his praise, and to seek to draw him, if it were* *possible, unto the archbishop; and, if not, yet at the least that he would be* *no enemy, if he would not nor could not be his friend.   You make me* *suspect that your praise is not hearty, but pretended, because you do so* *often and so bitterly speak against all those that will not receive the cap* *and surplice and other ceremonies, whereof M. Fox declareth his great* *misliking.   For answer unto the place, because I remember it not, nor* *mean not to read over the whole book to seek it, I say first, as I said* *before, that there may be something before or after, which may give the* 1. Tom. Act.   *solution to this place, especially seeing M. Fox in another place,* pag. 96.[7] *page 96., proving the epistles of Stephanus to be counterfeit, he* *useth this reason, because the fifth canon of the said epistles solemnly* *entreateth of the difference between primates, metropolitans, and arch-* *bishops; "which distinction," saith he, "of titles and degrees savour more of* *ambition than persecution*[8]*."   Moreover, I say that M. Fox, writing a* *story, doth take greater pain, and looketh more diligently to declare what* *is done, and in what time, and by whom, than how justly or unjustly,* *how conveniently or inconveniently it is done.   Last of all, if anything be* *spoken there to the hinderance of the sincerity of the gospel, I am well* *assured that M. Fox, which hath travailed so much and so profitably to* *that end, will not have his authority or name therein to bring any pre-* *judice.   Now will I also join with you, and leave it to the judgment* *of the indifferent reader, how well out of the scriptures, councils, writers* *old and new, you have proved either the lawfulness at all of the names of* *archbishops, patriarchs, archdeacons, primates, or of the lawfulness of the* *office of them, and of bishops which be in our times.*

Jo. Whitgift.

If you had so diligently read M. Fox his Book of Martyrs, as you boast and brag that you have done, then could not this place have been so strange unto you; for it is in the 20. page of his first tome, where he hath an whole treatise touching the supremacy of the bishop of Rome, and speaketh of this matter at large.   The words be his own, and express his own judgment of these degrees and offices in this church of England.   It had been some token of modesty so to have commended yourself and your own reading, that you had not depraved any other man's; but to commend yourself, and to

[5] Was a 180., Repl. 1 and 2.]   [6] Id. ibid. p. 58.]
[7] This reference is added from Repl. 2, which omits in the text *page 96.*]
[8] Id. ibid. p. 74 ; where *degrees and titles savouring,* and *of persecution.*]

detract from another, is either arrogant foolishness, or foolish arrogancy. I can bring forth good testimonies of my reading of these books, though I make no brag thereof or vain comparisons.

I have alleged none of " these epistles " otherwise than M. Fox himself hath alleged them.

M. Fox hath shewed himself (in the place by me cited out of his book) to be no "enemy" either "to archbishop, primate," or bishop; for I am sure he speaketh as he thinketh. He is not a man like to be "corrupted with praise;" and therefore in so saying you do us both great injury.

You may not judge my heart: I think of M. Fox as of one that I love and reverence; I will not utter all that I could, lest I should seem to flatter.

There is nothing that goeth either "before" that place, or followeth "after" it, that can procure any other sense to his words than that in the which I have set them down. I do not allege M. Fox for the original of these names and offices, but for the allowance of them. These words that I have recited are not spoken "in the way of any history," but of the order of government of this church, which he alloweth; and I dare say for him, that he hath herein spoken nothing which he thinketh may hurt "the sincerity of the gospel." And I am right well content to let the godly reader judge of both our proofs.

¶ The defence of the Answer of M. Jewel, concerning archbishops, &c., against the unreverend reply of T. C.

Chapter iv.   The First Division.

T. C. Page 91, Sect. 1.

And, forasmuch as I have purposed to answer in one place that which is scattered in divers, I will here answer half a sheet of paper which is annexed of late unto the[1] book, put forth in the name, and under the credit of the bishop of Sarisbury; wherein I will say nothing of those biting and sharp words which are given partly in the beginning when he calleth the propounders of the proposition which concerneth archbishops and archdeacons, novices, partly in the end, when he calleth them children, and the doctrine of the gospel wantonness, &c. If he had lived, for his

A shameless and wicked lie.

[1 This, Repl. 1 and 2.]

learning and gravity, and otherwise good deserts of the church, in de- M. Jewel's
fending the cause thereof against the papists, we could have easily borne it answer
at his hands: now he is dead and laid up in peace, it were against justified.
all humanity to dig or to break up his grave: only I will leave it to the
consideration of the reader, upon those things which are alleged, to judge
whether it be any wantonness or novelty which is confirmed by so grave
testimonies of the ancient word of God.

Jo. Whitgift.

If you doubt whether the bishop of Sarisbury were the
author of that half sheet of paper or no, you may see his own
hand-writing. If you call the words which he useth there
" biting " and " sharp," what shall we think of yours? we had
need term them " serpentine " or " viperous," or if there can
be any other name that better expresseth such immodest, contemptuous, and scoffing speeches. *Hypocrita, quid vides fes-*
tucam in oculo fratris tui, &c. But what are these " biting "
and " sharp " words that he useth? forsooth that he " calleth
the propounders of the proposition which concerneth archbishops and archdeacons, novices; and in the end he calleth
them children, and their doctrine wantonness." O these be Why T. C.
" biting and sharp words;" but wouldest thou know, good scorneth so
much at the
reader, why T. C. taketh these words so grievously? even be- words of the
cause they touch himself. For the man is of that humility and bishop.
patience, that, if there be never so little signification given of
any unskilfulness or lack of learning in himself, he roareth like
a lion, and swelleth like the sea; for none of that faction can The malici-
in any case abide to have their learning touched; and they ous nature of
that faction.
will not stick in commending themselves, to deface all other,
yea, even that notable Jewel, whose both labour and learning
they do envy, and among themselves deprave; as I have heard
with mine own ears, and a number more besides. For further
proof whereof, I do but refer you to the report that by this
faction was spread of him after his last sermon at Paul's Cross,
because he did confirm the doctrine before preached by a
famous and learned man, touching obedience to the prince and
laws. It was then strange to me to hear so notable a bishop,
so learned a man, so stout a champion of true religion, so
painful a prelate, so ungratefully and spitefully used, by a sort
of wavering, wicked, and wretched tongues. But it is their
manner, except you please their humour in all things, be you
never so well learned, never so painful, so zealous, so virtuous,

[WHITGIFT, II.]

M. Jewel's
answer
justified.

all is nothing with them, but they will deprave you, rail on you, backbite you, invent lies of you, and spread false rumours, as though you were the vilest persons in the whole earth.

The bishop
maliciously
slandered by
T. C.

And consider whether T. C. be not even now in that vein; for how maliciously doth he slander that so reverend bishop, saying that "he calleth the doctrine of the gospel wantonness," when he speaketh of their childish and fantastical devices, except all were "gospel" that they speak, or that cometh from them! Pardon me, though I speak something earnestly: it is in the behalf of a Jewel, that is contemned and defaced by contentious and ungrateful persons. If it had pleased God to have suffered him to live unto this day, in answering this Reply, he should no doubt have proved his "biting and sharp words" (as they be called) to be most true. But, seeing that he is at rest, and not here to answer for himself, though in respect of him I am far unmeet to intermeddle in his doings, yet in respect of the cause and adversary I will be bold to justify his answers.

Chapter iv.   The Second Division.

"¶ The Judgment of that reverend father, John, late bishop of Sarum, avouched by his own hand[1].

Novitiorum
assertio.

Archiepiscoporum et archidiaconorum nomina simul cum muneribus et officiis suis sunt abolenda.

The first Reason.

Prima ratio.

God so loved the church, that he left a perfect[2] pattern, orderly, &c. Ephes. iv. ; but there is named neither pope, nor archbishop, nor archdeacon.

The answer of the bishop of Sarisbury[3].

Ejus solutio.

How know you that the fourth chapter *ad Ephe.* is a perfect[2] pattern of all ecclesiastical government? We

The 4. Eph.
no perfect

have now neither apostles, nor evangelists, nor prophets;

[1 This "Judgment" of bishop Jewel is not in Answ. 1, and is placed nearly at the end of Answ. 2. Cartwright, as he has just before intimated, having left again the direct order of the Answer, Whitgift consequently follows him. Conf. Bp Jewel's Works, Park. Soc. Edit. Vol. IV. pp. 1299, 1300.]

[2 Perfite, Answ. 2.]   [3 Answ. 2 has not *of the bishop of Sarisbury*.]

and yet are they the chief in that pattern; neither have we there either bishop, or *presbyter*, or *diaconus*, or *catechista*, or *lector*; and yet are these necessary parts in ecclesiastical government; therefore that pattern is not perfect to hold for ever; neither were there then any public churches, or pulpits, or schools, or universities, &c. St Paul nameth neither pope nor archbishop, I grant; and the church is not governed by names, but by offices. Every bishop then was called *papa*; and Anacletus, that was next after Peter (if there be any weight in his words) nameth archbishops [4]."

T. C. Page 91, Sect. 1.

Unto the place of the iv. of the Ephesians before alleged, he answereth clean contrary to that which M. Doctor saith, that "we have now neither apostles, nor evangelists, nor prophets;" whereupon he would conclude that that place is no perfect pattern of the ministry in the church. Indeed it is true we have not, neither is it needful that we should. It was therefore sufficient that there were once, and for a time; so that the want of those now is no cause why the ministries there recited be not sufficient for the accomplishment and full finishing of the church, nor cause why any other ministries should be added besides those which are there recited.

Jo. Whitgift.

Not one word "contrary" to anything that I have spoken; for I told you before in what respect it may be said these offices to remain, and in what respect they be ceased [5]: there is now no planting of churches, nor going through the whole world, there is no writing of new gospels, no prophesying of things to come; but there is governing of churches, visiting of them, reforming of pastors, and directing of them, which is a portion of the apostolical function: there is preaching of the gospel, expounding and interpreting the scriptures, which be incident to the evangelist and prophet. Against this no learned man (as I think) speaketh.

But now to my lord of Sarisbury his argument, which is this: That, from the which somewhat must be taken, and unto the which somewhat must be added, is no perfect pattern; but apostles, evangelists, prophets, are taken away from the fourth

[4 Anaclet. Epist. ii. 1, 4. ad Episc. Ital. in Concil. Stud. Labb. et Cossart. Lut. Par. 1671-2. Tom. I. cols. 521, 4. See before, page 136, note 2.]

[5 See Vol. I. pages 492, &c.]

to the Ephesians, and deacons and elders (as you yourself say) must be added; *ergo*, it is no perfect pattern: neither do you, neither can you answer this argument. But I will come to your accustomed shifts.

Chapter iv.   The Third Division.
T. C. Page 91, Sect. 2.

Afterward he saith that neither bishop nor elder are reckoned in that place. The pastor is there reckoned up; and I have shewed that the pastor and bishop are all one, and are but divers names to signify one thing. And as for those elders which do only govern, they are made mention of in other places[1]; and therefore the bishop and elder are there contained[2]; which thing also M. Doctor granteth.

Jo. Whitgift.

If the bishop be contained under the pastor, why may not the archbishop be so likewise? but, if the elders ("which," you say, "do only govern") be not there contained, and yet a necessary function in the church (as you think), how can it then be a perfect platform? or why may not archbishops and archdeacons be also necessary, though they be not in that place named? But you say that "those elders be in other places mentioned." That is no answer to this place, but a reason rather to prove it no perfect pattern.

"M. Doctor granteth a bishop to be contained" under the name of a "pastor." But he doth not grant that your elder is so, or every "presbyter" (to whom the ministry of the word of God and sacraments is committed) to be a pastor.

Chapter iv.   The Fourth Division.
T. C. Page 91, Sect. 3.

After that he saith there is no catechista: *if there be a pastor, there[3] is one which both can, and ought to instruct the youth; neither doth it pertain to any other in the church and publicly to teach the youth in the rudiments of religion than unto the pastor; howsoever[4] in some times and places they have made a several office of it.*

[1 Here Repl. 2 inserts *the apostle's purpose being to reckon up here only those ministries, which are conversant in the word, as I have before alleged.*]

[2 Elder which with government teach also are there contained, Repl. 2.]

[3 Pastor or as some think doctor there, Repl. 2.]

[4 Pastor or doctor howsoever, Repl. 2.]

Jo. Whitgift.

If a "pastor" and a "catechist" may be in one[5], why may not a bishop and a governor also be one, and so your elders shut out of the doors? But you may learn in ancient writers, that the office of a "catechist" was necessary in the church, and distinct from the pastor. Origen was a catechist in the church of Alexandria; as Eusebius in his sixth book doth in sundry places declare[6]; and yet he was not then a pastor.

Chapter iv.　The Fifth Division.

T. C. Page 92, Sect. 1.

And, where he saith that there is neither deacon nor reader mentioned, for the deacon I have answered, that St Paul speaketh there only of those functions which are occupied both in teaching and governing the churches, and therefore there was no place there to speak of a deacon; and, as for the reader, it is no such office in the church, which the minister may not do. And, if either he have not leisure, or his strength and voice will not serve him first to read some long time, and afterward to preach, it is an easy matter to appoint some of the elders, or deacons, or some other grave man in the church, to that purpose; as it hath been practised in the churches in times past, and is in the churches reformed in our days, without making any new order or office of the ministry.

Jo. Whitgift.

This distinction helpeth not here; for, if you say the offices or names of deacons be left out in this place because St Paul speaketh not of such offices as be occupied only in government; first, I answer that the same may be said of archbishops and archdeacons, who have those names only in the respect of government. Secondly, I tell you that the office of a deacon is also to preach; as is hereafter proved. And, last of all, that the office of a deacon (especially as you restrain it) is neither office nor name of government, but of simple and absolute ministry and service.

Your starting-holes will not hide you; and this argument

[5 "Where I gave the catechizing unto the pastor, I will have it meant where there is no doctor; otherwise I have in the second edition amended that, assigning it as more proper to the D."—Sec. Repl. p. 634.]

[6 Euseb. in Hist. Eccles. Script. Amst. 1695-1700. Lib. vi. capp. viii. xix. pp. 169, 70, 8, &c.]

M. Jewel's answer justified.

of the bishop will not be answered.   You have said nothing to prove this place to be a perfect pattern of all ecclesiastical functions; neither do you say anything for omitting the names of "bishop," "deacon," "presbyter," &c., but we may say the same for the names of "archbishop," "archdeacon," &c.

The reader hath been counted a necessary office in the church[1], and is of great antiquity; and I know that "the deacon, or any other grave person" upon occasion may be admitted to read.   But, I pray you, where do you find any such thing in the scripture, especially of those which you call elders, which be in no degree of the ministry? for it is great presumption for you to appoint any such office in the church, not having your warrant in God's word; seeing you find such fault with whole churches for allowing offices used in the best time of the church, confirmed by the best councils, and approved by all ancient writers, because their names be not expressed in the scripture; and seeing also that you yourself a little before said that "only the pastor ought publicly in the church to teach the youth," and not a catechist; and I take public reading in the church to be as solemn a matter as catechizing the youth.   But you have liberty to coin what order you list, without either scripture, or any other approved writer: we must make you another Pythagoras.

T. C. taketh greater liberty to himself than he will allow to whole churches.

In times past it was a peculiar office; and he that had it was called *lector*; and therefore you cannot say, "as it hath been practised in times past," except you will confess that name and office of *lector*, and so also grant some name and office profitable for the church to be omitted in the fourth chapter to the Ephesians.

Chapter iv.   The Sixth Division.

T. C. Page 92, Sect. 1, 2.

Where he saith that by this reason we should have "no churches, pulpits, schools, or[2] universities," it is first easily answered that St Paul speaketh not in the fourth to the Ephesians of all things necessary for the church, but only of all necessary ecclesiastical functions, which do both teach and govern

---

[1 "That 'a reader hath been counted necessary' is said without proof; and, if it were, it was falsely counted; there being no necessary ministry not specified in the scripture."—Sec. Repl. p. 634.]

[2 Nor, Repl. 1, 2, and Def. A.]

in the church ; and then I have already shewed that there were both churches M. Jewel's answer justified.
and pulpits.

As for schools and universities, it is sufficient commandment of them, I grant, but not out of the 4. to the Ephe.
in that it is commanded that both the magistrates and pastors should be
learned ; for he that commandeth that they should be learned commandeth
those things and those means whereby they may most conveniently come to
that learning.   And we have also examples of them commended unto us in
Judg. v. 14.[3] *the old testament.   As in the book of the Judges, when Debora*
commendeth the university men, and those which handled the pen
of the writer, that they came out to help in the battle against the enemies of
1 Sam. xix. 19.[3] *God.   And in the first book of Samuel, and in the second[4]*
2 Kings ii. 3, 5, 7.[3] *book of the Kings[5], when[6] Naioth, and Bethel, Jericho, and a*
place beyond Jordan, are specified places which were schools or
universities, where the scholars of the prophets were brought up in the fear
of God, and good learning : the continuance of which schools and univer-
sities amongst the people of God may be easily gathered of that which
Acts vi. 9.[3] *St Luke writeth in the Acts ; where it may appear that in Jeru-*
salem there were certain colleges appointed for several country-
men ; so that there was one college to receive the Jews and proselytes which
came out of Cilicia, another for those that came out of Alexandria, &c., to
study at Jerusalem.   And, if any man be able to shew such evidence for
archbishops and archdeacons as these are for universities and schools, I will
not deny but it is as lawful to have them as these.

Jo. Whitgift.

Yet saith he truly ; for in those times in christian congregations there were neither " public churches, or pulpits, or schools,
or universities, &c. ;" and yet these do appertain to the government of the church.   Indeed, St Paul speaketh only there of
such ecclesiastical functions as do teach and preach the word,
and not of such as do only govern ; and therefore it cannot be
a perfect platform for ever ; as I have before declared ; and
yet divers of these things mentioned by the bishop of Sarisbury pertain both to the office of teaching and governing.

That which you say of schools and universities I mind
not to examine, because I know they be necessary for the
church, how aptly soever you prove them.   But this is the
matter : they be necessary in the church both for the office of
governing and teaching ; and yet they be not expressed in the
fourth to the Ephesians ; therefore in that fourth to the Ephe- The bishop is not an-
sians there is no perfect pattern of all ecclesiastical govern- swered.

[3 The verses are added to the references from Repl. 2.]
[4 And second, Repl. 1.]
[5 And in the book of Samuel and of the Kings, Repl. 2.]
[6 Where, Repl. 1 and 2.]

M. Jewel's
answer
justified.

ment; for that is the thing that the bishop of Sarisbury affirmeth; and thereunto you answer not one word.

Not one of these places that you allege proveth that in this text to the Ephesians either "schools or universities" be mentioned, though it be certain that they pertain both to teaching and governing; and therefore all this speech of yours is to no purpose, but only to dazzle the eyes of the reader, lest he should perceive how you offend *in ignorantia elenchi*, in not answering *ad idem*[1].

Ignorantia
Elenchi.

Chapter iv.   The Seventh Division.

T. C. Page 92, Sect. 3.

Furthermore he saith that "the church is not governed by names, but by offices;" so is it indeed. And, if the office of an archbishop or archdeacon can be shewed, we will not strive for the name; but, forsomuch as all the needful offices of the church, together with their names, are mentioned in the scripture, it is truly said that both the offices and names of archbishop and archdeacons[2], being not only not contained in them (but also condemned), ought to be banished out of the church.

Jo. Whitgift.

The office of
archbishops
and arch-
deacons con-
tained in
scripture.

I have before shewed that the office of visiting churches, of overseeing many pastors and bishops, of suppressing schisms, &c., was in the apostles, and is in the scriptures; but in these things doth the office of an archbishop consist, and in part of them the office of an archdeacon; therefore the offices of arch-bishops and archdeacons be contained in the scriptures, and were in the apostles' time. For, although (as I then said) that this part of the apostolical office, which did consist in planting and founding churches through the whole world is ceased, yet the manner of government by placing bishops in every city, by moderating and governing them, by visiting the churches, by cutting off schisms and contentions, by ordering ministers, remaineth still, and shall continue, and is in this

[1 Cartwright rejoins: "If the D. can shew one letter that I ever wrote or spake, that the place of the Ephes. 'containeth all things necessary for the church,' then this that he writeth may have place. If not, then he is unworthy to receive answer." He afterwards says: "I give the reader warning that Judg. v. 'of those said to handle the pen,' whilst I gave too much credit to translations, was not so fitly alleged to prove universities."—Sec. Repl. p. 635.]

[2 Archdeacon, Repl. 1 and 2.]

church in the archbishops and bishops, as most meet men to M. Jewel's answer justified.
execute the same. Wherefore, seeing the offices be in the
scriptures, there is no cause why the names should be misliked,
much less " banished and cast out of the church."

Chapter iv.   The Eighth Division.

T. C. Page 92, Sect. 4.

Last of all he saith that "Anacletus (if there be any weight in his words)
nameth an archbishop." I have before shewed what weight there is in his
words ; and I refuse not that he be weighed by[3] the bishop's own weights,
which he giveth us in the handling of the article of the supremacy, and in
the 223. and 224. pages[4], by the which weights appeareth that this Anacle-
tus is not only light, but a plain counterfeit.

Jo. WHITGIFT.

Yet you see that learned men are content to use such autho-
rity as occasion serveth ; as I have also before shewed other Supra, cap. 2, divis. 13.
learned men to do the like[5]. And, if it be so greatly to be
reproved, first smite at yourself, as most guilty in this point.

Chapter iv.   The Ninth Division.

" The second Reason.

The synagogue of the Jews was a figure of the church of Secunda ratio.
Christ. And God to the perfection of that church omitted
nothing.

The answer of the bishop[6].

I see not what you would conclude : perhaps you[7] Ejus solutio.
will say they had not the names of pope or archbishop.
So had they not this name *episcopus* in all Moses' law ;
yet were not all priests of like anciency in government.
They had other names that were equivalent with archbishops : as *principes synagogæ, principes sanctuarii, prin-*
cipes familiarum Leviticarum, principes familiarum sacer-
dotalium, principes sacerdotum, principes domus Dei, pon-
tifex, summus pontifex, summus sacerdos, &c. Therefore
this negative reason is but weak. Again, whereas it is

[3 With, Repl. 1 and 2.]
[4 See Bp Jewel's Works, Park. Soc. Edit. Vol. I. pp. 341, &c.]
[5 See before, page 137.]
[6 Answ. 2 omits *of the bishop*.]   [7 Ye, Answ. 2.]

M. Jewel's
answer
justified.
said that to the perfection of the synagogue there wanted nothing, it may be answered that to the perfection thereof there wanted many things ; as it is known and confessed. And, as the synagogue had not the names of pope and archbishop, so had it not the name of apostle, or evangelist, &c."

T. C. Page 92, Sect. 5.

The second reason which saith that the church of God under the law had all things needful appointed by the commandment of God, the bishop saith he knoweth not what could be concluded of it : I have shewed before that there is nothing less meant than that the church under the gospel should have all those things that that[1] church had, or should have nothing which that had not. But this thereupon is concluded, that the Lord, which was so careful for that as not to omit the least, would not be so careless for this church under the gospel as to omit the greatest.

Jo. Whitgift.

Tract. ii.
cap. 6. di-
vis. 3.
I told you before, that this which you call the perfection of the synagogue was rather a burden than a perfection[2] ; for God therefore prescribed unto them a prescript form of external things, that it might be a means to keep them from further inconvenience ; but to us in such things he hath left a greater liberty ; and the perfection of the church doth not consist in outward appearance, but in spiritual gifts; and therein hath the Lord much more plentifully and graciously shewed his care for the church under the gospel than he did for it under the law.

Touching external orders, both of ceremonies and government, he hath left the disposition thereof to his church in
Tract. ii.
many things ; as I have proved in the beginning of this book[3].

Chapter iv.   The Tenth Division.
T. C. Page 92, Sect. 6.

And, where he saith that there was then which was called high priest, and was over all the rest, he did well know that the cause thereof was be-
This was one
cause, but
not the only
cause.
cause he was a figure of Christ, and did represent unto the people chiefty and superiority of our Saviour Christ, which was to come; and that, our Saviour Christ being come, there is now no cause why there should be any such pre-eminence given unto one; and, further, that it is un-
A popish non
sequitur.
lawful that there should be any such, unless it be lawful to have one head

[1 The, Def. A. and B.]   [2 See Vol. I. page 267.]
[3 See Vol. I. pages 175, &c.]

bishop over all the church; for it is known that that priest was the head M. Jewel's
priest over all the whole church, which was during his time, unto our answer
Saviour Christ. justified.

Jo. Whitgift.

The "high priest was a figure of Christ:" so was David
and Salomon; but yet was the high priest also appointed to
govern other for order and policy; and so was David and
Salomon. The figure is taken away and the kind of sacrifice;
but the office of governing remaineth still, and is to be observed as the state of the church requireth. Christ being
come, the office of sacrificing ceaseth, but not the office of
governing; for Christ by his coming did not take away government and policy, no, not from the ecclesiastical state.

This reason of yours, "that that priest was the head A popish
priest over all the church; therefore, if by his example we will reason used
by the Re-
have an archbishop, he must be such a one as shall govern the plier.
whole church," is indeed a plain confirmation of the papists'
reason for the supremacy, who think that they may reason in
like manner. But I answer you, as M. Calvin answereth them,
Lib. Inst. cap. viii. sect. 87 : " There is no reason that com- Calvin.
pelleth to extend that unto the whole world which was profitable in one nation; nay, rather there is a great diversity
betwixt one nation and the whole world. Because the Jews
were compassed in on every side with idolaters, lest they
should be withdrawn through the variety of religion, God did
place the seat of his worship in the midst of the earth : there
he appointed over them one prelate, whom all should look
upon, that they might the better be contained in unity. Now,
when as true religion is dispersed throughout the whole world,
who doth not see it to be absurd that the government of both
the east and west should be given to one? it is like as if one
would say, because one precinct of ground hath not many
governors, therefore the whole world ought to be ruled of
one president or governor[4]."

[4 Primum, quod in natione una fuit utile, id in universum orbem extendere
nulla ratio cogit : imo gentis unius et totius orbis longe diversa erit ratio. Quia
undique ab idolatris septi erant Judæi, ne religionum varietate distraherentur,
cultus sui sedem in medio terræ sinu Deus collocavit : illic unum antistitem
præfecit, quem omnes respicerent, quo melius in unitate continerentur. Nunc ubi
vera religio in totum orbem diffusa est, uni dari Orientis et Occidentis moderatio-
nem, quis non videat esse prorsus absurdum? Perinde enim est acsi quis contendat totum mundum a præfecto uno debere regi, quia ager unus non plures
præfectos habeat. Sed est altera etiamnum ratio cur illud in imitationem trahi

I know that he maketh another answer likewise; even the same that you have borrowed of him, touching the figure; but his first answer is more direct, in my opinion.   And M. Nowel, against Dorman reasoning as you do, giveth him this answer:

"It agreeth very well with the estate of the Jews, that, as they being one nation had one chief priest, so is it good likewise that every christian nation have their chief priest or bishop.   It agreeth not that, because the Jews, one nation, had one high priest to govern them in doubts, therefore all nations through the world should have one high priest over all other; for not only the unlikelihood between these two, but the impossibility of the latter, is most evident[1]."   Other learned men also there be, as Hyperius, *Lib. iii. Method. Theolog.*, and divers others, who, answering this same argument of the papists, say that "by it we may well prove that one archbishop or metropolitan may govern one province, or one kingdom; but that it is too weak to prove that one pope may govern all the world[2]."   Howbeit you had rather give strength to the adversary than lack arguments to the defence of your cause.

Chapter iv.   The Eleventh Division.

T. C. Page 93, Line 1.

And, as for those titles, "chief of the synagogue," "chief of the sanctuary," "chief of the house of God," I say that that maketh much against archbishops and archdeacons; for, when as instead of the synagogue, and of the sanctuary, and of the house of God or temple, are come particular churches and congregations, by this reason it followeth that there should be some chief, not in every province or diocese, but in every congregation; and indeed so ought there to be certain chief in every congregation which should govern and rule the rest.   And, as for the "chief of the families of the Levites," and "chief of the families of the priests," the

non debeat.   Summum illum pontificem typum fuisse Christi nemo ignorat: nunc translato sacerdotio, jus illud transferri convenit.—Calvin. Op. Amst. 1667-71, Inst. Lib. iv. cap. vi. 2. Tom. IX. p. 295.]

[1 A Reprovfe, written by Alexander Nowell, &c. Lond. 1565. fol. 61.   See before, page 219, note 5.]

[2 ... Olim, inquiunt, apud Judæos summus sacerdos jussu ipsius Dei declaratus, et ab omnibus agnitus: quare etiam nunc in novo testamento par est, unum aliquem episcopum supremum constitui, quem omnes ubique venerentur, audiantque...Suaderi sane illo argumento queat, recte aliquem archiepiscopum sive metropolitanum uni dari provinciæ, sive regno aut principatui, nequaquam vero unum debere præfici toti orbi.—And. Hyper. Method. Theolog. sive præcip. Christ. Rel. Loc. Comm. Libr. Tres, Basil. 1574. Lib. iii. p. 682.]

same was observed in all other tribes of Israel[3]; and by all these princes M. Jewel's
over every tribe and family, as by the prince of the whole land, God did answer
as it were by divers lively pictures imprint in their understanding the justified.
chiefty and domination of our Saviour Christ. Besides this, the order
which was appointed in this point was observed in all the tribes[4].

Jo. Whitgift.

These titles be as glorious as any that are now remaining The Replier
in our church. And my L. of Sarum speaketh of names, to slippeth by
the which you do not answer one word, but seek out other the matter.
matter to blind the reader with, lest he should behold your
folly. But I will follow you. You say that "instead of the
synagogues, &c., are come particular churches and congregations, &c.;" and I say unto you, that they had then particular synagogues as well as we have now particular churches;
the which you yourself in effect have confessed before[5]. And Pag. 22,
you must understand that one christian commonweal is but line I.
one church, as it was among the Jews; and therefore such
offices of government may be such in the church as was among
the Jews, and such superiority among ministers as was then
amongst priests and Levites. And I marvel that you will deny
this, especially seeing that you would bind us to the civil law
of Moses, whereof this is a portion.

You add that "by all these princes over every tribe and
family, as by the prince of the whole land, God did as it
were, &c.:" all this maketh nothing against our offices, except
you will also take away the prince of the whole land.

As this order among the Jews was observed in all tribes,
so is it now in all provinces and dioceses. This is but slender
stuff you bring, and yet not to the purpose; for the Answer
speaketh of names; and you drive it to offices. Indeed you
almost in no place reason *ad idem;* which is a manifest argument that you are but a shifting caviller[6].

[3] Here Repl. 2 inserts *as a civil thing.*]
[4] This sentence is not in Repl. 2.]
[5] See Vol. I. page 269.]
[6] Cartwright in his rejoinder to this division says that Whitgift "as amazed
speaketh he cannot tell what;" that he asserts what "is untrue;" that he is
"ravished of all judgment;" that he is "frivolous," &c.—Sec. Repl. pp. 637, 8.]

Chapter iv.   The Twelfth Division.

T. C. Page 93, Line 13.

Moreover, these orders and policies touching the distribution of the offices of the Levites and priests, and touching the appoint- 2 Chron. *ment of their governors, were done of David by the advice of* xxix. 25.[1] *the prophets Gad and Nathan, which received of the Lord by commandment that which they delivered unto* [2] *David. And, if so be that it can be shewed that archbishops and archdeacons came into the church by any commandment of the Lord, then this allegation hath some force; but now, being not only not commanded, but also (as I have shewed) forbidden, every man doth see that this reason hath no place, but serveth to the utter overthrow of the archbishop and archdeacon. For, if David, being such a notable personage, and as it were an angel of God, durst not take upon him to bring into the church any orders or policies, not only not against the word of God, but not without a precise word and commandment of God, who shall dare be* [3] *so bold as to take upon him the institution of the chief office of the church, and to alter the policy that God hath appointed* [4] *by his servants the apostles?*

Jo. Whitgift.

You run away with the matter, as though all were clear, when as it is not so. You affirm that "David did appoint these orders and policies touching the distribution of the offices of the Levites and priests, &c., by the advice of Gad and Nathan, the prophets of God." And for proof hereof you quote in the margent 2 Chron. xix., where there is not one word for your purpose, or signifying any such thing. Indeed, in the 2 Chron. xxix. there is affirmed the like thing. But my L. of Sarisbury hath answered you, that such negative reasons are very weak [5]. And, if you will deny it to be a negative reason from authority, yet can you not deny but that it is as feeble an argument as almost can be. For what if David "did appoint these orders touching the distribution of the offices of the Levites and priests, &c.," doth it therefore follow that the church at no time may appoint such offices as shall be thought meet for the government of it, according to the time, places, and persons? where have you learned of a singular

[1 The verse is added, and the number of the chapter corrected, from Repl. 2: the other editions have erroneously *xix.*]

[2 To, Repl. 1 and 2.]

[3 Dare to be, Repl. 1 and 2.]   [4 Established, Repl. 1 and 2.]

[5 "So he bringeth him in answering this reason after his death; for in his life it was not propounded."—Sec. Repl. p. 638.]

example to make a general rule, or to frame an argument *ex solis particularibus?*

In the 2 Chron. xix., which you have quoted in the margent there is a notable place against you; for there express mention is made that Jehosaphat set in Jerusalem of the Levites, and of the priests, &c., for the judgment and cause of the Lord, and made Amariah the priest chief over them: neither were they judges for the city of Jerusalem only, but for the whole country. And yet we read not of any commandment that Jehosaphat had so to do[6].

M. Jewel's answer justified.

Scripture alleged against himself.
2 Chron. xix. vers. 8.

Chapter iv.   The Thirteenth Division.

T. C. Page 93, Sect. 1.

And, where the bishop saith, "it is known and confessed that there wanted many things to the perfection of the church of the Jews," truly I do not know, nor cannot confess that that church wanted any thing to the perfection of that estate which the Lord would have them be in, until the coming of our Saviour Christ. And, if there were anything wanting, it was not for want of good laws and policies, whereof the question is, but for want of due execution of them, which we speak not of.

This is directly contrary to yourself.

Jo. Whitgift.

Conveniet nulli, &c. How can he agree with any other man that doth not agree with himself? For before (after you have recited divers things left to the order of that church of the Jews for the which they had no express word) you say that you "will offer, for one that I bring that we have left to the order of the church, to shew that they had twenty which were undecided by the express word of God[7]." And here you say that it "wanted nothing to the perfection of that estate." How you will reconcile yourself, I know not: or whether it be your pleasure not to respect your own credit, so that you may seem to discredit that which that notable bishop hath spoken; but that which I have alleged of Jehosaphat, 2 Chron. xix., doth manifestly justify my lord of Sarisbury's saying, and condemneth yours. For there it is to be seen, that in matters of government orders were appointed which neither were commanded by any express commandment

T. C. contrary to himself.

Pag. 22, Sect. 1.

[6 "By the printer's small oversight, in putting 1. for 2., the D. hath stumbled upon 'a notable place &c.'"—Ibid. pp. 638, 9.]

[7 See Vol. I. page 270.]

of God, neither yet expressed in the word of God. But of this matter I have spoken before.

Chapter iv.   The Fourteenth Division.

"The third Reason.

Tertia ratio.   *Where the substance of anything is most perfite, there the accidents be most perfite; but the substance of true religion was most perfite in the primitive church; and yet there was then no archbishop; ergo.*

The answer of the bishop[1].

Ejus so-
lutio.   First, this *maxima* is not proved; for it may well be doubted whether the most perfite substance hath[2] evermore most perfite accidents. And again, the substance of religion is the same now that it was then : the difference, if there be any, standeth in accidents, and not in substance. Therefore this allegation of substance and accidents was not needful. In the primitive church God raised up apostles, and prophets, and gave them power extraordinary, as the gift of tongues, the gift of healing, the gift of government, &c. In place whereof he hath now given universities, schools, bishops, archbishops, &c. But you say there was then no archbishop. So may you say that before king Saul there was no king in Israel. So may you say that before of late times there was neither duke nor earl in England. So may you say that in the primitive church there was neither dean, nor parson, nor prebendary. And yet now both in ecclesiastical and civil government all these are thought necessary. Last of all, where you say there was no archbishop in the primitive church, it is written by many that St Paul made Titus archbishop of Creta.

Eras. in arg.
epist. ad Ti-
tum.   Erasmus saith : *Paulus Titum archiepiscopum Cretæ consecravit*[3]; and Lyra likewise saith: *Paulus instituit Titum archiepiscopum Cretensium*[4]. If these authorities like

---

[1 Answ. 2 omits *of the bishop*.]   [2 Have, Answ. 2.]
[3 Erasm. Op. L. Bat. 1703-6. In Epist. ad Tit. Arg. Tom. VII. cols. 1067, 8.
See before, page 132, note 2.]
[4 *Reliqui te Cretæ*, instituens te ibi archiepiscopum.—Bibl. cum Gloss. Ord.
et Expos. N. de Lyra, Basil. 1502. Ad Tit. cap. i. Pars VI. fol. 128.]

you not, Chrysostom saith : *Paulus Tito multorum epi-*
scoporum judicium commisit[5]. Now, having 'the government of many bishops,' what may we call him but an
archbishop ?"

T. C. Page 93, Sect. 2.

For the two last reasons against the archbishop and archdeacon, al-
though I be well acquainted with divers that favour this cause, yet I did
never hear them before in my life; and I believe they cannot be proved to
be his reasons whose they are supposed to be, and which did set down the[6]
proposition that the bishop confuteth. Notwithstanding, the former of these
two seemeth to have a good probability, and to be grounded of that place
of logic that sheweth that, according as the subject or substance of any-
thing is excellent, so are those things that are annexed and adjoined unto it.
But, because I would the simplest should understand what is said or written,
I will willingly abstain from such reasons the terms whereof are not easily
perceived but of those which be learned.

Jo. Whitgift.

Indeed you may disclaim what you list, for you could
never be brought before this time to set down your reasons
in writing; and there is no hold at your word; for you will
affirm and deny, even at your pleasure; and so will divers of
your companions, as experience hath taught. But yet you
think that this "former" reason "hath a good probability,
&c.;" howbeit you answer not one word to my L. of Sarum's
solution; which proveth it to be very fond.

Chapter iv.   The Fifteenth Division.

T. C. Page 93, Sect. 3.

And as for the answer which the bishop maketh, that, " in place of
apostles, prophets, the gifts of tongues, of healing, and of government,
are brought in universities, schools, bishops, and archbishops;" for schools
and universities, I have shewed they have been always, and therefore cannot
come in to supply the room of the apostles and prophets. And whether a
man consider the scholars that learn, or the schoolmasters which teach, or
the orders appointed for the government of the schools, they shall be found
to be rather civil than ecclesiastical, and therefore cannot come instead of
any ecclesiastical ministry. If the bishop do mean that they come in place

[5 Chrysost. Op. Par. 1718-38.   In Epist. ad Tit. cap. i. Hom. i. Tom. XI.
p. 727.]

[6 That, Repl. 1 and 2.]

of the gift of the tongues[1], and knowledge of the gospel that was first given miraculously, I grant it ; and then it maketh nothing to this question.

Jo. Whitgift.

You have not shewed that "schools and universities were always" in the church of Christ, nor you cannot shew that there were any universities or schools of Christians in the apostles' time. I am not disposed to contrary anything that is alleged for universities or schools; neither would I have you to deny this truth affirmed by my lord of Sarum; for it is certain that God worketh now in the church by means of universities and schools that which he wrought in the apostles' time miraculously by his apostles and prophets. And those gifts of tongues, healing, government, &c., which he then inspired at once without teaching, doth he now give by little and little, using the ministry of schools, universities, and such like; wherefore it is true that the bishop hath said.

And whereas you say that schools, "whether a man consider the scholars that learn, or the schoolmasters which teach, or orders appointed for the government of the schools, they shall be found rather civil than ecclesiastical:" if you speak of schools in a profane or heathenish commonwealth, it is true. But, if you speak of a christian kingdom, it is most untrue. For in a christian commonwealth schools are the first nurses that bring up children in the true knowledge of God, and of his word, and prepare many of them to the ministry; both which are ecclesiastical. Moreover, if you talk of universities, such especially as be in this realm of England, then, whether you consider either the masters, fellows, or scholars, or rules or orders appointed for the government of them, they be for the most part ecclesiastical; and therefore those things make greatly for the purpose; and you have said nothing that can overthrow them[2].

Chapter iv.   The Sixteenth Division.
T. C. Page 93, Sect. 4.

As for bishops, they cannot come in place of apostles or prophets, for-

---

[1 Of tongues, Repl. 2.]

[2 Cartwright calls this "poor divinity;" and adds: "for so a schoolmaster, teaching Terence, or professor reading Aristotle, is become an ecclesiastical officer."—Sec. Repl. p. 639.]

asmuch as they were when the apostles, evangelists, and prophets were, and M. Jewel's
are one of those ministries which St Paul mentioneth in the iv. to the Ephe- answer
sians, being the same that is the pastor. justified.

Jo. Whitgift.

I told you before, that that part of the apostles' office which consisted in government is now remaining in archbishops and bishops, as to visit churches, to reform disorders, to suppress contentions, and such like; which also they practised in the apostles' time, in such places as were committed unto them by the apostles, as it is evident in Timothy and Titus.

That bishops do succeed the apostles in this function of government it may appear by sundry learned writers. Cyprian, *Lib. iii. Epist.* 9., writeth thus: "But deacons must remember that the Lord hath chosen apostles, that is to say, bishops and chief governors; but the apostles, after the ascension of the Lord into heaven, did appoint unto themselves deacons, ministers of their bishopric and of the church[3]." And Ambrose, in *iv. ad Ephe.*, saith: *Apostoli episcopi sunt*[4]: "Apostles are bishops." Zuinglius also in his *Ecclesiastes* saith that "the apostles, when they left off going from place to place, and remained in one church, were no more called apostles, but bishops, as James at Jerusalem, and John at Ephesus[5]." Whereby it may appear that it seemeth strange neither to the old writers, nor to the new, to say that bishops succeed the apostles and come in place of them.

Bishops succeed apostles in government.
Cyprian.

Ambrose.
Zuinglius.

Chapter iv.   The Seventeenth Division.

T. C. Page 93, Sect. ult.

There remaineth therefore the archbishop, which if he came in place of

[3 Meminisse autem diaconi debent, quoniam apostolos, id est, episcopos et præpositos Dominus elegit: diaconos autem post ascensum Domini in cœlos apostoli sibi constituerunt episcopatus sui et ecclesiæ ministros.—Cypr. Op. Oxon. 1682. Ad Rogat. Epist. iii. p. 6.]

[4 Ambros. Op. Par. 1686-90. Comm. in Epist. ad Ephes. cap. iv. vv. 11, 12. Tom. II. Append. col. 241.]

[5 Simul etiam illud notari debet, &c. [See before, pages 302, 3, note 3]…. Idem de Joanne evangelista et Christi discipulo dicere possumus.—H. Zvingl. Op. Tigur. 581. Ecclesiast. Pars II. fol. 48.]

the prophets and apostles (as the bishop saith), how cometh it to pass that the bishop saith by and bye, out of the authority of Erasmus, that Titus was an archbishop? for at that time there was both apostles, prophets, and evangelists. If it be so, therefore, that the archbishop must supply the want of apostles, &c., how cometh it to pass he waiteth not his time whilst they were dead, but cometh in like unto one which is born out of time, and like the untimely and hasty fruit, which is seldom or never wholesome? And for one to come into the apostles' or prophets' place requireth the authority of him which ordained the apostles, &c., which is the Lord, and his institution in his word, which is that which we desire to be shewed. But hereof I have spoken before at large.

Jo. Whitgift.

It is not unknown to such as be willing to learn, that, where the apostles could not be present themselves, there they appointed some other to govern the churches for them; as the apostle Paul did Titus at Creta. Therefore this reason of yours is soon answered. And, in that that the apostles did appoint bishops in churches which they had planted, and gave unto them such authority, it is evident that therein they made them their successors; which they did not without sufficient testimony and warrant of the Spirit of God; and therefore you do but talk, you prove nothing.

Chapter iv.   The Eighteenth Division.
T. C. Page 94, Line 9; and Sect. 1, 2.

The necessity of deans I do not acknowledge, and I have already spoken of them. Touching prebendaries, I shall have occasion to speak a word hereafter. For earls, and dukes, and such like titles of honour, they are civil; neither doth it follow that, because there may new titles or new offices be brought into the civil government, that therefore the same may be attempted in the church. For God hath left a greater liberty in instituting things in the commonwealth than in the church.

For, forsomuch as there be divers commonwealths, and divers forms of commonwealths, and all good, it falleth out that the offices and dignities which are good in one commonwealth are not good in another; as those which are good in a monarchy are not good in aristocraty, and those which are good in aristocraty are not good in a popular state. But that cannot be said of the church, which is but one and uniform, and hath the same laws and form of government throughout the world.

In commonwealths also there are conversions, one form being changed into another; which cannot be in the true church of God.

Jo. Whitgift.

Your "acknowledging" or not acknowledging "the necessity of deans, &c." is not greatly material; they depend not upon you. To the example of king Saul, the first king of Israel, you say nothing[1]; and yet it is material. There is no such difference betwixt the civil government of the commonwealth and the external government of the church, but that the one in many things may be used as an example for the other. And it is untrue that the external form of government in the church ought to be one and the self-same throughout the world, in all times and places; as it shall hereafter more fully appear. But still I would have the reader to note what kind of government of the church you do allow, and join the same with that assertion of yours, that the government of the commonwealth must be framed according to the government of the church, as the hangings[2] to the house.

Tract. xvii.

Chapter iv. The Nineteenth Division.

T. C. Page 94, Sect. 2.

As for Erasmus' authority which saith that Titus was an archbishop, I have answered to it.

And, whereas Chrysostom saith that "the judgment of many bishops was committed to Titus," I have declared in what sort it[3] is to be understanded; and yet upon these[4] words the bishop can hardly conclude that which he doth, that Titus had "the government of many bishops." For it is one thing to say the judgment of many was committed unto Titus, and another thing to say that he had the government of many.

Untrue; for you have not as yet spoken one word of it.

Jo. Whitgift.

And shall the same answer serve for Lyra too? Well, I have answered your answer to Erasmus. And I trust that these authorities with the godly reader shall have the more credit, because this reverend father doth herein confirm their opinions; whose judgment, for his singular virtue and learning, ought to be more esteemed than a number such as you are.

[1 "In answering generally of all offices in the commonwealth, a man not utterly forsaken of his judgment must needs know that I had answered 'the example of Saul.'"—Sec. Repl. p. 640.]

[2 Hanging, Def. B.]   [3 That, Repl. 1 and 2.]

[4 Those, Repl. 1 and 2.]

M. Jewel's answer justified.

You neither have answered, nor do answer, nor can answer, these words of Chrysostom; and it is but a very poor shift to make such a distinction betwixt "judgment" and "government." For what is it else to "have the judgment of many bishops" committed unto him, but "to have the government?" Shew a difference if you can: no doubt you would have done it if you could. Wherefore this authority of Chrysostom remaineth untouched; and it confirmeth my answer to the Greek scholiast, who borrowed his words of him[1]. Neither would you have thus dallied in this place, if you had looked upon Chrysostom's words, who there affirmeth that Paul did commit to Titus the whole isle of Creta.

Chapter iv.   The Twentieth Division.

" The fourth Reason.

Quarta ratio.

The ecclesiastical and civil government may not be confounded, or be together in one person; but to be a chief or a ruler is a civil power; ergo, it cannot be exercised by any ecclesiastical person.

The answer of the bishop[2].

Ejus solutio.

Both these governments were confounded in Moses; therefore they may be confounded. And the priests of Israel had the judgment and government of the people. And St Augustine was troubled with hearing and determining of causes; as it appeareth by Possidonius[3].

And, where you say "to be a chief or a ruler is a civil government:" nay, in ecclesiastical causes it is ecclesiastical government, and not civil. And these differences of government may not so unadvisedly be confounded. This is the key of ecclesiastical correction, and belongeth only to the ecclesiastical officer, and to none other. Hereof St Paul saith: *Seniorem ne corripueris nisi sub &c. Tradidi illum Satanæ, &c.* This jurisdiction is not civil,

---

[1 See before, pages 284, 5.]

[2 Answ. 2 omits *of the bishop.*]

[3 August. Op. Par. 1679-1700. August. Vit. auct. Possid. cap. xix. Tom. X. Post-Append. cols. 270, 1.]

but ecclesiastical, and therefore may be exercised by any [4] ecclesiastical person."

T. C. Page 94, Sect. 3.

The answer of the bishop unto the fourth supposed reason pertaineth unto another question, that is, whether ecclesiastical persons ought to exercise civil jurisdiction; whereunto I will answer by God's grace when I come to speak upon occasion of M. Doctor's book of that question. In the mean time I will desire the reader to consider what weak grounds the archbishop and archdeacon stand upon, seeing that the bishop of Sarum, being so learned a man, and of so great reading, could say no more in their defence, which notwithstanding in the controversies against Doctor Harding is so pithy and so plentiful.

Jo. Whitgift.

The bishop of Sarum hath said much more than you have answered unto; and in the respect of the reasons he hath said fully enough. You may not think but that, if he had been disposed to have dealt of purpose in this cause, he could have said much more. But your secret and privy nips, whereby you insinuate to the reader that he would willingly defend a false cause, shall never be able to deface so worthy a prelate. You may perceive by this his conclusion (which toucheth you so near) that he took no great care or time for answering these weak reasons; for thus he concludeth:

"I beseech you to take these sudden answers in good part: as for these reasons, in my judgment they are not made to build up, and they are too weak to pull down. *Stultitia nata est in corde pueri; et virga disciplinæ fugabit illam. Proverb. xxii.* It is but wantonness: correction will help it."

Thus have I answered in his behalf, who both in this and other like controversies might have been a great stay to this church of England, if we had been worthy of him. But, whilst he lived, and especially after his notable and most profitable travails, he received the same reward of wicked and ungrateful tongues, that other men be exercised with, and all must look for, that will do their duty. But now again to T. C.

[4 An, Answ. 2.]

¶ The causes of Archbishops and of their prerogatives, and the estate of the old Bishops (assigned by T. C.), examined.

Chapter v.   The First Division.

T. C. Page 94, Sect. 4.

Now I have shewed how little those things which M. Doctor bringeth make for proof of that wherefore he allegeth them, I will, for the better understanding of the reader, set down what were the causes why the arch-bishops were first ordained, and what were their prerogatives and pre-eminences before other bishops, and the estate also of the old bishops which lived in those times; wherein although there were great corruptions, yet the church was in some tolerable estate; to the intent it may appear partly how little need we have of them now, and partly also how great difference there is between ours and them. Of the names of metropolitans[1] it hath been spoken, how that he should not be called the chief of priests, or the high priest, or bishop of bishops. Now I will set down their[2] office and power which they[3] had more than the bishops.

Jo. Whitgift.

If you have no more truth in your words following than you utter in the beginning of these, or if you deal no soundlier in them than you have done in the other, M. Doctor's proofs shall serve the turn. But it is in vain to answer words, I will therefore come to your matter.

Chapter v.   The Second Division.

T. C. Page 94, Sect. 5.

In the council of Antioch it appeareth that the bishop of the metropolitan seat called synods, and propounded the mat- Chap. 9.
ters which were to be handled, &c.[4] The archbishop doth not now call synods; but the prince doth; forasmuch as there is no convocation without a parliament; and he doth not propound the matters, and gather the voices, but another chosen, which is called prolocutor; therefore, in the respect that an archbishop and metropolitan was first ordained, we have no need of an archbishop or metropolitan. Again, another cause also appeareth there, which was to see that the bishops kept themselves within their own dioceses[5], and brake not into another's diocese; but first this may be done without an archbishop, and then it is not done of the arch-bishop himself, giving licences unto the wandering ministers to go through-out not so few as a dozen dioceses[5]; therefore the office of an archbishop

An untruth; for there is no such thing in that ninth canon.

Another untruth.

[1 Metropolitan, Repl. 2.]   [2 His, Repl. 2.]
[3 He, Repl. 2.]   [4 See below, page 362, note 1.]
[5 Diocese, Def. A. and B.]

is not necessary in this respect; and, if it were, yet it must be other than it is now.

Jo. Whitgift.

There is no council more flat against you than is that council of Antioch, nor any canon that overthroweth your assertion more directly than that ninth canon, the words whereof I have repeated before; but your untrue allegation in a manner compelleth me to repeat them again, that the reader may see before his eyes what truth there is in your doings. And, although it do pertain to the office of the metropolitan or archbishop " to call synods," yet is there not one word thereof in this canon, nor yet of " propounding any matters" in synods, or of "seeing bishops keep themselves within their own diocese;" as you do here avouch without all truth; and, notwithstanding, as I said before, those things do pertain to the office of the archbishop, yet, if they were also comprehended in that canon, it were rather a confirmation of that office, than otherwise.

The contents of that canon be only these; first, it saith that "it behoveth the bishops of every country or province to know their metropolitan bishop to have the care and oversight, or government, over the whole province." By the which words, the authority and name of a metropolitan or archbishop is most plainly confirmed, and proved to be a permanent office; secondly, this canon "willeth all those that have any business to do to resort to the metropolitan city." Whereby also is given to the metropolitan bishop great preeminence; and therefore it followeth immediately, that "he should excel all the rest in honour; and that the other bishops should do nothing of importance without him; according to the old rule made by their forefathers, but only those things which pertain to their own diocese, and those places and possessions that pertain unto the same." In which words who seeth not what pre-eminence is given to the metropolitan over all the bishops in his province, and what jurisdiction to the bishop in his own diocese and places pertaining unto it? where also it is to be noted that the council saith: *secundum antiquam a patribus nostris regulam constitutam:* "according to the ancient rule appointed of our forefathers." Which argueth a great antiquity of his office. Then it followeth: "For every bishop hath authority over his own diocese, to rule and govern it, *juxta reverentiam singulis competentem*: according to the reverence due unto every one of them, and that he hath especial care of that whole region that is subject to his city, so that he may ordain priests and deacons, *et singula suo judicio comprehendat*. But he may not attempt any other thing without the metropolitan bishop; nor the metropolitan do anything without the counsel of the other priests[1]."

What can be more plain, either for the authority of the archbishop, or jurisdiction of the bishop? and what one word of this canon have you truly alleged? and yet it is quoted in your margent.

But, if we imagine those things to be true which you say, how will you conclude? forsooth, that the metropolitan did then "call synods, and propounded the matters," but now he doth not "call synods and propound the matters;" therefore there is now no need of a metropolitan. First, it is untrue that metropolitans did then call either all synods, or that they called them of their own authority, without the consent of the prince and civil magistrate; which thing is evident when the magistrates were christened.

Councils summoned by princes. Eus. de Vita Constant. Lib. III.

The council of Nice was summoned by the commandment of Constantine the emperor, *Eusebius, de Vita Constanti. Lib. iii.*[2] Constantius[3] called the council which was in *Sardica civitate*[4]. The bishops in the council of Constanti. confess that they came together by the emperor's writ[5]. Ambrose, in the council of Aquileia, speaking of himself and of other bishops, saith that they were assembled out of Aquileia, by the commandment of the emperor[6]. The same doth Hierome testify concerning a council holden at Rome, *In Epita.*

[1 Concil. Antioch. can. 9. in Concil. Stud. Labb. et Cossart. Lut. Par. 1671-2. Tom. II. col. 565. See before, page 146, note 1.]

[2 Euseb. De Vit. Constant. in Hist. Eccles. Script. Amst. 1695-1700. Lib. III. cap. vi. p. 400.]   [3 Constantinus, Def. B.]

[4 ... ἔδοξε γνώμῃ τῶν βασιλέων [Κώνστα καὶ Κωνσταντίου], τοὺς ἀφ' ἑκατέρας ἀρχομένης ἐπισκόπους, εἰς ῥητὴν ἡμέραν καταλαβεῖν τὴν Σαρδώ.— Soz. in eod. Lib. III. cap. xi. p. 417.]

[5 Δεόμεθα τοίνυν τῆς σῆς εὐσεβείας ἐπικυρωθῆναι τῆς συνόδου τὴν ψῆφον· ἵν' ὥσπερ τοῖς τῆς κλήσεως γράμμασι τὴν ἐκκλησίαν τετίμηκας, οὕτω καὶ τῶν δοξάντων ἐπισφραγίσῃς τὸ τέλος.—Epist. ad Theodos. Imp. Nunc. præf. Cann. Concil. Constant. I. in Concil. Stud. Labb. et Cossart. Tom. II. col. 946.]

[6 ... nos...convenimus ad Aquileiensium civitatem, juxta imperatoris præceptum.—Ambros. Op. Par. 1686-90. Concil. Aquil. Gest. ap. Epist. Class. I. Tom. II. col. 788.]

Pauli.[7]   Pope Julio, *Epist.* 9. *ad Theodos.*, desireth the emperor, that by his authority there might be a council in Italy[8].
Zozomen., *Lib. vi. cap.* 7, sheweth how certain catholic bishops
intreated the emperor that they might have leave to gather
together for the redressing of certain errors[9].   But what
shall I need to labour in a matter most manifest?   No man
can be ignorant that readeth ecclesiastical stories, but that the
emperor's authority was required in summoning councils and
synods, not only general, but provincial also[10].   Secondly, it
is untrue that the metropolitan in this church doth not "call
synods, or propoundeth not the matters in them, &c."   For
he doth both, although he calleth no provincial synod without
the commandment of the prince, no more than other metropolitans have done in the best time of the church under christian princes.   Last of all, though all this were true, that is
here untruly affirmed, yet were the office of an archbishop
necessary, for it doth not only consist in calling synods, but in
sundry things beside; as I have shewed before, and this council
of Antioch manifestly declareth.   And, surely, if you would
prove anything hereof directly, it should be this, that either the
archbishop doth not exercise that jurisdiction which he ought
to do, or else cannot do that which pertaineth to his office;

[7 Quumque orientis et occidentis episcopos ob quasdam ecclesiarum dissen-
siones Romam imperiales literæ contraxissent.—Hieron. Op. Par. 1693-1706.
Epit. Paul. ad Eustoch. Epist. lxxxvi. Tom. IV. Pars ii. col. 671.]

[8 Unde si pietas vestra suggestioni ac supplicationi nostræ dignetur annuere,
ut intra Italiam habere jubeatis episcopale concilium.—Leon. Magni Op. Lut.
1623. Ad Theod. August. Epist. ix. col. 303. *Julio* in the text is obviously an
error for *Leo.*]

[9 ... οἱ...ἐπίσκοποι...προβάλλονται πρεσβεύειν ὑπὲρ αὐτῶν Ὑπατιανὸν τὸν
Ἡρακλείας τῆς Περίνθου ἐπίσκοπον. ὥστε ἐπιτραπῆναι συνελθεῖν ἐπὶ διορθώσει
τοῦ δόγματος· κ.τ.λ.—Soz. in Hist. Eccles. Script. Lib. vi. cap. vii. p. 525.
The history goes on to say that Valentinian replied that he as a layman had no
right to intermeddle in such matters; the bishops could meet wherever they
chose.]

[10 Cartwright rejoins that, "although some provincial councils were called
by the emperor, yet it is manifest both by the council of Nice and by this I alleged
...that the metropolitan with the bishops' advice might hold a provincial council.
It was done, I grant, by consent, and sometime by express confirmation of the
godly princes....This although it were 'not in the 9. canon,' yet when the D.
knew it was in that council (as appeareth by his precise denying of it to be in
'that canon,' where otherwise he would have said in that council) it appeareth that
he useth less sincerity in these holy matters than the heathen in their profane."
He goes on, in illustration of what he means, to refer to a passage in the life of
Alexander the Great, who said he would not "steal the victory."—Sec. Repl.
p. 641.]

and so should you speak for the amendment of the archbishop's jurisdiction.

Again, you say, "another cause appeareth there, which was to see that the bishops kept themselves within their own diocese, &c.; but first this may be done without an archbishop, &c." I tell you there is no such thing in that ninth canon; I say, further, that it may best and most orderly be done by an archbishop. Thirdly, I answer as before, that it is but one part of his office. Fourthly, I say unto you that this is a simple argument: the archbishop doth not keep such old canons as be not in use in this church; therefore there is no need of his office. Last of all, you ought to know that those whom you call wandering ministers be faithful preachers a number of them, and such as labour diligently in preaching the word, and have not a little profited the flock of Christ; so that your conclusion is not worth a straw.

Chapter v.   The Third Division.

T. C. Page 95, Sect. 1.

Again, the cause why the metropolitan differed from the rest, and why the calling of the synod was given to him, as it appeareth in the same council[1], was for that the greatest concourse was to that Chap. 9. *place, and most assembly of men; whereunto also may be added, for that there was the best commodity of lodging and of victualling; and for that, as it appeareth in other councils, it was the place and seat of the empire. But with us neither the greatest concourse nor assembly of men, nor the greatest commodity of lodging and victualling, neither yet the seat of the kingdom, is in the metropolitan city; therefore with us there is no such cause of a metropolitan or archbishop.*

Jo. Whitgift.

This is not alleged as a cause why there should be a metropolitan, or "why he differed from the rest, or why the calling of the synod was given unto him," but rather why he was placed in the chief city; so that these words touch not the metropolitan or his office, but the aptness of the place where he should continue. And yet, if credit be to be given either to interpreters or to the gloss in Gratian, *Caus. ix. quæst.* 3. *Per singulas,* the words be not as you interpret

[1 See before, page 362, note 1.]

them[2] ; for thus they be set down in the book of Councils, Tom. I. : *Propter quod ad metropolim omnes undique qui negotia videntur habere concurrant*[3] : " For the which let all that have any business have recourse from all places into the metropolitan city." Another translation is thus : *Propter quod ad metropolitanam civitatem ab his qui causas habent concurratur*[4]. And this last interpretation the authors of the Centuries do use, *Cent. iv.*[5] Of which words there can be no such thing gathered as you do imagine, but far otherwise. And the meaning of the council is, that such as have causes to be heard may resort to the metropolitan city where the metropolitan is.

And you must understand that it was in the power of the emperor and other princes to appoint the seat of the metropolitan where it pleased[6] them ; as it appeareth in the 12. chap. of the council of Chalcedon[7], and in the 17. Hom. of Chrysostom, *Ad populum Antiochenum*[8].

Chapter v.　The Fourth Division.
T. C. Page 95, Sect. 2.

In the council of Carthage, holden in Cyprian's time, it appeareth that no bishop had authority over another to compel another, or to condemn another, but every bishop was left at his own liberty to answer unto God, and to make his account unto Christ[9] *; and, if any thing were done against any bishop, it was done by the consent of all the bishops in the province, or as many as could conveniently assemble. Therefore Cyprian, which was the metropolitan bishop, had then no authority over the rest ; and yet then, there being no christian magistrate which would punish the disorders which were committed of the christian bishops, there was greatest need that there*

T. C. confesseth Cyprian to be a metropolitan.

[2 Corp. Jur. Canon. Lugd. 1624. Decret. Gratian. Decr. Sec. Pars, Caus. IX. Quæst. iii. can. 2. et not. ibid. cols. 872, 3.]

[3 Concil. Antioch. cap. 9. Edit. 1. in Crabb. Concil. Col. Agrip. 1551. Tom. I. p. 322.]

[4 Ibid. Edit. 2. ibid.]

[5 Centur. Eccles. Hist. Basil. 1560, &c. Cent. IV. cap. ix. col. 714.]

[6 Pleaseth, Def. B.]

[7 Ὅσαι δὲ ἤδη πόλεις διὰ γραμμάτων βασιλικῶν τῷ τῆς μητροπόλεως ἐτιμήθησαν ὀνόματι, μόνης ἀπολαυέτωσαν τῆς τιμῆς, κ. τ. λ.—Concil. Calched. can. 12. in Concil. Stud. Labb. et Cossart. Lut. Par. 1671-2. Tom. IV. col. 762.]

[8 ... διὰ ταῦτα ἀσχάλλεις, ἀγαπητέ ;...ἀλλ' ὅτι τὸ τῆς πόλεως ἀφεῖλεν [βασιλεὺς] ἀξίωμα, καὶ οὐκέτι καλεῖσθαι αὐτὴν μητρόπολιν εἴασεν ;—Chrysost. Op. Par. 1718-38. Ad Pop. Ant. Hom. xvii. Tom. II. p. 175.]

[9 Cypr. Op. Oxon. 1682. Concil. Carthag. pp. 229, 30. See before, page 208, note 3.]

should have been some one which might have had the correction of the rest.
If therefore, when there was most need of this absolute authority, there
neither was nor might be any such, it followeth that, now we have a christian
magistrate, which may and ought to punish the disorders of the[1] ecclesi-
astical persons, and may and ought to call them to account for their faults,
that there should be no such need of an archbishop.

Jo. Whitgift.

You here fall into the same fault that a little before you
ascribed unto me, for you come back from the council of Antioch, which was *anno* 360, to the council of Carthage, being
anno 260.[2]   I omit to tell you that that council concluded an
heresy for the which only it was assembled.   And therefore,
though it be in the book of the Councils, yet is it not reckoned
among the councils.   Only I demand the words of that council
that do signify one bishop not to have had authority over another.   I told you before, out of Cyprian himself, and out of
Gregory Nazianzene, that he had ample and large jurisdiction[3].   The words of Cyprian in that council, which seem to
touch the matter you talk of, I have expounded and answered
before :   they make not for your purpose.

It is no reason to prove that a bishop must not be subject
to any, because " he is left at his own liberty to answer unto
God, and to make his account unto Christ."   For by the
same reason he might be exempted from the authority of the
civil magistrate, and from all laws and orders touching church
matters; and so might every private man in like manner.   But
you must remember that a bishop is so " left to his own
liberty to answer unto God, and to make account unto
Christ," that he must also acknowledge his duty towards
man, and be subject to orders and laws.

What do you say for the freedom of a bishop from obedience unto the archbishop, but it may be said likewise of his
freedom from subjection to his prince in like matters; and of
every anabaptist, for his deliverance from subjection to all
superiors ?   Wherefore you wring Cyprian's words to an evil
sense.

You have been oft told that no archbishop hath such

[1 All, Repl. 1 and 2.]
[2 According to Labbe and Cossart, these councils were held in the years
341 and 256 respectively.]
[3 See before, page 164.]

power over either bishop or inferior minister, that of his own
authority he can do anything against them. The laws of the
realm will not suffer it, no, the canon law doth by no means
permit it; and therefore you do but dream of an authority
that is not.

Cyprian being a metropolitan had authority over the rest.

The civil magistrate doth govern the ecclesiastical state,
punisheth disorders among them, calleth them to account for
their faults by archbishops, bishops, and other officers, as he
doth the same in the civil state by civil magistrates. Your
meaning is not (I dare say) to have the prince hear all matters
herself; you will give her leave to appoint under-officers; as
Moses, David, Salomon, Jehosaphat, and other good kings,
have done. If you will not allow the magistrate so to do, let
us understand your reasons; for surely I believe there is some
such toy in your head.

Chapter v. The Fifth Division.

T. C. Page 95, Sect. 3.

*The moderation of their authority in the ancient times may appear first
by a canon which is falsely given to the apostles, being as it is*

34. Can.

like a canon of the council of Antioch; wherein although it This canon is
falsified both
ordaineth one primate in every nation over the rest, and will not suffer by adding
and de-
any great matter to be done without him, as also will not suffer him to do tracting.
*anything without the rest, yet every bishop might do that which appertained
unto his own parish without him, and he nothing to do with him in it. But,* This you
add unto
as it seemeth, the meaning of the canon was that, if there were any weighty the canon.
*matter to be concluded for all the churches in the nation, then the bishops
of every parish should not enterprise any thing without calling him to
counsel. Now we see that the archbishop meddleth with that which every
bishop doth in his own diocese, and hath his visitations for that purpose,
and will take any matter out of their hands, concludeth also of divers matters, never making the bishops once privy to his doings.*

Jo. WHITGIFT.

If it be a false canon or "falsely given to the apostles,"
why do you use it as a proof? I might say unto you as you said
before unto me: Have you such penury of proofs, that you are
constrained to allege false canons? if it be a canon of the
council of Antioch, shew what canon it is: if it be within that

council, undoubtedly it is the 9. canon before by you alleged;
and how much that proves your cause the very ignorant
reader may judge.

But let us hear this canon, be it true or false, and consider your collections of it: the words I have recited before,
but I will set them down again, that your pithy reasons

(reasoning altogether against yourself) may appear. "The
bishops of every nation or country must know who amongst
them is chief, whom they ought to esteem as their head, and
do nothing without his counsel, besides those things only
which belong unto their own parish, and the places which are
under it; neither ought he to do any thing without the advice
of them all; for so shall there be concord, and God shall be
glorified by Christ Jesus in the Holy Ghost, &c.[1]" Here first
there must be a primate or chief bishop (that is archbishop)
of every nation or country, whom the rest of the bishops must
acknowledge as it were for their head. Secondly, the bishops
must do nothing unaccustomed without him. Thirdly, that
the other bishops may do those things only *quæ ad parochiam
ejus, et regiones ei subditas pertinent*: "which pertain unto
his parish, and places subject unto it;" which last words you
leave out. Last of all, that this primate must do nothing
without their consents. What hath the archbishop lost by this
canon? surely not one jot: I think verily he doth not require so much. Every bishop may do as much in his own
diocese now (the authority of the prince and her laws reserved)
as he might do by that canon; for the archbishop doth not
rule by will, but by law, not of himself, but under the prince,
to whom both he and all other bishops be subject.

You hit nothing less than the meaning of the canon; nay,
undoubtedly you imagine a sense contrary to the express
words of the canon.

When the archbishop doth visit, it is not to make new
laws, or appoint new orders (except he be commanded so to
do by greater authority), but to see those orders and laws
kept that all bishops and other are bound unto; and therefore
he doth nothing in their diocese contrary to that which they
are bound to do, neither doth he conclude anything without

[1 Canon. Apost. 33. in Concil. Stud. Labb. et Cossart. Lut. Par. 1671-2.
Tom. I. col. 32.　See before, page 145, note 4.　Conf. Concil. Antioch. can. 9. ibid.
Tom. II. col. 565.　See before, page 146, note 1.]

them, which by their consent and authority of the law and prince is not given unto him [2].

Chapter v. The Sixth Division.
T. C. Page 95, Sect. 4.

Platina, cap. *Higinus, or as some think Pelagius (I speak here as Platina*
Higin.
reporteth, not thinking that in Higinus' time there was any metropolitan), ordained that " no metropolitan should condemn any bishop, unless the matter were first both heard [3] and discussed by the bishops of that province [4] ;" at what time, and after a great while, a bishop was the same we call a minister. Now the archbishop will, without any further assistance or discussion by others, suspend him, and in the end also throw him out of his charge; and, if he have the same authority over a bishop as a bishop over the minister (as it is said), he may do the like unto him also.

A gross petition of the principle, or rather an untruth.

Jo. Whitgift.

This is another forged witness (such sound proofs the man hath that reproves other men for the like); and yet God knoweth his witness maketh nothing for him [5]. For who giveth authority to the archbishop to deprive either bishop or inferior minister, without due proof and examination of the cause? touching consent of other, if he deal with him according to law, then dealeth he with the consent, not of the other bishops only, but of all the realm; because that which is done by law is done by the consent of all that consented either to the confirming or making of that law. Your glances by the way, that "there was then no metropolitan," that "then the same were bishops which we now call ministers," because they be but barely affirmed, it shall be sufficient as flatly to deny

---

[2 Cartwright, for proof of the assumption of authority by an archbishop, refers to "the book of the 70. archbishops, where Canterbury is made the head of all our churches, all bishops sworn to canonical obedience of that archbishop, &c.," and goes on to enquire, "if the lord bishops are his vassals, the poor ministers what place shall they have?"—Sec. Repl. p. 644. Conf. Parker, Antiq. Brit. Eccles. Hanov. 1605. pp. 25, &c.]

[3 Harde, Repl. 1 and 2.]

[4 Instituit præterea ne metropolitanus episcopum provinciæ suæ alicujus criminis reum faceret et damnaret, nisi prius a provincialibus episcopis causa discussa et cognita fuisset. Sunt tamen qui hoc postremum Pelagio pontifici ascribant.—Plat. De Vit. Pont. Col. 1551. Higin. p. 17.]

[5 "The authority out of the counterfeit Higinus...maketh for us more than if it had been out of the true Higinus ; considering that the archbishop in the counterfeit Higinus' time, being grown much out of fashion, was yet girded in less room than ours."—Sec. Repl. p. 644.]

them, and for proof thereof to refer the reader unto that
which hath been spoken before.

Chapter v.   The Seventh Division.

T. C. Page 95, Sect. 5.

No such
thing in the
17. canon.

The council of Antioch ordained that, if the voices of the Can. 17.[1]
*bishops were even, and that if half did condemn him, and half
clear him, that then the metropolitan bishop should call of the next province some other bishops, which should make an end of the controversy:
whereby appeareth that the metropolitan had so small authority and power
over and above the rest, that he had not so much as the casting voice when
both sides were even.   And therefore it appeareth that, besides the names of
metropolitan, there was little or no resemblance between those that were
then and those which be now.*

Jo. Whitgift.

You have written in the margent the 17. canon of that
council, in the which there are no such words, nor anything
tending to that purpose : it is the 14. canon that, I think, you
Conc. Antio.
can. 14. mean ; for in that canon it is thus determined, that, "if a
bishop be judged for certain crimes, and it happen that the
other bishops of the same province vary in judgment, some
thinking him to be innocent, some guilty, for the resolving of
all doubt it pleased the holy synod that the metropolitan
bishop shall call for other judges out of the next province, to
end the controversy, who, together with the bishops of the
same province, shall approve that which is just and right[2]."
Here is no mention of equality in voices, but only of disagree-
ing in judgment among the bishops of the same province.
Likewise in this canon it appeareth that a metropolitan had
authority over more provinces than one, for he might call the
bishops of another province to decide the matter, if the bishops
of the same province could not agree.

The au-
thority of I see not how this canon can anything help you ; for now

[¹ This reference is not printed in Repl. 1.]
[² Εἴ τις ἐπίσκοπος ἐπί τισιν ἐγκλήμασι κρίνοιτο, ἔπειτα συμβαίη περὶ
αὐτοῦ διαφωνεῖν τοὺς ἐν τῇ ἐπαρχίᾳ ἐπισκόπους, τῶν μὲν ἀθῶον τὸν κρινό-
μενον ἀποφαινόντων, τῶν δὲ ἔνοχον· ὑπὲρ ἀπαλλαγῆς πάσης ἀμφισβητήσεως,
ἔδοξε τῇ ἁγίᾳ συνόδῳ τὸν τῆς μητροπόλεως ἐπίσκοπον ἀπὸ τῆς πλησιοχώρου
ἐπαρχίας μετακαλεῖσθαι ἑτέρους τινὰς τοὺς ἐπικρινοῦντας, καὶ τὴν ἀμφισβή-
τησιν διαλύσοντας, τοῦ βεβαιῶσαι σὺν τοῖς τῆς ἐπαρχίας τὸ παριστάμενον.—
Concil. Antioch. can. 14. in Concil. Stud. Labb. et Cossart. Lut. Par. 1671-2. Tom.
II. col. 568.]

neither the metropolitan, nor all the bishops in the province, archbishops
and bishops
less than in
times past. can deprive any bishop without the consent of the prince; so that in that point the authority of the metropolitan is nothing increased, nor yet the authority of the bishops. For then, as it appeareth in the 12. canon of that council, "if a priest Can. 12. or a deacon had been condemned of his own bishop, or a bishop of a synod, it was not lawful for them to complain to the emperor:" if they had complained, it was determined in the same canon that they "should never be pardoned, nor have any place of satisfaction, nor hope of restitution[3]." But now it is far otherwise. The 11. canon of the same council Can. 11. is much to the same effect[4]. Wherefore the authority of the metropolitan and other bishops is not increased, as you pretend, but both the metropolitan and other bishops had as much authority then over other priests, ministers, and deacons, as they have now; as appeareth by sundry canons of the same council.

In the 4. canon it is decreed that, "if a bishop con- Canon 4. demned by a synod, or a priest or a deacon condemned by his own bishop, shall take upon him to exercise any ministry, he shall be without all hope of restitution; and whosoever doth communicate with him shall be excommunicated[5]." In the 5. canon it is thus determined: "If any priest Canon 5. or deacon, contemning his proper bishop, hath separated himself from the church, and, gathering people apart, hath erected an altar, and hath not obeyed the admonition of his bishop, neither hath consented and agreed unto him, calling him back divers times, let this man be condemned, and deposed by all means, and let him not obtain any remedy afterward, because he cannot receive again his dignity. But, if he per-

---

[3] Εἴ τις ὑπὸ τοῦ ἰδίου ἐπισκόπου καθαιρεθεὶς πρεσβύτερος, ἢ διάκονος, ἢ καὶ ἐπίσκοπος ὑπὸ συνόδου, ἐνοχλῆσαι τολμήσειε τὰς βασιλέως ἀκοὰς, δέον ἐπὶ μείζονα ἐπισκόπων σύνοδον τρέπεσθαι, καὶ ἃ νομίζει δίκαια ἔχειν, προσαναφέρειν πλείοσιν ἐπισκόποις, καὶ τὴν αὐτῶν ἐξέτασίν τε καὶ ἐπίκρισιν ἐκδέχεσθαι. εἰ δὲ τούτων ὀλιγωρήσας ἐνοχλήσειεν τῷ βασιλεῖ, καὶ τοῦτον μηδεμιᾶς συγγνώμης ἀξιοῦσθαι, μηδὲ χώραν ἀπολογίας ἔχειν, μηδὲ ἐλπίδα ἀποκαταστάσεως προσδοκᾶν.—Ibid. can. 12. ibid.]

[4] Ibid. cols. 565, 8.]

[5] Εἴ τις ἐπίσκοπος ὑπὸ συνόδου καθαιρεθεὶς, ἢ πρεσβύτερος, ἢ διάκονος ὑπὸ τοῦ ἰδίου ἐπισκόπου, τολμήσειέν τι πρᾶξαι τῆς λειτουργίας, εἴ τε ὁ ἐπίσκοπος κατὰ τὴν προάγουσαν συνήθειαν, εἴτε ὁ διάκονος· μηκέτι ἐξὸν εἶναι αὐτῷ, μηδ᾽ ἐν ἑτέρᾳ συνόδῳ ἐλπίδα ἀποκαταστάσεως, μήτε ἀπολογίας χώραν ἔχειν. ἀλλὰ δὲ τοὺς κοινωνοῦντας αὐτῷ πάντας ἀποβάλλεσθαι τῆς ἐκκλησίας, κ. τ. λ.—Ibid. can. 4. col. 564.]

sist to trouble the church, let him be corrected by the outward power as a seditious person[1]." By these canons it is
evident that the bishop of every several diocese had authority
by himself to excommunicate, to deprive, and to seclude from
the ministry any priest, deacon, or any other of the clergy, in
more ample and large manner than he hath at this day. The
which thing also may be seen in the 6.[2] and 12.[3] canons of
the same council; so that you have sought for help at the
council which is one of the greatest enemies to this your
assertion, and doth flatly condemn it. Divers canons of the
which council, if they were practised, would soon remedy the
sects and schisms which you have stirred[4].

Chapter v.   The Eighth Division.

T. C. Page 95, Sect. ult.

Now, to consider how the bishops which are now differ from the bishops
which were in times past, I must call to thy remembrance, gentle reader,
that which I have spoken before, which was that then there was, as ap-
peareth out of Cyprian, and Jerome, and others, one bishop in every parish
or congregation; now one is over a thousand: then every bishop had a
several church, where he preached and ministered the sacraments; now he
hath none: then he ruled that one church (as I shewed out of Jerome) in
common with the elders of the same; now he ruleth a thousand by himself,
shutting out the ministers, to whom the rule and government belongeth:
then he ordained not any minister of the church, except he were first chosen
by the presbytery, and approved by the people of that place whereunto he
was ordained; now he ordaineth where there is no place void, and of his
private authority, without either choice or approbation of presbytery or
people. Then he excommunicated not, nor received the excommunicated,
but by sentences of the eldership and consent of the people, as shall appear
afterward; now he doth both. And thus you see that, contrary to the
word of God, he hath gotten into his own hand and pulled to himself both
the pre-eminence of the other ministers, and the liberties of the church which
God by his word had given.

Many un-
truths heaped
together.

[1 Εἴ τις πρεσβύτερος, ἢ διάκονος, καταφρονήσας τοῦ ἐπισκόπου τοῦ ἰδίου,
ἀφώρισεν ἑαυτὸν τῆς ἐκκλησίας, καὶ ἰδίᾳ συνήγαγεν, καὶ θυσιαστήριον ἔστησεν,
καὶ τοῦ ἐπισκόπου προσκαλεσαμένου ἀπειθοίη, καὶ μὴ βούλοιτο αὐτῷ πείθε-
σθαι μηδὲ ὑπακούειν καὶ πρῶτον καὶ δεύτερον καλοῦντι· τοῦτον καθαιρεῖσθαι
παντελῶς, καὶ μηκέτι θεραπείας τυγχάνειν, μηδὲ δύνασθαι λαμβάνειν τὴν
ἑαυτοῦ τιμήν. εἰ δὲ παραμένοι θορυβῶν καὶ ἀναστατῶν τὴν ἐκκλησίαν, διὰ τῆς
ἔξωθεν ἐξουσίας ὡς στασιώδη αὐτὸν ἐπιστρέφεσθαι.—Ibid. can. 5. ibid.]

[2 Ibid. can. 6. ibid.]   [3 Ibid. can. 12. col. 568.]

[4 Cartwright acknowledges that he mistook the number of the canon he cited,
but still insists upon his point, that the authority of metropolitans and bishops
was then greater than in earlier times.—Sec. Repl. pp. 645, 6]

Jo. Whitgift.

There is scarce one word of all this true; and surely I much marvel that you dare be so bold so manifestly to speak against your own conscience and knowledge. I have before sufficiently proved all that is here by you avouched to be clean contrary for the most part. It shall be therefore sufficient as briefly now to answer as you do propound, Demetrius was bishop of all the diocese in Egypt and Alexandria, *Euseb. Lib. vi. cap.* 1.[5] Cyprian was bishop of Carthage, Numidia, Mauritania, *Cyprian, Lib. iv. Epist.* 8.[6] Timothy being bishop had the government almost of the whole country of Asia; as Chrysostom declareth upon the 1 Tim. v.[7], and 2 Tim. iv.[8] Titus was bishop of the whole isle of Creta; as the same Chrysost. testifieth, *ad Tit. i.*[9] I have before, by sundry examples and testimonies, by divers councils, and especially the council of Nice[10], detected the vanity and untruth of this that is here affirmed, that is, "that there was one bishop in every parish and congregation;" and the words of Cyprian and Jerome be clean contrary; for they both make a difference between a bishop to whom the government of many pastors is committed, and a pastor that hath but one several flock or charge. For further understanding whereof I refer the reader to that which is spoken before.

The bishops have now as several churches to preach and minister the sacraments in as they had then. They have no more authority in government now than they had at that time, nor so much; and yet, if they had more authority than they either have now, or had then, I think it were more for the commodity of the church, the state of time[11] and conditions of men considered.

As for ruling every several church by those which you call elders, you have shewed no such thing out of Jerome,

Eus. Lib. vi. cap. 1.

Cypr. Lib. iv. Ep. 8.

Chrysostom.

Idem.

[5] Euseb. in Hist. Eccles. Script. Amst. 1695-1700. Lib. vi. cap. ii. p. 164. See before, page 164, note 7.]

[6] Cypr. Op. Oxon. 1682. Ad Cornel. Epist. xlviii. p. 91. See before, page 164, note 5.]

[7] Chrysost. Op. Par. 1718-38. In i. Epist. ad Timoth. cap. v. Hom. xv. Tom. XI. p. 637. See before, page 284, note 2.]

[8] Ἄξιον ζητῆσαι πῶς καλεῖ τὸν Τιμόθεον πρὸς ἑαυτόν, εἴγε ἐκκλησίαν πεπιστευμένος ἦν, καὶ ἔθνος ὁλόκληρον.—Id. in ii. Epist. ad Timoth. cap. v. [iv.] Hom. x. ibid. p. 720.]

[9] Id. in Epist. ad Tit. cap. i. Hom. i. p. 729. See before, page 285, note 3.]

[10] See before, page 141, &c.]   [11] Of the time, Def. A.]

neither can you. For Jerome, in that place you mean, by *presbyteri* meaneth priests[1], as he doth in all other places that I remember. Neither doth he there speak of particular parishes.

Touching the electing and ordaining of ministers, sufficient hath been spoken before[2]. The bishop doth nothing therein, but that which he may justly by the word of God, and testimony of the best and most worthy writers.

Of excommunication we shall speak hereafter; you do glance at it now out of place. And thus he that is an indifferent reader may understand that the bishops in these days in this church of England have no other authority than the word of God doth give unto them, the bishops of the primitive church have practised, the liberty of the church well beareth, and the state of the time and condition of men requireth.

Chapter v.   The Ninth Division.

T. C. Page 96, Line 7.

And, as for the offices wherein there is any labour or travail, those they have turned unto the other ministers; as for example in times Hispal. conc. can. 7.[3] *past it was not lawful for him that was then an elder to preach or minister the sacraments in the presence of the bishop, because the bishop himself should do it; and now those which they call elders may preach and minister the sacraments by the bishop's good licence, although he be present.*

Jo. Whitgift.

There is no just cause of complaint for most of the bishops in that behalf. For I think the time hath not been wherein there were more preaching bishops than are at this day in this church. But do you think that a minister may not preach or minister the sacraments in the presence of the

bishop? or do you so well allow of that council and canon quoted in your margent? It was the second council called

Hispalense concilium, it was not general, but provincial, celebrated *Anno Dom.* 659.: the contents of the canon by you alleged are these: " That a priest may not consecrate altars, but only the bishop; that a priest and *chorepiscopi*

[1 See before, pages 221, note 5, 225, note 7.]
[2 See Vol. I. pages 296, &c.]   [3 Repl. 1 prints *Concil. c.* 7.]

may not consecrate virgins, erect altars, bless and anoint them,
hallow churches, make holy oil," and such like, but only the
bishop. Likewise that "no priest may baptize, say mass, teach
the people, or bless them in the presence of the bishop[4]."
Surely this is a worthy council, and a notable canon, especially
for you to allege, that have so depraved other worthy writers
for some imperfections found in them.

But what doth it make for your purpose? They might The council alleged a-gainst him-self.
both preach and minister the sacraments in the presence of
the bishop, if he willed them; and so is the canon. This law
was made for the increasing of the bishops' pomp and dignity;
for no man might presume to speak or do anything in their
presence, without their leave and licence: so were they
esteemed then, and such authority had they. But, if our
bishops should claim the like, you would say that it were an
untolerable arrogancy and pride.

I would to God all those that be deluded by you would
consider your allegations, and the grounds of your proofs.
Surely I would be loth to allege any council of that time to
prove anything in controversy. Much more loth would I be
to allege so corrupt a canon; but lothest of all to allege that,
which should be so flat against my cause, and prove the
clean contrary to that which I affirm, as this doth in your
cause.

And here I have one thing to tell you, that divers of T. C. charg-eth the office with the fault of the men.
those things, wherein you would make this difference betwixt
our bishops and those of the primitive church, if they were
true, yet were they no faults in the office, but in the men; as,
for example, this which you here set down. Will you make
a difference in the offices of our bishops and those of old time,
because some of them do not preach? This compareth the

[4 Nam quamvis cum episcopis plurima illis ministeriorum communis sit
dispensatio, quædam novellis et ecclesiasticis regulis sibi prohibita noverint : sicut
presbyterorum, et diaconorum, ac virginum consecratio ; sicut constitutio altaris,
benedictio vel unctio: siquidem nec licere eis ecclesiam, vel altarium [al. altaria]
consecrare, nec per impositionem manus fidelibus baptizatis, vel conversis ex hæresi
paracletum Spiritum tradere, nec chrisma conficere, &c., neque coram episcopo
licere presbyteris in baptisterium introire, nec præsente antistite infantem tingere
aut signare, nec pœnitentes sine præcepto episcopi sui reconciliare, nec eo præsente
sacramentum corporis et sanguinis Christi conficere, nec eo coram posito populum
docere, vel benedicere, aut salutare, nec plebem utique exhortari.—Concil. Hispal.
II. can. 7. in Concil. Stud. Labb. et Cossart. Lut. Par. 1671-2. Tom. V. col. 1666.
In Labbe and Cossart the date assigned to this council is A.D. 619.]

men together, not the offices, except you prove that it is forbidden or unlawful for one of our bishops to preach. There
are other such like, which I omit[1].

Chapter v.   The Tenth Division.

T. C. Page 96, Sect. 1.

Mark how
this is proved.
*Now if you will also consider how much the lordship, pomp, and state-
liness of the bishops in our days differ from the simplicity of them in times
past, I will give you also a taste thereof, if first of all I shew the beginning, or as it were the fountain, whereupon the pomp grew, which was
when, instead of having a bishop in every parish and congregation, they
began to make a bishop of a whole diocese, and of a thousand congregations.*

Jo. Whitgift.

If the pomp began as you say, then began it in the
apostles' time; for then began they to make one bishop over
a whole diocese, as Timothy almost over all Asia, and Titus
over all Creta; as I have declared. Which order hath been
from that day to this observed throughout all Christendom;
as it may appear by that which is already said.

Chapter v.   The Eleventh Division.

T. C. Page 96, Sect. 2.

It is an
epistle of
pope Za-
chary to
Boniface, not
of Zachary to
pope Boni-
face.
An untruth,
as will ap-
pear.

In an epistle of Zachary unto pope Boniface it is thus writ-   Conc. To. 3.
ten: "It hath been oftentimes decreed that there should not be a   Epist. Zach.
bishop appointed in every village or little city, lest they should   Boniface.
*wax vile through the multitude;" whereby it both appeareth that there was
wont to be a bishop in every parish, and upon how corrupt and evil consideration one bishop was set over a whole diocese. No doubt those that
were authors of this had learned too well our old proverb, "the fewer the
better cheer;" but, the more bishops, the merrier it had been with God's
people.*

Jo. Whitgift.

This epistle was written by pope Zachary to one Boniface,
which was bishop in France, and not to "pope Boniface:"
moreover it is in the 2. Tome of councils; and you have quoted
in your margent the third. But to the matter.

[1 Cartwright rejoins that what he had " alleged out of the council of Hispalis
...is in a council supposed more ancient than the first Nicene," viz. that of
Neocæsarea, and declares that there ought not to be one unpreaching bishop, for
such a one was " a monster."—Sec. Repl. pp. 646, 7.]

You have not one word in that epistle to prove that there was wont at any time "to be in every parish a bishop." And you have falsely alleged the words of the epistle; for these words, "lest they should wax vile through the multitude," are not there to be found. The words of the epistle be these: "For you must remember what we are commanded by the old canons to observe, that we ought not to ordain bishops in villages and small cities, lest the name of a bishop should wax vile[2]." What one word is there here of placing bishops in every parish? Zachary telleth Boniface that it is according to the old canons that bishops should not be placed in such small cities, but in more ample and large cities; because the contemptibleness of the place doth oftentimes bring contempt to the person; and a bishop ought to be esteemed and reverenced. If you had read the epistle, you should have perceived that this Boniface had lately converted to Christianity *interiorem Germaniam*, and that he had ordained among them certain bishops to govern them, whom he desired pope Zachary by his authority to confirm, to whom pope Zachary answering willeth him to consider whether the places be so convenient, or the number of the people so great, *ut episcopos habere mereantur. Meminerimus enim* (saith he) *quid in sacris canonibus &c.*; as I have rehearsed them before. And a little after he nameth the places where he will have the bishops' seats to be. So that there is nothing less meant than that there was "in every parish a bishop;" forsomuch as there was there before no bishop in any parish; but this is all that may be gathered, that the seats of bishops were by the old canons appointed to be in the best cities, and most famous places; which to be true you may soon perceive in those canons themselves, mentioned here by Zachary: they are to be found, *Dist.* 80.[3]

[2 Sed tua sancta fraternitas pertractet mature, et subtili consideratione discernat, si expedit, aut si loca vel populorum turbæ talia esse probantur, ut episcopos habere mereantur. Memineris enim quid in sacris canonibus præcipimur observare, ut minime in villulas vel in modicas civitates episcopos ordinemus, ne vilescat nomen episcopi.—Zach. Papæ Epist. ad Bonifac. Episc. in Crabb. Concil. Col. Agripp. 1551. Tom. II. p. 454. Boniface was an Englishman, who became archbishop of Mentz.]

[3 Corp. Jur. Canon. Lugd. 1624. Decret. Gratian. Decr. Prim. Pars, Dist. lxxx. cols. 381, &c. The rubric of the distinction is: Loca vero, in quibus primates, patriarchæ, archiepiscopi, episcopi, presbyteri sunt ordinandi, hæc sunt secundum Lucium papam, et Clementem, atque Anacletum. See before, page 118, note 2.]

Chapter v.   The Twelfth Division.

T. C. Page 96, Sect. 2.

And they might with as good reason hinder the sun from shining in all places, and the rain from falling upon all grounds, for fear they should not be set by, being common, as to bring in such a wicked decree, whereby, under pretence of delivering the bishop from contempt, they sought nothing else but an ambitious and stately lordship over those which had not that title of bishop that they had, although they did the office of a bishop better than they did.   And what intolerable presumption is this to change the institution of God, as though he, which ordained not one only, but some number more or less of bishops in every church, did not sufficiently foresee that the multitude and plenty of bishops could breed no contempt of the office!   And it may be as well ordained that the children of poor men should not call them that begat them fathers and mothers, but only the children of the rich and of the noble[1]; lest that, if every man that hath children should be called a father, fathers should be set nothing by.

When or where did God ordain this?

Jo. Whitgift.

It is a marvellous matter that you delight to run so fast upon a false string: I tell you, once again, that you never read that epistle, neither yet those canons that it speaketh of. If you had read them, you would never have affirmed (if there be any modesty left in you) that "the multitude of bishops is alleged there as a cause of contempt," no such thing being mentioned.   The canons have a very good consideration, and be not wicked, but wise and godly.   This superiority of bishops is God's own institution, and it hath a necessary use in the church of God; as is shewed before.   It hath been, and may be abused; and it is, and may be well used.   All these glorious words of yours are but very words; and therefore, as words, I will commit them to the wind.

But one bishop in a city.

This one thing I cannot let pass that you say, "God ordained not one only, but some number more or less of bishops in every church."   What scripture have you to prove that there should be more bishops than one in one church?   What one example in all the primitive church have you to warrant this your assertion?   Nay, you have the whole practice of the church to the contrary, even from the beginning.   James alone was bishop of Jerusalem, Timothy of Ephesus, Titus of Creta, Clemens of Rome, &c.; and it hath been always counted as monstrous to have two bishops of one city, as to have two

[1 Of noble, Repl. 2.]

heads of one body.   But such bold assertions without proof
are meet principles for such a ruinous and tottering platform
as you dream of.

Chapter v.   The Thirteenth Division.

T. C. Page 96, Sect. 2.

*And here let us observe by what degrees and stairs Satan lifted the
child of perdition unto that proud title of universal bishop.   First, where
the Lord did ordain that there should be divers pastors, elders, or bishops
in every congregation, Satan wrought first that there should be but one in
every church: this was no doubt the first step.   Afterwards he pushed
further, and stirred up divers not to content themselves to be bishops of one
church, but to desire to be bishops of a diocese; whereunto although it seemeth that there was resistance (in that it is said that " it was decreed often"),
yet in the end this wicked attempt prevailed; and this was another step:
then were there archbishops of whole provinces; which was the third stair
unto the seat of antichrist.   Afterwards they were patriarchs of one of
the four corners of the whole world, the whole church being assigned to the
jurisdiction of four, that is to say, of the Roman, Constantinopolitan,
Antiochene, and Alexandrine bishops; and, these four stairs being laid of
Satan, there was but an easy stride for the bishop of Rome into that chair
of pestilence wherein he now sitteth.*

> *In what place of scrip-ture?*
>
> *Is not this soundly proved?*

Jo. Whitgift.

All this is as coldly proved as it is boldly affirmed; for
here is neither scripture, doctor, story, council, or anything
else, but *ipse dixit.* How prove you that "the Lord ordained
that there should be in every congregation divers pastors,
elders, or bishops?" The place of scripture (if there be any)
had been soon quoted.   Or how prove you that "Satan
wrought first that there should be but one in every church?"
Is it Satan's work that one church should have but one
pastor? This is strange doctrine, and far from an apostolical
spirit; contrary to the practice of the apostles, and of the
church even from the beginning.   But, seeing you have so
barely set it down without any kind of proof, I will pass it
over, by putting you to your proof.   But yet, tell me, did
Satan stir up Timothy and Titus, who were bishops of one
whole diocese? Did he stir up the other ancient fathers and
godly bishops of whom I have spoken? Whither will this
slanderous mouth reach? whom will this venomous tongue
spare, if it speak so spitefully of such worthy pastors?

> *Satan not the cause of one bishop in one church.*

Your collection of "resistance" that hath been to such superiority (being grounded of the place that you never saw nor read) is rash and unadvised. For if you had seen either that epistle or those canons you would (or at the least you might) have learned another lesson.

"Archbishops," "patriarchs," &c., were allowed by the council of Nice, the godliest and the most perfect council (since the apostles' time) that ever was. And did Satan rule there also and prevail? O that Arius were alive to hear it! These steps, whereof you make Satan the author, and whereby you say, "the bishop of Rome hath ascended into the chair of pestilence, &c.," have been the best and most convenient kind of government that ever was in the church since the apostles' time; approved and allowed by the best councils, and the next means to have kept antichrist out of his seat, if in all places they had remained in their full force and authority.

But this I may not pass over, that you in effect confess your kind of government by elders to have ceased before the council of Nice, and also one bishop to have been over one whole diocese before that time[1], in that you say that the child of perdition was lifted up by these degrees, the last whereof was allowed in the Nicene council.

Chapter v.   The Fourteenth Division.

T. C. Page 96, Sect. 2.

Having now shewed how this lordly estate of the bishop began, and upon what a rotten ground it is builded, I come to shew how far the bishops in our time are for their pomp and outward stateliness degenerated from the bishops of elder times.

Jo. Whitgift.

A man would have thought that you, being so great an enemy to those degrees, would not have thus concluded upon so small proof, and the same utterly untrue; using only for your ground the epistle of pope Zachary, which maketh nothing for your purpose. Now let us see "how far the bishops of our time are for their pomp, &c., degenerated from the bishops of elder times."

[1 Cartwright declares this assertion to be "utterly untrue."—Sec. Repl. p. 647.]

Chapter v.   The Fifteenth Division.

T. C. Page 96, Sect. 3.

And here I call to remembrance that which was spoken of the poor estate of Basil and Theodoret; and, if M. Doctor will say (as he doth indeed in a certain place[2]) that then was a time of persecution, and this is a time of peace, it is easily answered that, although Basil were under persecution, yet Theodoret lived under good emperors.   But that shall appear better by the canons, which were rules given for the bishops to frame themselves by.

Jo. Whitgift.

It is for lack of other examples that you are constrained to repeat these: to the poorness of Theodoret I have answered: there may be as poor bishops now as there was then; and there might be as rich bishops then as there are now.   It is not one or two examples that can prove the contrary[3].

Chapter v.   The Sixteenth Division.

T. C. Page 97, Sect. 1.

14. Canon. *It calleth it hospitiolum.*   *In the iv. council of Carthage it is decreed that "the bishops should have a little house near unto the church[4]:" what is this compared with so many fair large houses, and with the princely* 15. Canon. *palace of a bishop? And in the same council it is decreed that he "should have the furniture and stuff of his house after the common sort, and that his table and diet should be poor, and that he should get him estimation by faithfulness and good conversation[5]."*

Jo. Whitgift.

In the 52.[6] and 53.[7] canons of the same council, clerks, how learned soever they be in God's word, are willed to get their living by some occupation, or by husbandry; but I think you

---

[2 See Vol. I. page 378.]

[3 "I grant...that they may be rich; but I deny that they ought to grow rich by the ministry."—Sec. Repl. p. 648.]

[4 Ut episcopus non longe ab ecclesia hospitiolum habeat.—Concil. Carthag. iv. can. 14. in Concil. Stud. Labb. et Cossart. Lut. Par. 1671-2. Tom. II. col. 1201.]

[5 Ut episcopus vilem supellectilem, et mensam ac victum pauperem habeat, et dignitatis suæ auctoritatem fide et vitæ meritis quærat.—Ibid. can. 15. ibid.]

[6 Clericus victum et vestimentum sibi artificiolo vel agricultura, absque officii sui detrimento, paret.—Ibid. can. 52. col. 1204.]

[7 Omnes clerici, qui ad operandum validiores sunt, et artificiola et literas discant.—Ibid. can. 53. ibid.]

will not have them so to do now at this time.   Wherefore you
must consider the diversity of the time and state of the church.
If God hath dealt now more bountifully with his church in external benefits, if he hath put into the hearts of christian
princes thus to deal with the ministers of the word, and if
this state and condition be necessary for this time and people,
why should you envy it?   Riches and fair houses be no hinderances, but helps, if they be used accordingly; and commonly hypocrisy and pride lieth hid under the name of poverty
and simplicity.

Chapter v.   The Seventeenth Division.

T. C. Page 95, Sect. 1.

No such thing in that place.

*And in another council, that the "bishops should not give
themselves to feasts, but be content with a little meat[1]." Let
these bishops be compared with ours, whose chambers shine
with gilt, whose walls are hanged with cloths of Auris, whose cupboards
are loaden with plate, whose tables and diets are furnished with multitude
and diversity of dishes, whose daily dinners are feasts—let them, I say, be
compared together, and they shall be found so unlike that, if those old
bishops were alive, they would not know each other.   For they would think
that ours were princes; and ours would think that they were some hedge-
priests, not worthy of their acquaintance or fellowship.*

5. Canon. Concil. Tyronens.

Jo. Whitgift.

If you mean the first *Tyronense concilium*, there is no
such thing found in the 5. canon of it, nor in the whole
council.   The fifth canon containeth a profitable admonition
for you and such as you are; for it forbiddeth, under the pain
of excommunication, that any, being a clerk, should leave off
his calling, and become a layman[2].   If you mean the second
Tyronense concilium, I make you the like answer.   Belike
your collector hath deceived you; but what if it were so?   This
only might be gathered that, unless bishops then had been
wealthy, there should not have needed a decree against feasting.   If our bishops should make the like now, it would be

[1 Episcopum non oportere nimium profusis incumbere conviviis: sed parco et
moderato contentus sit cibo, &c.—Concil. Turon. III. can. 5. ibid. Tom. VII.
col. 1262.]

[2 Si quis vero clericus, relicto officii sui ordine, laicam voluerit agere vitam,
vel se militiæ tradiderit, excommunicationis pœna feriatur.—Concil. Turon. I.
can. 5. ibid. Tom. IV. col. 1051.]

thought they did it for sparing. And I think that, and such like canons, meet not only for bishops, but for all states and degrees of men.

Riches and costly furniture be no impediment to a godly man for doing his duty. And in such external things the condition of the time, and state of the country, is to be observed. Let our bishops be compared with them in truth of doctrine, in honesty of life, in diligent walking in their vocation, and in knowledge (I speak of the most in both ages), and I think the difference will not be so great, but that they may both know one another, and very well agree among themselves; this only excepted, that the doctrine of the gospel is now much more purely professed by our bishops than it was at that time by them; for both the councils are in sundry points very corrupt[3].

Riches no impediment to godly men.

Wherein our bishops may be compared with the old bishops.

Chapter v.   The Eighteenth Division.

T. C. Page 97, Sect. 2.

Can. 34.   *In the same council of Carthage it was decreed that " no bishop sitting in any place should suffer any minister or elder to stand[4]." Now I will report me to themselves how this is kept, and to the poor ministers which have to do with them, and come before them.*

Jo. Whitgift.

A poor quarrel: though this humility is to be required in all bishops, yet is it to be used with discretion; for thus to deal with a proud and haughty stomach were but to give nourishment to arrogancy and contempt. It is meet that every man have that honour and reverence given unto him which his place, his office, and his person requireth. And, as it is humility in him to remit any part of it, even so it is an

---

[3 Cartwright makes a long reply to the 16th and 17th divisions, in which he maintains that, as the word is " clerks " in the canons referred to by Whitgift, readers, door-keepers, &c., were included, who " having light charges in the church" might very properly be required to spend part of their time in labour. He also charges Whitgift with absurdity and untruth, declares that bishops, instead of devouring all themselves, ought to maintain " a college of scholars in their houses," and adds that it was the 3rd " council of Tyron," which he had referred to.—Sec. Repl. pp. 648, &c.]

[4 Ut episcopus quolibet loco sedens, stare presbyterum non patiatur.—Concil. Carthag. iv. can. 34. in Concil. Stud. Labb. et Cossart. Lut. Par. 1671-2. Tom. II. col. 1203.]

intolerable contempt and pride for those that be inferiors so
to look for such equality, that in the mean time they refuse to
do that which civility, good manners, and duty, requireth. But
let all men consider those notes and tokens of your haughty
stomachs, and persuade themselves that it would not be long
before you would challenge the same equality with other states
and degrees in like manner[1].

Chapter v.   The Nineteenth Division.

T. C. Page 97, Sect. 3.

*The bishops in times past had no tail nor train of men after them, and
thought it a slander to the gospel to have a number of men before and*
behind them.   And therefore is Paulus Samosatenus noted as
one that brought religion into hatred, and as one that seemed
to take delight rather to be a capitain[2] of two hundred than a bishop, because he had gotten him a sort of serving men to wait on him[3].   Another
example, not unlike, and likewise reprehended, is in Ruffine, of
one Gregory a bishop.   Now in our days it is thought a commendation to the bishop, a credit to the gospel, if a bishop have 30. 40. 60.
or more waiting of him, some before, some behind; whereof three parts of
them (set apart the carrying of a dish unto the table) have no honest or
profitable calling to occupy themselves in two hours of the day, to the filling
of the church and commonwealth also with all kind of disorders and
greater incommodities than I mind to speak of, because it is not my purpose.*

*He was re-
proved for
using him-
self like a
capitain,
being accom-
panied with
a guard of
soldiers.*

*Gregory, for
George.*

*Euseb. Lib.
vii. cap. 30.*

*Ruf. Lib. i.
cap. 23.*

Jo. Whitgift.

In Eusebius it is said that Paulus Samosatenus used to
walk publicly in the market-places, reading letters, and boasting himself, being accompanied with "a number of soldiers,"
some before him and some behind him, more like to a capitain
than a bishop.   If any of our bishops walk in the streets to

*δορυφορού-
μενος:
that is, ac-
companied
with spear-
men and hal-
berts.*

[1 " But what if the bishop being proud the ministers be humble; surely by
this reason it should be rather in their discretion to make the bishop stand before
them."—Sec. Repl. p. 654.]

[2 Captain, Repl. 1 and 2.]

[3 ... ὡς ὑψηλὰ φρονεῖ καὶ ὑπερῆρται κοσμικὰ ἀξιώματα ὑποδυόμενος· καὶ
δουκηνάριος μᾶλλον ἢ ἐπίσκοπος θέλων καλεῖσθαι· καὶ σοβῶν κατὰ τὰς ἀγο-
ράς· καὶ ἐπιστολὰς ἀναγινώσκων καὶ ὑπαγορεύων ἅμα βαδίζων δημοσίᾳ καὶ
δορυφορούμενος· τῶν μὲν προπορευομένων, τῶν δὲ ἐφεπομένων πολλῶν τὸν
ἀριθμόν· ὡς καὶ τὴν πίστιν φθονεῖσθαι καὶ μισεῖσθαι διὰ τὸν ὄγκον αὐτοῦ καὶ
τὴν ὑπερηφανίαν τῆς καρδίας.—Euseb. in Hist. Eccles. Script. Amst. 1695-1700.
Lib. vi. cap. xxx. p. 229.]

be seen, or stand in the market-places, or other open and Honour-able titles of bishops.
public assemblies reading of letters, accompanied with soldiers
and men of war, then may it be truly said of them that is The example of P. Samo. unjustly ap-plied to our bishops.
here truly spoken of Paulus Samosatenus. But, if they, being
far from such vanity, keep that countenance and retinue of
men, which their place, the manner of their country, the
honour of the prince, the state of the church requireth, then
do you uncharitably and unjustly apply this example against
them. But, unless Paulus Samosatenus had been rich and
wealthy, how could this pomp of his have been maintained?
Wherefore this example is rather against you than for you;
neither doth it condemn wealth and riches in bishops, but
pride, vain-glory, and lightness. For they accuse him of
spoiling the church, and thereby enriching himself.

In the example of George, whom you call Gregory, mentioned in Ruffine, there is no word spoken of any "serving
men," or soldiers; only he is there reproved, because "he got Ruffin. Lib. i. cap. 23.
his bishopric by violence, and thought that the office of
judgment in civil causes was rather committed unto him than
the priesthood. &c.[4]" If any bishop offend in the like with
us, it is the fault of the man, not of the office. By this example also it may appear that bishops in those days had riches
and authority; for this abusing of their wealth and authority
doth argue that they had both, which they might have used
rightly and well[5].

Chapter v.   The Twentieth Division.

T. C. Page 97, Sect. 4.

*And here I will note another cause which brought in this pomp and
princely estate of bishops; wherein, although I will say more in a word for
the pompous estate than M. Doctor hath done in all his treatise, yet I
will shew that, although it were more tolerable at the first, now it is by no*
Theod. Lib. v. cap. 8. *means to be borne with. In the Ecclesiastical Story we read
that the inscriptions of divers epistles sent unto bishops were*

[4 ... apud Alexandriam vero Georgius satis procaciter ut raptum episcopatum
gerebat ita ut magis sibi juris dicendi creditos fasces quam sacerdotium ministran-
dum religiosis officiis æstimaret.—Hyst. Eccles. Par. Lib. x. cap. xxiii. fol. 115. 2.]

[5 Cartwright rejoins that the answer as to Paulus Samosatensis is "frivolous,"
and that Gregory "entered as well as George, and before him, with a troop of
men into the bishopric."—Sec. Repl. p. 655.]

Honourable titles of bishops.

τιμιωτάτοις κυρίοις[1]. *We read also of* ἀσπαστικὸν οἶκον: *"house* Lib. eodem, cap. 18. *of salutations," which Ambrose bishop of Millain had*[2]. *As for the title of "most honourable lords," it was not so great nor so stately as the name of a lord or knight in our country; for all those that know the manner of the speech of the Grecians do well understand how they used to call every one of any mean countenance in the commonwealth where he lived* κύριον, *that is, "lord;" so we see also the evangelists turn rabbi, which signifieth "master," by the Greek word* κύριος: *"lord;" as likewise in France*[3] *they call every one that is a gentleman*[4], *or hath any honest place, "Monsieur;" and so they will say also, "saving your honour." Now we know this word "lord" in our country is used otherwise to note some great personage, either by reason of birth or by reason of some high dignity in the commonwealth which he occupieth; and therefore those titles, although they were somewhat excessive, yet were they nothing so swelling and stately as ours are.*

Jo. Whitgift.

Prov. xxvii.

The wise man saith, " Let not thine own mouth praise thee;" but you, for lack of good neighbours, or else for too too much self-love, oftentimes forget this lesson, as in this place.

The title of most honourable lord.

Howsoever " the Grecians used to call every one of any mean countenance in the commonwealth where he lived κύριον: lord," yet did they not use to call him τιμιώτατον κύριον: "most honourable lord;" for that title was only given to such as were of great dignity and authority; as it is in the place of Theodoret (by you quoted) given to bishops; and therefore you have made an objection which you cannot answer. This word "lord" doth signify pre-eminence and superiority, and, having this title, "most honourable," joined with it, it cannot but signify some great state and degree of authority.

Rabbi.

The same I answer to that which followeth. And yet rabbi was a name given *primariis hominibus, et honore aliquo præditis:* " to the chief men, and those which were endued with some honour[5];" and, in that the evangelists do translate it " lord," it is manifest that this name " lord," sig-

[1 Κυρίοις τιμιωτάτοις, κ.τ.λ.—Theod. in Hist. Eccles. Script. Amst. 1695-1700. Lib. v. cap. ix. p. 208.]

[2 Ἐπειδὴ δὲ τοὺς ἱεροὺς περιβόλους κατέλαβεν, εἰς μὲν τὸν θεῖον οὐκ εἰσελήλυθε νεών. πρὸς δὲ τὸν ἀρχιερέα παραγενόμενος, ἐν δὲ τῷ ἀσπαστικῷ οἴκῳ οὗτος καθῆστο, ἐλιπάρει λυθῆναι τῶν δεσμῶν.—Id. ibid. cap. xviii. p. 221.]

[3 So we see also the evangelists use the word κύριος to note a mean person; as when Mary, in the xx. of John, thinking that our Saviour Christ had been the keeper of the garden, calleth him κύριον. So likewise in France, Repl. 2.]

[4 That is gentleman, Repl. 1 and 2.]

[5 " That every reader in the church was called Rabbi, those know which have any skill in the tongue from whence it was taken."—Sec. Repl. p. 655.]

nified then a degree of superiority; but, having, as I said, Honourable titles of bishops.
this title "most honourable" added unto it, as it is in that
place of Theodoret, it cannot but signify some especial pre-
eminence, and therefore equivalent with the titles now used.
Master Calvin, upon the xx. of John, verse 16., saith that Calvin.
"Rabboni," which is there interpreted "master," is *nomen ...
non modo honorificum* : "not only an honourable name," but
also [*quod*] *professionem continet obedientiæ*[6] : "such as
containeth a profession of obedience."

But do the titles of honour and dignity given unto bishops Very honourable titles to bishops.
so much trouble your haughty stomach? Surely you are not
then of that spirit that the old ancient fathers were, who dis-
dained not to call bishops by as honourable titles as we do.
Look in Atha. his ii. Apol.; you shall there find the synod Athan. Apol. 2.
gathered at Jerusalem writing to the priests of Alexand. call
Athanasius sundry times *dominum*, not as by a common title,
but a title of dignity, *quum vobis restituit pastorem vestrum
et dominum comministrum nostrum Athanasium*[7] : "when he
shall restore unto you your pastor and lord, our fellow-minister
Athanasius." In the same Apol., bishops are called *domini
preciocissimi*[8] : "most excellent or worthy lords." And it is
evident in the same book, that there was no other title given
to the emperor himself; for there he is only called "lord;" and
so were other of his nobles in like manner[9]. So that in those
days it was not grudged at to give unto bishops the same
titles of honour that was given to the emperor and other
nobles. The name of "most reverend" is as much as the
name of "most honourable," and yet was that name also given
unto bishops in Athanasius' time; as appeareth in the same
book in sundry places. For Athanasius himself is called by
his priests and deacons *reverendissimus episcopus*[10].

Eusebius Nicomed., writing to Paulinus, bishop of Tyrus,
useth this style, *Domino meo Paulino, &c.* : "To my lord
Paulinus," To. i. Con.[11]   But what should I labour to prove

[6 Calvin. Op. Amst. 1667-71. Comm. in Euang. sec. Joan. cap. xx. 16.
Tom. VI. p. 175.]

[7 Athanas. Op. Par. 1698. Apolog. adv. Arian. 57. Tom. I. p. 175.]

[8 Ibid. 77. p. 193.]

[9 Ibid. 76, 80. pp. 193, 7. The word here used is δεσπότης.]

[10 Ibid. 73. p. 189.]

[11 Epist. Euseb. Nicomed. ad Paulin. Episc. Tyr. in Crabb. Concil. Col.
Agripp. 1551. Tom. I. p. 245. Conf. Theod. in Hist. Eccles. Script. Lib. i. cap.
vi. p. 22.]

the antiquity of such titles, which cannot be unknown to such as be learned? I had more need to declaim against the pride and haughtiness of such as do disdain to use them; but I will not spend paper in words.

Chapter v.   The Twenty-first Division.

T. C. Page 97, Sect. 5, 6.

And, as touching Ambrose' house, albeit the word doth not imply[1] so great gorgeousness nor magnificence of a[2] house as the palaces and other magnifical buildings of our bishops, yet the cause whereupon this rose doth more excuse Ambrose, who, being taken from great wealth and government in the commonwealth, giving over his office, did retain his house and that which he had gotten.

It was the house belonging to the bishop.
A heap of slanders.

But our bishops do maintain this pomp and excess of the charges of the church, with whose goods a great number of idle loitering serving-men are maintained, which ought to be bestowed upon the ministers, which want necessary finding for their families, and upon the poor, and maintenance of the universities. As for these riotous expenses of the church-goods when many other ministers want, and of making great dinners and entertaining great lords and magistrates, and of the answer to them that say they do help the church by this means, I will refer the reader to that which Jerome writeth in an epistle Ad Nepotianum Monachum[3], *where this is handled more at large.*   Ad Nepotia-num Mona-chum[4].

JO. WHITGIFT.

Ambrose' house within the bounds of the church.

Your answer for Ambrose his house hath no probability in it; for the words of Theodoret in that place do plainly declare that it was near unto the church, yea, *infra septa ecclesiæ:* "within the bonds or close of the church;" and therefore most like to be the house pertaining to the bishopric, and not any part of Ambrose his former possessions. For, if you remember, you said a little before, that it was decreed in the iv. council of Carthage, can. 14, that a bishop should have his house near unto the church[5]. But wise men can consider from whence such unlikely assertions without any shew of proof do come.

Bishops defended against the slanderous Reply.

Bishops build not these great houses "of the church's goods," but receive them as left unto them by such as were

---

[1 Employ, Editt.]   [2 An, Repl. 1 and 2.]

[3 Hieron. Op. Par. 1693-1706. Ad Nepotian. de Vit. Cleric. Epist. xliv. Tom. IV. Pars II. cols. 256, &c.]

[4 This marginal reference is inserted from Repl. 2, which has in the text *Jerome writeth in a certain place where &c.*]

[5 See before, page 381, note 4.]

far from seeking a spoil: they use them according to the laws of the land; and their number of men can in no respect be discommended, tending to the defence and strength of the realm, the honour of the prince, and their own honest and good education. Our bishops therefore use the goods of the church according to the first institution and foundation; and I doubt not but they use them to more profit both of the church and commonwealth than they should be used if your fancies might take place.

Your complaint "for ministers, for the poor, &c.", may be otherwise satisfied than by a spoil; for, if benefices were rightly used, the ministers of this realm are better provided for than in any country or age: yea, there are more sufficient livings for them besides the bishoprics than can be supplied with able ministers. The poor also are well provided for (God be thanked) by sundry means, if laws made for the same were duly executed, and hospitals with such other provisions delivered from unreasonable leases, and bestowed upon the poor according to their first ordinances. Wherefore this clamour of yours is nothing but the voice of an envious spirit proclaiming the spoil of the church, to the decay of learning, and bringing in of barbarism, if it be not in time prevented. *Provision for ministers. Provision for the poor. Whereunto the Replier's clamour tendeth.*

The "universities" are much beholding to you for your care over them; but what reasons have you used against the livings and houses of bishops that may not also be used against their lands and colleges? for in times past, when that council of Carthage (before by you alleged) was holden, there were no such colleges endued with such possessions as there are now. Neither are there (as I have heard) in Christendom the like colleges, and the like livings for students, as are in this realm of England. Wherefore, if such examples and conditions of countries, times, and persons, be sufficient to overthrow bishops' houses and lands, I see not how colleges can stand long after them; and therefore we pray you speak for yourself; we require not the help of so evil a proctor. Would you seek to maintain learning with the spoil of the church, and the diminishing of the reward of learning? *An non vides, quam pugnantia loqueris?* *The same axe is lifted against universities, that hacketh at bishops' lands.*

By that "epistle of Jerome *ad Nepotianum*" it appeareth that the state of the clergy was not then so poor as you would seem to make it. Jerome reproveth the abuses of his

The thing must not be condemned for the abuse. time, as covetousness, gluttony, gorgeous and costly apparel, with such like, which at all times are in like manner to be condemned.   But doth he that reproveth the abuse condemn the thing ? It is a fault by covetous or unjust dealing to wax rich ; but yet it is no fault to be rich.   Pride in apparel is to be condemned ; but yet every man may lawfully wear that apparel that is meet for his degree.   No man alloweth gluttony or immoderate feasting ; neither doth any wise man condemn a plentiful table and good housekeeping.   It is not good dealing to apply that which is spoken against the abuse of a thing, to the condemning and quite overthrow of the thing itself ; as you do the words of Jerome in that epistle.

Chapter v.   The Twenty-second Division.

T. C. Page 98, Lin. 2.

By this which I have cited it appeareth what was one cause of this excess and stately pomp of the bishops, namely, that, certain noble and rich men being chosen to the ministry, and living somewhat like unto the former estates wherein they were before, others also assayed to be like unto them ; as we see in that point the nature of man is too ready to follow if they see any example before their eyes. But there is no reason, because Ambrose This is before answered. *and such like did so, therefore our bishops should do it of the church's costs: nor, because Ambrose and such like did tarry in their trim houses which they had built themselves of their own charge before they were bishops, that therefore they should come out of their chambers or narrow houses into courts and palaces builded of the church's costs.*

Jo. Whitgift.

Where have you shewed any such thing by Ambrose his example ? or how doth it appear that by such means "the pomp of the bishops" (as you call it) was brought in ? That which you speak of Ambrose' house is most untrue : it was pertaining to the bishop, and no part of Ambrose his proper possessions, as it is evident by this, that it was near unto the church, even within the limits of the church ; as I have said before.

Chapter v.   The Twenty-third Division.

T. C. Page 98, Sect. 1.

Another reason of this pomp and stateliness of the bishops was that which almost brought in all poison and popish corruption into the church, and that is a foolish emulation of the manners and fashions of the idolatrous nations.   For, as this was the craft of Satan to draw away the Israelites from the true service of God, by their fond desire they had to conform themselves to the fashions of the gentiles, so, to punish unthankful receiving of the gospel, and to fulfil the prophecies touching the man of sin, the Lord suffered those that professed Christ to corrupt their ways by the same sleight of the devil.

Jo. Whitgift.

If it be enough to say without any kind of proof, then you have said something; but, if words without proofs be but light, then are these words so to be esteemed, and not otherwise.   I know the papists, through foolish imitation of the gentiles, have brought in sundry superstitions of the gentiles. But I speak of the matter we have in hand, that is inequality of degrees and authority among the ministers of the church, and the names and offices of "archbishop," "bishop," "archdeacon," &c.; which you neither have shewed, nor can shew to be brought into the church, by any imitation of the gentiles; and therefore you do still *petere principium.*

T. C. still offendeth in petitione principii.

Chapter v.   The Twenty-fourth Division.

T. C. Page 98, Sect. 2.

Euseb. viii. cap. 15.

Galerianus Maximinus the emperor, to the end that he might promote the idolatry and superstition whereunto he was addicted, chose of the choicest magistrates to be priests, and, that they might be in great estimation, gave each of them a train of men to follow them ; and now the Christians[1] and christian emperors, thinking that that would promote the christian religion that promoted superstition, and not remembering that it is oftentimes abominable before God which is esteemed in the eyes of men, endeavoured to make their bishops encounter and match with those idolatrous priests, and to cause that they should not be inferior to them in wealth and outward pomp.   And therefore I conclude that, seeing the causes and fountains from whence this pomp and stateliness of bishops have come are so corrupt and naught, the thing itself which hath risen of such causes cannot be good.

A wrong collection.

Luke xvi.15.[2]

[1 And the Christians, Repl. 2.]
[2 This reference is inserted from Repl. 2.]

Jo. Whitgift.

There is no such thing in that place of Eusebius quoted in your margent; for in that book and chapter of Eusebius he only sheweth that enchanters and sorcerers were greatly esteemed of Maximinus, and that he builded churches of idols in every city, and appointed idolatrous priests in every place, also that he placed in every province one to be chief over the rest, and furnished him with soldiers and servants[1]; but there is not one word that any christian prince took any example of him to do the like in christianity. It rather appeareth that Maximinus did in this point imitate the Christians, who had their metropolitans, and one chief bishop in every province, long before this time; as I have declared before. And I see no cause why you should say that Christians did follow the gentiles rather in providing for the ministers of the gospel sufficiently, than in building of churches in every city and placing ministers in them; for Maximinus did this as well as he did the other. This I am well assured of, that there is no such signification in that place of Eusebius, that any christian prince should follow this example. And therefore your conclusion, being collected and gathered of such false and untrue conjectures, must needs be like unto them.

I do not speak to maintain any excessive or outrageous pomp, but I speak of the degrees in the ecclesiastical state, and of the manners[2] and conditions of the persons, as they be now according to the laws and customs allowed in this church of England.

Chapter v. The Twenty-fifth Division.
T. C. Page 98, Sect. 3.

And thus will I make an end[3], leaving to the consideration and indifferent weighing of the indifferent reader how true it is that I have before propounded, that our archbishops, metropolitans, archdeacons, bishops, have

[1 Μαντειῶν γοῦν δίχα καὶ χρησμῶν, οὐδὲ μέχρις ὄνυχος, ὡς εἰπεῖν, τολμᾶν τι κινεῖν οἷός τε ἦν. οὗ χάριν καὶ τῷ καθ᾽ ἡμῶν σφοδρότερον ἢ οἱ πρόσθεν καὶ πυκνότερον ἐπετίθετο διωγμῷ· νεώς τε κατὰ πᾶσαν πόλιν ἐγείρειν, καὶ τὰ χρόνου μήκει καθῃρημένα τεμένη, διὰ σπουδῆς ἀνανεοῦσθαι προστάττων· ἱερέας τε εἰδώλων κατὰ πάντα τόπον καὶ πόλιν· καὶ ἐπὶ τούτων ἑκάστης ἐπαρχίας ἀρχιερέα, τῶν ἐν πολιτείαις ἕνα γέ τινα τὸν μάλιστα ἐμφανῶς διὰ πάσης ἐμπρέψαντα λειτουργίας, μετὰ στρατιωτικοῦ στίφους καὶ δορυφορίας ἐκτάσσων· κ. τ. λ.—Euseb. in Hist. Eccles. Script. Amst. 1695-1700. Lib. VIII. cap. xiv. p. 254.]

[2 Manner, Def. B.]   [3 Make end, Def. B.]

besides the names almost nothing common with those which have been in elder times, before the sun of the gospel began to be marvellously darkened by the stinking mists which the devil sent forth out of the bottomless pit, to blind the eyes of men that they should not see the shame and nakedness of that purpled whore which, in the person of the clergy, long before she got into her seat, prepared herself by painting her writhen face with the colours of these gorgeous titles, and with the shew of magnifical and worldly pomp. For the devil knew well enough that, if he should have set up one only bishop in that seat of perdition, and left all the rest in that simplicity wherein God had appointed them, that his eldest son should neither have had any way to get into that; and, when he had gotten it, yet, being as it were an owl amongst a sort of birds, should have been quickly discovered.

Jo. Whitgift.

And I also leave it to the judgment of the learned and indifferent reader, to consider by that which I have said before, how untrue all this is that you here affirm (I speak of these degrees and offices as they be now used in this church of England); if there be any difference, it is because they have not so large and ample jurisdiction and authority now as they had then.

Satan worketh by sundry means, and spareth no fetches to bring to pass his purpose. Under the pretence of zeal, he hath engendered sects and schisms; under the title of purity and perfection, he hath brought in heresy; under the cloke of simplicity, he hath spread abroad many kinds of idolatry and superstition; under the shadow of humility, he hath covered untolerable ambition and marvellous arrogancy; and, whatsoever he bringeth to pass, commonly he doth it under the colour of virtue, and of that which is good; and therefore I think that even under the names and titles of lawful degrees and calling he hath established unlawful authority; but neither is true zeal, purity, perfection, simplicity, humility, nor yet lawful degrees and callings, therefore to be condemned. *Vitia* (as Cyprian saith) *vicina sunt virtutibus*[4] : "Vices be very nigh unto virtues;" and the one laboureth to imitate the other; but we must not therefore the less esteem of virtue, but rather learn prudently to discern what is the difference betwixt the one and the other. If we have not learned this

The subtlety of Satan in counterfeit godliness must not prejudice that which is true.

Discretion is very necessary.

[4 The editor has not discovered this sentiment in Cyprian : it is, however, to be found almost literally in Augustine. Thus : ... omnibus virtutibus non solum sunt vitia...contraria...verum etiam vicina quodam modo &c.—August. Op. Par. 1679-1700. Contr. Julian. Pelag. Lib. iv. cap. iii. 20. Tom. X. col. 595.]

lesson, what state in the commonwealth, what office, what degree of person, nay, what kind of government, shall we allow? It is the greatest folly in the world to condemn the thing itself because of the abuse.

Chapter v.   The Twenty-sixth Division.

T. C. Page 98, Sect. 3.

A proper caveat.

But I have done; only this I admonish the reader, that I do not allow of all those things which I before alleged in the comparison between our archbishops and the archbishops of old time, or our bishops and theirs. Only my intent is to shew that, although there were corruptions, yet in respect of ours they be much more tolerable, and[1] that it might appear how small cause there is that they should allege their examples, to confirm the archbishops and bishops that now are.

Jo. Whitgift.

You do well to work surely; for now shall no man take any great advantage of your words; howbeit it had been courteously done to have let us understand what you allow of this you have written, and what you allow not. For, in leaving the matter so rawly, you will make us suspect that you have spoken you know not what.

Other things concerning the offices and authority of our clergy, of inequality of degrees amongst ministers, &c., dispersed in other places of the Answer.

Chapter vi.   The First Division.

Answer to the Admonition, Page 75, Sect. ult.

Some civil offices meet for ministers[2].

Concerning the offices of an high commissioner and justice of peace, how necessarily they be committed to some of the best and wisest of the clergy, what vice by them is bridled, what inconvenience met with, what necessary discipline used, those know that be wise, and have experience in public affairs and government. There is no word of God to prove why these offices may not concur in one man. But it is the commission that troubleth these men; as for peace they are at defiance with it.

Read more at large hereof in the second part[2].

[1] *And* is repeated, Repl. 1.]
[2] These marginal notes are inserted from Answ. 2.]

T. C. Page 98, Sect. 4.

Concerning the offices of commissionership, and how unmeet it is that ministers of the word should exercise them, and how that the word of God doth not permit any such confusion of offices, there shall be by God's grace spoken of it afterward.

Jo. Whitgift.

And, until that "afterward" be performed will I also defer that which is further to be said in this matter.

Chapter vi.   The Second Division.

Answer to the Admonition, Page 76, Sect. 1, 2, 3, and Page 77, Sect. 1.

To be short, they say that all these offices be plainly in God's word forbidden, and they allege Matt. xxiii., Luke xxii., 1 Cor. iv., 1 Pet. v.   The places of Matthew and Luke be answered before [4].   Christ beateth down Tract. i.[3] ambition, and pride, and desire of bearing rule, as he did before, when he said, "Be ye not called Rabbi," and, "Call no man father," "Be not called doctors;" he doth not condemn the names, but the ambition of the mind.

In the 1 Cor. iv., it is thus written: "Let a man thus think of us as of the ministers of Christ, &c."   The ministers of the word indeed are not to be esteemed as gods, but as the ministers of God.   Some among the Corinthians gloried in their ministers, and attributed too much unto them.   Hereof came these factions: "I hold of Paul, I of Apollo, &c."   This teacheth your adherents and disciples not to attribute too much to you, and such as you are, or any other minister of God's word.   It maketh nothing against the names or authorities either of archbishop, lord bishop, or any other that you have named, who be the ministers of Christ, and ought so to be esteemed.

The place of St Peter, cap. v., is this: "Feed the flock of God, &c., not as though you were lords over the flock, &c."   Peter here condemneth haughtiness, contempt, and tyranny of pastors towards their flocks; he doth not take away lawful government.   The pastor

[3 This marginal reference is not in Answ.]
[4 See Vol. I. pages 148, &c.]

hath rule and superiority over his flock, but it must not be tyrannical.

These be but very slender proofs that the names and offices of archbishops, lord bishops, &c., be plainly forbidden by the word of God.

Surely you had thought that no man would have ever [1] taken pains to examine your margent.

T. C. Page 98, Sect. ult.

To your answer also unto the places of St Matthew and Luke the reply is made before. The place of the fourth of the first to the Corinthians is well alleged; for it teacheth a moderate estimation of the ministers, and a mean between the contempt and excessive estimation; neither can there be any readier way to breed that disorder which was amongst the Corinthians, as to say, I hold of such a one, and I of such a one, and I of such another, than to set up certain ministers in so high titles and great shew of worldly honour; for so cometh it to pass that the people will say, "I will believe my lord, and my lord archbishop, whatsoever our parson say; for they be wise men and learned;" as we see it came to pass amongst the Corinthians. For the false apostles, because they had a shew and outward pomp of speech, they carried away the people. For, although St Paul saith that some said, "I hold of Paul, I hold of Apollo, I of Cephas," yet, 1 Cor. iv. 6.2 *as it appeareth in his fourth chapter, they held one of this brave eloquent teacher, and[3] another of that. For he translated these speeches unto him and his fellows by a figure. All that rule is tyrannical which is not lawful, and is more than it ought to be. And therefore the place of St Peter is fitly alleged; whereof also I have spoken something before.*

Jo. Whitgift.

The Corinthians did not burst[4] out into these factions and parts-taking in respect of any title or office committed to any of their preachers; but it was a partial affection that they had towards their teachers in preferring them (for their supposed virtue and learning) before other of whom they had not conceived so good an opinion. A more lively example whereof cannot be than the dissension that is at this day; wherein some of your fautors, forgetting all modesty, do so greatly magnify you and your companions, that nothing may be heard that is spoken to the contrary; nay, in comparison, all other men be flatterers, worldlings, unlearned, dolts, and

---

[1 Ever have, Answ.]

[2 This reference is inserted from Repl. 2; which reads in the text *as it appeareth in another place.*]

[3 *And* is not in Repl. 1 or 2.]   [4 Brust, Editt.]

asses. So do some sort of men extol you, and contemn other:
so did the Corinthians extol and magnify their false prophets,
and deprave the true preachers. Wherefore, to take away
this partial affection and judgment, the apostle saith, *Sic nos
æstimet homo, &c.* : "Let a man so esteem of us as of the 1 Cor. iv.
ministers of Christ, &c." You will not, I am sure, acknowledge that at this time among the Corinthians there was any
such difference of titles or degrees of superiority. Wherefore
you cannot (speaking as you think) say that the apostle in
this place meaneth any such matter. But well you wot that
these affections (which I have spoken of) were rife among
them; and therefore it is most certain that the apostle
laboureth for the suppression of them. So that the interpretation, that I have given of this place in mine Answer, is
true; neither have you refelled it.

The rule that a bishop hath over other ministers in his
diocese is "lawful," neither is it such "tyrannical rule" as
the word κατακυριεύοντες (used by St Peter, and spoken of
before[5]) doth signify, that is, to rule with oppression; and
therefore the place is unaptly alleged[6].

Chapter vi.   The Third Division.

Answer to the Admonition, Page 77, Sect. 1.

I am of Hemingius' opinion in this point, that I
think this your assertion smelleth of plain anabaptism[7].

T. C. Page 99, Sect. 1.

*You are, you say, of Hemingius' mind, and think that this opinion
smelleth of anabaptism. I have shewed how you have depraved and corrupted Hemingius, and desire you to shew some better reason of your
opinion. αὐτὸς ἐφή will not suffice us.*

Jo. Whitgift.

And I have shewed how untruly you have reported of
me. Hemingius alloweth superiority, and degrees of dignity
among the ministers: he condemneth your confused equality,

[5 See Vol. I. pages 163, &c.]

[6 Cartwright calls Whitgift's argument in this division "frivolous," and adds,
"I say to all this beside wandering and unlikely slanders there is not a word."—
Sec. Repl. pp. 660, 1.]

[7 See before, pages 326, 7.]

and calleth it anabaptistical. Moreover, if you well mark the beginnings and proceedings of the anabaptists, you shall perceive that they first began with the ministry in the self-same manner and form that you now do.

Chapter vi.   The Fourth Division.
Answer to the Admonition, Page 77, Sect. 1.

Anabaptism feared[1].

And surely, if you had once made an equality (such as you fancy) among the clergy, it would not be long or you attempted the same among the laity. Let them take heed : *Tunc tua res agitur, &c.*[2]

T. C. Page 99, Sect. 1, 2, 3.

You say that, if we had once obtained equality amongst the clergy, we would attempt it in the laity.

In what star do you see that, M. Doctor ? Moses saith Deut. xviii. *that, "if a man speak of a thing to come, and it come not to* 22.[3] *pass as he hath spoken, that that man is a false prophet:" if your prophecy come not to pass, you know your judgment already out of Moses.*

The Pharisees, when our Saviour Christ inveighed against Luke xxiii. *their ambition, accused him that he was no friend to Cæsar,* 2.3 *and went about to discredit him with the civil magistrate : you shall apply it yourself : you will needs make the archbishop, &c., neighbours unto the civil magistrates ; and yet they almost dwell as far asunder as Rome and Jerusalem, and as Sion and St Peter's church there ; so that the house of the archbishop may be burnt stick and stone, when not so much as the smoke shall approach the house of the civil magistrate.*

Jo. Whitgift.

Equality of ministers will pull on the equality of other estates.

In the " star" that is in your forehead, in the accustomed practices of the anabaptists, in the places of scripture alleged by the Admonition for the equality of all ministers, which very same the anabaptists do also use against the civil magistrate[4]. To be short, I see it in your own words, where you

Pag. 144. Sect. 1.

say that " the government of the commonwealth must be framed according to the government of the church ;" and what kind of government you would have in the church who knoweth not? I do not take upon me to prophesy, but *ex*

[1 Anabaptism to be feared, Answ. 2.]   [2 Horat. Epist. Lib. i. xviii. 84.]

[3 The last reference and the verse of the former are inserted from Repl. 2.]

[4 "...let the reader judge...what a cunning star-gazer the D. is, which saw in the star of my forehead that the Admonition intended the overthrow of the civil magistrate."—Sec. Repl. p. 661.]

antecedentibus colligo consequentia: " I gather that we shall have storms, by the black clouds." You are not Christ; neither is your cause like unto his; and therefore you make a very unequal comparison. To whom the name of "Pharisee" doth most aptly agree is shewed in my Answer to the Admonition.

The self-same reasons overthrow the civil magistrate that overthroweth the ecclesiastical. And therefore the fire kindled against the one must needs be very dangerous for the other.

Chapter vi.　The Fifth Division

Admonition [5].

Rom. xii. 8.　*Instead of the [6] seniors in* [r]*every church, the pope hath brought in, and yet we* [7] *maintain the lordship of one man over sundry churches, yea, over many shires* [8].

Answer to the Admonition, Page 116, Sect. 1, 2.

I have proved before, in my answer to your 13. and 14. reason, that this lordship of one man (as you term it), but indeed lawful jurisdiction over sundry churches, was not the invention of any pope, but of great antiquity in the church of Christ, allowed by that famous council of Nice, and practised since of most godly and learned fathers [9].

In the 9. canon *Concil. Antioch.*, it is thus written: *Per singulas regiones episcopos convenit nosse metropolitanum episcopum solicitudinem totius provinciæ gerere, propter quod ad metropolim omnes undique qui negotia videntur habere, concurrant, unde placuit eum et honore præcellere, et nihil amplius præter eum cæteros episcopos agere, secundum antiquam a patribus nostris regulam constitutam, nisi ea tantum, quæ ad suam diœcesim pertinent, &c.* [11]: "It behoveth the bishops in every country to know

Concil. Antio. [10]
One minister above the rest [10].

[5] Here again, as Cartwright quits the order of the Answer in his Reply, Whitgift follows him. This sentence of the Admonition, with a paragraph of the Answer in reply, here omitted, will occur below, Tract. XVII. chap. i. Div. 7.]

[6] These, Adm. and Answ.]　　　　　　　　[7] We yet, Adm.]

[8] Over many churches, yea, over sundry shires, Adm.]

[9] See before, pages 118, &c.]

[10] These marginal notes are inserted from Answ. 2.]

[11] Concil. Antioch. can. 9. in Concil. Stud. Labb. et Cossart. Lut. Par. 1671-2. Tom. II. col. 565. See before, page 146, note 1.]

their metropolitan bishop to have care over the whole
province; and therefore all such as have any business
must come to their metropolitan city; wherefore it
pleaseth this council that he also excel in honour, and
that the other bishops do nothing without him, according to the ancient rule prescribed by our fore-fathers,
but those things only which pertain to his own diocese,
&c." This council was about the year of our Lord 345.

T. C. Page 99, Sect. 4, 5.

*In the 116. page for the authority of the archbishop is alleged the
9. canon of the council of Antioch, which I have before alleged to prove
how far different the authority of the metropolitan in those times was from
that which is now.   For there the council sheweth that every bishop in his
diocese hath the ordering of all the matters[1] within the circuit thereof, and
therefore the meaning of the council to be that, if there be any affairs that
touch the whole church in any land, that the bishops should do nothing
without making the metropolitan privy; as also the metropolitan might
do nothing without making the other bishops a council of that which he
attempted; which M. Doctor doth clean leave out.*

*And, if this authority, which the council giveth to the metropolitan, being
nothing so excessive as the authority of our metropolitans now, had not been
over much, or had been justifiable, what needed men father this canon
(which was ordained in this council) of the apostles; for the seeking falsely
of the name of the apostles to give credit unto this canon doth carry with
it a note of evil and of shame, which they would have covered as it were
with the garment of the apostles' authority.*

Jo. Whitgift.

There is no canon that maketh more directly against you
than this doth; all the shifts that you have to avoid it I have
answered before.   There is as great "authority" given to the
metropolitan in that canon as now he either useth or requireth.   For every bishop, observing the laws of the realm
and of the church, hath the ordering of all matters within his
diocese; and the metropolitan in this church may attempt no
new thing, or any matter of great importance, not already by
law established, though he have the consent of all the bishops;
so far is he from having authority to do any such thing without their consent.

That canon of the apostles is repeated and confirmed in

[¹ All matters, Repl. 2.]

this council; as divers canons of the council of Nice are in like manner repeated and confirmed by divers councils following. This is so far from discrediting that canon with wise men, that it rather addeth great authority unto it; but you keep your old wont, in discrediting the authority which you cannot answer.

Chapter vi.   The Sixth Division.

Admonition.

Now then, if you will restore the church to his ancient officers, this you must do. Instead of an archbishop, or lord bishop, you must make ˣ*equality of ministers.*

ˣ 2 *Cor. x.* 7.
  Coloss. i. 1.
  Phil. i. 1.[2]
  1*Thess.i.*1.[2]

Answer to the Admonition, Page 123.

I have proved before that as well the name as office of an archbishop is both most ancient, and also most necessary in the church of Christ; and that this equality of ministers, which you require, is both flatly against the scriptures, and all ancient authority of councils and learned men, and the example of all churches, even from Christ's time; as more plainly appeareth by these words of M. Bucer in his book *De regno Christi: Jam ex perpetua ecclesiarum observatione, ab ipsis jam apostolis videmus, visum et hoc esse Spiritui sancto, ut inter presbyteros, quibus ecclesiarum procuratio potissimum est commissa, unus ecclesiarum et totius sacri ministerii curam gerat singularem; eaque cura et solicitudine cunctis præeat aliis. Qua de causa episcopi nomen hujusmodi summis ecclesiarum curatoribus est peculiariter attributum: &c.*[4] "Now we see by the perpetual observation of the churches, even from the apostles themselves, that it hath pleased the Holy Ghost that, amongst the ministers to whom the government of the church especially is committed, one should have the chief care both of the churches, and of the whole ministry, and that he should go before all other in that care and diligence; for the which cause the name of a

Marginalia:
Equality of ministers flat against the scriptures[3].

Bucer.

One governor among ministers[3].

[² These last two references are inserted from Adm. They are not in the original edition of the Admonition.]

[³ These marginal notes are introduced from Answ. 2.]

[⁴ M. Bucer. De Regno Christi Libr. ii. Basil. 1557. Lib. ii. cap. xii. p. 98. See before, page 231, note 6.]

26

bishop is peculiarly given to such chief governors of churches, &c."

[*The same Bucer, upon the iv. to the Ephe., saith thus: "Paul in the Acts calleth the same men bishops and ministers, when he called for the ministers of Ephesus to Miletum; yet, because one among them did rule, and had the chief care of the church, the name of a bishop did properly belong unto him: neither was his age always considered, so that he were virtuous and learned; as we have an example in Timothy being a young man [1]."*] [2]

Furthermore I have declared that it engendereth schisms, factions, and contentions in the church, and bringeth in a mere confusion, and is a branch of anabaptism.

T. C. Page 99, Sect. 6, 7.

And in the hundred twenty and three page, to that which M. Bucer saith, that in the churches there hath been one which hath been chief over the rest of the ministers; if he mean one chief in every particular church, or one chief over the ministers of divers churches meeting at one synod, and chief for the time, and for such respects as I have before shewed, then I am of that mind which he is; and, if he mean any other chief, or after any other sort, I deny that any such chiefty was from the apostles' times, or that any such chiefty pleaseth the Holy Ghost; whereof I have before shewed the proofs.

And, whereas M. Bucer seemeth to allow that the name of a bishop, which the Holy Ghost expressly giveth to all the ministers of the word indifferently, was appropriated to certain chief governors of the church, I have before shewed by divers reasons how that was not done without great presumption and manifest danger, and in the end great hurt to the church.

Jo. WHITGIFT.

M. Bucer's words are plain: there is no cause why you should make such "ifs," but only that you may be thought able to say something, how contrary to truth and reason soever it be. Your own bare denial of M. Bucer's judgment will weigh little with any wise or learned man, considering what difference there is betwixt your knowledge and his, the trial that hath been of him and the trial that hath been of you, his experience and yours. But what should I compare together things so unlike? That M. Bucer is directly against

[1 Id. Prælect. in Epist. ad Ephes. Basil. 1562. cap. iv. p. 107. See before, page 231, note 7.]

[2 This paragraph is inserted from Answ. 2.]

you in this assertion of yours, it doth not appear only in these words of his, but in others also, which he speaketh to the like effect, as in the iv. to the Eph.; as I have before declared. And again, upon the same chapter he saith: "The third part of discipline is obedience, which is first to be rendered of all to the bishop and minister, then of every clerk to those that be in degree above him, and to such as may help him to the well executing of his ministry. Last of all, of bishops to synods, and to their metropolitan bishops, and to all other, to whom a more ample charge of the churches is committed³." And, in the same commentaries, after that he hath proved, by sundry examples and apt reasons, that this superiority among ecclesiastical persons is convenient and profitable, and shewed that these degrees in the church, bishop, archbishop, metropolitan, primate, patriarch, be not only most ancient, but also necessary, he concludeth on this sort: "Because it is necessary that every one of the clergy should have their rulers and governors, the authority, power, vigilancy, and severity of bishops, archdeacons, and all other, by what name soever they be called (to whom any portion of keeping and governing the clergy is committed), should or ought to be restored, lest there be any in this order out of rule, and without government⁴." How think you now of M. Bucer's judgment? Is it not directly against you? be not his words plain⁵?

Bucer in 4. Ephe.

Idem.

Chapter vi.   The Seventh Division.

Answer to the Admonition, Page 124, Sect. 1.⁶

Your places quoted in the margent to prove that there ought to be an equality of ministers sound nothing that way. 2 Cor. x. vers. 7, these be the words of the apostle: "Look ye on things after the appearance? If any trust in himself that he is Christ's, let him consider

Scriptures wrested to prove equality of ministers.

[³ Id. ibid. p. 129.   See before, page 331, note 1.]

[⁴ Id. ibid. p. 133.   See before, page 331, note 2.]

[⁵ Cartwright persists that "M. Bucer is wholly for us," and says, "that, if there be any difference here (touching these offices) between us and M. Bucer, it is only that, where we affirm it good that the presidentship should be chosen at every meeting, as that which cometh nearer the apostles' example, and more safe against tyranny, M. Bucer may seem to make it a standing and continual office settled in one man."—Sec. Repl. p. 662.]

[⁶ This paragraph is placed, in Answ., after that in page 406.]

this again of himself, that, as he is Christ's, even so are we Christ's." How conclude you of these words your equality? I promise you, it passeth my cunning to wring out of them any such sense: rather the contrary may be gathered out of the words following, which be these: " For though I should boast somewhat more of our authority, which the Lord &c., I should have no shame." M. Calvin expounding these words saith on this sort:

Calvin. " It was for modesty that he joined himself to their number, whom he did far excel; and yet he would not be so modest but that he would keep his authority safe; therefore he addeth that he spake less than of right he might have done. For he was not of the common sort of ministers, but one of the chief among the apostles; and therefore he saith, If I boast more, I need not be ashamed, for I have good cause [1]." And a little

Degrees of honour in the ministry. after: *Quamvis enim commune sit omnibus verbi ministris idemque officium, sunt tamen honoris gradus*[2]: "Although the self-same office be common to all the ministers of the word, yet there be[3] degrees of honour."

Thus you see Calvin far otherwise to gather of this place than you do.

T. C. Page 100, Sect. 1.

And, if M. Doctor delight thus to oppose men's authority to the authority of the Holy Ghost, and to the reasons which are grounded out of the scripture, M. Calvin doth openly mislike of the making of that name proper and peculiar to certain, which the Holy Ghost maketh common to more.

Here he defendeth not the Admonition, but shifteth it off by cavilling. *And, where as of M. Calvin's words which saith that " there be degrees of honour in the ministry," M. Doctor would gather an archbishop, if he had understanded that an apostle is above an evangelist, an evangelist above a pastor, a pastor above a doctor, and he above an elder that ruleth only, he needed never have[4] gone to the popish hierarchy to seek his diversities of degrees, which he might have found in St Paul. And, whereas upon M. Calvin's words, which saith that Paul was " one of the chief amongst the apostles," he would seem to conclude an archbishop amongst the bishops, he*

[1 Modestiæ fuit quod se adjunxit eorum numero, quos longe antecellebat: neque tamen ita modestus esse voluit, quin suam auctoritatem salvam retineret: ideo addit, minus dixisse, quam jure suo potuerit. neque enim erat ex vulgari ordine ministrorum, sed eximius etiam inter apostolos. Dicit ergo, Etiamsi amplius glorier, *non pudefiam*: erit enim justa materia.—Calvin. Op. Amst. 1667-71. Comm. in Epist. II. ad Corinth. cap. x. 8. Tom. VII. p. 261.]

[2 Id. ibid.]   [3 Is, Answ. and Def. A.]

[4 Never to have, Repl. 2.]

should have remembered that St Paul's chiefly amongst the apostles con-
sisted, not in having any authority or dominion over the rest, but in labour-
ing and suffering more than the rest, and in gifts more excellent than the
rest.

Jo. Whitgift.

I do not "oppose men's authority to the authority of the
Holy Ghost, and to the reasons which are grounded out of the
scripture;" but I oppose them to your authority, and to your
reasons, who spurn against that order which the Holy Ghost
hath placed in the church, and most shamefully abuse the
scripture to maintain your errors: an example whereof is this
present text alleged by the Admonition, which you pass over
in silence, condemning thereby their lewdness in abusing the
same. It is you and yours that abuse the name and authority
of the Holy Ghost: it is you that wring and wrest the
scriptures untolerably: it is you that falsify authorities of
learned men, and corruptly allege them: it is you, I say,
that deprave and discredit such writers as have been and be
notable instruments in the church of Christ; and all this you
do to maintain your erroneous opinions and false doctrine,
wherewith you endeavour to subvert this church of England.

M. Calvin's words be plain, and they directly overthrow
your equality of ministers, and shew the fondness of the Admonition in alleging that place of scripture to prove any such
equality. M. Calvin's words be these: *Quamvis commune sit*
omnibus verbi ministris idemque officium, sunt tamen honoris
gradus: "Although the self-same office be common to all the
ministers of the word, yet there are degrees of honour." Which
words disprove the equality of ministers by the Admonition
affirmed, and confirmed with this portion of scripture by
M. Calvin here interpreted, that is, 2 Cor. x. verse 7.

If there were degrees of honour in the apostles' time
among those which had *idem officium:* "the self-same office,"
as M. Calvin affirmeth, why should there not be so now likewise? But will you see how unlike you are unto yourself,
even in these few lines? first you say that M. Calvin's mean- T. C. con-
ing is "that an apostle is above an evangelist, an evangelist trary to
is above a pastor, &c.," and by and by after you confess that himself.
there was "chiefly even among the apostles, but it consisted
in labouring and suffering more than the rest, and in gifts
more excellent than the rest."

To omit these contrarieties of yours, into the which the plainness of Master Calvin's words hath driven you, this inequality that you confess to have been in these offices (which notwithstanding you speak of your own head, without any warrant of God's word) argueth that there may be superiority among the ministers of the church. And the degrees of honour that you acknowledge to have been among the apostles quite casteth down your confused equality. As for your salving the matter in saying that " this chiefty among the apostles consisted not in having any superiority above the rest, but in labouring, &c.;" it may please unskilful persons, but it will not satisfy men of discretion and wisdom. For it is to be thought that every one of the apostles laboured in their calling to the uttermost of their powers, that they suffered whatsoever God laid upon them, that they had all gifts most abundantly necessary for their functions. Wherefore in all these things there was *summa æqualitas*, and no man sought such pre-eminence, or received it being offered unto him; but according to their own doctrine every one thought of another better than of himself. Wherefore it could not be for this respect, but it was for order and policy to avoid confusion.

I have told you before why you labour so much to have honour and dignity distributed according to the excellency of gifts; for then you persuade yourself that the chiefty would light on your own neck; but you may peradventure be deceived.

Chapter vi. The Eighth Division.

Answer to the Admonition, Page 123, towards the end[1].

Why the Admonitors desireequality[2]. And now I add, that you desire this equality, not because you would not rule (for it is manifest that you seek it most ambitiously in your manner), but because you contemn and disdain to be ruled, and to be in subjection. Indeed your meaning is (as I said before) to rule and not to be ruled, to do what you list in your several cures, without controlment of prince, bishop, or any other. And therefore, pretending equality, most disorderly you seek dominion. I speak that I know by experience in some of you.

[1 See before, page 403, note 6.]   [2 This marginal note is not in Answ.]

T. C. Page 100, Sect. 2, 3.

Now, whereas he saith that we desire to pull the rule from others, that the rule might be in our hands, and we might do what we list, and that we seek to withdraw ourselves from controlment of prince and bishop, and all; first, he may learn, if he will, that we desire no other authority than that which is to the edifying of the church, and which is grounded of the word of God; which if any minister shall abuse to his gain or ambition, then he ought to abide not only the controlment of the other ministers, yea, of the brethren, but also further the punishment of the magistrates, according to the quantity of the fault.

And, seeing you charge the brethren so sore, you must be put in remembrance that this unreasonable authority over the rest of the ministers and clergy came to the bishops and archbishops, when as the pope did exempt his shavelings from the obedience, subjection, and jurisdiction of princes[3]. Now therefore that we be ready to give that subjection unto the prince, and offer ourselves to the prince's correction in things wherein we shall do amiss, do you think it an unreasonable thing that we desire to be disburdened of the bishops' and archbishops' yoke, which the pope hath laid upon our necks?

An untruth; for the lawful authority of bishops and archbishops was long before.

Jo. Whitgift.

Your answer maketh the matter more suspicious; for this authority you speak of, which you say "is to the edifying of the church, and grounded of the word of God," is as it pleaseth you to interpret it. For whatsoever you fancy, and whatsoever authority you usurp, shall have the same pretence; and, if the prince seek to restrain you, or to break your will, you and your seniors will excommunicate her if she be of your parish. Furthermore, the greatest pre-eminence she can have is to be one of your seigniory; and then must M. Pastor be the chief, and so in authority above the prince, and consequently a pope; but of this more in due place shall be spoken.

Excessive authority is sought under pretence of equality.

This authority, which the bishops and archbishops now exercise, came first from the apostolical church, then from the example of the primitive church for the space of five hundred years after the apostles' time; thirdly, from the councils of Nice, Antioch, Constantinople, and all the best and purest councils that ever were; and, last of all, from the authority of the prince, and by the consent of this whole church and realm of England, and therefore not from the pope, who hath rather diminished it (by taking all to himself) than in any respect increased it. Wherefore you also, in exempting your-

The authority of bishops and archbishops came not from the pope.

[3 Of the princes, Repl. 1 and 2.]

self from the authority and jurisdiction of the archbishop and bishop, resist God in his ministers, the prince in her officers, and the laws of the church and realm in their executors. And, as for your protested obedience, it is so enwrapped with conditions and provisos (as in other places of your book more plainly appeareth), that when it should come to the trial (if your platform were builded) it would prove as little as ever the popish bishops' was, in their greatest pride.

Chapter vi.   The Ninth Division.
Answer to the Admonition, Page 124, Sect. 2.

The place in the first to the Coloss. vers. 1, is this: "Paul an apostle of Jesus Christ by the will of God, and Timotheus our brother." Surely your mind was not of equality (I think) when you quoted these places to prove it. But it is your usual manner without all discretion and judgment to dally and play with the scriptures. For what sequel is there in this reason: Paul calleth Timothy brother; *ergo,* in all respects there must be equality? As though there were not[2] distinction of degrees even among brethren.

A weak proof[1].

Jo. WHITGIFT.

Magis mutus quam piscis, and by his silence the oversight confessed.

Chapter vi.   The Tenth Division.
Admonition.
[The fourteenth.

Their pontifical (which is annexed to the book of common prayer, and whereunto subscribing to the articles we must subscribe also), whereby they consecrate bishops, make ministers and deacons, is nothing else but a thing word for word drawn out of the pope's pontifical, wherein he sheweth himself to be antichrist most lively][3].

And, [g] *as the names of archbishops, archdeacons, lord bishops, chancellors, &c., are drawn out of the pope's shop, together with their offices, so the government which they use by the life of the pope, which is the canon law, is antichristian and devilish, and contrary to the scriptures.*

[g] Luke xxii. 25, 26. 1 Pet. v. 3, 4, 5. Matth. xx. 25, 26. Mat xxiii. 8, 11, 12. Gal. ii. 6. Hebr. v. 4. Luke xvi. 25. Ezek. xxxiv. 4. 2 Cor. i. 24.

[1 This marginal note is inserted from Answ. 2.]   [2 No, Answ. 2.]
[3 Here again Cartwright takes up quite a different part of Whitgift's Answer. This portion of Admonition and that below of Answer between the brackets are inserted from Answ.]

Answer to the Admonition, Page 208, Sect. 1.

[Now that you have spit out all your poison against the communion book, and poured down all your reasons, you come to the "pontifical," as you term it, that is, the book containing the order and manner of making of ministers, &c.: "this book," you say, "is word for word drawn out of the pope's pontifical, &c." Surely, if those things which were good in the pope's pontifical, and either contained in the scripture, or well used before in the ancient church, or well prescribed by general councils, be also in our pontifical, our pontifical is never the worse for having of them; for, if the thing itself be good and profitable, it forceth not from whom it was taken, or of whom it was used, so that now it be rightly used. But it is most false and untrue that the book of ordering ministers and deacons, &c., now used, is "word for word drawn out of the pope's pontifical," being almost in no point correspondent to the same; as you might have seen, if you had compared them together. But ignorance and rashness drives you into many errors.] The pope's pontifical not followed in the church.

Both of the names and also of the offices of arch- Scriptures wrested. bishops, archdeacons, lord bishops, &c., I have spoken before sufficiently, and fully answered those[4] places quoted in this margent, saving the ii. to the Galat. the v. to the Hebrews, Ezek. xxxiv., 2 Cor. i.; for these places have been found out since, and thought meet now to be alleged; but how discreetly by examination it will appear. The words of the apostle to the Galat. ii. verse 6 be these: "And of them which seemed to be great I was not taught (what they were in time passed, it maketh no matter to me, God accepteth no man's person); nevertheless they that are the chief did communicate nothing with me." The apostle in these words doth declare that he received not the gospel which he preached of men, no, not of the apostles, but of Jesus Christ, and that the gospel preached by him ought to be no less credited than the gospel preached by them. So that in those words he declareth that the truth of the doctrine doth not depend of any man's person. He

[[4] These, Answ.]

speaketh nothing against superiority, *quoad ordinem :* "concerning order," but doth rather acknowledge it; for he saith, "they that are the chief, &c." But it is true that Master Calvin noteth on this place: *Hic non est certamen ambitionis, quia nequaquam de personis agitur*[1] : "The contention is not for ambition, for it is not understanded of the persons." Now, I pray you, consider this argument : Paul received the gospel that he preached, not of the apostles, but of Christ; or : The gospel preached by Paul is equivalent with the gospel preached by other of the apostles; therefore "the names of archbishops, archdeacons, &c. are drawn out of the pope's shop together with their offices;" or this : Paul saith that they that were the chief did communicate nothing with him; *ergo*, "the names and offices of archbishops be taken out of the pope's shop."

T. C. Page 100, Sect. 4.

*And in the 207. page unto the midst of the 214. page, this matter is again handled; where first M. D*e*ctor would draw the place of Galatians*

the second *to prove an archbishop, and that by a false translation; for* οἱ δοκοῦντες, *which is, "they that seemed or appeared," he hath translated "they that are the chief;" and, although the place of the Galatians may be thought of some not so pregnant, nor so full against the archbishop, yet all must needs confess that it maketh more against him, than for him. For St Paul's purpose is to prove there that he was not inferior to any of the apostles; and bringeth one argument thereof, that he had not his gospel from them, but from Christ immediately; and therefore, if the apostles that were esteemed most of, and supposed by the Galatians and others to be the chief, had no superiority over St Paul, but were equal with him, it followeth that there was none that had rule over the rest. And, if there needed no one of the apostles to be ruler over the rest, there seemeth to be no need that one bishop should rule over the rest.*

This is an untruth; for it is only proved that the place is not against the archbishop, &c. Here you rashly accuse the translation of the bible printed at Geneva, and others.

Jo. Whitgift.

I have set down the words of the apostle as they be translated in the English bible printed at Geneva[2], not altering one tittle; and therefore, if there be any falsehood in the translation, it is in that bible, not in me. How truly you *οἱ δοκοῦν-* have translated οἱ δοκοῦντες, saying it signifieth "they that *τες trans-lated.*

[1 Calvin. Op. Amst. 1667-71. Comm. in Epist. ad Galat. cap. ii. 6. Tom. VII. p. 286.]

[2 See The Bible transl. according to the Ebrew and Greeke, Lond. 1578. Galat. chap. ii. v. 6. fol. 82.]

seemed or appeared," let the reader judge after he hath
considered these words of M. Beza upon the same words[3], *ad*
Galat. ii. verse 2 : "With those that are of reputation : τοῖς Beza.
δοκοῦσι, that is, τοῖς εὐδοκιμοῦσι, 'those which are well-esteemed
of,' the contrary whereof are οἱ ἀδοξοῦντες, 'they which are
without renown or estimation :' the common translation hath
'which seemed to be something,' τοῖς δοκοῦσι εἶναί τι ; which is
contrary to all our books, and unto Jerome's interpretation
also.   For thus he writeth, which thing Erasmus also doth
well note : ' I did very carefully search,' saith he, ' what that
should be that he said, *qui videbantur :* they which seemed.
But he hath taken away all doubt in that he addeth, *Qui*
videbantur esse columnæ : they which were accounted to
be pillars.' Hitherto Hierome ; whereby he doth evidently
declare that he had not read in this place εἶναί τι ; but in
such sort, notwithstanding, that he seemeth not to have
known τοὺς δοκοῦντας to have been called of the Grecians
absolutely τοὺς εὐδοκιμοῦντας, that is, 'those who are of great
estimation with all men.' And this ignorance of the Greek
tongue, as I think, was the cause that the old interpreter
(being more bolder than Hierome) did add *aliquid esse*[4]."
And Erasmus, in his annotations upon the same place, agreeth
with M. Beza herein : "δοκοῦντες,…*absolute dicuntur Græcis* Erasmus.
qui magnæ sunt auctoritatis[5] : "They which are of great
authority are of the Grecians absolutely called δοκοῦντες."
Budeus also saith that the apostle in this place taketh this Budeus.
word δοκῶ for ἔνδοξός εἰμι[6].   And both M. Beza himself and

[3 Word, Def. A.]

[4 Cum iis qui sunt in pretio, τοῖς δοκοῦσι. id est τοῖς εὐδοκιμοῦσι. quibus
opponuntur οἱ ἀδοξοῦντες. Vulg. Qui videbantur aliquid esse, τοῖς δοκοῦσιν
εἶναί τι, contra omnium nostrorum codicum fidem, et repugnante etiam Hieronymi
interpretatione.   Sic enim scribit, (quod et recte expendit Eras.) Solicitus, inquit,
requirebam quidnam esset quod diceret, Qui videbantur : sed nunc me omni
scrupulo liberavit, adjiciens, Qui videbantur columnæ esse.   Hæc Hieronymus
[Hieron. Op. Par. 1693-1706. Comm. Lib. ı. in Epist. ad Galat. cap. ii. Tom.'IV.
Pars ı. col. 241.], satis declarans se non legisse hoc in loco εἶναί τι. sed ita tamen
ut non videatur cognovisse τοὺς δοκοῦντας a Græcis vocari absolute τοὺς εὐδοκιμοῦντας. i. quorum apud omnes præclara est existimatio. Eadem (ut opinor) Græci
sermonis imperitia fecit ut vetus interpres, Hieronymo audacior, aliquid esse,
adjiceret.—Nov. Test. cum Interp. et Annot. Th. Bezæ, H. Steph. 1565. Epist.
ad Galat. cap. ii. v. 2. pp. 351, 2.]

[5 Erasm. Op. L. Bat. 1703-6. Adnot. in Epist. ad Galat. cap. ii. v. 2. Tom.
VI. col. 805.]

[6 Est etiam δοκῶ τὸ ἔνδοξος ϊγίνομαι, cui ἀδοξῶ opponitur,…Apostolus hoc
verbo usus est, ἐμοὶ γὰρ οἱ δοκοῦντες οὐδὲν προσανέθεντο, mecum enim ii qui

Erasmus translate it as it is in the Geneva bible. Wherefore here your cunning faileth you; and you had not well considered the matter before you entered this accusation of falsifying[1].

The true sense and meaning of this place to the Galat. I have set down in my Answer; and it is according to the interpretation of the best writers, justified by the words of M. Calvin there alleged, and not confuted by you. Wherefore the conclusion remaineth as it did.

That there was superiority among the apostles, *ordinis et politiœ causa*, I have shewed before.

This place to the Galatians is not brought in by me to prove the authority of the archbishop (although it might well be alleged to prove degrees of honour in the ministry), but it is quoted in the Admonition fondly and foolishly, to prove that the "names of archbishops, archdeacons, lord bishops, &c., are drawn out of the pope's shop, together with their offices." And of this dallying with the scriptures you speak not one word; for you care not how they be profaned, so it be for the maintenance of your own cause.

Chapter vi.   The Eleventh Division.

Answer to the Admonition, Page 208, Sect. ult.

The words in the v. to the Hebrews, verse 4,[2] be these: "And no man taketh this[3] honour to himself, but he that is called of God, as Aaron was[4]." The apostle here sheweth that Christ was a lawful priest, because he was thereunto called by God, as Aaron was. What is this to archbishops, &c. ? This place teacheth that no man ought to intrude himself to any function, except he be thereunto called by God. But what maketh this against any lawful function or authority, or what conclusion call

Weak arguments[5].

existimatione præditi erant, consilia non communicarunt.—G. Budæi Op. Basil. 1557. Comm. Ling. Græc. Tom. IV. col. 500.]

[1 Cartwright still presses his notion of the meaning of οἱ δοκοῦντες, but adds, "Howbeit I confess that, if I had known that I had in this point to do with the Geneva, M. Beza's and Erasmus' translation, and Budies' authority, I would (for reverence of their learning) have used an easier word in dissenting."—Sec. Repl. p. 663.]

[2 4. verse, Answ.]   [3 His, Def. B.]
[4 As was Aaron, Answ.]   [5 Arguments very weak, Answ. 2.]

you this: Christ did not take upon[6] him that office
whereunto he was not called; or: No man must take
upon him that whereunto he is not called; *ergo,* "archbishops, &c., and their offices came out of the pope's
shop"? you should first prove that which ought to be
your minor.

T. C. Page 100, Sect. 4.

But that I run not back to that I have handled before, I will not here A cleanly
so much urge the place, as I will not do also that of the Hebrews which shift.
followeth; and yet the argument is stronger than that M. Doctor could
answer. For, if the writer to the Hebrews do prove our Saviour Christ's
vocation to be just and lawful, because his calling was contained in the Untrue.
scriptures, as appeareth in that[7] *5. and 6. verse, then it followeth that the*
calling of the archbishop, which is not comprehended there, is neither just
nor lawful. "For that no man (saith the apostle) taketh the[8] *honour unto*
himself but he that is called of God, &c." But I say, having before suffi-
ciently spoken of the reasons which overthrow the archbishop, I will let
pass these and other places, answering only that which M. Doctor bringeth
for the establishment of them.

Jo. WHITGIFT.

This is a cleanly and handsome shift to avoid the defence The Replier
of these gross and unapt allegations of scriptures. I have proveth not
                                                              that which is
answered the argument grounded upon the v. to the Hebrews, denied.
and required the proof of the minor, which is this, that
archbishops, lord bishops, &c., intrude themselves into their
offices without any lawful calling, which both they and you
have omitted; and therefore I have answered sufficiently,
until you have proved that which is by me denied.

It is not true that the apostle to the Hebrews " proveth
the vocation of our Saviour Jesus Christ to be just and
lawful, because his calling was contained in the scriptures;" he
only sheweth by evident testimonies of the scriptures that Christ
did not intrude himself, but was called of God. And, if you
will have no man to execute any function in the church but
him that hath such special and personal testimonies of the
scriptures to shew for himself, I see not how any man can
justify his calling. It is therefore sufficient if his calling be
generally contained in the scripture; as all lawful and ordinary functions are, even the offices of archbishops and lord
bishops, &c.

[6] Unto, Answ. and Def. A.]
[7] The, Repl. 1 and 2.]   [8] That, Repl. 2.]

Chapter vi.   The Twelfth Division.

Answer to the Admonition, Page 209, Sect. 1, 2, 3, and Page 210, Sect. 1.

Scriptures
wrested [1].

In the xvi. of Luke, verse 25, it is thus written : "But Abraham said, Son, remember that thou in thy life-time receivedst thy pleasures, and likewise Lazarus pains : now therefore is he comforted ; and thou art tormented." The rich glutton in his life received pleasure, and therefore was after in hell tormented : Lazarus received pains, and after was comforted ; therefore "archbishops, &c., and their offices come out of the pope's shop." These fellows neither care for major, minor, nor conclusion, so they say something, and vainly paint their margent with shamefully abusing the scriptures.

The words of Ezek. chap. xxxiv. verse 4, be these : "The weak have ye not strengthened, the sick have ye not healed, neither have you bound up the broken, &c." In the which place the prophet speaketh against such kings, magistrates, and rulers, as despise the people of God, and use themselves cruelly towards them. This doth as well condemn kings and magistrates as it

Abuse of offices condemned, not the offices.

doth archbishops ; although indeed it condemneth no office or superiority, but the abuse of the same, that is, the man abusing the office, and not the office itself.

In the 2 Cor. i. verse 24, the apostle speaketh thus unto them : "Not that we have dominion over your faith, but we are helpers of your joy ; for by faith you stand." St Paul here saith that he hath no authority to alter true religion, or to rule over their consciences ; but how proveth this that "archbishops, &c., came out of the pope's shop"?   Paul saith that he had no power over the consciences of the Corinthians ; therefore "archbishops, &c., and their offices were drawn out of the pope's shop." If you had been more studious when you were a sophister (if ever you were any), you would have learned better to frame an argument, and have had better judgment in the sequel of the same. If you had not troubled your margent with these quotations, you had less uttered your folly.

[1 This marginal note is not in Answ.]

So much of the canon law as is contrary to the Canon laws
not alto-
gether con-
demned. scriptures is antichristian and devilish; but there be divers canons in it very good and profitable, which may well be retained. Good laws may be borrowed even of Turks and heathenish idolaters; and why not of papists also? I have told you before, that the thing itself is to be considered, not the inventor: if it be good and profitable, it may be used, whosoever did invent it.

Jo. Whitgift.

Not one word answered to all this.

Chapter vi.   The Thirteenth Division.

Admonition [2].

And as safely may we by the warrant of God's word subscribe to allow the dominion of the pope universally to reign over the church of God, as of an archbishop over a [3] whole province, or a lord bishop over [4] a diocese, which containeth many shires and parishes. For the dominion that they exercise, the archbishop above them, and they above the rest of their brethren, is unlawful, and expressly forbidden by the word of God.

Answer to the Admonition, Page 210, Sect. 2.

In that you say that you "may as safely by the warrant of God's word subscribe to allow the dominion of the pope universally to reign over the church of God, as of an archbishop over an whole province, &c.;" you express but your heat; I suppose you think not so. Can the pope as well govern the whole church as the archbishop one province, and a lord bishop one diocese? Is one king as well able to govern the whole world as he may be to govern one kingdom? Or, because you can rule one parish well, can you therefore in like manner well govern twenty parishes? Surely an archbishop An archbi-
shop may go-
vern one
province, but
the pope not
all the world. may well govern one province; but the pope can never well govern the whole church. And yet an archbishop hath not the charge of government over the whole province generally, but only in cases exempted, and therefore may do it more easily.

[2 This paragraph is placed in Answ. immediately after those printed above, page 408.]

[3 An, Adm. and Answ. 1.]   [4 A lordship over, Answ. 2.]

T. C. Page 100, Sect. 4.

He saith therefore afterward, that, although one man be not able to be bishop over all the church, yet he may be bishop over a whole diocese, or of a province. Now, if I would say the one is as impossible as the other, and for proof thereof allege that which the philosophers say, that, as there are no degrees in that which is infinite, so that, of things which are infinite, one thing cannot be more infinite than another, so there are no degrees of[1] impossibility, that, of things which are impossible, one thing should be more impossible than another—if I should thus reason, I think I should put you to some pain. But I will not draw the reader to such thorny and subtil questions; it is enough for us that the one and the other be impossible, although one should be more impossible than the other. And that it is impossible for one man to be bishop over a whole province, or over a whole diocese, I leave it to be considered of that which is before said in the description of the office of a bishop, pastor, or minister, where I speak of the necessity of the residence of the bishop in his church.

Jo. Whitgift.

In so saying I say but as other learned men have said, and especially M. Calvin, in the place afterward alleged in my Answer[2]; and as the practice of the church hath been in the best state, and under the best bishops; as it may appear by that which hath been hitherto spoken. Your philosophical argument is soon answered without any great pain. For to govern one province in that manner and form that is required of an archbishop is neither "infinite" nor "impossible." But it is great lack of judgment to think that, because one man cannot well govern the whole world, therefore he cannot well govern a province or diocese. I have shewed the practice of the church to be contrary in the apostles' time, and since their time.

Chapter vi. The Fourteenth Division.
T. C. Page 101, Sect. 1.

As a prince may rule a whole realm, such as France or England, so

This is absurdissimum; as M. Calvin saith, Instit. cap. 8. Sect. 92.

may he rule the whole world by officers and magistrates appointed underneath him. And there have been divers princes which have had as many lands under their power as the pope hath had churches; and, although it be somewhat inconvenient, yet I know not why they might not so have, coming lawfully by them. Now I would gladly hear whether you would say the same of a bishop; and, if you dare not, then why do you bring the similitude of the government of a prince over a land to prove that an archbishop may be over an[3] whole province? M. Doctor dare boldly say

[1] In, Repl. 1, 2, and Def. A.]   [2] See below, page 419.]
[3] A, Repl. 1 and 2.]

that there may be one bishop over a whole province, but he dare not say
that there may be a bishop over the whole church.   But what better
warrant for the one than for the other?   Again, if the whole church be   If the sky
in one province, or in one realm, which hath been, and is not impossible to   fall, &c.
                                                                                 Yes, surely,
be again, if there may be now one bishop over a realm and[4] province, then   as the state
there may be one bishop over all the church; so that in travailing with an   is now.
archbishop he hath brought forth a pope.

Jo. Whitgift.

The self-same reason you had before; and I answer it   Supra, cap.
                                                           3, divis. 31,
now as I did then[5].   The causes by me there alleged be suf-   32, 33.
ficient to prove the difference betwixt the government of a
prince and the government of a bishop.   And yet no man
will deny but that one prince shall better be able to govern
one kingdom than the whole world.   And to affirm that the
whole world may be contained in one monarchy, learned men
say is *multis modis absurdissimum*[6] : "in divers respects   Calv. Inst.
                                                                 cap. 8,
most absurd."   I bring the example of a king, because other   sect. 92.
writers use the like examples in the like matters to confute
such unlikely reasons, and namely M. Calvin in the words
following.

That which M. Doctor affirmeth, of "one bishop over one
whole province," and of "one bishop over the whole world,"
no man will deny.   A warrant for the one are the examples of
Timothy and Titus, and the continual practice of the church
without contradiction in the best times; but there is no warrant for the other of any credit or sufficiency, being only in
the most corrupt time of the church, and contrary to all
former examples and canons.

You say, "if the whole church be in one province, &c.;"
I say that if the sky fall you may catch larks, as the common
proverb is.   Moreover, if it were possible so to be (as now it
is not), then it were no absurdity the bishop of that province
still to remain bishop of the same.   But what moveth you to
such strange suppositions?   I might as well say, if the whole   The Replier's
                                                                  "if" turned
church were in one city, or town, or parish, as it was in Jeru-   upon him-
                                                                  self.
salem after Christ's ascension, and one bishop or pastor might
be over that city, or town, or parish, then one bishop or pastor
should be over the whole church; and so you likewise, " in   The church
                                                              cannot be

[4 Or, Repl. 1, 2, and Def. A.]   [5 See before, pages 244, &c.]
[6 Calvin. Op. Amst. 1667-71. Inst. Lib. iv. cap. vi. 9. Tom. ix. p. 296.
See before, page 264, note 2.]

travailing with a pastor to be in one church," at the length
" bring forth a pope." But do you not know that the church
of Christ is dispersed throughout the whole world, and cannot
now be shut up in one kingdom? much less in one province?
except you will become Donatists. He that is not wilfully
blind may see into what straits you are driven, when you are
constrained to utter such impossibilities for reasons.

Chapter vi.   The Fifteenth Division.
T. C. Page 101, Sect. 2.

*But he saith that an archbishop hath not the charge of government over
the whole province generally, but in cases exempted, and so may do it
more easily.   But he should have remembered that he assigned before the
offices of archbishop and bishop to be in all those things which other
ministers are, and that beside[1] those offices he giveth them particular
charges.   So that, where the office of the minister is but to preach, pray,
and minister the sacraments in his parish, the office of archbishop and
bishop is to do the same, and more too in the whole province or diocese;
and so it followeth that it is easier for a minister to discharge his duty in
his parish than for an archbishop or bishop to discharge their duties in
any one parish of their province or diocese; for they have in every parish
more to do and greater charge than the minister of the parish hath, then
much less are they able to do their duties in all the parishes of their provinces or diocese.*

Jo. Whitgift.

I speak of the office of government, and so be my words.
Every particular parish hath a particular pastor " to preach,
pray, and minister the sacraments." The bishop hath to procure
(so much as lieth in him) that all things be done in his diocese
according to the laws and orders of the church.   The archbishop hath not only to see that the bishops do their duties,
but to help them in reforming that which by themselves they
cannot do.   The office of preaching they exercise where and
when they see it most convenient.   The whole charge of
preaching and of governing resteth neither upon the archbishop, neither upon the bishop; but the one is a help unto
the other; and they together with the pastors teach the flock
of Christ faithfully and truly, and govern them according to
the laws prescribed.   And therefore the whole government
of the province doth not rest in the archbishop; for the which

[1 Besides, Repl. 1 and 2.]

cause he may with less difficulty execute that that doth appertain to[2] him.

Whatsoever any other minister may do, the same may the archbishop do also; but it doth not therefore follow that he is bound to the same particular parish. The pastor may preach; so may the archbishop; but the pastor's charge is particular; the archbishop's more general. And this is a very evil consequent: the archbishop may minister the sacraments, and preach the word; therefore he must do it in every particular congregation.

Chapter vi.　The Sixteenth Division.

Answer to the Admonition, Page 211, Sect. 1, 2.

You borrowed these arguments from the very papists, who by the self-same reasons go about to prove the pope's supremacy; for thus they argue.

Among the Israelites there was one high priest, which had authority over the rest; therefore there must be one high priest (which is the pope) over the whole church of Christ. Master Calvin, in his Institutions, chap. viii., doth answer this reason on this sort: *Quod in una natione fuit utile, id in universum orbem extendere nulla ratio cogit: imo gentis unius et totius orbis longe diversa erit ratio*[4]: "That which is profitable to[5] one nation cannot by any reason be extended to the whole world; for there is great difference betwixt the whole world and one nation." And a little after: *Perinde enim est ac si quis contendat totum mundum à præfecto uno debere regi, quia ager unus non plures præfectos habeat*[6]: "It is even as though a man should affirm that the whole world may be governed of one king, because one field or town hath but one ruler or master."

[*Hype., *Lib. iii. Metho. Theolo.*, making mention of this argument (there was an high priest among the Jews; *ergo*, there ought to be one pope over all Christendom), saith that it is "a good argument to prove that one arch-

Arguments borrowed of the papists.

Calvin.[3]

---

[2] Unto, Def. A.]
[3] This word is not in Answ.]
[4] Calvin. Op. Amst. 1667-71. Inst. Lib. iv. cap. vi. 2. Tom. IX. p. 295. See before, page 245, note 3.]
[5] In, Answ.]　　　　　[6] Id. ibid.]

bishop or metropolitan may well govern one province or one kingdom; but too weak to prove that one bishop may govern all the world"*[1].][2]

T. C. Page 101, Sect. 3, and Page 102, Sect. 1.

After M. Doctor translateth out of M. Calvin the papists' reasons for the supremacy of the pope, and M. Calvin's solutions. For what purpose he knoweth: I cannot tell, unless it be to blot paper; I know not what he should mean; and the quarrel also which he picketh, to translate this place, is yet more strange. For he saith that the authors of the Admonition "borrowed their arguments from the papists," when the contrary is true, that they use the reasons, which they of the gospel use against the supremacy of the pope, to overthrow the archbishop. And M. Doctor doth use reasons to defend the archbishop which the papists use to maintain the pope. For M. Doctor would prove that, for because there is one king over a realm, therefore there may be one bishop over a province; and the papists use the same reason to prove the pope to be a bishop of the whole church. Shew now one reason that the authors of the Admonition brought of the papists to prove that there should be no archbishop. But now I perceive his meaning, and that is, that he thought to get some comfort for the archbishop in M. Calvin's solutions made unto the papists' reasons for the supremacy. And therefore he hath haled and pulled in as it were by the shoulders this disputation between the protestants and the papists touching the supremacy. And what is it that M. Calvin saith for the archbishop? It hath been before shewed what his judgment was touching having one minister over all the ministers of a province, and that he doth simply condemn it in his commentary upon the first chap. of the Philip.[3] Now let it be considered, whether in these sentences he hath said anything against himself. The papists object that, forsomuch as there was one high priest in Jewry over all the church, therefore there should be one bishop over all. To whom M. Calvin answereth, that the reason followeth not; for, saith he, "there is no reason to extend that to all the world which was profitable in one nation[4]." Hereupon M. Doctor would conclude that M. Calvin alloweth one archbishop over a whole province.

If one going about to prove that he may have as many wives as he list would allege Jacob for an example, which had two wives, and M. Doctor should answer and say that, although he might have two wives, yet it followeth not that he may have as many as he list, would not M. Doctor think that he had great injury, if a man should conclude of these words that his opinion is that a man may have two wives? I think that he

(margin left, upper) It is not picked, but offered.

(margin left, lower) Being truly alleged. In alleging them falsely. Untrue, for he never used that for a reason.

[[1] And. Hyper. Method. Theolog. sive præcip. Christ. Rel. Loc. Comm. Libr. Tres, Basil. 1574. Lib. III. p. 682. See before, page 348, note 2.]

[[2] This paragraph is inserted from Answ. 2.]

[[3] Calvin. Op. Amst. 1667-71. Comm. in Epist. ad Philip. cap. i. 1. Tom. VII. p. 358. See before, page 324, note 1.]

[[4] Id. Inst. Lib. IV. cap. vi. 2. Tom. IX. p. 295. See before, page 419, note 4.]

would suppose that he had great wrong; and yet thus would he conclude of M. Calvin's words in this first sentence; whereas indeed M. Calvin declareth a little after a special reason why there was but one high priest in the whole land of Jewry, which is because he was a figure of Christ, and that thereby should be shadowed out his sole mediation between God and his church[5]; and therefore sheweth that, forsomuch as there is none to represent or figure our Saviour Christ, that his judgment is that, as there should be no one over all the churches, so should there be no one over any nation.

Falsification; for he sheweth no such thing.

Jo. Whitgift.

The authors of the Admonition say that they "may as safely by the warrant of God's word subscribe to allow the dominion of the pope universally to reign over the church of God, as of an archbishop over an whole province, or a lord bishop over a diocese, which containeth many shires and parishes." This I confute by M. Calvin's answer to the arguments of the papists; wherein appeareth evidently how far from reason this and such like assertions are, that there may as well be "one pope over the whole church, as one bishop over one province or diocese."

Now therefore you may see, if you list, that I have "translated these reasons and solutions out of M. Calvin" to some purpose. And, although I might have had the same solutions out of other learned writers, yet I thought it best to use M. Calvin, as one of whom you have conceived a better opinion.

I may truly say that the authors of the Admonition borrowed this of the papists, that there may be "as well one pope over the whole world, as one bishop over one province or diocese."

The reasons that I use for the defence of the archbishop are the solutions of the arguments used for the pope; and such solutions as are used by all learned men that write against the pope (as the solution of the places of Cyprian before mentioned, and now these that follow) to the strongest arguments of the papists. Wherefore I confess that I use some of the same arguments, but not to the same end, nor in

The reasons for the archbishop are solutions against the pope.

[5 *Summum, &c. convenit. Ad quem...? Non ad papam...sed ad Christum, qui ut solus munus ipsum sine vicario aut successore sustinet, ita honorem alteri nemini resignat.*—Id. ibid. See before, pages 347, 8, note 4.]

like manner. For they use them untruly, against reason, and the true meaning of the author: I use them truly, according to reason, and their proper sense. And my using of them to the purpose that I do is the direct answer and plain overthrow of all the arguments of the papists. It is not therefore good dealing to make the simple believe that the same arguments confirm the pope that confirm the archbishop, when as the application of them to the one is the quite overthrow of the other.

M. Doctor never went about to prove that, "because there is one king over a realm, therefore there may be one bishop over a province;" and, in uttering these and such like untruths willingly and wittingly as you do, you declare of what spirit you are. But M. Doctor hath reasoned clean contrary, that it is no good argument to say that, because one king may well rule one kingdom, therefore he may also well rule the whole world; or, because one bishop may be over one province, therefore one pope may be over all Christendom. These be papistical reasons: these M. Doctor dissolveth and confuteth; neither can you be ignorant of it; but malice is blind. God forgive you; for your whole drift is to bring M. Doctor into hatred and contempt by such lying means; but God that seeth the hearts of all will one day detect your deep dissembled hypocrisy, and reveal that lump of arrogancy and ambition, which is now cloaked with a counterfeit desire of reformation.

I have told you for what purpose I have used these solutions of M. Calvin's, whose opinion also I have shewed before concerning those names and offices.

Calvin alloweth one to rule over the rest of ministers.

In the place to the Philippians now again repeated (and yet this Replier can abide no repetitions in others, though he use almost nothing else himself), M. Calvin overthroweth your equality, for thus he saith: "Truly I grant that (as the manners and conditions of men are) there can no order remain among the ministers of the word except one do rule over the rest[1]." And he addeth that he speaketh *de singulis corporibus, non de totis provinciis, multo autem minus de orbe universo:* "of several bodies, not of whole provinces, much less of the whole world;" meaning, as I suppose, such pro-

[1 Id. Comm. in Epist. ad Philip. cap. i. 1. Tom. VII. p. 358. See before, page 324, note 1.]

vinces as be under divers governors; for one province in one *What is meant by a body in Calvin.* particular church, in one kingdom, under one prince, is but one body; and therefore M. Calvin saith nothing to the contrary but that one may *præesse reliquis ministris:* "rule over the rest of the ministers" in such a province.   Undoubtedly he cannot mean that in every several parish or town there should be one *qui præsit reliquis,* because the most parishes and towns have but one minister; and he that ruleth must have some to rule over.   If you will say that M. Calvin meaneth of such ministers as be in cities, where there be many, and not of the country, where there is in every several town but one; then I answer that it were against reason to bring the ministers of the city under the government of one, and to suffer the ministers of the country to live as they list.   The same causes, that require a ruler or governor for the one, requireth the same also for the other; except you would have uniformity in the city and confusion in the country.   Wherefore M. Calvin's meaning is as I have said.   But you have subtilly kept in his words, both here and before, because you know that they made much more against your equality than they do against the archbishop.   It had been uprighter dealing to have set down his words; but you will neither use that plainness yourself, nor allow of it in other men.

M. Calvin useth two answers to that objection of the papists; the first whereof is this that I have reported in my Answer.   And surely he would never have used that solution, and caused it to be printed, if he had not allowed it, and thought well of it.   And not he alone, but other of singular religion and zeal have used the same; as Hyperius in the place before by me alleged: so doth M. Nowel against Dorman in his first book, fol. 60.; whose words (because they be wholly to my purpose, and an evident declaration that such testimonies may lawfully be used for the authority of the bishops, that are unlawfully abused for the authority of the pope) I have set down before[2].   Whereby also the reader *Supra, cap. 3, the 15. divis.* may understand how we agree both among ourselves and to ourselves, which are desirous to keep the peace of the church; and that these places now used in the defence of the archbishop's and bishop's authority are no otherwise applied by us than they were before any such controversy began.

M. Calvin maketh no doubt of the matter, but setteth it

[2 See before, page 219.]

down as an apt answer, and by him allowed. And therefore your objection of "Jacob's two wives" may serve for a jest, but little to the purpose.

It followeth not that if a man make two answers to one argument he disalloweth the one; for they may both be true. Touching M. Calvin's second answer, I have spoken before, and declared wherein that high priest was a figure of Christ. M. Calvin in that place hath not these words, "that his judgment is that, as there should be no one over all churches, so should there be no one over any nation." And therefore you keep your accustomed manner of falsifying.

Chapter vi. The Seventeenth Division.

Answer to the Admonition, Page 211, Sect. 3.

Another of their reasons is this : Peter was the chief among the apostles; therefore there ought to be one chief over the whole church. The same M. Calvin, in the book and chapter before rehearsed, maketh this one answer to that argument : *Unus inter apostolos summus fuit, nempe quia pauci erant numero. Si unus duodecim hominibus præfuit, an propterea sequetur unum debere centum millibus hominum præfici* [2] *?* "There was one chief among the apostles, because they were but few in number; but, if one man rule over twelve, shall it therefore follow that one man may rule over an [3] hundred thousand?" And a little after : *Quod inter paucos valet, non protinus trahendum est ad universum terrarum orbem* [4], *ad quem regendum nemo unus sufficit* [5] *:* "That which is of force among few may not by and by be drawn to the whole world; the which no one man can govern." Every hive of bees hath one chief master-bee : every company of cranes hath one principal guide; must there be therefore but one bee and one crane, to direct all the bees and the cranes that be in the world [6]? You see therefore how weak this reason is. The rest of this reason I have answered before.

[1] This reference is not in Answ.]

[2] Calvin. Op. Amst. 1667-71. Inst. Lib. iv. cap. vi. 8. Tom. IX. p. 296. See before, page 247, note 5.]

[3] One may rule over a, Answ.]   [4] *Orbem terrarum*, Answ.]

[5] Id. ibid. See before, page 245, note 5.]   [6] The whole world, Answ.]

T. C. Page 102, Sect. 1.

To the papists, objecting for the supremacy that St Peter was the
prince and chief of the apostles, M. Calvin answereth, first by denying
that Peter was so, and bringeth many places to prove that he was equal
to the other apostles; afterward he saith, although it be granted that Peter
was chief, yet followeth it not, because one may bear rule over twelve, being
but a few in number, that therefore one may rule over an hundred
thousand, and that it followeth not, that that which is good amongst a few
is forthwith good in all the world. Now let all men judge with what
conscience and trust M. Doctor citeth M. Calvin for to prove the office of
the archbishop.

Jo. Whitgift.

M. Calvin in the same place hath these words : " It is not
to be marvelled that the twelve had one amongst them that
might govern the rest. For this thing doth nature allow, and
the disposition of man require, that in every society, though
all be equal in power, yet some should be as it were moderator of the rest, upon whom the other might depend. There
is no court without a consul, no session of judges without a
prætor or justice, no college without a governor, no society
without a master : so should it not be any absurdity if we
should confess that the apostles gave such pre-eminence unto
Peter[7]." Now let the reader judge whether it be Calvin's
meaning in good earnest, or no, that there was one chief
among the apostles; which being true (as it is), M. Doctor
may with good " conscience" use this answer of M. Calvin,
both against the papists, and the authors of the Admonition
also, reasoning not much unlike unto them.

Calvin. Inst.
cap. 8.

Chapter vi.   The Eighteenth Division.
T. C. Page 102, Sect. 1.

But I marvel that he could not also see that which M. Calvin writeth
in the next sentence almost, where he saith that Christ is only the head of
the church, and that the church doth cleave unto another[8] under his do-
minion; but by what means? "According (saith he) to the order and form
of policy which he hath prescribed;" but he hath prescribed no such form of
policy, that one bishop should be over all the ministers and churches in a
whole diocese, or one archbishop over all the ministers and churches in a
whole province; therefore this form of policy which is by archbishops, and
such bishops as we have, is not the means to knit us one to another in unity

[7 Quod &c. societas. Sic nihil absurdi esset si fateremur apostolos detulisse Petro talem primatum.—Id. ibid. See before, page 231, note 5.]

[8 Cleave one to another, Repl. 2.]

under the dominion of Christ. Touching the titles and names of honour which are given to the ecclesiastical persons with us, and how that princes and civil magistrates may and ought to have the title which cannot be given to ministers[1], I have spoken before. And therefore of archbishops, archdeacons, and the lord bishops, thus far.

Jo. Whitgift.

M. Calvin, in the next section, after that he hath answered

Calvin. Inst.
cap. 8.

to other arguments of the papists, saith thus: " But let it be as they would have it, that it is good and profitable that the whole world should be contained in one monarchy, which notwithstanding is most absurd, but let it be so: yet I will not therefore grant that it doth likewise hold in the government of the church. For the church hath Christ her only head, under whose government we are knit together according to that order and form of policy which he himself hath prescribed. Wherefore they do Christ notable injury, which under this pretence will have one man to rule over the whole church, because she cannot want a head; for Christ is the head whereby the whole body, being compacted and coupled by every joint of government, doth, according to the operation in the measure of every member, increase to a perfect body[2]." All which I agree unto as most true, but nothing at all pertaining to your purpose. He saith that "under the government of Christ we cleave together among ourselves, according to that order and that form of policy which he hath himself prescribed." And who denieth this? But *Quorsum?* This he speaketh of the spiritual regiment and policy, not of the external; and yet that external regiment and policy is also prescribed by him, which is profitable for his church according to time, place, and persons, though it be not particularly expressed in his word; as partly hath been declared before, and shall be hereafter more at large upon particular occasion.

Thus have you (after so many years travail in this controversy) uttered all your skill against the archbishop, poured

---

[1 To the ministers, Repl. 1, 2, and Def. A.]

[2 *Verum &c. valere.* Habet enim illa Christum unicum suum caput, sub cujus principatu omnes inter nos cohæremus, secundum eum ordinem et eam politiæ formam quam ipse præscripsit. Insignem itaque injuriam Christo faciunt quum eo prætextu volunt hominem unum præesse ecclesiæ universæ, quia hæc capite carere non possit. *Christus enim caput est, ex quo totum corpus compactum et connexum per omnem juncturam subministrationis, secundum operationem in mensura cujusque membri, augmentum corporis facit.*—Id. ibid. 9. ibid. See before, page 264, note 2.]

out all your malice, exercised your gibes and jests, whetted
your slanderous tongue; and yet, besides corrupt and false
allegations of writers, fond and toyish distinctions of your own,
contrary to all practice and learning, unchristian speeches
and heathenish flouts and frumps, you have uttered nothing.
And I protest unto the whole church before God, that your
unfaithfulness in handling the matter, your vain and frivolous
reasons, have much more animated me to the defence of those
ancient, reverend, profitable, and necessary offices. I speak
of the offices as they be used in this church. And I shall
most heartily desire the reader to weigh and consider the
authorities and reasons on both parties indifferently, and to
judge thereof according to the truth.

¶ A brief collection of such authorities as are used in this
Defence of the authority of archbishops and bishops.

Chap. vii.

Timothy was bishop of Ephesus; and Chrysostom saith, in
1 Ti. v., that *gens fere tota Asiatica:* "almost the whole country
of Asia was committed to him[3]." And upon the 2. to Timothy,
chap. iv., he saith that Paul had committed to Timothy *guber-
nacula ecclesiæ gentis totius*[4]: "the government over the
church of the whole nation," meaning Asia.

Titus was bishop of Creta, not of one city only, but of the
whole isle. So saith Chrysostom in his commentaries upon
the first to Titus[5]. And Lyra[6], Erasmus[7], Pellican[8], and others
write that St Paul made him archbishop of Creta. And
Illyricus calleth him and Timothy *multarum ecclesiarum
episcopos*[9]: "bishops of many churches."

St John (as Eusebius reporteth, *Lib. iii. cap.* 23.), after

Testimonies of the apostles' times, and thereunto adjoining.

[3 Chrysost. Op. Par. 1718-38. In i. Epist. ad Timoth. cap. v. Hom. xv.
Tom. XI. p. 637.]

[4 Id. in ii. Epist. ad Timoth. cap. iv. Hom. x. p. 720.]

[5 Id. in Epist. ad Tit. cap. i. Hom. i. p. 729. See before, page 285, note 3.]

[6 Bibl. cum Gloss. Ord. et Expos. N. de Lyra, Basil. 1502. Ad Tit. cap. i.
Pars VI. fol. 128. See before, page 352, note 4.]

[7 Erasm. Op. L. Bat. 1703-6. In Epist. ad Tit. Arg. Tom. VII. cols. 1067, 8.
See before, page 132, note 2.]

[8 C. Pellican. Comm. in Omn. Apost. Epist. Tigur. 1539. In Epist. ad Tit.
Arg. p. 577. See before, page 132, note 3.]

[9 Nov. Test. ex Vers. Erasm. cum Gloss. Comp. Flac. Illyr. Basil. 1570.
In Quatr. Epist. Timoth. &c. inscr. Præf. p. 1036. See before, page 298,
note 3.]

his return from Pathmos, did govern the churches in Asia, and ordained ministers and bishops[1].

James was made by the apostles bishop of Jerusalem; and the government of that church was committed to him. *Euseb. Lib. ii. cap.* 23.[2]

The 33. or, as some count, 34. of the canons attributed to the apostles, appointeth "one head and chief bishop" to be in every nation or country, to whom all other bishops of the same nation must be subject[3].

Dionysus Areopagita was archbishop of Athens, appointed thereunto by St Paul; as Volusianus, a godly and learned writer, testifieth[4].

Polycarpus was by St John made bishop of Smyrna. *Tertull. De Præscript.*[5]

In the church of Alexandria, from the time of St Mark, the ministers had always a bishop to govern them. *Hiero. ad Evagrium*[6].

Ignatius, who lived in the apostles' time, doth call a bishop *principem sacerdotum :* "the prince of priests," *in Epist. ad Smyrnenses*[7].

Testimonies of the times next after the apostles.

Anno 180.

In Eleutherius his time, which was *anno* 180., when this realm of England was first converted to Christianity, there was appointed in the same three archbishops, and 28. bishops. M. Fox, Tom. i. pag. 146.[8]

191.

Demetrius, who lived *anno* 191., was bishop of Alexandria, and of Egypt. *Euseb. Lib. vi. cap.* 1.[9]

235.

Cyprian, who was *anno* 235., being bishop of Carthage, had under him Numidia and Mauritania; as he himself saith,

---

[1] Euseb. in Hist. Eccles. Script. Amst. 1695-1700. Lib. iii. cap. xxiii. p. 73. See before, page 140, note 3.]

[2] Id. ibid. Lib. ii. cap. xxiii. p. 50. See before, page 136, note 4.]

[3] Canon. Apost. 33. in Concil. Stud. Labb. et Cossart. Lut. Par. 1671-2. Tom. I, col. 32. See before, page 145, note 4.]

[4] Volus. Epist. ii. in Fox, Acts and Monuments, Lond. 1684. Vol. II. p. 396. See before, page 130, note 2.]

[5] Tertull. Op. Lut. 1641. De Præscr. Hæret. 32. p. 243. See before, page 119, note 4.]

[6] Hieron. Op. Par. 1693-1706. Ad Evang. Epist. ci. Tom. IV. Pars ii. col. 803. See before, page 222, note 3.]

[7] Ignat. Interp. Epist. ad Smyrn. 9. in Coteler. Patr. Apost. Amst. 1724. Vol. II. p. 87. See before, page 304.]

[8] Fox, Acts and Monuments, Vol. I. p. 118. See before, p. 128, note 5.]

[9] Euseb. in Hist. Eccles. Script. Lib. vi. cap. ii. p. 164. See before, page 164, note 7.]

Lib. iv. Epist. 8.[10]   And Gregory Nazianzene, in an oration
that he made of Cyprian, saith that he ruled and governed
not only the churches of Carthage and Afric, but of Spain
also, and of the whole east church[11].   And for this cause doth
Illyricus call him a metropolitan[12]; the which name T. C.
also doth give unto him in his Reply, pag. 95. sect. 2.[13]

Dionysius called Alexandrinus, who lived *anno* 250., being   250.
bishop of Alexandria, had also under his jurisdiction all the
churches in Pentapolis; as Athanasius testifieth in a certain
epistle, *Apol. ii.*[14]; and yet had these churches their proper
bishop; as Eusebius doth witness, *Lib. vii. cap.* 26.[15]   Wherefore the bishop of Alexandria did govern them as archbishop.

Gregory, being bishop, did govern all the churches through   270.
Pontus, *anno* 270.   *Euseb. Lib. vii. cap.* 14.[16]

Epiphanius, *Lib. ii. To.* 2. *Hær.* 68., maketh mention of one   304.
Peter, who lived *anno* 304., whom he calleth archbishop of
Alexandria, and declareth that Meletius, then bishop in Egypt,
was under him; where also he hath these words: *Hic enim
mos*[17] *obtinet ut Alexandriæ episcopus totius Ægypti, ac The-
baidis, Mariotæque ac Lybiæ, Ammonicæque ac Mariotidis,
ac Pentapolis ecclesiasticam habeat administrationem*[18]:
"For this custom hath prevailed, that the bishop of Alexandria should have the ecclesiastical government of all Egypt,
Thebais, Mariota, Lybia, Ammonica, Mariotis, and Pentapolis."   And, *Hær.* 69., he saith: *Quotquot enim ecclesiæ in
Alexandria catholicæ ecclesiæ sunt, sub uno archiepiscopo
sunt*[19]: "For all the churches in Alexandria that be catholic
are under one archbishop."

The same Epiphanius in the same place doth call Meletius   304.
archbishop of Egypt, but yet he saith that he was subject to

[10] Cypr. Op. Oxon. 1682. Ad Cornel. Epist. xlviii. p. 91. See before, page
164, note 5.]

[11] Gregor. Naz. Op. Par. 1778-1840.   Orat. xxiv. 12. Tom. I. p. 445.   See
before, page 164, note 6.]

[12] Catalog. Test. Genev. 1608. col. 118.   See before, page 194, note 5.]

[13] See before, page 365.]

[14] Athanas. Op. Par. 1698. Epist. de Sentent. Dionys. 5. Tom. I. p. 246.
See before, page 165, note 8.]

[15] Euseb. in Hist. Eccles. Script. Lib. VII. cap. xxvi. p. 226. See before,
page 165, note 9.]

[16] Id. ibid. Lib. VI. cap. xxx. p. 187.   See before, page 165, note 10.]

[17] *Nos,* Def. B.]

[18] Epiph. Op. Par. 1622. Adv. Hær. Lib. II. Tom. II. Hær. lxviii. 1. Tom. I.
p. 717.   See before, page 160, note 3.]

[19] Id. ibid. Hær. lxix. 1. p. 727.   See before, page 161.]

the archbishop of Alexandria[1]. And this Meletius lived also *anno* 304.

330.   The council of Nice, *anno* 330., in the 4. canon, saith that the confirmation of bishops doth pertain to the metropolitan of every province[2]; and, in the 6., mention is made of metropolitans to be in every province, and that *secundum antiquum morem*: "according to the old custom." And it is further said that the bishop of Alexandria hath the regiment of Lybia and Pentapolis in Egypt[3].

335.   In the 6. and 37. canons of the second council of Arelat., it is decreed that no bishop may be ordained without the consent of the metropolitan; nor anything to be attempted against the great synod of the metropolitan[4].

344.   The council of Antioch, in the 9. canon, willeth that in every province the bishops be subject to their metropolitan bishop, which hath the care of the whole province, &c. And in that canon is this clause also, *Secundum antiquam a patribus nostris regulam constitutam*[5]: "according to the ancient rule appointed by our forefathers."

Athanasius was archbishop of Alexandria, and had jurisdiction over the rest of the clergy, to whom also Mariotes was subject. *Athana. Apo. ii.*[6]

Amphilochius, metropolitan of Lycaonia, governed the whole country. *Theod. Lib. iv. cap.* 11.[7]

Zozomen, *Lib. vii. cap.* 19., writeth that, though there be many cities in Scythia, yet they have but one bishop[8].

Aurelius, bishop of Carthage, in the council of Africa saith that he had the oversight and care of many churches[9].

Ambrose, *Lib. de Dig. Sacer. cap. v.*, maketh mention of

[1 Id. ibid. 3. p. 729. See before, page 161, note 5.]

[2 Concil. Nic. can. 4. in Concil. Stud. Labb. et Cossart. Lut. Par. 1671-2. Tom. II. col. 29. See before, page 158, note 4.]

[3 Ibid. can. 6. ibid. col. 32. See before, page 144, note 1.]

[4 Concil. Arelat. II. cans. 6, 56. ibid. Tom. IV. cols. 1012, 17. See before, page 159, note 10. It may be doubted whether Whitgift, though following other authorities, interprets these canons quite correctly. The metropolitans were to do nothing in opposition to "the great synod," i. e. of Nice.]

[5 Concil. Antioch. can. 9. ibid. Tom. II. col. 565. See before, page 146, note 1.]

[6 Athanas. Op. Par. 1698. Apolog. contr. Arian. 74, 85. Tom. I. pp. 190, 1, 200. See before, pages 162, 3.]

[7 Theod. in Hist. Eccles. Script. Amst. 1695-1700. Lib. IV. cap. xi. pp. 163, 4. See before, page 165, note 12.]

[8 Soz. in eod. Lib. VII. cap. xix. p. 595. See before, page 165, note 11.]

[9 Cod. Canon. Eccles. Afric. can. 55. in Concil. Stud. Labb. et Cossart. Tom. II. cols. 1078, 9. See before, page 165, note 13.]

archbishops[10], and he himself was a metropolitan, having charge and government of many churches; as the authors of the Centuries testify in their fourth Century[11].

Simeon was archbishop of Seleucia. *Zozo. Lib. ii. cap.* 8.[12] He lived about the time of the Nicene council. Basil, metropolitan of Cappadocia. *Zozo. Lib. iii. cap.* 16.[13]

In the council of Constantinople, which is one of the 4. general councils, in the 2. and 5. canons, this authority and regiment of primates, metropolitans, and archbishops, is contained. Which thing also Socrates doth note in the same council. *Lib. v. cap.* 8.[14] An. 383.

In the 2. council of Carthage, canon 12. &c., it is evident that in every province there was a primate[15]. An. 415.

In the council of Chalcedon, Flavianus is called archbishop of Constantinople; Dioscorus, archbishop of Alexandria; Leo, archbishop of Rome; and the authorities of these offices and degrees in[16] divers points specified[17]. An. 453.

In the first canon of the council of Ephesus, it may manifestly be gathered that all other bishops of the same province were then subject to their metropolitan bishop[18]. An. 463.

Hierome, *ad Rusticum Monachum*, saith: *Singuli ecclesiarum episcopi, singuli archipresbyteri, singuli archidiaconi, &c.*[19] I omit his other places *ad Lucif., ad Titum, &c.*[20]

[10] Ambros. Op. Par. 1686-90. De Dign. Sacerdot. cap. v. Tom. II. Append. cols. 362, 3. See before, page 153, note 7.]

[11] Centur. Eccles. Hist. Basil. 1560, &c. Cent. IV. cap. x. col. 1150. See before, page 155.]

[12] Soz. in Hist. Eccles. Script. Lib. II. cap. ix. p. 371. See before, page 166, note 2.]

[13] Id. ibid. Lib. III. cap. xvi. pp. 427, 8. See before, page 166, note 3.]

[14] Socr. in eod. Lib. v. cap. viii. pp. 217, 8. Conf. Concil. Constant. cans. 1, 2, 3. in Concil. Stud. Labb. et Cossart. Tom. II. cols. 946, 7. See before, page 163, notes 9, 10.]

[15] Concil. Carthag. II. can. 12. ibid. Tom. II. cols. 1162, 3. Conf. Cod. Canon. Eccles. Afric. can. 13. ibid. col. 1055. See before, page 159, note 12, page 160, note 1.]   [16] Degrees there in, Def. A.]

[17] Concil. Calched. Act. I. ibid. Tom. IV. cols. 148, 9, 52.]

[18] Εἴτις ὁ μητροπολίτης τῆς ἐπαρχίας ... προσέθετο τῷ τῆς ἀποστασίας συνεδρίῳ,...οὗτος κατὰ τῶν τῆς ἐπαρχίας ἐπισκόπων διαπράττεσθαί τι οὐδαμῶς δύναται, κ. τ. λ.—Concil. Ephes. can. 1. ibid. Tom. III. col. 803. The dates of the councils here cited are, according to Labbe and Cossart, somewhat different from those assigned by Whitgift. The councils of Arles, Antioch, Constantinople, Carthage, Chalcedon, and Ephesus are placed respectively A.D. 452, 341, 381, 390, 451, 431.]

[19] Hieron. Op. Par. 1693-1706. Ad Rustic. Monach. Epist. xcv. Tom. IV. Pars II. col. 775.]

[20] Id. adv. Lucifer. Tom. IV. Pars II. col. 295. See before, page 222, note 5.

Ambrose, *in iv. ad Ephe.*, saith that all orders be in a bishop, because he is *primus sacerdos, hoc est, princeps sacerdotum*[1]: "the chief priest, that is, prince of priests."

Augustine, in his questions *in Vetus et Novum Test. cap. ci.*, saith: *Quid est . . . . episcopus, nisi primus presbyter, hoc est, summus sacerdos*[2]?

Chrysostom, being archbishop of Constantinople, did also govern the churches in Thracia, Asia, and Pontus. *Theod. Lib. v. cap.* 28.[3] The authors of the Centuries affirm the same, and call him archbishop. *Cent. v. cap.* 10.[4]

Theodoret, being bishop of Cyrus, had under his government 800. churches; as he himself testifieth in his epistle to Leo[5].

Gennadius, bishop of Constantinople, writeth to the bishop of Rome thus: *Curet sanctitas tua universas tuas custodias, tibique subjectos episcopos*[6].

Ruff. Lib. i. cap. 29. Infinite testimonies and examples there are of this sort; and no man that is of any reading can be ignorant but that these degrees of superiority, and this kind of regiment, hath been in the church continually, even from the apostles' time[7].

M. Bucer, upon the fourth to the Ephe., sheweth that these degrees in the church, bishop, archbishop, metropolitan, primate, patriarch, be not only most ancient, but also necessary[8].

M. Calvin, in his *Instit. cap. viii. sect.* 52., upon the place of Hierome in the epistle *ad Evagrium*, saith that in the old time there was to every city appointed a certain region, province, or diocese, *quæ presbyteros inde sumeret, et velut cor-*

Id. Comm. in Epist. ad Tit. cap. i. Tom. IV. Pars i. col. 413. See before, pages 221, 2, note 5.]

[1] Nam in episcopo omnes ordines sunt; quia primus sacerdos est, hoc est, princeps est sacerdotum.—Ambros. Op. Par. 1686-90. Comm. in Epist. ad Ephes. cap. iv. vv. 11, 12. Tom. II. Append. col. 241.]

[2] August. Op. Par. 1679-1700. Quæst. ex utroq. mixt. Quæst. ci. Tom. III. Append. col. 93.]

[3] Theod. in Hist. Eccles. Script. Amst. 1695-1700. Lib. v. cap. xxviii. pp. 235, 6. See before, pages 312, 13, note 5.]

[4] Centur. Eccles. Hist. Basil. 1560, &c. Cent. v. cap. x. col. 1171. See before, page 316, note 2.]

[5] Theod. Op. Lut. Par. 1642-84. Ad Leon. Episc. Rom. Epist. cxiii. Tom. III. pp. 986, 7. See before, page 320, note 5.]

[6] Gennad. Epist. Synod. in Concil. Stud. Labb. et Cossart. Lut. Par. 1671-2. Tom. IV. col. 1030.]

[7] ...ex concilii decreto Asterio ceterisque qui cum ipso erant orientis injungitur procuratio, occidentis vero Eusebio decernitur.—Hyst. Eccles. Par. Lib. x. cap. xxix. fol. 116. 2.]

[8] M. Bucer. Prælect. in Epist. ad Ephes. Basil. 1562. cap. iv. pp. 131, 2, 3.]

pori illius ecclesiæ accenseretur, and that the same also was
under the bishop of the city. *Quod si amplior erat ager,
qui sub ejus episcopatu erat, quam ut sufficere omnibus
episcopi muniis ubique possit, per ipsum agrum designa-
bantur certis locis presbyteri, qui in minoribus negotiis ejus
vices obirent: eos vocabant chorepiscopos, quod per ipsam
provinciam episcopum repræsentabant* [9].

M. Beza, *Lib. Conf. cap.* 7., calleth the names of archbishops, bishops, &c., " holy names ;" for thus he saith : " That
pastors in process of time were distinct into metropolitans,
bishops, and those whom they now call curates (that is, such
as be appointed to every parish) was not in the respect of the
ministry of the word, but rather in respect of jurisdiction and
discipline.   Therefore, concerning the office of preaching the
word and administering the sacraments, there is no difference
betwixt archbishops, bishops, and curates ; for all are bound to
feed their flock with the same bread ; and therefore by one
common name in the scriptures they be called pastors and
bishops.   But what impudency is there in those men (meaning
the papists) to use those holy names, and therefore to glory
of the succession of the apostles and true bishops [10] !"   In the
same chapter he maketh two kinds of degrees used in the papistical church ; the one unknown to the apostles and to the
primitive church, the other taken out of the word of God,
and from the primitive church ; in the second order he placeth
archbishops, curates, canons, seniors, or ministers, archdeacons,
deans, subdeacons, clerks [11].

But what should I stand longer in this matter ?   There is
not one writer of credit that denieth this superiority to have
been always among the clergy, and these degrees to come
even from the best time of the church since the apostles, and
to be both most ancient and general.   Wherefore I cannot but
count such as deny so manifest a truth either unlearned and
unskilful persons, or else very wranglers, and men desirous of
contention [12].

[9 Calvin. Op. Amst. 1667-71. Inst. Lib. IV. cap. iv. 2. Tom. IX. p. 286;
where *ecclesiæ illius,* and *posset.*]

[10 Th. Bezæ Confess. Christ. Fid. Genev. 1587. cap. vii. 12. p. 238. See
before, page 333, note 3.]

[11 Id. ibid. pp. 230, 1.   See before, page 332, note 2.]

[12 " Thus we are (by the grace of God) come to an end of this treatise, wherein
let the reader judge whether it hath been proved that the offices of archbishops and
archdeacons be unlawful, that they came not into the church 300. years after the

28

A brief comparison betwixt the bishops of our time, and the
bishops of the primitive church.

Chap. viii.

I know that comparisons be odious, neither would I use
them at this time, but that I am thereunto (as it were) compelled by the uncharitable dealing of T. C., who, by comparing
the bishops of our time with the bishops in the old church,
hath sought by that means to disgrace them, if it were possible. I may peradventure in this point seem to some to
flatter, but the true judgment thereof I leave to him that
knoweth the secrets of the heart. In the meantime I will
affirm nothing which is not evident to all those that be learned
divines, and not overruled with affection. My comparison
shall consist in these three points; truth of doctrine, honesty
of life, and right use of external things.

Touching the first, that is, truth of doctrine, I shall not
need much to labour. For I think T. C. and his adherents
will not deny but that the doctrine taught and professed by
our bishops at this day is much more perfect and sounder
than it commonly was in any age after the apostles' time.
For the most part of the ancientest bishops were deceived with
that gross opinion " of a thousand years after the resurrection,
wherein the kingdom of Christ should here remain upon earth."
The fautors whereof were called *Millenarii*. Papias, who

Euse. Lib. III.
cap. 39, & 35. lived in Polycarpus and Ignatius his time, being bishop of Jerusalem[1], was the first author of this error[2]; and almost all the
most ancient fathers were infected with the same.

ascension of our Saviour Christ; that their names are likewise unlawful by the
word, forbidden by ancient councils, not to be found in any ancient writing before
400. years approached. Further, whether that every congregation ought to have a
bishop; that one only may have two or more; that they ought all to have like
titles and authority. Saving that in their meetings for order's sake one by consent
of the rest governeth that action in such sort as is declared. That all these points
of the bishop have ground of the word of God, and most of them shewed to have
remained some time after the apostles, and the traces long after. Finally,
whether that even the elder bishops when they were declined from the sincerity
of God's ordinance, and the archbishops and archdeacons which he never
ordained, were much more tolerable than ours; as those whose authority was
without comparison less, and pomp none at all."—Sec. Repl. p. 666.]

[1 " ... his [collector] deceived him, and was herein somewhat too well skilled
in Greek; which, for Hierapolis a city in Phrygia, whereof Papias was bishop, told
him that he was 'of Jerusalem.' "—Ibid. p. 654.]

[2 ... χιλιάδα τινὰ φησὶν [ὁ Παπίας] ἐτῶν ἔσεσθαι μετὰ τὴν ἐκ νεκρῶν
ἀνάστασιν, σωματικῶς τῆς τοῦ Χριστοῦ βασιλείας ἐπὶ ταυτησὶ τῆς γῆς ὑπο-

Cyprian and the whole council of Carthage erred in Tom. Conc. I.
Lib. epi. ii.
epi. 3. " re-baptization[3];" and Cyprian himself also was greatly over- seen in making it a matter so necessary in the celebration of the Lord's supper to have water mingled with wine, which was, no doubt, at that time common to more than to him ; but the other opinion which he confuteth, of using water only, is more absurd[4]; and yet it had at that time patrons among the bishops.

How greatly were almost all the bishops and learned writers of the Greek church, yea, and the Latins also, for the most part, spotted with doctrines of free-will, of merits, of invocation of saints, and such like? Surely you are not able to reckon, in any age since the apostles' time, any com- pany of bishops that taught and held so sound and perfect doctrine in all points as the bishops of England do at this time.

If you speak of ceremonies, and of the sincere adminis- tration of the sacraments, you shall find the like difference ; for, compare the ceremonies that Tertullian saith, *Lib. de Coro. Mil.*, then to be used in the church about the sacraments, and otherwise[5]; or those that Basil rehearseth, *Lib. de Sancto Spi.*[6]; or such as we may read to have been in St Augustine's time[7], with those that we now retain in this church, and you cannot but acknowledge that therein we are come to a far greater perfection.

I mean not to stand in particulars; I think T. C. and his companions will not contend with me in this point ; for, if they do, it is but to maintain contention. Seeing then that in the truth of doctrine, which is the chief and principal point, our bishops be not only comparable with the old bishops, but in many degrees to be preferred before them, we think there is too too great injury done unto them, and to this doctrine which they profess, when as they are so odiously compared,

σστησομένης.—Euseb. in Hist. Eccles. Script. Amst. 1695-1700. Lib. III. cap. xxxix. p. 90.]

[3 Cypr. Op. Oxon. 1682. Concil. Carthag. pp. 229, &c. Conf. Crabb. Concil. Col. Agrip. 1551. Tom. I. pp. 143, &c.]

[4 Id. ad Cæcil. Epist. lxiii. pp. 148, &c.]

[5 Tertull. Op. Franek. 1597. De Cor. Mil. 3. p. 180.]

[6 Basil. Op. Par. 1721-30. Lib. de Spir. Sanct. cap. xxvii. 66. Tom. III. pp. 54, &c.]

[7 August. Op. Par. 1679-1700. Ad Inq. Januar. Lib. II. seu Epist. lv. cap. xix. 35. Tom. II. col. 142.]

and so contemptuously intreated by T. C. and his colleagues.

2. Touching honesty of life, which is the second point, I will not say much; I do not think but that therein they may be compared with the old bishops also, and in some points preferred. Every age hath some imperfections in it; and the best men are most subject to the slanderous tongue. Great contention there was among the bishops in the council of Nice; insomuch that even in the presence of the emperor they ceased not to libel one against another[1]. What bitterness and cursing was there betwixt Epiphanius and Chrysostom! what affectionate[2] dealing of Theophilus against the same Chrysostom[3]! what jarring betwixt Hierome and Augustine[4]! But I will not prosecute this. Men, be they never so godly, yet they be men; and the common sort of people, when they wax weary of the word of God truly preached, then do they begin to deprave the true and chief ministers of the same.

3. For the third point, that is, the use of external things, if the bishops now have more land and living than bishops had then, it is the blessing of God upon his church; and it is commodious for the state and time. If any man abuse himself therein, let him be reformed; let not his fault be made a pretence to cloak a mind desirous to spoil. I see not how those lands and livings can be employed to more benefit of the church, commodity of the commonwealth, and honour of the prince, than they be now in state and condition wherein they remain. Bishops shall not now need to live by pilling and polling, as it seemed they did in Cyprian's time; for he complaineth thereof, *Ser. de Lapsis*[5]. Nor as some did in Ambrose[6] or Augustine's[7]. They have (God be thanked) living sufficient without any such unlawful means; and I doubt not but, if their expenses shall be compared with their pre-

Amb. de Dig. Sacerd.
August. Lib. iii. advers. Parmen.

---

[1] Euseb. in Hist. Eccles. Script. Amst. 1695-1700. De Vit. Constant. Lib. III. cap. xiii. p. 404.]

[2] Affectionate: passionate.]

[3] Chrysost. Op. Par. 1718-38. Vit. Chrysost. Tom. XIII. pp. 141, &c.]

[4] August. Op. Par. 1679-1700. Vit. August. Lib. IV. cap. xiii. Lib. V. capp. ix. xii. Tom. XI. cols. 196, &c., 254, 270, &c.]

[5] Cypr. Op. Oxon. 1682. De Laps. pp. 123, 4.]

[6] Ambros. Op. Par. 1686-90. De Dign. Sacerdot. capp. v. vi. vii. Tom. II. Append. cols. 362, &c.   See before, page 153, note 7.]

[7] August. Op. Contr. Epist. Parmen. Lib. III. cap. ii. 7, &c. Tom. IX. cols. 60, &c.]

decessors', it shall appear that they be according to the proportion that God hath limited unto them[8]. But an eye, dimmed with malice, or bent to the spoil, can see nothing that may hinder the desired purpose. God root out of the hearts of men such ravening affections and greedy desires.

[8 " It is high time that he were (to speak no grievouslier) unbishoped, which will take occasion of pillage, having to live on a hundred pound a year."—Sec. Repl. p. 649. The Second Reply goes no farther than the end of this Tractate. Cartwright's observations on the succeeding portion of the Defence are contained in "The Rest of the Second Reply." See Vol. I. page 3, note 3.]

¶ Of the Communion Book.

Tract. IX.

The general faults examined wherewith the public service is charged by T. C.

Chapter i.   The First Division.

T. C. Page 102, Sect. 2.

Before I come to speak of prayers, I will treat of the faults that are committed almost throughout the whole liturgy and public service of the church of England; whereof one is that which is often objected by the authors of the Admonition, that the form of it is taken from the church of antichrist, as the reading of the epistles and gospels so cut and mangled, as the most of the prayers, the manner of ministering the sacraments, of marriage, of burial, confirmation, translated as it were word for word, saving that the gross errors and manifest impieties be taken away. For, although the forms and ceremonies which they used were not unlawful, and that they contained nothing which is not agreeable to the word of God (which I would they did not), yet, notwithstanding, neither the word of God, nor reason, nor the examples of the eldest churches, both Jewish and christian, do permit us to use the same forms and ceremonies, being neither commanded of God, neither such as there may not as good as they, and rather better, be established.

Jo. Whitgift.

In these words are contained two false principles: the one is that " the form " and manner of prayer used in the church of England "is taken from the church of antichrist ;" the other, that it is not lawful " to use the same forms (of prayer) and ceremonies" that the papists did. This latter I have already proved to be otherwise, in the beginning where I spake of ceremonies[1], and intend hereafter to answer such arguments as shall be used to prove the contrary : the first will appear to be most untrue, being manifest that such things as we now use in the book of common prayer (though some of them have been used in the time of papistry) were appointed in the church by godly and learned men, before the pope was antichrist, or the church of Rome greatly corrupted; as " the reading of the epistle and gospel," which is of very long continuance in the church, even whilst the church of Rome was as yet, in the principal points of doctrine, pure, being also chosen places of scriptures, apt for the time, and most to

Tract. VII. cap. 5. divis. 3, 4, &c.

Reading of gospels and epistles very ancient.

[1 See before, pages 31, &c.]

edifying, which no honest heart and godly-disposed person can discommend.

If in "the administration of the sacraments, celebration of marriage, burying of the dead, confirmation," those things that are good and profitable be retained, and "the gross errors and manifest impieties taken away," as you say they be, why do you then on this sort trouble the church for using that which is good, and refusing that which is evil? Is papistry so able to infect the word of God, godly prayers, and profitable ceremonies, that they may not be used in the church reformed, the errors and impieties being taken away? Why do we call our churches reformed churches, rather than newly builded, or as it were wholly transformed, but that we retain whatsoever we find to be good, refuse or reform that which is evil? But of these matters more is to be spoken as occasion is offered. Hitherto you use but words, which have no weight without good and sound reasons.

Things abused may be used, impieties being taken away.

The church is reformed, not transformed.

Chapter i.   The Second Division.

T. C. Page 102, Sect. 3.

For the word of God I have shewed before, both by the example of the apostles conforming the gentiles unto the Jews in their ceremonies, and not contrariwise the Jews to the gentiles, and by that the wisdom of God hath thought it a good way to keep his people from the infection of idolatry and superstition, to sever them from idolaters by outward ceremonies, and therefore hath forbidden them to do things which are in themselves very lawful to be done.

Acts xv. 20.[2]

Jo. Whitgift.

What you have spoken in any place of your book concerning this matter is there answered where it is spoken; but you have not as yet, to my remembrance, anywhere shewed that God ever hath "forbidden his people to do things in themselves very lawful to be done," because the same were used by idolaters: I have before proved the contrary, both by the manifest words of the scripture, and by the testimony of St Augustine and divers other learned writers[3].

Tract. VII. cap. 5.

[2 This reference is inserted from Repl. 2.]
[3 See before, pages 31, &c.]

Chapter i.   The Third Division.

T. C. Page 102, Sect. 4.

*Now I will add this further, that, when as the Lord was careful
to sever them by ceremonies from other nations, yet was he not
so careful to sever them from any as from the Egyptians,
amongst whom they lived, and from those nations which were
next neighbours unto them, because from them was the greatest
fear of infection.   Therefore, by this constant and perpetual
wisdom which God useth to keep his people from idolatry,
it followeth that the religion of God should not only in matter
and substance, but also, as far as may be, in form and fashion, differ
from that of the idolaters, and especially the papists, which are round
about us and amongst us.   For indeed it were more safe for us to conform our indifferent ceremonies to the Turks which are far off, than to
the papists which are so near.*

Levit. xix.
27.[1]
Deut. xxii.
11, 12.[1]
Levit. xi.[1]
Deut. xiv.[1]
Eph. ii. 14.[1]
Levit. xviii.
3.[1]
Deut. xvii.
16.[1]

An unad-
vised as-
sertion.

Jo. Whitgift.

The gentiles
and papists
not like in
all respects.

The Egyptians and idolatrous gentiles neither worshipped,
nor pretended to worship, the God of Israel, and therefore no
marvel though in rites and ceremonies they were utterly
severed from them; but the papists either worship, or pretend
to worship, the same God which we do; and therefore there is
no such cause in all points of rites and ceremonies to differ
from them.   And it is most untrue that God so severed his
people from the Egyptians or other nations near adjoining,
that they had nothing common with them, or no ceremonies
like unto theirs; for they were like in many things touching
the external form.   The gentiles had sacrifices; and so had
they: the gentiles in worshipping their gods used external
pomp of garments, of golden and silver vessels, and such like;
and so did they; yea, divers learned men be of this judgment,
that God did prescribe unto the Israelites that solemn manner
and form of worshipping him by external rites and ceremonies
shortly after their return out of Egypt, that they, being therewith not only occupied, but also delighted, should have no
desire to return into Egypt, or to worship their gods whom
they had seen with great solemnity of ceremonies and external
rites adored.   And therefore you ground your talk upon false
principles, which you have not proved, but imagined.

The Jews and
the gentiles
in some re-
spect agreed
in cere-
monies.

Now, if we may have ceremonies common with them, or
like unto them, from whom we wholly differ in matter and

[¹ These references are inserted from Repl. 2.]

substance of religion, as we do from the gentiles, and from the Turks, much more may we have ceremonies common with them, or like unto them, from whom we do not wholly differ in matter and substance, but in certain material and substantial points. As for this your saying, "That it were better for us to conform our indifferent ceremonies to the Turks which are far off, than to the papists which are so near," I take it to be but spoken in a heat, and that you will otherwise think when you have better considered the matter; the one being a professed enemy unto Christ, and the name of Christ, the other pretending the contrary. But, to put you out of doubt, we do not in any kind of ceremonies conform ourselves to the papists, but, using christian liberty in external things, and knowing that "all things be clean to those that be clean," such things as we find instituted by learned and godly men, and profitable to the church as pertaining to edifying, or comeliness and order (though abused of the papists), we retain in our churches, and restore to the right use; as our forefathers did the temples of idols, turning them to christian churches, and revenues consecrated to idols, transposing them to find the ministers of the church, and such like; as I have declared in another place[2].

We conform not ourselves to the papists in ceremonies.

Tit. i.

Tract. VII. cap. 5. divis. 3, 4, &c.

Chapter i. The Fourth Division.
T. C. Page 103, Sect. 1.

Common reason also doth teach that contraries are cured by their contraries: now christianity and antichristianity, the gospel and popery, be contraries; therefore antichristianity must be cured not by itself, but by that which is (as much as may be) contrary unto it. Therefore a meddled[3] and mingled estate of the order of the gospel and the ceremonies of popery is not the best way to banish popery; and therefore as, to abolish the infection of false doctrine of the papists, it is necessary to establish a divers doctrine, and, to abolish the tyranny of the popish government, necessary to plant the discipline of Christ, so, to heal the infection that hath crept into men's minds by reason of the popish order of service, it is meet that the other order were put in place[4] thereof.

Jo. Whitgift.

"Contraries must be cured by contraries" in all things wherein they be contrary. "Christianity and antichristianity,

How contraries must be cured by contraries.

[2 See before, pages 31, &c.]
[3 So that a meddled, Repl. 2.]   [4 In the place, Repl. 1 and 2.]

the gospel and popery," be not in all things contrary, touching outward profession; and therefore no necessity of abandoning all things from "christianity" that was used "in antichristianity." So much of the papistical doctrine as is contrary to the gospel, that kind of government in the pope's church that is repugnant to the word of God, all such order of service or kind of prayer as is ungodly and superstitious, is to be removed and cured with the contrary; but, as they have some truth in doctrine, so have they some lawful kind of government, and good and godly prayers; all which, being restored to their own purity, are to be retained; for no abuse can so defile anything that is good, that the same thing may not be used, the abuse being taken away.

The order of popish service clean altered in this church.

And yet, if you would speak the truth, you cannot say but that the order of the popish service is clean altered in this church; for what similitude hath the vulgar tongue with a tongue unknown? What likelihood is there betwixt the multitude of ceremonies used by the papists and the fewness of such as are now retained? How much doth the simplicity used in our service differ from the pomp and gorgeousness used in theirs! How contrary is our communion to their mass! What diversity is there in the celebration of our sacraments and theirs! To be short, the difference is as much as either the word of God or the state and condition of the church requireth: the which you might see if you were disposed; but, as I have said before, *Cæca malitia non videt apertissima:* "Blind malice seeth not those things that are most manifest."

Chapter i.   The Fifth Division.
T. C. Page 103, Sect. 1.

Philosophy, which is nothing else but reason, teacheth that, if a man will draw one from vice which is an extreme unto virtue which is the mean, that it is the best way to bring him as far from that vice as may be, and that it is safer and less harm for him to be led somewhat too far than he should be suffered to remain within the borders and confines of that vice wherewith he is infected.   As if a man would bring a drunken man to sobriety, the best and nearest way is to carry him as far from his excess in drink as may be; and, if a man could not keep a mean, it were better to fault in prescribing less than he should drink, than to fault in giving him

A crooked rule.

more than he ought; as we see, to bring a stick which is crooked to be straight, we do not only bow it so far until it come to be straight, but we bend it so far until we make it so crooked of the other side as it was before of the first side, to this end that at the last it may stand straight, and as it were in the midway between both the crooks; which I do not therefore speak as though we ought to abolish one evil and hurtful ceremony for another, but that I would shew how it is more dangerous for us that have been plunged in the mire of popery to use the ceremonies of it, than of any other idolatrous and superstitious service of God.

Jo. Whitgift.

"Philosophy" also "teacheth" that both the extremes be vices; and therefore your rule doth teach that a man must go from one vice to another, if he will come to virtue, which is a mean; but St Paul teacheth the contrary, saying, *Non est faciendum malum, ut inde veniat bonum:* "We must not do evil that good may come thereof." Wherefore, as your rule is heathenish and naught, so do you as naughtily follow it. Is there no way for the prodigal man to come to liberality, but by covetousness? no way for the glutton to come to temperance, but by pining himself? no way for the presumptuous person to come to the true fear and love of God, but by desperation? no way to come from popery to the gospel, but by confusion, and overthrow of all good order and government? Is this divinity? Indeed such divinity it is that Aristotle, a profane philosopher, doth teach in his Ethics, but not that Christ and his apostles do teach in the gospel. *The Replier prescribeth a heathenish rule of reformation.* *Rom. iii.*

The ordinary means, whereby a Christian man must come from vice to virtue, from an extreme to a mean, is the diligent reading and hearing of the word of God, joined with earnest and hearty prayers. The best way therefore to "bring a drunken man to sobriety" is not to persuade him to a superstitious kind of abstinence or fasting, but to lay before him out of the word of God the horribleness of that sin, and the punishment due unto the same. The similitude of a crooked stick is apt to set forth so crooked a precept, but not so apt to make manifest the way unto virtue. But I may not blame you for using and allowing those profane rules, which you so aptly follow, and so commonly practise in all your doings[1]. *The ordinary means to draw men from vice.*

[1 "… he disputeth against me, as though I allowed that a man might run from one vice for remedy against the other; which is an open untruth and untolerable, seeing I added expressly that I did 'not allow it, but only that of two evils it was the less;' whereunto he could not answer."—The Rest of Sec. Repl. p. 174.]

Chapter i.   The Sixth Division.

T. C. Page 103, Sect. 1, 2.

*This wisdom of not conforming itself unto the ceremonies of the idola-
ters in things indifferent hath the church followed in times passed.*

 Tertullian saith, " O," saith he, "better is the religion of the Lib. de
heathen; for they use no solemnity of the Christians, neither the Idolatria.
*Lord's day, neither the Pentecost; and if they knew them they would have
nothing to do with them; for they would be afraid lest they should seem
Christians; but we are not afraid to be called heathen."*

JO. WHITGIFT.

Tertullian in that place speaketh against such Christians
as celebrated the feast of the gentiles together with them, remaining in their wicked abuse; as it appeareth in the words

Lib. de Ido-
latria.

that go before, which are as followeth : *Nobis, quibus sabbata
extranea sunt et neomenia et feriæ aliquando a Deo dilectæ, Saturnalia et Januariæ et Brumæ et Matronales fre-
quentantur, munera commeant, strenæ consonant, lusus, con-
vivia constrepunt. O melior fides nationum in suam sectam,
&c.[1]:* "The feasts of Saturn, of Janus, of Bacchus, and of
Juno, are frequented of us, unto whom the sabbaths, new
moons, and holy-days sometimes beloved of God, are strange,
gifts and presents are very rife, sports and banquets keep a
stir. O better is the faith of the gentiles in their sect, &c."
Wherefore this saying of Tertullian may aptly be alleged
against those that frequent the popish solemnities together
with them, come to their churches, communicate with them in
worshipping their idols, and yet profess the knowledge of the
gospel; but it can by no means be drawn unto such as, withdrawing themselves from such kind of communicating with
them, do in their several churches use those good things well
which the papists have abused; as the scripture, the sacraments, prayers, and such like. Wherefore you do not well to
allege Tertullian's words, omitting the circumstances which
declare his meaning.

A man being present at idolatrous service must needs give
great suspicion that he is an idolater; and therefore no man

[1 Nobis &c. a Deo aliquando dilectæ, &c. sectam : quæ nullam solennitatem
Christianorum sibi vindicat, non dominicum diem, non pentecosten. etiamsi
nossent, nobiscum non communicassent ; timerent enim ne Christiani viderentur.
Nos ne ethnici pronunciemur, non veremur.—Tertull. Op. Franek. 1597. De
Idol. 14. p. 155.]

ought to be present at it which in heart condemneth it. But, as there is no honest and godly man, which can call our service idolatrous or papistical, so is there none that can suspect us to be idolaters or papists; the whole world knowing that both our practice and profession is to the contrary.

Chapter i.   The Seventh Division.
T. C. Page 103, Sect. 3.

Euseb.
Lib. iii.
cap. 17.

Constantine the emperor, speaking of the keeping of the feast of Easter, saith "that it is an unworthy thing to have anything common with that most spiteful company of the Jews." And a little after he saith that "it is most absurd and against reason that the Jews should vaunt and glory that the Christians could not keep those things without their doctrine[2]." And in another place it is

Socrat. i.
Lib. cap. 9.

said after this sort · "It is convenient so to order the matter that we have nothing common with that nation[3]."

Jo. Whitgift.

"Constantine speaketh of the feast of Easter," which he would not have observed according to the manner of the Jews; and yet you know that the churches in Asia, following the examples of Philip and John the apostles, and of Polycarpus, and many other godly men, did celebrate that feast together with the Jews; as it is to be seen in the fifth book of Eusebius' Eccle. History[4]. Wherefore the matter was not of so great importance, before it was for quietness' sake determined by the church; neither doth Constantine in either of the places mean that we should have nothing common with the Jews, but only that we should have no such things common with them as are repugnant to christian liberty, or to the truth of the gospel, or such as may confirm them in their obstinacy and error. For, if his meaning had been generally and simply, then might he have utterly abrogated the feast of

Euseb. Lib. v.
cap. 23, 24,
& 25, 26.

[2 Καὶ πρῶτον μὲν ἀνάξιον ἔδοξεν εἶναι, τὴν ἁγιωτάτην ἐκείνην ἑορτὴν τῇ τῶν Ἰουδαίων ἐπομένους συνηθείᾳ πληροῦν·...μηδὲν τοίνυν ἔστω ἡμῖν κοινὸν μετὰ τοῦ ἐχθίστου τῶν Ἰουδαίων ὄχλου...ἔστι γὰρ ὡς ἀληθῶς ἀτοπώπατον, ἐκείνους αὐχεῖν ὡς ἄρα παρεκτὸς τῆς αὐτῶν διδασκαλίας ταῦτα φυλάττειν οὐκ εἴημεν ἱκανοί.—Euseb. in Hist. Eccles. Script. Amst. 1695-1700. De Vit. Constant. Lib. III. cap. xviii. pp. 405, 6.]

[3 Ὅθεν ἐπειδὴ τοῦτο οὕτως ἐπανορθοῦσθαι προσῆκεν, ὡς μηδὲν μετὰ τοῦ τῶν πατροκτόνων τε καὶ κυριοκτόνων ἐκείνων ἔθνους εἶναι κοινόν.—Socr. in eod. Lib. I. cap. ix. p. 28.]

[4 Euseb. in eod. Lib. v. capp. xxiii. xxiv. xxv. pp. 154, &c.]

Easter, being no commandment for it in the new testament. As therefore Constantine thought that the church had not the feast of Easter common with the Jews, not because the thing itself was abrogated, but the day altered; even so the church of England cannot be said to have anything common with the papistical church, though it retain something used in the same, because the manner is changed, and certain circumstances altered; for, whereas before it was in a strange tongue, now it is in a tongue known; and, whereas it was before abused and mixed with superstition, now it is rightly used and purged from all corruption. And therefore, although the thing remain, yet, because the circumstances be altered, it is not the same, no more than our sabbath is the Jews' sabbath, and our Easter the Jews' Easter.

Chapter i.   The Eighth Division.

T. C. Page 103, Sect. 4, 5, 6.

The councils, although they did not observe themselves always in making of decrees this rule, yet have kept this consideration continually in making their laws, that they would have the Christians differ from others in their ceremonies.

The council of Laodicea, which was afterward confirmed by the sixth general council, decreed that the Christians should not take unleavened bread of the Jews, or communicate with their impiety[1]. Tom. i. Conc. Laod. cap. 38.

Also it was decreed in another council, that they should not deck their houses with bay leaves and green boughs, because the pagans did use so, and that they should not rest from their labours those days that the pagans did, that they should not keep the first day of every month as they did[2]. ii. Tom. Braccar. can. 73.

Jo. Whitgift.

What is all this to your purpose[3]? Who saith that either we must use all things that the Jews and gentiles did, or that the church hath not authority to take order therein as shall be thought most convenient? The church at this time did perceive inconveniences in these customs and ceremonies, and therefore did by ordinary authority abrogate them. In like manner, and upon like consideration, hath this church of England abandoned great numbers of papistical rites and ceremonies;

[1 See below, note 4.]   [2 See below, note 5.]
[3 "... you know full well that these go to the heart of your cause."—The Rest of Sec. Repl. p. 176.]

but, because it refuseth some, may it therefore retain none ?
or, because it rejecteth those which be wicked and unprofitable,
may it not therefore keep still such as be godly and pertain
to order and decency ?

The canon of the council of Laodicea is this : *Non opor-*   Canon. 38.
tere a Judæis azyma accipere, aut communicare impietati-
bus eorum [4] *:* "That we ought not to take unleavened bread
of the Jews, or communicate with their impiety." And surely
I marvel what you can conclude of it ; for no man (as I suppose) doth think that we may use ceremonies proper to the
Jews, and abrogated by Christ, or that it is lawful to communicate with their impiety.

That canon which you call 73. of the council of Bracar. is
not to be found in any such council ; for there are not so many
canons in any council so called ; but the canon that you mean,
as I think, is among the canons collected out of the Greek
synods, by St Martin, and in number 74. The words be
these : " Let it not be lawful to use wicked observations of the
calends, and to keep the gentiles' holy-days, nor to deck
houses with bays or green boughs ; for all this is an heathenish
observation [5] ."

To what purpose do you allege this canon ? what doth it
prove ? Christians are inhibited from observing days, and
times, and other frivolous superstitions, after the manner of
the gentiles. But what is this to godly prayers grounded
upon the word of God, or comely and decent orders and
ceremonies ?

Chapter i.   The Ninth Division.

T. C. Page 103, Sect. ult.

Afric. Conc.   *Another council decreed that the Christians should not cele-*   A manifest
ca. 27 [6].   *brate feasts on the birth-days of the martyrs, because it was the*   untruth.
manner of the heathen : whereby it appeareth that, both of singular men,
and of councils in making or abolishing of ceremonies, heed hath been

---

[4 Concil. Laod. can. 38. in Concil. Stud. Labb. et Cossart. Lut. Par. 1671-2.
Tom. I. col. 1504.]

[5 Non liceat iniquas observationes agere Kalendarum, et otiis vacare gentili-
bus, neque lauro aut viriditate arborum cingere domos. Omnis hæc observatio
paganismi est.—Capit. Martin. Episc. Brac. 73. in eod. Tom. V. col. 913.]

[6 17, Def. B.]

taken that the Christians should not be like unto the idolaters, no, not in those things which of themselves are most indifferent to be used or not used.

Jo. Whitgift.

It is marvellous to behold your dealing, and to consider how, under the pretence of avoiding I know not what, in reciting the words of such authors as you allege, you delude the reader with an untrue sense; as it evidently appeareth in this canon of the council of Afric; the words whereof be these: " This is also to be desired (of the emperors) that such feasts as contrary to the commandments of God are kept in many places, which have been drawn from the error of the gentiles (so that now Christians are compelled by the pagans to celebrate them, whereby another persecution in the time of christian emperors seemeth covertly to be raised), might be by their commandment forbidden, and the pain laid upon cities and possessions prohibited ; especially, seeing they are not afraid to commit such things in some cities, even upon the birth-days of blessed martyrs, and in the holy places. Upon which days also (which is a shame to tell) they use most wicked dancings throughout the streets; so that the honour of matrons, and the chaste shamefastness of many women which come devoutly unto that holy-day, is by their lascivious injuries invaded, insomuch that those religious meetings are almost shunned[1]." In these words the heathenish feasts of the gentiles, which are against the commandment of God, being full of impiety and uncleanness, are forbidden to be used of Christians in the birth-days of martyrs, or at any other time. How this can be applied to your purpose I know not, except that you count all that for fish that comes to net.

Now let the reader consider what weighty reasons you

Conc. Afric. can. 27.

[1 Κἀκεῖνο ἔτι μὴν δεῖ αἰτῆσαι παρὰ τῶν χριστιανῶν βασιλέων, ἐπειδὴ παρὰ τὰ θεῖα παραγγέλματα ἐν πολλοῖς τόποις συμπόσια οὕτως ἐπιτελοῦνται ἐκ τῆς ἐθνικῆς πλάνης προσενεχθέντα, ὡς καὶ χριστιανοὺς τοῖς Ἕλλησι λάθρα προσσωνάγεσθαι ἐν τῇ τούτων τελετῇ· ἵνα κελεύσωσι τὰ τοιαῦτα κωλυθῆναι καὶ ἐκ τῶν πόλεων καὶ ἐκ τῶν κτήσεων· μάλιστα, ὅτι καὶ ἐν αὐτοῖς τοῖς γενεσίοις τῶν μακαρίων μαρτύρων ἀνά τινας πόλεις καὶ εἰς αὐτοὺς τοὺς ἱεροὺς τόπους τὰ τοιαῦτα πλημμελήματα φωρῶνται· ἐν αἷς ἡμέραις, ὅπερ καὶ λέγειν αἰσχύνη ἐστὶν, ὀρχήσεις μυσαρὰς εἰς τοὺς ἀγροὺς καὶ εἰς τὰς πλατείας ἐκτελοῦσι, ὥστε τῇ τῶν οἰκοδεσποινῶν τιμῇ, καὶ ἄλλων ἀναριθμήτων γυναικῶν τῇ αἰδοῖ τῶν εὐλαβῶν εἰς τὴν ἁγίαν ἡμέραν παραγενομένων, λάγναις ὕβρεσιν ἐφορμᾶν· ὡς καὶ αὐτῆς τῆς ἁγίας πίστεως σχεδὸν φεύγεσθαι τὴν προσέλευσιν.—Cod. Canon. Eccles. Afric. can. 60. in Concil. Stud. Labb. et Cossart. Lut. Par. 1671-2. Tom. II. col. 1086.]

have hitherto used against our order of prayer; nay, rather how unaptly you have alleged both your reasons and authorities. And, whereas you seem to insinuate that the things you have spoken of be "most indifferent;" that is nothing so: for the most of those things prohibited by these canons be things least indifferent; as it may appear by that which is already spoken of them, and even in the very canons themselves.

Chapter i.   The Tenth Division.

T. C. Page 104, Lin. 1.

It were not hard to shew the same considerations in the several things which are mentioned of in this Admonition: as for example in the cere-
Lib. de Anima. *monies of prayer, which is here to be handled, we read that Tertullian would not have the Christians sit after they had prayed, because the idolaters did so. But, having shewed this in general to be the policy of God first, and of his people afterward, to put as much difference as can be commodiously between the people of God and others which are not, I shall not need to shew the same in the particulars.*

Jo. Whitgift.

If "it were not too hard," I doubt not but that you would say something more in the matter than you have done. I know not to what purpose you have alleged Tertullian for not "sitting after prayer, &c.," except your meaning be that we shall not kneel in praying because the papists did use that gesture. Howbeit there is no such thing to be found in that book of Tertullian. Wherefore you are too careless in alleging your authors, and give too much credit, as it should seem, to other men's collections. In his book *De Oratione* he reproveth certain that used to sit after prayer, alleging for their author Hermas, to whom the book called *Pastor* is ascribed: he sheweth that no such thing can be gathered of Hermas his words; and further addeth that this gesture is to be reproved, not only because idolaters did use it in worshipping their idols, but also because it is an unreverent gesture. His words be these: *Eo apponitur et irreverentiæ* Tertullian. *crimen, &c.*[2]: "Hereunto is added the fault of unreverence, that

[2 Item quod adsignata oratione assidendi mos est quibusdam, non perspicio rationem, nisi si Hermas ille, cujus scriptura fere Pastor inscribitur, transacta oratione non super lectum assedisset, verum aliud quid fecisset, id quoque ad observationem vindicaremus...Imo contra scripturam fecerit, si quis in cathedra,

might be understood even of the gentiles themselves, if they were wise; for it is an unreverent thing to sit in the sight and against the face of him whom thou wouldest especially reverence and worship: how much more is this deed most profane in the sight of the living God, his angel being as yet present at this prayer." Truly, your general reasons hitherto used are neither of sufficient policy nor might to deface a book with so great wisdom, learning, and zeal collected and approved. If your particular reasons be no better, a small confutation will serve.

Chapter i.   The Eleventh Division.

T. C. Page 104, Sect. 1.

Furthermore, as the wisdom of God hath thought it the best way to keep his people from infection of idolatry to make them most unlike the idolaters; so hath the same wisdom of God thought good that, to keep his people in the unity of the truth, there is no better way than that they should be most like one to another, and that, as much as possibly may be, they should have all the same ceremonies. And therefore St Paul, to establish this order in the church of Corinth, that they should 1 Cor. xvi. 1.[1] *make their gatherings for the poor upon the first day of the sabbath (which is our Sunday), allegeth this for a reason, that he had so ordained in other churches; so that, as children of one father, and servants of one family, he will have all the churches not only have one diet, in that they have one word, but also wear (as it were) one livery in using the same ceremonies.*

Jo. Whitgift.

You take upon you to tell what "the wisdom of God is," without any warrant of God's word, which is presumption[2].

aut subsellio sederit. Porro cum perinde faciant nationes adoratis sigillaribus suis residendo, vel propterea in nobis reprehendi meretur quod apud idola celebratur. Eo apponitur et irreverentiæ crimen, etiam ipsis nationibus, si quid saperent, intelligendum. Siquidem irreverens est assidere sub conspectu contraque conspectum ejus, quem cum maxime revereris ac venereris: quanto magis sub conspectu Dei vivi angelo adhuc orationis astante factum istud irreligiosissimum est, nisi exprobramus Deo quod nos oratio fatigaverit.—Tertull. Op. Franek. 1597. De Orat. 12. p. 123.]

[1 The verse is added from Repl. 2.]

[2 Cartwright asserts that he had taken one of his reasons out of St Paul, and therefore censures Whitgift for that "in his answer he feareth not to say that I 'speak without any warrant of God's word.' As if St Paul's authority were no word of God with him; which if I had abused, why did he not convince me?"—The Rest of Sec. Repl. p. 182.]

I told you before, that in outward shew and form the Israelites had many things like unto the gentiles, which cannot be denied. Unity of ceremonies is to be wished in all churches, though it be not so necessary; for from the beginning there hath been therein great variety; but, seeing it is a thing so greatly to be desired, why are you an occasion of the contrary? why do you not submit yourself[3] to the church, that unity in all things may be observed?

Chapter i.   The Twelfth Division.
T. C. Page 104, Sect. 2.

Conc. Nic.
can. 20.

This rule did the great council of Nice follow, when it ordained that, where certain at the feast of Pentecost did pray kneeling, that they should pray standing; the reason whereof is added, which is that one custom ought to be kept throughout all the churches[4]. It is true that the diversity of ceremonies ought not to cause the churches to dissent one with another, but yet it maketh much to the avoiding of dissension, that there be amongst them an unity, not only in doctrine but also in ceremonies.

Jo. Whitgift.

This is to be wished throughout the whole church of Christ, if it were possible; but, as it never was hitherto, so will it not be as long as this world lasteth; and, lest it should be in this particular church of England, Satan hath stirred up instruments to procure the contrary; wherefore in these words, as I think, you condemn yourself and all other disturbers of the church for external rites and ceremonies.

Chapter i.   The Thirteenth Division.
T. C. Page 104, Sect. 2.

Now we see plainly that, as the form of our service and liturgy cometh too near that of the papists, so is[5] it far different from that of other churches reformed, and therefore in both these respects to be amended.

Jo. Whitgift.

From what "reformed church doth it so far differ?" or to which "reformed church" would you have it framed? or

[3 You self, Def. B.]

[4 Ἐπειδή τινές εἰσιν ἐν τῇ κυριακῇ γόνυ κλίνοντες, καὶ ἐν ταῖς τῆς πεντηκοστῆς ἡμέραις ὑπὲρ τοῦ πάντα ἐν πάσῃ παροικίᾳ φυλάττεσθαι, ἑστῶτας ἔδοξε τῇ ἁγίᾳ συνόδῳ τὰς εὐχὰς ἀποδιδόναι τῷ Θεῷ.—Concil. Nic. can. 20. in Concil. Stud. Labb. et Cossart. Lut. Par. 1671-2. Tom. II. cols. 37, 40.]

[5 It is, Repl. 1 and 2.]

To frame all churches after one is dangerous.

why should not other "reformed churches" as well frame themselves unto us? for we are as well assured of our doctrine, and have as good grounds and reasons for our doing as they have; except you will bring in a new Rome, appoint unto us another head church, and create a new pope, by whom we must be in all things directed, and according to whose usage we must frame ourselves.

You know what M. Calvin saith in the argument upon the epistle to the Galatians, speaking of those that came from Jerusalem to other churches: "Many were puffed up (saith he) with vain-glory, because they were familiar with the apostles, or at the least were instructed in their school; therefore nothing pleased them but that which they had seen at Jerusalem: all other rites that were not there used they did not only refuse, but boldly condemn. Such a kind of frowardness is a most pestilent mischief, when as we will have the manner of one church to be in place of an universal law. But this ariseth of a preposterous zeal, whereby we are so affected towards one master or place, that without judgment or consideration we would bind all men and places unto the opinion of one man, and unto the orders of one place, as unto a common rule. Albeit there is always mixed ambition: yea, rather always too much frowardness is ambitious[1]." The like saying he hath upon the xv. of the Acts: "Luke doth not express by what affection these varlets were moved; yet is it very like that a preposterous zeal was the cause that they set themselves against Paul and Barnabas; for there are froward wits, whom nothing but their own can please. They had seen at Jerusalem circumcision and other rites of the law to be observed; and whithersoever they come they can abide no new thing or divers; as if the example of one church did bind all other churches, as with a certain law. But, although such men are led with a preposterous zeal to move tumults, yet in-

Calv. in argu. in Epist. ad Gal.

A pestilent mischief.

Preposterous zeal.

Ambitious frowardness.

Idem in 15. Act.

Froward wits.

Ambition.

[1 Sed multi erant stulta gloria inflati, quod familiares fuissent apostolis, vel saltem in eorum schola instituti. Ideo nihil illis placebat, nisi quod Jerosolymis vidissent: alios omnes ritus illic non usitatos, non tantum respuebant, sed audacter etiam damnabant. Talis morositas, deterrima est pestis: quum morem ecclesiæ unius volumus pro universali lege valere. Nascitur autem ex præpostero zelo, quum erga magistrum aliquem vel locum ita sumus affecti, ut sine judicio loca omnia et omnes homines velimus ad unius hominis sensum, ad unius loci instituta, tanquam ad commune præscriptum adigere. quanquam semper admista est ambitio: imo semper nimia morositas est ambitiosa.—Calvin. Op. Amst. 1667-71. Arg. in Epist. ad Galat. Tom. VII. p. 278.]

wardly their ambition moveth them, and a certain kind of contumacy pricketh them forward. In the meantime, Satan hath that which he desireth, that the minds of the godly, being darkened with the smoke and mists that he casteth, can scant discern black from white. Therefore this mischief is first to be avoided, that none prescribe unto other a law of their custom; lest the example of one church be prejudicial to the common rule. Then another caution must be added, lest the estimation of men's persons do either hinder or obscure the search and inquiry of the matter and cause. For, if Satan do transform himself into an angel of light, and if he oftentimes usurp with wicked audacity the holy name of God; what marvel is it if through the same wickedness he delude with the names of godly men[2]?"

To frame all churches after one is dangerous.

A necessary caution.

M. Gualter also upon these words, 1 Cor. xiv., *An a vobis sermo Dei profectus est?* writeth thus: "Who can think their insolency to be tolerable, that usurp authority over all churches, and will have them servilely to be subject unto them? Therefore that which Paul here presently saith to the Corinthians, the self-same may at this day with better right be spoken to the Romish clergy, which will have all men subject to their laws, and say that it is necessary unto salvation that all souls should be subject to the bishop of Rome. These things may also be applied against those which compel every man to swear unto the opinion of their master, as though it were sin never so little to disagree from those things which he hath once uttered. And their ambition also is no less here reproved, which go about to bring all churches unto the form of their order and discipline, and cry out that there is no

Gualter in 1 Cor. xiv.

[2 Non exprimit quidem Lucas quo affectu impulsi fuerint isti nebulones: verisimile tamen est κακοζηλίαν in causa fuisse, ut se Paulo et Barnabæ opponerent. sunt enim morosa quædam ingenia, quibus nihil placet, nisi suum. Jerosolymæ circumcisionem, et alios legis ritus viderant servari: quocunque veniant, nihil possunt novum aut diversum ferre: quasi unius ecclesiæ exemplum reliquas omnes certa lege obstringat. Etsi autem tales præpostero zelo feruntur ad movendas turbas: intus tamen sua eos sollicitat ambitio, et contumacia quædam instigat. Interea habet Satan quod cupit, ut fumorum objectu confusæ piorum mentes vix nigrum ab albo discernant. Cavenda igitur primum hæc pestis, ne legem alii aliis ex suo more perscribant: ne unius ecclesiæ exemplum communis regulæ præjudicium sit. deinde adhibenda altera cautio, ne hominum personæ, rei et causæ disquisitionem vel impediant, vel obscurent. nam si Satan se transfigurat in angelum lucis, et si sanctum Dei nomen sacrilega audacia sæpe usurpat: quid mirum est, si eadem improbitate sanctorum virorum nominibus illudat?—Id. Comm. in Act. Apost. cap. xv. 1. Tom. VI. p. 134.]

To frame all churches after one is dangerous. discipline where all things are not correspondent to their orders and statutes; but these men receive a just reward of their arrogancy, when as they which come from them to other countries do go beyond all other in saucy malapertness; neither bring they anything with them from home, but a vain and untolerable contempt of all good men; neither can they abide that they should be corrected by any admonition of others. &c. [1]"

Beware of ambitious morosity, and take heed of a new popedom. I think no church is so bound to the example of another, but that in external rites and ceremonies there is free liberty given unto it to appoint what shall be for the present state and time most convenient. You may not bind us to follow any particular church, neither ought you to consent to any such new servitude [2].

Chapter i.   The Fourteenth Division
T. C. Page 104, Sect. 3.

Another fault there is in the whole service or liturgy of England, for that it maintaineth an unpreaching ministry; and so consequently an unlawful ministry; I say it maintaineth, not so much in that it appointeth a number of psalms and other prayers and chapters to be read, which may occupy the time which is to be spent in preaching, wherein notwithstanding it ought to have been more wary, considering that the devil under this colour of long prayer did thus in the kingdom of antichrist banish Argu. a non causa. *preaching—I say not so much in that point, as for that it requireth*

[1 Aut quis tolerabilem putet esse eorum insolentiam, qui sibi ipsis in omnes ecclesias jus sumunt, et eas sibi serviliter subjectas esse volunt? Quod ergo in præsenti Paulus Corinthiis dicit, hoc ipsum hodie meliori jure Romanensibus dici poterat, qui suis legibus omnes subjici volunt, et de necessitate salutis esse dicunt, ut omnes animæ Romano pontifici subjiciantur. Sed et in eos ista conveniunt, qui quosvis in sui magistri verba jurare cogunt, quasi nefas sit ab iis vel latum unguem discedere, quæ ille semel effutivit. Nec minus illorum quoque ambitio hic arguitur, qui omnes ecclesias ad suæ œconomiæ sive disciplinæ formam reducere conantur, et disciplinam illic nullam haberi clamant, ubi non omnia ipsorum traditionibus sive statutis respondent. Sed iidem dignas suæ arrogantiæ pœnas exolvunt, quando qui ab illis veniunt ad exteros, petulantia quosvis alios superant, nec aliquid domo secum adferunt, quam immanem et intolerabilem optimorum quorumque contemptum, neque ullis aliorum admonitionibus sese coerceri sinunt. &c.—R. Gualther. In Prior. ad Corinth. Epist. Hom. Tigur. 1578. Hom. lxxvi. fol. 223. 2.]

[2 "That out of M. Calvin, and Gualter, only serveth for filling. For we confess that for indifferent ceremonies neither the churches ought to fall out with themselves, nor any member sever himself from the church."—The Rest of Sec. Repl. p. 183.]

necessarily nothing to be done by the minister which a child of ten year old cannot do as well and as lawfully as that man wherewith the book contenteth itself.

To frame all churches after one is dangerous.

Jo. Whitgift.

This is a strange collection, that the book of common prayer " maintaineth an unpreaching ministry," because " it appointeth a number of psalms and other prayers and chapters to be read, which may occupy the time that is to be spent in preaching." Would you have preaching only, and neither reading nor praying in the public congregation? or do you think that the chapters and prayers that are read occupy too long time? or are you persuaded that there cometh no profit by reading and praying?   If you mean the first, you have the examples of the churches in all places, and at all times against you; if you mean the second, the time is not so long that is spent in praying and reading, but that there may be preaching also: the longest time (if there be no communion) is not more than an hour; and can you spend that hour better than in praying and hearing the scriptures read[3] ? If you mean the third, I shall have occasion to speak more of it hereafter.

But you say it doth not so much maintain an unpreaching ministry in that point, " as for that it requireth nothing necessarily to be done by the minister which a child of ten years old cannot do as well and as lawfully as that man wherewith the book contenteth itself."   It requireth of him (besides plain and distinct reading) the administration of the sacraments; and may a child of ten years old do that also[4] ? Who seeth not that you are of purpose set to deface the book, though it be with childish reasons?   Because a child may read the book, doth it therefore maintain an unpreaching ministry? you might as well say that, because a child of ten years old can read the bible translated into English, therefore the bible translated into English maintaineth an unpreaching ministry.   This argument is *a non causa.*

T. C. seeketh to deface the book without reason.

[3 " Whereunto I answer that, if with that hour he allow another for the sermon, the time will be longer than the age of some, and infirmities of other some, can ordinarily well bear.   Whereunto also if another hour, at the least, be added for the celebration of the holy communion, he may see that either the preaching must be abridged, or not so due regard had of men's infirmities."—Ibid. pp. 184, 5.]

[4 " No forsooth, but yet as well as he which can but barely read, if he have the same calling; which, being that which I affirmed, he is not able to move with one word of reason."—Ibid. p. 185.]

Some may
minister
the sacra-
ments
which do
not preach.

Chapter i.　The Fifteenth Division.

T. C. Page 104, Sect. 3.

*Neither can it be shifted in saying this is done for want of able men to
be ministers; for it may be easily answered that first the want of sufficient
ministers ought to be no cause for men to break the unchangeable laws of
God, which be, that none may be made minister of the church which cannot
teach, that none minister the sacraments which do not preach. For,
although it might be granted (which thing I would not deny, no, not when
there are enough sufficient ministers) that they may appoint some godly
grave man which can do nothing else but read to be a reader in the
church, yet that may not be granted that they may make of one that can
do nothing but read a minister of the gospel, or one which may have
power to minister the sacraments.*

Jo. Whitgift.

Some may
minister the
sacraments
which do not
preach.

Where is that "unchangeable law of God, that none may
minister the sacraments which do not preach?" what scripture
or authority have you for it? Chrysostom, Hom. 3. 1 Cor. i.,
upon these words: *Non enim misit me Christus ut bapti-*

Chrysost.

zarem, &c., saith thus: "He saith not, I was forbidden, but I
am not sent to do this, but to do that which was more
necessary. *Evangelizare enim perpaucorum est, baptizare
autem cujuslibet, modo fungatur sacerdotio*[1]: for few can
preach the gospel; but every man may baptize that is a
priest."

And Ambrose, upon the same words and chapter, saith thus:

Ambrose.

*Non omnis qui baptizat idoneus est…evangelizare; verba
enim solennia sunt quæ dicuntur in baptismate. &c.*[2]: "Every
one which baptizeth is not apt to preach the gospel; for the
words that are spoken in baptism are usual: to conclude, the
apostle Peter commanded other to baptize Cornelius, neither
did he vouchsafe to do it himself, other ministers being present; &c."

[1 Οὐ γὰρ εἶπεν, ὅτι ἐκωλύθην, ἀλλ', ὅτι οὐκ ἀπεστάλην ἐπὶ τούτῳ, ἀλλ'
ἐπὶ τῷ ἀναγκαιοτάτῳ. τὸ μὲν γὰρ εὐαγγελίζεσθαι, ἑνός που καὶ δευτέρου, τὸ
δὲ βαπτίζειν, παντὸς ἂν εἴη τοῦ τὴν ἱερωσύνην ἔχοντος.— Chrysost. Op. Par.
1718-38. In Epist. i. ad Corinth. Hom. iii. Tom. X. p. 18.]

[2 … non &c. baptismate. Denique apostolus Petrus credentem Cornelium
cum suis jussit baptizari, nec dignatus est, ministris adstantibus, hoc opus facere;
&c.—Ambros. Op. Par. 1686-90. Comm. in Epist. ad Corinth. prim. cap. i. v. 17.
Tom. II. Append. col. 114.]

Peter Martyr, writing upon the same words of the _{Some may minister the sacraments which do not preach.} apostle, saith likewise : " Therefore the office of baptizing was committed to every one in the church, but not the office of preaching.   Neither is it to be doubted but the apostles them- _{Peter Martyr.} selves would have baptized if there had lacked other mi- nisters.   But, seeing there was many whom they might win to the gospel by preaching, they committed them to other to be baptized[3]."

So saith M. Calvin also upon the same words : "Few there _{Calvin.} were to whom the office of preaching was committed, but to baptize was committed to many : &c.[4]"

Zuinglius, in his book *De Baptismo*, of this matter speaketh thus : "The disciples administered the external bap- _{Zuinglius.} tism once, with doctrine and the Spirit; for Christ taught; and they did baptize ; as it appeareth, Joh. iv.   And Paul said, 'Christ sent me not to baptize, but to preach ;' therefore some taught ; and other some baptized[5]."

Musculus also, in his Common-places, declareth that "in _{Musculus in Loc. Com. de cœna Domini.} some churches some were admitted to minister the sacraments that were not admitted to preach[6]."   And he doth not dis- allow that manner, but alloweth it.

And M. Beza, *Lib. Conf. cap. v.*, saith that "it was the _{Beza.} office of pastors and doctors generally to dispense the word, and to pray ; under the which also we comprehend the admi- nistration of sacraments and the celebration of marriage, according to the continual custom of the church ; although deacons in these things oftentimes supplied the offices[7] of

[3 Munus tingendi cuivis in ecclesia committi potest, non item munus evange- lizandi.   Nec dubium est, quin si alii ministri defuissent, apostoli profecto bap- tizassent. At quando illorum copia erat, ut hinc videre licet, quos Christo lucri- fecerant sua prædicatione, aliis tingendos delegabant.—P. Martyr. Comm. in D. Pauli prior. ad Corinth. Epist. Tigur. 1572. cap. i. fol. 9. 2.]

[4 ... sed quum paucorum esset docere, pluribus autem baptizare datum foret: &c.—Calvin. Op. Amst. 1667-71.   Comm. in Epist. i. ad Corinth. cap. i. 17. Tom. VII. p. 116.]

[5 Baptismum externum, qui aqua fit, citra omnem doctrinam et spiritum, discipuli olim contulerunt.   Hi enim Christo docente, sed non baptizante, baptiza- runt, quemadmodum ex Joan. 4. et 1 Corinth. 1. paulo ante demonstravimus. Paulus enim, Non misit me, inquit, Christus, ut baptizarem, sed ut evangeliza- rem. Alii ergo docebant, alii vero baptizabant.—H. Zvingl. Op. Tigur. 1581. De Bapt. Lib. Pars II. fol. 61. 2.]

[6 Scio quibusdam ecclesiis hoc esse in more, ut ministri verbi loco fungantur prophetarum et doctorum, et interim *parœcis* ac *plebanis*, ut vocant, cum diaconis sacramentorum administrationem relinquant. &c.—Wolfg. Muscul. Loc. Comm. Theolog. Basil. 1599. De Cœn. Dom. p. 369.]   [7 Office, Def. A.]

pastors[1]." And to prove this he quoteth 1 Cor. i. verse 14, 15, &c., and John iv. verse 2.

So do other learned men in like manner; who also bring for their purpose that which is written, 1 Tim. v.: *Qui bene præsunt presbyteri, &c.* So that you may understand that learned men be of this judgment, that some may be admitted to administer the sacraments which are not admitted to preach.

I know it to be true that there may be some appointed to read in the church, which be not admitted either to preach or to administer the sacraments. For so it was in the primitive church; as it is to be seen in ancient stories and writers. But, because you would have nothing used in the church, especially no office appointed without a commandment in the word of God, I pray you, tell where you have either commandment or example for such kind of readers. I do but demand this, that the reader may understand what liberty you challenge unto yourself of allowing and disallowing what you list, and when you list, without that warrant of God's word, to the which you so straitly bind all other.

Chapter i.   The Sixteenth Division.

T. C. Page 104, Sect. 4.

Besides that, how can they say that it is for want of sufficient ministers, when as there be put out of the ministry men that be able to serve God in that calling, and those put in their rooms which are not able, when there are numbers also which are fit to serve, and never sought for, nor once required to take any ministry upon them? If therefore it were lawful to plead want of able ministers for this dumb ministry, which is altogether unlawful, yet would this plea never be good until such time as both those were restored which are put out, and all other sought forth, and called upon which are fit for that purpose.

Jo. Whitgift.

Confess.
Helv. You know what was before alleged out of the confession of the churches of Helvetia, that "the harmless simplicity of some shepherds in the old church did sometimes more profit

---

[1 Horum doctorum [pastorum et doctorum] officium est in genere, administrando sermoni, et precibus habendis incumbere, sub quibus etiam comprehendimus sacramentorum administrationem, et nuptiarum benedictionem ex perpetuo ecclesiæ usu, quamvis sæpe diaconi in his rebus suppleverint pastorum vices.—Th. Bezæ Confess. Christ. Fid. Genev. 1587. cap. v. 25. p. 238.]

the church than the great, exquisite, or fine or delicate, but a little too proud, learning of some others[2]." A great sort think too well of themselves, and be of nature unquiet; such of necessity (if by no means they can be kept in order) must be removed; for the church may not for their sake be rent and torn in pieces; neither must you that so well allow of discipline burden other men with it, and cast it off yourselves. There is none in this church of England removed from his ministry but upon just causes; and ministers must be subject to laws and orders.

Unquiet natures must be removed.

Those that be willing to come into the ministry lack no provoking nor moving thereunto, if they be known; but it is you and your company which labour by all means possible to dehort men from the ministry, persuading them that the calling is not ordinary and lawful. And surely your meaning is to make this church destitute of ministers, that it may of necessity be driven to admit your platform and government. But you shall never be able to bring it to pass: the more you labour, the more you are detected. And those wise men that seek the truth in sincerity of conscience will espy your purposes daily more and more, and be moved to a just misliking of them.

The ministry hindered, and by whom.

The restitution of those that " be put out of the ministry " I think is soon obtained, if they will submit themselves to the order of the church, which they ought of duty to do, both the laws of God and man requiring the same.

Chapter i.   The Seventeenth Division.
T. C. Page 104, Sect. ult.

Again, it cannot be said justly that they have taken these reading ministers until such time as better may be gotten; for, if the church could procure able ministers, and should desire that they might be ordained over them, they cannot obtain that, considering that these reading ministers have a freehold and an estate for term of their lives in those churches of the which they are such ministers; so that by this means the sheep are not only committed to an idol shepherd, I might say a wolf, and speak no otherwise than Augustine speaketh[3], in that a not preaching minister hath

[2 Confess. et Expos. Fid. Christ. cap. xviii. in Corp. et Syntagm. Confess. Fid. Genev. 1654. p. 38. See Vol. I. page 338, note 1.]

[3 Videtis quam sit tacere periculosum? Moritur ille, et recte moritur: in impietate sua et peccato suo moritur; negligentia enim ejus [pastoris] occidit eum.—August. Op. Par. 1679-1700. Serm. xlvi. 20. De Past. in Ezek. xxxiv. Tom. V. col. 235. This is the passage which Cartwright (Sec. Repl. p. 373) declares he meant.]

entrance into the church, but the door also is shut upon him and sparred[1] against any able minister that might happily[2] be found out.

Jo. WHITGIFT.

And would you so gladly intrude yourselves into some of their rooms? Surely I believe it; and it is not unknown but that some of you have laboured to do it. Well, I have before told you the judgment of the reformed churches touching such ministers as be not able to preach, being otherwise virtuous and godly. I have also set down the opinion of divers learned and godly men concerning ministers admitted to minister the sacraments, which notwithstanding cannot preach. If any man use himself in his ministry lewdly, or otherwise than beseemeth him, "his estate for term of life" is not so sure, but that he may be dispossessed of the same. Otherwise, if he use himself honestly, and as it becometh him, though he have not the gift of preaching (which notwithstanding is to be wished), God forbid that either you or any man else should seek to displace him, that you might enjoy the room yourselves. And surely, if the minister were but tenant at will, or of courtesy (as you would seem to have him), his state should be most slavish and miserable, and he and his family ready to go a begging whensoever he displeaseth his parish.

If you had told me where Augustine speaketh that, I should have quickly let you understand his meaning; but his books be many and large, the sentence you allege short, and therefore it were too much for me to search it out. Moreover, it improveth nothing now in question. But with what face can you flout and jest at me for once or twice not quoting the chapter or leaf, yourself so often offending in quoting neither chapter, leaf, book, nor tome?

Chapter i.   The Eighteenth Division.
T. C. Page 105, Sect. 1.

There is a third fault which likewise appeareth almost in the whole body of this service and liturgy of England, and that is that the profit which might have come by it unto the people is not reaped; whereof the cause is for that he which readeth is not in some places[3] heard, and in the most places not understanded of the people, through the distance of place between the people and the minister; so that a great part of the people

[1] Sparred or speared : closed, fastened.]   [2] Haply, Answ. 2.]
[3] Place, Def. A. and B.]

*cannot of knowledge tell whether he hath cursed them or blessed them,
whether he hath read in Latin or in English; all the which riseth upon the
words of the book of service, which are that the minister should stand in
the accustomed place; for thereupon the minister in saying morning and
evening prayer sitteth in the chancel with his back to the people, as though
he had some secret talk with God which the people might not hear. And
hereupon it is likewise, that, after morning prayer, for saying another
number of prayers he climbeth up to the further end of the chancel, and
runneth as far from the people as the wall will let him, as though there
were some variance between the people and the minister, or as though he
were afraid of some infection of plague; and indeed it reneweth the
memory of the Levitical priesthood, which did withdraw himself from the
people into the place called the holiest place, where he talked with God and
offered for the sins of the people.*

Jo. Whitgift.

This nothing toucheth the order or substance of the book,
and therefore no sufficient reason against it, if it were true.
But you herein deal as you have done in other matters, that
is, corruptly and untruly. For you do not report the words Corrupt
dealing.
of the book concerning this matter as they be indeed; and
it is wonderful, and argueth great impudency, that you are
not ashamed to report untruly in so public a cause. The
words of the book be these: " The morning and evening
prayer shall be used in the accustomed place of the church,
chapel, or chancel, except it shall be otherwise determined by
the ordinary of the place." And you, leaving out all the rest,
say that "the words of the book of service are that the
minister should stand in the accustomed place;" as though it
bound him of necessity to the chancel, which is nothing so.
But you must be borne with; your errors and disorders cannot Errors and
disorder
maintained
by falsifying.
otherwise be maintained but by falsifying. I think there are
but few churches in England where the bishops have not
taken a very good order for the place of prayer: if any bishop
have neglected it, the fault is in the bishop, not in the book.

But still I must desire the reader to note the weightiness
of the reasons whereby you go about to deface the book of
common prayer.

Chapter i.   The Nineteenth Division.

T. C. Page 105, Sect. 2.

*Likewise for marriage he cometh back again into the body of the
church, and for baptism unto the church-door: what comeliness, what*

decency, what edifying is this?   Decency (I say) in running and trudging from place to place: edifying, in standing in that place, and after that sort, where he can worst be heard[1] and understanded.   St Luke sheweth that in the primitive church both the prayers and preachings, and the whole exercise of religion, was done otherwise.   For he sheweth how St Peter, sitting amongst the rest, to the end he might be Acts i. 15.[2]
the better heard, rose, and not that only, but that he stood in the midst of the people, that his voice might as much as might be come indifferently to all their ears, and so standing both prayed and preached.   Now, if it be said for the chapters and litany there is commandment given that they should be read in the body of the church, indeed it is true; and thereof is easily perceived this disorder which is in saying the rest of the prayers, partly in the hither end, and partly in the further end of the chancel ; for, seeing that those are read in the body of the church, that the people may both hear and understand what is read, what should be the cause why the rest should be read further[3] off?   Unless it be that either those things are not to be heard of them, or, at the least, not so necessary for them to be heard as the other which are recited in the body or midst of the church. And, if it be further said that the book leaveth that to the discretion of the ordinary, and that he may reform it if there be anything amiss, then it is easily answered again that, besides that it is against reason that the commodity and edifying of the church should depend upon the pleasure of one man, so that upon his either good or evil advice and discretion it should be well or evil with the church—besides this (I say), we see by experience of the disorders which are in many churches and dioceses in this behalf, how that, if it were lawful to commit such authority unto one man, yet that it is not safe so to do, considering that they have so evil quitten themselves in their charges, and that in a matter, the inconvenience whereof is[4] so easily seen and so easily reformed, there is notwithstanding so great and so general an abuse.

JO. WHITGIFT.

Weighty reasons against the book.

These be passing weighty arguments to overthrow the book, and come from a deep and profound judgment : if I should use the like, you would wipe them away with scoffing. The book appointeth that the " persons to be married shall come into the body of the church, with their friends and neighbours, there to be married;" and what fault can you find in this? Is not the midst of the church the most meet place for such a matter? The book speaketh neither of the coming back of the minister, nor his going forward; these be but your jests; and yet must he go both backward and forward, if he

[1 Hard, Repl. 1 ; harde, Repl. 2.]
[2 This reference is inserted from Repl. 2.]
[3 Farther, Repl. 1 and 2.]   [4 Being, Repl. 2.]

will either come into the church, or go out of it. For baptism
the book appointeth no place; but, because there is no just
cause known why the font should be removed, therefore the
minister doth stand where that is placed, which is somewhere
in one place, somewhere in another; for I know divers places
where it is in the midst of the church, some place where
it is in the nethermost part; I know no place where it standeth at the church-door.   And therefore in saying that "for
baptism the minister goeth to the church-door," you do but
counterfeit.

No man denieth but that both praying and preaching, &c.,
ought to be in that place where it may be best heard of all;
and therefore the book doth prudently leave it to the discretion of the bishop.   But the midst is not the fittest place
for that purpose. He that standeth in the midst of the
church hath some behind him, some before him, and some of
each side of him : those which be behind, or on the sides, cannot so well hear as those that be before; as experience teacheth in sermons at the Spittle, at the cross in Paul's, and
other places.   Wherefore in my opinion that place in the
church is most fittest, both for praying and preaching, where
the minister may have the people before him, except the church
be so great and the people so many that he cannot be heard
of them, then there ought to be some regard thereof.

St Luke telleth what St Peter did in the congregation,
he doth not prescribe any general rule : every circumstance
that is told in the scriptures is not straightway to be made
an inviolable rule of all men to be followed. The place is not
material; so that it be such as the people may well hear and
understand that which is read and preached.

Concerning the lessons which are to be read, the book
prescribeth no place, only it willeth the minister "to stand
and to turn him so as he may best be heard of all such as be
present:" and are you offended at that? Neither doth the
book appoint any certain place for the litany to be said in.
And therefore you do but dally and trifle.

The ordinary is the meetest man to whose discretion those
things should be left, both for his learning and wisdom, and
also that there may be one uniform order in his diocese : if
any ordinary be careless in such matters, if you will complain
of him, I am sure you shall be heard. But your delight and

pleasure is to be girding at bishops, though the cause be forged[1].

Chapter i.   The Twentieth Division.
T. C. Page 105, Sect. 3.

Untrue.

And the end of the order in the book is to be observed, which is to keep the prayers in the accustomed place of the church, chapel, or chancel; which how maketh it to edification? And thus for the general faults committed either in the whole liturgy, or in the most part of it, both that I may have no need to repeat the same in the particulars, and that I be not compelled always to enter a new disputation, so oft as M. Doctor saith,

These be not my words.

very unskilfully and unlike a divine, whencesoever this or that come, so it be not evil, it may be well established in the church of Christ.

Jo. Whitgift.

What is "the end of the book" in that matter? why do you not express it? But you say it "is to keep the prayers in the accustomed places, &c." If this be the end, why doth the book admit alteration? do you not see yourself manifestly convinced by the book? I believe, and I am well assured, that the end is edification, whatsoever you imagine to the contrary. And undoubtedly you have found out marvellous weighty and witty reasons against "the whole liturgy, or the most part of it;" and the faults you have noted be very many and exceeding great. But have you no conscience in calling good evil? or are you not afraid upon so light quarrels to make such a schism in the church, and to bring so worthy a book into so great contempt? Well, you will one day be better advised, I doubt not; which truly I wish for, and hope for, how uncourteously soever you have used me.

[1 " ... he answereth nothing worth the naming. But the sum of his defence is, that the 'bishop hath power to order it, to the most edification.' Wherein how unlawful it is that he alone should have the order hereof is before declared; and how dangerous it is, let the practice in this point be judge. For I am assuredly persuaded that the tenth church in England hath not all the service said in that place where the whole church may best hear it; and withal note (as I said) what a shameful disorder is committed in a matter so easily remedied. The place of St Luke is an unchangeable rule to teach...His cavil of the place of the font, said of me to 'be at the church-door,' instead that I should have said, 'over against the church-door,' is unworthy the answer, especially considering that I spake more favourably for the book than he which by this answer sendeth the minister for baptism beneath the church-door...And this both separation of the minister by chancel, as 'monkish,' as also the often shifting of the minister's place, as a thing 'very absurd,' M. Bucer, both generally in all places, and particularly in our church, doth condemn."—The Rest of Sec. Repl. pp. 186, 7.]

That which M. Doctor saith so "unskilfully and unlike a divine" he hath learned of better and more skilful divines than either of us both be; that is, of Ambrose, and of Calvin; for the one saith : *Omne verum a quocunque dicitur a Spiritu sancto est*[2] : "All truth, of whomsoever it is spoken, is of the Holy Ghost;" the other: *Purus est multarum rerum usus,* Calvinus in *quarum vitiosa est origo*[3] : "The use of many things is pure, 5. Matt. vers. 37. whose beginning is vicious and unpure." But M. Doctor's bare affirmation (if he had so used it) is of as good credit as your bare negation; but, when he hath learned men of his opinion and judgment, for you thus to shift it off is but to bewray your unableness to disprove it, either by authority or reason. You should at the least have made true report of my words, which you have not done, but dealt therein according to your accustomed manner; for my words be these, fol. 82.[4]: "It Pag. 82, sect. 2. maketh no matter of whom it was invented, in what book it is contained, so that it be good and profitable, and consonant to God's word;" and you report them thus : "Whencesoever this or that come, so it be not evil, it may be well established in the church of Christ." If you have the truth, why do you thus go about to maintain it with lies? In so doing you hurt not me, but yourself, and your cause.

¶ An examination of the particular faults, either in matter or form, wherewith the Book of Common Prayer is charged.

Chapter ii.   The First Division.

T. C. Page 105, Sect. 3.

Now I come to the form of prayer which is prescribed, wherein the authors of the Admonition declare that their meaning is not to disallow of prescript service of prayer, but of this form that we have; for they expound A proper ex- *themselves in the additions unto the first part of the Admonition.* cuse.

Jo. Whitgift.

Indeed they have retracted it in some point, which argueth they writ their book at the first with small advice, and less

---

[2 ... quidquid enim verum a quocumque dicitur, a sancto dicitur Spiritu.—Ambros. Op. Par. 1686-90. Comm. in Epist. ad Corinth. prim. cap. xii. v. 3. Tom. II. Append. col. 150.]

[3 Calvin. Op. Amst. 1667-71. Comm. in Harm. Euang. Matt. v. 37. Tom. VI. p. 73.]

[4 See below, Tractat. x. chap. ii. div. 8.]

[WHITGIFT, II.]

30

discretion. It is no " exposition," but a retractation or recan-
tation; for the places of scripture which they quoted, and their
very words, declare that they meant the contrary, and so doth
their practice in secret conventicles.   But now you come to
my Answer, wherein you take what you list, and leave what
you list, as you have hitherto done.

Chapter ii.   The Second Division.

Admonition.

The fourteenth.

Then ministers were not so tied to any form of prayers
invented by man, but, as the Spirit [g] *moved them, so they poured*
forth [2] *hearty supplications to the Lord.   Now they are bound*
of necessity to a [h]*prescript order of service and book of*
common prayer [3].

> [g] Rom. viii.
> 26 [1].
> 1 Tim. i. 2.
> [h] Damasus
> the first in-
> ventor of
> this stuff,
> well fur-
> thered by
> Gregory
> the seventh.

Answer to the Admonition, Page 77, Sect. 3.

To prove that " ministers were not so tied to any form
of prayer, invented by man, but that as the Spirit moved
them, &c.," you quote Rom. viii. and the 1 Tim. i.   In
the eighth to the Romans the words be these : " Likewise
also the Spirit helpeth our infirmities; for we know not
what to pray as we ought; but the Spirit itself maketh
request for us with sighs which cannot be expressed."
This place speaketh nothing against any prescript form
of prayer, for then it should disallow the Lord's prayer;
but it teacheth us that it is the Spirit of God that stir-
reth us up to pray, and maketh us earnestly pour out
our supplications unto God.   And thus [4] the Spirit

A prescript
order of
prayer in
the church [5].

worketh as well by prescript prayers as by prayers suddenly invented.   The words to Timothy, Epist. i. ca. i,
vers. 2, are far-fetched, and nothing to the purpose : the
words be these : " Unto Timothy, my natural son in the
faith, grace, mercy, and peace from God our Father, and
from Christ Jesu our Lord."   What maketh these words
against any prescript form of prayers? peradventure you

[1 Adm. omits this reference.]

[2 Any one form of prayers but as the Spirit moved them and as necessity of
time required so they might pour forth, Adm.]

[3 Here Answ. continues the sentence of Adm. which is found below, page
495, and subsequently.]

[4 This, Answ.]   [5 This marginal note is inserted from Answ. 2.]

would have alleged the 1 to Timo. ii. "I exhort therefore that, first of all, supplications, &c.;" which maketh
directly against you.

Jo. Whitgift.

Nothing answered to this.

Chapter ii.   The Third Division.

Answer to the Admonition, Page 78, Sect. 1.

If you mean by "prayers invented by man" such
prayers as man inventeth against the word of God, as
prayer for the dead, prayer unto saints, and such like,
then it is true that you say.   But, if you mean such
prayers as by godly men be framed according to the
holy scriptures, whether they be for matters pertaining to
the life to come, or to this life, then you shew your ignorance; for it is manifest, that there hath been always in
the church of Christ a prescript form of public prayer;
as it appeareth in Justinus Martyr, *Apol. ii. pro Chris-* Justinus
tianis, and other ancient fathers: neither did ever any Martyr.
learned or godly man, or reformed church, find fault
herewith, or not greatly commend the same, except only
the sect of anabaptists.

T. C. Page 105, Sect. ult., and Page 106, Sect. 1.

*It is not to any purpose that M. Doctor setteth himself to prove that
there may be a prescript order of prayer by Justin Martyr's testimony,
which notwithstanding hath not one word of prescript form of prayers;
only he saith there were prayers; he saith indeed the ancient fathers say
that there hath been always such kind of prayers in the churches; and,
although they do say so, yet all men may understand easily that M. Doctor
speaketh this rather by conjecture, or that he hath heard other men say so;
forsomuch as that doctor which he hath chosen out to speak for all the
rest hath no such thing as he fathereth on him.   He saith that "after they
have baptized they pray for themselves, and for him that is baptized, and
for all men, that they may be meet to learn the truth, and to express it in
their honest conversation, and that they be found to keep the commandments, that they may attain to eternal life;" but is this to say that there was
a prescript form of prayer, when he sheweth nothing else but the chief
points upon the which they conceived their prayers?   If you had alleged
this to prove what were the matters or principal points that the primitive
church used to pray for, you had alleged this to purpose; but to allege it*

30—2

for a proof of a prescript form of prayer, when there is not there men-
tioned so much as the essential form of prayer (which is the asking of our
petitions in the name and through the intercession of our Saviour Christ),
without the which there is not, nor cannot be, any prayer, argueth that
either you little know what the form of prayer is, or that you thought (as
you charge the authors of the Admonition so often) that this gear of yours
should never have come to the examination.

But, forasmuch as we agree of a prescript form of prayer to be used
in the church, let that go: this that I have said is to shew that, when
M. Doctor happeneth of a good cause, which is very seldom in this book,
yet then he marreth it in the handling.

JO. WHITGIFT.

I have the less laboured in this point, because it is a
thing so generally allowed of in all churches, in all times, and
so unlearnedly impugned by the authors of the Admonition.

Justinus Martyr maketh much for my purpose; for, in that
he doth rehearse those chief points of their prayers then used,
it is manifest that they had a prescript order and form of
prayer; the which no man can deny that readeth the place[1].
I grant that these words, " prescript form of prayer," are not
there to be found; yet is there a prescript order and form by
him generally described; whereby it is more than probable that
at that time there was used a prescript form of prayer.   In the
3. council of Carthage we find this canon: " Let no man use
the forms of prayer which he hath framed to himself, without
conference with brethren that are better learned[2]."   Whereby
it may evidently be gathered, that at that time there was a
prescript form of prayer used, and that it was not lawful to
use any new form of private prayers, except the same were
allowed by the brethren.   But, forasmuch as in this point you
consent with me, and grant that there may be a prescript
form of prayer, I will omit whatsoever I had purposed to have
said more in that matter; and so I will do also your taunts
respecting the matter, rather than Lucian's rhetoric.

Conc. Carth.
III. Can. 23.

[1 Just. Mart. Op. Par. 1742. Apol. I. 65, 7. pp. 82, 3. See Vol. I. page 215,
note 4.]

[2 Et quicumque sibi preces aliunde describit, non eis utatur, nisi prius eas
cum instructioribus fratribus contulerit.—Concil. Carthag. III. can. 23. in Concil.
Stud. Labb. et Cossart. Lut. Par. 1671-2. Tom. II. col. 1170.]

Chapter ii.   The Fourth Division.

Answer to the Admonition, Page 78, Sect. 2, 3.

Damasus was a good bishop, and therefore no good thing by him appointed to be disallowed; but he did not first ordain a prescript form of public prayers, he only added something thereunto; as *Gloria Patri, &c.*, to the end of every psalm; and decreed that psalms should be sung as well in the night-time as in the day-time in every church[4]; but they were sung in the church before; and, as I have said, there was a prescript form of prayer in Justinus Martyr's time, who was long before Damasus.

Damasus added Gloria Patri, &c.[3]

Gregory added the litany only[5].   I muse what you mean to write so manifest untruths.

Gregory made the litany.

Jo. Whitgift.

Nothing answered to this.

Chapter ii.   The Fifth Division.

Answer to the Admonition, Page 79, Sect. 1.

You note not here (neither are you able) any prayer in the whole communion-book, wherein there is any thing not agreeable to God's word. We may say as St Augustine[6] saith in his 121. epistle written *ad Probam viduam: Etsi per omnia precationum sanctarum verba discurras, quantum existimo nihil invenies, quod non ista dominica contineat et concludat oratio.   Unde liberum est aliis atque aliis verbis eadem tamen in orando dicere; sed non debet esse liberum alia dicere*[7]: " And, if thou runnest through all the words of the holy prayers, I suppose thou shalt find nothing which the Lord's prayer doth not contain and comprehend; therefore we may in

Augustine.

[3 Answ. has not &c.]

[4 ... ut psalmi quoque alternis vicibus in ecclesia canerentur, in fineque eorum verba hæ[c] ponerentur, Gloria Patri et Filio et Spiritui Sancto, instituit.—Plat. De Vit. Pont. Col. 1551. Damas. I. p. 48.]

[5 Præterea vero supplicationes majores, quas Græci letanias vocant, primus instituit.—Id. ibid. Gregor. I. p. 73.]

[6 Austine, Answ.]

[7 August. Op. Par. 1679-1700. Ad Prob. Epist. cxxx. cap. xii. 22. Tom. II. col. 391 ; where *quod in ista dominica non contineatur et concludatur oratione.*]

other words speak the same things in our prayers, but we may not speak contrary things."

T. C. Page 106, Sect. 1, 2.

After he affirmeth that there can be nothing shewed in the whole book which is not agreeable to[1] *the word of God.*

I am very loth to enter into this field, albeit M. Doctor doth thus provoke me, both because the papists will lightly take occasion of evil-speaking when they understand that we do not agree amongst ourselves in every point, as for that some few professors of the gospel being private men, boldened upon such treatises, take such ways sometimes, and break forth into such speeches as are not meet nor convenient.

Jo. Whitgift.

In so saying, I do fully agree with such as have learnedly and truly written against the common adversaries of this book; among whom there is one that wrote a book entituled, "A sparing Restraint of many lavish Untruths which M. Doctor Harding doth challenge in the first Article of my lord of Sarisbury's Reply." The author of that book writeth thus :

A sparing Restraint.

"O M. Harding, turn again your writings, examine your authorities, consider your councils, apply your examples, look if any line be blameable in our service, and take hold of your advantage. I think M. Jewel will accept it for an article." And a little after : "Our service is good and godly, every tittle grounded on holy scriptures; and with what face do you call it darkness[2] ?" This was his opinion then of our service. And it both was then, and is now my full persuasion; and I will (God willing) perform that against you which be offered in M. Jewel his name against Harding.

The Replier his words contrary to his deeds.

Your "lothness to enter into this field" is but dissembled; your continual barking against the state and form of this church of England doth convince you of the contrary. Neither have you any respect or regard for giving occasion of evil speech to the papists, much less of provoking your adherents to undutiful speeches (as you pretend), your book tending wholly to the contrary.

[1 Unto, Repl. 1 and 2.]

[2 A sparing Restraint, of many lauishe Vntruthes, which M. Doctor Harding dothe chalenge, in the first Article of my Lorde of Sarisburies Replie. By Edward Dering, Lond. p. 5; where *again to your writings, it as an article*, and *do ye call it*.]

Chapter ii.   The Sixth Division.
T. C. Page 106, Sect. 3.

Notwithstanding, my duty of defending the truth, and love which I have first towards God and then towards my country, constraineth me being thus provoked to speak a few words more particularly of the form of prayer, that when the blemishes thereof do appear it may please the queen's majesty and her honourable council, with those of the parliament whom the Lord hath used as singular instruments to deliver this realm from the hot furnace and iron yoke of the popish Egypt, to procure also that the corruptions which we have brought from them (as those with which we being so deeply dyed and stained have not so easily shaken off) may be removed from amongst us, to the end that we, being nearlier both joined unto the sincerity of the gospel, and the policy of other reformed churches, may thereby be joined nearer with the Lord, and may be set so far from Rome that both we may comfort ourselves in the hope that we shall never return thither again, and our adversaries which desire it, and, by this too much agreement with them, and too little with the reformed churches, hope for it, may not only be deceived of their expectation, but also, being out of all hope of that which they do desire[3], may the sooner yield themselves unto the truth whereunto they are now disobedient.

Jo. Whitgift.

What "duty" can there be in defacing a known and received truth? what "love," in slandering your country unjustly, and renting it in pieces with sects and schisms, and provoking the subjects to have misliking of their magistrates, and such as be placed in authority over them? these be but cloaks to cover an evil and ungodly purpose. If you shall be able to shew any such blemishes in the book of common prayers, they shall not be covered for me; but if not, then are you not a man to be credited.

I have told you M. Calvin's and M. Gualter's opinion touching the ambitious morosity of such as would have all churches framed after the example of some one[4]; and now I tell you again, that there is no cause why this church of England, either for truth of doctrine, sincerity of public divine service, and other policy, should give place to any church in Christendom; and sure I am, that we are as near joined with the Lord our God as the members are to the body, and the body to the head.

Supra, cap. 1. the 13. division.

[3 They desire, Repl. 1, 2, and Def. A.]   [4 See before, pages 452, &c.]

Our "adversaries" have no such "hope" upon any such occasion as you pretend; if their hope be any, it is especially in your contentions.

Wherein do we agree with the papists? or wherein do we dissent from the reformed churches? with these we have all points of doctrine and substance common; from the other we dissent, in the most part both of doctrine and ceremonies. From what spirit come these bold and untrue speeches?

Chapter ii.   The Seventh Division.
T. C. Page 106, Sect. 4.

And, as for the papists' triumph in this case, I shall not greatly need to fear it, considering that their discords and contentions are greater, and that our strife is because we would be farther from them.   For the other that profess the gospel, I will desire in the name of God that they abuse not my labour to other end than I bestow it, and that they keep themselves in their callings, commit the matter by prayer unto the Lord, leaving to the ministers of the word of God, and to the magistrates, that which appertaineth unto them.

Jo. Whitgift.

It is true of the papists; but they deal in their controversies more circumspectly and warely, though they dissent in matters of far greater importance, and in the chief points of their own religion.

To the professors of the gospel you give better counsel than you have taken yourself; and you shew an example contrary to your words; and therefore how shall they believe you? But now to the matter; for hitherto you have uttered nothing but words.

Chapter ii.   The Eighth Division.
T. C. Page 106, Sect. ult.

To come therefore to touch this matter, I answer, that there is fault in the matter, and fault in the form.   In the matter, for that there are things there that ought not to be, and things there are wanting in the order that should be.   Of the first sort is "that we may evermore be defended from all adversity."   The Collect of Trinity Sunday.

Jo. Whitgift.

The first fault that you find in the matter of prayer is a portion of the collect of Trinity Sunday, wherein we pray

"that we may evermore be defended from all adversity."
And is this the matter you mislike? let us then consider your
reason.

Chapter ii.   The Ninth Division.
T. C. Page 107, Sect. 1.

*Now, forasmuch as there is no promise in the scripture that we should
be free from all adversity, and that evermore, it seemeth that this prayer
might have been better conceived, being no prayer of faith, or of the which
we can assure ourselves that we shall obtain it. For, if it be said that by
the word "adversity" is meant all evil, we know that it hath no such signification, neither in this tongue of ours, neither in other tongues which use
the same word in common with us; but that it signifieth trouble, vexation,
and calamity; from all the which we may not desire always to be delivered.
And, whatsoever can be alleged for the defence of it, yet every one that is
not contentious may see that it needeth some caution or exception.*

Jo. Whitgift.

I think no man will contend with you for the signification
of this word "adversity;" for it properly signifieth all affliction or trouble that pertaineth either to the body or to the
mind. And it is *species mali:* "a kind of evil;" for *malum*
doth contain not only vice and sin, but adversity also and
affliction.

But to come to your reason: you say [1], "there is no pro- *The argu-ment re-torted.*
mise in scripture that we should be free from all adversity;"
and therefore we may not pray to be free from all adversity.
If this be a good argument, then will I also reason thus:
there is no promise in scripture that we should be free from
all sin; therefore we may not pray that we should be free
from all sin. There is no promise in scripture that we should
be free from persecution, but the contrary rather; and therefore we may not pray against persecution. Likewise, there is
no promise that we shall be always delivered from poverty,
and from divers other particular evils. To be short, if this
rule and reason be good, then must we pray for nothing,
except first we search in the scriptures whether there be any
promise for the same or no.

But you and all Christians ought to understand that our *Our prayers and faith are grounded upon pro-mises. John xiv.*
prayers, and faith annexed to them, are grounded upon these
promises: "Whatsoever you ask in my name, that will I
do." And again: "If you ask anything in my name, I will
do it," John xiv. And in the xvi. chap., "Verily, verily, I *John xvi.*

[1 Say you, Def. B.]

say unto you, whatsoever you shall ask my Father in my name, he will give it you." Upon these promises is both our

A condition annexed to petitions for external things.
faith and prayer[1], grounded. But, for because in asking of external things we be uncertain whether they be profitable for us or no, therefore we ask them with a condition (which although it be not expressed, yet it is always understood) "if it be God's will;" being certainly persuaded that, if those things we ask be profitable for us, we shall obtain them for his promise' sake. And, forasmuch as all good things come of God, whether they pertain to the body or to the soul, and at all times "to be delivered from adversity" is one of his singular benefits, we may, no doubt, beg the same at his hands, referring, notwithstanding, the granting of it to him, who knoweth what is better for us than we do ourselves. If you will spoil us of this liberty in praying, you shall not only bring prayer into a narrow room, but deprive us of one of the greatest and most singular consolations that a christian man can have in this world. We cannot assure ourselves that we shall obtain any external benefits by prayer at God's hands, because we know not whether that which we ask be profitable for us or no; and yet God forbid that we should cease from

2 Sam. xv. praying even for such things. David, being put out of his kingdom by his son Absolon, was not assured that he should be restored again, and yet did he pray for it, with this con-

Matt. xxvi. dition, "if it pleased God." Christ himself prayed to have the cup of his passion removed from him, which undoubtedly he knew before would not be granted unto him. Many examples there be in the Psalms of prayers made for external things; of the obtaining whereof the prophet could not assure

Augustine. himself. Well saith St Augustine: "When thou dost ask of God health of the body, if he know it be profitable for thee he will give it unto thee; if he give it not, then it is not profitable for thee to have it[2]." Therefore we may lawfully ask any external benefit at God's hand, because he hath willed us so to do; and the same petition or prayer is a prayer of faith, because it hath a promise in the scripture to ground

[1 Prayers, Def. A.]

[2 The idea is frequent in Augustine. The following passage exhibits nearly the words of the text. Quis enim sanitatem non petat, cum ægrotat? Et tamen forte adhuc ægrotare ei utile est. Potest fieri ut hinc non exaudiaris : non tamen exaudiaris ad voluntatem, ut exaudiaris ad utilitatem.—August. Op. Par. 1679-1700. Enarr. in Psalm. lix. 7. Tom. IV. col. 580. Conf. Enarr. in Psalm. lxxxv. 9. cols. 906, 7.]

upon, which is, " Whatsoever you shall ask my Father in my John xvi.
name, &c.," and such like. But the success of our prayer we
must commit to him of whom we ask ; as David did.

And why should this manner of speaking seem so strange
unto you ? do we not read in the xci. psalm that a promise is
made to those that love God in this manner : " There shall Psal. xci.
no evil come unto thee ; neither shall any plague come nigh
unto thy dwelling"? Is not this as much as though he should
have said, Thou shalt ever " be defended from all adversity "?
for, as learned interpreters say, *dictione mali omnis generis
afflictiones, miserias, et ærumnas, complectitur:* "The psalm-
ist in that place by this word 'evil' doth comprehend all kind
of afflictions, miseries, and calamities ;" so that you have here
the very words expressed that you find fault with in the
prayer used on Trinity Sunday. Wherefore they may still
remain without any " caution or exception." And I would to
God you were as far from contention as those be that think so.

I might here add and say that we are " delivered from
all adversity" after two sorts, that is, bodily and spiritually ; Deliverance
bodily, when we are not temporally and externally afflicted from adver-
with them ; spiritually, when we are not overcome by them, sorts.
or caused to decline from God, or to mistrust in his mercies.
That we may pray to be delivered from all adversity in the
first signification, I have proved ; that we ought so to do in
the latter signification, there is no christian man that doubteth[4].

Chapter ii.   The Tenth Division.

T. C. Page 107, Sect. 2.

*In the collect upon the twelfth Sunday after Trinity Sunday, and
likewise in one of those which are to be said after the offertory (as it is
termed) is done, request is made that God would give " those things which
we for our unworthiness dare not ask;" for it carrieth with it still the
note of the popish servile fear, and savoureth not of that confidence and*

[3 See for a very similar interpretation Psalmor. Libr. Quinque Explan. eluc.
per Aret. Felinum (M. Bucer). Argent. 1529.   Psalm. xci. fol. 307.]

[4 Cartwright rejoins that, " seeing our prayers made without faith be abominable, and no faith is able to be grounded but upon the word of promise, it must
needs follow that the prayer conceived without promise is likewise abominable."
He hence insists that we may not pray to be free from all sin in this life, and considers the example of Christ alleged by Whitgift inapposite ; for, " as touching
his humanity, he knew not the most infinite and extreme weight of sufferances,
which God his heavenly Father had measured unto him, or, knowing them, had
through the unspeakable force of the pangs ' which he then was in' forgotten
them."—The Rest of Sec. Repl. pp. 200, 1.]

reverent familiarity that the children of God have through Christ with their heavenly Father ; for, as we dare not without our Saviour Christ ask so much as a crumb of bread, so there is nothing which in his name we dare not ask, being needful for us ; and, if it be not needful, why should we ask it ?

Jo. Whitgift.

Humility in prayer.
Luke xviii.

I pray you, whether doth the prayer of the Pharisee, that so extolled himself, or of the publican that so humbled himself, like you better ? belike you prefer the Pharisee's prayer, else would you never find fault with us for acknowledging our own unworthiness, which is the root and ground of humility, one of the principal ornaments of prayer. We are not worthy of the least benefit that God bestoweth upon us. And therefore duty requireth that we should not for desert desire anything at his hands ; and humility saith that in desiring we ought to acknowledge our own unworthiness. If a man be desirous to obtain anything at his father or friend's hand, of whom he hath received many things, and not recompensed the least, is not this a meet kind of speech for him to use ? There is something necessary for me to have, but I dare not ask it at your hands for my unworthiness, who have received so much already without any kind of recompence : surely this is both the next way for him to obtain that which he desireth, and a good token not of servile fear, but of true humility, and of that due reverence that a good child oweth to a most natural and loving father. " The publican durst not come nigh, nor lift up his eyes :" so did he acknowledge his unworthiness, such was his humility. And yet you know what Christ did pronounce of him, and what general rule he groundeth Luke xviii. upon that example, even this : *Omnis qui se exaltat &c.:* " Every one that exalteth himself shall be brought low, &c." You know also what the prodigal son said to his own father, Luke xv. after his father had embraced him, and received him into mercy : *Neque posthac sum dignus qui vocer filius tuus:* "And I am no more worthy to be called thy son."

God forbid that we should so presume of ourselves, that we should shut humility, and the acknowledging of our own unworthiness, from faithful and hearty prayer. In that therefore we say, " for our own unworthiness we dare not ask it," we both ask it, and yet with all humility acknowledge our own unworthiness ; which, if it be spoken unfeignedly, cannot

be but greatly accepted of God. And surely this kind of
begging is most effectual, and it is used towards those to
whom we think ourselves most bound, and whom (for their
benefits bestowed upon us) we love most dearly. Neither
doth this kind of prayer savour of mistrust, but rather of
great confidence, in the mercy of God, at whose hands we
crave those things which we are of ourselves unworthy to
ask or receive[1].

Chapter ii.   The Eleventh Division.

Admonition.

[2] *They pray that they[3] may be delivered from thundering and tempest,
when no danger is nigh: that they sing* Benedictus, Nunc dimittis, *and*
Magnificat, *we know not to what purpose, except some of them were ready
to die, or except they would celebrate the memory of the virgin, and John
Baptist, &c. Thus they profane the holy scripture*[4].

Answer to the Admonition, Page 202, Sect. 4.

You mislike also that we should "pray to be delivered from thundering and tempest, when there is no
danger nigh." You broach many strange opinions. May
not we pray to be delivered from perils and dangers,
except they be present, and known to be at hand? where
find you that? Christ teacheth us to say in our daily
prayer, *Libera nos a malo :* "Deliver us from evil." What
know we when there is any danger of thundering and
lightning? have we not examples of divers that have
suddenly perished with the same? Is it not therefore
necessary to pray for deliverance from thunder and
lightning, as well as from other dangers, though they be
not present? Well, men may see whereunto this gear
tendeth, if they be not blind. *Benedictus*, also, *Nunc
dimittis*, and *Magnificat*, be great motes in your eyes; but
you shew no reason worthy to be answered; only in
derision you say, "except some of them were ready to

*Prayer to be
delivered
from thun-
der, good[5].*

*Magnificat
and Nunc
dimittis, &c.[6]*

[1] Cartwright rejoins that "the very similitudes" which Whitgift uses "condemn him," and that, "instead of teaching true humility, he openeth a school to
hypocrisy, which the Lord detesteth."—The Rest of Sec. Repl. p. 203.]

[2] This is part of a paragraph, the consideration of the other portions of which
comes long after. See Tractat. XXI. chap. vii. div. 1, 2.]

[3] They pray that all men may be saved and that they, Adm. and Answ.]

[4] Scriptures, Adm.]

[5] Prayers to be delivered from thunder &c. good, Answ. 2.]

[6] Singing of *Magnificat*, &c. Answ. 2.]

die, or would celebrate the memory of the virgin, or
John Baptist." As though these hymns or psalms were
not profitable for all men, as the rest of the holy scripture is, but these especially, because they contain the
mystery of our salvation, and the praise of God for the
same. By this your reason we may not use any of the
psalms until we be in like case as David was, or other,
when they were first made. But I think now the time
is come when those shall correct *Magnificat, qui nesciunt
quid significat.* Truly this your doing is a mere profanation of holy scriptures.

*Absurdity
consequent 1.*

T. C. Page 107, Sect. 2.

*And, if all the prayers were gathered together, and referred to these
two heads of God's glory, and of the things which pertain to this present
life, I can make no geometrical and exact measure, but verily I believe
there shall be found more than a third part of the prayers, which are not
psalms and texts of scripture[2], spent in praying for, and praying against
the incommodities[3] of this life; which is contrary to all the arguments or
contents of the prayers of the church which are set down in the scripture,
and especially of our Saviour Christ's prayer[4], by the which ours ought to
be directed, which of seven petitions bestoweth one only that ways. And
that[5] these foresaid prayers do[6] not only in general words, but by deduct-
ing the commodities and incommodities of this life into their particular
kinds; and that we[7] pray for the avoiding of those dangers which are
nothing near us, as from lightning and thundering in the midst of winter,
from storm and tempest when the weather is most fair, and the seas most
calm, &c. It is true that upon some urgent calamities prayer[8] may and
ought to be framed which may beg either the commodity for want whereof
the church is in distress, or the turning away of that mischief which either
approacheth, or which is already upon it; but to make those prayers which
are for the present time and danger ordinary and daily prayers, I cannot
hitherto see any either scripture or example of the primitive church. And
here, for the simple's sake, I will set down after what sort this abuse crept
into the church.*

Jo. Whitgift.

I think you do confess and acknowledge that it is lawful
to pray for things which pertain to this present life: if you

[1] This marginal note is inserted from Answ. 2.]

[2] Scriptures, Repl. 2.]

[3] Praying for and praying against the commodities and incommodities,
Repl. 2.]

[4] Prayers, Def. A. and B.]   [5] This, Repl. 1 and 2.]

[6] Go, Def. B.]   [7] And we, Repl. 1 and 2.]

[8] Calamity a prayer, Repl. 1 and 2.]

should deny it, I could confute you by the prayer that Jacob made to be delivered from the hands of his brother Esau, Gen. xxxii., and by sundry of the psalms, and divers examples in the gospel, of such as craved the like things at Christ's hands, and obtained their desire: how many such prayers be in the book of common prayer, it skilleth not, so long as you cannot prove them to be other than godly and necessary.

If in every prayer we make some petition for temporal things, we do but imitate and follow that prayer which Christ hath prescribed unto us, both as a most necessary prayer, and as a rule also to frame and form all our prayers by. You might as well prove that we ought not so often to ask remission and forgiveness of our sins, because of seven petitions there is but one only bestowed that way. How far therefore this reason is from godliness and reason, the godly and reasonable reader may judge.

All things we pray for tend to the glory of God, who is the author and giver of all things, both eternal and temporal. Things that are to be prayed for are of two sorts, the one temporal, the other eternal; but they both pertain to the glory of God, though not equally and in like manner. *All things to be prayed for tend to the glory of God.*

The wise man saith: "In the days of prosperity think of adversity, &c." Christ, Matt. xxiv., forewarning his disciples of the external afflictions and evils which should happen as well before the destruction of Jerusalem, as the end of the world, willeth them to pray before the danger be present, saying: "Pray that your flight be not in winter, nor upon the sabbath;" and will you not have us to pray for deliverance from such perils and dangers whereunto we be subject, except they be present? Shall we not pray "to be delivered from thundering and lightning, storm and tempest, plague and pestilence," and such like, except we be in manifest peril and danger, these things being in God's hands to punish us with, even in a moment, and when we think it most unlike? Have we not sundry examples of such as have suddenly perished with thundering and lightning, and some sithence the publishing of your book? What scripture have you or authority of any learned man to the contrary? Will you be credited upon your bare word against so many grave, learned, wise and godly men, that had the penning and allowing of that *Prayers before danger. Ecclus. xi.* *Matt. xxiv.* *The presumption of the Replier.*

book? Surely that were against all order and reason; and it is too great presumption for you with so light and slender reasons to go about the overthrow of that which so many godly and learned men have both liked and allowed, except they had allowed that which the scriptures do disallow[1].

Chapter ii.   The Twelfth Division.

T. C. Page 107, Sect. 3.

There was one Mamercus, bishop of Vienna, which, in the time of great earthquakes which were in France, instituted certain supplica- Plat. cap. *tions, which the Grecians, and we of them, call the litany*[2], Leo. *which concerned that matter; there is no doubt but, as other discommodities rose in other countries, they likewise had prayers accordingly. Now pope Gregory either made himself, or gathered the supplications that were made against the calamities of every country, and made of them a great litany or supplication, as Platina calleth it*[3], *and gave it to be used in all churches; which thing albeit all churches might do for the time, in respect of the case of the calamity which the churches suffered, yet there is no cause why it should be perpetual that was ordained but for a time, and why all lands should pray to be delivered from the incommodities that some land hath been troubled with.*

Jo. Whitgift.

As though we were not at all times subject to these perils and dangers, and as though we ought not, by the calamity of other nations, to be moved earnestly to pray against the like, which might also happen to us.

It is not to be doubted but that the prayer of the just is acceptable to God, and that of his mercy he, being thereby moved, doth stay from plaguing us with earthquakes, thundering and lightning, and such like calamities, wherewith he would otherwise punish us.

The reason used against the litany is of the same force against the psalms.

Truly your reasons be marvellous profane, and they might as well be alleged against any of the psalms, which all were made at the first upon some special occasion, and yet are profitable for ever, in all states of the church to be used.

[1 Cartwright in his rejoinder to this division calls it "idle," "frivolous," "nothing to purpose," and declares that Whitgift "doth but abuse the time."— The Rest of Sec. Repl. pp. 204, 5.]

[2 Primus enim Mamercus (ut aiunt) supplicationes, quas Græci litaneias vocant, instituit ob frequentes terræ motus, qui tum maxime Gallias vexabant.— Plat. De Vit. Pont. Col. 1551. Leo I. p. 58.]

[3 Id. ibid. Gregor. I. p. 73. See before, page 469, note 5.]

Whatsoever good and godly prayer in the time of any common misery and calamity hath been invented, the same is at other times profitable to be used in the church, because the like punishments and plagues are in God's hands at all times to execute upon sinners, and therefore continually to be prayed against.

Chapter ii.   The Thirteenth Division.

T. C. Page 107, Sect. 4.

The like may be said of the Gloria Patri, *and the Athanasius' creed: it was first brought into the church, to the end that men thereby should make an open profession in the church of the divinity of the Son of God, against the detestable opinion of Arius and his disciples, wherewith at that time marvellously swarmed almost the whole Christendom; now that it hath pleased the Lord to quench that fire, there is no such cause why these things should be in the church, at the least why that* Gloria Patri *should be so often repeated.*

A weak reason.

Jo. Whitgift.

Even as convenient now as it was then; for it is as necessary to maintain truth, and make it known, as it is to suppress errors; and yet it is not unknown that even in our days, and in this church, there have been Arians; and I pray God there be none still. I much suspect the matter, not well understanding whereunto these glances of yours at "*Gloria Patri*, and Athanasius' creed," do tend. *Gloria Patri*, besides that it containeth a brief confession of the Trinity, and of the divinity of Jesus Christ, it is a magnifying and glorifying of the Father, the Son, and the Holy Ghost, three Persons and one God; and Athanasius' creed is not only an excellent confutation of Arius' heresy, but a plain declaration of the mystery of the Trinity, such as is necessary for all christian men to learn and know; and therefore he that is offended with the oft repetition or saying of either of them, I cannot tell what I should judge of him. But undoubtedly there is great cause why I should suspect him at the least of singularity and unquietness. Shall we not oftentimes rehearse the articles of our belief in God the Father, the Son, and the Holy Ghost, because all men be now persuaded therein, and none known that maketh any doubt? The reason is all one, and prevaileth as well against the repeating of this,

The manifestation and maintenance of truth as necessary as the suppression of errors.

Gloria Patri.

Athanasius' Creed.

as of the other. I think your meaning is, that we know too much, and therefore now we must learn to forget.

Well, your authority is little, and your reasons much less; and therefore they are like to stand in *statu quo;* and this is most sure, that harm they do none, but much good, because a good thing cannot be too oft said or heard[1].

Chapter ii.   The Fourteenth Division.

T. C. Page 107, Sect. ult.

Moreover, to make Benedictus, Magnificat, *and* Nunc dimittis *ordinary and daily prayers seemeth to be a thing not so convenient, considering that they do no more concern us, than all other scriptures do, and than doth the* Ave Maria, *as they called it. For, although they were prayers of thanksgiving in Simeon, Zachary, and the blessed virgin Mary, yet can they not be so in us, which have not received like benefits; they may be added to the number of psalms, and so sung as they be; but to make daily and ordinary prayers of them is not without some inconvenience and disorder.*

Jo. Whitgift.

Here is no reason shewed, nor anything answered to that I have alleged to prove the contrary.   Your objection of the *Ave Maria* is vain, for it pertaineth to the virgin only, and is spoken to her person.   But, if it were not so, what kind of reasoning call you this?   The church doth not use daily in public prayer to say *Ave Maria; ergo,* it may not say *Benedictus, Magnificat,* or *Nunc dimittis.*   These three are most meetest for us, for "they contain," as I have said in my Answer, "the mystery of our salvation, and the praise of God for the same," and therefore cannot be too often either said or sung.

Chapter ii.   The Fifteenth Division.

T. C. Page 108, Sect. 2.

Very slenderly; and, if you had said less of them, you had said nothing at all.

And so have I answered unto those things which are contained in the 202. 203. *pages; saving that I must admonish the reader that, whereas you will prove that we ought to have an ordinary prayer to be delivered from danger of thunder, lightnings, &c., because there are examples of certain that have been killed thereby, you might as well bring in a prayer*

[1 "To prove that '*Gloria Patri* &c. may be oft repeated at one meeting,' he answereth that 'a good thing cannot be too oft said.'   Which...is as much to say that a man cannot take too many purgations."—The Rest of Sec. Repl. p. 206.]

that men may not have falls from their horses, may not fall into the
hands of robbers, may not fall into waters; and a number such more
sudden deaths, wherewith a greater number are taken away than by thun-
derings or lightnings, and such like; and so there should be never any end
of begging these earthly commodities; which is contrary to the form of
prayer appointed by our Saviour Christ.

Jo. Whitgift.

The punishment of God by thundering and lightning is
more notorious and terrible, not by any help of man to be
repelled; whereas the other things that you speak of come
oftentimes and most commonly through negligence, wilfulness,
unruliness, too much boldness, indiscreetness of the parties
themselves. Besides this, there are ordinary means to avoid
them. And yet I think it most convenient that we should pray
against those evils; and so doth the church daily in the last
collect used in the morning prayer; which thing also is most
consonant to the Lord's prayer, petitions to the like end and
purpose being there expressed.

Chapter ii.   The Sixteenth Division.
T. C. Page 108, Sect. 2.

And, whereas you allege the petition of the Lord's prayer, "Deliver us
from evil," to prove this prayer against thunder, &c.; besides that all the
commodities and discommodities of this life are prayed for and prayed
against in that petition, whereby we desire our daily bread, it is very
strange to apply that to the thunder that is understanded of the devil, as
the article ἀπὸ τοῦ πονηροῦ doth declare; and it is a marvellous conclu-
sion that, forsomuch as we ought daily and ordinarily and publicly desire
to be delivered from the devil; ergo, we ought daily and [2] ordinarily and
publicly desire to be delivered from thunder.   It is one thing to correct
Magnificat, *and another thing to shew the abuse of it.   And therefore I*
see no cause why you should use this allusion between magnificat *and*
significat; *unless it be for that you, purposing to set out all your learn-*
ing in this book, would not so much as forget an old rotten proverb,
which trotted amongst the monks in their cloisters; of whom I may justly
say which Tully said in another thing: Nec quicquam ingenuum potest monasterium [3]: *that is, "the cloister could never bring forth any witty*
Rhyme with- *thing;" for here, although there be* rythmus, *yet it is* sine
out reason.   ratione.

[2 Add, Repl. 1.]
[3 Nec enim quidquam ingenuum potest habere officina.—Cic. Op. Lond.
1681. De Offic. Lib. I. 42.   Tom. IV. pp. 409, 10.   Def. A. has ingenium, following probably Repl. 2, which however corrects the reading in the list of errata.]

Jo. Whitgift.

All men may see that you hunt for contention and strife, and not for the truth; otherwise you would be more upright and sincere in your dealing. The effect of my Answer to the Admonition is that, forasmuch as this word *malum* in the last petition of the Lord's prayer doth contain all kind of evil, whether it pertain to the body or to the mind, therefore all such prayers as are for our deliverance from external perils and dangers, being grounded upon that petition, are lawful, whether they be daily used or otherwise; in which sort and kind those prayers are wherein we desire to be delivered from thundering and lightning, the dangers thereof being so frequent, and so terrible.

The interpretation of the last petition.

And, whereas you say that the word "evil" doth there signify the "devil," and therefore not adversity, and external evil that happeneth to the body, you shall understand your error, by the expositions both of the old and new writers. Cyprian, in his exposition upon the Lord's prayer, interpreting these words, saith thus: "In the last place we put, 'But deliver us from evil;' comprehending all kind of adversities which the enemy worketh against us in this world." And a little after: "But when we say, 'Deliver us from evil,' there remaineth nothing which ought further to be desired, seeing we pray at once for the protection of God against evil; which being obtained, we stand secure and safe against all things which the world and devil worketh[1]."

Cyprian.

Augustine likewise, in his epistle *ad Probam viduam*, in number 121. and *cap.* 11., expoundeth the same words in like sort: "When we say, 'Deliver us from evil,' we admonish to consider that we are not as yet in that good (estate) where we shall suffer no evil; and this, which is last placed in the Lord's prayer, is extended so far, and so plainly, that a christian man moved with any kind of tribulation may in this petition sigh, in this shed his tears, begin herein, continue herein, and end his prayer herein[2]."

Augustinus.

[1] In novissimo enim ponimus: *Sed libera nos a malo*, comprehendentes adversa cuncta, quæ contra nos in hoc mundo molitur inimicus;...Quando autem dicimus: sed libera nos a malo, nihil remanet quod ultra adhuc debeat postulari: quando semel protectionem Dei adversus malum petamus, qua impetrata contra omnia quæ diabolus et mundus operantur, securi stamus et tuti.—Cypr. Op. Oxon. 1682. De Orat. Domin. p. 151.]

[2] Cum dicimus, *Libera nos a malo;* nos admonemus cogitare, nondum nos

M. Bucer, expounding the same words in his commentaries upon the vi. of Matthew, saith: " Satan is therefore Bucer. called a tempter, because he doth tempt and exercise us; especially labouring for this, that he may withdraw us from a right faith in God; but, if he cannot bring that to pass (such is his hatred) then he doth rejoice in afflicting and molesting us with external evils; as we read that he hath done against Job and other holy men." And a little after: " Wherefore, forasmuch as Satan is as it were our tormenter, by whose ministry God doth also outwardly exercise us, in this respect the prayer, ' to be delivered from bodily evils,' is included in this last petition[3]." In like manner doth Musculus expound the same[4]. And do you think that these men did not understand their *Pater-noster* ? You see therefore that, although the word signify the " devil," yet it nothing hindereth my interpretation, but maketh much for it; because the devil is the author of all evil that cometh either to the body or to the soul; and therefore, being delivered from him, there is no cause why we should be any longer careful.

There is no " abuse of *Magnificat* " as yet shewed, but there is a very unlearned reason in the Admonition put why it should not be used, to the answer whereof you have not replied; and therefore I may justly say of their correcting of *Magnificat* that which I have said; and the proverb is meet for such unskilful persons; but your childish or rather profane jests and scoffs be not seeming for a divine, and him that would be counted so greatly learned and mortified.

esse in eo bono, ubi nullum patiemur malum. Et hoc quidem ultimum quod in dominica oratione positum est, tam late patet, ut homo christianus in qualibet tribulatione constitutus in hoc gemitus edat, in hoc lacrymas fundat, hinc exordiatur, in hoc immoretur, ad hoc terminet orationem.—August. Op. Par. 1679-1700. Ad Prob. Epist. cxxx. cap. xi. 21. Tom. II. col. 390.]

[3 Tentator enim Satanas ideo dicitur, quod nos tentat et exercet, potissimum quidem hoc agens, ut a recta in Deum fide nos detorqueat, si tum id ei non succedit, quo est in nos odio, gaudet malis externis nos obruere et excruciare, uti contra Iiob egisse legimus, et sanctos alios....Quatenus igitur Satanas velut tortor noster est, cujus ministerio etiam externe nos Deus exercet, eatenus et corporalium malorum deprecatio, huic ultimæ petitioni inclusa est.—M. Bucer. Enarr. Perp. in Quat. Evang. Argent. 1530. In Evang. Matt. cap. vi. fol. 67.]

[4 Wolfg. Muscul. Comm. in Matt. Evang. Basil. 1611. cap. vi. Tom. I. pp. 135, 6.]

Chapter ii.   The Seventeenth Division.

T. C. Page 108, Sect. 3.

As these are divers things more than ought to be conveniently, so want there some things in the prayers: there are prayers set forth to be said in the common calamities and universal scourges of the realm, as plague, famine, &c.   And indeed so it ought to be, by the word of God, joined with a public fast commanded, not only when we are in any calamity, but also when any the churches, round about us, or in any country, receive any general plague, or grievous chastisement at the Lord's hand.   But, as such prayers are needful whereby we beg release from our distresses, so there ought to be as necessarily prayers of thanksgiving when we have received those things at the Lord's hand which we asked in our prayers.

Great faults in little matters. *And thus much touching the matter of the prayers, either not altogether sound, or else too much or too little.*

Jo. Whitgift.

If anything lack in the book, that derogateth nothing from that which is good and godly in the same; neither is it any cause why any man should deprave it or make such a stir and schism in the church for it.

It is meet that we should as well give thanks for the benefits received, as to pray for the receiving of them; neither is the book void of any such kind of prayers.   These be but very small quarrels against the book, and slender faults (if they were faults) to make so great a schism for.   But, as I said with St Augustine, against the authors of the Admonition, Aug. Epist. 121. so say I unto you: "If thou runnest through all the words of the holy prayers, I suppose thou shalt find nothing which the Lord's prayer doth not contain; therefore we may in other words speak the same things in our prayers, but we may not speak contrary things[1]."   You have not as yet, neither will you ever be able to shew one line in any prayer contained in that book to be contrary to the word of God, or not consonant or agreeable unto the same.   And this dealing of yours against it upon so weak reasons (or rather none at all) argueth that you seek only contention, and that your chief quarrel is at the maintainers of the book, and not at the matter.

[1 August. Op. Par. 1679-1700. Ad Prob. Epist. cxxx. cap. xii. 22. Tom. II. col. 391. See before, page 469, note 7.]

Chapter ii.　The Eighteenth Division.

T. C. Page 108, Sect. 4.

Concerning the form, there is also to be misliked: a great cause whereof is the following of the form used in popery; against which I have before spoken. For, whilst that service was set in many points as a pattern of this, it cometh to pass that, instead of such prayers as the primitive churches have used, and those that be reformed now use, we have divers short cuts and shreddings, which may be better called wishes than prayers. And, that no man think that this is some idle fancy, and that it is no matter of weight what form of prayer we use, so that the prayers be good, it must be understanded that, as it is not sufficient to preach the same doctrine which our Saviour Christ and his apostles have preached, unless the same form of doctrine and of teaching be likewise kept, so is it not enough that the matter of our prayer be such as is in the word of God, unless that the form also be agreeable unto the forms of prayers in the scripture. Now we have no such forms in the scripture as that we should pray in two or three lines, and then, after having read awhile some other thing, come and pray as much more, and so to the xx. and xxx. time, with pauses between.*

These are unseemly terms for godly prayers, be they never so short.

Where learn you that?

The Lord's prayer is not much more: the prayers of the publican, of Stephen, and of Christ, are much less.

Jo. Whitgift.

You have very aptly answered yourself, though you would seem to make it an objection, and to wipe it away; for undoubtedly, when you thought that other men would count this device of yours "an idle fancy," you thought truly, and your own thought therein condemneth you. But I add that it is not only "an idle fancy," but an untrue surmise; for, first, which be those "prayers that the primitive church used, instead whereof we have but short cuts and shreddings?" Why do you not name them? Will you still speak without proof? Will you raise up a general slander, and shew no particulars?

Touching your charging us with "following of the form used in popery," I have answered before, where you have in like manner objected it, and only objected it.

How prove you that "it is not sufficient to preach the same doctrine that our Saviour Christ and his apostles have preached, unless the same form of teaching be likewise kept?" For I take that to be "an idle fancy," and utterly untrue. I am persuaded that, if the same doctrine be preached, the manner and form of preaching is left for every one to use according to the gift that God hath given unto him, as he shall think it to be most expedient to edifying; but this is an old

The fancy of the Replier concerning the form of preaching.

[² Of Christ on the cross are, Def. A.]

" fancy " of yours, partly grounded upon an arrogant opinion of yourself, whose manner and form of preaching you would bind all men unto ; partly of emulation and envy, because you have perceived other men's manner and kind of preaching to have been much better liked than yours. But, to let this pass, Christ and his apostles did not usually pray before nor after their sermons, or at the least it is not expressed in scripture that they did ; they, when they preached, did not usually take any one certain place or portion of scripture to entreat of [1] ; and it is manifest that they used not any uniform manner of preaching, but they spake as God gave them utterance ; neither did they labour or study for their sermons, but preached as present occasion served ; and therefore, for my part, until I hear very good reasons of this new device, I must needs account it a very fond imagination.

Shew me wherein the form of our prayers doth differ from the manner and form of praying contained in the scripture. Or shew me in the scripture any prescript form of public and daily prayers commanded, the Lord's prayer only excepted. Or let me understand what scripture you can allege why in the public congregation we may not sometime pray, and sometimes read the scriptures. And what do we else in the whole order of our service ? Will you still more and more utter your contempt against God, against his church, against a most pure and godly kind of public prayer and service, and that with such unreverend speeches ? But I omit them : it is enough to have noted them in the margent, for they are confutation to themselves.

Chapter ii.   The Nineteenth Division.

T. C. Page 108, Sect. ult.

If a man should come to a prince, and keep such order in making his petitions unto him that, having very many things to demand, after he had demanded one thing, he would stay a long time and then demand another, and so the third, the prince might well think that either he came to ask before he knew what he had need of, or that he had forgotten some

[1 " ... that of our Saviour ' Christ's and the apostles' usual preaching without texts ' hath no ground. That of their ' preaching without prayer before or after their sermons ' is a shameful untruth. For, prayer being assigned for a piece of the duty of the ministry (Acts vi. 4), although it had been never (as sometime (John xvii. 1) it is) expressed, yet it must of necessity be intended."—The Rest of Sec. Repl. p. 211.]

piece of his suit, or that he were distracted in his understanding, or some other such like cause of the disorder of his supplication. And therefore how much more convenient were it that, according to the manner of the reformed churches, first the minister, with an humble and general confession of faults, should desire the assistance of the Lord for the fruitful handling and receiving of the word of God; and then, after that we have heard the Lord speak unto us in his word by his minister, the church should likewise speak unto the Lord, and present all those petitions and suits at once, both for the whole church and for the prince, and all other estates, which shall be thought needful.

Jo. Whitgift.

As much difference as there is betwixt man and God, so far is your similitude from proving your purpose; except you will admit the like similitude used by the papists, to prove praying to saints; for the one hath as much strength to prove anything as the other, and yet neither of them both worth a rush. And here you do injury to God, to compare him to an earthly prince, especially in this behalf. For what prince would not think himself abused if a man should daily and hourly sue unto him? But it is not so with God; for we have a commandment to pray continually, Luke xviii.; 1 Thess. v.; and he doth not respect the form of words, but the affection of the heart. And in very deed it is most convenient that reading of the scriptures and praying should be intermingled.

The dissimilitude of the Replier's similitude.

All the scripture that you have to allege is "the reformed churches:" let other men think what they will, I verily believe that in our manner and kind of worshipping God in our public and common prayers, there is no cause why we should think ourselves one whit inferior unto them: they also, or the most part of them, have allowed the same order of ours, at what time the like contention was about the same book among our Englishmen which were in Q. Mary's time banished for the gospel[2].

Chapter ii. The Twentieth Division.

T. C. Page 109, Sect. 1.

And, if any will say that there are short prayers found in the Acts, it may be answered that St Luke doth not express the whole prayers at

[2 This contention broke out among the exiles at Frankfort. There is an account of it in " A brieff discours off the troubles begonne at Franckford in Germany Anno Domini 1554." 1575; a work subsequently reprinted.]

large, but only set down the sums of them, and their chief points. And,
further, it may be answered that always those prayers were continued
together, and not cut off and shred into divers small pieces.

Jo. Whitgift.

How know you that "St Luke doth not express the
whole prayers at large, but only set down the sums of them
and their chief points?" What scripture have you that
teacheth you so to think? and, if this be a sufficient answer to
say, the "scripture hath not expressed the whole, &c.," why
is it not also a sufficient answer for me to that which followeth,
that the scripture hath not expressed any certain or deter-
minate form of public prayer to be used in all churches (as indeed it hath not), but only in the Lord's prayer given certain
general points according to the which all our prayers must
be framed? Surely your fancy is strong; but your arguments
be exceeding weak. For tell me, I pray you, where have
you in the whole new testament (the Lord's prayer only
excepted) any form of public prayer used in the church
described? If you cannot shew this, why do you so childishly
dally?

The scripture hath not pre-scribed any form of public prayer.

Chapter ii.   The Twenty-first Division.

T. C. Page 109, Sect. 2.

Another fault is that all the people are appointed in divers places
to say after the minister, whereby not only the time is unprofitably wasted,
and a confused voice of the people, one speaking after another, caused,
but an opinion bred in their heads, that those only be their prayers which
they say and pronounce with their own mouths; which causeth them to
give the less heed to the rest of the prayers which they rehearse not after the
minister; which, notwithstanding, are as well their prayers as those which
they pronounce after the minister, otherwise than the order which is left
unto the church of God doth bear. For God hath ordained the minister
to this end, that, as in public meetings he only is the mouth of the Lord
from him to the people, even so he ought to be only the mouth of the people
from them unto the Lord, and that all the people should attend to that
which is said by the minister, and in the end both declare their consent to
that which is said, and their hope that it should[1] so be and come to pass
which is prayed, by the word "Amen;" as St Paul declareth 1 Cor.xiv.16.[2]
in the epistle to the Corinthians, and Justin Martyr sheweth 2. Apol. pro
to have been the custom of the churches in his time[3]. Christianis.

Untruth.

[1 Shall, Repl. 1, 2, and Def. A.]   [2 The verse is added from Repl. 2.]
[3 Just. Mart. Op. Par. 1742. Apol. i. 65. p. 82. Conf. 67. p. 83. See Vol.
I. page 215, note 4.]

Jo. Whitgift.

God be thanked that the book is so perfite that you are constrained, for saving your credit with your disciples, thus triflingly to deal with it.   You unchristianly say that "the time is unprofitably wasted" which is spent in prayer; you imagine that of the people that never entered into their thoughts; you call it "a confused voice," that is a most acceptable sound unto the Lord; and, if to surmise or to imagine be sufficient, then may we imagine your doctrine to tend to the contempt of prayer, and the over-thwarting of all good and godly order.   But you must know that there is more special cause why the people should rather rehearse after the minister those things that the book appointeth them so to do, than the other prayers, because they contain a general confession of sins, which all Christians together, as well in voice as in heart, ought to confess; neither doth the book prescribe the people to say anything after the minister (the Lord's prayer after the communion only excepted) but these general and public confessions; and yet, if it did, I see not how you can justly therefore reprove it.   Musculus, expounding these words: *Et cum hymnum cecinissent, &c.*, thinketh it not un- Muscul. in
26. Matth. likely *ipsum .... ita prœloquutum esse, ut verba ipsius ab illis sint excepta et vicissim reddita*[4]: "That Christ did in that order speak before his disciples, that they repeated his words after him."   Whereby it appeareth that he was so far from thinking this order to be "an unprofitable wasting of time," that he doubteth not to ascribe it to our Saviour Christ and his apostles.   But, if it be such "an unprofitable wasting of time" to rehearse prayer after the minister, how happeneth it that you and all other your partners that be preachers use to cause the people to pray after you in your sermons[5]? Is it lawful for you so to do in the pulpit, and is it not lawful for the minister to do the same in the church? Belike nothing is well done that you do not yourselves, or are not the authors of.

But here I cannot omit that which you so boldly affirm of The minister
not the only
mouth of the
people.

[4 Wolfg. Muscul. Comm. in Matt. Evang. Basil. 1611. cap. xxvi. Tom. III. p. 524.]

[5 "'That I used that form in my sermons' (for anything that I know) I learned it of the book ; which use, forsomuch as some years after, whilst I yet preached, I corrected in myself, it declareth that I first misliked and condemned myself in that point, or ever I found fault with the book."—The Rest of Sec. Repl. p. 213.]

the minister, whom you say "God hath ordained to be the *only* mouth of the people from them unto the Lord in public meetings :" are you of that opinion, that the people may join with the minister in pronouncing public prayers at no time ? Or that they should only "attend to that which is said by the minister, and in the end give their consent by this word, Amen ?" Hath God ordained this ? I pray you, where find you this ordinance ? Sure I am that the place by you alleged doth not prove it. For, although it be true that the minister is the mouth of the people to God, yet doth it not follow that he is the "*only* mouth of the people unto the Lord ;" and, although we read that the people used to give their consent unto the prayer pronounced of the minister by this word, "Amen ;" yet, if you will hereof conclude that they ought only to say "Amen," and at no time join as well in voice as in heart with the minister (which you seem to affirm in saying he is the only mouth), then, besides the weakness of your conclusion, the practice of the church of God will sufficiently confute you. We read that, when Peter and John were let go, after their examination before the priests and elders, for healing the man that was lame from his mother's womb, they came to the rest of his disciples, and declared to them what had

Acts iv.

happened ; "and, when they heard that, they lift up their voices to God with one accord, and said, Lord, thou art God, &c." So that the minister here was not "the only mouth of the people," but the whole company that was assembled joined together in this prayer, lifted up their voices and spake with one accord. And surely it is not unlike that they used herein that order which you before accounted " an unprofitable wasting of time ;" for, seeing that this prayer was framed according to the present occasion, I am persuaded that the rest did rather repeat the words after him that conceived the prayer, than that they all miraculously joined upon the sudden in one

Plinius Epist. Lib. x.

and the same form of words[1]. Pliny, in an epistle to Trajan the emperor, concerning the Christians, writeth that their custom was *stato die ante lucem convenire, carmenque Christo quasi Deo dicere secum invicem: &c.*[2] : " to meet together

[1 " The Greek is they ' with one accord lifted up a voice to God,' not ' voices ;' so that St Luke noteth that there was but one ' voice' amongst them all ; which, because it was with consent, he doth aptly call the voice lifted up of them all, and wherewith they all prayed : &c."—Ibid. p. 212.]

[2 C. Plin. Secund. Epist. Lib. x. Epist. xcvii.]

early at an appointed day, and to sing together a song unto
Christ, as unto God." Chrysostom, going about to prove that
in some respect there is no difference betwixt the priest and
people, useth this for an example, that in public prayer they
sometime join together. His words be these: *Quin et preci-* Chrysost.
Hom. 18, in
bus &c.[3] : "A man may also see the people to offer many 2. Cor.
prayers together, for those that are possessed and peniten-
tiaries (as they term them); for common supplications are
made both of the priest, and of them, and they all say one
prayer, &c." And again: *Quid miraris si cum sacerdote
populus loquitur*[4]*?* "Why dost thou marvel if the people
speak together with the priest? &c." You cannot be ignorant,
I am sure, that Basil likeneth "the sound of men, women, Basil.
Hex. 4.
and children, praying in the church, to the roaring of the
waves against the sea-banks[5]." This might you have seen
also even in that place of Justin Martyr which you quote; for
there, describing the liturgy, he saith that, after the exhortation or sermon, *omnes surgimus et comprecamur*[6] : "we do Apol. 2.
all rise and pray together, &c." This you skipped over,
and took that which followed, because it made more for
your purpose; for indeed Justin doth describe both, that is,
both the prayer of the whole church together, and of the
bishop alone, the people giving their consent by this word
"Amen." I need not to use more testimonies: these may suffice
to declare by the practice of the church, that "the minister is"
not "the only mouth of the people in public meetings," which
you have only set down without any proof, for what purpose
you know best yourself, surely I cannot conjecture, except it
be that the people should wholly depend upon the minister's
words, and as it were hang upon his lips, which whereunto it
would in time grow, wise men can consider.

But what need I to stand so long upon this point, seeing The Replier
contrary to
you yourself afterward affirm as much? For, finding fault himself.
with the order of singing psalms side by side, you have these

---

[³ ... καὶ ἐν ταῖς εὐχαῖς δὲ πολὺ τὸν λαὸν ἴδοι τις ἂν συνεισφέροντα. καὶ
γὰρ ὑπὲρ τῶν ἐνεργουμένων, ὑπὲρ τῶν ἐν μετανοίᾳ, κοιναὶ καὶ παρὰ τοῦ ἱερέως,
καὶ παρ᾽ αὐτῶν γίνονται αἱ εὐχαί· καὶ πάντες μίαν λέγουσιν εὐχὴν, κ.τ.λ.—
Chrysost. Op. Par. 1718-38. In Epist. II. ad Corinth. Hom. xviii. Tom. X. p. 568.]

[⁴ Καὶ τί θαυμάζεις, εἴ που μετὰ τοῦ ἱερέως ὁ λαὸς φθέγγεται, κ.τ.λ.—Id. ibid.]

[⁵ ...πῶς οὐχὶ καλλίων ἐκκλησίας τοιαύτης σύλλογος, ἐν ᾗ συμμιγὴς ἦχος,
οἷόν τινος κύματος ἠιόνι προσφερομένου, ἀνδρῶν καὶ γυναικῶν καὶ νηπίων,
κατὰ τὰς πρὸς τὸν Θεὸν ἡμῶν δεήσεις, ἐκπέμπεται.—Basil. Op. Par. 1721-30.
In Hexaem. Hom. iv. Tom. I. p. 39.]

[⁶ Just. Mart. Op. Par. 1742. Apol. I. 67. p. 83.]

Pag. 163. in
the midst.

words : " From whencesoever it came, it cannot be good, considering that, when it is granted that all the people may praise God (as it is in singing of psalms), there this ought not to be restrained unto a few, and, where it is lawful both with heart and voice to sing the whole psalm, there it is not meet that they should sing but the one half with their heart and voice, and the other with their heart only. For, where they may both with heart and voice sing, there the heart is not enough." Than the which what can be more contrary to this, that "the minister ought to be the only mouth of the people to the Lord?" For here you affirm that all the people may praise God, and sing psalms, not with heart only, but with voice, and so to be their own mouth unto the Lord. How you can reconcile this gear I see not; sure I am that truth is not contrary to itself.

Chapter ii.   The Twenty-second Division.
T. C. Page 109, Sect. 3.

Conscientia
mille testes.

Although these blots in the common prayer be such as may easily enough appear unto any which is not wedded to a prejudicate opinion, and that there is no great difficulty in this matter; yet I know that this treatise of prayer will be subject to many reprehensions, and that there will not be wanting some probable colours also whereby these things may be defended, if men will set themselves to strive and to contend. Yet, for the desire that I have that these things should be amended, and for the instruction of the simple[1] which are studious of the truth, I have been bold to utter that which I think, not doubting also but that the light of the truth shall be able to scatter all those mists of reasons which shall go about to darken the clearness thereof.

Jo. Whitgift.

Surely if the "blots" be so manifest as you would seem to make them, it is not wisely done of you so slenderly to pass them over.

The pith of
the reply
concerning
prayer.

You do well to think that "this treatise" of yours "touching prayer will be subject to many reprehensions;" and why should it not? What is there in it worthy of commendation? What learning? what reason? what truth? what godliness? except vain words be learning, fancies reason, lies truth, contempt of good laws and orders, with unseemly jests, be godliness; for what is there else in this treatise? Truly, if you had not settled yourself to strive and to contend, and had not

[¹ Simpler, Repl. 1 and 2.]

been desirous to pervert the simple, rather than to instruct them, you would never, upon so weak a ground, and with so feeble reasons, or rather vain fancies, have gone about to deprave so worthy a book; in the which, as I have said before, you are not able to shew anything, especially touching the order, manner, and matter of prayer, that is not consonant to the word of God. Neither have you, for all that is spoken against the form of prayer, alleged one text of scripture, or one sentence of any one ancient or late writer; and do you think that men will believe you upon your bare words, against so many martyrs and learned men as have allowed and do allow that book? Your credit is not so great as you think it is; and that which you have, when you are accordingly detected, will utterly vanish and fade away.

Of baptism by women, wherewith the communion book is falsely charged.

Chapter iii. The First Division.

Admonition.

In which a great number of things contrary to God's word are contained, as baptism [1] by women.

[1] *Matt.xxviii. 19; 1 Cor. xiv. 35.*

The first appointer hereof was Victor I.[2] Anno 198.

Answer to the Admonition, Page 79, Sect. 2, 3, 4, 5.

But you say, "a number of things contrary unto God's word are contained in this book, as baptism by women, &c.[3]"

All prayers good in the communion book.

Here is not one prayer in all the communion book[4] found fault with; and yet your quarrel is against a prescript form of prayers invented by man.

You marvellously forget yourself, and confusedly go from matter to matter, without any consideration.

Digressing, therefore, from prayers contained in the communion book, you come to other matters in the same, against God's word (as you say); and first you allege baptizing by women.

I deny baptizing by women to be expressed in that

[2] See below, page 507, note 3.]

[3] Here Answ. proceeds with the sentence which is continued subsequently.]

[4] The whole communion book, Answ.]

book; and, when you have proved it to be necessarily gathered out of the same, then shall you hear my judgment thereof.

T. C. Page 109, Sect. 4.

Master Doctor requireth that it should be proved unto him that by private baptism is meant "baptism by women." First, it is meant that it should be done by some other than the minister, for that the minister is bid to give them warning that they should not baptize the child at home in their house without great cause and necessity; secondarily, I would gladly ask him who they be that are present when the child is so shortly after it is born in great danger of death; and, last of all, Master Doctor doth not see how he accuseth all the magistrates of this realm of the neglect of their duty, in that they allow of the daily practising by women in baptizing children, if so be that the book did not so appoint it, or permit it. If he meant plainly herein, there needed not so much ado.

JO. WHITGIFT.

Here is nothing said which the authors of the Admonition have not alleged before, either in their book or in their additions; and therefore the same answer that was made unto them will serve for you. I told you there that the book of common prayer doth call it "private baptism," in respect of the place, which is a private house, and not in respect of the minister; which evidently appeareth in these words, which you yourself allege in this place, that is, that "the minister is bid to give them warning that they should not baptize the child at home in their houses, &c.;" but you cannot thereof conclude the meaning of the book to be, that women should baptize; for even in that necessity the curate may be sent for, or some other minister that may sooner be come by.

Your question is soon answered; for no man doubteth of the persons that be present at such a time; but I have told you that, when such necessity requireth, the curate, or the next minister, is soon sent for, as oftentimes he is in as great extremities as that; and what a reason call you this: Women be present when the child that is born is in great danger of death; therefore the minister cannot be sent for to baptize the child?

To your objection of "the magistrates allowing the practice of baptizing by women," I answer, first, that your general proposition is untrue (as I think); for all the magistrates of this realm do not so. Secondly, that, if they did, yet it followeth

(marginal note:) Why baptism is called private.

not that they do it by the authority of the book; for many things be permitted as tolerable, which are not established by any law: and therefore, if you had done well, you should rather have reproved the custom that doth use it, than the book that speaketh never a word of it.

I deal as plainly as I can, for I keep me to the book. But your vain conjectures and frivolous reasons against that book may not be yielded unto, but opened, that they may appear in their colours.

Chapter iii.　The Second Division.
Answer to the Admonition, Page 79, Sect. ult.

Your places of scripture alleged against it are not of sufficient force to prove your purpose. Christ, in the xxviii. of Matthew, said to his disciples, "Go and teach all nations, baptizing them in the name of the Father, &c.;" *ergo*, women may not baptize. I say this argument followeth not, no more than this doth; *ergo*, pastors may not baptize; for it is manifest that an apostle is distinct from a pastor.

Feeble arguments.

T. C. Page 109, Sect. 5.

Chap. xxviii. 19.[2]

The place of the xxviii. of St Matthew[1] *is as strong against women's baptizing as it is against their preaching. For the ministry of the word and sacraments cannot be pulled in sunder, which the Lord hath joined together from time to time. For Noah, which was a preacher unto the old world of the will of God, was ordained also of*

Untruth, as hath been proved.

These examples prove not the purpose.

2 Pet. ii. 5.[2]
Gen. vi. 14.[2]

God to make the ark, which was a sacrament and seal of his preaching, touching the destruction of the world. And Abra-

Gen. xviii. 19.[2]

ham, whom the Lord would have to be the doctor of his church, which was then in his family, was also commanded

Gen. xvii. 23.[2]

to minister the sacrament of circumcision unto his family.

The priests and Levites, which were appointed to teach the people, were also appointed to sacrifice, and to minister other sacraments in the church. Likewise the same prophets, which God stirred up to preach, he also ordained to confirm the same by signs and sacraments.

Luke ix. 1.[2]
Luke x. 1, 17.[2]

The same may be also drawn throughout the new testament, as unto every of the twelve, and afterward to the seventy, power was given both to preach the gospel, and also to confirm with signs

Acts xxii. 15.[2]
1 Cor. i. 17.[2]

and miracles, which were seals of their doctrine. And St Paul, by the commandment that our Saviour Christ gave him to preach, undertook also to baptize, although there were no express words

[1 The place of St Matthew, Repl. 2.]
[2 These marginal references are inserted from Repl. 2.]

that licensed him thereunto; for he knew right well that it was the per-
petual ordinance of God that the same should be the ministers of the
word and sacraments.   Whereupon it followeth that, forasmuch as women
may not preach the gospel, no, not by the laws of the realm, that they ought
not to minister baptism.

Jo. Whitgift.

My reason alleged in my Answer to the Admonition, why
this place doth not make any necessary conclusion against the
baptizing by women, is not answered; but there is a new
collection made of the same place, which is of as great force
as the other; for you might as well conclude thus; *ergo*, pastors
may not preach, because pastors be not apostles. I speak of
the argument, not of the thing. For I would not have the
scriptures abused to confirm, no, not a truth, lest it make
men the bolder to wrest them at their pleasure, and for the
confirming of error. M. Zuinglius, in his book *De Baptismo*,
saith that "Christ did not in this place of Matthew institute
baptism, nor prescribe either time, place, or any other circumstance, pertaining to the same[1]."

I have proved before that the adminstration of the sacraments may be committed to some to whom the public preaching of the word is not committed[2]; and your examples here
alleged do not prove the contrary, except you will have us
to ground points of doctrines upon bare examples; which if
we should do, many inconveniences would follow, yea, even
baptizing by women, which you so greatly mislike. *A facto
ad jus*, or *a non facto ad non jus*, be the usual reasons of the
anabaptists, but of no force[3].

The example of Noah helpeth you not, except you will
either allegory, or prove that the minister of the word may
make sacraments, because "Noah made the ark." The ark
cannot be properly termed a sacrament in the signification

(margin: Zuinglius.)

(margin: Tract. IX. cap. 1. sect. 15.)

[1 Christus enim eo in loco [Matt. cap. xxviii.] nec baptismum instituit, nec
de ordine baptismi et doctrinæ disputat.—H. Zvingl. Op. Tigur. 1581. De Bapt.
Lib. Pars II. fol 92. 2.]

[2 See before, pages 456, &c.]

[3 "As for M. Calvin, he useth this place expressly, which the Adm. doth, to
prove that women ought, at no hand, to baptize, but 'only the ministers ordained
to preach the gospel:' [Calvin. Op. Amst. 1667-71. Inst. Lib. IV. cap. xv. 22.
Tom. IX. p. 354.]...Neither is it anything excused by Zuinglius. For, although
'baptism be not instituted here,' which was instituted in the ministry of John
Baptist, 'nor here be mentioned any circumstance;' yet the minister of that institution, which is no 'circumstance,' but a subordinate efficient cause, may well be
appointed."—The Rest of Sec. Repl. p. 117.]

that ours be; for it had no promise of eternal life annexed unto it; neither was it any seal of God's promise, but a means to save Noah and his family from perishing by the waters, and a type and figure of the church of Christ; as you have before confessed[4].

Pag. 63, sect. 1.

Your examples which follow (although some of them be very unapt, for miracles be no sacraments, neither yet every kind of signs and wonders) may, as examples, shew that the administration of the sacraments was committed to such as were preachers of the word. But they cannot prove that it was only committed unto them, and to no other. It is not required of you to prove whether he that may preach may also administer the sacraments, but whether it be of necessity that none should be admitted to minister the sacraments, except the same also be admitted to preach; the contrary whereof I have shewed before.

T. C., omitting the purpose, proveth that which is not denied.

Chapter iii.　The Third Division.

Answer to the Admonition, Page 80, Sect. 1.

The second place you do allege is 1 Cor. xiv.; where Paul saith " it is a shame for women to speak in the congregation." Paul saith not, it is[5] a shame for women to speak at home in private houses; for women may instruct their families, yea, and they may speak also in the congregation in time of necessity, if there be none else there that can or will preach Christ; and hereof we have examples.

T. C. Page 110, Lin. 13, and Sect. 1.

But M. Doctor riseth up, and saith that " a woman in time[6] of necessity, and where[7] there is none other that either can or will preach, may preach the gospel in the church."

This is strange doctrine, and such as strengtheneth the anabaptists' hands, and savoureth stronger that ways than any one thing in all the Admonition, which is so often condemned of anabaptism. His first reason to prove it is that there are examples thereof. When we allege the examples of all the churches of the apostles' times to prove the election of the minister by the church, and in other cases, which are general examples, approved and executed by the apostles, contrary to no commandment nor institution of God; yea, and, as hath been proved, according to the com-

How vain this brag is, hath been shewed, Tract. III.[8]

[4 See before, page 92.]
[5 Saith not that it is, Answ.]
[6 In the time, Repl. 1 and 2.]
[7 When, Repl. 1 and 2.]
[8 See Vol. I. pages 339, &c.]

mandment of God, M. Doctor giveth us our answer in a word, that ex-
amples prove not.   Now that the question is to make good women's preach-
ing in the church, examples I will not say of all churches, but of no one
church, only of a few singular persons, not according to the command-
ment of the word of God, but clean contrary to the prescript   1 Cor.xiv.34.[1]
word of God—I say now examples, and such singular ex-   1 Tim. ii.12.[1]
amples, are good proofs and strong arguments.

Jo. Whitgift.

In what point doth he "strengthen the anabaptists?" If
you could have told, I trust it should not have been kept in
silence.   I have charged the authors of the Admonition with
nothing but I have shewed my author for it; deal you with
me in like manner, and spare not; otherwise your words do
What force
is in exam-
ples.
but savour choler.   Examples without precepts make no
general or necessary rule; but they sometimes declare what
was done, and what may be done extraordinarily, upon like
occasion, and the same circumstances, if they be commendable
examples[2].

Matt. xxviii.
John xx.
John iv.
Women were the first that preached Christ's resurrection;
a woman was the first that preached Christ in Samaria,
John iv.; and yet undoubtedly none of these did contrary to
the prescript word of God.   Women may not speak ordinarily
in the congregation, nor challenge any such function unto
themselves; but upon occasion they may speak; as I have said
in my Answer.

Chapter iii.   The Fourth Division.
T. C. Page 110, Sect. 2.

A cavil.
Now, if the speech be a true messenger of the heart, I perceive Master
Doctor is of this mind, that he would have women preach in the church
of England at this time; for he cannot deny, and he also confesseth it

---

[1 The verses are added from Repl. 2.]
[2 "But note, I beseech you, what horrible confusion he bringeth into the
world by this saying.   For, if extraordinary examples do prove that 'such things
may be done in such cases,' then may private men execute malefactors, because
Phinees did so; and men may borrow and never pay, as did the Israelites.   If he
say that he addeth 'upon like occasion and circumstance,' it is true, but thereby
he meaneth, if like need or necessity be.   For, if he mean as he ought, having a
particular commandment of God by word, or a rare and extraordinary instinct by
the Spirit of God, his answer is nothing to purpose, considering that he will not, I
think, say that the midwives have any of these two; and, if they had, they do it
not in respect of the former example, but only by reason of the extraordinary
either commandment or motion."—The Rest of Sec. Repl. p. 122.]

*sometimes, that this is the time of necessity; and indeed it must be needs
an extreme necessity that driveth to make one man pastor of two churches,
especially so far distant; that driveth to make men, which are not able to
teach, ministers; and divers more things, which are contrary to the word
of God. Therefore, this being a time of necessity, by M. Doctor's judgment
we ought to have women to preach. Besides this, he saith, " if neither none
other can or will preach," that then women may preach; but in the most
churches of this realm there is none that either can or will preach; therefore there, and in those churches, women (at the least if they be able) may
preach the gospel, and consequently minister the sacraments.*

Jo. Whitgift.

You wander from the matter, and do but seek occasion to
quarrel; there is no such necessity in this church (God be
thanked) as M. Doctor speaketh of; for there is none in any
place or corner thereof that be ignorant of Christ, or do not
profess the name of Christ. In all places they have the scriptures read unto them, which contain matter sufficient to salvation; and therefore there is no cause why women should take
upon them to preach in the congregation; neither doth M.
Doctor mean any such thing, as you know very well, but that
it is your pleasure to dally. He meaneth such places where
all be infidels, where they have neither heard of Christ, nor
have his word, neither yet any other means to come by the
knowledge of the same; which is nowhere in this church.

In what time
a woman
may preach
Christ.

Chapter iii.   The Fifth Division.

Admonition[3].

h 1 Cor. xiv.
34.
1 Tim.ii.11.

*Women, that may [h]not speak in a congregation, may yet,
in time of necessity, minister the sacrament of baptism, and
that in a private house.*

Answer to the Admonition, Page 186, Sect. ult.

You say, "women, that may not speak in a congregation, may yet, in time of necessity, minister the sacrament of baptism, and that in a private house." And to
prove that women may not speak in a congregation you
quote 1 Cor. xiv., 1 Tim. ii.; whereas you should rather
have proved that women may not, in time of necessity,
minister baptism, for that is the question, and not the
other. Women may speak in the congregation, if neces-

[3 The order of the Admonition and Answer is again interrupted.]

Women may
speak in the
church some-
times[1].

sary occasion do require; as M. Calvin teacheth in his
Institutions, chap. xiii. sect. 32.[2]

T. C. Page 110, Sect. 3.

In the 187. page he citeth M. Calvin, in the 13. chap. section 32., to
prove that women may teach; wherein I marvel what he meaneth so to

An argument
of your ig-
norance.

allege M. Calvin continually: he allegeth the 13. chap. and no book, as
though he had written but one book; and indeed there is no such thing in
no such chapter [3] of any book of his Institutions, or in any other place
throughout his whole works, as I am persuaded. If this fault had been
but twice or thrice, I would have thought it had been the printer's; but now
that it is continual, and so oftentimes, surely he giveth great suspicion that
either somebody hath mocked him with these places, or else he would abuse
others, and especially him that should answer his book, setting him to seek
that he should never find.

Jo. Whitgift.

Pag. 19,
sect. 2.

You plead ignorance of such an edition of M. Calvin's Institutions; but it is because you cannot answer the place (for
other places which I have in like manner alleged, for the
which you might have any colour of answering, you have
found out at the first; yea, and the self-same place now in
question); but, when there is no shift to avoid that which is
alleged, then you quarrel with the book, and suspect "that
either somebody hath mocked him, or that he would abuse
others, &c." No, no, T. C., I thank God I use no such dealing;
I do allege nothing which I have not read in the authors
themselves. I study not to encumber the Answerer; for either
I set down the whole place, or else quote it so that it may
easily be found. Touching this book of Institutions of M.
Calvin's, which I now follow, I have spoken before, and
declared why I do use it rather than any other[4]; I have
laboured it, noted it, I am acquainted with it, and belike, I
read it before you knew whether there was any such book or
no; and, if there be no such book of M. Calvin's Institutions,
only divided into chapters and sections, and not into books,
I will give you all M. Calvin's works, because you so complain
of lack of books.

But, to come to the thing itself, M. Calvin, in that place

[1 This marginal note is inserted from Answ. 2.]

[2 Calvin. Op. Amst. 1667-71. Inst. Lib. iv. cap. x. 31. Tom. IX. p. 323.
See Vol. I. pages 245, 6, note 3.]

[3 Chapiter, Repl. 1.]

[4 See before, pages 268, 9, also page 326, note 1.]

speaking of such laws and orders in the church, as are not perpetual, but alterable as occasion serveth, useth this commandment of St Paul's touching the silence of women in the church, for one example to make the matter more manifest: his words be these: " Or is the commandment touching her *Chap. 13. sect. 32.* silence such as it may not be broken without wickedness ?" And a little after : *Et est, ubi loqui non minus opportunum illi sit, quam alibi tacere* [5] : " And there is a time and place when and where it is as fit for her to speak as elsewhere to hold her peace." These words be plain, and do sufficiently answer all that you can object to the contrary.

Chapter iii.   The Sixth Division.
T. C. Page 110, Sect. 4.

iv. Lib. Insti- tut. cap. 15. sect. 20. As for *M. Calvin's judgment what it is of women's preaching, it may appear by that he will not by no* [6] *means, no, not in time* [7] *of necessity (as they term it), suffer either woman or any layman to baptize or minister any sacrament, and therefore not to preach* [8].

Jo. Whitgift.

I doubt not of M. Calvin's judgment in that point, and yet I know other learned and notable men that think otherwise, and namely Zuinglius, in his book *De Baptismo* [9] ; neither do I go about to teach that women may preach. I tell you only what extreme necessity may extraordinarily permit, without just cause of reprehension.

Chapter iii.   The Seventh Division.
T. C. Page 110, Sect. ult.

And, as for the examples of Mary the sister of Moses, of Olda, of Anna, and the daughters of Philip the evangelist, which are all called prophetesses (for I think M. Doctor meaneth these examples); as for them, I say it will be hard for to shew that they ever prophesied or taught openly in any public meeting or congregation. But the surer answer is that, although the Lord do sometimes, not being under any law, change the order which he hath set, in raising up certain women, partly to the shame of men and to humble them, partly to let them understand that he can, if he would, want their ministry ; yet it is not lawful for us to draw that

[5 See above, note 2.]   [6 Any, Repl. 2.]   [7 In the time, Repl. 1 and 2.]

[8 Hoc etiam scire ad rem pertinet, perperam fieri si privati homines baptismi administrationem sibi usurpent: ... Neque enim aut mulieribus aut hominibus quibuslibet mandavit Christus ut baptizarent : sed quos apostolos constituerat, iis mandatum hoc dedit. &c.—Calvin. Op. Inst. Lib. IV. cap. xv. 20. Tom. IX. p. 354.]

[9 H. Zvingl. Op. Tigur. 1581. De Bapt. Lib. Pars II. fol. 96. 2. See below, page 511, note 7.]

into example, and to follow it ; or that, forasmuch as he breaketh the law which is not subject unto it, and which he made not for himself, that therefore we may break the law whereunto we be subject, and to whom it is given. But we must go in the broad high-way of the commandment, and of the ordinary usage of God in governing his church, and not in the bypath of certain singular examples, which have been in divers ages. And, as often as God hath used this extraordinary means of the ministry of women, so often also hath he confirmed their calling either by miracle, or some wonderful issue, or with some other singular note and mark, whereby he hath made their calling, otherwise strange and monstrous, most certain and undoubted to all men.

Jo. Whitgift.

There be other examples also besides these, and yet these be sufficient to prove anything that I have spoken touching this matter: he that well considereth what is written of Mary the sister of Moses, *Num.* xii., or of Olda, 2 *Reg.* xxii., will not doubt whether they spake "openly in the congregation," or no; but you will not stick upon this point. And in your second answer I agree with you in this, that we must make no general rule of these particular examples; and that women may not presume to preach in the congregation, except they be extraordinarily called thereunto, and have certain and sure signs of their calling. And surely I muse what you mean to spend so much labour about this matter, wherein there is no controversy. I might say unto you, as it hath pleased you to say unto me, that you have some old rusty notes which you would gladly utter, and you know not how otherwise to make merchandize of them than by picking such a quarrel to utter them.

Chapter iii.   The Eighth Division.
T. C. Page 111, Sect. 1.

There is a greater difficulty than M. Doctor mentioneth in the words of St Paul, where he saith, "a woman praying or prophesying ought to be veiled, and have her head covered;" in which words 1 Cor. xi. 5.[1] *it seemeth that the apostle licenseth a woman to prophesy, so that she do it with her head covered. But to him that shall diligently consider the place, it shall appear that the women of Corinth did pass the bounds of modesty and of shamefastness two ways; whereof one was that they came into the congregation, contrary to the custom of those countries, with their heads and faces uncovered; another was that they also took upon them to speak in the congregation; both which faults St Paul condemned, but in their*

[1 The verse is added from Repl. 2.]

several and proper places. Although therefore, speaking against the abuse
of uncovering their head, he doth not condemn their boldness in teaching,
yet he did not therefore approve it ; the confutation whereof he reserved
to a more commodious place.

Jo. Whitgift.

To what end bring you in this saying of St Paul? I do
not remember that I have at any time used it for any proof;
and yet you have objected more than you can well answer.
Howbeit, because it pertaineth not to improve anything that I
affirm, I will not examine your answer (and yet not yours, but
M. Calvin's[2]), nor trouble the reader with frivolous and vain
digressions.

Chapter iii. The Ninth Division.

Answer to the Admonition, Page 80, Sect. 2, 3.

If women do baptize, they baptize in private houses,
not in the congregation.

Surely you are able to mar a good matter for lack
of skilful handling.

T. C. Page 111, Sect. 1, 2.

But saith he, "if women do baptize, it is in private houses." I have
shewed before that they may not baptize at all, therefore not in private
houses ; besides that that I have in the reply unto the section in the one-
and-twenty page shewed how it is not lawful neither to preach the word,
nor to minister the sacraments in private corners[3].

Jo. Whitgift.

I answer to their argument, and go not about to confirm
the baptizing by women. I say this argument followeth not :
St Paul forbiddeth them to speak in the congregation ; *ergo,*
they may not baptize ; for they baptize in private houses, not
in public places ; and St Paul doth bid them to speak in private places. Whatsoever you have replied unto, I have there
answered where you have replied ; and it is manifest that
both the word may be preached, and the sacraments ministered
in private places, upon just occasion.

[2 Nam quum reprehendit quod prophetabant nudo capite, non tamen illis
permittit prophetare alio quovis modo : quin potius hujus quoque vitii reprehen-
sionem in alium locum differt, nempe in caput 14.—Calvin. Op. Amst. 1667-71.
Comm. in Epist. ad Corinth. cap. xi. 5. Tom. VII. p.178.]

   [3 See Vol. I. pages 207, &c.]

Chapter iii.   The Tenth Division.

T. C. Page 111, Sect. 2, 3, 4.

For the which matter of not ministering the sacraments in private houses, to the authors of the Admonition, citing the eleventh chapter of the first epistle unto the Corinthians, M. Doctor answereth that he reproveth the profanation of the supper, by banqueting and contempt of their brethren, and exhorteth to tarry one for another.

But what is this to the purpose? we ask not M. Doctor the interpretation of this place, as we do not of all the rest which he interpreteth, where there is no occasion in the world to interpret them, being of themselves very clear; and the interpretation which is brought never almost making anything for the solution of that which is objected; which I desire the reader to mark throughout his whole book. For what if St Paul reprove the profanation of the supper of the Lord? doth it follow therefore that he doth not give to understand that the sacrament should be administered in a common assembly? What if he exhort to tarry one for another? therefore doth he not dehort from celebrating of the sacrament in a private house?

And surely methink you cannot be so ignorant as you make yourself, that you should not understand their argument; and therefore I think you do rather dissemble it, as you do in divers other places; for all men may easily perceive that, as St Paul opposeth the supper of the Lord to the common supper, his banquet to the common banquet, so he opposeth there manifestly the church and congregation unto the private house, and declareth that, as the common supper or banquet ought to be kept 1 Cor. xi. *at their houses, so the Lord's supper and his banquet ought* 20, 21, 22.[1] *to be celebrated in the congregation.*

The places be interpreted to shew how far out of square they be alleged in the Admonition.

Jo. Whitgift.

I think indeed that M. Doctor's interpretations trouble you shrewdly; for they detect much of your vanity, and make manifest the lack of discretion and learning in the authors of the Admonition. I say lack of discretion and learning; for otherwise so evidently and so oft to abuse the scriptures were great dishonesty, or rather impiety. If I have missed in interpreting, or wrongfully accused them, why do not you make it known as occasion is offered? It stands you upon, for it is much to your dishonesty, and a great discredit to your whole cause.

Touching this place of St Paul, 1 Cor. xi., I say as I said before; and I add that he only reproveth such abuses as were used among them in their public assemblies; he speaketh not of celebrating the communion in private places.

[[1] This reference is introduced from Repl. 2.]

St Paul maketh no such opposition in that place as you speak of, neither doth he speak anything sounding that way, only he reproveth the abuse which was then crept into the supper of the Lord among the Corinthians : *Quod sacro et* Calv. in 1 Cor. xi. *spirituali epulo profana symposia permiscerent, idque cum pauperum contumelia[2] :* "In that they mingled profane banquets with that holy and spiritual feast, and that with the contumely of the poor;" as M. Calvin saith. Wherefore it appeareth that either you are disposed to make good whatsoever they have written, be it never so absurd, or else you wittingly dissemble the true sense and meaning of this place.

Chapter iii. The Eleventh Division.

Answer to the Admonition, Page 80, Sect. 4.

You say in your margent, that Victor, *anno* 198., did first appoint that women might baptize. By this you[3] add more credit to the cause than you are aware of; for Victor was a godly bishop, and a martyr, and the church Victor a good bishop and at that time was in great purity, not being long after martyr. the apostles' time. But truly I can find no such thing in all his decrees, only this he saith, that "such as be converted of the gentiles to the faith of Christ in time of necessity, or at the point of death, may be baptized at any time in any place, whether it be in the sea, or in a river, or in a pond, or in a well, so that they make a confession of their faith[4] :" he maketh no mention at all of any baptizing by women; and therefore you have done your cause great injury.

Jo. Whitgift.

Nothing answered hereunto.

[2 Calvin. Op. Amst. 1667-71. Comm. in Epist. I. ad Corinth. cap. xi. 20. Tom. VII. p. 180.]

[3 Ye, Answ.]

[4 Et constituit, ut necessitate faciente, ubicumque inventus fuisset quicumque hominum ex gentibus veniens, sive in flumine, sive in mari, sive in fonte, sive in stagno, baptizaretur : tantum christianæ credulitatis confessione declarata, integer efficeretur Christianus.—Ex Lib. Pont. in Concil. Stud. Labb. et Cossart. Lut. Par. 1671-2. Tom. I. col. 591.]

¶ Of ministering the sacraments in private places.

Chapter iv.   The First Division.

Admonition.

Then they were ministered in public "assemblies, now in "Mar. i. 5.
private houses[1].   1 Cor.xi.18.

Answer to the Admonition, Page 92, Sect. 2.

The places of scripture, whereby you prove that

Baptism ministered in private places[2].

sacraments were then ministered in public assemblies, be
taken out of the first of St Mark and 1 Cor. xi.; which
places of scripture prove that John did baptize openly,
and that the Lord's supper was ministered in the public
congregation; but neither of them both conclude that
these sacraments may not also be ministered upon any
occasion in private houses; for what sequel is there in
this reason? "All the country of Judea, and they of Jeru-

Arg. non[3] sequitur.

salem, went out unto him, and were baptized of him in
the river of Jordan, confessing their sins;" *ergo,* baptism
may not be ministered upon any occasion in private
houses: you may as well conclude that none ought to
be baptized but in the river of Jordan, and none but such
as be able to confess their sins; and so you should seclude
children from baptism, as the anabaptists do.

T. C. Page 111, Sect. ult.

To the Admonition objecting, in the ninety-and-two page, that John
baptized openly amongst the congregation, he answereth and Mark i. 5.[4]
saith, that it may be as well concluded that we should baptize
only in the river of Jordan, and none but those that be of age; by which
saying he giveth to understand that to baptize in the church hath no

Nay, I give you to understand the fondness of the argument.

greater necessity than the baptizing in Jordan; nor it skilleth no more
whether baptism be ministered in the public assembly than it is necessary
or skilleth whether we be baptized in the river of Jordan; and that the
baptism of young infants hath no better grounds than private baptism
hath.   The latter[5] whereof (both being absurd) is too too injurious unto the
baptism of young infants.   For, as of our Saviour Christ's preaching[6] in

---

[1] This is a sentence from a paragraph of the Admonition, the rest of which is
considered below, Tractat. XII. Answ. repeats it at the head of the portion which
here follows, with the introduction: *The second general reason is this: Then*
sacraments were ministered &c.]

[2] This marginal note is not in Answ.]   [3] *Non* is not printed in Answ.]
[4] This marginal reference is inserted from Repl. 2.]
[5] Later, Repl. 1 and 2.]   [6] Preachings, Repl. 1 and 2.]

public places, and refusing private places, we do gather that the preaching
of the word ought to be public; even so of St John's preaching and bap-
tizing in open meetings we conclude that both preaching and baptizing
ought to be in public assemblies.

Jo. Whitgift.

I refer it to the learned reader to judge whether this be
a good argument or no : John baptized openly in the river
Jordan ; *ergo,* baptism may at no time upon any occasion be
ministered in a private house.   And, if any will judge it to be
good, then will I demand of them, why this should not be as
good : John did baptize in Jordan ; *ergo,* none ought to be
baptized but in the river Jordan.   Or this : John baptized
such as confessed their sins ; *ergo,* none must be baptized but
such as are able to make a confession of their sins.   This is
that unskilful kind of reasoning that Zuinglius so oft reproveth the anabaptists for, and he calleth it an argument *a
facto ad jus*[7].   I do not in any respect speak against baptizing in the church, but do greatly commend it, as a thing
most convenient; but I do not so tie the sacrament to the
place, or public congregation, that I make it of the necessity
of the sacrament, so that it may not upon any occasion be ministered in a private house.   I compare not baptizing in the
church and in the river Jordan together; neither do I say
that baptizing of young infants "hath no better grounds than
private baptism hath ;" but I disallow this kind of proof,
which the Admonition useth ; and I see not why it is not of
like force in all other the circumstances of that place, and
those examples that I have alleged.

Christ preached both privately and publicly, in the
temple and in private families, in great assemblies and
severally to his own disciples, and at all times as occasion
served ; and therefore you cannot conclude by the example of
Christ that the preaching of the gospel ought only to be
public in the open congregation, and at no time private upon
any occasion.

Chapter iv.   The Second Division.

T. C. Page 112, Sect. 1.

And, although to some one action there concur divers things, which

[7 H. Zvingl. Op. Tigur. 1581. Elench. contr. Catabapt. Pars II. fol. 9. 2. See
Vol. I. page 353, note 7.]

partly are not to be followed at all, partly are indifferent to be followed or
not followed, yet neither the unlawfulness of the one to be followed, nor the
indifferency of the other can hinder, but there are some other things[1] in
the same action necessary to be followed, which may be considered both of

It is said, but
not proved.

the place of the Acts, touching the election, where I have proved
some things there mentioned to be necessary to be done in   *Acts i.[2]*
elections, although other some be not convenient nor fit for us to follow.
And I have shewed it also by M. Calvin, which M. Doctor allegeth for

A digression
from the
matter to the
person.

himself, and by Cyprian[3], whose authority he would be loth to reject, I am
sure, lest he should lose the opinion of his studiousness of the old writers,
which he hunteth so diligently after in this book, and whereof he maketh the
authors of the Admonition so great contemners. And it is not hard to
shew the same in twenty places more, as in the tenth of St   *Matt. x.[2]*
Matt.[4], and St Luke; where, as there are divers things not   *Luke ix.[2]*
   Luke x.[2]
to be followed of the ministers now, other things indifferent to
be followed, so are there also other things that be as well commanded
to all the ministers that now are as they were then either to the 12. or
70. disciples.

Jo. Whitgift.

And of those circumstances whereof there is no commandment, how prove you which be "indifferent," which be unlawful or "not convenient to be followed," which "necessary?"
why is it not as necessary by this example of John that
they should be baptized in Jordan, or that they should confess their sins before they be baptized, as it is that they
should be publicly baptized? If you take upon you to interpret without authority and ground of scripture, it is meet
that you should shew very good and substantial reason. I
demand the like touching the places alleged out of the Acts,
where you retain what you list, refuse what you list, alter as
you list, as though you were lord over the scripture, and had
omnia jura tam divina quam humana in scrinio pectoris[5]:
"all laws as well divine as human in the coffer of your
breast," like to the pope. But to these places of the Acts I
have answered in their due place. Your scoffs make not your
cause one whit the better.

Of "twenty places," you recite not one; and of "divers
things, some indifferent, some not to be followed, other some

[1 Are other some things, Repl. 1 and 2.]
[2 These marginal references are inserted from Repl. 2.]
[3 See Vol. I. pages 297, 358.]   [4 As in St Matthew, Repl. 2.]
[5 ... pontifex (qui jura omnia in scrinio pectoris sui censetur habere) &c.—
Corp. Jur. Canon. Lugd. 1624. Sext. Decretal. Lib. I. Tit. ii. cap. 1. col. 11.]

commanded to all ministers, spoken to the twelve or seventy
disciples in the x. of Matthew, and Luke, you name none:"
speaking without ground or reason is but prattling. I know
that in one action there be divers circumstances, of divers conditions and natures; but, if any of them be necessary at all Necessary
circum-
times to be observed, the same is contained in some command- stances are
commanded.
ment in the scriptures; and therefore well saith Zuinglius that
an argument *a facto ad jus* is then strong, when as we are
able to shew that that which is done is done according to
some rule or commandment[6]. Now, if you can shew me either
rule or commandment in scripture, that upon no occasion we
may preach or baptize in private families, I yield unto you.
But, if you cannot this do, your examples prove what was then What ex-
amples do
done, and what in the like cause may be done now, but they prove with-
out com-
make not any general and perpetual rule. mandment.

Now touching these and such like circumstances, in my
opinion M. Zuinglius, in his book *De Baptismo*, maketh a full
resolution, which may satisfy any reasonable man. His words
be these: "There is here three errors about circumstances, Zuinglius.
that is, the elements of the world. The first is of the time;
for they thought that baptism was not rightly administered,
except it were in the first day; for the time is of no great
weight, so that we take diligent heed of this, that none rashly
or negligently defer it longer than is convenient, for by this
occasion it may come to pass that the baptism of children
might be taken away. Another error is touching the circumstance of the person; for they thought that baptism could not
be administered of no other than of a priest; when as notwithstanding every man may minister it, even a woman, if
necessity require. The third error is in the circumstance of
the place, because it is not necessary that the infant should
only be baptized in the church[7]."

[6 H. Zvingl. Op. Tigur. 1581. Elench. contr. Catabapt. Pars II. fol. 9.2.
See Vol. I. page 353, note 7.]

[7 Triplex enim hic circa circumstantias, id est, elementa mundi error ver-
satur. Primus enim temporis erat, quo baptismum non nisi primo die rite conferri posse arbitrabantur: cum temporis ratio non adeo multum hic momenti
habeat, modo hoc caveatur sedulo, ne quis temere vel negligenter rem hanc diutius,
quam par sit, differat. Facile enim hujusmodi occasione fieri posset, ut parvulo-
rum baptismus e medio tolleretur. Alter error circa personæ circumstantiam
versabatur, quod baptismum a nemine alio, quam a solo sacerdote, conferri posse
putarent, cum interim quivis hominum hoc facere possit, imo fœmina quoque, si
quando necessitas sic postulare videatur. Tertio in loci circumstantia non minus

Chapter iv.   The Third Division.

Answer to the Admonition, Page 92, Sect. 3, 4.

Baptism was ministered in Cornelius' house, Acts x.
The place is not of the substance of the sacraments.

Baptism in
an house. To the 1 Cor. xi. it is answered before.   Surely this
church of England doth not permit the sacraments to
be ministered in private-places, except there be a congregation, and then not usually, but only in certain cases.

T. C. Page 112, Sect. 1.

*Another reason he addeth there, that St Peter baptized in Corne-
lius' house.   But M. Doctor maketh not the best choice of his arguments.
For St Paul's baptizing in the house of the jailor had been more*
fit for him.   For unto his place it may be easily answered, that   Acts xvi. 33.[1]
*Cornelius, having so great a family as it is like he had, and besides that
divers soldiers underneath him, and, further, his friends and his acquaintance which he had called, had a competent number, and as many as would
make a congregation, and as could commodiously be preached unto in one
place.   But the answer to both these examples, and other such like, as that
St Paul baptized in the house[2] of Stephana, is easy.   For, there*
being persecutions at that time, so that it was not safe neither   1 Cor. i. 16.[1]
*for the minister nor for the people to be seen, it was meet that they
should do it in houses, which otherwise they would have done in open
places; and then those houses which receive the congregation are not[3],
as I have shewed, for the time to be counted private houses; and, further,
in places where the gospel hath not been received, nor no church gathered,
but one only household embracing the gospel, I say in such a case, and
especially in the time of persecution, where should the ministers preach, or
minister the sacraments, more conveniently than in that house where those
professors of the gospel be?   Now, to draw this into our churches which may
safely come into open places, and where the church and congregation
standeth of divers households, is a token of great want of judgment in
shuffling those things together which, for the great diversity of their natures,
will not be mingled.*

Jo. Whitgift.

The example of Peter's baptizing in Cornelius' house is
sufficient to prove that then it was lawful to baptize in

quam primis istis, errabatur, eo quod non opus erat, infantem in templo tantummodo baptizari.—Id. De Bapt. Lib. Pars II. fol. 96. 2.]

[[1] These references are added from Repl. 1 and 2 : the former does not give
the verses.]

[[2] Baptized the house, Repl. 1 and 2.]

[[3] Received the congregation were not, Repl. 2.]

private families : the example of Paul baptizing the jailor and his family proveth the same; but it ministereth a more ready answer to a quarreller, because Paul, then being prisoner, had not such liberty to make choice of his place as Peter had. But they are both very fit examples for my purpose : the bigness of Cornelius' family or the smallness is not material to this question ; for we speak of the place, not of the persons. And, whereas you say that in Cornelius' house "there was a competent number, and as many as would make a congregation," I answer that so it is with us when baptism is ministered in private families; for, " wheresoever two or three be gathered together in the name of Christ," there is a congregation. Matt. xviii.

To your second answer of the difference of time, " because that was in time of persecution, &c.," I say that, as persecution was then a cause why baptism was usually ministered in private houses, so necessity is now the cause why the same is ministered sometimes in private families. Neither do I maintain or allow the administering of the sacraments in private families to be usual, or without urgent cause, but only upon extreme necessity of sickness, peril of death, and such like. In which cases, as never any learned man misliked ministering of the sacraments in such places, so are not you able to shew either scripture, doctor, or reason to the contrary ; and, whatsoever you say of the time of persecution touching the matter, the same may be said of the time of necessity also. But here I would have the reader to note, that you are now driven to confess a difference in the church betwixt the time of persecution and the time of prosperity, and that to be convenient in the one which is not convenient for the other ; which distinction and diversity of times you would not before acknowledge to make any difference in the election of ministers, and government of the church ; and yet the case is all one.

Chapter iv.   The Fourth Division.
Admonition.

They should first prove that[4] . . . private communion, &c. are agreeable to the written word of God[5].

[4 Prove by the word that, Adm.; prove by the word of God that, Answ.]

[5 Adm. and Answ., instead of &c., have the enumeration of several other things, and conclude *word of the Almighty.* The paragraph appears below, page 562; also Tractat. xxi. Chap. i. Div. 4.]

Answer to the Admonition, Page 152, Sect. 2.

Of the communion ministered in private places[1]. If you mean by "private communion" the communion ministered to one alone, there is no such allowed in the book of common prayers; but, if you call it private, because it is ministered sometimes[2] in private houses to sick persons, then have we the example of Christ, who ministered the supper in a private house, and inner parlour, Mark xiv. Luke xxii. Matt. xxvi.; we have also the example of the apostles themselves, who did minister the supper in private houses, especially if that place be understanded of the supper which is in the second of the Acts, and before alleged of you to prove that common and usual bread ought to be in the supper; likewise of the primitive church; as appeareth in the second apology of Justinus Martyr, Tertull. *De Corona Militis*, and others[3].

T. C. Page 112, Sect. 2.

And in the page 152. *he bringeth other reasons to prove that the sacraments may be ministered in a private house; whereof the first is that our Saviour Christ celebrated his supper in a private house, and in an inner parlour; the reason whereof is easily to be known; for the law of God ordained that every householder in his house should eat the passover with his own family, if it were so great as that they might well eat up a whole lamb.*

Jo. Whitgift.

That is a reason why Christ did eat the passover in a private house; but it is no reason why he did celebrate his supper there in like manner. Wherefore my reason holdeth as yet.

Chapter iv.   The Fifth Division.
T. C. Page 112, Sect. 3.

Our Saviour Christ therefore with his household observeth this law, and, for because he would declare that the passover had his end, and that his holy sacrament should come in place thereof, he doth forthwith celebrate

[1 Communion in private houses, Answ. 2.]   [2 Sometime, Answ.]
[3 Just. Mart. Op. Par. 1742. Apol. i. 65, 7. pp. 82, 3; Tertull. Op. Franek. 1597. De Cor. Mil. 3. p. 180.   In these places descriptions are given of the christian rites then celebrated; but it seems doubtful whether private houses were used as the places of ministration. See Bingham, Orig. Eccles. Book VIII. chap. i. sectt. 13, &c.]

his supper in the same place[4], *which if he had not done, neither could he
have done it at all, the hour of his apprehension then approaching; neither
should it so lively have appeared that either the passover was abolished, or
that the supper came in place of it, being celebrated both at another time,
and in another place.*

Jo. Whitgift.

Our Saviour Christ's example of instituting and ministering
his supper in a private family, giving afterward no commandment to the contrary, is a manifest proof that the place is not
of the substance of the sacrament, and that upon occasion it
may be ministered in a private house.   You shew a reason
why Christ, at that time and in that place, did minister his
supper, but you shew no reason why we may not in like
manner upon necessary occasion celebrate the communion in
the like place.

Unnecessary proof.

Chapter iv.   The Sixth Division.
T. C. Page 112, Sect. ult.

*For the celebrating of the supper in houses in the apostles' times, and in
Justinus'*[5] *and Tertullian's times, which were times of persecution, I have
spoken before; where also I declared that such houses for the time are not
private, but public.*

Jo. Whitgift.

This answer is as fit for me as it is for you; for admit
that the sacraments may be administered in private families in
the case of necessity, and I ask no more.   For, if persecution
be a necessary cause, why is not sickness and peril of death
so in like manner? again, if a private house be "no private"
but a "public" place, when for the fear of persecution the sacraments be ministered in it, why is it not so likewise when they be
there ministered for extremity of sickness and fear of death?
the reason is all one, and the case of necessity like; and therefore you have not said anything against me, but with me.

Chapter iv.   The Seventh Division.
T. C. Page 113, Sect. 1.

*And these are his reasons wherewith he would prove that the sacraments,
and therefore also the sacrament of baptism, may be ministered in a private
house.*

[4 And that his holy sacrament of the supper should come in place thereof he
doth forthwith celebrate it in the same place, Repl. 2.]

[5 Justins, Repl. 1 and 2.]

JO. WHITGIFT.

And these reasons have you confirmed rather than confuted; but to the contrary you have shewed no reason at all; and therefore these stand in full force; to the which I might add that circumcision was celebrated in private families; as M. Calvin truly gathereth, upon the 58. verse of the first chapter of Luke[1]; which is a better argument to prove that the sacraments may be ministered in private places, than you have shewed any to the contrary.

[Admonition.

The seventh.

And as for private baptism, that will abide the touchstone. "Go ye," saith Christ, *"and teach, baptizing them, &c.*[g]*" Now teaching* gMatt.xxviii. 19. *is divorced from communions and sacraments. They may go alone without doctrine.*]

[Answer to the Admonition.]

[Of private baptism I have spoken before: here is nothing alleged against it but the xxviii. of Matt.: "Go ye and teach, baptizing them, &c.;" which text doth prove that it was a portion of the apostles' office to baptize, but in what place, at what time, how many at once, is not there prescribed; and therefore "private baptism" may "abide this touchstone" for any thing that I see to the contrary.

*The anabaptists use this text, Matt. xxviii, *Euntes docete omnes gentes, baptizantes eos, &c.*, to improve the baptism of infants; because he saith in that text *docete*, before he saith *baptizantes, &c.*; and "infants cannot be taught," as that learned man Zuinglius declareth in his book *De Baptismo*, fol. 64. and 65.; where also he saith that "Christ did not in this place institute baptism, nor prescribe either time, place, or any other circumstance pertaining to the same;" as appeareth in divers other places of that book[2]. But, because this text is shamefully abused of the anabaptists, to overthrow the baptizing of infants, even as it is also abused of these men, both against

[1 Colligimus ex Lucæ verbis, quamvis domi circumciderent suos infantes, non tamen id facere solitos sine hominum frequentia et conventu.—Calvin. Op. Amst. 1667-71. Comm. in Harm. Euang. Luc. i. 58. Tom. VI. p. 16.]

[2 See before, p. 498, note 1.]

private baptism, and also to prove that preaching of necessity must go before baptism, which tendeth to the same end the anabaptists use it for, therefore I will set down the very words of Zuinglius touching that text. In his book *De Baptismo* he saith thus : " The first foundation that those bring for themselves which deny baptism to infants is the words of Christ, Matt. xxviii.: ' Go and teach all nations, baptizing them, &c.' For they urging the bare order of words cry this one thing, *Docete et baptizate :* ' Teach and baptize, &c.'" And a little after : " Although we grant you this order of words to be something, yet they pertain not so to children and infants, but that they may be baptized before doctrine. For these words pertain to them that may be taught. But it is certain that infants cannot be taught ; and therefore these words cannot prove that they may not be baptized. But the anabaptists do object, if these words pertain not to infants, then infants ought not to be baptized ; for Christ did here institute the sign and use of baptism. You are far deceived, not understanding the scriptures ; for the institution of baptism is not begun in this place ; the ignorance whereof hath made you fall into this error. &c. Neither can you prove anything, although the order of words be taken according to the letter. The order of words prove nothing ; for, if we shall admit that, there is many places of scripture that we shall be compelled to take in a preposterous and false sense ; which I could prove by divers examples. In the first of John, John Baptist, pointing to Christ with his finger saith, ' Behold the Lamb of God, which taketh away the sins of the world ;' and a little after he saith, ' And I knew him not.' How shall it be said that he knew him not, when as he testified before, that he was the Lamb of God ? Likewise Paul in the tenth to the Romans saith, ' If thou shalt confess with thy mouth the Lord Jesus, and believe in thine heart that God raised him from death, thou shalt be saved.' In the which words we see the confession of the mouth to be put in the first place, the which, notwithstanding, is vain and unprofitable, without the inward faith of the mind ; and therefore the order of words in this place of Matthew is

not so stiffly to be urged[1]." Furthermore the same
Zuinglius in the same book declareth how that preaching before baptism is necessary when such are baptized
as have discretion, and may be taught, but not when
children and infants be baptized to whom preaching can
do no good[2]. But of this matter I will say no more
until I understand further of your meaning. In the
meanwhile you give great cause for a man to suspect
that you would have none baptized but such as be taught;
which is to seclude children from baptism*.

Slanderous speech.

You say untruly when you do affirm that "teaching
in this church is divorced from communions and sacraments;" but such forged slanderous speeches be usual
to you. Of this matter also I have spoken in the former
part.][3]

[1 E quibus primum esto, quod pro sese adducere solent, qui infantibus baptismum negant. Christus Jesus apud Matthæum cap. 28. ait, Euntes docete omnes
gentes, baptizantes eos &c....Nudum enim verborum ordinem urgentes hoc unum
clamitant, Docete et baptizate...Nam etiamsi demus vobis, hunc verborum ordinem aliquid hoc loco posse, ad parvulos tamen et infantes hæc nequaquam pertinent, quo minus ante doctrinam baptismo initiari debeant. Verba enim hæc ad
eos pertinent, qui doctrina verboque externo instituuntur. Parvulos autem non
doceri certo constat. Verba ergo hæc ad illos referri non possunt, quo minus baptizari debeant. Sed objiciunt hic nobis catabaptistæ, Si ad infantes hæc referri non
possunt, infantes quoque baptizandi non sunt. Christus enim hoc loco baptismi
signum et usum instituit. Toto cœlo erratis, o viri, non intelligentes scripturas...
Nec enim hoc loco baptismi institutio cœpta est : cujus ignorantia vobis erroris
vestri causam præbuit....Nec enim quicquam efficietis, etiamsi verborum ordo juxta
nudam literam alicujus momenti hoc loco esse queat. Sed ordinis ratio nihil
urget. Si enim hoc admiserimus, jam plures sunt scripturæ loci, quos præpostero
et fallaci omnino sensu recipere cogemur. Cujus rei exempla plura proferre
possum. Apud Joannem enim capite i. Baptista servatorem Christum digito
demonstrans, dicit, Ecce Agnus ille Dei, qui tollit peccatum mundi. Et paulo
post idem ille inquit, Et ego non noveram eum. Qua autem ratione eum non
novisse dicetur, cum antea testatus sit, ipsum esse Agnum Dei ? &c. Item Paulus
ad Romanos scribens, cap. x. ait, Si confessus fueris ore tuo Dominum Jesum, et
credideris in corde tuo quod Deus illum excitavit a mortuis, salvus eris. In quibus
verbis oris confessionem primo loco poni videmus, quæ tamen, nisi fides animi
interna accedat, vana est et inutilis. Non igitur verborum ordo in hoc Matthæi
loco pertinaciter urgendus est.—H. Zvingl. Op. Tigur. 1581. De Bapt. fol. 64.
2, 65.]

[2 Interim tamen hoc illis non inviti concedimus, doctrinam et institutionem
baptismo præmittendam esse si quando incredulos perveniamus. &c.—Id. ibid.
fol. 92. 2.]

[3 The portions of Admonition and Answer between brackets do not appear in
the Defence : it is thought desirable to introduce them here. The piece of the
Admonition, p. 516, immediately precedes that in page 501 : the paragraph of
Answer between the asterisks is only in Answ. 2.]

¶ The sacraments ministered by other than
ministers.

Chapter v.   The First Division.

Admonition.

ᵂMatt.xxviii.   *Then by ministers ᵂonly, now by midwives and deacons*
19.
1 Cor. iv. 1.   *equally[4].*

Answer to the Admonition, Page 93, Sect. 2.

That then the sacraments were ministered only by
ministers, you allege the xxviii. of Matt.; which place is
answered before.   Likewise 1 Cor. iv.: "Let a man so
think of us as of the ministers of Christ, and disposers
of the mysteries of God."   Here is not one word for
your purpose, except you take mysteries for sacraments,
which if you do, you are much deceived; for by the
word "mysteries" here he understandeth the word of
God, and gospel of Christ; as all learned writers do interpret it.

*Whether any
may minister
the sacra-
ments besides
the minister[5].*

*What mys-
teries be[6].*

Jo. Whitgift.

Nothing answered to the unapt allegation of the 1 Cor. iv.

Chapter v.   The Second Division.

Answer to the Admonition, Page 93, Sect. 2.

We read in the eighth of the Acts, that Philip, a
deacon, did baptize; we read also that Moses' wife did
circumcise.   But where doth this church of England
allow any woman to baptize, or deacon to celebrate the
Lord's supper?   And, if it did, the dignity of the sacraments do not depend upon the man, be he minister or
not minister, be he good or evil.   [*Well saith Master Calvin in his Institutions, *cap.* 17 : "Now, if it be true that we
have set down, the sacrament is not to be esteemed of his
hand by whom it is ministered, but as it were of the hand

*Philip, dea-
con, baptized.
Moses' wife
did circum-
cise.*

[4 This is a sentence from a paragraph in Adm. and is repeated at the head of
the portion of the Answer which here follows, with the introduction : *The third
general reason is this.*]

[5 This marginal note is not in Answ.]   [6 Mysteries what they be, Answ. 2.]

[7 Philip being a, Answ.]

of God from whom it certainly cometh: hereof we may
gather that nothing is added or taken from the dignity
of it by him by whom it is ministered. And therefore, as
among men if an epistle be sent, so that the hand and seal
be known, it skilleth not who or what manner of person
carrieth it; even so it is sufficient for us to know the hand
and seal of the Lord in his sacraments, by whomsoever
they be delivered. Hereby is the error of the Donatists
confuted, who measured the virtue and worthiness of the
sacrament by the worthiness of the minister. Such be
now-a-days our anabaptists, which deny us to be rightly
baptized, because we were baptized by wicked and idolatrous persons in the pope's church. And therefore
they furiously urge re-baptization; against whose folly
we shall be sufficiently defended, if we think that we
were baptized not in the name of any man, but in the
name of the Father, and of the Son, and of the Holy
Ghost, and therefore baptism not to be of man, but of
God, by whomsoever it be ministered[1]." *Hæc Calvinus.* 🖎]² Let³ every one take heed that they do not
usurp that authority whereunto they be not called.

[These be your general reasons, which indeed be no
reasons, but bare words. Your particular reasons, whereby
you seem to prove that neither of the sacraments be
sincerely ministered, be these that follow. And first concerning the Lord's supper you reason on this sort.]⁴

[¹ Porro si verum est quod constituimus, sacramentum non ex ejus manu æsti-
mandum esse a quo administratur, sed velut ex ipsa Dei manu, a quo haud dubie
profectum est: inde colligere licet nihil illi afferri vel auferri ejus dignitate per
cujus manum traditur. Ac perinde atque inter homines, siqua missa epistola
fuerit, modo satis et manus et signum agnoscatur, minime refert quis aut qualis
tabellarius fuerit: ita nobis sufficere debet manum et signum Domini nostri in
sacramentis suis agnoscere, a quocunque tandem tabellario deferantur. His Do-
natistarum error pulchre refutatur, qui vim ac pretium sacramenti metiebantur
ministri dignitate. Tales hodie sunt catabaptistæ nostri, qui rite nos baptizatos
pernegant, quod ab impiis et idololatris in regno papali baptizati sumus: itaque
anabaptismum furiose urgent. Adversus quorum ineptias satis valida ratione
muniemur, si cogitemus nos baptismo initiatos, non in nomen alicujus hominis,
sed in nomen Patris, et Filii, et Spiritus sancti: ideoque baptismum non esse
hominis, sed Dei: a quocunque tandem administratus fuerit.—Calvin. Op. Amst.
1667-71. Inst. Lib. IV. cap. xv. 16. Tom. IX. p. 353.]

[² This portion between the brackets is inserted from Answ. 2.]

[³ But let, Answ. 2.]

[⁴ This paragraph is inserted from Answ. The last words are introductory to
the matters treated on in Tractat. xv.]

T. C. Page 113, Sect. 1, 2, 3.

He hath certain other to prove that women may baptize, whereof the Untruth; for
first is in the 93. page; and that is, that Sephora, Moses' wife, circumcised I use no rea-
her child; whereunto I have answered partly before, that particular ex- sons to that
amples, especially contrary to general rules, are not to be followed; and end.
*will further answer, if I first admonish the reader whereupon this baptism
of midwives and in private houses rose, that, when we know of how rotten
a stock it came, the fruit itself may be more loathsome unto us. It first
therefore rose upon a false interpretation of the place of St John: " Un-*
John iii. 5.[5] *less a man be born again of water and of the Spirit, he cannot
enter into the kingdom of heaven." Where certain do interpret
the word "water" for the material and elemental water wherewith men are
washed, when as our Saviour Christ taketh water there, by a translation
or borrowed speech, for the Spirit of God, the effect whereof it shadoweth*
Matt. iii. 11.[5] *out. For, even as in another place by the fire and Spirit[6]
he meaneth nothing but the Spirit of God, which purgeth and
purifieth as the fire doth; so in this place by the water and the Spirit he
meaneth nothing else but the Spirit of God, which cleanseth the filth of sin,
and cooleth the broiling heat of an unquiet conscience, as water washeth
the thing which is foul, and quencheth the heat of the fire. Secondarily,
this error came by a false and unnecessary conclusion drawn of that place.
For, although the scripture should say that none can be saved but those
which have the Spirit of God, and are baptized with material and elemental water, yet ought it to be understanded of those which can conveniently*
John iii. 18.[5] *and orderly be brought to baptism; as the scripture, saying
that whoso doth not believe the gospel is already condemned,
meaneth this sentence of those which can hear the gospel, and have discretion to understand it when they hear it, and cannot here shut under this
condemnation either those that be born deaf, and so remain, or little infants
or natural fools, that have no wit to conceive what is preached.*

106. Epist. ad *And hereupon St Augustine concludeth that all not baptized*
Bonifac.
In Lib. De *are condemned; which is as absurdly concluded of him as that*
Meritis et Re- *of our Saviour Christ's words, " Except one eat the flesh of*
miss. Peccat.
i. cap. 24. *the Son of man he hath not life," he concludeth that whatso-*
ever he be which receiveth not the sacrament of the supper is damned[7].

*Upon this false conclusion of St Augustine hath risen this profanation
of the sacrament of baptism in being ministered in private houses, and by
women or laymen; as also upon his other absurd conclusion sprung a horrible abuse of the Lord's supper, whilst they did thrust the bread and wine
into young infants' mouths; for that men were persuaded that otherwise, if
their children should die before they were baptized, or had received the sup-*

---

[5] The verses are supplied from Repl. 2.]
[6] And the Spirit, Repl. 1 and 2.]
[7] Si ergo ut tot et tanta divina testimonia concinunt, nec salus nec vita æterna
sine baptismo et corpore et sanguine Domini cuiquam speranda est, frustra sine
his promittitur parvulis.—August. Op. Par. 1679-1700. De Pecc. Mer. et Remiss.
Lib. I. cap. xxiv. 34. Tom. X. cols. 19, 20. Conf. ad Bonifac. Episc. Epist. xcviii.
10. Tom. II. col. 268.]

per, that[1] *they were damned for ever.   And what better token can there be that this was the cause of this blind baptism, than that the papists, from whom this baptism by women is translated, were of the same judgment, and for that cause brought in their baptism by women.   Hereunto may be added another cause, which is that, as (when the church began not only to decline, but to fall away from the sincerity of religion) it borrowed a number of other profanations of the heathen, so also it borrowed this. For, as the heathen had women priests, so it would have also her women priests; and that this was another occasion of bringing in the baptism by women it appeareth by your Clement*[2], *if he can speak any* Lib. iii. cap. 9. *truth.*

JO. WHITGIFT.

It is untrue that I use any reasons at all " to prove that women may baptize:" only I bring this and such like examples to improve this general assertion of the Admonition, that " then sacraments were ministered by ministers only, and not by midwives or deacons." For deacons then did baptize ; and Moses' wife long before that time did circumcise. I know

Particular examples may sometimes be followed.

that " particular examples" make no general rules ; but you are not ignorant that particular examples may in the like cases and circumstances be followed, when there is no rule to the contrary.

The place in the iii. of John by you alleged hath divers interpretations ; and the most part of the ancient writers do take water in that place for material and elemental water ;

Chr. in 3. Jo. iii. Lib. de Spirit. sanct. Lib. ii. de Abraham. pa- triare. Cyri. in 3 Jo.

as Augustine[3], Chrysostom[4], Ambrose[5], Cyril[6], and sundry others, even as many of the ancient fathers as I have read upon that text. But, because I do mislike as much as you the opinion of those that think infants to be condemned which are not baptized, therefore I will not contend with you, either in the interpretation of that place, or in any other thing that you have spoken touching this error : only this I say, that you must take heed lest, in avoiding an error, you fall into an heresy, and give place to anabaptists in not baptizing in-

[1 *That* is not in Repl. 2.]

[2 ... τοῦτο γὰρ τῆς τῶν Ἑλλήνων ἀθεότητος τὸ ἀγνόημα, θηλείαις θεαῖς ἱερείας χειροτονεῖν· ἀλλ' οὐ τῆς Χριστοῦ διατάξεως.—Const. quæ trib. Apost. Lib. III. cap. ix. in Concil. Stud. Labb. et Cossart. Lut. Par. 1671-2. Tom. I. col. 315.]

[3 August. Op. Par. 1679-1700. In Johan. Evang. cap. iii. Tractat. xi. xii. Tom. III. Pars II. cols. 374, &c. Conf. De Bapt. Parvul. Serm. ccxciv. 8. Tom. V. cols. 1186, 7.]

[4 Chrysost. Par. Op. 1718-38. In Joan. Hom. xxv. Tom. VIII. p. 144.]

[5 Ambros. Par. Op. 1686-90. De Spir. Sanct. Lib. III. cap. x. 63, &c. Tom. II. cols. 677, 8. Conf. De Abrah. Lib. II. cap. xi. 79, 84. Tom. I. cols. 348, 50, 1.]

[6 Cyril. Alex. Op. Lut. 1638. Comm. in Joan. Evang. Lib. II. cap. i. Tom. IV. p. 147.]

fants.   And I know not what you can say against private
baptism, in that case of necessity, which they do not in like
manner allege against the baptizing of young infants.   Master
Calvin, in his Introduction *adversus Anabap.*, though he allow
not this error, which condemneth children not baptized, yet
doth he approve and allow the necessity of baptizing infants:
his words be these: "But some man will say, that the grace Calvin. ad-
vers. Ana-
of God towards us is not diminished if infants be not ad- bapt.
mitted to baptism, so that it be not denied that God is as
merciful unto them as unto the children of the Jews; but I will
shew that it is much diminished; for we must esteem the
grace of God especially by the declaration thereof which he
maketh both by his word and sacraments.   Seeing therefore
baptism is now ordained, that the promise of salvation may be
sealed in our bodies, as it was in times past in the people of
the Jews, Christians should be deprived of a singular consolation, if their children should be secluded from this confirmation, which all the faithful have at all times enjoyed, that
they should have the visible sign whereby the Lord doth shew
and witness that he receiveth their children into the communion and fellowship of the church[7]."

If the authors of the Admonition say truly, that Victor,
who lived *anno* 198., did first appoint that women might baptize, then came it neither from the papists, nor yet from the
gentiles[8].   But, whensoever this began, or from whomsoever
it was taken, the baptizing of infants hath always been thought
necessary in the church, by all such as have not divided themselves by any schism or heresy from the same.

[7 At dicet quispiam, non imminui gratiam Dei erga nos, si infantes ad baptismum non admittentur: modo non negetur Deum ipsos pari misericordia pro-
sequi, qua liberos Judæorum.   Ego vero valde imminui ostendo.   Nam gratiam
Dei præcipue æstimare debemus ex declaratione, quam tum verbo, tum sacramentis facit.   Quum igitur baptismus hodie institutus sit, ut promissio salutis in
corporibus nostris obsignetur, ut olim in populo Judaico fiebat: singulari conso-
latione privarentur Christiani, si hæc confirmatio liberis suis adimeretur, qua
semper potiti sunt fideles omnes: ut visibile signum haberent, quo Dominus
ostendit ac testatur se liberos ipsorum in ecclesiæ communionem recipere.—Calvin.
Op. Amst. 1667-71. Instr. adv. Anabapt. Art. i. Tom. VIII. p. 358.]

[8 " It may well stand that this ' profanation came from the gentiles, from Victor,
and from the papists;' Victor borrowing it of the heathen, and the papists of him.
For both popery is like a bundle of corruptions, which, being picked out of
sundry times and places, it hath cocked up together; and the pope is like a hog,
which when he cometh into a garden, leaving the sweet flowers, taketh himself
always to that which is most filthy in all the place."—The Rest of Sec. Repl.
p. 125.]

Chapter v.   The Third Division.

T. C. Page 113, Sect. 4.

Now I return to the example of Sephora, and say that the unlawfulness of that fact doth appear sufficiently, in that she did it before her husband Moses, which was a prophet of the Lord, and to whom that office of circumcision did appertain; so that, unless M. Doctor would have midwives baptize in the presence of the bishop or the minister, there is no cause why he should allege this place. Besides that, she did cut off the[1] foreskin of the infant, not of mind to obey the commandment of God, or for the salvation of the child, but in a choler only, to the end that her husband might be eased, and have release; which mind appeareth in her, both by her words and by casting away in anger the foreskin which she had cut off. And, if it be said that the event declared that the act pleased God, because that Moses forthwith waxed better, and was recovered of his sickness, I have shewed before how, if we measure things by the event, we shall oftentimes justify the wicked, and take the righteousness of the righteous from them.

Moses by reason of sickness was not able to do it himself. This is contrary to that he hath, pag. 170, sect. 1.

Jo. Whitgift.

Pag. 170, sect. 1.

In the 170. page of your book, you say that "God took the priesthood from Moses, and gave it to Aaron," and now you seem to affirm the contrary in saying that "Moses was a prophet of the Lord, to whom that office of circumcision did appertain;" for hereby you do insinuate that Moses was a priest[2]. Moreover, Moses at this time was extremely sick, and therefore could not execute that office himself. And in the Geneva bible there is this note: that it "was extraordinary; for Moses was sore sick; and God even then required it[3]." Sephora therefore did circumcise in a point of extremity, and not wilfully or of purpose; and that circumcision was a true circumcision, though it were not done ordinarily: even so baptism is true baptism, though it be sometimes ministered by such as be not ordinary ministers.

Baptism true though not ordinarily ministered.

The event doth oftentimes declare the thing: *Exitus acta probat*, though not necessarily; but this is certain, that these events are better reasons to justify the fact, than you can shew any out of that place to the contrary.

[1 That, Repl. 2.]

[2 Cartwright calls this a "foul oversight." For "the time of the deliverance over of the priesthood unto Aaron was long after the time here spoken of."—Ibid. p. 127.]

[3 The Bible, transl. according to the Ebrew and Greeke. Lond. 1578. Exod. iiii. v. 24. fol. 23.]

Chapter v.   The Fourth Division.

T. C. Page 113, Sect. ult.; and Page 114, Sect. 1.

Another reason he hath, which is that the dignity of the sacraments doth not depend upon the man, whether he be minister or no minister, good or evil.

Indeed, upon this point, whether he be good[4] or an evil minister, it dependeth not; but on this point, whether he be a minister or no, dependeth not only the dignity, but also the being of the sacrament; so that I take the baptism of women to be no more the holy sacrament of baptism, than I take any other daily or ordinary washing of the child. Neither let any man think that I have at unwares slipped into this asseveration, or that I have forgotten that soon after the times of the apostles it was the use of certain churches that deacons should baptize in the time of necessity (as they call it); for, as for the baptism of deacons, I hold it to be lawful, for because, although (as it is with us) they give him the name of deacon, yet indeed he is, as he then was in the elder times, a minister, and not a deacon. And, although he did then provide for the poor, and so had two functions (which was not meet), yet his office ought to be esteemed of the principal part of his function, which was preaching and ministering of the sacraments in certain cases. And, as for the baptizing by laymen, considering that it is not only against the word of God, but also founded upon a false ground, and upon an imagined necessity (which is none indeed), it moveth me nothing at all, although it be very ancient; forsomuch as the substance of the sacrament dependeth[5] chiefly of the institution and word of God, which is the form, and, as it were, the life of the sacrament, of which institution this is one, and of the chief parts, that it should be celebrated by a minister.

A strange assertion avouched without proof.

Urge hoc, &c.

Jo. Whitgift.

If this be true and sound doctrine, then is there many that go under the name of Christians which were never baptized; for, besides divers that have been baptized by women, some there are, and not a few, that have been baptized by such as have taken upon them the ministry, not being thereunto either ordinarily or extraordinarily called; and it may so be that T. C. hath hereby proved himself to be no Christian[6].

The inconvenience of the Replier's doctrine.

[4 Be a good, Repl. 1 and 2.]   [5 Depended, Repl. 2.]

[6 " In another place he said (see below, page 538) 'that it is a probable sign of reprobation, if children die without baptism;' but here he setteth down flat, that 'they be no Christians which are not baptized.' So that the children of the faithful by his doctrine are not Christians, before they be baptized; and consequently condemned. Whereas the truth is otherwise, that, if he be not a Christian before he come to receive baptism, baptism can make him no Christian, which is only the seal of the grace of God before received."—The Rest of Sec. Repl. p. 134.]

The assertion
hath no suffi-
cient patrons. And surely, if you peruse all the writings of the ancient fathers, and of the late writers in like manner, I believe that you shall not find the like proposition affirmed; for, although divers, both old and new, do not allow that laymen should be suffered to baptize, yet is there none of them (such only ex-

Baptism by laymen. cepted as err in re-baptization) that think "the being of the sacrament so to depend upon the minister, that it is no sacrament if it be not celebrated by a minister." Tertull., in his

Tertull. book *De Baptismo*, saith that "laymen may baptize[1]."

Ambrose. Ambrose, in the fourth *ad Ephes.*, saith that "in the beginning it was lawful for all men to baptize[2]." Hierome, *ad*

Hierome. *Luciferianos*, affirmeth that "it is lawful for laymen to baptize, if necessity do require[3]." And hereunto also doth St

Augustine. Augustine agree, in his second book against the epistle of Parmenian, the xiii. chapter[4]. M. Zuinglius, in the place be-

Zuinglius. fore by me alleged, writeth that "the second error in the circumstances of baptism is about the person, because they think that baptism cannot be given of any but of a priest only; whereas, if necessity do require, any man may do it[5]." And a little after he saith that "this and such like circumstances are not *de ipsa baptismi essentia*[6]: not of the being of the sacrament." Which is directly contrary to your assertion. M. Calvin also, in his Institutions, *cap. xvii. sect.* 16, doth suf-

Calvin. ficiently confute this error in these words: "Now, if it be true that we have set down, the sacrament is not to be esteemed of his hand by whom it is ministered, but as it were of the hand of God, from whom it certainly cometh: hereof we may gather that nothing is added or taken from the dignity of it by him by whom it is ministered. And therefore among men, if an epistle be sent, so that the hand and seal be known, it skilleth not who or what manner of person carrieth it; even so it is

[1 Proinde et baptismus æque Dei census ab omnibus exerceri potest :...sufficiat scilicet in necessitatibus ut utaris, sicubi aut loci, aut temporis, aut personæ conditio compellit. &c.—Tertull. Op. Franek. 1597. Lib. de Bapt. 17. p. 225.]

[2 Primum enim...omnes baptizabant, &c.—Ambros. Op. Par. 1686-90. Comm. in Epist. ad Ephes. cap. iv. vv. 11, 12. Tom. II. Append. col. 241.]

[3 Quod frequenter [jus baptizandi], si tamen necessitas cogit, scimus etiam licere laicis.—Hieron. Op. Par. 1693-1706. Adv. Lucif. Tom. IV. Pars II. col. 295.]

[4 August. Op. Par. 1679-1700. Contr. Epist. Parm. Lib. II. cap. xiii. 29. Tom. IX. col. 44. See below, page 532, note 1.]

[5 H. Zvingl. Op. Tigur. 1581. De Bapt. Lib. Pars II. fol. 96. 2. See before, page 511, note 7.]

[6 Hujusmodi circumstantiæ omnes non sunt de ipsa baptismi essentia.—Id. ibid.]

sufficient for us to know the hand and seal of the Lord in his
sacraments, by whomsoever they be delivered.   Hereby is the
error of the Donatists confuted, who measured the virtue and
worthiness of the sacrament by the worthiness of the minister.
Such be now-a-days our anabaptists, which deny us to be
rightly baptized, because we were baptized by wicked and
idolatrous persons in the pope's church.   And therefore they
furiously urge re-baptization; against whose folly we shall sufficiently be defended, if we think that we were baptized not in
the name of any man, but in the name of the Father, of the
Son, and of the Holy Ghost, and therefore baptism not to be
of man, but of God, by whomsoever it be ministered[7]."   *Hæc
Calvinus.*

Undoubtedly, if this your assertion were true, there had
need be some general re-baptization throughout all Christendom, as well of men as of children; for certain it is that that
sacrament hath been ministered to many by such as be in no
degree of the ministry.

Your opinion of a deacon, that he should nothing differ
from a minister, is very strange, and unheard of in any
writer old or new.   Shew any author, any example, any scripture that proveth or alloweth it: *diaconus* and *presbyter* or
sacerdos be distinct in all authors.   But I know wherefore
this is affirmed of you, even to stop a gap; but it will not
serve.   I will say no more: the opinion is very absurd and
unlearned, contrary to the scriptures and all learned authors.
Neither do you shew any reason of your paradox, which you
ought to do, seeing it is *contra opinionem omnium:* " contrary
to all men's opinions," not one excepted.

Against "baptizing by laymen" in time of necessity you
have no scripture.   But for the allowing of it you have the
authority of learned men, even such as were far from the
opinion of Augustine in condemning infants not baptized; as
namely Zuinglius, who also in the place before recited sufficiently answered whatsoever is here by you barely without
any kind of proof set down.

Baptism by laymen not condemned in scripture.

You have also examples thereof in ecclesiastical histories.
Socrates, *Lib. i. cap.* 14, and Sozom., *Lib. ii. cap.* 17, write
that "Alexander, bishop of Alexandria, together with the rest

Examples of baptism by laymen. Socrates. Sozomen.

[7 Calvin. Op. Amst. 1667-71. Inst. Lib. IV. cap. xv. 16.   Tom. IX. p. 353.
See before, page 520, note 1.]

of the clergy, determined that baptism which was ministered

Athanasius
being a
child bap-
tized.

by Athanasius, being but a child, to certain other children, to
be true baptism, and not to be iterated, because after examination he was found to have used the words and right form of
baptism[1]." Whereby it is plain that the opinion of the
church at that time was, the minister not to be of the substance

Cent. ii.
cap. 6.

or being of baptism. There is recited a story in the Centuries, of a Jew baptized in the case of necessity by laymen,
and with sand, because there was no water. Afterward the
bishop of Alexandria, being demanded of the matter, *De sententia ecclesiæ respondit, baptizatum esse Judæum si modo
aqua denuo perfunderetur*[2]: "He answered by the judgment
of the church, that the Jew was baptized, if so be he were
again sprinkled with water." This argueth that the church
then made no doubt in the respect of the persons that ministered this baptism, but only because there lacked water. This
story is cited out of Nicephorus, *Lib. iii. cap.* 37, and alleged
by the authors of the Centuries, to prove the simplicity of the
church at that time about baptism; neither do they in any
respect shew any misliking of it. And surely I know not
wherein this opinion of yours doth differ from the Donatists,
or anabaptists, except it be in this, that you speak of laymen,
and they of ministers.

The Replier
in so weighty
a matter
useth no
proofs.

And, whereas you say that "the minister is one of the
chief parts, and as it were of the life of the sacrament," in
so weighty a cause, and great a matter, it had been well if you
had used some authority of scripture, or testimony of learned
author; for, so far as I can read, the opinion of all learned
men is that the essential form, and as it were the life of bap-

The essential
point of bap-
tism.

tism, "is to baptize in the name of the Father, of the Son, and
of the Holy Ghost;" which form being observed, the sacrament
remaineth in full force and strength, of whomsoever it be min-

---

[1 ... ἐπιμείναντος δὲ αὐτοῦ τῇ βασάνῳ, κατεμήνυσαν ἐπίσκοπον μὲν καὶ
ἀρχηγὸν γενέσθαι τὸν Ἀθανάσιον. βαπτισθῆναι δὲ παρ' αὐτοῦ τινὰς τῶν
ἀμυήτων παίδων· οὓς ἐπιμελῶς ἀνέκρινεν Ἀλέξανδρος, τί μὲν αὐτοὺς ἤρετο ἢ
ἐποίησεν ὁ τῆς παιδιᾶς ἱερεύς· τί δέ αὐτοὶ ἀπεκρίναντο ἢ ἐδιδάχθησαν· ἀνευ-
ρὼν δὲ πᾶσαν τὴν ἐκκλησιαστικὴν τάξιν ἀκριβῶς ἐπ' αὐτοῖς φυλαχθεῖσαν,
ἐδοκίμασεν ἅμα τοῖς ἀμφ' αὐτὸν ἱερεῦσι βουλευσάμενος, μὴ χρῆναι ἀναβαπ-
τίσαι τοὺς ἅπαξ ἐν ἁπλότητι τῆς θείας χάριτος ἀξιωθέντας.—Soz. in Hist.
Eccles. Script. Amst. 1695-1700. Lib. ii. cap. xvii. p. 380. Conf. Socr. ibid.
Lib. i. cap. xv. p. 37.]

[2 Centur. Eccles. Hist. Basil.1560,&c. Cent. ii. cap. vi. col. 110. Conf. Niceph.
Eccles. Hist. Lut. Par. 1630. Lib. iii. cap. xxxvii. Tom. I. pp. 276, 7.]

istered, or howsoever by ceremonies or other additions it is corrupted. This I am sure is the answer of Zuinglius, both in his book *De Baptismo*, and in his *Elench. contra Anabap.*, to the anabaptists, who would have them all to be re-baptized that have been baptized in the pope's church[3]. And the same is the opinion of M. Calvin in the place before recited[4], and of all other learned men that I have read.

And certainly, if "the being of the sacrament" depended upon man in any respect, we were but in a miserable case, for we should be always in doubt whether we were rightly baptized or no; but it is most true that the force and strength of the sacrament is not in the man, be he minister or not minister, be he good or evil, but in God himself, in his Spirit, in his free and effectual operation. And therefore saith St Paul, "What is Paul, what is Apollo? &c." This I speak not to bring confusion into the church (for, as I said before, let men take heed that they usurp not an office whereunto they be not called; for God will call them to an account for so doing), but to teach a truth, to take a yoke of doubtfulness from men's consciences, and to resist an error, not much differing from Donatism and anabaptism[5].

The force of baptism dependeth not upon man, but upon God.

1 Cor. iii. Confusion and disorder is not maintained.

Chapter v.   The Fifth Division.

T. C. Page 114, Sect. 1.

For, although part of the institution, in that the name of the holy Trinity is called upon, be observed, yet, if the whole institution be not, it is no more a sacrament than the papists' communion was, which, celebrating it in one kind, took a part of the institution, and left the other.

Jo. Whitgift.

If you can shew as manifest scripture that the minister is of the substance of baptism, as I can do that the cup is one of the essential parts of the supper, then it is something that you say; but, if there be no likelihood betwixt the one and the

---

[3 H. Zvingl. Op. Tigur. 1581. Elench. contr. Catabapt.; De Bapt. Lib. Pars II. foll. 19. 2, 20, 83. 2.]

[4 See before, page 520, note 1.]

[5 Cartwright makes a long rejoinder to this division of Whitgift, in order, as he says, "to cut his comb, that he crow not so loud hereafter." He accuses him of "untruth," of "a plain asking of that in controversy," and maintains that his authorities "for the most part are idly set down."—The Rest of Sec. Repl. pp. 127, &c.]

other, then can you not want just reprehension, for so confidently avouching that which you cannot prove.

The distribution of the cup in the Lord's supper is commanded in manifest and express words as a part of the supper; but you cannot shew me the like commandment that only a minister shall celebrate baptism, or else that it is no baptism. We know that circumcision, the figure of baptism, was ministered sometimes by such as were no priests, and yet right and true circumcision.

Chapter v.   The Sixth Division.

T. C. Page 114, Sect. 1.

And, forasmuch[1] as St Paul saith that a man cannot Rom. x. 15.[2]

This is added to the text. *preach which is not sent, no, not although he speak the words of the scripture and interpret them; so I cannot see how a man can baptize unless that he be sent to that end, although he pour water and rehearse the words which are to be rehearsed in the ministry of baptism.*

Jo. Whitgift.

St Paul, in that x. chap. to the Rom., speaketh of the extraordinary calling to the office of preaching; so saith M. Martyr in his commentaries upon this place: "And, although Paul intreateth in this place of calling, and sending, and this is, as I said, ordinary and extraordinary; there is no doubt but that he now speaketh of the extraordinary calling, &c.[3]" And M. Calvin likewise, upon the same place, saith that Paul doth not there speak, *de legitima cujusque vocatione[4]:* "of the lawful calling of every man." Wherefore, if you will ground any such reason upon this place, it must be thus: St Paul saith that a man cannot preach which is not sent; and he meaneth of an extraordinary sending; therefore no man may preach unless he be extraordinarily called thereunto; and so consequently not minister baptism, except he be called in like manner.   If you will reason thus, then do you confirm the

Martyr.

Calvin.

[1 And for so much, Repl. 1 and 2.]

[2 The verse is supplied from Repl. 2.]

[3 Et licet Paulus hoc loco de vocationibus et missione agat, eaque, ut dixi, ordinaria sit et extraordinaria, dubium non est, quin loquatur modo de extraordinaria, &c.—P. Martyr. Comm. in Epist. ad Rom. Basil. 1568. cap. x. p. 473.]

[4 Quia autem hic nequaquam de legitima cujusque vocatione agit Paulus, &c.—Calvin. Op. Amst. 1667-71. Comm. in Epist. ad Rom. cap. x. 15. Tom. VII. p. 74.]

baptizing by laymen, who do it not ordinarily, but extraordinarily, upon necessity.

St Paul doth not say, "that a man cannot preach which is not sent, no, not although he speaketh the words of the scripture, and interpret them." These words be so added by you, that the simple and ignorant may think they be the words of St Paul. "He that speaketh the words of the scripture, and doth interpret them," preacheth, though he be not thereunto called; and it is the true word of God he preacheth, if he truly interpret, but he intrudeth himself into a vocation whereunto he is not called, and therefore offendeth God; but that doth derogate nothing from the word preached. The same reason is of the administration of the sacraments; for, as the word of God is the word of God, by whomsoever it be preached, minister or other, so is the sacrament of baptism true baptism, by whomsoever it be celebrated : the usurper of the office hath to answer for his intrusion; but the sacrament is not thereby defiled.

The Replier addeth to the text, and for what purpose.

Usurpers both in preaching and ministering the sacraments offend God.

It is no hard matter to shew that in the primitive church laymen were suffered to preach : you know that Euseb. saith that Origen being a layman was sent into Arabia to preach the gospel; which he also did, both before and after in the church of Alexandria, and likewise in Cæsarea. And, although Demetrius, then bishop of Alexandria, found fault that Origen being a layman should preach in the presence of bishops at Cæsarea; yet is it manifest that he allowed laymen to preach if bishops were not present. And in the same chapter by divers examples it is shewed (as of Euelpis at Laranda, of Paulinus at Iconium, of Theodorus at Synada) that the custom of the churches both then and before that time was, that laymen might preach even in the presence of bishops[5]; so that you have erred both in applying the place of St Paul, and in saying that laymen may not preach the word upon occasion, and so consequently baptize.

Laymen suffered to preach. Euseb. Lib. vi. cap. 20.

Chapter v.   The Seventh Division.

T. C. Page 114, Sect. 1.

I know there be divers difficulties in this question, and therefore I was loth to enter into it, but that the Answerer setteth down so confidently that

The more to blame you are without proof to enter into such difficulties.

[5 Euseb. in Hist. Eccles. Script. Amst. 1695-1700. Lib. vi. cap. xix. p. 180.]

it maketh no matter for the truth of baptism, whether he be minister or no minister, and so whether one have a calling or no calling; wherein, notwithstanding, he doth not only by his often handling of one thing confound his reader, but himself also, and forgetteth that he is in another question than which is propounded. For, although it should be granted him that the sacrament doth not depend upon that, yet hath he not that which he would have, that women may baptize. For it is one thing to say the baptism which is ministered by women is good and effectual, and another thing to say that it is lawful for women to minister baptism. For there is no man doubteth but that the baptism which is ministered by an heretical minister is effectual; and yet I think that M. Doctor will not say that therefore an heretical minister may baptize, and that it is lawful for heretics to baptize in the church. And therefore men must not only " take heed (as M. Doctor saith) that they usurp not that which they are not called unto," but they must also take heed that they receive not functions and charges upon them whereof they are not capable, although they be thereunto called.

This is not intended.

Jo. Whitgift.

There are more "difficulties" in this question than you can well determine; and therefore it had been best, either not to have spoken of it at all, or else to have handled it more substantially; but the scarcity of matter and reasons argueth the weakness and faintness of the cause. I pass over your words. I go not about to prove "that women may baptize," only I withstand this error, that "the substance and being of the sacraments dependeth upon the man" in any respect. I say that baptism ministered by women is true baptism, though it be not lawful for women to baptize, as the baptism also ministered by heretics is true baptism, though they be usurpers of that office. And the same St Augustine affirmeth of baptism by laymen in the place before alleged: "Although " (saith he) " it be usurped without necessity, and is given of any man to any man, that which is given cannot be said not to be given, although it may be rightly said not to be rightly given[1]." And I further say that, if " the baptism, ministered by heretical ministers," which be no members of the church, be notwithstanding good and " effectual," I see

Baptism true baptism, though unlawfully ministered.

August. Lib. ii. contr. Epist. Parmen. cap. 13.

[1 Quamquam etsi laicus aliquis pereunti dederit necessitate compulsus, quod cum ipse acciperet, quomodo dandum esset addidicit, nescio an pie quisquam dixerit esse repetendum...Sed et si nulla necessitate usurpetur, et a quolibet cuilibet detur, quod datum fuerit non potest dici non datum, quamvis recte dici possit illicite datum.—August. Op. Par. 1679-1700. Contr. Epist. Parm. Lib. ii. cap. xiii. 29. Tom. IX. col. 44.]

no cause why it should not be so rather if it be ministered
by laymen, which are members and parts of the church[2].

Chapter v.   The Eighth Division.

Answer to the Admonition, Page 153, Sect. 2.

[If you mean by "private baptism" baptism minis- Private baptism.
tered in private houses and families, you have thereof
example in the scriptures, Acts x.: other private baptism
allowed in the church of England I know none.][3]

M. Bucer, in his Censure upon the communion-book,
speaking of the order appointed in the same for private
baptism, writeth thus: "In this constitution all things Bucer.
are godly appointed; I would to God they were so ob-
served, and especially this, that the baptism of infants be Deferring of
baptism not
expedient.
not deferred; for thereby is a door opened unto the
devil, to bring in a contempt of baptism, and so of our
whole redemption, and communion of Christ, which
through the sect of anabaptists hath too much prevailed
with many[4]."

[For women to baptize we have no rule that I know
in the whole communion-book, but in scripture we have
an example of Moses' wife that did circumcise; and
circumcision is correspondent to baptism.   But I know
no general doctrine can be grounded of a singular example; and therefore most of your arguments be very
feeble.][3]

T. C. Page 114, Sect. 2.

*In the 153. page, M. Bucer's Censure upon the communion-book is
cited for the allowance of that it hath touching private baptism, and
consequently of the baptism by women.   It may be that, as M. Bucer,* This is but
gross cour-
although otherwise very learned, hath other gross absurdities, so he may tesy.
have that.   But it had been for the credit of your cause, if you had shewed

---

[2 " ... a foul error."—The Rest of Sec. Repl. p. 131.]

[3 These paragraphs are introduced from Answ.]

[4 In hac constitutione sunt omnia sancte proposita, utinam ita serventur: et
maxime illud, ne baptisma infantium differatur.   Nam eo patefit diabolo ostium
introducendi contemptum ecclesiæ, ac ita totius redemptionis et communionis
Christi; quod per sectam anabaptistarum nimis optate obtinuit opinionem apud
quamplurimos.—M. Bucer. Script. Anglic. Basil. 1577. Censur. in Ordinat. Eccles.
cap. xv. p. 481.]

that out of those writings which are published and known to be his, and not out of those whereof men may doubt whether ever he wrote any such or no ; and, if he wrote, whether they be corrupted by those into whose hands they came. And, if you would take any advantage of M. Bucer's testimony, considering that a witness is a public person, you should have brought him out of your study into the stationer's shop where he mought have been common to others as well as to you, whereby his style and manner of writing, as it were by his gestures, and countenances, and by those things that go before and come after, as it were by his head, and by his[1] feet, we might the better know whether it were the true Bucer or no.

Jo. Whitgift.

The reverence which T. C. giveth to learned men.

It is very gross courtesy that you shew to so worthy and learned a man : modesty and charity would not have been so rash as to answer that which he well speaketh, in opprobriously objecting unto him his other errors, which you call "gross absurdities[2]." But this is the reverence that you give to all learning, and learned men, that are contrary to your opinions. I have sometimes heard a papist burst out into this rage against M. Bucer, being pressed with his authority ; but you are the first professor of the gospel that ever I heard so churlishly to use so reverent, so learned, so painful, so sound a father, being also an earnest and zealous professor. It causeth me the less to regard what you speak of me, when I hear such bitternesss against all other, be they never so zealous and excellent. Well, Bucer's reasons (which touch the quick) would have been reasonably answered without spite; and you should rather have considered them than the author. There is nothing in these words by him affirmed which is not in as plain terms avouched by Zuinglius in the words before recited[3]. The book of M. Bucer's is forthcoming to be shewed; and he affirmeth nothing therein contrary to his books published : he had more special occasion here offered to speak both of this and other matters now in controversy, and therefore the more he is to be credited.

[1 And his, Repl. 2.]

[2 "And, if it be judged of the godly that I might have spared that speech, it is a thing wherein I will not stand against them in mine own defence."—The Rest of Sec. Repl. p. 132.]

[3 See before, page 511, note 7.]

Chapter v. The Ninth Division.

T. C. Page 114, Sect. 2.

For, although I will not say but that this may be Bucer's doing, yet it seemeth very strange that Bucer should not only, contrary to the learned writers now, but also contrary to all learned antiquity, and contrary to the practice of the church, whilst there was any tolerable estate, allow of

De Virgin. Velan. *women's baptizing. Tertullian saith "it is not permitted to[4] a woman to speak in the church, nor to teach, or[5] to baptize, nor to do any work of a man, much less of a minister[6]." And in*

Lib. De Baptis. *another place, although he do permit it to be done by[7] laymen in the time of necessity (as it is termed), yet he giveth not that*

Epiph. Li. i. contra, Hæres. Lib. ii. Ubi de Phrygib. et Priscil. Lib. iii. *licence to the woman[8]. Epiphanius upbraideth Marcion that he suffered women to baptize[9]. And in another book he derideth them that they made women bishops[10]. And in another book he saith it was not granted unto the holy mother of Christ to baptize her Son[11].*

Jo. Whitgift.

M. Bucer speaketh not one word in this place of baptizing by women, but of private baptism; which neither Tertullian nor Epiphanius in these places by you alleged do disallow.

Chapter v. The Tenth Division.

T. C. Page 115, Line 6.

i. Li. de Merit. et Remis. Peccat. 24. cap. *Augustine, although he were of that mind that children could not be saved without baptism[12], yet in the time of neces-* An untruth. *sity (as it is called) he doth not allow either of baptism in private houses, or by women, but when there was danger the women hasted to carry the children unto the church; and, although he do seem to allow of the baptism of a layman in the time of necessity, yet there also he mentioneth not women's baptism. And further he doubteth*

[4 Unto, Repl. 1 and 2.]   [5 Nor, Repl. 2.]

[6 Non permittitur mulieri in ecclesia loqui, sed nec docere, nec tinguere, nec offerre, nec ullius virilis muneris, nedum sacerdotalis officii sortem sibi vendicare.—Tertull. Op. Franek. 1597. De Virg. Veland. 9. p. 192.]

[7 Of, Repl. 1 and 2.]

[8 Petulantia autem mulierum quæ usurpavit docere, utique non etiam tinguendi jus sibi pariet, &c.—Id. Lib. de Bapt. 17. p. 225. See before, page 526, note 1.]

[9 Δίδωσι καὶ ἐπιτροπὴν γυναιξὶ βάπτισμα διδόναι.—Epiph. Op. Par. 1622. Adv. Hær. Lib. I. Tom. III. Hær. xlii. 4. Tom. I. p. 305.]

[10 Ἐπίσκοποί τε παρ' αὐτοῖς γυναῖκες, καὶ πρεσβύτεροι γυναῖκες, καὶ τὰ ἄλλα.—Id. ibid. Lib. II. Tom. I. Hær. xlix. 2. p. 418.]

[11 Ἀλλ' οὐδὲ βάπτισμα διδόναι πεπίστευται [Μαρία].—Id. ibid. Lib. III. Tom. II. Hær. lxxix. 3. p. 1059.]

[12 August. Op. Par. 1679-1700. De Pecc. Mer. et Remiss. Lib. I. cap. xxiv. 34. Tom. X. cols. 19, 20. See before, page 521, note 8.]

whether the child should be baptized again which was baptized by a layman.

Contra Epist. Parmen. Lib. ii. 13. cap.

Jo. Whitgift.

Where doth St Augustine disallow baptism by women, or in private houses? he uttereth no such thing in any of the places quoted in the margent. Will you still counterfeit? is there no end with you of falsifying? In his second book *Contra Epistolam Parmeniani, cap.* 13, he doth not only say that a layman may baptize in the time of necessity, but he also addeth that, if it be ministered without necessity, yet notwithstanding that it is baptism; as appeareth in these words (as I have before said): " But, although it be usurped (he meaneth baptism by laymen) without necessity, and is given of any man to any man, that which is given cannot be said not to be given, although it may be rightly said that it is not lawfully given[1]." And he doth make the same manifest by two pretty similitudes following, which I omit for to avoid tediousness. The learned reader may in that place of Augustine soon perceive what an error this is to say, that " the minister is of the substance and being of the sacrament;" neither doth he, in either of the places, either disallow " baptism by women, or in private houses," as you affirm, but *ad Fortunatum* he saith thus : " In necessity, when the bishops, or priests, or any other minister cannot be found, and the danger of him that requireth doth constrain, lest he should depart this life without this sacrament, we have heard that even laymen have given this sacrament that they have received[2]."

August. Lib. ii. contra Epist. Parm. cap. 13.

Aug. ad Fortunatum.

Chapter v. The Eleventh Division.

T. C. Page 115, Line 12.

And in the fourth council of Carthage it is simply decreed[3] that " a woman ought not to baptize."

Tom. i. Conc. ca. 100.

[1 Id. contr. Epist. Parm. Lib. ii. cap. xiii. 29. Tom. IX. col. 44. See before, page, 532, note 1.]

[2 In necessitate, cum episcopi, aut presbyteri, aut quilibet ministrorum non inveniuntur, et urget periculum ejus, qui petit, ne sine isto sacramento hanc vitam finiat, etiam laicos solere dare sacramentum, quod acceperunt, solemus audire.—Id. ad Fortunat. in Corp. Jur. Canon. Lugd. 1624. Decret. Gratian. Decr. Tert. Pars, De Consecr. Dist. iv. can. 21. col. 1933.]

[3 Simply without exception decreed, Repl. 1 and 2.]

Jo. Whitgift.

This canon in Gratian, *De Conse. Dist.* 4, is thus reported : *Mulier, quamvis docta et sancta, viros in conventu docere, vel aliquos baptizare non præsumat, nisi necessitate cogent[e]*[4]: " Let not a woman, although learned and godly, presume to teach men in an assembly, or to baptize any, except necessity constrain." So that the canon inhibiteth women to preach or to baptize in the open church and public assemblies. And this is a sufficient answer to this place, neither doth it impugn anything affirmed in the Answer.

Chapter v. The Twelfth Division.
T. C. Page 115, Line 13.

The authors of the Admonition object that necessity of salvation is tied to the sacraments by this means, and that men are confirmed in that old error, that no man can be saved without baptism; which indeed is true. For must it not be thought to be done of necessity, and upon great extremity, for the doing whereof the orders that God hath set, that it should be done in the congregation, and by the minister of the gospel, are broken? Yes, verily. And I will further say that, although that the infants which die without baptism should be assuredly damned (which is most false), yet ought not the orders which God hath set in his church to be broken after this sort. For, as the salvation of men ought to be dear unto us, so the glory of God, which consisteth in that his orders be kept, ought to be much more dear, that, if at any time the controversy could be between his glory and our salvation, our salvation ought to fall that his glory may stand.

Jo. Whitgift.

Yet the avoiding of that error is no sufficient cause to debar infants from baptism; except you will therein join with the anabaptists. The outward sacramental signs are seals of God's promises, and whosoever refuseth the same shall never enjoy the promises; and, although the necessity of salvation is not so tied to the sacraments, that whosoever hath the external signs shall therefore be saved, yet is it so tied unto them, that none can be saved that willingly and wittingly is void of them, and not partakers of them. Circumcision, which is a figure of baptism, had that necessity joined unto it, that whosoever lacked it was not counted nor c koned amongst the people of

There is necessity of baptism, though the necessity of salvation be not tied to the sacraments.

Gen. xvii.

[4 Ex Concil. Carthag. iv. cap. 99 et 100. ibid. can. 20. ibid. Conf. Crabb. Concil. Col. Agrip. 1551. Tom. I. p. 441. It would seem that the last three words are the addition of Gratian, or some other. Lombard, Lib. iv. Dist. vi. has them.]

Mark xvi.

The doctrine tendeth to the derogation of the sacraments.

God. It is not nothing that Christ saith : *Qui crediderit et baptizatus fuerit, &c.*   But your manner of doctrine is such that it maketh men think that the external signs of the sacraments are but bare ceremonies, and in no sense necessary to salvation; which must in time bring in a contempt of the sacraments, and especially of baptism for infants.

M. Zuinglius, Bucer, and Calvin, as you heard before, although they do not think children without baptism to be damned, yet do they judge the baptism of children to be necessary, and that for just causes; as is before declared[1]. And what Christian would willingly suffer his child to die without the sacrament of regeneration, the lack whereof (though it be not a necessary) yet may it seem to be a probable token and sign of reprobation.

What either "order of God," or commandment, is broken in private baptism? or where hath God appointed that baptism must be ministered "in the open congregation" only, and not upon any cause in private families? Will you yet deal on this sort without ground or proof? In private baptism used upon necessity there is neither order nor commandment of God broken. If there be, shew it.

Chapter v.   The Thirteenth Division.

The Admonition.

And yet this is not to tie necessity of salvation to the sacraments, nor to nousel men up in that opinion.   This is agreeable with the scriptures, and therefore, when they bring the baptized child, they are received with this special commendation : "I certify you that you have done well and according to[2] due order, &c."

But now we speak in good earnest; when they answer this let them tell us how this gear agreeth with the scriptures, and whether it be not repugnant or against the word of God.

Answer to the Admonition, Page 187, Sect. 1.

"And yet (you say) this is not to tie necessity of salvation to the sacraments, nor to nousel men up in that opinion, &c.[3]" No surely, no more than it is to teach that children ought to be baptized, and not to tarry until such time as they be able to answer for themselves. [You should have proved this to be re-

[1 See before, pages 511, 23, 33.]   [2 Unto, Adm.]   [3 &c. is not in Answ.]

pugnant to the scriptures (because you say it is), and therefore you refuse to subscribe. When you set down the scriptures to the which it repugneth, if it fall out so indeed, you shall have me a conformable adversary: I will say with St Augustine: *Errare possum, hæreticus esse nolo*[4]: "Err I may, an heretic I will not be;" and I would to God you could learn that lesson.][5]

Error and heresy differeth.

T. C. Page 115, Sect. 1.

Now, in the 187. page M. Doctor answereth hereunto, that this implieth no more that the salvation is tied to the sacraments than[6] when it is taught that infants must be baptized, and not tarry until they come to the age of discretion. The[7] which, how truly it is spoken, when as the one hath ground of the scripture, the other hath none, the one approved by the continual, and almost the general practice of the church, the other used only in the corrupt and rotten estate thereof, let all men judge.

Jo. Whitgift.

This verifieth my saying; for, if baptism of children be grounded upon the scriptures, as it is, then is the necessity of baptizing them the more; so that, if not for fear of damnation, yet because of God's commandment and institution, children are of necessity to be baptized; and this is a received opinion in the church, even from the beginning; and therefore laymen in the time of necessity, from the beginning, have been permitted to baptize; as may appear by the authors before alleged.

Chapter v. The Fourteenth Division.
T. C. Page 115, Sect. 1.

Therefore, forsomuch as the ministry of the word and sacraments go together, and that the ministry of the word may not be committed unto women, and for that this evil custom hath risen first of a false understanding of the scripture, and then of a false conclusion of that untrue understanding, which is that they cannot be saved which are not baptized; and for that the authors themselves of that error did never seek no remedy of the mischief in women's or private baptism; and last of all, for that, if there were any remedy against the[8] mischief in such kind of baptism, yet it ought not to be used, being against the institution of God and his glory, I conclude that the private baptism, and by women, is utterly unlawful.

[4 See Vol. I. page 8, note 4.]
[5 This is inserted from Answ. The translation of the sentence cited from St Augustine is omitted in Answ. 1.]
[6 That, Def. B.]   [7 Repl. 2 omits *the*.]   [8 That, Repl. 2.]

Jo. Whitgift.

These be all petitions of principles, or the most of them; for I have shewed before that the administration of baptism hath been and may be committed to some, even in the public congregation, to whom the preaching of the word is not committed; and now in like manner I have proved that laymen in the time of necessity may baptize; which both are denied by you without any kind of proof. I have also shewed how that the necessity of baptizing infants is vehemently defended of those that be not of St Augustine's judgment touching their damnation[1] if they be not baptized, and I have set down their words which contain their reasons. Last of all, I have put you to prove that private baptism in time of necessity is against any commandment or institution of Christ; for I deny it. So that, notwithstanding I suspend my judgment for baptizing by women, yet I am out of doubt for private baptism[2].

¶ Of private communion, wherewith the Admonition chargeth the book of common prayer.

Chapter vi.   The First Division.
Admonition.

[3]*Now they are bound to the book of common prayer, in which a great number of things contrary to the word of God*[4] *are contained, &c., as* [k]*private communion*[5]*, &c.*   [k] *1Cor. xi. 18.*

[1 See before, pages 511, 23, 33.]

[2 Cartwright sums up his rejoinder on the ministering of baptism by private persons : "Seeing then they only are bidden in the scripture to administer the sacraments, which are bidden to preach the word, and that the public ministers have only this charge of the word; and seeing that the administration of both these are so linked together that the denial of licence to do one is a denial to do the other, as of the contrary part licence to one is licence to the other; considering also that to minister the sacraments is an honour in the church which none can take unto him but he which is called unto it as was Aaron; and, further, forasmuch as the baptizing by private persons, and by women especially, confirmeth the dangerous error of the condemnation of young children, which die without baptism; last of all, seeing we have the consent of the godly-learned of all times against the baptism by women, and of the reformed churches now against the baptism by private men, we conclude that the administration of this sacrament by private persons and especially by women, is merely both unlawful and void."—The Rest of Sec· Repl. p. 142.]

[3 This sentence was begun above, page 446, and has been continued in fragments, with occasionally a connecting word or two introduced.]

[4 God's word, Adm. and Answ.]

[5 Private communions, Adm. and Answ.]

Answer to the Admonition, Page 81, Sect. 1, 2.

[The second thing you mislike is private communions. And you quote the 1. Cor. xi. In which chapter St Paul reproveth the profanation of the supper
among the Corinthians by banqueting and contempt of
their brethren, and he exhorteth one of them to tarry
for another. But how can you apply this to your purpose?][6]

I know not what you mean by private communion: Of[7] private
communion.
if you mean the receiving of one alone, there is none
such allowed in the book: if you mean because it is
ministered sometime upon occasion in private houses,
I see not how you can call it private in respect of the
place, if the number of communicants be sufficient. You
must explicate yourself before I can tell what you mean.

There is nothing in the communion-book touching
the communion, contrary to the[8] place of St Paul by 1 Cor. xi. 18.[9]
you quoted, to my knowledge.

T. C. Page 105, Sect. 1.

*There followeth the private communion, which is found fault with,
both for the place wherein it is ministered, and for the small number of
communicants which are admitted by the book of service. Touching the
place, before is spoken sufficiently: it resteth to consider of the number. But
before I come to that I will speak something of the causes and beginning
of receiving in houses, and of the ministering of the communion unto sick
folks. It is not to be denied but that this abuse is very ancient, and was
in Justin Martyr's time, in Tertullian's and Cyprian's time, even as also
there were other abuses crept into the supper of the Lord, and that very
gross, as the mingling of water with wine, and therein also a necessity and
great mystery placed; as it may appear both by Justin Martyr[10] and
Cyprian[11]; which I therefore by the way do admonish the reader of, that
the antiquity of this abuse of private communion be not prejudicial to the
truth, no more than the mingling of water with that opinion of necessity
that those fathers had of it is, or ought to be, prejudicial to that that we
use in ministering the cup with pure wine, according to the institution.*

[6 This is inserted from Answ.]　　　[7 Answ. 2 omits *of*.]
[8 That, Answ.]　　　　　　　　[9 This reference is not in Answ.]
[10 Just. Martyr. Op. Par. 1742. Apol. I. 65, 7. pp. 82, 3.]
[11 ... videmus in aqua populum intelligi, in vino vero ostendi sanguinem
Christi.—Cypr. Op. Oxon. 1682. Ad Cœcil. Epist. lxiii. pp. 153, 4.]

Jo. Whitgift.

The usual answering of T. C.

This is your accustomed manner (but it is besides all good manners), to wipe away ancient and learned authority, by objecting unto the authors some imperfection in their writings, or errors in their times. Is this a good reason? water was of necessity required in Cyprian's time in the administration of the supper; and that was an error; therefore the communion at that time, and long before, ministered unto the sick, and carried to private persons being absent, was unlawful. Such be your arguments, and this is your kind of answering; which may be plausible to the ignorant people, but nothing pleasant to such as be learned. This one thing I will desire the reader to consider (that seeing our sacraments now be more sincerely ministered than they were in Justin's, Tertullian's and Cyprian's time, being so near the apostles), what cause there should be for you so bitterly to inveigh against this church in that respect.

More sincerity in the ministration now than in the ancient church.

Chapter vi. The Second Division.
T. C. Page 115, towards the end.

I say, therefore, that this abuse was ancient, and rose upon these causes. First of all, in the primitive church, the discipline of the church was so severe, and so extreme, that, if any which professed the truth, and were of the body of the church, did through infirmity deny the truth, and joined himself unto the idolatrous service, although he repenting came again unto the church, yet was he not received to the communion of the Lord's supper any more. And yet, lying in extremity of sickness, and ready to depart this life, if they [1] did require the communion in token that the church had forgiven the fault, and was reconciled altogether unto that person that had so fallen, they granted that he might be partaker of it; as may appear by the story of Serapion [2]. Euseb. Lib. vi. cap. 43.

Jo. Whitgift.

All this is true, for sometime they had three, six, or ten years' space of repentance before they were admitted to the sacrament; and, after that time was expired, they came as other did to the communion, if they lived to it; if not, they received it on their death-bed. This is for my purpose; for it manifestly declareth that then the communion was min-

[1 He, Repl. 2.]
[2 Euseb. in Hist. Eccles. Script. Amst. 1695-1700. Lib. vi. cap. xliv. pp. 200, 1.]

istered unto the sick, which is our question; it can by no means be drawn against me.

Chapter vi.　The Third Division.
T. C. Page 116, Line 2.

Another cause was that which was before alleged, which is, the false opinion which they had conceived that all those were condemned that received not the supper of the Lord; and therefore, when as those that were, as they called them, Catechumeni, which is, young novices in religion, never admitted to the supper, or young children fell sick dangerously, they ministered the supper of the Lord unto them, lest they should want their voyage victual (as they termed it); which abuse, notwithstanding, was neither so ancient as the other, nor so general.

Jo. Whitgift.

This was the cause that moved some so to do; howbeit, neither was it the only cause, neither the general and usual cause; but the general and usual cause was the institution of Christ, and the fruits and effects of that supper, the which whosoever doth consider accordingly will neither cease from requiring it in time of extremity, neither withhold it from such as faithfully and earnestly desire the same; and it is an easy matter to shew that this manner of communicating in private families is of very great antiquity, even in Justinus Martyr's time; as appeareth in his second Apology[3], and is by you confessed.

Chapter vi.　The Fourth Division.
T. C. Page 116, Line 8.

And there wanted not good men which declared their misliking, and did decree against both the abuses, and against all manner communicating in private houses. As in the council of Laodicea it was or-
Tom. i. *dained that "neither bishop nor elder should make any oblation,"*
can. 58. *that was, minister any communion in houses[4].*

Jo. Whitgift.

This council doth speak against the usual manner of celebrating the communion in private houses, without any respect

[3 Just. Martyr. Op. Par. 1742. Apol. i. 65, 7. p. 83.]

[4 Ὅτι οὐ δεῖ ἐν τοῖς οἴκοις προσφορὰς γίνεσθαι παρὰ ἐπισκόπων ἢ πρεσβυτέρων.—Concil. Laod. can. 58. in Concil. Stud. Labb. et Cossart. Lut. Par. 1671-2. Tom. I. col. 1505.]

of necessity ; which abuse was grown in some places in the time of Hierome and Damasus, about whose time this council was ; but there is neither council nor learned father that ever opened their mouths against ministering the communion to the sick in private families, or upon any other urgent or necessary occasion. The 12. canon of the council of Nice doth determine directly that the communion ought to be ministered to the sick [1].

The communion ministered to the sick.

In the Greek it is the 13. canon.

Chapter vi.　The Fifth Division.
T. C. Page 116, Line 12.

Besides, therefore, that I have before shewed the unlawfulness generally of ministering the sacrament in private places, seeing that the custom of ministering this supper unto the sick rose upon corrupt causes and rotten foundations ; and considering also (God be praised) in these times there are none driven by fear to renounce the truth, whereupon any such excommunication should ensue, which in the extremity of sickness should be mitigated after this sort (for no man now that is in extreme sickness is cast down, or else assaulted with this temptation, that he is cut off from the church)— I say, these things considered, it followeth that this ministering of communion in private houses, and to the sick, is unlawful, as that which rose upon evil grounds ; and, if it were lawful, yet that now in these times of peace, and when the sick are not excommunicated, there is no use of it. And so it appeareth how little the custom of the old church doth help M. Doctor in this point.

Jo. Whitgift.

This was one cause, but not the only cause why the communion was ministered to the sick ; the chief and principal cause was (as I have said) the fruits and effects of that sacrament, which is remission of sins, peace of conscience, and effectual applying of the death and passion of Christ unto the communicants, and an assurance of God's promises, whereof that sacrament is an effectual seal.

[1 Καθόλου δὲ καὶ περὶ παντὸς οὑτινοσοῦν ἐξοδεύοντος, αἰτοῦντος τοῦ μετασχεῖν εὐχαριστίας, ὁ ἐπίσκοπος μετὰ δοκιμασίας ἐπιδότω.—Concil. Nic. can. 13. ibid. Tom. II. col. 36.]

Chapter vi.   The Sixth Division.

Answer to the Admonition, Page 81, Sect. 3.

The communion exhibited unto[2] sick persons is allowed both of Peter Martyr and Bucer, as in the other treatise I have declared, and consonant to the custom of Christ's church, even from the apostles' time, as is to be seen in the old[3] writers.

Sick persons receive the communion.

T. C. Page 116, Sect. 1.

And as for that he saith Peter Martyr and Bucer do allow the com-munion exhibited to the sick persons, when he sheweth that he shall have answer. For, where he saith he hath declared it in another treatise, either the printer hath left out that treatise, or M. Doctor wonderfully forgetteth himself, or else he meaneth some odd thing that he hath written, and laid up in some corner of his study; for surely there is no such saying in all his book before, nor yet after, as[4] far as I can find.

Jo. Whitgift.

M. Bucer, in his Censures upon the communion-book, speaking of this part of it saith thus: "And those things which are commanded in this behalf do well enough agree with the holy scriptures; for to receive the communion of the Lord, and to be partaker of his table, doth not a little avail unto the comfort of afflicted consciences, if it be received according to the Lord's institution[5]."

Bucer.

M. Martyr's allowing of the same is added in that place[6].

M. Musculus, in his Common-places, *Titul. de Cœna Domini,* saith that *privata et extrema ægrotantium commu-nio, &c. :* "private and last communion ministered to the sick is retained in divers reformed churches, for this end, that the sick persons thereby may be strengthened in faith, made stronger against the temptations of Satan, and the better armed to bear the pains of death[7]."   Neither do I see any

Musculus.

[2 To, Answ.]   [3 In old, Answ.]   [4 So, Repl. 1 and 2.]

[5 Et quæ hic præcipiuntur, sunt divinis scripturis satis consentanea. Com-munionem enim sumere Domini, et de mensa ejus, ad consolandum perturbatas conscientias non parum valet : si ea ut Dominus instituit, sumatur.—M. Bucer. Script. Anglic. Basil. 1577. Cens. in Ordinat. Eccles. cap. xxii. p. 489.]

[6 Martyr agrees generally with Bucer : only he objects to the order in that book for carrying the sacrament from the church on communion days to the sick person. His letter to Bucer is preserved in Corpus Christi college library, Cam-bridge (cxix. 39, Nasm. Catalog.). It is printed by Strype, Cranmer, Append. No. lxi. Conf. Park. Soc. Liturgies of Edw. VI. p. 141.]

In evangelicis vero nonnullis ecclesiis, licet explosa sit papistarum opinio,

reason (if the superstitious opinion of the papists be rooted out) why any man in that case should be deprived of these benefits.

Chapter vi.   The Seventh Division.
T. C. Page 116, Sect. 2.

Now remaineth to be spoken of the number of communicants, and that there is fault in the appointing of the service-book, not only for that it admitteth in the time of plague that one with the minister may celebrate the supper of the Lord in the house, but for that it ordaineth a communion in the church, when of a great number which assemble there it admitteth three or four. The abuse and inconvenience whereof may thus be considered. The holy sacrament of the supper of the Lord is not only a seal and confirmation of the promises of God unto us, but also a profession of our conjunction as well with Christ our Saviour and with God, as also (as St Paul teacheth) a declaration and profession that we are at one with our brethren; so that it is first a sacra- 1 Cor. x. 17.[1] *ment of the knitting of all the body generally, and of every member particularly, with the head, and then of the members of the body one with another. Now, therefore, seeing that every particular church and body of God's people is a representation, and, as it were, a lively portraiture of the whole church and body of Christ, it followeth that[2] which we cannot do with all the church scattered throughout the whole world, for the distances of places whereby we are severed, we ought to do with that church whereunto God hath ranged us, as much as possibly or conveniently may be. The departing, therefore, of the rest of the church from those three or four is an open profession that they have no communion, fellowship, nor unity with them that do communicate; and, likewise, of those three or four, that they have none with the rest that join not themselves thereunto; when as, both by the many grapes making one cup, and corns making one loaf, that whole church, being many persons, are called as to the unity which they have one with another, and altogether among[3] themselves, so to the declaration and profession of it, by receiving one with another, and altogether amongst themselves. And as, if so be that we do not celebrate, as we may possibly and conveniently, the supper of the Lord, we thereby utter our want of love towards the Lord which hath redeemed us; so, if we do not communicate together with the church so far forth as we may do conveniently, we betray the want of our love that we have one towards another. And therefore St Paul, driving hereunto, wisheth[4] that one should tarry for another, reprehending that when one preventeth and* 1 Cor. xi. 33.[1] *cometh before another, saying that that is to take every man his own supper, and not to celebrate the Lord's supper; not that, so many*

retinetur tamen privata et extrema ægrotantium communio, ad hoc, ut per corpus ac sanguinem Domini confirmatiores in fide, et ad resistendum tentationibus Satanæ, sustinendosque mortis dolores, instructiores reddantur.—Wolfg. Muscul. Loc. Comm. Theolog. Basil. 1599. De Cœn. Dom. p. 370.]

[1 The verses are added from Repl. 2.]   [2 Followeth that that, Repl. 2.]
[3 Amongst, Repl. 1 and 2.]   [4 Willeth, Repl. 1 and 2.]

men or women as there came, so many tables were, for that had not been
possible in so great assemblies, but that they sorted themselves into certain
companies, and that they came scattering one after another, and that,
instead of making one supper of the Lord, they did make divers.

JO. WHITGIFT.

You cannot be ignorant that the whole drift of the communion-book is to move all men to oft communicating, and
that together, as it manifestly appeareth in the first exhortation in the book, prescribed to be read when the curate shall
see the people negligent in coming to the communion; the
which if you had well perused, you would have (as I think)
cut off much of this talk. If the book should appoint that
three or four should communicate together, and no more, or if
it did not allow that communion best wherein most of the
church do participate, then were your reasoning to some
end; but, seeing that it is appointed that there should not be
fewer than three or four, to the end that it might be a communion, and have no similitude with the papistical mass, there
is no cause why you should take this pains. And surely he
that shall compare that exhortation in the book with this discourse of yours, it will be no hard matter for him to judge
how much more pithily and effectually this matter is there
handled, than it is here by you. But that three or four
should be a sufficient number to communicate if other will not,
there is good[5] cause; for, seeing the holy sacrament is a seal
and confirmation of God's promises, and an effectual applying
of the death and passion of Christ unto us, and therefore a
singular comfort and relief to the afflicted conscience and mind
touched with the feeling of sin, why should those that be desirous of it, being a congregation (as three or four is, according
to the saying of Christ: "where two or three be gathered together in my name, &c."), be debarred from their godly desire,
and that singular comfort, for the carelessness, security, negligence, or lack of such feeling of others? Shall none communicate because all will not? Or shall not three or four
because the rest refuse? Or is it lack of love towards our
neighbour, or any token thereof, if we resort to the Lord's
table when other will not? Where learn you that?

The place of St Paul, 1 Cor. xi., is not aptly applied. For
the apostle in that place reproveth only such as contemptu-

The intent of the book is to move all men to communicate.

Three or four a sufficient number, if other will not communicate.

Three or four a congregation. Matt. xviii.

[5 Is no good, Def. B.]

ously or contentiously did separate themselves from other as well in the public feasts, called "love-feasts," and then used in the church, as in the supper of the Lord.   But he rather meaneth of the first than of the latter; and therefore saith M. Martyr upon that place: "The supper is here called private, either because some did challenge to themselves privately that which belonged to all, or else because every one after the receiving of the holy mysteries did take again to himself those things which he had offered at the Lord's table, and made that his own which by right belonged to all." And, again, he saith that the Corinthians be there reproved, "because they pampered their belly, and contemned their brethren[1]." I told you before what M. Calvin thought of this place[2]: it can in no respect tend to the disallowing of any order appointed in the book of common prayer, because no man is secluded from the communion that will come, and those that come, when other men will not, do it not of contempt or of contention, but of conscience and piety.   Moreover, we have no such banquets or feasts, either before or after the communion, as the Corinthians had; and therefore in that respect there can be no such abuse as the apostle there reproveth.

Chapter vi.   The Eighth Division.

Admonition.

Sixthly, in this book three or four are allowed for a fit number to receive the communion; and the priest alone, together with one more, or with the sick man alone, may in time of necessity, that is, when there is any common plague, or in time of other visitation, minister it to the sick man, and, if he require it, it may not be denied.   This is not, I am sure, like in effect to a private mass: that scripture, f *"Drink ye all of this,"*   f Matt. xxvi. *maketh not against this, and private communion is not against*   27. *the scriptures.*   Mark xiv. 23.

[1 Coena hic dicitur propria: vel quia quod erat omnium, aliqui privatim sibi vendicabant: vel quod ea quæ obtulisset quisque ad mensam Domini, sibi rursus post sacra percepta resumebat, et quod jure omnium esse debuisset, suum ipsius faciebat...Accusat Paulus eos, tanquam helluones, qui viderentur tantummodo ventrem colere...Non tantum lædebantur pauperes, quod eis cibus deficeret, sed etiam quod afficerentur contumelia, cum despicerentur.—P. Martyr. Comm. in D. Paul. prior. ad Corinth. Epist. Tigur. 1572. cap. xi. vv. 20, 21. fol. 155. 2.]

[2 See before, page 507, note 2.]

Answer to the Admonition, Page 185, Sect. 1.

How untruly these men charge the church with private communions I have shewed before. The place of scripture here alleged to prove that three or four be not a sufficient number to communicate is this: "Drink ye all of this," Matt. xxvi. Mark xiv.; which may as well be applied to prove that ten, twenty, forty, is no sufficient number. I know not what your meaning is, except you think no number sufficient, unless all do communicate together, because Christ said: "Drink ye all of this[3]." This text proveth that all ought to be partakers of the Lord's cup, but it doth not determine any certain number of communicants. I know there be some of the old fathers, as Basilius Magnus, which would not have fewer communicants than xii.[4]. But of the number of communicants there is nothing determined in scripture, neither is it material, so that there be a number that it may be a communion.

No number determined to be at the communion.

Basil would have xii. at the least.

T. C. Page 117, Sect. 1.

These things being considered, the reason which the Admonition useth in the 185. page, where this matter is spoken of, which is: "Drink you all of this," is not so ridiculous as M. Doctor maketh it. For, although it[5] do neither prove that 12. or 20. or any other definite number must of necessity receive, yet it proveth that, as all they which were present did communicate, so[6] as many as in the church are fit to receive the sacraments, or may conveniently receive them together, should follow that example in celebrating the supper together.

Jo. Whitgift.

The book of common prayer doth greatly commend and like the receiving of the whole church together, but, if that cannot be obtained (as it cannot, and they will not have men compelled unto it), it secludeth not those that be well disposed, so they be a competent number. And the book doth exhort those to depart which do not communicate, with a warning from whence they depart; so that you may well understand that the meaning of the book is that all that be present

[3 The last two words are not in Answ.]

[4 Et quemadmodum spiritualis lex non pauciores quam duodecim esse vult mysticum pascha comedentes: sic &c.—Basil. Op. Lat. Basil. 1540. Exerc. ad Piet. Serm. iv. Tom. III. p. 425.]

[5 For although that it, Repl. 1 and 2.]   [6 And so, Repl. 2.]

should communicate.   Neither can this place of scripture be
drawn to improve the decree of the church therein.   For
Christ had 70. other disciples, and his mother, with divers
other which followed him, that were not present at that
supper; as no doubt they should have been if by that example he had meant to have made a law that there may be
no communion unless the whole congregation of every particular church do communicate together.

Chapter vi.   The Ninth Division.

T. C. Page 117, Sect. 1.

*And it is probably to be thought that, if our Saviour Christ had not
been restrained by the law of God touching the passover* Exod. xii. 3.¹
unto his own family, being twelve, and therefore a compe-
tent number to eat up² a lamb by themselves, that he would have cele-
They were *brated his supper, not only amongst his xii. disciples, which afterward he*
made apo- *made apostles, but also³ amongst other of his disciples and professors of*
stles before, *his doctrine.   But, forsomuch as it was meet that he should celebrate his*
and so called. *supper there and then, where and when he did celebrate his passover, for*
the cause before by me alleged, it pleased him to keep his first supper with
twelve only, for that the law⁴ of communication unto the passover, which
was joined with the supper, would not admit any greater number of
communicants, they being sufficient and enough to eat up⁵ the passover.

Jo. Whitgift.

This is only a conjecture, but it overthroweth your argument; for, by your saying, Christ had his twelve apostles
there at supper, because the law touching the passover did
bind him thereunto, not because he would signify that there
should be no communion except the whole church do communicate.

The disciples were "made apostles" before the institution
Matt. x.   of the supper; and were so called, as it is evident, Matt. x.
Mark iii.   and Mark iii.; and therefore I marvel what you mean in say-
ing, "which afterwards he made apostles."

[¹ This reference is inserted from Repl. 2.]
[² Unto his own family and to as many only as would serve to eat up, Repl. 2.]
[³ The words from *supper* are omitted in Repl. 2.]
[⁴ With the fewer for that the law, Repl. 2.]
[⁵ Communicants than was sufficient to eat up, Repl. 2.]

Chapter vi.　The Tenth Division.

T. C. Page 117, Sect. 2.

And, although it be clear and plain that, when it is said: "Drink ye all of this," and: "Tarry one for another," these sayings are meant of that particular congregation or assembly which assemble themselves together to be taught by one mouth of the minister, yet I have therefore put this caution of [6] *"as much as may be possible," lest any man should cavil, as though I would have no communion until all the godly through the world should meet together. Likewise I have put this caution "as much as may be conveniently;" for, although it be possible that any* [7] *particular church may communicate at one table, in one day, and together, yet may the same be inconvenient for divers causes. As if the number should be very great, so that to have them all communicate together it would require such a long time, as the tarrying out of the whole action would hazard either the life or at least the health of divers there. Again, forasmuch as, other some being at the church, it is meet that other should be at home, upon occasion of infants and such like things as require the presence of some to tarry at home. In these cases, and such like, the inconveniences do deliver us from the guilt of uncharitableness, and forsaking the fellowship of the church, for that we do not here sever ourselves, but are by good and just causes severed; which guilt we shall never escape, if besides* [8] *such necessary causes we pretend those that are not, or, having not so much as a pretence, yet, notwithstanding, separate ourselves; as the daily practice through* [9] *the church doth shew.*

Jo. Whitgift.

If you be content to admit so many "cautions" and exceptions, then is the question soon decided, and you make it no such commandment but that upon occasion it may be altered. Indeed the words of Christ do signify that the cup of the supper and the whole supper is common to all, as well of the laity (as we term them) as of the clergy, but it doth not prescribe what number shall be present at every several communion. I do not excuse those that withdraw themselves from that supper, except it be upon necessary and just occasion, but I deny that the negligence or lawful occasion of some ought to hinder or stay other from communicating: this you should have proved; but you do not, and your "cautions" and exceptions (which I very well allow) declare the contrary.

[6 Repl. 2 omits *of*.]　　　　　　　[7 A, Repl. 2.]
[8 Beside, Repl. 1 and 2.]　　[9 Thorough out, Repl. 2, throught, Repl. 1.]

Chapter vi.   The Eleventh Division.

T. C. Page 117, Sect. 3.

But it may be objected, that in this point the book of common prayer is not in fault, which doth not only not forbid that all the church should receive together, but also by a good and godly exhortation moveth those that be present that they should not depart, but communicate all together. It is true that it doth not forbid, and that there is godly exhortation for that purpose; but that, I say, is not enough; for neither should it suffer that three or four should have a communion by themselves (so many being in the church meet to receive, and to whom the supper of the Lord doth of like right[1] appertain), and it ought to provide that those which would withdraw themselves should be by ecclesiastical discipline at all times, and now also under a godly prince by civil punishment, brought to communicate with their brethren.   And this is the law of God, and this is now, and hath been heretofore, the practice of the churches[2] reformed.   All men understand that the passover was a figure of the Lord's supper, and that there should be as strait bonds to bind men to celebrate the remembrance of our spiritual deliverance as there was to remember the deliverance out of Egypt.   But whosoever did not then communicate with the rest, at that time when the passover was eaten, was excommunicated; as may[3] appear in the Numbers[4], where he saith that, whosoever did not communicate, being clean, his soul should be cut off from amongst the people of God.   Therefore this neglect, or contempt rather, of the Lord's supper ought to be punished with no less punishment, especially when as (after the church hath proceeded in that order which our Saviour Christ appointeth of admonishing) they be not sorry for their fault, and promise amendment.   And that this was the custom of the churches it may appear by the 9. of those canons which are fathered of the apostles; where it is decreed that "all the faithful that entered into the congregation and heard the scriptures read, and did not tarry out the prayers and the holy communion, should be, as those which were causers of disorders in the church, separated from the church," or (as it is translated of another) "deprived of the communion[6]."   Also in the council of Braccara it was decreed that, " if any entering into the church of God heard the scriptures, and afterward of wantonness or looseness withdrew himself from the communion of the sacrament, and so brake the rule of discipline in the

This is clean contrary to the Admonition, pag. 109.

This is not excommunication, but putting to death.

Num. ix. 13.[5]

Conc. Apo. can. ix.

Conc. ii. Bracca. cap. 83. Tom. ii.

[1 Of right, Repl. 2.]   [2 Of churches, Repl. 1, 2, and Def. A.]
[3 As it may, Repl. 1, 2, and Def. A.]
[4 In the book of Numbers, Repl. 2.]
[5 The verse is added from Repl. 2.]
[6 Πάντας τοὺς εἰσιόντας πιστοὺς, καὶ τῶν γραφῶν ἀκούοντας, μὴ παραμένοντας δὲ τῇ προσευχῇ καὶ τῇ ἁγίᾳ μεταλήψει, ὡς ἀταξίαν ἐμποιοῦντας τῇ ἐκκλησίᾳ, ἀφορίζεσθαι χρή.—Canon. Apost. 9. in Concil. Stud. Labb. et Cossart. Lut. Par. 1671-2. Tom. I. col. 28.]

reverend sacraments, should be put out of the church till such time as he had by good fruits declared his repentance[7]."

Jo. Whitgift.

I do not much disagree from this, saving that I see no reason that three or four should be debarred from so comfortable and fruitful a sacrament, either for the negligence or necessary impediments of others; except also your misunderstanding of the ix. of Numbers; for *delere animam ejus de populis suis* is there not "to excommunicate," as you interpret it, but "to put to death," and "to kill;" which were a hard punishment for such as be negligent in coming to the communion. Convenient discipline I think very necessary in this point, and therefore I will not stand with you in other circumstances of this portion; only I will desire the reader to note how far the authors of the Admonition vary from you in this assertion, who, page 102., say that we "thrust them in their sin to the Lord's table," and, page 109., that it should be provided that "papists nor other neither constrainedly nor customably[8] communicate in the mysteries of salvation;" which cannot otherwise be meant, than that we compel them by punishments to come to the Lord's table. But how much more cause should they have so to say, if we were as severe in punishing as you here require? But the negligence of the common sort, in not oftener frequenting the Lord's supper, is lamentable, the punishment appointed for such in all places not so well executed; and therefore, as I said before, I think convenient discipline, and due execution of the same, very necessary.

Another thing also I would have the reader to mark, that you here allege for proof the canons of the apostles, which are as much doubted of to have been the apostles' as the epistles either of Clement or Anacletus.

The Admonition and the Reply agree not.

[7 Si quis intrat ecclesiam Dei, et sacras scripturas non audit, et pro luxuria sua avertit se a communione sacramenti, et in observandis mysteriis declinat constitutam regulam disciplinæ, istum talem projiciendum de ecclesia catholica esse decernimus, donec pœnitentiam agat, et ostendat fructum pœnitentiæ suæ; &c.— Capit. Martin. Episc. Bracar. 83. in eod. Tom. V. col. 914.]

[8 Customable, Def. A.]

Chapter vi.   The Twelfth Division.

T. C. Page 118, Sect. 1.

But here also may rise another doubt of the former words of Moses in the book of Numbers.   For, seeing that he maketh this exception, "if they be clean," it may be said that those that depart do not feel themselves meet to receive, and therefore depart, the other three or four, or more, feel themselves meet and disposed for that purpose; whereupon it may seem that it is neither reason to compel those to come which feel not themselves meet, nor to reject them that feel that good disposition and preparation in themselves.   For answer whereunto we must understand that the uncleanness which Moses speaketh of was such as men could not easily avoid, and whereunto they might fall sometimes by necessary duty, as by handling their dead, which they were by the rule of charity bound to bury, sometimes by touching at unwares a dead body, or by sitting in the place where some unclean body had sitten, or by touching such things which the law judged unclean; which thing cannot be alleged in those which are now of the church; for as many as be of it, and withal of such discretion as are able to prove and examine themselves, can have no excuse at all if they may be at the church to withdraw themselves from the holy supper of the Lord. For, if they will say that they be not meet, it may be answered unto them that it is their own fault, and, further, if they be not meet to receive the holy sacrament of the supper, they are not meet to hear the word of God, they are not meet to be partakers of the prayers of the church, and if they be for one they are also for the other; for with that boldness, and with that duty or lawfulness (I speak of those which are of the church and of dis-

This is not true; as shall be shewed.

cretion to examine themselves)—I say, with what lawfulness they may offer themselves to the prayers and to the hearing of the word of God, they may also offer themselves unto the Lord's supper.   And, to whomsoever of them the Lord will communicate himself by preaching the word, unto the same he will not refuse to communicate himself by receiving of the sacraments. For whosoever is of God's household and family, he need not be afraid to come to the Lord's table, nor doubt but that the Lord will feed him there; and whatsoever he be that is a member of the body of Christ may be assured that he receiveth life from Christ the head, as well by the arteries and conduits of the supper of the Lord as by the preaching of the word of God; so that it must needs follow that the not receiving of those which depart out of the church when there is any communion celebrated proceedeth either of vain or[1] superstitious fear, growing of gross ignorance of themselves and of the holy sacraments, or else of an intolerable negligence, or rather contempt; of the which neither the one nor the other should be either borne with or nourished, either by permitting three or four to communicate alone, or else in letting them which depart go so easily away with so great a fault, which ought to be severely punished.

[¹ And, Repl. 1, 2, and Def. A.]

Jo. Whitgift.

Neither do I differ from you in the substance of this that
you here set down, which is (as I take it) to cut off frivolous
and vain excuses, used by such as either neglect or contemn
the holy communion; but in certain circumstances here used I
do not altogether agree with you. For, first, the uncleanness
that Moses speaketh of is but ceremonial and external, and
therefore may more easily be avoided; but weakness of faith
and uncleanness of life (which may and ought for a time withdraw men from the communion) is natural and inward, and
therefore with greater difficulty shunned.

Secondly, a christian man and a true member of the
church may take benefit by prayer and hearing of the word
of God, which yet for divers respects is not meet to receive
the holy communion; and indeed praying and preaching be
means to prepare men, and make them apt to communicate:
besides this, he that is weak in faith, corrupt in judgment,
ignorant in the right use of the sacrament, may be admitted
to prayer, and to the hearing of the word, that he may be
instructed (for *fides ex auditu :* "faith cometh by hearing"); so
may he not to the receiving of the supper. Thirdly, no man
may presume to receive the supper except he hath first tried
and examined himself; but he ought to come to the hearing
of the word of God, that he may first learn how to examine
himself. Wherefore this is not true, that, "with what lawfulness they may offer themselves to the prayers and to the
hearing of the word of God, they may also offer themselves
unto the Lord's supper." And you affirm the contrary,
pag. 35.[2] For there you say that the magistrate ought to
compel such as be papists and excommunicate persons to hear
sermons, and, pag. 133., you affirm the same in plainer words,
shewing a reason why such may be admitted to the hearing of
the word, and yet not to the participation of the Lord's supper.
Lastly, I deny that any such persuasion is nourished in them,
by suffering three or four to communicate, but the contrary
rather; for the godly example of these few may either provoke
the rest to the like diligence, or else confound them and make
them ashamed; especially if either that godly exhortation contained in the book be read unto them, or they be otherwise

Men not meet to communicate may be admitted to the hearing of the word and prayers.

Rom. x.

T. C. contrary to himself, pag. 35, line 10, and pag. 133, lin. 19.

[2 See before, Vol. I. page 366.]

put in mind of their slackness by a godly and careful minister. These circumstances excepted, in the rest of the matter in this part I agree with you.

Chapter vi.   The Thirteenth Division.
T. C. Page 118, Sect. 1.

And upon this either contempt or superstitious fear drawn from the papists' lenten preparation of forty days, earshrift, displing[1], &c., it cometh to pass that men, receiving the supper of the Lord but seldom, when they fall sick must have the supper ministered unto them in their houses, which otherwise being once every week received before should not breed any such unquietness in them when they cannot come to receive it, although, as I have before shewed, if they had never received it before, yet that private receiving were not at any hand to be suffered. And thus, having declared what I think to be faulty in the communion-book in this point, and the reasons why, and withal answered to that which either M. Doctor allegeth in this place of the 80. and 81., and likewise in the 152. and 185. pages touching this matter, I come now unto that which is called the "Jewish purifying" by the Admonition, and by the service-book aforetime "The purification of women."

Jo. Whitgift.

I see not how this in any point is true; for "lenten fast" was then used when the communion was most diligently and often frequented, and indeed the rare and seldom receiving came in with private massing, which had the beginning long after the "lenten fast."

To "receive once every week" is a thing to be wished, if it might conveniently be. And yet, notwithstanding, were not the communion to be denied to the sick; for it oftentimes cometh to pass, that men through infirmity and sickness are not able to come to the church in whole months and years, whom this weekly communicating could nothing help; and it were against all reason to debar them of this seal of God's promises, this effectual manner and kind of applying of the death of Christ unto themselves, this assurance of the forgiveness of sins, and this sacrament of comfort, especially in time of extremity and sickness, if they be desirous of it. And thus you "have declared what" you "think to be faulty in the communion-book in this point, and the reasons why;" but of what force your reasons are, and how justly in this point you charge the book, the reader may now judge.

[1 Displing: discipline.]

Of the churching of women.

Chapter vii.   The First Division.

T. C. Page 118, Sect. ult.

Now to the churching of women, in the which title yet kept there seemeth Strife about words.
to be hid a great part of the Jewish purification; for, like as in
Levit. xii. *the old law she that had brought forth a child was holden*
2, 4, 6.[2] *unclean, until such time as she came to the temple to shew her-*
self, after she had brought forth a man or a woman; so this term
of "churching of her" can seem to import nothing else than a banishment,
and as it were, a certain excommunication from the church during
the space that is between the time of her delivery and of her coming
unto the church. For what doth else this churching imply but a
restoring her unto the church, which cannot be without some bar or
shutting forth presupposed? It is also called "the thanksgiving," but the
principal title, which is the directory of this part of the liturgy, and
placed in the top of the leaf as that which the translator best liked of, is
"churching of women." To pass by that, that it will have them come
as nigh the communion-table as may be, as they came before to the high
altar (because I had spoken once generally against such ceremonies), that of
all other is most Jewish, and approacheth nearest to[3] the Jewish purifica-
tion, that she is commanded to offer accustomed offerings. Wherein, besides
that the very word "offering" carrieth with it a strong scent and suspicion
of a sacrifice (especially being uttered simply without any addition), it can-
not be without danger that the book maketh the custom of the popish church
(which was so corrupt) to be the rule and measure of this offering. And,
although the meaning of the book is not that it should be any offering for
sin, yet this manner of speaking may be a stumbling-stock in the way of
the ignorant and simple, and the wicked and obstinate thereby are con-
firmed and hardened in their corruptions. The best which can be answered
in this case is that it is for the relief of the minister; but then it should be
remembered, first, that the minister liveth not any more of offerings; secon-
darily, that the payment of the minister's wages is not so convenient, either
in the church or before all the people; and, thirdly, that thereby we fall
into that fault which we condemn in popery, and that is that, besides the
ordinary living appointed for the service of the priests in the whole, they
took for their several services of mass, baptism, burying, churching, &c.,
several rewards; which thing being of the service-book well abolished in
certain other things, I cannot see what good cause there should be to retain
it in this and certain other.

Jo. Whitgift.

It is the property of quarrellers, and of men naturally bent Strife of words proper to quarrellers.
to contention, to strive about words and terms, when they

[2 The verses are added from Repl. 2.]   [3 Unto, Repl. 1 and 2.]

cannot reprove anything in the matter itself.   For in all these faults here pretended there is not one that toucheth the matter of the book: only "the title in the top of the leaf," "the coming of women so near to the communion-table," "the paying of the accustomed offerings to the curate," are in this place reproved, as matters of great importance, being all of themselves not worth the talking of; and yet, being (as comely and decent orders) prescribed by the church, may not be contemned and despised, without the crime of stubbornness and disobedience.   But, that your quarrelling may the rather appear, I will answer your cavils in as few words as I can. And first for the title, which is this : " The thanksgiving of women after child-birth, commonly called the churching of women."   Now, sir, you see that the proper title is this : "The thanksgiving of women after child-birth."   The other

The people hardly brought to leave accustomed terms.

is the common name customably used of the common people, who will not be taught to speak by you, or any man, but keep their accustomed names and terms ; therefore they call the Lord's day "Sunday," and the next unto it "Monday," profane and ethnical names, and yet nothing derogating from the days and times.   Likewise they call the morning and evening prayer "mattins" and "evensong," neither can they be brought to the contrary ; and yet the prayers be not the worse: so they call the day of Christ's nativity "Christmas," &c.: what is this to condemn the things themselves ?

But you say, "this term doth import nothing else than a banishment from the church, &c.;" so might you say that these names Sunday and Monday do import that we dedicate those days to the sun and moon ; and so likewise might you say of the other names retained in the common and usual speech ; but all men would then espy your folly, even as they may do now, if they be disposed.   The absence of the woman after her delivery is neither banishment nor ex-

The true cause of the absence of the woman after her deliverance.

communication (as you term it), but a withdrawing of the party from the church by reason of that infirmity and danger that God hath laid upon womankind in punishment of the first sin, which danger she knoweth not whether she shall escape or no ; and therefore, after she hath not only escaped it, but also brought a child into the world, to the increase of God's

The cause of her thanksgiving.

people, and after such time as the comeliness of nature may bear, she cometh first into the church to give thanks for the same, and for the deliverance by Christ from that sin, whereof that infirmity is a perpetual testimony. And, this being done, not Jewishly, but christianly, not of custom, but of duty, not to make the act of lawful matrimony unclean, but to give thanks to God for deliverance from so manifold perils, what christian heart can for the name's sake thus disallow of it, as you do?

The "coming so near to the communion-table" is a very small matter to carp at; it is thought to be the most convenient place, both for the minister and for the woman, especially if she be disposed to receive the holy communion. But such trifling quarrels argue an extreme penury of good and substantial reasons.

The "paying of her accustomed offerings," which you seem most to mislike (as yourself confess the meaning of the book to be), hath no such purpose and intent as you would make the reader to believe, neither can it; for she neither offereth "lamb," "turtles," or young "pigeons," as the law re- *Levit. xii.* quireth, but payeth to the curate his accustomed duty, which both she may as lawfully give and he receive, as the other tenths may be paid and received. It is a portion of the pastor's living appointed and limited unto him by the church; and therefore he may lawfully receive it, as it is appointed unto him. And all your objections to the contrary are hereby answered fully.

Chapter vii.   The Second Division.

Admonition.

In which book[1] *a great number of things contrary to God's word are* *b Acts xv. 10.* *contained, as Jewish* *b purifyings, &c.*[2]

Answer to the Admonition, Page 81, Sect. 4.

The third is the "Jewish purifyings;" as you term *Churching of* it. You cite for that purpose Acts xv., where Peter, *women.*[3] speaking against certain of the Pharisees which believed and taught that it was needful for the gentiles which were converted to be circumcised, and to observe

---

[1 *Book* is not in Adm. or Answ.]
[2 See before, page 540, note 3.]
[3 This marginal note is inserted from Answ. 2.]

Moses' law, saith on this sort: "Now therefore why tempt ye God, to lay a yoke on the disciples' necks, &c.?" How anything here contained prohibiteth women, after they be delivered from the great danger and pains of child-bearing, to give in the congregation thanks for their deliverance, let the godly reader judge. Surely this is no Jewish purifying, but christian giving of thanks, most consonant and agreeable to the word of God. But hereof also something more is to be spoken in another place.

T. C. Page 119, Line 24.

Now, whereas M. Doctor saith that the place of the xv. of the Acts, alleged by the Admonition, maketh nothing against this, he should have considered that if it be a Jewish ceremony (as they suppose it) it is to be abolished utterly. For, it being shewed there that all the ceremonial law of Moses is done away through our Saviour Christ, this also a part thereof must needs be therein comprised.

Jo. Whitgift.

The place nothing pertaineth to this purpose, neither is giving of thanks a Jewish ceremony; and therefore their supposition is but vain.

Chapter vii. The Third Division.
T. C. Page 119, in the midst.

And, whereas he saith that it, being nothing else but a thanksgiving for her deliverance, cannot be therefore but christian and very godly; I answer that, if there should be solemn and express giving of thanks in the church for every benefit, either equal or greater than this, which any singular person in the church doth receive, we should not only have no preaching of the word, nor ministering of the sacraments, but we should not have not so much leisure as to do any corporal or bodily work, but should be like unto those heretics which were called of the Syriac word Messalians, or continual prayers, and which did nothing else but pray. Theod. Li. iv. cap. 11.

Jo. Whitgift.

Truth is never contrary unto itself: before, you reproved the book of common prayer for want of thanksgiving for benefits received[1], and now you reprove it for appointing thanks to be given for deliverance from sin, from manifold perils and

[1 See before, page 486.]

dangers, and for the increase of God's people; all which things are public, although thanks be given by a private person; for indeed the punishment and danger laid upon all womankind for the disobedience[2] is not only common, but very notorious, and a perpetual testimony of our subjection unto sin, and therefore requireth a solemn thanksgiving at such time as it pleaseth God to shew his mercy therein, and to deliver from it. And yet, if it were not so, where read you that any private person is forbidden to give thanks in the public congregation for some especial benefit received, namely if the church think it convenient, and agree thereunto, as it doth to this?

Theodoret saith that the Messalian heretics had these errors: first, they, being possessed with a devil, which they thought to be the Holy Spirit, did condemn all bodily labour as wicked; secondly, they, being given to much sleep, did name the visions of their dreams prophecies; thirdly, they said that the supper of the Lord and baptism did neither good nor harm to any man; fourthly, when they were charged with such things, they would not stand to them, but impudently deny them; last of all, they taught that every man when he is born doth take of his parents, as the nature, so likewise the servitude of devils, which being driven out by diligent prayer, the Holy Spirit entered in, &c.[3] This is all that Theodoret in that place reporteth of those heretics; the which how much it maketh against either diligent or continual prayers or thanksgiving for benefits received, the reader may consider. Christ and the apostle St Paul require continual prayer and thanksgiving, but not in same sense and meaning that the Messalians did.

The errors of the Messalians. Theod. Lib. iv. cap. 11.

Luke xviii. Rom. xii. Eph. vi. Col. iv.

[2 For disobedience, Def. A.]

[3 Ἐνθουσιασταὶ γὰρ καλοῦνται, δαίμονός τινος ἐνεργείας εἰσδεχόμενοι, καὶ Πνεύματος ἁγίου παρουσίαν ταύτην ὑπολαμβάνοντες. οἱ δὲ τελείαν τὴν νόσον εἰσδεδεγμένοι, ἀποστρέφονται μὴν τὴν τῶν χειρῶν ἐργασίαν ὡς πονηράν. ὕπνῳ δὲ σφᾶς αὐτοὺς ἐκδιδόντες, τὰς τῶν ὀνείρων φαντασίας προφητείας ἀποκαλοῦσι...οὐδὲν οὔτε ὀνίνασθαι οὔτε λωβᾶσθαι φάσκοντες τὴν θείαν τροφὴν,...κρύπτειν δὲ τὴν νόσον πειρώμενοι, καὶ μετὰ ἐλέγχους ἀναιδῶς ἐξαρνοῦνται,...ἔφη μηδεμίαν μὴν ἐκ τοῦ θείου βαπτίσματος ὠφέλειαν τοῖς ἀξιουμένοις γίνεσθαι· μόνην δὲ τὴν σπουδαίαν εὐχὴν τὸν δαίμονα τὸν ἔνοικον ἐξελαύνειν. ἕλκειν γὰρ ἕκαστον τῶν τικτομένων ἔλεγεν ἐκ τοῦ προπάτορος, ὥσπερ τὴν φύσιν, οὕτω δὴ καὶ τὴν τῶν δαιμόνων δουλείαν. τούτων δὲ ὑπὸ τῆς σπουδαίας ἐλαυνομένων εὐχῆς, ἐπιφοιτᾷ λοιπὸν τὸ πανάγιον Πνεῦμα, κ.τ.λ.—Theod. in Hist. Eccles. Script. Amst. 1695-1700. Lib. iv. cap. xi. pp. 163, 4.]

Chapter vii.   The Fourth Division.

Admonition.

They should first prove . . . . that churching of women, coming in veils, abusing the psalm to her: "I have lifted up mine eyes unto the hills, &c.," and such other foolish things, are agreeable to the written word of the Almighty[2].   Psalm cxx.[1]

Answer to the Admonition, Page 155, for the which T. C. hath noted 153, Sect. 2.

The cxxi. Psalm (for I think your printer was over-seen in that quotation): "I have lifted up mine eyes, &c.," teacheth that all help cometh from God, and that the faithful ought only to look for help at his hands, and therefore a most meet psalm to be said at such time as we being delivered from any peril come to give thanks to God.

[What mean you to add "and such other foolish things"? What foolishness, I beseech you, can you find in this so godly a psalm? O where are your wits? Nay, where is your reverence you ought to give to the holy scriptures? * But still I say with Zuinglius, you do require that of other, which you ought to perform yourselves; for you ought to prove all these things which you condemn to be against the scriptures. *][3]

T. C. Page 119, somewhat past the midst.

For the Psalm cxxi., spoken of in the 155.[4] *page, it being shewed that it is not meet to have any such solemn thanksgiving, it is needless to debate of the psalm wherewith the thanksgiving should be made.*

Jo. Whitgift.

A short answer, and to small purpose: the psalm is most apt to that end, and thanksgiving in such cases most godly; as I have declared both in my Answer to the Admonition, and to your Reply.

[1] Psal. cxxi., Adm.; but the first edition, as above, *Psalm cxx.*]

[2] This paragraph is composed of fragments of the whole that is contained in Adm. and Answ.; see before, page 513. It is printed afterwards more fully, in Tractat. xxi.]

[3] This is inserted from Answ., the last sentence being in Answ. 2 only.]

[4] 153, Repl. 1.]

Chapter vii. The Fifth Division.
Admonition.

The twelfth.

Churching of women after child-birth smelleth of Jewish purification :
their other rites and custom[5] in their lying-in and coming to church is
foolish and superstitious, as it is used. She must lie in with a white sheet
upon her bed, and come covered with a veil, as ashamed of some folly.
She must offer ; but these are matters of custom, and not in the book ; but
_{o Psalm cxxi.} *this psalm (as is noted before) is childishly abused. " I ^ohave*
    lifted[6] up mine eyes unto the hills, from whence cometh my
help." " The sun shall not burn thee by day, nor the moon by night."

Answer to the Admonition, Page 155 and 202; for the which
   T. C. hath quoted 101 and 102 page.

In the hundred fifty-five these be my words:

That women should come in veils is not contained in
the book, no more indeed is the wafer-cake ; and therefore you might well have left these two out of your
reason, being thrust in without all reason.

To the which nothing is answered.

In the 202. page thus I say :

[Of the churching of women, I have spoken before,
and also of the cxxi. Psalm : " I have lifted up mine eyes
to the hills, &c."][7]

For their lying-in I can say little. I am not skilful
in women's matters, neither is it in the book, no more
is her white sheet, nor her veil : let the women themselves answer these matters.

T. C. Page 119, Line 38.

And, whereas in the 101.[8] and 102. pages, unto the Admonition
objecting that the coming in the veil to the church more then than at other
times is a token of shame, or of some[9] folly committed, M. Doctor
jestingly leaveth the matter to the women's answer ; a little true knowledge
of divinity would have taught him that the bringing in or usurping with-
out authority any ceremony in the congregation is both an earnester matter
than may be jested at, and a weightier than should be permitted unto the

[5 Customs, Adm.]
[6 Lift, Adm.]   [7 This sentence is inserted from Answ.]
[8 In 101, Repl. 1 and 2.]   [9 Or some, Repl. 1 and 2.]

discretion of every woman, considering that the same hath been so horribly abused in the time[1] of popery.

Jo. Whitgift.

The woman's veil a civil custom, not a ceremony of the church.
The answer is fit for so frivolous an objection; and a little true reason void of malicious carping would have taught you that this is rather a civil manner and custom of our country, than a ceremony of the church; and the wearing of new gloves (as many at that time, and especially at the time of marriages do) is as much a ceremony as this; for the wearing of the veil first began of that weakness and sickness that nature in that danger doth bring most women unto, thereby to keep them the more from the air; and therefore (as I have said) in this country it was taken up as a custom of the people, and not as a ceremony of the church. But I perceive you will play small game before you sit out, and pick out very small trifles (though without the book) to brawl and bark at, rather than you would lack matter.

[1 In time, Repl. 1 and 2.]

Of Holy-days.

Tract. x.

Of holy-days in general, that they may be appointed by
the church ; and of the use of them.

Chapter i.   The First Division.

Admonition.

In which a great number of things are contained contrary to the
^m Exod. xx.
9.   *word of God[2], as observing of* ^m *holy-days, &c., patched (if not
altogether, yet the greatest piece) out of the pope's portuis[3].*

Answer to the Admonition, Page 81, Sect. 5, 6.

Fourthly, you mislike observing of holy-days, and Holy-days.
you allege Exod. xx.: " Six days shalt thou labour, and
do all thy work."

To observe any day superstitiously, or to spend any
day unprofitably, is flat against not this commandment
only, but others also in the holy scriptures. And I would
to God it were better looked unto.   But to abstain any Good use of
day from bodily labour, that we may labour spiritually holy-days.
in hearing the word of God, magnifying his name, and
practising the works of charity, is not either against
this, or any other commandment. For I think the meaning of this commandment is not so to tie men to bodily
labour, that they may not intermit the same to labour
spiritually.   For then how could we preachers and students excuse ourselves?   How might the people lawfully come to our sermons and lectures in any of the
six days?   But of this thing also occasion will be ministered to speak more hereafter [in the second part,
where I have spoken of it at large[4]].

T. C. Page 119, Sect. 1.

*The holy-days follow, of which M. Doctor saith that so they be not used
superstitiously or unprofitably they may be commanded.   I have shewed
before that they were.   If they were so indifferent as they are made, yet,
being kept of the papists, which are the enemies of God, they ought to be
abolished.   And, if it were as easy a matter to pull out the superstition of*

[2 Contrary to God's word are contained, Adm. and Answ.]
[3 See before, page 540.]
[4 The words between brackets are added from Answ. 2.]

the observing of those holy-days out of men's hearts, as it is to protest and to teach that they are not commanded for any religion to be put in them, or for any to make conscience of the observing of them, as though there were some necessary worship of God in the keeping of them; then were they much more tolerable; but, when as the continuance of them doth nourish wicked superstition in the minds of men, and that the doctrine which should remedy the superstition, through the fewness and scarcity of able ministers, cannot come to the most part of them which are infected with this disease, and that also where it is preached the fruit thereof is in part hindered, whilst the common people attend oftentimes rather to that which is done than to that which is taught, being a thing indifferent (as it is said), it ought to be abolished, as that which is not only not fittest to hold the people in the sincere worshipping of God, but also as that which keepeth them in their former blindness and corrupt opinions which they have conceived of such holy-days.

Jo. Whitgift.

Profitable things must not be refused for the abuse.

Things that be good and profitable, and have a necessary use, tending to the edifying of the church, and the worshipping of God, are not to be utterly removed for the abuses crept in; but the abuse must be taken away, and the thing still remain. If all things should be abrogated because they were kept of the papists, there would be a marvellous alteration both in the church and in the commonweal. But I have

Tract. VII. cap. 5.

shewed before how far this is from the truth, even in some things invented by popes, much more in such things as were agreed upon in the primitive church (as many of the holy-days were), before the pope's tyranny, though afterwards greatly abused[1].

The use of our holy-days a stop to superstition.

Holy-days, as they be now used, be rather means to withdraw men not only from superstition of the days themselves, but from all other kinds of superstition whatsoever: for then is God in the public congregation truly worshipped, the sacraments rightly ministered, the scriptures and other godly homilies read, the word of God faithfully preached; all which be the chief and principal means to withdraw men, not only from superstition, but all kind of error likewise.

Chapter i.　The Second Division.

T. C. Page 120, Line 2.

And, if they had been never abused neither by the papists nor by the Jews (as they have been and are daily), yet such making of holy-days is

[1 See before, pages 30, &c.]

never without some great danger of bringing in some evil and corrupt opinions into the minds of men.

Jo. Whitgift.

Imaginations and guesses may not go for reasons; and I have shewed before that the holy-days now observed in the church of England be means to root evil and corrupt opinions out of the hearts of men; so far are they from engendering the contrary.

Chapter i. The Third Division.
T. C. Page 120, Line 5.

I will use an example in one, and that the chief of holy-days, and most generally and of longest time observed in the church, which is the feast of Easter, which was kept, of some more days, of some fewer. How many thousands are there, I will not say of the ignorant papists, but of those also which profess the gospel, which, when they have celebrated those days with diligent heed taken unto their life, and with some earnest devotion in praying and hearing the word of God, do not by and by think that they have well celebrated the feast of Easter, and yet have they thus notably deceived themselves. For St Paul teacheth the[2] cele-

1 Cor. v. 8.[3]

brating of the feast of the Christians' Easter is not as the Jews' Easter was, for certain days, but sheweth that we must keep this feast all the days of our life, in "the unleavened bread of sincerity and of truth;" by which we see that the observing of the feast of Easter for certain days in the year doth pull out of our minds, or ever we be aware, the doctrine of the gospel, and causeth us to rest in that near consideration of our duties for the space of a few days, which should be extended to all our life.

Jo. Whitgift.

What? do you condemn the feast of Easter also? would you have it abrogated because it hath been abused? do you not know that the apostles themselves observed it, and the church ever sithence their time? read Eusebius, *Lib. v. cap.* 23, and you shall find it to be a tradition of the apostles; peruse the 24. and 25. chapter of the same book, and you shall understand, by the testimony of Polycrates, and all the other bishops in Asia, that Philip the apostle, John the evangelist, Polycarpus his scholar, and other bishops likewise of greatest antiquity, kept solemnly the feast of Easter[4]. But

The apostles observed Easter.

Euseb. Lib. v. cap. 23, 24, 25.

[2 Teacheth that the, Repl. 2.]
[3 The verse is added from Repl. 2.]
[4 Euseb. in Hist. Eccles. Script. Amst. 1695-1700. Lib. v. capp. xxiii. xxiv. xxv. pp. 154, &c.]

why should I labour to prove that that all histories, all ancient fathers, all late writers, all learned men, confess? and especially seeing that St Augustine, *ad Janu.* 119., saith that the observation of Easter hath "the authority from the scriptures[1];" and seeing also that the same feast with others is allowed by the confession of the churches in Helvetia? The words of which confession be these: "Moreover, if churches, as they may by christian liberty, keep religiously the remembrance of Christ his birth, circumcision, passion, resurrection, ascension into heaven, and sending his Holy Ghost unto his disciples, we well allow it[2]." Therefore I cannot but marvel that you so boldly, without ground, for abuse' sake, condemn even the feast used and allowed by the apostles, and continued in the church without contradiction of any one worthy of credit to this day. Surely you may as well reason that the scriptures are not to be read because that heretics have so greatly abused them.

Confess.
Helve.

The place of St Paul, 1 Cor. v., is nothing to your purpose; for, though he borrow a metaphor of the Jews' passover, to move the Corinthians to pureness and integrity of life, yet doth he not abrogate the feast of Easter; if he had meant any such thing (as he did not), yet must it have been understanded of the Jews' passover, not of celebration of the memory of Christ's resurrection, which we commonly call Easter. Doth he that saith the whole life of a christian man ought to be a perpetual fast deny that there may be any day or time appointed to fast in? A christian man must ever serve God and worship him; shall there not therefore be certain days appointed for the same? This is a very simple argument: St Paul willeth us "to purge out the old leaven, that we may be a new lump, &c.;" also, "to keep the feast, not with old leaven, neither with the leaven of maliciousness, &c.;" therefore we may not celebrate the feast of Easter once a year. I deny this argument.

The observing of Easter doth rather put us in mind of the

[1] Hæc et ex auctoritate divinarum scripturarum, et universæ ecclesiæ...consensione, per anniversarium pascha celebrantur, &c.—August. Op. Par. 1679-1700. Ad Inq. Januar. Lib. ii. seu Epist. lv. 27. Tom. II. col. 138.]

[2] Præterea si ecclesiæ, pro christiana libertate, memoriam dominicæ nativitatis, circumcisionis, passionis et resurrectionis, ascensionis item in cœlum, et missionis sancti Spiritus in discipulos, religiose celebrent, maximopere approbamus. Festa vero hominibus, aut divis instituta, non probamus.—Confess. Fid. Christ. cap. xxiv. in Corp. et Syntag. Confess. Fid. Genev. 1654. p. 54.]

doctrine of the gospel, and draw us to a more near consideration of the benefits that we have received by the death, passion, and resurrection of Christ; and I suppose that there are few godly-disposed Christians that do not think it most convenient and profitable that such feasts especially should be in the church retained; neither is every contentious person's imagination and surmise what may happen to be so greatly regarded, that it should be sufficient to condemn anything that may have a profitable use in the church, by whomsoever it is invented, much less if it hath been used of the apostles themselves, and ever sithence their time continued in the church; as I have shewed this feast to have been. The weakness of man is great; therefore, as he is continually to be taught that he should at all times remember his duty, so is it very necessary to have certain feasts, wherein by the reading and hearing of the scriptures men may be particularly stirred to the remembrance and deep consideration of the principal parts of our religion, and the good and godly examples of the saints of God in doing their duty therein.

Chapter i.   The Fourth Division.

T. C. Page 120, Line 18.

But, besides the incommodities that rise of making such holy-days, and continuing of those which are so horribly abused, where it is confessed that they are not necessary—besides this, I say the matter is not so indifferent as it is made: I confess that it is in the power of the church to appoint so many days in the week or in the year, in the which the congregation shall assemble to hear the word of God and receive the sacraments and offer up prayers unto God, as it shall think good, according to those rules which are before alleged.   But that it hath power to make so many holy-days (as we have), wherein no man may work any part of the day, and wherein men are commanded to cease from their daily vocations of ploughing and exercising their handicrafts, &c., that I deny to be in the power of the church.   For proof whereof I will take the fourth commandment, and no other interpretation of it than M. Doctor alloweth of in the 174. page[3], which is, that God licenseth and leaveth it at the liberty of every man to work six days in the week, so that he rest the seventh day. Seeing that therefore that the Lord hath left it to all men at liberty that they might labour, if they think good, six days; I say, the church, nor no man, can take away this liberty from[4] them, and drive them to a necessary rest of the body.

You draw from the magistrate his lawful authority, and give to the people too much carnal liberty.

[3 See below, page 595.]

[4 Take this liberty away from, Repl. 1 and 2.]

Jo. Whitgift.

The same God that gave that liberty in that commandment did appoint other solemn feast-days besides the sabbath; as the feast of Easter, of Pentecost, of tabernacles, &c.; without any restraint of this liberty. Therefore the interpretation given by me, page 174., of that place doth not leave it to every private man's free liberty, against the authority of the magistrate, or of the church, but it giveth liberty rather to such as be in authority, and to the church, to appoint therein what shall be convenient.

The magistrate hath authority to abridge external liberty.

What liberty cannot be taken away.

The magistrate hath power and authority over his subjects in all external matters, and bodily affairs; wherefore he may call them from bodily labour or compel them unto it, as shall be thought to him most convenient. The liberty that God giveth to man, which no man ought to take from him, nor can if he would, is liberty of conscience, and not of worldly affairs. In bodily business he is to be governed by magistrates and laws. This doctrine of yours is very licentious, and tendeth too much to carnal and corporal liberty, and indeed is a very perilous doctrine for all states. Not one tittle in God's word doth restrain either the magistrate, or the church, from turning carnal liberty to the spiritual service of God, or bodily labour to divine worship, as those do that cause men to abstain from corporal labour, that they may hear the word of God, and worship him in the congregation.

And why may not the church as well restrain them from working any part of the day, as it may do the most part of it? for you " confess that it is in the power of the church to appoint so many days in the week, or in the year, in the which the congregation should assemble to hear the word of God and receive the sacraments, and offer up prayers unto God, as it shall think good, according to those rules which are before alleged;" and this it cannot do, unless in the same days during all that time (which is no small portion of the day) it restrain them from bodily labour.

Wherefore, this being no commandment, that they shall labour six days in the week, but a signification that so many days they may labour; as the same God that gave this commandment hath done before in the old law, so may the churches likewise, for the increase of godliness and virtue, and edification, appoint some of those six days to be bestowed in prayers, hearing the word, administration of the sacraments, and other holy actions.

Chapter i.   The Fifth Division.

T. C. Page 120, about the midst.

And, if it be lawful to abridge the liberty of the church in this point, and, instead that the Lord saith, " Six days thou mayest labour," if thou wilt, to say, Thou shalt not labour six days; I do not see why the church may not as well, where as the Lord saith, " Thou shalt rest the seventh day," command that thou shalt not rest the seventh day; for, if the church may restrain the liberty that God hath given them, it may take away the yoke also that God hath put upon them.

Jo. Whitgift.

The church is not abridged of her liberty in this point, but useth her liberty in appointing some of these days to the worshipping of God, and the instruction of his people; which should not be counted a bondage or servitude to any man.

To rest the seventh day is commanded; to labour six days is but permitted[1]; he that forbiddeth rest on the seventh day doth directly against the commandment; so doth not he that restraineth men from bodily labour in any of the six days; and therefore the reason is not like.   And yet the commandment of bodily rest upon the seventh day in sundry cases may of a man's self, much more at a lawful commandment of a magistrate, in necessity be broken.

In things indifferent private men's wills are subject to such as have authority over them; therefore they ought to consent to their determination in such matters, except they will shew themselves to be wilful; which is a great fault, and deserveth much punishment.

But hitherto you have not replied to any Answer made to the Admonition.

[1 " ... his answer that the ' one is a commandment, the other a permission,' is nothing worth. For, as the commandment of resting the seventh day must, because of God's authority, abide in the nature of a commandment; so the permission to work the six days, warranted by the same authority, must abide in the nature of a permission."—The Rest of Sec. Repl. p. 193.]

Chapter i.   The Sixth Division.

Answer to the Admonition, Page 173, in the latter end.

This is no restraint for any man from serving of God any day in the week else. For the Jews had divers other feasts which they by God's appointment observed, notwithstanding these words: "Six days &c."

T. C. Page 120, Sect. 1.

And, where as you say, in the 173. page, that, notwithstanding this fourth commandment, the Jews had certain other feasts which they observed; indeed the Lord which gave this general law might make as many exceptions as he thought good, and so long as he thought good; but it followeth not because the Lord did it that therefore the church may do it, unless it hath commandment and authority from God so to do. As when there is any general plague or judgment of God, either upon the church, or coming towards it, the Lord commandeth in such a case that they should sanctify a general fast, and proclaim ghnatsarah, *which signifieth a prohibition or forbidding of ordinary works,* Joel ii. 15.[1] *and is the same Hebrew word wherewith those feast-days are noted in the law wherein they should rest; the reason of which commandment of the Lord was that, as they abstained that day as much as might be conveniently from meat, so they might abstain from their daily works, to the end they might bestow the whole day in hearing the word of God, and humbling themselves in the congregation, confessing their faults, and desiring the Lord to turn away from his fierce wrath. In this case, the church, having commandment to make a holy-day, may and ought to do it; as the church which was in Babylon did during the time of their captivity. But, where it is destitute of a commandment, it may not presume by any decree to restrain that liberty which the Lord hath given.*

JO. WHITGIFT.

When you are convinced by manifest scripture, as you are in this matter, then you fly to your newly-devised distinctions, as you do in this place, saying; "The Lord which gave this general law might make as many exceptions as he thought good;" but to no purpose; for you cannot shew in the whole scripture where God hath made any law or ordinance against his own commandment[2]. And surely in this point you have

---

[1 The verse is added from Repl. 2.]

[2 "His fear, that God 'should be thus contrary to himself,' is causeless: no more than the father is to be holden unconstant, which, when his son cometh to man's estate, freeth him of the obedience unto his servant, under which he cast him in his tender years; or than the physician, which, according to the state of the patient's body, prescribeth not only a divers, but a quite contrary diet."—The Rest of Sec. Repl. p. 190.]

greatly overshot yourself, being content rather to grant contrariety to be in the scripture, than to yield to a manifest and known truth. The church, in appointing holy-days, doth follow the example of God himself, and therefore hath sufficient ground and warrant for her doings; and of the authority of the church in such matters I have spoken in another place[3]; Tract. II. and I have also a little before declared what kind of liberty the church may not restrain; and I add that every private man's consent is in the consent of the church, as it is in the consent of the parliament; and therefore no man's liberty No man's liberty restrained. otherwise restrained than he hath consented unto.

That in the second of the prophet Joel maketh against The Replier bringeth authority against himself. you directly; for it sheweth that upon just occasion the church may inhibit men from labour even in the six days, notwithstanding it be said: "Six days thou shalt labour, &c." And to the intent no man should doubt of the liberty of the church herein, or of the practice of this liberty, let the ninth chapter of Esther be perused, and therein it will appear that, in remembrance of their great delivery from the treason of The Jews appointed to themselves holy-days. Haman, the Jews, by the commandment of Mordecai, did solemnize and keep holy-day the fourteenth and fifteenth day of the month Ader, every year. But, if neither the ordinances of God himself, nor the words of his prophets, nor the examples of his apostles, nor the practice of his church from the beginning, will take any place with you, you are no man for me to deal with.

¶ Of saints' days.

Chapter ii.   The First Division.

T. C. Page 120, Sect. ult.

Now that I have spoken generally of holy-days, I come unto the apostles' and other saints' days, which are kept with us. And, though it were lawful for the church to ordain holy-days to our Saviour Christ, or to the blessed Trinity, yet it is not therefore lawful to institute holy-days to the apostles and other saints, or to their remembrance. For, although I confess as much as you say in the 153. page, that the church of England doth not mean by this keeping of holy-days that the saints should be honoured, or, as you allege in 175.[4] and 176. pages[5], that with us the saints are not prayed unto, or that it doth propound them as meritorious, yet that is not enough. For, as we reason against the popish purgatory,

[3 See Vol. I. pages 175, &c.]   [4 In the 175, Repl. 1 and 2.]
[5 See below, pages 592, 5.]

Saints'
days.

Argum. ab
authoritate
negative.

*that it is therefore naught, forasmuch as, neither in the old testament, nor
in the new, there is any mention of prayer at any time for the dead, so
may it be reasoned against these holy-days ordained for the remembrance
of the saints that, forsomuch as the old people did never keep any feast or
holy-day for the remembrance either of Moses, or Daniel, or Job, or Abraham, or David, or any other, how holy or excellent soever they were; nor the
apostles, nor the churches in their time, never instituted any, either to keep
the remembrance of Stephen, or of the Virgin Mary, or of John Baptist,
or of any other notable and rare personage, that the instituting and
erecting of them now, and this attempt by the churches which followed,
which have not such certain and undoubted interpreters of the will of God,
as the prophets and apostles were which lived in those churches, is not
without some note of presumption; for that it undertaketh those things
which the primitive church in the apostles' times (having greater gifts of
the Spirit of God than they that followed them had) durst not venture
upon.*

Jo. Whitgift.

"Purgatory" is made a matter of salvation or damnation,
as all other doctrines of the pope's be; and therefore a negative reason (such as you use) is sufficient enough to improve
it. But holy-days in our church have no such necessity ascribed
unto them, only they are thought very profitable to the edifying of God's people; and therefore such negative reasons prevail not against them; no more than they do against other
constitutions of the church pertaining to edifying, order, or
comeliness, whereof there is no mention made in the word of
God. And therefore nothing that is here spoken by you can
take any hold.

Chapter ii.   The Second Division.

Answer to the Admonition, Page 175, Sect. 1.

Why the
name of
saints are
given to our
holy-days[1].

Neither are they called by the name of any saint in
any other respect than that the scriptures which that
day are read in the church be concerning that saint,
and contain either his calling, preaching, persecution,
martyrdom, or such like[2].

T. C. Page 121, Sect. 1.

Moreover, I have shewed before what force the name of everything

[1 This marginal note is not in Answ.]

[2 This paragraph follows at some interval that in page 572. In fact, Cartwright, as Whitgift complains just afterwards, has so "dismembered" the
Answer, that it is perplexing, and of little use, to note all the variations from the
original order.]

hath, to cause men to think so of everything as it is named ; and therefore, Saints'
although you say in the 175. page that, in calling these holy-days the days days.
of such or such a saint, there is nothing else meant but that " the scrip-
tures which are that day read concern that saint, and contain either his
calling, preaching, persecution, martyrdom, &c. ;" yet every one doth not
understand so much.   For, besides that the corrupt custom of popery hath
carried their minds to another interpretation, the very name and appella-
tion of the day teacheth otherwise.   For, seeing that by the[3] *days dedicated*
to the Trinity, and those that are consecrate to our Saviour Christ, are, in
that they be called Trinity day, or the Nativity day of our Saviour Christ,
by and by taken to be instituted to the honour of our Saviour Christ, and of
the Trinity, so likewise the people, when it is called St Paul's day, or
the blessed Virgin Mary's day, can understand nothing thereby, but
that they are instituted to the honour of St Paul, or of the Virgin
Mary, unless they be otherwise taught.   And, if you say, let them so
be taught, I have answered that the teaching in this land cannot by
any order which is yet taken come to the most part of those which have
drunk this poison; and, where it is taught, yet were it good[4] *that the names*
were abolished, that they should not help to unteach that which the
preaching teacheth in this behalf.

Jo. Whitgift.

You have so dismembered my book, in taking here a piece, and there a piece, to answer as it pleaseth you, and in leaving out what you list, that you rather make a new discourse of your own, than a reply to any thing that I have set down.

Touching the names of the holy-days (which you mislike), I have told the cause why they be so called, which cause you cannot improve, and therefore you fall again to your accustomed conjectures and suppositions, which are but very simple and slender arguments.   What if " every one doth not understand so much ?" must the church alter her decrees and orders for every particular man's abusing or not understanding them ? He that is most ignorant may learn and know why they be so called, if he be disposed : if he be not, the fault is his own; the name of the day is not the worse to be liked.   You might much better reason against the names of Sunday, Monday, and Saturday, which be heathenish and profane names[5]; yet I

[3 That the, Repl. 2.]   [4 Taught it were good, Repl. 2.]

[5 " ... our people hath not been nusled up in that filth of worshipping the sun and moon, as they have been of the saints : insomuch as (the learned set apart) there are few, which know that there were ever any days observed in the honour of the sun or moon. If they had been so nusled, who seeth not but that it had been most convenient, for the rooting out of that idolatry, to have made a change of these names?"— The Rest of Sec. Repl. p. 195.]

suppose that there is no man so mad as to think that those days be instituted and used of Christians to the honour of the sun, of the moon, and of Saturn[1]. This is but to play the part of a quarreller (as I have sundry times told you), to cavil at the name, when you cannot reprove the matter. Those days be rather retained in the church to root out such superstitious opinions, by the preaching of the word, and the reading of the scriptures; neither can any man that understandeth English, and frequenteth the common and public prayers in those holy-days (except he be wilful), be so affected as you seem to suspect.

Trinity Sunday, the Nativity of our Saviour Christ, and such like, although we honour the Trinity, and our Saviour Christ in them, as we do in all other, yet have they their names especially, because the scriptures then read in the church concern the Trinity and the Nativity of our Saviour Christ. Augustine, *ad Januar.* 119., saith thus of the day of the Nativity of Christ: "Here first it behoveth that thou know the day of the nativity of the Lord not to be celebrated in a sacrament or figure, but only that it is called back into remembrance that he is born; and for this there needeth nothing but that the day yearly be signified by solemn devotion wherein the thing was done[2]."

There is no place in this land so destitute of instructions, either by preaching or reading, that any man can justly plead ignorance in such matters. And therefore, seeing you have no other arguments against holy-days but conjectures and surmises, and they false and untrue, or at the least not sufficient to alter a profitable order in the church, holy-days may still remain and stand in their former force and strength.

[1 "And here it is to be noted that the D. is taken in his own nets. For he defendeth the keeping holy of these saints' days, as they were used in the elder churches, and as Jerome and Augustine maintain them. Now himself hath for his defence alleged out of Jerome, that these days are 'observed to the martyrs;' and out of Augustine, that in them 'we honour the memories of martyrs' [See below, pages 579, 80]. Therefore his escape, that 'no man is so mad' as to think that 'by these days we do any honour unto the saints,' is not only an open untruth, but directly contrary to that himself maintaineth."—Ibid. p. 196.]

[2 Hic primum oportet noveris diem natalem Domini non in sacramento celebrari, sed tantum in memoriam revocari quod natus sit, ac per hoc nihil opus erat, nisi revolutum anni diem, quo ipsa res acta est, festa devotione signari.—August. Op. Par. 1679-1700. Ad Inq. Januar. Lib. II. seu Epist. lv. cap. i. 2. Tom. II. col. 128.]

Chapter ii.   The Third Division.

T. C. Page 121, Sect. 2.

*Furthermore, seeing the holy-days be ceremonies of the church, I see
not why we may not here renew Augustine's complaint, that the estate of
the Jews was more tolerable than ours is* [3] *(I speak in this point of holy-
days) ; for, if their holy-days and ours be accounted, we shall be found to
have more than double as many holy-days as they had. And, as for all the
commodities which we receive by them, whereby M. Doctor goeth about to
prove the goodness and lawfulness of their institution, as that the scriptures
are there read and expounded, the patience of those saints in their persecution and martyrdom is to the edifying of the church remembered and
yearly renewed—I say that we might have all those commodities without
all those dangers which I have spoken of, and without any keeping of
yearly memory of those saints, and as it falleth out in better and more
profitable sort. For, as I said before of the keeping of Easter, that it
tieth and (as it were) fettereth a meditation of the Easter to a few days,
which should reach to all our age and time of our life ; so those celebra-
tions of the memories of saints and martyrs straiten our consideration
of them unto those days, which should continually be thought of, and daily
as long as we live. And, if that it be thought so good and profitable a
thing that this remembrance of them should be upon those days wherein
they are supposed to have died, yet it followeth not therefore that, after this
remembrance is celebrated by hearing the scriptures concerning them, and
prayers made to follow their constancy, that all the rest of the day
should be kept holy in such sort as men should be debarred of their
bodily labours and of exercising their daily vocations.*

*It will be
found other-
wise.*

*Very ab-
surdly.*

Jo. Whitgift.

Augustine speaketh not of holy-days in that place, but of
other unprofitable ceremonies used in particular churches,
neither grounded of the scriptures, determined by councils,
nor confirmed by the custom of the whole church. But the
holy-days that we retain, being not only confirmed by the
custom of the whole church, but also profitable for the instruction of the people, and used for public prayer, administration of the sacraments, and preaching the word, cannot
be called burdens, except it be a burden to serve God in
praying, in celebrating his sacraments, and in hearing his
word.

Epist. ad Ja.
119.

[3 ... ipsam tamen religionem...servilibus oneribus premunt, ut tolerabilior
sit conditio Judæorum, qui etiamsi tempus libertatis non agnoverunt, legalibus
tamen sarcinis, non humanis præsumtionibus subjiciuntur.—Id. ibid. cap. xix.
35. col. 142.]

And, whereas you say that, "if their holy-days and ours
be accounted, we shall be found to have more than double as
many holy-days as they had," you speak that which you
are not able to justify.   In the xxiii. of Leviticus there is appointed unto the Jews the feast of Easter; the feast of unleavened bread; the feast of first-fruits; Whitsuntide; the
feast of trumpets; the feast of reconciliation; and the feast of
tabernacles; whereof the feast of unleavened bread and the
feast of tabernacles had each of them seven days annexed
unto them.   And, if you will add these, Judith's feast, chap.
xvi.; the Maccabees' feast, 1 Macca. iv., which continued eight
days together; and Hester's feast, chap. ix., which continued
two days, you shall find that our holy-days be somewhat
short in number of theirs: so far are we from having "more
than double as many as they had."   But your spirit is acquainted with such untrue assertions.

But you say, "we might have all these commodities
without all those dangers, &c.;" and why not as well this
way which the whole church hath from time to time allowed,
as that way which certain particular persons of their own
heads have devised?   There is nothing that you have to say
against these days, but only their names, and that "those
memories of martyrs straiten our consideration of them
unto those days, &c.," and that "men be inhibited from
bodily labour" to serve God; all which I have answered
before, and the latter in part you confess; for you would
have certain days appointed for public prayer, the celebration
of the sacraments and hearing the word, and you seem not
to deny but that the remembrance of saints and martyrs may
be kept, only you mislike that "in the rest of the day men
should be debarred from their bodily labours, and exercising
their daily vocations."   Well, I perceive that something you
would find fault with if you knew what.   They are not so
bound from labour (as it appeareth in the laws of this church)
but that they may do their necessary business; and indeed
they are so far from scrupulosity in this point, that all the
punishments appointed cannot keep a number of them from
their worldly affairs, not in the very time of public prayers
and preaching of the word; and yet I see no cause why they
may not justly be wholly debarred (except some urgent
occasion require sometime the contrary) from their bodily

labours in such days; for are not the householders bound of Saints'
duty as well to instruct their families, as the pastor is bound days.
to instruct them? and when is there a more convenient time
than in such days? If you have such a regard to their
worldly affairs, is it not more commodious for them to abstain
wholly from work upon these holy-days, when they fall, than
twice or thrice every week half the day? Therefore this
reason of yours as it is worldly, so is it weak, both in the
respect of God, and of the world also.

Your imagination that "the keeping of Easter doth fetter A vain rea-
the meditation of Easter to a few days, &c.," and so likewise son.
the rest of the holy-days, I have answered before: it is a most
vain reason, and you might as well say that there ought to
be no certain times appointed for the receiving of the holy
communion, because the meditation of the death and passion
of Christ, and the application of the same, is fettered to
these certain days, which should continually be thought of,
and daily as long as we live. The same might you say
likewise of the sabbath-day. But you ought to know that
the especial celebrating of the memory of Christ's resurrection
once in the year is no more a fettering of our meditation
thereof to that day only, than the receiving of the communion
once in the month is a straiting of our consideration of
the death and passion of Christ to that time only wherein
we receive the holy sacrament. By this reason of yours we
must either have such memories celebrated at all times, or at
no time. But wise men can consider how far you wander
for want of reason.

Chapter ii.   The Fourth Division.

Answer to the Admonition, Page 176, Sect. 3, 4, 5.

Jerome, writing upon the iv. chap. to the Gala-
tians, saith on this sort: "If it be not lawful to observe Jerome.
days, months, times, and years, we also fall into the like
fault which observe the passion of Christ, the sabbath-
day, and the time of Lent, the feasts of Easter and of
Pentecost, and other times appointed to martyrs, according to the manner and custom of every nation; to the
which he that will answer simply will say that our observing of days is not the same with the Jewish observ-

ing; for we do not celebrate the feast of unleavened
bread[1], but of the resurrection and death of Christ.
&c.   And, lest the confused gathering together of the
people should diminish the faith in Christ, therefore
certain days are appointed that we might all meet together in one place, not because those days be more
holy, but to the intent that in what day soever we meet
we may rejoice to see one another. &c.[2]"

Augustine in like manner, *Lib. xviii. de Civitate Dei,*

Augustine.   *cap.* 27, saith that "we honour the memories of martyrs as of holy men, and such as have striven for the
truth, even to death, &c.[3]"

The same Augustine, in his book *contra Adamantum
Manichæi Discip. cap.* 16, expounding the words of the
apostle, "Ye observe days, years, and times," writeth

Idem[4].   thus: "But one may think that he speaketh of the sabbath: do not we say that those times ought not to be
observed, but the things rather that are signified by
them? for they did observe them servilely, not understanding what they did signify and prefigurate: this is

Paul ex-   that that the apostle reproveth in them, and in all those
pounded[5].   that serve the creature rather than the Creator; for we
also solemnly celebrate the sabbath-day, and Easter,
and all other festival days of Christians; but, because we
understand whereunto they do appertain, we observe

[1 Unleavened or sweet bread, Answ.]

[2 Dicat aliquis: Si dies observare non licet, et menses, et tempora, et annos,
nos quoque simile crimen incurrimus quartam sabbathi observantes; et parasceven;
et diem dominicam; et jejunium quadragesimæ; et paschæ festivitatem; et pen-
tecostes lætitiam: et pro varietate regionum, diversa in honore martyrum tempora
constituta. Ad quod qui simpliciter respondebit, dicet: non eosdem Judaicæ
observationis dies esse quos nostros. Nos enim non azymorum pascha celebramus,
sed resurrectionis et crucis. &c. Et ne inordinata congregatio populi fidem mi-
nueret in Christo, propterea dies aliqui constituti sunt; ut in unum omnes pariter
veniremus. Non quo celebrior sit dies illa qua convenimus: sed quo quaquumque
die conveniendum sit, ex conspectu mutuo, lætitia major oriatur.—Hieron. Op.
Par. 1693-1706. Comm. Lib. ii. in Epist. ad Galat. cap. iv. Tom. IV. Pars i.
col. 271.]

[3 Honoramus sane memorias eorum [martyrum] tamquam sanctorum hominum Dei, qui usque ad mortem corporum suorum pro veritate certarunt, &c.—
August. Op. Par. 1679-1700. De Civ. Dei, Lib. viii. cap. xxvii. 1. Tom. VII.
col. 217.]

[4 *Idem* is not in Answ.; but instead *Gal. iv.* 10.]

[5 This is inserted from Answ. 2.]

not the times, but those things which are signified by
the times[6]. &c.[7]

T. C. Page 122, Sect. 1.

*Now, whereas M. Doctor citeth Augustine and Jerome to prove that in
the churches in their times there were holy-days kept besides the Lord's day,
he might have also cited Ignatius, and Tertullian, and Cyprian, which
are of greater anciency[8], and would have made more for the credit of his
cause, seeing he measureth all his truth almost through the whole book
by the crooked measure and yard of time. For it is not to be denied
but this keeping of holy-days (especially of the Easter and Pentecost) are very ancient, and that these holy-days for the remembrance of
martyrs were used of long time. But these abuses were no ancienter
than other were, grosser also than this was; as I have before declared,
and were easy further to be shewed if need required. And therefore
I appeal from these examples to the scriptures, and to the examples of*
the perfectest church that ever was, which was that in the apostles' times.

An un-
learned shift.

Jo. Whitgift.

I know that I might have alleged many other authorities
for the proof of this matter, but I thought these two sufficient
(as they be indeed) in such a matter as this is; and your
lightly rejecting of them will win no credit to your cause
among wise and learned men. You may easily perceive by
the words of both these authors that these days in their time
were rightly and without all superstition used. But you do
well to appeal from these examples and from all other ancient
authority of learned men; for you know full well your lack
of ability to maintain this and other your opinions by the testimonies of ancient writers: nay, you cannot but confess that
the old learned fathers are utterly against you, which is the
cause why you appeal from them; but it is an unlearned
shift[9].

The Replier
appealeth
from ancient
authority.

[6 Time, Answ. 2.]

[7 Sed putat esse de sabbato dictum? Numquid et nos non dicimus ista non
esse observanda, sed illa potius quæ his significantur? Illi enim ea serviliter
observabant, non intelligentes ad quarum rerum significationem et prænuntia-
tionem pertinerent. Hoc in eis culpat apostolus, et in omnibus qui serviunt
creaturæ potius quam Creatori. Nam nos quoque et dominicum diem et pascha
sollemniter celebramus, et quaslibet alias christianas dierum festivitates. Sed
quia intelligimus quo pertineant, non tempora observamus, sed quæ illis significantur temporibus. &c.—Id. Lib. contr. Adimant. Manich. cap. xvi. 3. Tom. VIII.
col. 135.]

[8 Anciency, Repl. 1 and 2.]

[9 "In the next division there is nothing but a manifest pillar of popery, with
shameful outrage unto the Holy Ghost; in that he calleth the appeal to the

Saints' days.

Chapter ii.　The Fifth Division.

T. C. Page 122, Sect. 1.

And yet also I have to say that the observation of those feasts first of all was much better than of later times.　For Socrates, con- Lib. v. cap. *fessing that "neither our Saviour Christ, nor the apostles, did* 22. *decree or institute any holy-days, or lay any yoke of bondage upon the necks of those which came to the preaching," addeth, further,* Socrates' words un- truly re- ported. *that "they did use first to observe the holy-days by custom, and that as every man was disposed at home;" which thing if it had remained in that freedom, that it was done by custom, and not by commandment, at the will of every one, and not by constraint, it had been much better than it is now, and had not drawn such dangers upon the posterity as did after ensue and we have the experience of.*

Jo. Whitgift.

Surely they were never better, nor more pure from all superstition and other errors than they be now in this church; and therefore in that respect there is no cause to complain.

You do not truly report Socrates' words, nor yet his meaning; for he doth not say that " every man at home kept Socrat. Lib. v. cap. 22. those days as he was disposed;" but thus he saith : " Wherefore neither the apostle, nor the gospel, do at any time lay a yoke of bondage upon them which come unto the preaching of the gospel ; but men themselves every one in their country, according as they thought good, celebrated the feast of Easter, and other holy-days of custom, for the intermission of their labours and remembrance of the healthful passion[1] :" his meaning is not that every private man in his own house kept Easter, and the other feasts, as him listed, but that every church appointed such an order and time for the same as it thought convenient ; and that this is his meaning, that which followeth in that chapter, and expresseth his own opinion of this matter, doth evidently declare.　His words be these :

scriptures and example of the apostles, from certain customs of the churches, which were more than a hundred years after Christ, ' an unlearned shift.' "—The Rest of Sec. Repl. pp. 197, 8.]

[1 ... οὐδαμοῦ τοίνυν ὁ ἀπόστολος, οὐδὲ τὰ εὐαγγέλια, ζυγὸν δουλείας τοῖς τῷ κηρύγματι προσελθοῦσιν ἐπέθηκαν....ὅθεν ἐπειδὴ φιλοῦσι τὰς ἑορτὰς οἱ ἄνθρωποι, διὰ τὸ ἀνίεσθαι τῶν πόνων ἐν αὐταῖς, ἕκαστοι κατὰ χώρας ὡς ἐβουλήθησαν, τὴν μνήμην τοῦ σωτηριώδους πάθους ἐξ ἔθους τινὸς ἐπετέλεσαν· οὐ γὰρ νόμῳ τοῦτο παραφυλάττειν ὁ Σωτήρ, ἢ οἱ ἀπόστολοι ἡμῖν παρήγγειλαν.—Socr. in Hist. Eccles. Script. Amst. 1695-1700. Lib. v. cap. xxii. p. 232.]

" Surely I am of this opinion, that, as many other things in Saints' days. divers places have been brought in of custom, so the feast of Easter had a private or peculiar observation with every particular people of custom; because none of the apostles (as I have said) did make any law hereof: &c.[2]"   For his whole drift is to prove that the feast of Easter, concerning the day and time, was diversly observed in divers churches and countries; but he neither can prove, nor goeth about to prove, that there was any church wherein it was not observed. And I have before declared that the feast of Easter was observed by the apostles, and sithence that time continued.

Chapter ii.   The Sixth Division.

Answer to the Admonition, Page 177, Sect. 1; and Page 178, Sect. 1, &c.

Other reformed churches also have days ascribed to saints as well as we; as it may appear by these words of Bullinger writing upon the xiv. to the Rom.: " In the Bullinger. ancient writers, as Eusebius and Augustine, thou mayest find certain memorials appointed to certain holy men, but after another manner, not much differing from ours Observing of holy-days in other reformed churches. which we as yet retain in our church of Tigurie; for we celebrate the nativity of Christ, his circumcision, resurrection, and ascension, the coming of the Holy Ghost, the feasts also of the Virgin Mary, John Baptist, Magdalene, Stephen, and the other apostles; yet not condemning those which observe none, but only the sabbath-day. For, perusing old monuments, we find that this hath always been left free to the churches, that every one should follow that in these things that should be best and most [3]convenient[4]."

[2 'Εμοὶ δὲ φαίνεται, ὅτι ὥσπερ ἄλλα πολλὰ κατὰ χώρας συνήθειαν ἔλαβεν, οὕτω καὶ ἡ τοῦ πάσχα ἑορτὴ παρ' ἑκάστοις ἐκ συνηθείας τινὸς, ἰδιάζουσαν ἔσχε τὴν παρατήρησιν, διὰ τὸν μηδένα τῶν ἀποστόλων, ὡς ἔφην, μηδενὶ νενομοθετηκέναι περὶ αὐτῆς· κ. τ. λ.—Id. ibid.]

[3 Most best and convenient, Def. A. and B.]

[4 Apud veteres quidem, Eusebium in primis et Augustinum, invenias memorias quasdam piis quibusdam institutas fuisse hominibus, sed longe alia ratione ac modo, nimirum parum differente a nostro ritu, quo adhuc in ecclesia nostra Tigurina, nativitatis, circumcisionis, resurrectionis et ascensionis Domini, missionisque sancti Spiritus, deiparæ virginis, Joannis Baptistæ, Magdalenæ, Stephani,

M. Bucer, in his epistle to Master Alasco, speaking of holy-days, saith that " in the scriptures there is no express commandment of them : it is gathered notwithstanding," saith he, " from the example of the old people, that they are profitable for us, to the increase of godliness ; which thing also experience proveth[2]."

To be short, Illyricus, writing upon the fourth to the Galat., maketh this division of observing days and times :

1.   " The first is natural ; as of summer, spring-time, winter, &c., time of planting, time of sowing, time of reaping, &c.

2.   The second is civil.

3.   The third, ecclesiastical ; as the sabbath-day, and other days, wherein is celebrated the memory of the chief histories or acts of Christ, which be profitable for the instruction of the simple, that they may the better remember when the Lord was born, when he suffered, when he ascended up into heaven, and be further taught in the same.

4.   The fourth, superstitious ; when we put a necessity, worshipping, merit, or righteousness, in the observing of time ; and this kind of observing days and times is only forbidden in this place[3]."

Thus you see, by the judgments of all these learned

---

et apostolorum Domini festa celebramus, neminem interim eorum damnantes, qui post dominicam, aliam nesciunt festivitatem.   Videmus enim veterum monumenta perlustrantes liberum hoc ecclesiis semper fuisse, ut quæque quod hisce in rebus minutilis videretur optimum et ad pietatem conservandam commodissimum, sequeretur.—H. Bullinger. Comm. in Omn. Apost. Epist. Tigur. 1539. In Rom. cap. xiv. p. 108.]

[1 Bucer's opinion also, Answ. 2.]

[2 For there is no express commandment by word in the holy scriptures of these things [churches and holy-days] : it is gathered &c.—Bucer to Alasco at the end of A briefe examination for the tyme, &c. Lond. Jugge. fol. D 1.]

[3 Est vero quadruplex observatio temporum, physica, civilis, ecclesiastica, et superstitiosa.   Physica ut æstatis, veris, hyemis, &c. cum qua sunt conjuncti motus stellarum : quæ est necessaria ad multa rustica, politica et œconomica,... ecclesiastica, quæ etiam decoro et bono ordini servit, quo facit quoque dies dominica et tempora præcipuarum historiarum, aut factorum Christi, quæ prosunt ad ædificationem rudium, ut rectius meminerint, quando sit Dominus natus, passus, et quando in cœlum ascenderit, ac de singulis illis historiis suo tempore tanto commodius instituantur,...Postrema est superstitiosa, cum ponimus necessitatem, cultum, meritum, aut justitiam in observatione temporum :...Hanc ultimam ac superstitiosam damnat hic apostolus, non illas tres priores.—Nov. Test. cum Gloss. Comp. M. Flac. Illyr. Basil. 1570. Galat. cap. iv. p. 899.]

men, that days ascribed unto[4] saints is no such matter Saints' days. as ought to make men separate themselves from the church, and abstain from allowing by subscription so worthy and godly a book as the book of common prayer is, much less to make a schism in the church for the same.

T. C. Page 122, Sect. 2 and 3.

As touching M. Bucer's, M. Bullinger's, and Illyricus' allowance of them, if they mean such a celebration of them as that in those days the people may be assembled, and those parts of the scriptures, which concern them whose remembrance is solemnized, read and expounded, and yet men not debarred after from their daily works, it is so much the less matter; if otherwise, that good leave they give the churches to dissent from them in that point, I do take it granted unto me, being, by the grace of God, one of the church.

Although as touching M. Bullinger, it is to be observed, since the time that he wrote that upon the Romans, there are about 35. years, sithence which time, although he hold still that the feasts kept[5] unto the Lord, Confessio Ecclesiæ Tigur. et aliarum Eccles. cap. 24. *as of the Nativity, Easter, and Pentecost, dedicated unto the Lord may be kept, yet he denieth flatly that it is lawful to keep holy the days of the apostles; as it appeareth in the confession of the Tigurine church joined with others[6].*

JO. WHITGIFT.

How perfect an answer this is to these learned men's authorities, let the learned reader judge. You are not a church, but a member of the church; and therefore, seeing the matter is such as the church may take an order in, you ought to submit yourself to the determination of that church in such matters, whereof you are a member.

What M. Bullinger hath in any other place consented unto I know not, but certain it is that these be his own words, and that when he writ them he was of the same opinion that we are at this time in this church of England[7].

[4 To, Answ.]

[5 Dedicated, Repl. 2; which omits *dedicated unto the Lord* in the next lines.]

[6 Confess. Fid. Christ. cap. xxiv. in Corp. et Syntag. Confess. Fid. Genev. 1654. p. 54. See before, page 568, note 2.]

[7 Cartwright rejoins: "if the learned reader look the later edition of M. Bullinger's commentary upon the Romans, he may, peradventure, find his former judgment alleged by the D. corrected." He goes on to cite Musculus and bishop Hooper as decidedly condemning saints' days [Conf. Wolfg. Muscul. Loc. Comm. Theolog. Basil. 1599. De Præc. Decalog. Præc. iv. p. 75; Bp. Hooper's Works, Park. Soc. Edit. Declarat. of Commandments, Comm. iv. Vol. I. p. 347].—The Rest of Sec. Repl. pp. 198, 9.]

Chapter ii.   The Seventh Division.

Answer to the Admonition, Page 177, Sect. 2.

Calvin[1].

Calvin, in like manner writing upon the fourth to the Galatians, doth not disallow this kind of observing days: his words be these: "When as holiness is attributed to days, when as one day is discerned from another for religion' sake, when days are made a piece of divine worship, then days are wickedly observed. &c. But, when we have a difference of days, laying no burden of necessity on men's consciences, we make no difference of days, as though one were more holy than another, we put no religion in them, nor worshipping of God, but only we observe them for order and concord' sake; so that the observing of days with us is free, and without all superstition[2]." And again upon the ii. to the Coloss.: "But some will say that we as yet have some kind of observing days: I answer that we observe them not as though there were any religion in them, or as though it were not then lawful to labour, but we have a respect of policy and orders, not of days[3]." And in his Institutions, upon the fourth commandment: "Neither do I so speak of the seventh day, that I would bind the church only unto it; for I do not condemn those churches which have other solemn days to meet in; so that they be void of superstition, which shall be if they be ordained only for the observing of discipline and order[4]."

[1 Calvin's opinion thereof, Answ. 2.]

[2 Quando itaque diebus per se tribuitur propria sanctitas, quando discernitur dies a die religionis causa, quando feriæ pars divini cultus esse censentur : tum dies perperam observantur. &c. nos hodie quum habemus dierum discrimen, non induimus necessitatis laqueum conscientiis, non discernimus dies, quasi alius alio sit sanctior, non constituimus illic religionem et cultum Dei : sed tantum ordini et concordiæ consulimus. Ita libera est apud nos, et omni superstitione pura observatio.—Calvin. Op. Amst. 1667-71. Comm. in Epist. ad Galat. cap. iv. 10. Tom. VII. p. 303.]

[3 Atqui, dicet quispiam, nos adhuc retinemus aliquam dierum observationem. Respondeo, nos dies nequaquam servare, quasi in feriis aliqua sit religio, aut quasi fas non sit tunc laborare : sed respectum haberi politiæ et ordinis, non dierum.— Id. Comm. in Epist. ad Coloss. cap. ii. 16. pp. 395, 6.]

[4 Neque sic tamen septenarium numerum moror, ut ejus servituti ecclesiam astringam : neque enim ecclesias damnavero, quæ alios conventibus suis solennes dies habeant, modo a superstitione absint. Quod erit, si ad solam observationem disciplinæ et ordinis bene compositi referantur.—Id. Inst. Lib. ii. cap. viii. 34. Præcept. Quart. Tom. IX. p. 100.]

T. C. Page 122, Sect. 4.

*As for M. Calvin, as the practice of him and the church where he
lived, was and is, to admit no one holy-day besides the Lord's day, so can
it not be shewed out of any part of his works (as I think) that he
approved those holy-days which are now in question. He saith, indeed, in
his Institution, that he will not condemn those churches which use them;
no more do we the church of England, neither in this nor in other things
which are meet to be reformed. For it is one thing to mislike, another
thing to condemn; and it is one thing to condemn something in the
church, and another to condemn[5] the church for it. And as for the
places cited out of the epistle[6] to the Galatians and Colossians, there is
no mention of any holy-days either to saints, or to any other, and it
appeareth also that he defendeth not other churches but the church of
Geneva, and answereth not to those which object against keeping[7] of
saints' days or any holy-days (as they are called) besides the Lord's day,
but against those which would not have the Lord's day kept still as a day
of rest from bodily labour; as it may appear both by his place upon the
Colossians, and especially in that which is alleged out of his Institutions.
And that he meaneth nothing less than such holy-days as you take upon
you to defend, it may appear first in the place of the Colossians, where he
saith that the days of rest which are used of them are used for policy' sake.
Now it is well known that, as it is policy and a way to preserve the estate
of things, and to keep them in a good continuance and success, that as well
the beasts, as the men which labour six days, should rest the seventh; so it
tendeth to no policy nor wealth of the people, or preservation of good
order, that there should be so many days wherein men should cease from
work, being a thing which breedeth idleness and consequently poverty,
besides other disorders and vices, which always go in company with idleness. And in the place of his Institutions he declareth himself yet more
plainly when he saith that those odd holy-days then are, without superstition "when they be ordained only for the observing of discipline and
order;" whereby he giveth to understand that he would have them no further
holy-days than for the time which is bestowed in the exercise of the discipline and order of the church, and that for the rest they should be altogether as other days, free to be laboured in. And so it appeareth that the
holy-days ascribed unto[8] saints by the service-book is a just cause why a
man cannot safely, without exception, subscribe unto the service-book[9].*

Jo. Whitgift.

Whatsoever M. Calvin's practice was in the church of
Geneva, yet in these places doth his judgment evidently
appear; neither doth a man always use that himself which he

[5 Another thing to condemn, Repl. 1 and 2.]
[6 Epistles, Repl. 1 and 2.]
[7 Against the keeping, Repl. 1, 2, and Def. A.]
[8 To, Repl. 1 and 2.]   [9 Repl. 2 omits *book*.]

alloweth in another; for there may be circumstances to make that commendable in one place that is not so in another.

He that condemneth the thing as unlawful must also condemn the churches that use the same, though not wholly, yet in that point. Forasmuch therefore as M. Calvin did not condemn other churches for observing such days, it is a manifest argument that he condemneth not the observing of those days in those churches. Indeed, "it is one thing to mislike, and another thing to condemn;" but he that maketh such a stir in the church for these matters as you do, and that so disorderly, cannot be said only "to mislike," but also "to condemn."

The place of M. Calvin, out of the epistle to the Galat. is not meant only of the Lord's day, but of other days also observed in other reformed churches; and in that place he maketh a general answer as it were for them all; as it is soon perceived by such as will read that place. He also, that shall peruse his words upon the second chapter to the Colossians, shall find the like sense in them. In that he saith they be used for order and policy, we do not dissent from him, but think so in like manner; howbeit we understand as he doth ecclesiastical order and policy; for, in the words that go before the place to the Galatians, he saith

Calv. in iv.
Gal.

that "the observing of days doth also pertain *ad regimen ecclesiæ:* to the government of the church[1]." What better order and policy can there be than to have certain days appointed wherein the people may rest from bodily labour, to labour spiritually, to hear the word of God, &c., which M. Calvin calleth order and policy, and not the external rest of the sabbath-day, which is a commandment of God, and no constitution of the church; neither hath the church any respect to worldly policy in appointing of holy-days, but to ecclesiastical policy, which consisteth in hearing the word, ministering the sacraments, public prayers, and other such-like godly actions?

The place in his Institutions convince all your shifting conjectures of mere folly; for therein he plainly declareth his allowing in other churches of more holy-days than the Sunday,

---

[1 Jam observatio civilis, tam agriculturæ, quam politiæ et œconomiæ servit. ad ecclesiæ quoque regimen extenditur.—Calvin. Op. Amst. 1667-71. Comm. in Epist. ad Galat. cap. iv. 10. Tom. VII. p. 303.]

which you have denied to be his opinion in the former two
places.   I have told you what he meaneth by discipline and
order or policy; whereby he giveth to understand nothing
less than that which you would conclude, being but your
own device to serve for a poor shift at a need.   And, although
the matter is not great whether they labour or no, yet the
law of the prince and the order of the church is to be
observed.   And so it appeareth that there is no reasonable
cause as yet proved why you ought not to subscribe to the
service-book.

Chapter ii.   The Eighth Division.

Answer to the Admonition, Page 82, Sect. 1, 2.

In the end you add: "patched if not altogether,
yet the greatest piece, out of the pope's portuis."

To this I answer briefly, it maketh no matter of
whom it was invented, in what book it is contained; so
that it be good and profitable, and consonant to God's
word. Well saith Ambrose: *Omne verum a quocunque* A notable
dicitur a Spiritu sancto est[2]: "All truth, of whomsoever saying of
it is spoken, is of the Holy Ghost." Ambrose[3].

T. C. Page 123, Lin. 6.

*Now, whereas M. Doctor saith, "it maketh no matter whether these
things be taken out of the portuis, so they be good, &c.;" I have proved
first they are not good, then, if they were, yet being not necessary, and
abused horribly by the papists, other being as good and better than they,
ought not to remain in the church.*

Jo. Whitgift.

Your reasons be not sufficient to prove them not to be good:
the abuse hath not been such but that, it being removed, the
thing may still remain as profitable and convenient: the judg- The judgment of the church in determining what is best and most church is to
fittest in matters of order, policy, and government (not being to private
against the word of God), is to be preferred before any pri- ment.
vate man's opinion and imagination.

[2 Ambros. Op. Par. 1636-90. Comm. in Epist. ad Corinth. prim. cap. xii. v. 3.
Tom. II. Append. col. 150. See before, page 465, note 2.]
 [3 This is inserted from Answ. 2.]

Chapter ii.   The Ninth Division.
T. C. Page 123, Lin. 10.

*And as for Ambrose saying, " All truth, of whomsoever it be said, is
of the Holy Ghost," if I were disposed to move questions, I could demand
of him which careth not of whom he have the truth, so he have it, what
our Saviour Christ meant to refuse the testimony of devils* Mark i. 24.[1]
when they gave a clear testimony that he was the Son of God Luke iv. 41.[1]
and the Holy One : and what St Paul meant to be angry, Acts xvi. 17.[1]
*and to take it so grievously, that the pythoness said he and his companion
were the servants of the high God, which preached unto them the way of
salvation. Here was truth, and yet rejected; and I would know whether
M. Doctor would say that these spake by the Spirit of God. Thus, whilst
without all judgment he snatcheth here a sentence, and there another, out
of the doctors, and that of the worst, as if a man should of purpose
choose out the dross and leave the silver, within a while he will make
no great difference, not only between the prophets and apostles and profane
writers, as Aristotle and Plato, but not between them and those which*[2]
*speak not by the conduit and leading of the Holy Ghost, but by the violent
thrusting of the wicked spirit.*

Jo. Whitgift.

Christ liked not the truth being uttered of the devil,
because he spake it of an evil meaning ; but he liked very
well the same testimony of truth afterwards uttered by Peter
sincerely, Matt. xvi. Mark viii. Neither did he mislike the
words because they were abused by the devil before. But I
will leave devils, and speak of men, of whom I think Ambrose
meant; although the truth is truth, of whomsoever it is uttered;
but, to answer for Ambrose, he hath said nothing in that
sentence which may not be justified.

M. Calvin (upon these words, 1 Corinth. xii.: "And no
man can say that Jesus is the Lord, but by the Holy Ghost")
saith thus : "It may be demanded whether the wicked have
the Spirit of God, seeing they sometime testify plainly and
well of Christ : I answer that there is no doubt but that
they have, so much as concerneth that effect ; but it is another thing to have the gift of regeneration, than to have the
gift of bare understanding, wherewith Judas was endued when
he preached the gospel[3]."

[1 The second reference and the verses of the others are inserted from Repl. 2:
Repl. 1 has *Mark. iv.*]

[2 Between them which, Repl. 2.]

[3 Quæritur hic, quum impii præclare interdum de Christo et splendide disse-

M. Martyr also, upon the same words, after he hath re- Saints' days. P. Martyr. cited the opinions of other, maketh this resolution: " But, when I weigh this matter with myself, I perceive that the apostle here doth speak, not of the Spirit which doth rege- nerate, or of that grace which justifieth, but of the gifts which are freely given, which may happen as well to the good as to the evil. Therefore I think that Paul spake simply, that he might declare that, by what means soever we speak well of Christ, it is of the Holy Ghost, of whom cometh *Omne verum a Spiritu sancto est.* all truth ; as all untruth proceedeth of the devil, who is the father of lies[4]." You see therefore that Ambrose is not of this judgment alone, and that his saying is very true.

The doctors that I have used in this cause be Jerome and Augustine, which be not the worst, but comparable with the best. I have rehearsed out of them whole sentences, and perfite, the which you are not able to answer: the rest of your opprobrious words, wherewith you conclude this question of holy-days, I leave for other to consider of, as notes of your spirit.

And, to the intent that the reader may understand that it was not for nought that you set not down my book together with your Reply, I will here set down such portions of my book touching this matter as you have not answered unto, but closely passed over, not thinking that any man should have espied your lack of ability to answer them.

Chapter ii.　The Tenth Division.

Admonition.

They should first prove ... that holy-days ascribed to saints, prescript services for them, &c., are agreeable to the written word of the Almighty [5].

rant, an habeant Dei Spiritum. Respondeo, eos proculdubio habere, quod ad effectum illum spectat : sed aliud est donum regenerationis, aliud donum nudæ intelligentiæ, qua Judas quoque præditus fuit quum evangelium prædicaret.— Calvin. Op. Amst. 1667-71. Comm. in Epist. I. ad Corinth. cap. xii. 3. Tom. VII. p. 186.]

[4 Cæterum cum ego rem mecum expendo, sermonem hic ab apostolo video institutum esse non de regenerante Spiritu, aut gratia justificante, verum de charismatibus gratuito concessis, quæ tam bonis quam malis obvenire possunt. Ideo Paulum simpliciter loquutum existimo, ut ostenderet, quocunque modo bene de Christo loquamur, id esse a Spiritu sancto, a quo est omne verum, quem- admodum omne mendacium a diabolo, qui pater est mendacii.—P. Martyr. Comm. in I. Epist. ad Corinth. Tigur. 1572. cap. xii. v. 3. fol. 171. 2.]

[5 See before, page 513, note 5.]

Answer to the Admonition, Page 153, Sect. 4;
and Page 154, Sect. 1.

Holy-days[1].

"Holy-days ascribed to saints," wherein not the saints but God is honoured and the people edified, by reading and hearing such stories and places of scripture as pertain to the martyrdom, calling, and function of such saints, or any other thing mentioned of them in scripture, must needs be according to God's word. For to honour God, to worship him, to be edified by the stories and examples of saints out of the scripture, cannot be but consonant to the scripture. The prescript service for them is all taken out of God's word, and not one piece thereof but it is most consonant unto the same. If there be any that is repugnant, set it down that we may understand it.

I told you before that, touching the days and times and other ceremonies, the church hath authority to determine what is most convenient, as it hath done from time to time. St August., in his epistle *ad Janu.*, in

Augustine.

the place before of me recited, saith that "the passion of Christ, his resurrection, his ascension, and the day of the coming of the Holy Ghost, (which we commonly call Whitsuntide) is celebrated, not by any commandment written, but by the determination of the church[2]." And it is the judgment of all learned writers that the church hath authority in these things; so that nothing be done against the word of God. But of this I have spoken partly before, and intend to speak more largely thereof in the place following, where you again make mention of it.

Admonition.

In this book days are ascribed unto saints, and kept holy with fasts on their evens, and prescript service appointed for them; which, beside that they are of many superstitiously kept and observed, and[3] also contrary to the commandment[z] of God: "Six days thou shalt labour[4];" and therefore we, for the superstition that is put in them, dare not subscribe to allow them.

[z] Exod. xx. 9.
Exo. xxiii.
12.
Deut. v. 13.
Esa. i. 10,
13, 14.
Lev. xxiii.
3.
2 Esd. i. 13.
Rom. xiv.
6.[5]
Ga. iv.1 0,
11.

[1] This is inserted from Answ. 2.]

[2] August. Op. Par. 1679-1700. Ad Inq. Januar. Lib. i. seu Epist. liv. cap. i. 1. Tom. II. col. 124. See Vol. I. page 230, note 4.]

[3] Are, Adm.]   [4] Shalt thou labour, Adm.]   [5] Rom. xvi. 6. Adm.]

Answer to the Admonition, Page 173, Sect. 2 ; and Page 174,
175 ; and Page 176, Sect. 1, 2.

[This is contained in your first reason, and there
answered.][6] Your collection hangeth not together; for
how followeth this? These holy-days be superstitiously
observed of some; therefore you may not allow them.
Why should other men's superstition hinder you from
lawfully using a lawful thing? The sabbath-day is su- Abuse of things doth
perstitiously used of some; so is the church, so is the not condemn the things.
creed, and the Lord's prayer, and many things else; and
yet I hope you will subscribe to them. You heap up a
number of places in the margent to prove that which no
man doubteth of, that is, this portion of the commandment : "Six days shalt thou labour, &c.;" the meaning of
which words is this, that, seeing God hath permitted
unto us six days to do our own works in, we ought the
seventh day wholly to serve him[7].

Every man hath not bodily labour to do, but may
serve God as well in these six days as in the seventh.
And certainly he doth not by any means break this
commandment, which abstaineth in any of these six days
from bodily labour to serve God. For this is the commandment : "Remember that thou keep holy the sabbath-day;" as for this : "Six days thou shalt work," is
no commandment, but tendeth rather to the constitution
of the sabbath than to the prohibiting of rest in any
other day appointed to the service of God; and it is
as much as if he should say, "Six days thou mayest
work ;" and so do some translate the Hebrew word.

The place alleged out of the first of Esay is far from
the purpose; there is not one word there spoken of any
holy-days dedicate[8] to saints, but only the Lord signifieth
that their sacrifices and feast-days were not acceptable
unto[9] him, because they were done in hypocrisy, and Esay con-demneth the
without faith; so that he reproveth *modum* not *factum*, manner of sa-crificing[10].
their manner of sacrificing, that is, their hypocritical

[6 This is inserted from Answ.]
[7 Here in Answ. comes in the portion inserted before, page 572.]
[8 Dedicated, Answ.]   [9 To, Answ.]
[10 Answ. 2 goes on *and not the deed.*]

[WHITGIFT, II.]   38

38

kind of worshipping him [and not the worship or the
deed done.]¹

In the second of Esdras i.², in the place by you quoted,
I see not one word that may serve for your purpose: the
words you quote be these: " I have led you through the
sea, and have given you a sure way since the beginning;
I gave you Moses for a guide, and Aaron for a priest."

In the xiv. to the Ro., the apostle speaketh nothing of our holy-days, but of such as were observed
among the Jews and abrogated by the coming of Christ.
And yet in that place the apostle exhorteth that we
which be strong should not despise them that are weak,
nor condemn them, though they use not the christian
liberty in days and meats.

That in the fourth to the Galat.: " Ye⁴ observe days,
months, and times, and years, &c.," St Augustine, *ad*
Januar. Episto. 119, expoundeth on this sort: *Eos in-
culpat qui dicunt, Non proficiscar, . . . quia posterus dies est,
aut quia luna sic fertur; vel, Proficiscar ut prospera cedant,
quia ita se habet positio siderum: Non agam hoc mense com-
mercium, quia illa stella mihi agit mensem; vel, Agam, quia
suscepit mensem⁵.* ["The apostle blameth those which say,
This day I will not travel or journey, for that the day is
unlucky and unfortunate, or for that the moon is in this
or that course; or, This day I will not proceed my purposed journey, that my affairs may happily come to pass,
because that the planets do so much import and foreshew.
Or, I will not in this month traffic, because that this or
that star and planet governeth the month; or, I will buy
and sell in this month, because it doth govern the same."]⁶
I know there be other that do otherwise expound that
place (and that truly), even as they do also that in the
xiv. to the Rom., of certain Jewish feasts, as sabbaths,
new moons, the feasts of tabernacles, the year of jubilee,
and such like, abrogated by the gospel, and yet superstitiously observed of some. But these places can by

[¹ The last eight words are introduced from Answ. 2.]
[² In the 2 Esdras i., Answ.]   [³ These notes are not in Answ.]
[⁴ You, Answ. 2.]
[⁵ Eos enim culpat &c.—August. Op. Par. 1679-1700. Ad Inq. Januar. Lib.
II. seu Epist. lv. cap. vii. 13. Tom. II. col. 133.]
[⁶ This translation is introduced from Answ. 2.]

no means be understood of the days observed by us, and called by the names of saints' days; for they were ordained since the writing of this epistle.

And, that you may understand the difference betwixt the festival days observed of the papists, and the days allowed now in this church, it is to be considered, first, that their saints' days were appointed for the honouring and worshipping of the saints, by whose names they were called; ours be ordained for the honouring of God, for public prayer, and edifying the people by reading the scriptures, and preaching[8]. *Difference betwixt the papists' holy-days and ours.* *Saints[7].*

2. The papists in their saints' days prayed unto the saints: we only pray unto God in Christ's name.

3. They had all things done in a strange tongue without any edifying at all: we have the prayers and the scriptures read in a tongue known, which cannot be without great commodity to the hearers.

4. To be short, they in observing their days think they merit thereby something at God's hands: we in observing our days are taught far otherwise.

The church even from the beginning hath observed such feasts; as it may appear in good writers.

[9]Page 179, Sect. 1.

Touching fasting on the evens of such feasts, or rather abstaining from flesh, you know it is not for religion, but for policy, and as I think the same is protested in that act, where such kind of abstaining is established[10]; and therefore these be but slender quarrels picked to disallow such a book[11].

Jo. Whitgift.

All this have you overskipped: for what cause you know best yourself.

[7 This word is inserted from Answ. 2.]

[8 Here in Answ. comes the sentence printed before, page 574.]

[9 Def. B. prefixes here *T. C.*]

[10 Statutes at large, Lond. 1763, &c. Vol. II. pp. 545, 7.   Conf. Bp. Jewel's Works, Park. Soc. Edit. Vol. IV. pp. 1141, 2.]

[11 This paragraph follows in Answ. those printed page 579-81, 583-5, 6.]